W9-DED-089

Natural Resource Economics

NEW HORIZONS IN ENVIRONMENTAL ECONOMICS

General Editor: Wallace E. Oates, *Professor of Economics, University of Maryland*

This important new series is designed to make a significant contribution to the development of the principles and practices of environmental economics. It will include both theoretical and empirical work. International in scope, it will address issues of current and future concern in both East and West and in developed and developing countries.

The main purpose of the series is to create a forum for the publication of high quality work and to show how economic analysis can make a contribution to understanding and resolving the environmental problems confronting the world in the late 20th century.

Innovation in Environmental Policy
Edited by T.H. Tietenberg

Environmental Economics
Policies for Environmental Management and Sustainable Development
Clem Tisdell

The Economics of Solid Waste Reduction
The Impact of User Fees
Robin R. Jenkins

Fair Principles for Sustainable Development
Essays on Environmental Policy and Developing Countries
Edited by Edward Dommen

The Economics of Project Appraisal and the Environment
Edited by John Weiss

Economics and Environmental Policy
T.H. Tietenberg

Environmental Problems in the Shortage Economy
The Legacy of Soviet Environmental Policy
Ann-Mari Sätre Åhlander

Environmental and Resource Economics
Selected Essays of Anthony C. Fisher
Anthony C. Fisher

Natural Resource Economics
Selected Papers of Allen V. Kneese
Allen V. Kneese

Environmental Policy with Political and Economic Integration
The European Union and the United States
Edited by John B. Braden, Henk Folmer and Thomas S. Ulen

Principles of Environmental and Resource Economics
A Guide for Students and Decision-Makers
Edited by Henk Folmer, H. Landis Gabel and Hans Opschoor

Natural Resource Economics

Selected Papers of Allen V. Kneese

Allen V. Kneese

Senior Fellow, Resources for the Future, U.S.A.

NEW HORIZONS IN ENVIRONMENTAL ECONOMICS

Edward Elgar
Aldershot, UK • Brookfield, US

© Allen V. Kneese 1995

Published by
Edward Elgar Publishing Limited
Gower House
Croft Road
Aldershot
Hants GU11 3HR
UK

Edward Elgar Publishing Company
Old Post Road
Brookfield
Vermont 05036
US

British Library Cataloguing in Publication Data
Kneese, Allen V.
  Natural Resource Economics: Selected
  Papers of Allen V. Kneese. – (New
  Horizons in Environmental Economics
  Series)
  I. Title II. Series
  333.7

Library of Congress Cataloguing in Publication Data
Kneese, Allen V.
    Natural resource economics: selected papers of Allen V. Kneese.
      p. cm. — (New horizons in environmental economics)
    Includes bibliographical references and index.
    1. Natural resources. 2. Sustainable development. I. Title.
  II. Series.
  HC55.K64   1995
  333.7—dc20   95–7200
                                                                      CIP

ISBN 1 85898 173 5

Printed and bound in Great Britain by
Hartnolls Limited, Bodmin, Cornwall

Contents

Acknowledgements   vii
Introduction   ix

PART ONE   PERSPECTIVES

1   'The Economics of Natural Resources' in *Population and Resources
    in Western Intellectual Traditions* (eds. Michael S. Teitelbaum and
    Jay M. Winter), 1989, The Population Council, 281–309.   3
2   'Ethics and Environmental Economics' (with William D. Schulze) in
    Handbook of Natural Resource and Energy Economics Volume One
    (eds. Allen V. Kneese and James L. Sweeney), 1985, Elsevier
    Science Publishers B.V., 191–220.   32
3   'The Sustainable Economy' (with Robert U. Ayres) in *Frontiers in
    Social Thought – Essays in Honor of Kenneth E. Boulding*, 1976,
    Elsevier Science Publishers B.V., 183–214.   62
4   'Environmental Quality and the Optimal Jurisdiction' (with Edwin T.
    Haefele) in *Urban and Social Economics in Market and Planned
    Economies: Housing, Income and Environment Volume 2* (eds. Alan
    A. Brown, Joseph A. Licari and Egon Neuberger), 1974, Praeger
    Publishers Inc., 280–99.   94
5   'The Faustian Bargain', *Resources*, **44**, September 1973, 1–5.   114

PART TWO   WATER RESOURCES AND BENEFIT–COST ANALYSIS

6   'Economics and Water Resources' in *Water Resources Administration
    in the United States: Policy, Practice and Emerging Issues* (ed.
    Martin Reuss), 1993, Michigan State University Press, 23–35.   125
7   'Reallocation by Markets and Prices' (with Kenneth D. Frederick) in
    Climate Change and U.S. Water Resources (ed. Paul E. Waggoner),
    1990, John Wiley & Sons Inc. for the American Association for the
    Advancement of Science, 395–419.   138
8   'Hypothetical Shocks to Water Allocation Institutions in the Colorado
    Basin' (with Gilbert Bonem) in *New Courses for the Colorado River:
    Major Issues for the Next Century* (eds. Gary Weatherford and F.
    Lee Brown), 1986, University of New Mexico Press, 87–108.   163

9   'Establishing the Scientific, Technical and Economic Basis for
    Coastal Zone Management' (with Clifford S. Russell), *Coastal Zone
    Management Journal*, **1**(1), 1973, 47–63.   185
10 'Israel's Water Policy' in *Arid Zone Settlement Planning* (ed. Gideon
    Golany), 1979, Pergamon Press Inc., 357–92.   202
11 'The Future of Arid Lands' (with Jennifer E. Zamora) in *Salinity in
    Irrigation and Water Resources* (ed. Daniel Yaron), 1981, Marcel
    Dekker Inc. 379–405.   238

PART THREE   ENVIRONMENTAL ECONOMICS AND POLICY

12 'Background for the Economic Analysis of Environmental Pollution'
    in *The Economics of Environment – Papers from Four Nations* (eds.
    Peter Bohm and Allen V. Kneese), 1971, The Macmillan Press Ltd,
    1–24. Reprinted from *The Swedish Journal of Economics*, **73**(1),
    March 1971.   267
13 'Production, Consumption, and Externalities' (with Robert U.
    Ayres), *The American Economic Review*, **59**(3), June 1969, 282–97.   291
14 'Measuring Social and Economic Change: Benefits and Costs of
    Environmental Pollution' (with Orris C. Herfindahl) in *The
    Measurement of Economic and Social Performance* (ed. Milton
    Moss), 1973, Columbia University Press, 441–508.   307
15 'Environmental Policy' in *The United States in the 1980s* (eds. Peter
    Duignan and Alvin Rabushka), 1980, Hoover Institution Press,
    253–83.   375
16 'State Liability for International Environmental Degradation: An
    Economic Perspective' (with Ralph C. d'Arge), *Natural Resources
    Journal*, **20**, July 1980, 427–50.   406
17 'Bribes and Charges in Pollution Control: An Aspect of the Coase
    Controversy' (with Karl-Göran Mäler), *Natural Resources Journal*,
    13(4), October 1973, 705–16.   430
18 'Pollution, Prices, and Public Policy' (with Charles L. Schultze),
    Policy Studies Review Annual (ed. Stuart S. Nagel), 1977, Sage
    Publications Inc., 634–60.   442
19 Review of *The economy of the earth: Philosophy, law and the
    environment* by Mark Sagoff, *Journal of Economic Literature*,
    XXVII, December 1989, 1674–6.   469

Name index   475

Acknowledgements

The publishers wish to thank the following who have kindly given permission for the use of copyright material.

American Economic Association for articles: 'Production, Consumption, and Externalities' (with Robert U. Ayres), *The American Economic Review*, **59**(3), June 1969, 282–97; Review of *The economy of the earth: Philosophy, law and the environment* by Mark Sagoff, *Journal of Economic Literature*, **XXVII**, December 1989, 1674–6.

Elsevier Science Publishers B.V. for articles: 'Ethics and Environmental Economics' (with William D. Schulze) in *Handbook of Natural Resource and Energy Economics Volume One* (eds. Allen V. Kneese and James L. Sweeney), 1985, 191–220; 'The Sustainable Economy' (with Robert U. Ayres) in *Frontiers in Social Thought – Essays in Honor of Kenneth E. Boulding*, 1976, 183–214.

Gideon Golany for article: 'Israel's Water Policy' in *Arid Zone Settlement Planning* (ed. Gideon Golany), 1979, Pergamon Press Inc., 357–92.

Greenwood Publishing Group Inc. for article: 'Environmental Quality and the Optimal Jurisdiction' (with Edwin T. Haefele) in *Urban and Social Economics in Market and Planned Economies: Housing, Income and Environment Volume 2* (eds. Alan A. Brown, Joseph A. Licari and Egon Neuberger), 1974, Praeger Publishershers, 280–99.

Hoover Institution Press for article: 'Environmental Policy' in *The United States in the 1980s* (eds. Peter Duignan and Alvin Rabushka), 1980, 253–83.

John Wiley & Sons Inc. for article: 'Reallocation by Markets and Prices' (with Kenneth D. Frederick) in *Climate Change and U.S. Water Resources* (ed. Paul E. Waggoner), 1990, 395–419.

The Macmillan Press Ltd for article: 'Background for the Economic Analysis of Environmental Pollution' in *The Economics of Environment – Papers from Four Nations* (eds. Peter Bohm and Allen V. Kneese), 1971, 1–24.

Marcel Dekker Inc. for article: 'The Future of Arid Lands' (with Jennifer E. Zamora) in *Salinity in Irrigation and Water Resources* (ed. Daniel Yaron), 1981, 379–405.

Michigan State University Press for article: 'Economics and Water Resources' in *Water Resources Administration in the United States: Policy, Practice and Emerging Issues* (ed. Martin Reuss), 1993, 23–35.

National Bureau of Economic Research for article: 'Measuring Social and Economic Change: Benefits and Costs of Environmental Pollution' (with Orris C. Herfindahl) in *The Measurement of Economic and Social Performance* (ed. Milton Moss), 1973, Columbia University Press, 441–508.

Natural Resources Journal for articles: 'State Liability for International Environmental Degradation: An Economic Perspective' (with Ralph C. d'Arge), **20**, July 1980, 427–50; 'Bribes and Charges in Pollution Control: An Aspect of the Coase Controversy' (with Karl-Göran Mäler), **13**(4), October 1973, 705–16.

The Population Council for article: 'The Economics of Natural Resources' in *Population and Resources in Western Intellectual Traditions* (eds. Michael S. Teitelbaum and Jay M. Winter), 1989, 281–309.

Sage Publications Inc. for article: 'Pollution, Prices, and Public Policy' (with Charles L. Schultze), *Policy Studies Review Annual* (ed. Stuart S. Nagel), 1977, 634–60.

Taylor & Francis Ltd. for article: 'Establishing the Scientific, Technical and Economic Basis for Coastal Zone Management' (with Clifford S. Russell), *Coastal Zone Management Journal*, **1**(1), 1973, 47–63.

Introduction

Edward Elgar requested that I make the introduction to this volume of selected papers 'personal'. I take this to mean that I am requested to put the papers reprinted in this volume into a broader perspective as to the overall development of the field of natural resource economics, much of which took place at Resources for the Future (RFF), or was stimulated by RFF, and in much of which I had a hand. Also that I need not avoid personal, but I hope informed, opinion.

I came to RFF in 1960 to initiate a program of work on water quality economics and management, and the economics of water resources more generally. I have been there since, with the exception of teaching and research stints at Stanford University and the University of New Mexico. The latter happens to be in my favorite State.

From 1963 to 1967, I was Director of the Water Resources Program at RFF. This program dealt with both water quantity and water quality issues and fed my long standing and continuing interest in water resource matters. From 1967 to 1978, I was Director of the Quality of the Environment Division at RFF. Most of my professional life has been spent in helping to develop the, now thriving, field of environmental economics. In 1978, after a stint at the University of New Mexico, I returned to RFF a Senior Fellow, a position I still hold. The papers selected for reprinting here were published between 1960 and 1993 and reflect the range of research I conducted, directed, or participated in, over more than three decades.

The volume is divided into three parts: (a) Perspectives, (b) Water Resources and Benefit–Cost Analysis, and (c) Environmental Economics and Policy.

Part One: Perspectives

The first category contains five chapters that attempt to provide a description of some of the main issues and ideas of natural resource economics and present a rather broad perspective on some of them. The first chapter 'The Economics of Natural Resources' provides a non-technical introduction to the field. It discusses in a summary manner a number of issues, some of which are addressed in more detail in other papers in the volume, for example, benefit–cost analysis and the ethical foundations of environmental economics. While the discussion in this paper is non-technical, professional economists who have reviewed the paper found the compact but rather comprehensive discussion of the field useful, so have students.

The second chapter 'Ethics and Environmental Economics' addresses the ethical issues in much more detail. Welfare economics, one of the foundations of conventional environmental economics, can be thought of as being an enormous elaboration of the moral philosophy developed by Bentham, Mill and others in the eighteenth and nineteenth centuries. There are, however, rival ethical systems that also put forward rules for individual and social moral behavior that are different from those of utilitarian approaches. The paper explores the implications of applying alternative ethical rules to some difficult environmental economic problems.

Chapter 3, 'The Sustainable Economy', so far as I know, coined the term 'sustainable economy', a term now used almost universally in discussions of environment, resources, and economic development. The essay considers the question of whether humanity can converge to an indefinitely sustainable economy in a way that is reasonably orderly, peaceful and safe, or whether it is on a one-way track to disaster. The paper stresses the complexity of this issue pointing out that conventional economic growth theory and ordinary projection procedures cannot even come close to answering the question. Conclusions of the paper about the question stress the uncertainty inherent in it but are rather pessimistic, 'What does seem clear is that humanity faces a future full of stresses and strains and that life will not be comfortable for any persistent periods for a long long time to come – if ever'. This paper was written nearly twenty years ago, but, aside from revising somewhat downward world population projections, I would not change it much today.

Chapter 4, 'Environmental Quality and the Optimal Jurisdiction', addresses the difficult problem of the normative characteristics of alternative institutional and legal arrangements for environmental management. There are three main types of collective choices to be made for environmental management. First is the choice of what level of environmental quality should be achieved. The second is about the income distribution issue as it relates both to benefits and to costs. Finally, management instruments must be chosen collectively.

The paper endeavors to answer the question, with these three main types of collective choices to be made, how do we decide which collectivity makes them? The problem is greatly complicated by the fact that air sheds and water sheds will not usually be coterminous and solid waste disposal may have effects on land use at great distances. Furthermore, the residuals management problem is but one public service problem, and it must compete for a share of a limited public purse. The paper first reviews the received theory of 'optimal jurisdiction' most of which is based on what is called the Tiebout 'Voting with the feet' hypothesis. This theory is found wanting and the paper proposes and defends the establishment of general purpose representatives in a region or metropolitan area. This defense is based on an aspect of collective choice theory.

The final chapter in this section is called 'The Faustian Bargain'. The paper argues that benefit–cost analysis, despite efforts to use it in evaluating the desirability of developing a large scale fission based economy cannot, by itself, answer the most important policy questions. The paper deals with the issues surrounding whether the society should strike what Alvin M. Weinberg called the Faustian bargain with the nuclear scientists and engineers to attempt to insure safe applications of nuclear technology. The answer of the paper is a resounding 'no'. Again this paper was written about twenty years ago. Unfortunately, most of the things it argued and feared might happen have happened, and the nuclear industry is dead or dying except for a few places where it continues, driven by a sense of desperation.

Part Two: Water Resources and Benefit–Cost Analysis

As mentioned, I directed the RFF water program for several years in the middle 1960s. At that time the program was concerned mostly with water quantity as opposed to water quality issues although, ultimately, I did much more work on water quality matters, especially during my tenure as Director of the Quality of the Environment Division. Still my interest in water quantity issues persists. On these most of my work has been in two areas. One is the application of benefit–cost analysis to water development and management issues and the second area involves issues of water allocation in the arid west.

Benefit–cost analysis is an applied welfare economics technique that played a very large role in water resource economics, especially in the evaluation of federal water resource projects. In more recent times its application, as explained in Chapter 6, 'Economics and Water Resources', in this volume, has been expanded greatly to other issues such as federal environmental regulations. These newer applications stretch the procedure to, or beyond, its limits. Many of those applying or advocating the technique are unaware of its theoretical foundations and history. The opening paper in this section presents, to my knowledge, the most comprehensive and up to date discussion of these aspects of the technique that exists.

The second issue, water allocation, is also discussed in this paper and in more detail in the next one, Chapter 7, 'Reallocation by Markets and Prices'. There are basically no more unallocated supplies of water in the American arid west. This means attention is shifting away from development projects and associated economic evaluation problems to the efficient and equitable allocation and reallocation of existing supplies. Western water allocation institutions need to evolve toward greater reliance on economic incentives through the formation of markets and the improvement of pricing policies for publicly supplied water. Evidence shows that water use is sensitive to price, and demand-side management is increasingly important for balancing demand with supplies. These themes are developed in detail in this paper.

Chapter 8 discusses hypothetical, but not necessarily improbable, shocks to the water allocation institutions in the Colorado River Basin. The flow of the Colorado is an important source of municipal and industrial water supplies, and especially irrigation water supplies in the states of Colorado, Utah, Arizona, New Mexico, and California. But water from the river is overallocated. In other words more 'paper rights' to water exist than there is water available over the long run. The reasons for this are indicated in the paper, and the whole situation is clouded by the existence of unquantified but potentially very large Indian water rights, especially on the Navajo reservation. A shock not considered in this paper, because at the time the paper was written it was not apparent how important it would be, is protection of threatened and endangered species under the Endangered Species Act. But the matter is considered in the final section of Chapter 6 in this volume. It now appears that efforts to enforce this act, however important that it may be, will cast a pall of uncertainty over all water allocation arrangements throughout the west for years to come.

In most countries that have a coastline, coastal zones are heavily populated and industrialized and important for recreational and environmental use which often conflicts. In the United States, nearly half of industrial employment is in the coastal zones. Chapter 9 deals with establishing the scientific, technical and economic basis for coastal zone management. It has three major aims: first, to put the management problems in perspective, second to set out a general framework for consideration of coastal zone management problems, and third to discuss institutional problems.

Because of the central role that water resource development has had in the overall development, especially the early development, of Israel, the water policies established there are of special interest. In 1976 the Israeli Water Commission asked me to do a broad examination of Israeli water policy and of decision-making processes and administrative practices with respect to water resources development, use, and management in Israel. In doing this I was greatly assisted by the Water Commission staff and by TAHAL (the Israeli water planning agency). I made this examination from the viewpoint of an economist and with an emphasis on efficiency considerations, but also recognizing the broader social, ideological (very important, especially in the earlier years), and security goals which have been major forces in the way water development and allocation occurred in the State of Israel. Chapter 10, 'Israel's Water Policy', in this volume presents the results of this investigation.

The final chapter in Part Two 'The Future of Arid Lands' aims to provide a broad perspective on the situation of the world's arid lands, the trends affecting them, and possible future developments affecting them. I found that for various reasons they are currently suffering severe stresses and strains, in many instances not for the first time in their history. The paper starts with a modest statistical analysis testing various hypotheses about relationships between economic development and climates. Here it develops the concept of 'arid hinterlands'. It then proceeds to a fairly detailed, but, given the sparse data, somewhat anecdotal, discussion of tendencies that will adversely affect the future of the arid lands. These include, among others, desertification, deterioration of mountain environments, increasing salinity of surface and ground water, and siltation of scarce reservoir sites. On balance the conclusions are rather pessimistic.

Part Three: Environmental Economics and Policy

I have had an interest in, and worked on, a variety of natural resource problems, as I hope the papers in Parts One and Two show, but by far my greatest professional time and effort went into helping to establish and develop the field of environmental economics. Most of this activity took place during the 1960s and 1970s and was greatly assisted by the associate director of the Quality of the Environment Division, Blair Bower. Blair made many valuable contributions.

Chapter 12 presents needed background information on the effects of human activities on the environment and how they can be managed. This may be a suitable place to state that environmental economics is inherently interdisciplinary. To some, including me, that is a major part of its attraction. 'Background for the Economic Analysis of Environmental Pollution' is naturally a bit dated but, interestingly, the issues remain largely the same. The paper also provides a suitable background and introduction to the next two papers which discuss what I would regard as the centerpieces of the Division's efforts during the late 1960s and throughout the 1970s. These are the spelling out of the implications of the first law of thermodynamics for environmental economics and the development of a regional residual management model incorporating mass balances and methods and data from economics, engineering, ecology, and political science. Because of the importance I attach to the papers discussing work on these matters, I will provide a rather extended introduction to them that contains background information beyond what is included in the papers themselves.

Research on environmental problems at Resources for the Future, as already pointed out, was at first an outgrowth of an older water resources research program. Study of the conditions of water supply and demand in the United States soon led to the conclusion that in many regions of the United States deterioration of water quality was at least as important a problem as the adequacy of supply. Moreover, it became clear that these two problems were often tightly interconnected. Starting in 1960, a series of theoretical, case, and comparative international studies on water quality problems was launched. This phase of research culminated in 1968 with a summary and interpretive volume, *Managing Water Quality: Economics, Technology, Institutions*, by myself and Blair Bower and published by RFF.

Prior to the completion of this set of studies the first statement of a broader research program was developed in a book by myself and Orris Herfendahl in *Quality of the Environment: An Economic Approach to Some Problems in Using Land, Water, and Air* (RFF–1965). This provided the basis for a new program of studies at RFF, launched in 1965 as the Quality of the Environment Program. This program initially focused individually on problems associated with airborne, waterborne, and solid wastes. At the outset these different residuals and the different environmental media were treated as separate categories of problems – even though researchable within a similar conceptual framework. It soon became clear, however, that there were many tradeoffs among the airborne, waterborne, and solid waste streams. For example – and one could cite many examples – when dissolved organic material and suspended solids are removed from liquid residuals stream in a sewage treatment plant, a semisolid sludge results, thereby causing a solid residual disposal problem. If the sludge is incinerated, certain gaseous residuals are generated, thereby transferring the original liquid waste problem into a possible air quality problem. Conversely, scrubbing particulates from a gas stream by aqueous solutions transfers the pollutants from air to water. Or, the modification of a production process to reduce the generation of waterborne wastes may involve use of additional energy, thereby resulting in the generation of additional gaseous wastes and waste heat.

At the same time that this early empirical work was going on, theoretical research was proceeding on a conceptual framework for more sophisticated work in the area. Chapter 13 'Production, Consumption and Externalities' sets forth a formal model of the role of materials balance (first law of thermodynamics) in externality problems. It does this by incorporating mass balance into a general equilibrium model of the economy.

While the model itself is somewhat technical, the basic ideas are rather simple. The relationships between pollution and economic activity can be described by a simple materials balance model such as that portrayed in Figure 1. In that diagram, all of the production activities of the economic system are represented by the box labeled 'production sector'. Located in this box are all of the mines, factories, warehouses, transportation networks, and public utilities, for instance, that are engaged in the extraction of materials from the environment, their processing, refinement, and rearrangement into marketable goods and services, and their transportation and distribution throughout the economy to the point of ultimate use.

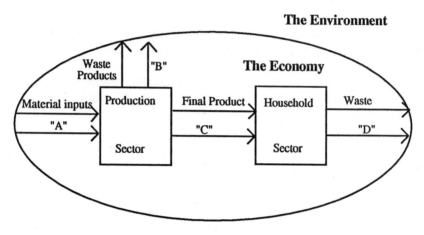

Figure 1   Materials Balance and the Economy

Whatever is produced in the production sector of this model economy goes to individuals acting as consumers. They are represented by the box labeled 'household sector'. Together, these two boxes make up what is usually called the economic system. Conventional portrayals of the economic system show a circular flow of money accompanied by an opposite flow of goods and services and productive factors between the household sector and the production sector. The household sector provides factor inputs: that is, capital and labor in return for money payments or income. In turn, the production sector provides its goods and services output to the household sector in return for money payments. Thus, the circular flow is completed. However, from the perspective of the materials balance model, such a view of the economic system is misleading because it ignores important flows of materials and the basic laws of physics governing them. Given that goods and services are made out of 'something', the conventional model fails to indicate where that something comes from and where it goes.

In the materials balance model, the environment can be viewed as a large shell surrounding the economic system. It has the same relationship to the economy as does a mother to an unborn child – it provides sustenance and carries away wastes. These input and waste flows are also portrayed in the figure. Raw materials flow from the environment, are processed in the production sector (that is, converted into consumer goods), and then, at least in part, pass on to the household sector. The materials returning to the environment from the household sector are residuals. They are the unwanted by-products of the consumption activities of households. Similarly, not all of the material inputs that enter the production sector are embodied in the consumption goods flowing on to the household sector. These are the residuals from production. Thus, there is a flow of residuals from both the production and consumption sectors back to the environment.

These materials flows must obey the basic law of physics governing the conservation of matter. In an economy with no imports or exports, and where there is no net accumulation of stocks (plant, equipment, inventories, consumer durables, or residential buildings), the mass of residuals returned to the natural environment must be equal to the mass of basic fuels, food, minerals, and other raw materials entering the processing and production system, plus gases taken from the atmosphere. This is the principle of materials balance. This principle must hold true for each sector of the economic system taken separately, and for the economic systems as a whole. Thus, in the absence of inventory accumulation, the flow of consumer goods from the production sector to the household sector must be matched by an equal mass flow back to the environment.

From this simple model, it is clear that the environment is of considerable value to man as a source of material inputs for production and consumption. However, it has not been as widely recognized – at least until recently – that the environment is also valuable as a receptor for the corresponding residuals flows. Indeed, the environment has a capacity to accept, absorb, and assimilate most of the types of returning materials. But when this absorptive and assimilative capacity is overused or misused, pollution and environmental degradation is the result.

One of the lessons learned from this materials balance model is that the common economic usage of the terms 'input', 'output', and 'consumption' are misleading. For example, the input–output relationships of the production sector are more accurately described as processes of throughput. Similarly, the household sector may use the services of the goods it receives or it may transform these goods by mechanical, chemical, or biological processes; but it never consumes them in a physical sense. After the household sector is through with a good, there is still something left and it must be disposed of, somehow and somewhere. Thus the processes of resource use, production, and consumption (as the economist usually uses that term) can better be described as processes of materials and energy throughput and balanced materials flows. More importantly, these processes are intimately bound together with the problems of residuals disposal – and hence of air, land, and water pollution.

Given the population, industrial production, and transport services in an economy (a regional rather than a national economy would normally be the relevant unit), it is possible to visualize combinations of social policy which could lead to quite different relative burdens placed upon the environment as a whole. To take one extreme, a region which went in heavily for electric space heating and wet scrubbing of stack gases (from stream plants and industries), which ground up its garbage and delivered it to the sewers and then discharged the raw sewage to watercourses, would protect its air resources to an exceptional degree. On the other hand, a region which treated municipal and industrial liquid residuals streams to a high level but relied heavily on the incineration of sludges and solid residuals would protect its water and land resources but at the expense of discharging residuals predominantly to the air. Finally, a region which practiced high-level recovery and recycling of residuals and fostered low residuals production processes to a far-reaching extent in each of the economic sectors would discharge few residuals to any of the environmental media.

Considerations like these led to the decision to construct a Regional Environmental Quality Management Model by the Quality of the Environment Division at RFF. This model, which came to be known as the Russell/Spofford model, after the scholars who developed the details of the model, along with some other macroeconomic consideration is discussed in Chapter 14 'Measuring Social and Economic Change: Benefits and Costs of Environmental Pollution' in this volume. The paper provides a good discussion of the structure and methods of the model but it does not include a discussion of the actual regional application and its results because this information was not yet available when the paper was prepared. Therefore I will present a brief review here.

The Lower Delaware Valley region, chosen for this application, is a very complex one with many individual point and non-point sources of residuals discharges. The region includes, but is larger than, the Delaware Estuary area. Overall, the population of the area was a little more than five and a half million in 1970. Of this, 35 percent is accounted for by Philadelphia alone, with a further 5 percent found in Trenton, Camden and Wilmington. However, other parts of the region are also heavily urbanized and industrialized.

The region as a whole contains an abundance of manufacturing plants. In fact, it is one of the most heavily industrialized areas in the United States. It has, for example, seven major oil refineries, five steel plants, sixteen major pulp and paper or paper mills, fifteen important thermal power generating facilities, numerous large and small chemical and petrochemical plants, foundries, and large assembly plants for the auto and electronic industries. This, of course, made the task of identifying sources of residuals discharges, estimating the costs of discharge reduction for them, and including them in the regional model, an enormous one. The model used contains 125 industrial plants, 44 municipal sewage treatment plants, and 23 municipal incinerators, all dealt with as point sources. In addition, there are 57 home and commercial heating sources with controllable discharges, each of which is treated as an area source, i.e. not tied to a specific stack location. Other point and non-point sources not distinguished in the region are incorporated as background discharges.

The large population of the region naturally produces vast quantities of residuals from consumption activities, requiring correspondingly large facilities for their handling and disposal. There are seven municipal sewage treatment plants with flows greater than ten million gallons per day (m.g.d.) and seventeen with flows greater than one m.g.d. On the major tributaries to the estuary and the Schuylkill River, there are more than 120 municipal treatment plants of widely varying sizes. For the disposal of solid residuals, there are seventeen incinerators currently operating with an aggregate capacity of about 6,000 tons per day, and many major and minor landfill operations. Together, on an annual basis, the heating of homes and commercial buildings is responsible for about a quarter of the total discharges of sulfur dioxide and 10–15 percent of the particulate discharges in the region.

Without dwelling on the structure and function of the model, which, as mentioned, are well explained in Chapter 14, I will sample a few quantitative results. First, the model shows that in this realistic setting of an actual case there are significant linkages among the management of different residuals types. Tighter ambient standards for the atmosphere do significantly affect the cost of maintaining water-quality standards and vice versa. This can be seen by considering the results in Table 1 from production runs of the Lower Delaware Valley integrated (Russell/Spofford) residuals management model.

Table 1   Additional Daily Costs of Meeting Water Quality Standards

	Easy Ambient Standards – AIR	Tight Ambient Standards – AIR
Easy Ambient Standards – Water	$395,640	$1,064,892
Tight Ambient Standards – Water	$422,031	$1,309,271

High-quality landfill required in all runs.

All the numbers in the table refer to total additional costs to the region of meeting environmental standards, in dollars per day. The numbers are based on prices of the early 1960s and would be much higher today, but the relationships among them might remain about the same. The runs show that going from easy (relatively low) water standards to tight (relatively high) water quality standards costs about $16,000 per day when only easy air standards are imposed. If, however, tight air standards are imposed, going from easy to tight quality water standards costs about $244,000 – almost ten times as much.

Secondly, there appears to be a variety of strategies for meeting the environmental quality standards that do not differ very much in overall total costs to the region. This is interesting in that it suggests that distributional issues will be an important consideration in environmental quality management in the region.

Finally, and perhaps most important, the Lower Delaware Valley application indicates that it is possible to develop an integrated residuals management model for a large region at a manageable cost. The cost of this model (granted that much of the basic data had been collected already) was about ten man-years of effort on the part of the senior researchers, plus some research assistance, plus perhaps a hundred thousand dollars worth of computer time at commercial rates. In dollar terms the cost could be put at roundly a million dollars, or about the same as the extra cost to the region of operating with tight environmental standards for one day.

The last five chapters in this volume, numbers 15 through 19, deal with one or another aspect of environmental policy. Chapter 15 'Environmental Policy' starts with the premise that the state of natural resources in the United States, including policy at the national level with respect to them, is a matter for deep concern. The policies are fragmented, suffering from multiple schizophrenia, and grossly over dependent upon direct regulation rather than on modification of the defective system of economic incentives, which is a primary source of resources and environmental problems in the first place. The paper explores this proposition using the concepts of mass balance and common property resources introduced in Chapter 13. It goes on to explore in some detail ways in which the defective system of economic incentives could be corrected including changes in natural resources tax policy and fees for the use of common property resources.

Chapter 16 'State Liability for International Environmental Degradation: An Economic Perspective' deals with an aspect of environmental policy about which there is relatively little literature, principles of state liability for damages occurring outside its borders but resulting from activities within them. State responsibility and liability are not clearly defined with respect to environmental degradation. Given this, the paper defines and analyses four major possible principles of assigning state responsibility and discusses the economic meaning of those principles based on the criterion of economic efficiency.

In the 1960s an extensive debate occurred as to the neutrality of property rights as regards resource allocation. This came to be known as the 'Coase controversy'. As it happens a fairly casual set of remarks in a publication of mine became one epicenter of this debate. The remarks were contained in a publication considering among other things the traditional Pigovian solution of taxing an externality-causing activity, in this case the discharge of water pollutants. The question arose as to whether a system of subsidy payments (later termed bribes in the literature) could be made equivalent to changes or taxes as regards allocative effects. I claimed that in principle it could but the information requirements for doing so were impossibly large and therefore it was not interesting as a practical policy alternative. A number of papers appeared later in the literature disputing that even in principle the two could be made equivalent. Chapter 17 'Bribes and Charges in Pollution Control: An Aspect of the Coase Controversy' restates my argument in some detail, including the use of a general equilibrium model. The conclusion I stated earlier holds.

Chapter 18 'Pollution, Prices and Public Policy' presents data, analysis, and research results in support of a proposed 'positive program' for environmental management in the United States. It examines alternative strategies based explicitly upon the recognition that at their core, pollution problems result from the failure of the market system to generate the proper incentives for the allocation and management of a particular type of resources – those with common property characteristics. It starts with water and air pollution and then considers the failure of incentives in environmental management in general. The centerpiece of the 'positive program', proposed in this paper, is point four of the nine point program. Point four states 'of substances whose discharge is not absolutely forbidden, or whose use is not controlled by input taxes, levy national effluent or emission taxes at levels that provide a genuine incentive for control. Special provision could be made to assist firms that suffer particularly adverse effects that they can demonstrate. Where emission taxes cannot practically be collected, taxes should fall on inputs leading to discharge of deleterious substances. It must be recognized, however, that placing the tax on anything but the pollutant itself narrows the range of possible responses'. While there was only modest support for the use of fees and taxes in environmental policy at the time these words were written, there is now intense interest and discussion, worldwide, of such approaches. It currently often proceeds under the rubric 'green taxes'.

The final paper in this part and in this volume, is a rather extended review of a book 'The Economy of the earth' by a notable moral philosopher. The stated objective of the book is to 'bury' environmental and resource economics. It is a frontal attack on resources and environmental economics and all of its many practitioners, with a number of references specifically to my work. In the review I find his analysis severely lacking being largely based on a fundamental misconception of how representative government works. I conclude: 'Economists as well as philosophers and political scientists understand that, in the final analysis, in a democracy, choices about the level of provision of public goods must be made politically. But in this process, cost is always important and benefit information, where it can usefully be developed, is also important, especially since we appear to be on the steep slope of the marginal cost curve for many of our environmental programs. In this context, environmental and natural resource economics seems more relevant than ever, not irrelevant as the author claims to have shown'.

This is perhaps a suitable note on which to conclude this introduction except to observe that my opinion seems to be borne out by the boom in interest in resource and environmental economics in academic and research institutions and in government, worldwide.

PART I

Perspectives

[1]

"The Economics of Natural Resources," by Allen V. Kneese, is reprinted, with permission, from Population and Resources in Western Intellectual Traditions, edited by Michael S. Teitelbaum and Jay M. Winter (New York, The Population Council, 1989), pp. 281-309. A supplement to Population and Development Review vol. 14.

The Economics of Natural Resources

ALLEN V. KNEESE

ECONOMISTS HAVE STUDIED NATURAL RESOURCES from the earliest days of the profession and for good reason. Resources are seen as the basis for national prosperity, power, and wealth. For example, the ability to harness energy resources in new ways is recognized as perhaps the major factor underlying the industrial revolution. Even more fundamental, food supplies depend on forests, fisheries, and agricultural land.

Yet only relatively recently have broad theories been developed specific to natural resources and energy economics. Previously, examination of these fields relied upon the general economic theories used to analyze other commodities. Now, however, economists recognize that certain special characteristics of natural resources require theories that account explicitly for these characteristics.

Only in the last generation have agricultural land, forests, and fisheries been perceived and described as renewable resources. Of course, this does not imply unconditional renewal. Such resources are self-renewing at a limited rate, which may itself depend on the size of the stock in existence at any given time and on the extent and nature of human intervention into the stock dynamics. Regardless, *renewable resources* is an apt and useful term.

In contrast, minerals and many energy commodities now are seen as depletable or nonrenewable resources—resources for which only a limited, concentrated stock exists for allocation over all time. For these resources, a central issue involves when they should be extracted and used. Using a given portion of a stock at one time precludes the option of using that portion at another time.

Even more recently have the environmental resources—air, water, open space—also been seen as renewable or, in some cases, depletable resources. The image of environmental resources, fisheries, and wild animal stocks as common property resources owned by everyone and hence by no one has played an enormous role in economic reasoning about these resources in recent decades. Furthermore, economists systematically have in-

281

corporated concepts of materials balance into theories of the flow of physical materials from the natural environment, through the economy, and back into the natural environment. And only since the early 1970s have energy resources been given major attention as a matter for theorizing, empirical testing, and policymaking.

Thus, there now exists a set of concepts that unite the field of natural resource economics. While these concepts also are finding application in other branches of economics, their formalization has been motivated by the need to better understand natural resource issues.

Economics may be necessary to understand the use and abuse of natural resources, but it is not sufficient. Indeed, most important energy and natural resource issues are inherently interdisciplinary, requiring integration of information from some combination of physics, engineering, chemistry, biology, ecology, political science, and law.

Current theories reflect this interdisciplinary reality. Materials balance concepts from physics now are fundamental to economic theories of the environment. Population dynamics concepts from biology and ecology are intertwined with economic concepts in renewable resources theories. Thermodynamic concepts and concepts of energy conservation are basic to theoretical work on natural resources.

Resource economics: The state of the art

The study of resource economics thus has required and motivated researchers to reach out beyond their own disciplines and to integrate ideas from other fields. In some of the most recent work this has extended, at least in an experimental manner, to such fields as formal ethical theory and concepts from information theory.

I address these ideas in the second part of this essay, which deals with frontier issues in the field. In that section I hope to show that the era of theory building is not over in resource economics, that in fact the field is in a considerable state of ferment.

In the first part of this essay I discuss what I see as a half dozen of the main themes in the received body of resource and environmental economics. The underlying problem that animates all of them is a concern with resource scarcity. Indeed, all of economics is concerned with scarcity, for in a world without scarcity (of labor, capital, information, natural resources) there is no economic problem. The problem of scarcity of natural resources may be exacerbated by rapid population growth. Let us start therefore with a classical statement of the problem of scarce natural resources.

1 Diminishing returns and resource scarcity: The Malthusian debate

Thomas Malthus could be viewed as the first natural resource economist, even though he is most widely known for his work on population. In 1798, he published his *Essay on Population*, a clear and forceful version of the seminal idea of diminishing returns to increased effort in the presence of a scarce resource. The scarce resource, in his view, was the stock of agricultural land, which he took to be absolutely limited. (David Ricardo later built a theory of scarcity on the assumption that land was not absolutely limited but progressively declined in quality as more of it was exploited.)

Harold Barnett and Chandler Morse (1963) succinctly state the basic Malthusian proposition:

> Malthus' famous *Essay on Population* may be credited with having widely propagated the belief that natural resource scarcity impairs economic growth. His doctrine is based on presumed natural law. That natural resources are limited and population multiplies continuously, subject to a biological restriction, are taken as nature-given facts. In the absence of social preventive checks, population increases to the limits of subsistence. The limits of nature constitute scarcity. The dynamic tendency of population to press continually to the borders of subsistence is the driving force. The incompatibility of a finite amount of agricultural land with provision of subsistence to a continually increasing population entails an eventual decline in output per capita and cessation of growth. This is the economic scarcity effect. (p. 52)

The idea of diminishing returns to effort expended upon the land became generally accepted in economics. The concept was accepted for generations as intuitively obvious. Perhaps the most famous English economist of the late nineteenth and early twentieth century, Alfred Marshall (1920), wrote:

> . . . our law [of diminishing returns] states that sooner or later (it being always assumed that there is meanwhile no change in the arts of cultivation) a point will be reached after which all further doses will obtain a less proportionate return than the preceding doses. (p. 153)

But by the middle of the twentieth century, it became clear that a great deal of growth in fact had occurred in the developed world without an apparent diminishing return to effort. Part of this growth was simple expansion as new geographic regions were occupied and developed and labor and capital were applied to them. But it also was apparent that the "arts of cultivation" or, more generally, technological progress in man's ability to find and exploit resources had much to do with it. In 1963, Barnett and Morse's

Scarcity and Growth was published, to less notice than it merited. In this now classic work, the authors explored the importance of technological change and resource substitution in combating resource scarcity. They also reported an empirical test to determine whether real resource costs have risen over the long term, which would indicate scarcity in an economic sense. Their methods and data need not detain us here, but the authors concluded:

> Our empirical test has not supported the hypothesis—let us call it the "strong hypothesis"—that economic scarcity of natural resources, as measured by the trend of real cost of extractive output, will increase over time in a growing economy. Observing the extractive sector in the United States from 1870 to 1957, we have found that the trend in the unit cost of extractive goods as a whole has been down—not up. (p. 199)

A later extension of the time series confirms the conclusion (Barnett, 1979, p. 175).

Thus, one main theme in resource economics involves the question of whether resources are becoming more scarce. Almost two centuries ago, Malthus and others thought such increasing scarcity to be imminent and obvious. But so far, in an economic sense (rising real cost of resources), this scarcity is not apparent. Whether one believes it will become so in the future depends heavily on whether one views the world through the eyes of a technological optimist or a technological pessimist. But in the very long run, as I point out in the Frontiers section, even technological optimists must contemplate profound changes in the way natural resources are used.

2 Optimal depletion

As suggested, the economic theory of natural resource use commonly distinguishes between depletable or exhaustible resources and nondepletable or renewable resources. But the distinction is not always clear. A renewable resource can be exhausted, as with the extinction of a species. Indeed, Hans Landsberg has argued that when time, space, quality, and considerations of reversibility are taken into account, few if any resources are inexhaustible (Landsberg, 1983). But the distinction has played a large role in economic theorizing concerning natural resources, and I will adhere to it, at least for now.

In the late nineteenth century, the problem of resource depletion came to the attention of economists in a somewhat different context than it had to Malthus, as Britain, France, Germany, and Russia competed ever more strenuously to establish colonies and spheres of influence. In considerable measure, colonialism sought to gain control over resources seen to be inherently scarce. The question then raised by economists was: Is there an optimal depletion path for an exhaustible resource? The models developed in this field of study were, and are, "macro" in the sense that typically it is assumed that there is a single undifferentiated resource stock (perhaps of varying quality) for an entire economy. Alternatively, it may be assumed that there is a single extractive industry composed entirely of identical competitive firms.

In the first reasonably widely known article on the economics of exhaustible resources, L. C. Gray (1914), using the graphical methods characteristic of the time, recognized that a depletable resource was different from an ordinary good in that it is limited in total quantity and is not producible. As we have seen, one outcome of this point is that a unit of such a resource used today leaves a unit less of it to use tomorrow. In other words, using it today involves not only the cost of contemporary extraction but also an additional cost—that of not having it available for use in the future. This additional opportunity cost is referred to variously in the literature, perhaps most commonly as a user cost. The practical result of defining such a cost is that unlike a producible resource, for which the efficiency condition is that price equal incremental production cost, the condition for an exhaustible resource is that price equal incremental production cost plus user cost. But how should user cost vary over time? Gray perceived that the answer hinged, in a key way, on the interest rate or, equivalently, on the rate of discount. He anticipated a general result for the simplest case. Given a well-defined quantity of the exhaustible resource, assuming extraction costs do not rise with increased extraction, and assuming demand continues until exhaustion, user cost must rise over time at the rate of interest.

To see this, consider the following situation. If user cost—the difference between incremental production cost and price—rises less than the rate of interest in period two, it would have paid to increase extraction in period one and to invest the additional proceeds at the market rate of interest. Conversely, if user cost promised to rise at a rate higher than the rate of interest, it would pay to reduce production in the present period and to borrow money at the rate of interest to increase production in the second period. Equilibrium occurs when the two rates are equal.

For this extraordinarily simple example, intuition seems adequate to derive the answer. But more realistic cases require more powerful methods. For example, what happens when extraction costs increase as the resource is depleted and the quality of the remaining stock declines? The method of calculus of variations was applied to this type of question by Harold Hotelling (1931) in a classic article. The problem of optimal depletion addressed by Hotelling is one of a class of optimization problems in which the quest is not for a number (scalar) but for an optimal path (function) through time or across space. Hotelling's approach and results were relatively neglected until

recently, probably because the mathematics were difficult and most economics curricula did not include much mathematical training for at least a generation after his article appeared. His work and most subsequent work
assumed no technological change.

Economists revived interest in the matter of optimal depletion theory
in the 1960s, and this interest greatly accelerated in the 1970s. Most newer
work addresses the "optimal-path" problem using contemporary mathematical (optimal control) methods. A key question in the newer work is how to
handle technological change. I will return to this subject in the section on
Frontiers.

3 How quickly to use a renewable resource

Living natural resources experience a life cycle. In some cases, as with most
field crops, this cycle is annual and not much under the control of man. With
others, like fish or, particularly, forests, the life span is longer and the stock is
manageable through the scheduling of harvest. In the classic example of
when to cut a standing forest, the manager faces conflicting choices. If the
forest is not mature and still growing, he can wait another year and produce
more lumber from a given stand. But if he does this he will forgo the interest
he could have earned on the income he would receive if he cut now.
Moreover, he would forgo interest on all earnings from future cuttings that
would be similarly delayed if harvesting is done in a succession of cycles of
equal length.

The problem is, given that the forest tends to grow more slowly as it
ages, when is the optimum time to cut if one wishes to maximize the present
value (discounted future income) from managing the forest? In a seminal
1849 paper, Martin Faustmann derived the solution for a simple situation in
which the forest is used exclusively for timber production, and with prices,
costs, the growth function, and the interest rate known and unchanging over
time. The rigorous derivation requires the use of calculus. But if we simplify
the problem further by concentrating on a single harvest and neglect all costs
and gains that may occur in the future as a result of the harvest decision, the
solution becomes intuitive. Again, as in the case of optimal depletion, the
solution depends in a pivotal way on the interest rate.

Under the circumstances postulated, the manager should harvest at the
time (year) at which the additional gain from delay—the value of additional
timber growth—exactly equals the interest he could earn on the money he
gets for harvesting now, minus harvesting costs. The period from the start of
regeneration of a harvested forest to another harvest is known as the rotation
period. When future forgone interest is considered, the solution indicates a
slightly shorter rotation time.

Over the years, the Faustmann solution has, until quite recently, stood fast along with several published interpretations and extensions (Gaffney, 1957; Samuelson, 1979). For example, in analyzing the Faustmann solution vis-à-vis the maximum sustained yield criterion beloved of foresters, Paul Samuelson defined maximum sustained yield as based on the assumption of an even flow of harvest aimed at producing the greatest average flow of value per year. He showed that such a policy results in the selection of longer rotation periods than the economically optimum policy and amounts to ignoring the interest rate.

Despite its long tenure, the Faustmann solution has only very limited relevance to the conditions under which multiple-use forestry management is conducted by public agencies in the United States. One of the main reasons is that the managers of these lands must, in addition to considering timber harvests, consider the various nonmarket amenity services such as recreation, water flow, and wildlife that are influenced by alterations in the standing stocks of timber. When these are considered, the problem becomes immensely more complicated.

Michael Bowes and John Krutilla (1985) have recently addressed the problem of multiple use. Their methodology, which involves a rather advanced mathematical technique known as dynamic programming, produces conclusions that are interesting, if somewhat disillusioning, in the light of Faustmann's simple and straightforward outcome:

> The general multiple use harvesting policy is seen to be complex. No simple rule of thumb is likely to describe the harvest. We see that sometimes younger stands are harvested, leaving older ones uncut. We may choose to briefly delay regeneration. We rarely cut a particular stand at the same age twice in succession during the initial periods. The forest areas may be managed with some areas set aside for specialized purposes—old growth or clearing for wildlife. We may choose to specialize over time with the land producing high timber yields in some periods and high recreation benefits in others. Even flow policies are not inherently desirable long-run goals. The optimal harvest age is unlikely to be at the age of maximum sustained yield. Indeed, long even flow rotations, far from being the desirable compromise policy for multiple use management, may simply provide both uneconomic timber and a poor balance of age classes for nontimber use. Perhaps most importantly we see, from these examples, that the harvesting decision can be extremely sensitive to factors about which we have little empirical knowledge. (p. 566)

4 Models of economic growth and natural resources

The development of economic growth models is among the more significant accomplishments by economists, including some resource economists, since

World War II. These models are "aggregative" in the sense that they deal with total measures of such variables as labor, capital, income, saving, investment, and (sometimes) resource depletion for entire national economies.

Some early versions of aggregative growth models are often referred to as Keynesian because a number of the seminal ideas underlying them stem from J. M. Keynes's great work, *The General Theory of Employment, Interest, and Money.* Keynes himself did not advance a formal model of economic growth, but basic ideas of the early aggregative growth models, like the "multiplier" and the "accelerator," stemmed from his thought.

The first generation of such models are usually referred to as Harrod–Domar models.[1] They were based on what Lawrence Klein (1962) has called "the great ratios of economics," including the savings–income ratio (propensity to save) and the capital–output ratio (acceleration principle).

It is not my intent to review these early efforts in detail, but merely to give the reader unfamiliar with them an impression of their nature. A basic proposition of the Harrod–Domar models is that a change in the rate of investment flow will have two effects. On the one hand, it will affect aggregate demand through its effect on national income (the multiplier effect); on the other hand, it will affect the productive capacity of the economy (the acceleration effect).

In this type of model, equilibrium is defined as a situation in which investment stimulates aggregate demand just enough to use up the potential capacity it generates. In other words, generated demand must equal productive capacity and vice versa. The basic question for this type of model is the following: Is there a time path of investment that will satisfy this equilibrium requirement, and, if so, what is it? The basic result of the Harrod–Domar models is proof that such time paths do exist and can be defined for various capacity–capital ratios and marginal propensities to save.

These early, highly simplified models could be criticized on a number of grounds. One is that they do not take into account the time lags—for example, between investment and capacity expansion—that characterize the real world and that may give rise to cyclical phenomena. One line of further development, therefore, was to build models containing explicit time lags and employing difference equation techniques for their solution.

Another line of early criticism pertained to the extremely simple form of the production function (that is, the mathematical function relating outputs to inputs) embodied in the model, which simply posits production capacity to be proportional to invested capital. One result of this simplistic assumption is an inherent instability in the behavior of the Harrod–Domar models. To avoid either surpluses or shortages of productive capacity, investment growth must be carefully guided along a "razor's edge."

In later work, Robert Solow (1956) showed that the razor's edge result is an artifact of the particularly simple (and unrealistic) form of the production function in Harrod–Domar models. Because output in the model is stated as a function of capital alone, it is implicitly assumed that labor is combined with capital in a fixed proportion. Solow analyzed a growth model in which labor and capital can be combined in varying proportions. Thus, in general form his production function is

$$\pi = f(K, L)$$

where π is aggregate output, K is the capital stock, and L is the labor force. Solow showed that for a linearly homogenous production function (in which an increment of a fixed set of inputs always yields the same increment in output regardless of the scale of output) containing both labor and capital, a growth pattern of investment could result that represents an equilibrium with inherent stability properties. For present purposes, it is important to note that natural resources played no role in the Harrod–Domar models.

The traditional economic view, as exemplified by the Harrod–Domar models (and their relatives and offspring), and building on the much older concept of a production function, attributes output to "factors of production," notably labor and capital. Resource flows are not normally regarded as essential factors of production. Yet, this seems to flagrantly contradict the fact that the economic system could not function for a minute without a large flow of available energy (essergy)[2] and materials.

Some economists have faced this issue and offered a rebuttal of sorts. They argue that one can suppose without major error that resources are, in effect, infinitely substitutable by labor and/or capital. This assumption is, in fact, implied by the choice of two favorite forms (Cobb–Douglas and constant elasticity of substitution—CES) of production functions. Moreover, an important attribute of the assumed free market is that impending scarcity "casts a shadow," so to speak, in the form of rising prices. This, in turn, automatically triggers technological substitution of capital—or of other resources—for the scarce resource on the supply side and the altered consumption patterns on the demand side. Increased supply, coupled with decreased demand, brings supply and demand back into balance, and the market clears. Thus, actual shortages never occur in a perfectly functioning free market, provided the elasticity of substitution between reproducible capital and exhaustible resources is sufficiently large. It follows, incidentally, that in the received paradigm, economic growth can, in principle, continue indefinitely without resource constraints. Certainly there are many well-documented historical examples of technological substitutions that have "come to the rescue" in the above sense. Moreover, plausible nonscarce substitutes for most—if not all— so-called scarce resources can be identified by any competent technologist. (For instance, see the well-known article "The age of substitutability," by H. E. Goeller and Alvin Weinberg, 1976).

But the standard view of the resource situation noted above is not shared by all economists. For instance, it has been noted by Robert Ayres (1978) and others that substitution of capital for scarce resources has physical limits if scarce resources (either mass or energy) must be embodied in the capital itself. They show that if energy is embodied in capital, the first law of thermodynamics—conservation of mass/energy—precludes boundless economic growth unless a limitless supply of energy (essergy) is available. On the other hand, if the production function is constrained by the availability of some scarce material species, even constant consumption is impossible unless the critical scarce materials can be recovered and recycled with 100 percent efficiency either from waste or from the Earth's crust. The former possibility appears to be ruled out by the second (entropy) law of thermodynamics. Indeed, it is on this basis that Nicholas Georgescu-Roegen (1979a and b) denies even the possibility of a steady-state economy in the long run, still less a perpetually growing one. These considerations take us to the boundaries of our understanding of relationships between scarce resources and economic growth.

I will discuss these issues further in the section on Frontiers. But before doing so, I will address two more main themes. One is the emergence of environmental economics, as a part of natural resource economics, and its relation to classical welfare theory. The second is the application of an applied economics technique, benefit–cost analysis, to resource and environmental issues.

5 Economic welfare and the emergence of environmental economics

Coincident with the rise of the modern national state there arose a body of doctrine called mercantilism, which held that money was a store of wealth and that the overriding object of a state was to earn money abroad by importing as little as possible. The mercantilists sought to serve the purposes of monarchies, which in turn sought the political and economic supremacy of their nation.

In the eighteenth, nineteenth, and twentieth centuries, however, especially in Britain, France, the Scandinavian countries, and the United States, a body of economic doctrine arose that called into question the main premises of mercantilism. Moreover, this body of thought has displayed an enduring fascination with market processes. The result is an elaborate structure of theory that explains and evaluates the functioning of market processes under highly idealized conditions. Today, therefore, when economists speak of the market, they usually have a particular intellectual construct in mind—not the corner grocery store or even the stock exchange. This conceptual, or in recent decades, mathematical, model is the product of an evolutionary process going back at least as far as Adam Smith's *Wealth of Nations,* which was published at the close of the eighteenth century.

The model derived from the observation of a curious phenomenon. Economic activities such as farming, mining, industrial production, selling, and finance were unplanned and, on the surface at least, apparently entirely uncoordinated. Yet, in the end there seemed to be order in the results (the often-used modern illustration of this rather amazing situation is that the right number of cartons of milk wind up in the right number of households in New York every day, yet the whole process starts with the conception of a calf, perhaps in Wisconsin). Adam Smith saw clearly that prices—the powerful signaling and incentive (information) forces generated by private exchange in markets—were at the core of a process that, through the decisions of many independent economic units, transformed resources into products and distributed them to consumers: hence, his famous reference to "the invisible hand." Clearly, in spite of occasional spectacular failure, markets do display an orderly and directed production process. But economists also have been very interested to discover whether this order was purely orderly or whether it might have other desirable or normative properties as well.

Welfare economics, which has nothing to do with welfare programs in the ordinary sense, concerns itself with such questions. Its practitioners have found that the results of an ideal market process are not only efficient but also desirable if a basic value judgment is accepted and if the market-exchange economy has certain structural characteristics.

The value judgment is that the personal wants of the individuals in a society should guide the use of society's resources. This is also the premise at the root of Anglo-American political theory.

The three structural characteristics are that:

1 All markets are competitive: no particular firm or individual can affect any market price significantly by decreasing or increasing the supply of goods and services offered. In this sense, all participants in the market-exchange process must be small units. A good example is an individual grain grower. He can sell or hold his crop as he wishes, his decision having no effect on the market price for grain.

2 All participants in the market are fully informed about the quantitative and qualitative characteristics of goods and services and the terms of exchange. This can, of course, be only approximately true in any market.

3 And, as is usually implicit, all valuable assets can be individually owned and managed without violating the competition assumption. This, plus competitive market exchange, implies that all costs of production and consumption are borne by the producer and consumer.

If these conditions hold, it could be concluded that the best social solution to the problem of allocating society's scarce resources to alternative

ends is to limit the role of government to deciding questions of income distribution, providing rules of property and exchange, and enforcing competition, while allowing exchange of privately owned assets in markets to take
care of the rest.

Market exchange, under these circumstances, with each participant
pursuing his own private interest, will lead to a "Pareto optimum," named
for the Italian economist and sociologist who first stated it. Perhaps the simplest way of intuitively grasping the meaning of such an optimum is to regard
it as a situation where all possible gains from voluntary exchange have been
exhausted. Money is the medium of exchange, and prices are the terms of
exchange at which real goods and services of all kinds are traded. Under the
conditions postulated, an exchange takes place only when both parties feel
they benefit by it. When no one can be better off without someone else being
worse off, the optimum has been reached. Pareto optimality has been demonstrated to result from exchange in theoretical competitive market models
that contain labor markets, markets for intermediate goods, and markets for
consumer goods—or, in other words, from a reasonably complete if highly
abstract characterization of the functions performed in an actual market
economy. The proof that ideal markets can achieve a Pareto optimum may be
regarded as the basic theorem of modern welfare economics.

We must be careful to note the exact sense in which a Pareto optimum
can be equated with a maximum position of economic welfare in a society. A
Pareto optimum is efficient in fulfilling consumer wants. This means, to put
it in a slightly different way, that if the use of any productive service were
changed, or if any consumer good or service were made available to a consumer other than the one who had a claim to it, someone would have to be
made worse off. This concept of the efficiency of a whole economic system is
a rather subtle idea but a vastly important one. But we must be clear that a
Pareto optimum is the highest welfare position for the society only in relation
to the particular distribution of rights to assets that exists. It says nothing
about the justice of the distribution of claims. I will return to this point in the
Frontiers section.

For some decades a few economists, voices in the wilderness, argued
that while the model provided a highly useful insight into the functioning of
market processes, in reality there were serious departures from the model. Of
particular pertinence for environmental concerns, they claimed (although
they did not quite put it that way in their day), was that the third structural
assumption indicated above—the holding of all valuable assets in discrete
units of private property—was a severe simplification of reality for existing
economies. At the turn of the present century, Alfred Marshall in his *Principles
of Economics* (already cited under theme 1) had introduced, along with most
of the other major ideas found in contemporary market theory, the notion of
external costs and benefits. These terms describe instances in which the activ-

ities of one fiscally independent economic unit, let us say a firm, directly affected the position of another fiscally independent unit, say a consumer, without the intervention of the market. Early examples were offered that were environmental in nature—sparks from a locomotive engine setting fire to a farmer's field, or, on the external benefit side, a beekeeper's bees pollinating an orchard owner's apple trees. In the last four or five decades, writers like A. C. Pigou, in Britain, and William Kapp and William Baumol, in the United States, called attention to what they regarded as the importance of such phenomena in actual economic systems.

While well taken, it is fair to say that their warnings carried very little weight within the profession. Perhaps it was because the structure of market theory—welfare economics—was so tightly and elegantly developed that there was a great reluctance to modify it, especially if those modifications were to be "messy."

During the 1960s and especially toward the end of that decade, a number of economists began to come to grips with environmental problems. A fair amount of theoretical development ensued, as well as a substantial amount of applied work. Both lines of activity have continued to accelerate in the 1970s and the 1980s. What happened to make people, including economists, suddenly so acutely aware of environmental pollution? I believe three things that have come upon us slowly, but more or less simultaneously, are chiefly responsible.

First, recent decades have seen immense increases in industrial production and energy conversion. Associated with these are massive flows of materials and energy from concentrated states in nature to degraded and diluted states in the environment. This has begun to alter the physical, chemical, and biological quality of the atmosphere and hydrosphere on a truly massive scale. Furthermore, scientists and technicians now have the means to detect even very small changes in these natural systems so that we are much more aware of what is happening.

Second, "exotic" materials are being introduced into the environment. The near-alchemy of modern physics and chemistry has recently subjected the world's biological systems to strange, unnatural inputs to which they cannot adapt (or at least not quickly); or adaptation may occur in some species but not in others, and thus the balance of species is upset.

Third, because of general affluence, ordinary folk have come to expect standards of cleanliness, safety, and wholesomeness in their surroundings that were the exclusive province of the well-born or rich in earlier times.

What is to be done in the face of these profound new forces in the world? And why did existing market institutions not cope with them at all well? To answer, we must try to understand the basic causes of the pollution problems that affect the economies of most of the nonsocialist industrialized world (the socialist world has its own set).

As a first step toward gaining insight into the origins of this growing divergence between private ends and social ends, it is useful to invoke one of the most basic physical principles—that of mass balance (the first law of thermodynamics).[3] When minerals, fuels, gases, and organic materials are extracted and harvested from nature and used by producers and consumers, their mass is not altered except in trivial amounts. The mass of material residuals (commonly, wastes or by-products) generated in production and consumption activities must be about equal to that extracted initially from nature.

Market exchange works to allocate the services of material objects to those who desire them most, but their physical substance remains intact. This fact has important implications for the allocation of resources in a market system: namely, while most extractive harvesting, processing, and distributional activities can be conducted relatively efficiently through the medium of exchange of private ownership rights, the inevitable residual mass returned to the environment goes heavily into what economists call common property resources. The same is true of residual energy. Common property resources are those valuable natural assets that cannot, or can only imperfectly, be reduced to private ownership. Examples are the air mantle, watercourses, the oceans, complex ecological systems, large landscapes, and the electromagnetic spectrum. The nature of all these resources violates the third structural assumption for an efficient market—that all valuable assets can be individually owned and managed without violating the competition assumption.

One need not ever have heard of the discipline of economics to know what will happen when open and unpriced access to such resources is permitted, and careful study of particular common property or common pool problems confirms that intuition: unhindered access to such resources leads to overuse, misuse, and the degradation of quality. Market forces are marvelously efficient in allocating owned resources, but they work to damage or destroy common property resources.

The laws of conservation of mass and energy have always existed. But at lower levels of population and economic activity, the return of "used" materials and energy to the environment has only local effects, most of which can be dealt with by local government measures to improve sanitation in the immediate vicinity of cities. Thus, butchers can be moved, sewers can be installed, and streets can be cleared of trash and offal.

But, as economic development proceeds, more and more material and energy are returned to the environment. Indeed, some forces press in the direction of increasing the proportion of residual waste to final usable output; the need to mine progressively lower quality ores or to use shales for the production of oil is a case in point. Larger areas or "problem sheds" are affected, and greater numbers of people more remotely located in both space and time suffer adverse impacts. Common property assets, which cannot enter into market exchange, are progressively degraded because industries and individuals use them as dumps at no cost to themselves, even though important assets associated with other uses are degraded or destroyed.

In summary, a great asymmetry has developed in the effectiveness and efficiency of economic incentives inherent in market systems. On the one hand, the market works well in stimulating the exploitation of basic resources and in processing and distributing them, but it fails completely in the efficient disposal of residuals to common property resources.

Seen from this perspective, it is clear that Marshall's external costs are not freakish random effects. They are a systematic part of the economic development process in economies where common property resources have become increasingly scarce, and they present a problem of collective management that different governments have undertaken in various ways.

What I have described here could fairly be represented as today's conventional view of environmental economics. In the Frontiers section I will raise some questions about this viewpoint.

6 Benefit–cost analysis

An applied welfare economics technique called benefit–cost analysis has played a very large role historically in natural resource economics and, more recently, in environmental economics as well. This mode of analysis initially was developed to evaluate water resources investments made by federal water agencies in the United States, principally the US Bureau of Reclamation and the US Army Corps of Engineers. The general objective of benefit–cost analysis in this application was to provide a useful picture of the costs and gains from making investments in water development. The intellectual father of the technique is often said to be Jules Dupuit, who in 1844 wrote a frequently cited study, "On the measure of the utility of public works." In this remarkable article, Dupuit recognized the concept of consumer's surplus[4] (a central concept in the modern application of benefit–cost analysis) and saw that consequently the benefits of public works are not necessarily equal to the direct revenues that the public works projects will generate.

Early contributions to benefit–cost analysis generally came from the federal agencies responsible for water development. In fact, such agencies have long been aware of the need for economic evaluation of projects, and the benefit–cost procedure is now embodied in agency policy and in government legislation. As examples, in 1808 Albert Gallatin, President Jefferson's secretary of the treasury, issued a report on transportation programs for the new nation in which he stressed the need to compare the benefits and the costs of proposed waterway improvements. The Federal Reclamation Act of 1902, which created the Bureau of Reclamation and was aimed at opening the American West to irrigation, required analysis to establish the repayment capacity of projects. The Flood Control Act of 1936 proposed a feasibility test based on utilitarian welfare economics that requires that the benefits to "whomsoever they accrue" must exceed costs. This directive told the agencies to ignore the distribution of benefits and costs and give attention only to their total amounts.

In 1946, the US Federal Interagency River Basin Committee appointed a subcommittee on benefits and costs to reconcile the practices of federal agencies in making benefit–cost analyses. In 1950, the subcommittee issued a landmark report entitled "Proposed practices for economic analysis of river basin projects." While never fully accepted either by the parent committee or the federal agencies, this report was remarkably sophisticated in its use of economic analysis and laid such an intellectual foundation for research and debate as to set it apart from other major reports in the realm of public expenditures. This document also provided general guidance for the routine development of benefit–cost analysis of water projects that persists to the present day.

Following this report came some outstanding publications from the research and academic communities. Several books appearing over the past quarter century have clarified the welfare economics concepts applicable to water resources development and use and have explored the fundamental rationale for government activity in the area. For example, Otto Eckstein's 1958 book, *Water Resources Development: The Economics of Project Evaluation*, is outstanding for its careful review and critique of federal agency practice with respect to benefit–cost analysis.

A clear exposition of principles together with applications to several important cases was prepared by Jack Hirschleifer and collaborators in 1960. Other reports appeared during the early 1960s. One, which was especially notable for its deep probing into applications of systems analysis and computer technology within the framework of benefit–cost analysis, was published in 1962 by a group of economists, engineers, and hydrologists at Harvard University (Maass et al.). The intervening years have seen considerable additional work on the technique and its gradual expansion to areas outside the field of water resources.

The most striking development in benefit–cost analysis in recent years has been its increasing application to the environmental consequences of new technologies and scientific and regulatory programs. For instance, the Atomic Energy Commission used the technique to evaluate the fast breeder reactor research and development program, and the technique has also been applied to other potential sources of hazard and environmental pollution. Its development and application to environmental issues were accelerated by a Reagan administration directive requiring the benefit–cost analysis of "major" federal regulations.

Even while benefit–cost analysis was limited largely to the relatively straightforward problem of evaluating investment in water resources, economists actively debated the proper way of handling both empirical and conceptual difficulties with the technique. Some of the discussion centered primarily on such technical issues as ways of computing consumer surplus and how best to estimate demand functions for various outputs. Other issues were more clearly related to questions of value and equity, including whether the distribution of benefits and costs among individuals needed to be accounted for or whether it was adequate to consider, as the Flood Control Act directed, only aggregates, and the question of the appropriate rate of time discount to use on water projects.

Application of the technique to issues like the development of nuclear energy, the storage of atomic waste, man-induced climate change, and the regulation of toxic substances complicates both the empirical and value issues found in water resource applications. There are several reasons for this.

First, while water resource applications often involve the evaluation of public goods[5] (in the technical economic sense of goods exhibiting jointness in supply), most outputs pertain to such things as irrigation, navigation, flood control, and municipal and industrial water supplies, which usually can be reasonably evaluated on the basis of market price information. But in the newer applications, we are dealing almost entirely with public goods, where market surrogates are much more difficult to establish—for example, a magnificent vista obscured by air pollution.

Second, such matters as nuclear radiation and toxic materials relate to exposure of the entire population or large subpopulations to very subtle influences of which they may be entirely unaware. It is difficult to know what normative value individual preferences (upon which the economic theories of demand and consumer surplus are built) have under these circumstances.

Third, the distributional issues involved in these applications entail not only monetary benefits and costs, but also the distribution of actual physical hazard. While it is not impossible that monetary equivalents to these risks could be developed, the ethical issues appear to be deeper than just the economic returns involved. This is especially so if compensation is not actually paid to losers, as in practice it is unlikely to be.

Fourth, we are in some cases dealing with long-term effects that could extend to hundreds of thousands of years and to great numbers of human generations. This raises the question of how the rights and preferences of future generations can be represented in the decision process. Realistically, the preferences of the existing generation must govern. The question is whether simple desires of existing persons are to rule or whether it is necessary to persuade the present generation to adopt some ethical rules of a constitutional nature in considering costs imposed on future generations.

The new applications of benefit–cost analysis bristle with ethical and value issues. I turn to a further discussion of these in the next section.

Frontier issues in resource economics

7 Ethical foundations

Much of the recent questioning by resource economists about the ethical foundations of their subject (see, for example, Page, 1977 and Kneese and Schulze, 1985) stems from the types of concerns just expressed. For instance, standard benefit–cost analysis discounts the future and therefore gives little regard to events beyond a few decades hence. This has led economists and (lately) moral philosophers to question the nature of our obligations to future generations in the face of resource depletion and potential environmental degradation. These concerns fall under the heading of sustainability.

The idea of managing resources so as to maintain a sustainable yield has appealed to many conservationists, but the concepts they have put forward have often drawn the criticism of economists, as is explained under theme 3 above. Some economists, however, have been attracted to close relatives of the sustainable yield concept in considering questions about our obligations to the "further future," as some philosophers put it. In an early instance, S. V. Ciriacy-Wantrup (1952) advocated requiring a "safe minimum standard of conservation" as a matter of resource and environmental policy: "A safe minimum standard of conservation is achieved by avoiding the critical zone—that is those physical conditions, brought about by human action, which would make it uneconomical to halt and reverse depletion" (p. 253).

In more recent writings, Talbot Page (1982) has elaborated a related idea. He argues that preserving opportunities for future generations is a commonsensical minimal notion of intergenerational justice. He writes:

> It seems sensible to focus on and limit our responsibility to what we can foresee and control. As future opportunity is more in our control than future utility, it would seem that opportunity is a more sensible object of intergenerational justice. With some effort we can control the form of the heritage to be passed on to the next generation. It is beyond the control of the present generation to ensure that the next one will be happy or hardworking. It is beyond our control to increase their welfare; we can only assure them of certain opportunities for happiness that we foresee will be essential. But we *can* preserve certain essentials, such as the valuable parts of the cultural and natural resource base. If we cannot ensure that these will in fact be passed on to future generations, we can at least keep from ensuring that they will not be passed on. (pp. 53–54)

From his writings, it is clear that Page includes environmental resources in his concept of the "resource base."

The idea of sustainability might also find support in the ideas of the moral philosopher John Rawls, whose *A Theory of Justice* (1971) has been exceptionally widely noted and commented upon. Rawls's just society is based on principles contracted with the mutual consent of all of society in an "original position," behind what he calls a "veil of ignorance." Behind the veil, everyone has the general knowledge for determining what principles of justice will regulate society, but lacks knowledge about his own individual case. Rawls writes:

> [N]o one knows his place in society, his class position or social status; nor does he know his fortune in the distribution of natural assets and abilities, his intelligence and strength, and the like. Nor, again, does anyone know his conception of the good, the particulars of his rational plan of life, or even the special features of his psychology such as his aversion to risk or liability to optimism or pessimism. More than this, I assume that the parties do not know the particular circumstances of their own society. That is, they do not know its economic or political situation, or the level of civilization and culture it has been able to achieve. The persons in the original position have no information as to which generation they belong. (p. 137)

Rawls goes on to formulate principles of justice that he thinks would be chosen by society behind the veil of ignorance, so that: "each person is to have an equal right to the most extensive basic liberty compatible to similar liberty for others"; and "social and economic inequalities are to be arranged so that they are both: (a) reasonably expected to be to everyone's advantage, and (b) attached to offices and positions open to all" (p. 150).

These are principles for intragenerational justice. To the extent that he treats the intergenerational question at all, Rawls views it primarily in terms of the present generation's duty to save. But this is unsatisfactory because in an intergenerational context, one of the important ideas of the "original position" is that it links all generations together with a common perspective. In the original position, there is no shift in time perspective from one generation to another. It seems plausible that if those in the original position did not know which generation they were going to be part of, they would emphasize intergenerational equity for the same reasons that Rawls supposed that they would do so in developing principles of intragenerational justice. Rawls's theory may be taken to imply an egalitarian system of values.

I proceed now to a discussion of two other systems of ethical beliefs that have dominated the discussion of welfare and justice in economics. These are utilitarianism in its various forms and the Pareto criterion or libertarianism.

In classical utilitarianism, individual or collective actions were to be taken in such a manner as to maximize the good of the whole society. Thus, it is quite possible that a person would be called upon to take an action

injurious to himself for the good of the whole. By contrast, neoclassical utilitarianism requires that the individual maximize only his own utility. As indicated under theme 6, neoclassical welfare economics demonstrates that,
under certain very restrictive conditions, this results in a welfare maximum
for the whole economic system, for a given distribution of claims to assets.
Thus, neither classical nor neoclassical utilitarianism is concerned with the
distribution of income, but they are indifferent to it in distinct ways. Classical
utilitarianism is indifferent to the overall distribution of income as long as
measured utility is maximized; neoclassical utilitarianism does not claim to
be able to measure utilities or to compare them across individuals. Therefore,
neoclassical utilitarianism must take the distribution of income as fixed in
proving its welfare theorem and must also admit that there is a welfare maximum that corresponds to every conceivable income distribution and, as
such, it cannot choose among them. Choice of income distribution must be
based on concepts other than utility, such as justice. Page (1982) comments
on these matters in an illuminating way:

> To state the matter a little more soberly, many economists rejected classical
> utilitarianism in favor of its neoclassical version when they decided that utility
> was entirely nonobservable. At the same time it became clear that most of the
> structure in economics could be preserved by thinking in terms of preference
> orderings instead of quantitative utilities. Preference orderings have the advan-
> tage of being, at least in principle, observable by choices actually made.
>
> If interpersonal comparisons of utility are impossible, then we are no longer
> able to maximize the sum of utilities across people. So the neoclassical utilitar-
> ian defends a weaker kind of maximization process in which each one maxi-
> mizes his own utility. The classical utilitarian's moral principle, which says to
> maximize the sum of utilities, is strong in the sense that it sometimes directs
> people to act against their own selfish interests. The corresponding, weaker
> neoclassical utilitarian's moral principle says that we should move toward Par-
> eto optimality. This principle is weaker in not requiring individuals to act
> against their own selfish interests. It is also weaker because in many situations
> it does not tell us what to do (it is a partial ordering). (p. 45)

Thus, the most modern versions of economic welfare theory are said to
be ordinal utility theories, while the classical utility theories assume measurable or cardinal theory. It is now possible to see where benefit–cost analysis (theme 6) sits in all this. Actually, it is an amalgam of classical and
neoclassical ideas. It is neoclassical in assuming the maximization of individual utilities rather than the utility of the whole, but it is classical in that in
actual quantitative application it must, contrary to the neoclassical tradition,
assume both measurable and comparable utility. However, it cannot actually
measure utility, and to get around this fact—to exclude considerations of income distribution and to maintain its logical integrity—it must make some

very strong assumptions. For example, in its simplest form benefit–cost analysis must assume that the marginal utility of income is constant and equal for everyone. Under this assumption, in terms of maximizing net total utility, it does not matter who gets a dollar's worth of benefit or who bears a dollar's worth of costs. In this simple but very unrealistic case, the to-whomsoever-they-accrue criterion of the Flood Control Act corresponds to neoclassical welfare maximization.

The second ethical system is an amalgam of a number of ethical principles embodied in part in a Christian ethic (the Golden Rule) as well as in the US Constitution (individual freedoms prevail except where other persons may be harmed). These views emphasizing individual rights have been formalized by Robert Nozick (1974) in a strict libertarian framework. We are not concerned here with changing the initial position of individuals in society to some ideal or at least acceptable state, as was the case in the ethical systems discussed earlier, but rather in benefiting all or at least preventing harm to others, even if those others are already better off. This ethic has often been embodied by economists in the form of a criterion requiring "Pareto superiority"—that is, an unambiguous improvement in welfare requires that all persons be made better off by a change in resource use or at least as well off as before. Any act is then immoral or wrong if anyone is worse off because of it. Any act that improves an individual's (or several individuals') well-being and harms no one is then moral or "right."

This criterion, while seemingly weak—it does not call for redistribution—can block many possible actions if they redistribute income so as to make anyone worse off, however slight the effect may be and regardless of intent. To satisfy a libertarian or Pareto criterion requires that gainers from a particular social decision must actually compensate losers. In practice, this rarely occurs in public policy decisions, at least not fully, and in some important situations it is technically impossible. This criterion, while appealing strongly to a sense of fairness, is often rejected because it tends to paralyze public decisionmaking.

In a recent article, William Schulze and I (Kneese and Schulze, 1985) define these utilitarian, neo-utilitarian, and libertarian ethical systems more rigorously, developing a model that permits their illustrative application to some large issues in environmental economics. The one we chose to elaborate was the storage of nuclear wastes. The most we can claim is to have taken a step toward making ethical issues an explicit and integral part of the economic analysis of resource problems. This is truly a frontier area.

8 Economics, thermodynamics, and information

Economists normally do not think of economic activities and relationships in thermodynamic terms. When economists talk about equilibrium, they refer to a balance between supply and demand, or (looking at it another way) between prices, wages, and profits. Neoclassical economic models consider labor, capital goods, and services to be abstractions (see theme 3). The exception is resource/environmental economics, where some physical properties (e.g., mass, toxicity), as we have seen, cannot be neglected (see theme 4).

The proof of the existence of a static equilibrium (conjectured by Leon Walras and finally proven by Kenneth Arrow and Gerard Debreu), as I have also noted under theme 4, is one of the great achievements of neoclassical economics because it seems to provide a theoretical explanation of Adam Smith's price-setting "invisible hand." Unquestionably, the operation of a money-based free competitive market generates a kind of coherence, or long-range order, in contrast to the unstable price/wage anarchy that prevails, for instance, in a barter society. The static competitive free-market–based economic system described in textbooks does reflect a kind of order very similar to cooperative phenomena in physics and other realms of reality. It has also been proven, again as noted under theme 4, that an idealized market-based system tends toward a Pareto optimum—a situation where no one can be better off without making somebody else worse off—although it does not necessarily allocate resources equitably. (Equity, as indicated, is a moral concept.) Finally, the market system is, in theory, self-regulating and capable of recovering from a perturbation in demand, for instance.

Even this very abstract model of the economic system depends on resource inputs, although in most general equilibrium models, resources are assumed to be generated by labor and capital or neglected altogether. Thus, the neoclassical system is, in effect, a perpetual-motion machine. (This was emphatically pointed out in 1922 by F. Soddy, a chemist, who was ignored or ridiculed by virtually all economists of his time.) Among the first economists to stress the dissipative nature of the economic system was Georgescu-Roegen. The relevance of mass/energy conservation to environmental and resource economics was emphasized particularly by Kneese, Ayres, and d'Arge (1971).

In reality, the resource inputs to the economic system are physical: they include air, water, sunlight and material substances, fuels, foods, and fiber crops, all of which embody thermodynamically available work (essergy). Outputs, on the other hand, are "final goods" whose utility is ultimately used up and thrown away or, sometimes, recycled. Available work is expended at every stage—extraction, refining, manufacturing, construction, and even final consumption. Although total energy is always conserved, essergy, as we have seen, is not. Energy inputs like fossil fuels are rich in essergy, while energy residuals are mostly in the form of low-temperature waste heat, oxidation products, or degraded materials. Thus, the economic system in reality is absolutely dependent on a continuing flux of essergy from the environment and knowledge from structures, centrally including man. In preindustrial times, the sun provided almost all essergy in the form of wood, food crops, animals, water power, or windpower. Today, the major source, by far, is fossil fuels: petroleum, natural gas, and coal from the Earth's crust. These resources are of course exhaustible.

Evidently, the real economic system looks somewhat like a "dissipative structure," in the sense described by Ilya Prigogine and Isabelle Stengers (1984): it depends on a continuous flow of essergy (the sun or fossil fuels) as well as information in more familiar form—not instantly recognized as essergy (although the two can be proven to be equivalent). And the system exhibits coherent, orderly behavior. In fact, it is self-evidently capable of growth. Economic growth can be of two distinct kinds. First, an economic system can, in principle, expand like a balloon without technological or structural change. It simply gets bigger, as capital and labor inputs increase proportionally. This kind of quasi-static growth can lead to increased final consumption per capita while maintaining its equilibrium, but only by producing more of everything, in fixed ratios. (This is possible only if there are no economies or diseconomies of scale, which is an unrealistic but common economic assumption.) Also, there has to be a nonscarce input, "nature," in order for this process to continue indefinitely. (Most growth models, as we have seen, contemplate this kind of growth.)

The second kind of economic growth adds evolutionary changes in structure. These changes are driven by innovations—new products, new processes—that result not only in quantitative increases in per capita consumption, but also in qualitative changes in the mix of goods and services generated by the economy. In general, this kind of growth involves increased complexity and organization.

Quasi-static growth of the first kind can be modeled theoretically as an optimal control problem with aggregate consumption (or welfare) as the objective function. The control variable is the rate of savings diverted from immediate consumption to replace depreciated capital and add new capital to support a higher level of future consumption. The rate of growth in this simple model is directly proportional to the rate of savings, which, in turn, depends on the assumed depreciation rate and an assumed temporal discount rate to compare present and future benefits. Note that assumptions about the operation of the market play almost no role in this type of growth model. Savings, in this model, can be voluntary or enforced by government. These are the types of growth models discussed under theme 3.

It is noteworthy (and unfortunate) that most economic development programs in the Third World for at least two decades following World War II were based on the generalized Harrod–Domar models; this approach assumed a primary role for aggregate capital investment and depended on central planners to maintain balance between the capital needs of various sectors. Harrod himself called this balancing process "walking on the razor's edge." As I noted, however, Solow later showed that the Harrod–Domar models' extreme sensitivity to balancing is an artifact of their particular choice of production function. But empirical research carried out as early as the 1950s by Moses Abramovitz, Solomon Fabricant, Robert Solow, and others established quite clearly that economic growth in the United States cannot be accounted for primarily in terms of increased capital inputs. In fact, the linked notion of increased factor productivity as a reflection of technological progress was introduced into economics at this time, for example by John Kendrick. The relatively poor performance of most centrally planned economic development programs is probably due in part to their focus on investment per se, to the neglect of structural adjustments and innovation (production and embodiment of knowledge).

Dynamic growth of the second, evolutionary, kind is less dependent on savings and/or capital investment. It cannot occur, however, without capital investment because new production technologies, in particular, are largely embodied in capital equipment. Technological innovation drives this kind of dynamic growth. There is ample evidence that technological progress is not an autonomous (self-organizing) process, as often assumed in economic growth models (when it has been included at all). On the contrary, knowledge and inventions are purposefully created by individuals and institutions in response to incentives and signals generated within and propagated by the larger socioeconomic system.

An actual example of the importance of knowledge and intelligence, as I have defined them, in economic development may be illuminating. This is the so-called German economic miracle following World War II. In less than a decade, the German economy recovered fully from a condition so severe that many doubted it could ever again compete in the world economy. This recovery was made possible by knowledge and intelligence, in the information theory sense, embodied in human skills, organizations, and infrastructure. Far greater amounts of capital became available to other countries—such as Iran—with far different results. This illustrates that financial capital and raw labor (the focus of most economic models) are feeble engines of development compared with embodied knowledge and skills.

It is axiomatic that technological progress is based mainly on an expanding knowledge base embodied in structures, including man. Several themes following from the prior discussion can now be summarized in terms of their implications for economic growth. First, because the economy is a dissipative structure, it depends on continuous energy (essergy) and material flows from (and back to) the environment. Such links are precluded by closed neoclassical general equilibrium models, whether static or quasi-static. Second, the energy and physical materials inputs to the economy have shifted, over the past two centuries, from mainly renewable sources to mainly nonrenewable sources. Third, dynamic economic growth is driven by technological change (generated, in turn, by economic forces or deliberate government policy) that also results in continuous structural change in the economic system. It follows, incidentally, that a long-term survival path must sooner or later reverse the historical shift away from renewable resources. This will be feasible only if human technological capabilities rise to levels much higher than current ones. But, since technological capability is endogenous, it will continue to increase only if the pace of deliberate investment in research and development is continued or even increased. In short, the role of knowledge-generating activity in retarding the global entropic increase seems to be growing in importance.

In a recent article, Robert Ayres (1987) develops a formal model that endeavors not only to include central concepts from thermodynamics and information into economic growth theory but also to move them to center stage. As we try to explain long-term growth in modern economic systems, such concepts are much more deserving of attention, in my view, than are the static or quasi-static traditional concepts of capital and labor that have dominated the economic growth and natural resources literature. A step has been made in this direction, but we still are at the frontiers of understanding.

A closing comment

Natural resource economics is an enormous subject, and I have merely sampled from it, but I trust not randomly. I hope, as a result, that the reader will see that resource economics displays plenty in the way of ideology and intellectual traditions, as well as more than a little science.

In addition to theory, a vast body of empirical work exists in the area of natural resource economics. I have chosen to neglect this almost entirely (the exception is the discussion of Barnett and Morse under theme 1, where the concern about natural resource scarcity stemmed directly from population growth) since our main concern here has been with ideas and principles, but the reader should be aware of this additional dimension.

Notes

In the preparation of this essay, the author acknowledges a special debt to Robert Ayres (Carnegie-Mellon University and International Institute for Applied Systems Analysis) and William Schulze (University of Colorado). Both have been frequent collaborators with me in various writings (published and unpublished), and I have borrowed freely from them in this article.

1 The basic publications on which this designation is based are R. F. Harrod (1936, Chapter 2) and E. D. Domar (1956). The mid-1930s also saw the development of "sectoral" growth models that disaggregate the economy by industrial sector. The basic article was published by the Hungarian-born John von Neumann in 1937; an English version appeared in 1945 (von Neumann, 1945).

2 Essergy is a relatively new concept in thermodynamics, although it is a close relative of some older ones. It depends on a set of subtle ideas about the nature of energy. Suffice it to say, it is a measure of energy available to do "work." Work in this conception is inherently a dissipative process (see Prigogine and Stengers, 1984). Therefore, while energy is strictly conserved, because of entropy, essergy is not. If full thermal equilibrium is achieved, no energy is lost but essergy becomes zero and no work can be performed because there can be no heat gradients. Rudolf Clausius, one of the originators of the entropy concept, envisaged a cosmology in which the entire universe would reach equilibrium and the result would be the famous *Wärmetod*, or heat death of the universe.

3 One speaks freely of "conservation of mass," as I have just done, although it is now realized that mass per se is not rigorously conserved. In fact, mass is totally interconvertible with energy via Einstein's famous equation $E = mc^2$. In practice, however, mass–energy conversion is insignificant except in nuclear reactions or at relativistic velocities close to the speed of light. Hence, since total energy is conserved and the mass–energy interconversion is negligible under normal terrestrial circumstances, mass can also be regarded as a separately conserved quantity in virtually all cases of economic interest.

4 The basic idea of consumer's surplus is that, if a consumer pays a price for a good or service that yields an amount of revenue less than he would have been willing to pay rather than go without the good or service, he gets an extra benefit from that good or service not reflected in the revenue yield; and that an effort should be made to include this extra benefit in the evaluation of public works.

5 Economists distinguish between private goods and public goods. Private goods exhibit a quality known as separability. To take a mundane example, if I buy and eat a banana you cannot buy and eat that same banana. The most extreme example of a public good is national defense. If it is provided for one citizen, it is simultaneously and unavoidably provided to all others in the same amount. This phenomenon, termed "jointness in supply," is the central characteristic of public goods. Many aspects of environmental quality exhibit jointness in supply.

References

Arrow, K. J., and G. Debreu. 1964. "Existence of an equilibrium for a competitive economy," *Econometrica* 22, no. 3: 265–290.

———. 1968. "Applications of control theory to economic growth," in *Mathematics of the Decision Sciences*, ed. G. Dantzig and A. Veinott. American Mathematical Society.

Anderson, K. 1972. "Optimal growth when the stock of resources is finite and depletable," *Journal of Economic Theory* 4 (April): 251–267.

Atkins, P. W. 1984. *The Second Law.* Scientific American Library (distributed by W. H. Freeman and Company).

Ayres, Robert U. 1978. *Resources, Environment and Economics.* New York: John Wiley and Sons.

———. 1987. "Optimal growth paths with exhaustible resources: An information-based model." Laxenberg, Austria: International Institute for Applied Systems Analysis, mimeographed.

———, and A. V. Kneese. 1969. "Production, consumption and externalities," *American Economic Review* 69 (June): 282–297.

Barnett, Harold J., and Chandler Morse. 1963. *Scarcity and Growth: The Economics of Resource Scarcity.* Baltimore: Johns Hopkins University Press, for Resources for the Future.

Barnett, Harold J. 1979. "Scarcity and growth revisited," in *Scarcity and Growth Revisited*, ed. V. Kerry Smith. Baltimore: Johns Hopkins University Press, for Resources for the Future.

Baumol, William J., and Wallace E. Oates. 1975. *The Theory of Environmental Policy: Externalities, Public Outlays, and the Quality of Life.* Englewood Cliffs, N.J.: Prentice-Hall.

Bentham, Jeremy. 1789. *Introduction to the Principles of Morals and Legislation.* London.

Berndt, E. R., and D. W. Jorgenson. 1973. "Production structure," in *U.S. Energy Resources and Economic Growth*, Ford Foundation Energy Policy Project, October.

Berry, R. S., Geoffrey Heal, and Peter Salamon. 1978. "On a relation between economic and thermodynamic optima," *Resources and Energy* 1 (October): 125–127.

Bowes, Michael D., and John Krutilla. 1985. "Multiple use management of public forest lands," in *Handbook of Natural Resources and Energy Economics*, ed. Allen V. Kneese and James L. Sweeney, Vol. 2. Amsterdam: North Holland.

Brillouin, Leon. 1956. *Science and Information Theory.* New York: Academic Press.

Ciriacy-Wantrup, S. V. 1952. *Resource Conservation: Economics and Policies.* Berkeley and Los Angeles: University of California Press.

Committee of the National Academy of Sciences. 1974. "Air quality and automotive emissions control," in vol. 4, *The Costs and Benefits of Automotive Emissions Control*, serial no. 19-24. Washington, D.C.: US Government Printing Office.

Daly, Herman. 1973. *Toward a Steady State Economy.* San Francisco: W. H. Freeman.

Dasgupta, P., and G. Heal. 1974. "The optimal depletion of exhaustible resources," *Review of Economic Studies*, Symposium on the Economics of Exhaustible Resources.

———, G. Heal, and M. Majundar. 1977. "Resource depletion and research and development," in *Frontiers of Quantitative Economics*, ed. M. Intrilligator. North Holland Press.

Denison, E. F. 1967. *Why Growth Rates Differ.* Washington, D.C.: Brookings Institution.

Domar, E. D. 1956. "Capital expansion, rate of growth and employment," *Econometrica* 14:137–147.

Dorfman, Robert, Paul Samuelson, and Robert Solow. 1958. *Linear Programming and Economic Analysis.* New York: McGraw-Hill.

Eckstein, Otto. 1958. *Water Resources Development: The Economics of Project Evaluation.* Cambridge, Mass.: Harvard University Press.

Ehrlich, P. R., and A. H. Ehrlich. 1970. *Population, Resources, Environment: Issues in Human Ecology.* San Francisco: W. H. Freeman.

Faustmann, Martin. 1849. "On the determination of the value which forest land and timber stands possess for forestry," English version in M. Gane (ed.) 1968, *Martin Faustmann and the Evolution of Discounted Cash Flow*, Institute Paper 42, Commonwealth Forestry Institute, Oxford University.

Fisher, I. (n.d.). *Nature of Capital and Income.* New York: A. M. Kelley.

Fisher, A. C., J. V. Krutilla, and C. J. Cicchetti. 1972. "Alternative uses of natural environments: The economics of environmental modification," in *Natural Environments: Studies in Theoretical and Applied Analysis*, ed. J. V. Krutilla. Washington, D.C.: Resources for the Future.

———. 1981. *Resource and Environmental Economics.* Cambridge: Cambridge University Press.

Forrester, J. W. 1971. *World Dynamics.* Cambridge, Mass.: Wright-Allen.

Frautschi, S. 1982. "Entropy in an expanding universe," *Science* 217 (August): 593–599.

Gaffney, M. M. 1957. "Concepts of financial maturity of timber and other assets," Agricultural Economics Information Series no. 62, North Carolina State College, Raleigh.

Georgescu-Roegen, N. 1971. *The Entropy Law and the Economic Process.* Cambridge, Mass.: Harvard University Press.

———. 1979a. "Energy analysis and economic valuation," *Southern Economic Journal* (4 April).

———. 1979b. "Comments," in *Scarcity and Growth Reconsidered*, ed. V. K. Smith. Washington, D.C.: Resources for the Future.

Goeller, H. and A. Weinberg. 1976. "The age of substitutability," *Science* 191 (February): 560–567.

Gray, L. C. 1914. "Rent under the assumption of exhaustibility," *Quarterly Journal of Economics* 28: 466–489.

Guggenheim, E. A. 1949. "Statistical basis of thermodynamics," *Research* 2: 450–454.

Harrod, R. F. 1936. *The Trade Cycle.* Oxford: Oxford University Press.

Herfindahl, O. 1967. "Depletion and economic theory," in *Extractive Resources and Taxation*, ed. M. Gaffney. Madison: University of Wisconsin Press.

Hirschleifer, Jack, James De Haven, and Jerome Milliman. 1960. *Water Supply: Economics, Technology, and Policy.* Chicago: University of Chicago Press.

Hotelling, H. 1931. "The economics of exhaustible resources," *Journal of Political Economy* 39: 137–175.

Huettner, David A. 1976. "Net energy analysis: An economic assessment," *Science* 192 (April): 101–104.

Jackson, Clement, et al. 1976. "Benefit–cost analysis of automotive emissions reductions," General Motors Research Laboratory GMR 2265.

Jaynes, E. T. 1957. "Information theory and statistical mechanics, I," *Physical Review* 106: 620.

Kamien, M., and N. Schwartz. 1978. "Optimal exhaustible resource depletion with endogenous technical change," *Review of Economic Studies* 45.

Kantor, F. W. 1977. *Information Mechanics.* New York: John Wiley and Sons.

Khinchin, A. L. 1957. *Mathematical Foundations of Information Theory.* New York: Dover.

Klein, L. R. 1962. *An Introduction to Econometrics.* Englewood Cliffs, N.J.: Prentice-Hall.

Kneese, A. V., and B. T. Bower. 1968. *Managing Water Quality: Economics, Technology, Institutions.* Baltimore: Johns Hopkins University Press.

———, R. Ayres, and R. d'Arge. 1971. *Economics and the Environment.* Baltimore: Johns Hopkins University Press.

———, and B. T. Bower. 1979. *Environmental Quality and Residuals Management.* Baltimore: Johns Hopkins University Press.

———, and W. P. Schulze. 1985. "Ethics and environmental economics," in *Handbook of Natural Resources and Energy Economics,* ed. Allen V. Kneese and James L. Sweeney, Vol. 1. Amsterdam: North Holland.

Knight, F. H. 1921. *Risk, Uncertainty, and Profit.* New York: A.M. Kelley.

Krutilla, John V. 1972. *Multiple Purpose River Development Studies in Applied Economic Analysis.* Baltimore: Johns Hopkins University Press.

———, and Anthony C. Fisher. 1975. *The Economics of Natural Environments: Studies in the Valuation of Commodity and Amenity Resources.* Baltimore: Johns Hopkins University Press.

Lansberg, Hans H. 1983. "Some thought on exhaustibility," unpublished manuscript, Resources for the Future, Washington, D.C.

Maass, Arthur, et al. 1962. *Design of Water Resource Systems.* Cambridge, Mass.: Harvard University Press.

Mäler, Karl-Goran. 1974. *Environmental Economics: A Theoretical Inquiry.* Baltimore: Johns Hopkins University Press.

Malthus, T. R. 1826. *An Essay on Population,* reprint of 6th ed. London: Ward, Lock and Company.

Manne, Alan S., Richard G. Richels, and John Weyant. 1979. "Energy policy modelling: A survey," *SRSA Journal* (January–February): 1–36.

Marshall, Alfred (1890) 1920. *Principles of Economics,* 8th ed. London: Macmillan.

Meadows, D., et al. 1972. *The Limits to Growth: A Report for the Club of Rome's Project on the Predicament of Mankind.* Universe Books.

Nicolis, Gregoire, and Ilya Prigogine. 1977. *Self Organization in Non-Equilibrium Systems.* New York: John Wiley and Sons.

Nozick, Robert. 1974. *Anarchy, State, and Utopia.* New York: Basic Books.

Odum, Howard T. 1971. *Environment, Power and Society.* New York: John Wiley and Sons.

Page, Talbot. 1977. *Conservation and Economic Efficiency.* Baltimore: Johns Hopkins University Press, for Resources for the Future.

———. 1982. "Intergenerational justice as opportunity," in *Energy and the Future,* ed. Douglas MacLean and Peter Brown. Totowa, N.J.: Rowman and Littlefield.

Pielou, E. C. 1969. *An Introduction to Mathematical Ecology.* New York: Wiley-Interscience.

Pigou, A. C. 1920. *The Economics of Welfare,* 1st ed. London: Macmillan and Company, Ltd.

———. 1952. *Economics of Welfare.* London: The Macmillan Company.

Prigogine, Ilya, and Isabelle Stengers. 1984. *Order out of Chaos.* New York: Bantam Books.

Ramsey, F. P. 1928. "A mathematical theory of saving," *Economic Journal* 38, no. 152 (December): 543–559.

Rawls, John. 1971. *A Theory of Justice.* Cambridge, Mass.: Harvard University Press.

Rifkin, Jeremy. 1980. *Entropy: A New World View.* New York: Viking Press.

Samuelson, P. A. 1979. "Wildlife habitats in managed forest: The Blue Mountains of Oregon and Washington," Agricultural Handbook no. 533. Washington, D.C.: US Department of Agriculture, Forest Service.

Shannon, C. E., and W. Weaver. 1949. *The Mathematical Theory of Information.* Urbana: University of Illinois Press.

Siebert, Horst. 1981. *Economics of the Environment.* Lexington, Mass.: D.C. Heath.

Soddy, F. 1922. *Cartesium Economics.* London: Hendersons.

Solow, R. M. 1956. "A contribution to the theory of economic growth," *Quarterly Journal of Economics* 70 (February): 65–95.

———. 1974a. "The economics of resources or the resources of economics," *American Economic Review* 64, no. 2 (May): 1–14.

———. 1974b. "Intergenerational equity and exhaustible resources," *Review of Economic Studies:* 29–45.

Stiglitz, J. 1974. "Growth with exhaustible natural resources: Efficient and optimal growth paths," *Review of Economic Studies* 41: 25–36.

———. 1979. "A neoclassical analysis of the economics of natural resources," in *Scarcity and Growth Revisited,* ed. V. K. Smith. Baltimore: Johns Hopkins University Press, for Resources for the Future.

Theil, H. 1967. *Economics and Information Theory.* Amsterdam: North Holland.

Tribus, M., P. T. Shannon, and R. B. Evans. 1966. "Why thermodynamics is a logical consequence of information theory," *American Institute of Chemical Engineering Journal* 244 (March): 55–67.

———, and E. C. McIrvine. 1971. "Energy and information," *Scientific American* 225 (September): 179–188.

US Atomic Energy Commission, Division of Reactor Development and Technology. 1972. *Updated 1970 Cost–Benefit Analysis of the US Breeder Reactor Program.* Washington, D.C.

von Neumann, J. 1945. "A model of general economic equilibrium," *Review of Economic Studies* 13:1–9.

Wan, H. J. 1971. *Economic Growth.* New York: Harcourt Brace Jovanovich.

Wicksteed, Philip. 1894. *An Essay on the Coordination of the Laws of Distribution.* London: Macmillan and Company.

Wright, P. G. 1970. "Entropy and disorder," *Contemporary Physics* 2, no. 6: 581–588.

[2]

Chapter 5

ETHICS AND ENVIRONMENTAL ECONOMICS

ALLEN V. KNEESE

Resources for the Future, Washington

and

WILLIAM D. SCHULZE

University of Colorado, Boulder

> The moral problem is a conflict that can never be settled. Social life will always present mankind with a choice of evils. No metaphysical solution that can ever be formulated will seem satisfactory for long. The solutions offered by economists were not less illusory than those of the theologians that they displaced.
>
> All the same, we must not abandon the hope that economics can make an advance toward science, or the faith that enlightenment is not useless. It is necessary to clear the decaying remnants of obsolete metaphysics out of the way before we can go forward   [Robinson (1963, p. 146)].

1. Introduction

Welfare economics, one of the foundations of conventional environmental economics, can be thought of as being an enormous elaboration of the utilitarian moral philosophy developed by Bentham, Mill, and others in the eighteenth and nineteenth centuries. There are, however, rival ethical systems that also put forward rules for individual and social moral behavior that are different from those of utilitarianism.

But why be concerned with moral philosophy in a book on environmental economics? There are two main reasons, one having its origins in economics and the other in philosophy. The first stems from the increasingly strained applications of benefit–cost analysis to large environmental issues and the concerns this raises about the adequacy, in these applications, of its conceptual, as well as empirical, basis. From the side of moral philosophy, there has been a great upsurge of interest by philosophers in the ethical implication of man's impacts on the environment. One result has been a spate of writings endeavoring to develop a nontheological, nonhumanistic, environmental ethic. The ideas of these philosophers, if accepted, would have large implications for environmental economics

Handbook of Natural Resource and Energy Economics, vol. I, edited by A.V. Kneese and J.L. Sweeney
© *Elsevier Science Publishers B.V., 1985*

which, because of its basis in welfare economics, is intensely humanistic in its orientation.[1]

In the next two sections, we elaborate first on the concerns emanating from the economic side and then from the standpoint of the new naturalistic philosophers.

Following that, we discuss several efforts by economists and others to develop criteria of "sustainability" with respect to both particular resources and the whole economic system. These are meant to provide ethical guidance concerning appropriate behavior where resource depletion or environmental degradation threaten to reduce the welfare of future generations. Particularly, we discuss the ideas of the economist Page and their relationship to the writings of the philosopher Rawls.

Then we consider a critique of all the major humanistic ethical ideas in Western philosophy after Aristotle. This critique is contained in an important recent book by the philosopher MacIntyre. This assessment sets the stage for a statement about our own stance concerning the alternative humanistic ethical systems we analyze further on in terms of their implications for environmental economics.

To permit this latter analysis to proceed with some rigor, it is necessary to state the alternative ethical ideas in their simplest possible terms. Therefore, they can in that form be linked only in a loose sense to the writings of any particular philosopher.

Having accomplished this epitomization, we apply several examples of the alternative humanistic ethics we have formalized to some particularly vexing problems in environmental economics. These are the analysis of environmental risks and the problems associated with discounting of environmental benefits and costs over long periods of time. We combine these problems in an illustrative analysis of the problem of storing radioactive nuclear wastes. Because of limitation of information, many questionable assumptions have to be made and the analysis should be taken as being nothing more than an effort to add a certain amount of concreteness to an otherwise very abstract discussion.

We close with a section that, in a sense, takes us back to the opening parts of the chapter. Here we consider a policy issue, the use of economic incentives in environmental policy, that has divided economists who emphasize economic efficiency from many environmentalists who take a different ethical view of environmental policy. This discussion focuses on an important recent book about environmental economics and ethics by political scientist Kelman. It also provides us with a vehicle for a closing statement of perspective on ethics and environmental economics.

---

[1] It is worth noting, however, in passing, that Bentham's utilitarianism was not anthropocentric. He wrote, " the French have already discovered that the blackness of the skin is no reason why a human being should be abandoned without redress to the caprice of a tormentor. It may come one day to be recognized, that the number of legs... or the termination of the os sacrum are reasons equally insufficient for abandoning a sensitive being to the same fate" [Bentham (1789), quoted in Passmore (1974 p. 14)].

In closing the present section of this chapter, we want to remark that we set out on the tasks just outlined with humility. Neither one of us is a trained philosopher, and we feel sure that professional philosophers reading this chapter would find many of the things we say, at least, simplistic. Still, we think the issues are potentially so important for the future of environmental economics that we feel the attempt must be made.

2. Ethical concerns of benefit–cost analysis

Benefit–cost analysis is discussed in other parts of this Handbook. Our intent here is not to instruct about its application, but rather to provide a brief historical perspective on why some of its newer applications are raising increasingly large ethical concerns among some economists.

Benefit–cost analysis was developed initially to evaluate water resources investment made by the federal water agencies in the United States, principally the United States Bureau of Reclamation and the United States Corps of Engineers. The general objective of benefit–cost analysis in this application was to provide a useful picture of the costs and gains from making investments in water development. The intellectual "father" of the technique is often said to be Jules Dupuit, who in 1844 wrote a frequently cited study "On the Measure of the Utility of Public Works". In this remarkable article, he recognized the concept of consumer's surplus and saw that consequently the benefits of public works are not necessarily the same thing as the direct revenues that the public works projects will generate.

Early contributions to development of benefit–cost analysis generally did not come from the academic or research communities but rather from government agencies. The agencies responsible for water development in this country have for a long time been aware of the need for economic evaluation of projects and the benefit–cost procedure is now embodied in agency policy and in government legislation. In 1808, Albert Gallatin, Jefferson's Secretary of the Treasury, produced a report on transportation programs for the new nation. He stressed the need for comparing the benefits with the costs of proposed waterway improvements. The Federal Reclamation Act of 1902 which created the Bureau of Reclamation, and was aimed at opening western lands to irrigation, required economic analysis of projects. The Flood Control Act of 1936 proposed a feasibility test based on utilitarian welfare economics which requires that the benefits to whomsoever they accrue must exceed costs. This directive told the agencies to ignore the distribution of benefits and costs and give attention only to their total amounts.

In 1946, the Federal Interagency River Basin Committee appointed a subcommittee on benefits and costs to reconcile the practices of federal agencies in making benefit–cost analyses. In 1950, the subcommittee issued a landmark report entitled "Proposed Practices for Economic Analysis of River Basin Projects". While never fully accepted either by the parent committee or the federal agencies, this report was remarkably sophisticated in its use of economic analysis and laid the intellectual foundation for research and debate which set it apart from other major reports in the realm of public expenditures. This document also provided general guidance for the routine development of benefit–cost analysis of water projects which persists to the present day.

Following this report came some outstanding publications from the research and academic communities. Several books appearing over the past quarter century have gone much further than ever before in clarifying the welfare economics concepts applicable to our water resources development and use and in exploring the fundamental rationale for government activity in the area. Otto Eckstein's (1958) book is particularly outstanding for its careful review and critique of federal agency practice with respect to benefit–cost analysis. While naturally a bit dated, this book is still well worth reading.

A clear exposition of principles together with applications to several important cases was prepared by Jack Hirschleifer and collaborators in 1960. Other reports appeared during the early 1960s. One, which was especially notable for its deep probing into applications of systems analysis and computer technology within the framework of benefit–cost analysis, was published in 1962 by a group of economists, engineers, and hydrologists at Harvard [Maass et al. (1962)]. The intervening years have seen considerable further work on the technique and a gradual expansion of it to areas outside the water resources field.

The most striking development in benefit–cost analysis in recent years has been an increasing application of the technique to the environmental consequences of new technologies and scientific programs. For example, the U.S. Atomic Energy Commission (1972) (before ERDA and the DOE were created) used the technique to evaluate the fast breeder reactor research and development program. It has also been applied to other potential sources of environmental pollution and hazard. Two studies which come to quite contrary conclusions have been made of the Automotive Emissions Control Program. The first was prepared by a Committee of the National Academy of Sciences (1974). The other study is by the research arm of a major automotive producer [Jackson et al. (1976)]. Still other studies have been or are being conducted in the area of water quality analysis, emissions from stationary sources, and toxic substances including nuclear waste disposal.

Even while the benefit–cost technique was limited largely to the relatively straightforward problem of evaluating water resources investments, there was much debate among economists about the proper way of handling both empirical and conceptual difficulties with it. Some of the discussion surrounded primarily technical issues, e.g. ways of computing consumer surplus and how best to estimate demand functions for various outputs. Others were more clearly value and equity issues, e.g. whether the distribution of benefits and costs among individuals needed to be accounted for or whether it was adequate to consider, as the Flood Control Act directed, only aggregates, and what is the appropriate rate of time discount to use on water projects.

Application of the technique to issues such as nuclear energy development programs, the storage of atomic waste, man-induced climate change, and the regulation of toxic substances aggravate both the empirical and value issues which existed in water resource application. There are several reasons for this.

First, while water resource applications often involve the evaluation of public goods (in the technical economic sense of goods exhibiting jointness in supply) the bulk of outputs pertain to such things as irrigation, navigation, flood control, and municipal and industrial water supplies which usually could be reasonably evaluated on the basis of some type of market information. In the newer applications, we are dealing almost entirely with public goods where market surrogates are much more difficult to establish.

Secondly, such matters as nuclear radiation and toxic materials relate to exposure of the whole population or large subpopulations to very subtle influences of which they may entirely unaware. It is difficult to know what normative value individual preferences have under these circumstances.

Thirdly, the distributional issues involved in these applications entail not only monetary benefits and costs, but the distribution of actual physical hazard. While it is not out of the question that monetary equivalents to these risks could be developed, the ethical issues appear to be deeper than just the economic returns which are involved. This is especially so if compensation is not actually paid to losers, as it is in practice unlikely to be.

Fourthly, we are in some cases dealing with long-lived effects which could extend to hundreds of thousands of years and many, many human generations. This raises the question of how the rights and preferences of future generations can be represented in this decision process. Realistically, the preferences of the existing generation must govern. The question is whether simple desires of existing persons are to rule or whether it is necessary to persuade the present generation to adopt some ethical rule or rules of a constitutional nature in considering questions of future generations.

The new applications of benefit–cost analysis bristle with ethical and value issues. These are the concerns raised from the side of economics.

3. The new naturalistic ethics

Some philosophers have recently chosen to address the difficult issues of ethics and policy presented by environmental concerns by abandoning humanistic philosophy altogether. These have been referred to as the "new naturalistic philosophers" [Marietta (1982)]. This group is rapidly producing a large new literature.

Actually, in many cases the discussion starts with the question of what is the nature and extent of man's obligation to nonhuman creatures – there is by now a large "animal rights" literature. From there, by some, extensions are made to nonliving entities, and by yet others, ideas having originated in humanistic philosophy are abandoned entirely and a purely naturalistic view of the ethical aspects of man in nature is advocated.

In a few instances the writing is rather hysterical and reminiscent of the more extreme kind of environmentalist prose of the later 1960s and early 1970s. For example, the main themes of a book, *Why the Green Nigger? Re-mything Genesis* [Gray (1979)] is stated by a reviewer [Shute (1980)] as follows:

> In *Why the Green Nigger?* Elizabeth Dodson Gray attempts to show that it has been the use of a male-constructed, hierarchical picture of the world (with men at the top) that has been responsible for making nature a "green nigger." Possessing no rights, feminine and inferior nature is mastered, manipulated and oppressed by superior men. This male-constructed hierarchical picture of reality, Gray says, is posing a threat to the survival of life on the planet Earth. But Gray sees hope for changing the status and treatment of nature if we understand that reality is not hierarchical, but is a "complex and dynamic web of energy" (p. 67) which men are not only dependent upon, but in which they are inextricably enmeshed as beings with value no greater than that of anything else.

Most of the writing, however, has been a sober and well-intentioned attempt by the pertinent group of moral philosophers to tussle with some hard issues. There is no hope in the scope of a chapter to comprehensively survey all the contributions to this literature, but the interested reader can find a concentrated supply of articles from it in the journal *Environmental Ethics*. We choose a few of what we take to be among the best efforts of this genre and try to state the main ideas succinctly. We start with one that is a "slight" extension of some typical humanistic type arguments, then go through one that tries to extend man's obligations to all living things, a possible rationale for Albert Schweitzer's famous "respect for life", to a further one that extends ethical standing even to nonliving things, and finally to a set of writing that abandons the humanistic anchors altogether.

The first piece is by philosopher Richard A. Watson (1979). The idea of reciprocity is frequently invoked in the philosophical discussion of morality, and Watson uses a reciprocity framework to try to explain and justify the attribution of moral rights and duties.

We pause to note that the reciprocity is used in two separate senses in the literature under consideration. In the first it refers to the possibility of *actual* reciprocal action between or among agents. In the second it is used more in the "golden rule" sense of doing to others of what you would have them do unto you.

A related idea is Kant's categorical imperative that views ethical behavior as being that which the acting party believes should be universalized into a rule so that it would apply to everyone else, including their actions toward him. The second version does not necessarily imply that real reciprocal action is possible and therefore, as can be seen in the paper following Watson's, may apply to a broader range of phenomena.

Another pause is merited to explain a further distinction. In the pertinent literature, "right" (as in "animal rights") is taken to have at least two meanings. There can be "legal rights", and there can be moral rights or "inherent rights". That nonhuman entities can have legal rights is, of course, manifest. Corporations have rights in the legal sense as do wilderness areas and laboratory animals, although in the last case, enforcement is virtually nil. The real issue is whether nonhuman entities can have intrinsic rights inherent in the thing itself (das Ding an sich).

Now to return to Watson. He claims that to say that an entity has rights makes sense only if that entity can fulfill reciprocal duties, i.e. can act as a moral agent. To be such, again he claims, an entity must be (1) self-conscious, (2) understand general principles, (3) have free will, (4) understand the given principles, (5) be physically capable of acting, and (6) intend to act according to or against the given principles. So far, this line of argument would not be surprising to a conventional ethical philosopher even though he might not necessarily agree with it. It could be taken to define a human milieu which is moral as contrasted with a nonhuman one which is not.[2]

But Watson goes on to argue that a few animals besides humans, especially chimpanzees, gorillas, dolphins, and dogs, "...which, in accordance with good behavioral evidence, are moral entities, and sometimes moral agents. On the grounds of reciprocity, they merit, at a minimum, intrinsic or primary rights to life and to relief from unnecessary suffering" [Watson (1979, p. 99)].

Again, an interpretive note. Having heard an argument of this nature, it seems that many, if not most, economists would be puzzled as to why the philosopher making it should expect anyone else to believe him. By what authority can you, the philosopher, tell me what is morally right or morally wrong? A theological explanation, which is not invoked in humanistic philosophy, might not be believed, but it would probably be regarded as an understandable argument. But this attitude misunderstands the point of view of at least some, perhaps most, ethical philosophers. They do not appeal to higher authority, but believe that if they are clever enough and think hard enough about a moral problem, they should be able to come up with principles or rules that will persuade anyone else,

---

[2] It should be noted, however, that those who argue from *real* reciprocity seem to have a lot of trouble with the rights of very young children, the insane, hopeless idiots, and the helpless old.

or at least those who have an informed and sensitive moral intuition, of their validity.

With this background, and a set of arguments that gives "moral standing" to a few chimps and such, let us turn to a set of arguments that opens a much wider field of beings to moral claims. In a widely respected, which is not necessarily the same as to say widely agreed with, article, philosopher Kenneth E. Goodpaster (1978) approaches the question of man's responsibility to nature in a different way. Instead of addressing questions raised by the inherent rights concept, he asks the question, what makes a being morally "considerable"? The issue is one raised in an earlier book by philosopher G.J. Warnock (1971). Warnock asks what is the condition of having a claim to be "considered" by rational agents to whom moral principles apply. Goodpaster rephrases Warnock's question, "...for the terminology of R.M. Hare (or even Kant) the same questions might be put thus: In universalizing our putative moral maxims, what is the scope of the variable over which universalization is to range?", and a little further on, "For all A, X deserves moral considerations from A where A ranges over rational moral agents and moral 'consideration' is construed broadly to include the most basic forms of practical respect (and so is not restricted to 'possession of rights by X')" [Goodpaster (1978, pp. 308–309)].

Still further on, he states the conclusion to which his thoughts about this question have led him. "Neither rationality not the capacity to experience pleasure and pain seem to me necessary (even though they may be sufficient) conditions of moral considerability. And only our hedonistic and concentric forms of ethical reflection keep us from acknowledging this fact. Nothing short of the condition of being alive seems to me to be a plausible and nonarbitrary criterion" [Goodpaster (1978, p. 310)].

Having as he said, "put his cards on the table", and having further introduced distinctions and terminology we do not have space to explain (thus our characterization will necessarily do offense to the richness of his arguments and ideas), he begins with a critique of how Warnock answered his own question. As a matter of deserving moral consideration, Warnock rejects the reciprocity argument used by Watson, as explained above, at least partly based on the "infants and imbeciles" argument suggested in Watson (1979, p. 99). Instead, Warnock proposes that the criterion of moral considerability arises from the capacity to suffer.

Or stated in the more formal manner introduced earlier: for all A, X deserves moral considerations from A if and only if X is capable of suffering pain (or experiencing enjoyment).

Note that this may sound utilitarian, but unlike utilitarianism, it does not provide a criterion for action, but merely for consideration, by moral agents. While according to Goodpaster, Warnock in some places writes as though he is only including humans, but by the end of the book, he has broadened his scope to include nonhumans. Still, the operative idea is sentience.

Goodpaster is not convinced. He writes, "Biologically, it appears that sentience is an adaptive characteristic of living organisms that provides them with a better capacity to anticipate, and so to avoid threats to life. This at least suggests, though of course it does not prove, that the capacities to suffer and to enjoy are ancillary to something more important rather than tickets to considerability in their own right" [Goodpaster (1978, p. 316)]. He continues, "Nor is it absurd to imagine that evolution might have resulted (indeed might still result?) in beings whose capacities to maintain, protect and advance their lives did not depend upon mechanisms of pain and pleasure at all" [Goodpaster (1978, p. 317)].

Following this line of thinking, he proposes, but does not claim to have proved, that the quality of being alive is a better claim to moral considerability than sentience.

He then considers some possible objections, especially on the part of those who have claimed that sentience is the key and therefore moral considerability should be limited to humans and a few of the higher animals. In particular, he discusses a paper by Feinberg (1974) which he takes to be the best representative of that point of view. The main point argued by Feinberg is that a being cannot intelligibly be said to deserve moral considerability unless it satisfies the "interest principle". Feinberg notes,

> The sorts of beings who can have rights are precisely those who have (or can have) interests. I have come to this tentative conclusion for two reasons: (1) because a rightholder must be capable of being represented and it is impossible to represent a being that has no interests, and (2) because a rightholder must be capable of being a beneficiary in his own person, and a being without interests is a being that is incapable of being harmed or benefited, having no good or "sake" of its own [Feinberg (1974, p. 51)].

Goodpaster objects to the claim that "interests" logically presupposes desires or wants or aims, the equipment for which is not available to plants. He states that there is no absurdity or unintelligibility in imagining the representation of the needs of a tree for sun and water in the face of a proposal to cut it down or pave its surrounding space for a parking lot. Because of plants' clear tendencies to maintain and heal themselves, he finds it very difficult to reject the idea of interests on their part in staying alive. This he contrasts with "mere things" that are not alive and therefore have no interests.

But in commenting on Goodpaster's article, philosopher W. Murray Hunt (1980) claims that even the condition of living is too narrow a criterion for moral considerability, and that "being in existence" is *at least* as plausible and nonarbitrary a criterion as is life. Hunt's argument rests on two main bases. The first is the "continuity" between living and nonliving things. The second is a counter-example to the proposition that the consideration of "being alive" is sufficient for moral considerability. His example is the problem of fulfilling the wishes of a person who has died. The being alive criterion would imply that such wishes have no moral standing, an implication that Hunt says would not be acceptable to most ethicists. He argues that if the response is that this is because he once was alive, then the criterion would have to be amended to "being alive or once having been alive". In this case, moral consideration would have to be given to "mere things", like coal, since the material composing it was once alive. Essentially, Hunt argues that having started on the "slippery slope" of abandoning strict adherence to humanism, there is no stopping point short of according moral considerability to everything in existence.

Finally, we turn to a very brief discussion of the work of some philosophers who do not even start with humanistic traditions. These are the true "new naturalistic philosophers". Aldo Leopold (1949) is the father of naturalistic ethics, and his famous statement from *A Sand County Almanac*, "A thing is right when it tends to preserve the integrity, stability, and beauty of the biotic community. It is wrong when it tends otherwise", is frequently quoted in this literature. The Summer 1982 (vol. 4, no. 2) of *Environmental Ethics* is a symposium issue, "Environmental Ethics and Contemporary Ethical Theory". In it are contained several papers of this genre. We quote the succinct description of them given in the introduction to the volume by the journal editor:

In the first paper, Peter Miller argues that psychologically based environmental ethics are ill suited to characterize natural intrinsic value. To solve this problem Miller proposes the acceptance of a metaphysical or metaethical category of richness. In the next paper, Donald Scherer argues that natural value need not depend on psychologically based judgments of human beings. Scherer imagines a series of planets with ever more highly organized levels of life, each of which yield new forms of value. These values are, Scherer argues, neither anthropocentric nor holistic. Holmes Rolston, III develops a position similar to Scherer's, but he finds value in nature beyond life: in geological, tectonic and entropic nature as well. Rolston is concerned with establishing the objective existence of nonpsychological values although he allows that there is a subjective (psychological) component as well, and finds a place for it in his view.

In closing this section, we must reiterate that we have been able to give the reader no more than a glimpse at the new literature in environmental ethics. But we trust it will give the economist reader a feel for the types of arguments made. Whether one is inclined to accept them or not, it is clear that these ideas are much too abstract, or insufficiently formed, to mesh tightly with actual public policy issues or with economic concepts. For the remainder of this chapter, with the exception of the last section, we return to the humanistic fold, and explore some of the implications for environmental economics of ideas stemming from that tradition. But first we develop a perspective on Western humanistic moral philosophy to which we hold for the remainder of this chapter.

4. A plague on all your houses, and a perspective

As our discussion so far should indicate, unanimity of view is not one of the stronger characteristics of environmental ethicists. One might think that might be true primarily of those whom their more orthodox brethren would take to be on the fringe of the discipline, such as the new naturalistic philosophers. But this is not the case. Disagreement abounds among those who espouse utilitarian views on the one hand and libertarian views on the other. The one looks to actions that maximize the good of the whole, and the other to individual rights. Others still are Kantians or Rawlsians, both emphasizing universibility, but in different contexts. Other views exist in addition. In an important recent book, philosopher Alasdair MacIntyre (1981) has performed a critical evaluation of all of the major ethical views in Western philosophy over the last few centuries and found them all wanting. To him they are a combination of fragments of the "older" (aristotelean) tradition and certain modern "novelties". He writes,

> It follows that our society cannot hope to achieve moral consensus. For quite non-Marxist reasons Marx was in the right when he argued against the English trade unionists of the 1860s that appeals to justice were pointless, since there are rival conceptions of justice formed by and informing the life of rival groups. Marx was of course mistaken in supposing that such disagreements over justice are merely secondary phenomena, that they merely reflect the interests of rival economic classes. Conceptions of justice and allegiance to such conceptions are partly constitutive of the lives of social groups, and economic interests are often partially defined in terms of such conceptions and not vice versa. None the less Marx was fundamentally right in seeing conflict and not consensus at the heart of modern social structure. It is not just that we live too much by a variety and multiplicity of fragmented concepts; it is that these are used at one and the same time to express rival and incompatible social ideals and policies *and* to furnish us with a pluralist political rhetoric whose function is to conceal the depth of our conflicts [MacIntyre (1981, p. 235)].

We share MacIntyre's skepticism about man's efforts to find principles of morality through the exercise of his powers of reason and, in his detailed analyses, he makes a convincing case that expressions of ethical views are intertwined with other less minded interests. At the same time, we find his own prescriptions, which would require re-establishment of something like an Athenian city state, equally unconvincing.

If this is the case, one may well ask, why bother with this ethical exercise at all? There are reasons. First, it is indisputably true that most people have moral beliefs and concerns. Perhaps that is what distinguishes them most from even the other higher animals. We think it is very much worthwhile to examine what implementation of those beliefs would imply for environmental economics and decisions on environmental problems – a task to which we turn in succeeding sections. Second, we have a different view of pluralistic society and the function of political processes than expressed in the quotation from MacIntyre. We believe that the pluralism of modern society is simply a fact and that the development of political processes to peacefully and reasonably fairly resolve value conflicts is a high achievement. We also believe that economic-ethical analysis can make an important contribution to informing those processes about implications of viewing things from different moral perspectives. Finally, the philosophical foundation of modern neoclassical economic thought is the ethical doctrine of utilitarianism, albeit in considerably amended form from classical utilitarianism (as we will explain subsequently). We feel that it is worthwhile to try to understand what implications other competing ethical ideas might have for the economic analysis of environmental problems. On this we also hope to make some progress in succeeding sections. Before proceeding, however, to the comparative analysis of several competing ethical systems in the context of some large questions in environmental economics, we turn briefly to the ideas of a few economists who have stepped partly out of the utilitarian framework to consider one such large question. That is our obligation to future generations in the face of resource depletion and potential environmental degeneration.

5. Sustainability

The idea of managing resources in such a way as to maintain a sustainable yield has had appeal to many conservationists. The concepts they have put forward have often drawn the criticism of economists as is explained in Chapters 2, 12 and 14 of this Handbook. However, some economists have been drawn to close relatives of the sustainable yield concept in considering questions about our obligations to the "further future", as some philosophers put it. An early instance was S.V. Ciriacy-Wantrup. In a classical book [Ciriacy-Wantrup (1952)] he advocated the idea of requiring a "safe minimum standard of conservation" as a matter of resources and environmental policy. He wrote "a safe minimum standard of conservation is achieved by avoiding the critical zone – that is those physical conditions, brought about by human action, which would make it uneconomical to halt and reverse depletion" [Ciriacy-Wantrup (1952, p. 253)].

In recent writings, economist Talbot Page (1977, 1982) has elaborated a related idea. He argues that preserving *opportunities* for future generations is a common sense minimal notion of intergenerational justice. He writes,

It seems sensible to focus on the limit our responsibility to what we can foresee and control. As future opportunity is more in our control than future utility, it would seem that opportunity is a more sensible object of intergenerational justice. With some effort we can control the form of the heritage to be passed on to the next generation. It is beyond the control of the present generation to ensure that the next one will be happy or hardworking. It is beyond our control to increase their welfare; we can only assure them of certain opportunities for happiness that we foresee will be essential. But we *can* preserve certain essentials, such as the valuable parts of the cultural and natural resource base. If we cannot ensure that these will in fact be passed on to future generations, we can at least keep from ensuring that they will not be passed on.

From his writings, it is clear that Page includes environmental resources in his concept of the "resource base".

While appealing to common sense, Page, however, also makes appeal to the ideas of two moral philosophers John Locke and John Rawls. Locke's ideas, especially that of "just acquisition" are also incorporated into modern libertarian thought. Page writes:

The most absolute claim of just acquisition is an individual's claim to work wholly created by himself. Thus, Byron had a right to burn his books, but his wife did not, without his permission. (The classical utilitarian would not see the point of this distinction and might deny Byron the right to burn his own books.) The next strongest claim of just acquisition is by an individual who "produces" an object by mixing his labor with a resource of which there is "enough and as good" left for others. The last claim, in fact no claim at all, of just acquisition [for it] concerns the resource base passed into the hands of the present generation by the mere passage of time.

By this argument, the present generation does not have a right to deplete the opportunities afforded by the resource base since it does not "own" it. This is not to say that the resource base, including environmental resources, must be held physically intact, but that when there is depletion, is must be compensated for by technological development or capital investment.

The other ethical philosopher to whose ideas Page appeals is John Rawls (1971). Rawls' book, *A Theory of Justice*, has been exceptionally widely noted and commented upon.

Rawls' just society is based on principles contracted with the mutual consent of all society in an "original position", behind what he calls a "veil of ignorance". Behind the veil, everyone has the general knowledge for determining what principles of justice will regulate society, but lacks knowledge about his own individual case. Rawls writes:

No one know his place in society, his class position or social status; nor does he know his fortune in the distribution of natural assets and abilities, his intelligence and strength, and the like. Nor, again, does anyone know his conception of the good, the particulars of his rational plan of life, or even the special features of his psychology such as his aversion to risk or liability to optimism or pessimism. More than this, I assume that the parties do not know the particular circumstances of their own society. That is, they do not know its economic or political situation, or the level of civilization and culture it has been able to achieve. The persons of the original position have no information as to which generation they belong [Rawls (1971, p. 139)].

Rawls goes on to formulate principles of justice that he thinks would be chosen by society behind the veil of ignorance so that: (1) "each person is to have an equal right to the most extensive basic liberty compatible to similar liberty for others"; (2) "social and economic inequalities are to be arranged so that they are both: (a) reasonably expected to be to everyone's advantage, and (b) attached to offices and positions open to all" [Rawls (1971, p. 68)].

These are principles for intragenerational justice. To the extent that he treats the intergenerational question at all, and his treatment is very limited, he views it primarily in terms of the present generation's duty to save. Page finds this argument unsatisfactory. To him, one of the important ideas of the original position is that it links all generations together with a common perspective [Page (1977, p. 203)]. In the original position, there is no shift in time perspective from one generation to another. It seems plausible that if those in the original position did not know which generation they were going· to be part of, they would emphasize intergenerational equity for the same reasons that Rawls supposed that they would do in developing principles of intragenerational justice.

We now proceed to the task of taking five humanistic criteria, utilitarian, benefit–cost analysis (which is an application of a special case of neo-utilitarianism), egalitarian, libertarian, and elitist, and simplifying and defining them in such a way that they can be used in a reasonably rigorous manner for analyzing large problems in environmental economics. This is not an exhaustive list of possible criteria, but they do reasonably span the range of the essence of ideas advocated by humanistic philosophers in the last few centuries. Later we will show how three of these (utilitarian and libertarian as compared to benefit–cost analysis) can be applied to the problem of storing radioactive wastes.

6. Comparative analysis of ethical systems

6.1. Introduction

As we have already said, developing these criteria for analysis involves some radical simplification of the complex frameworks developed by actual moral philosophers. We turn first to utilitarianism. We discuss it somewhat more fully than our other systems. There are two reasons for this: (1) a highly evolved (neo-classical) utility theory is the basis for modern welfare economics and, to an extent, its applied arm, benefit–cost analysis, and (2) the other ethical systems we present are in our version much less complex.

6.2. Utilitarian

In *classical* utilitarianism, individual or collective actions were to be taken in such a manner as to maximize the good of the whole society. Thus, it is quite possible that a person would be called upon to take an action injurious to himself for the good of the whole. *Neoclassical* utilitarianism requires that the individual maximize only his own utility. Neoclassical welfare economics demonstrates that, *under certain very restrictive conditions*, this results in a welfare maximum for the whole economic system, *for a given distribution of claims to assets*. Therefore, neo-classical utilitarianism must take the distribution of income as fixed in proving its welfare theorem and admit that there is also a similar welfare maximum that corresponds to every conceivable income distribution and, as such, it cannot choose among them. Choice of income distribution must be based on concepts other than utility, e.g. justice. Page comments on these matters in an illuminating way:

> To state the matter a little more soberly, many economists rejected classical utilitarianism in favor of its neoclassical version when they decided that utility was entirely nonobservable. At the same time it became clear that most of the structure in economics could be preserved by thinking in terms of preference orderings instead of quantitative utilities. Preference orderings have the advantage of being, at least in principle, observable by choices actually made. This rejection of classical, quantitative utility has two repercussions noteworthy for our purposes.
>
> First, if interpersonal comparisons of utility are impossible, then we are no longer able to maximize the sum of utilities across people. So the neoclassical utilitarian defends a weaker kind of maximization process in which each one maximizes his own utility. The classical utilitarian's moral principle, which says to maximize the sum of utilities, is strong in the sense that it sometimes directs people to act against their own selfish interests. The corresponding, weaker neoclassical utilitarian's moral principle says that we should move toward Pareto optimality. This principle is weaker in not requiring individuals to act against their own selfish interests. It is also weaker because in many situations it does not tell us what to do (it is a partial ordering).
>
> Second, the rejection of observable utilities leads toward a behaviorist or black-box theory of the mind. The only evidence allowed for inferences about happiness or satisfaction is observable behavior: for example, actual purchases

in markets. Evidence from introspection is looked upon with suspicion, as are surveys of stated preferences. The situation is a little like trying to infer the structure of a car's motor by observing the car's operation. With this black-box approach it is not surprising that we might be limited to simple concepts of the motor [Page (1982)].

Thus, the most modern versions of economic welfare theory are said to be *ordinal* utility theories while the classical utility theories assume measurable or cardinal theory. It is now possible to see where benefit–cost analysis sits in all this. Actually, it is an amalgam of classical and neo-classical ideas. It is neo-classical in that it assumes the maximization of individual utilities rather than the utility of the whole, but it is classical in that in actual quantitative application it must, contrary to the neo-classical tradition, assume both measurable and comparable utility. However, it cannot *actually* measure utility, and to get around this fact, to exclude considerations of income distribution, and to maintain its logical integrity, it must make some very strong assumptions; for example, that the marginal utility of income is constant and equal for everyone.[3] Under this assumption, in terms of maximizing net total utility, it does not matter who gets a dollar's worth of benefit or who bears a dollar's worth of costs.

But before turning to our next ethical system, which emphasizes the *justice* of income distribution rather than the maximization of utility (although the principle can, as we shall see, be interpreted in utility terms), it will be a useful lead in to discuss the income distribution question a little more formally. Here we assume, as does benefit–cost analysis, that utility is cardinal and maximized by individuals. However, we assume, consistent with the classical utilitarian view, that marginal utility diminishes with increased income for each individual and may differ between individuals.

First, we will examine the case, consistent, for example, with the view of Pigou (1920), where all individuals have (about) the same relationship between utility and income. Thus, for example, if two individuals, A and B, have utility U_A and U_B, respectively, derived from incomes Y_A and Y_B, respectively, and if Mr. B is initially wealthier than Mr. A., $Y_B^0 > Y_A^0$, then B has a higher total utility level than A. But given the traditional utilitarian assumption of diminishing marginal utility, that the utility curves in Figure 5.1 flatten out as income increases, it is easy to show that society's total utility could be enlarged by giving A and B the same income, $\overline{Y}$. This follows because, by raising A's income from Y_A^0 to $\overline{Y}$, we get a gain in utility of ΔU_A compared to the loss in utility ΔU_B to B, resulting from lowering B's incomes from Y_B^0 to $\overline{Y}$. Note that $Y_B^0 - \overline{Y} = \overline{Y} - Y_A^0$, so we take income away from B to give to A to get a gain in total utility, $U_A + U_B$, since $|\Delta U_A| > |\Delta U_B|$, or A's gain exceeds B's loss.

---

[3] Although it must be pointed out that benefit–cost analysis may be defensible in logically looser ways.

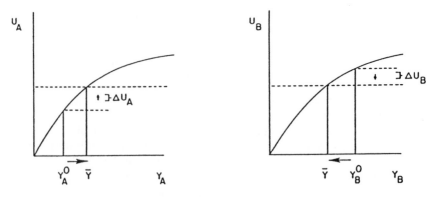

Figure 5.1. Utility as a function of income for two hypothetical individuals.

The same solution results from solving the following problem:

$$\max U_A(Y_A) + U_B(Y_B)$$
s.t.
$$Y_A + Y_B = Y_A^0 + Y_B^0,$$

which implies at the optimum that $\Delta U_A/\Delta Y_A = \Delta U_A/\Delta Y_B$, or that the rate of increase of utility with income (marginal utility) must be equal for the two individuals. Since the two individuals in our example have similar utility functions, marginal utilities are equated where incomes are the same, $Y_A = Y_B = \overline{Y}$.

But, on the other hand, we can assume different individuals have different utility functions. For example, Edgeworth (1967), in *Mathematical Psychics* (first published in 1881) argues that the rich have more sensitivity and can better enjoy money income than the poor. We then end up with a situation like that shown in Figure 5.2. Y_A^* and Y_B^* are utility maximizing incomes for A and B because the marginal utilities of income are equated. Mr. A gets more income then Mr. B because he obtains more utility from income than B does. In Edgeworth's view, Mr. A by his sensitivity should have more money to be used in appreciating fine wine than Mr. B who is satisfied with common ale. In the extreme case, Mr. A might be a "utility monster", i.e. his marginal utility of money income might everywhere exceed Mr. B's marginal utility of income, in which case all of society's income should go to Mr. A.

Clearly, then, in the utilitarian framework, depending on beliefs about the particular nature of utility functions, any distribution of income can be justified, ranging from an egalitarian viewpoint (Pigou) to an elitist viewpoint (Edgeworth).

There do exist ethical systems which are totally egalitarian on the one hand, and totally elitist on the other. These diametrically opposed ethical systems are described next. We realize that probably very few people, if pushed to the wall,

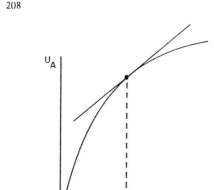
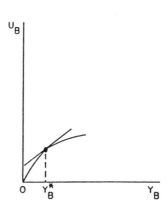

Figure 5.2. Society maximizes total utility by giving more income to A than to B.

would actually support the implementation of either of these extreme systems in its pure form. But is is useful to analyze them as representing the ends of the spectrum.

6.3. Egalitarian

The egalitarian view holds that the well-being of a society is measured by the well-being of the worst off person in that society. This criterion would, if fully adopted, lead to a totally equal distribution of utility.[4]

The egalitarian criterion can be expressed mathematically in economic terms as follows: for two individuals A and B, where utility is denoted U, if $U_A < U_B$, we maximize U_A subject to $U_A \leq U_B$; if $U_B < U_A$, then we maximize U_A subject to $U_B \leq U_A$. If we reach a state where $(U_A = U_B$, then we maximize U_A subject to $U_A = U_B$. The implication of this for redistribution of income is that we begin by adding income to the worst off individual (taking income away from wealthier individuals) until he catches up with the next worst-off individual. We then add income to both individuals until their utility levels (well-being) have caught up to the third worst off, etc. Eventually, this process must lead to a state where $U_A = U_B = U_C = U_D \ldots$ for all individuals in a society, where all utilities are identical, or to a state where further redistributions will make everyone worse off, e.g. through negative impacts on incentives. This criterion can be written more

---

[4] Contemporary egalitarianism is often associated with the writing of John Rawls but it should be clear from even our brief earlier discussion of his ideas that his theory of just distribution is much more complex than the simple egalitarian criterion we analyze here.

compactly for a two-person society as max min $\{U_A, U_B\}$, so we are always trying to maximize the utility of the individual with the minimum utility. Implicit also in the argument is the assumption that the individuals' utility functions with respect to income are about the same. Thus, this ethical criterion would work toward a relatively equal distribution of income among individuals in a single generation or, in an intergenerational situation, across generations.

6.4. Elitist

An elitist criterion can be derived as the precise opposite of the egalitarian criterion. The well-being of society is measured by the well-being of the best off individual. Every act is "right" if it improves the welfare of the best off and "wrong" if it decreases the welfare of the best off.[5]

We discuss this criterion primarily to display the polar opposite of the egalitarian case. But it should be mentioned elitist arguments are sometimes made and action taken on them even in our society. The gasoline shortage of the summer of 1979 moved Senator Hiyakawa of California to comment: "The important thing is that a lot of the poor don't need gas because they're not working." Economic productivity can in this sense rationalize a defined "elite". Thus, concepts of merit can be elitist in nature, e.g. those who produce the most "should" have the largest merit increases in salary (even though they may already have the highest salaries).

The income distribution implied by this criterion is not simply to give all of society's wealth to the best off. This is true because, if between two individuals A and B we are attempting to

$$\max \max \{U_A, U_B\},$$

or to maximize the utility of the individual who can attain the greatest utility, we must first find the solution for $\max U_A$, and then separately for $\max U_B$, and then pick whichever solution gives the greatest individual utility. Obviously, it will usually be better to keep B alive to serve A, i.e. to contribute to his well-being than to give B nothing if A is to be best off. Thus, subsistence (which in a broader context might include minimal education, health care, etc.) is typically required for B. Similarly, if we have two succeeding generations, it may well be "best" for the first generation to save as much as possible to make the next generation better off. This attitude has been manifest among many immigrants to the United States with respect to their children. Thus, an elitist viewpoint may support altruistic behavior.

---

[5] The elitist view is often associated with the writing of Fredrich Nietzsche, *Beyond Good and Evil* (1886). But, as noted in connection with Rawls, Nietzsche's ideas are much more complex than the simple criterion adopted here.

The ethical systems we have considered so far have been in one way or another concerned with the welfare or the "goodness" of the whole society. There is another class of ethical systems that concerns itself not with society at large, but with protecting individual rights. In regard to public policy issues, as we will see, the two are usually in conflict.

6.5. Pareto criterion

The fourth ethical system is an amalgam of a number of ethical principles embodied in part in a Christian ethic (the Golden Rule) as well as in the U.S. Constitutional viewpoint that individual freedoms prevail except where others may be harmed. These views which emphasize individual rights have been formalized by Nozick (1974) in a strict libertarian framework. We are not here concerned with changing the initial position of individuals in society to some ideal state, as were all the ethical systems discussed earlier, but rather in benefiting all or at least preventing harm to others, even if those others are already better off. This ethic has been embodied often by economists in the form of a criterion requiring "Pareto superiority", that is, an unambiguous improvement in welfare requires that all persons be made better off by a change in resource use or at least as well off as before. Any act is then immoral or wrong if anyone is worse off because of it. Any act which improves an individual's or several individuals' well-being and harms no one is then moral or "right".

If, for example, Mr. A and Mr. B initially have incomes Y_A^0 and Y_B^0, then we require for any new distribution of wealth (Y_A, Y_B) – for example, if more wealth becomes available and must be distributed – that

$$U_A(Y_A) \geq U_A(Y_A^0)$$

and

$$U_B(Y_B) \geq U_B(Y_B^0),$$

or each individual must be at least as well off as he initially was. Any redistribution, e.g. from wealthy to poor or vice versa, is specifically proscribed by this criterion. Thus, this criterion, while seemingly weak – i.e. it does not call for redistribution – can block many possible actions if they do as a side effect redistribute income to make *anyone* worse off, however slight the effect may be. Often, then, to satisfy a libertarian or Pareto criterion requires that gainers from a particular social decision must *actually* compensate losers. In practice, in public policy decisions, this rarely occurs, at least fully, and there are some important situations where it is technically impossible.

7. An application to the problem of nuclear waste storage

This section is an attempt to look beyond traditional benefit–cost analysis to consider long-term nuclear waste storage from both an ethical and an economic perspective. The problem of nuclear waste storage exemplifies the type of problem where benefit–cost analysis has most often been criticized. We conjecture that the dual problem of valuing risk to life of future generations motivates these criticisms. To address these issues, we develop formal economic models of alternative decision criteria for nuclear waste storage which are based, at least loosely, on alternative ethical positions. In particular, two of the alternative ethical positions outlined above are contrasted with each other and then with standard benefit–cost analysis.

First, the utilitarian ethic is used to explore the notion that the proper goal for society is to pursue the good of the whole both across individuals and more importantly across time. Second, we focus on the Pareto or libertarian criterion where the protection of individual rights both across individuals and across generations is more important than the good of the whole. It should be noted that these criteria share two characteristics. First, in each, man is the measure of all things. Thus, in contrast to the naturalistic ethic the only value of the natural environment is the value human beings place on it, and so nonhuman objects have no intrinsic value. Second, these criteria are consistent with the neo-classical notion of economic efficiency and are consequentialist in nature – focusing on outcomes of the decision process. It should be noted that philosophers view any consequentialist analysis to be at least utilitarian in spirit as opposed to other humanistic ethics which focus on procedures or due process.

Given the formalization of the Utilitarian and Pareto ethics presented in the previous section, we can model the choice to store nuclear wastes using an expected utility framework as follows: we assume that there are only two generations. Generation one, the current generation, has to decide whether or not to develop nuclear facilities. Utility of generation one, $U_1(Y_1)$ depends on generation one's income, Y_1, which initially is $\overline{Y}_1$. For this illustrative example we assume that generation of one's income can be augmented by utilizing nuclear power which adds B dollars in net to income (net benefits to generation one of nuclear power) but in turn depends on generating nuclear wastes of w tons. Thus, B is an increasing function of w, $B(w)$. Income to generation one is then $\overline{Y}_1 + B(w)$. However, generation one may decide to compensate the future generation, generation two, for the hazards of nuclear waste storage imposed on them. Thus, generation one might reduce their income by C dollars to be invested for the benefit of generation two, leaving a net income of $Y_1 = \overline{Y}_1 + B(w) - C$. Generation two, with an initial income of $\overline{Y}_2$, may then receive an income of $Y_2 = \overline{Y}_2 + (1 + r)C$ if generation one invests C dollars at a rate of return r for the period of time between the two generations. If, however, the two generations are separated by 10 000 years, it is highly doubtful that compensation is possible, i.e. the odds are zero that a financial institution will survive over such a period to accumulate compound interest at rate r. Of course, we still may properly assume that risk of death to individuals in generation two, $\Pi_2(w)$, is a function of the quantity of nuclear wastes created by generation one, since nuclear wastes will still be radioactive even after 10 000 years have passed. We assume, to focus just on the intergenerational risk issue, that risks to generation one are fixed at Π_1^0. Utilizing the two ethical criteria, we will now explore under what decision rule nuclear power should be pursued by generation one, thus transferring nuclear waste to generation two.

We can summarize the notation outlined above as follows:

Π_i = probability of death in generation i,

U_i = utility in generation i where $U_i' > 0$; $U_i'' < 0$,

Y_i = income in generation i,

$B(w)$ = net benefits (additional income) of having nuclear power, an increasing function of the quantity of nuclear waste (w),

r = interest rate,

C = compensation from generation one to generation two: $C \geq 0$.

For generation one, expected utility (E_1) is equal to the probability of death times the utility obtained from initial income ($\overline{Y}_1$) plus the benefits associated with nuclear power, minus compensation paid (if any) to the future generation:

$$E_1 = \left(1 - \Pi_1^0\right)U_1\left(\overline{Y}_1 + B(w) - C\right). \tag{1}$$

The second generation's expected utility is dependent upon the probability of death as a function of the amount of nuclear waste times the utility from initial income ($\overline{Y}_2$) plus compensation paid (if any) compounded at the rate of interest, r:

$$E_2 = \left(1 - \Pi_2(w)\right)U_2\left(\overline{Y}_2 + (1 + r) \cdot C\right). \tag{2}$$

The Utilitarian criterion states that the sum of the total expected utilities of both generations, T, should be maximized;

$$\max_{w,C} T = E_1 + E_2, \tag{3}$$

where the choice variables are the levels of compensation (C) and generation of nuclear waste (w). We make the following assumptions of symmetry between generations: (1) $U_1(Y) \equiv U_2(Y)$ or both generations have the same utility functions; (2) $\overline{Y}_1 = \overline{Y}_2$ or both generations have the same initial income; and (3) $\Pi_1^0 = \Pi_2^0$ or both generations have the same initial risk. Thus, we explore an

Natural Resource Economics

egalitarian formulation of the Utilitarian ethic similar to that associated with Pigou in the preceding section.

The first-order conditions are:

$$\partial T/\partial C = -(1 - \Pi^0)U_1' + (1 - \Pi_2)U_2'(1 - r) \leq 0 \tag{4}$$

and

$$\partial T/\partial w = (1 - \Pi^0)U_1'B' - \Pi_2'U_2 \leq 0. \tag{5}$$

The decision of whether or not to build nuclear power plants thus generating nuclear wastes can be analyzed in two contexts. The first situation is that where compensation between generations is impossible or undesirable ($C = 0$) so (4) holds with inequality. The second case is where compensation is possible and desirable ($C > 0$) so (4) holds with equality. We will evaluate whether or not nuclear facilities should be built, generating waste, by evaluating $\partial T/\partial w$ at the point where $w = 0$. Rearranging (5) yields:

$$B'(0) \gtrless \frac{\Pi_2'U_2}{(1 - \Pi_1^0)U_1'}, \quad \text{for} \quad \left.\frac{\partial T}{\partial w}\right|_{w=0} \gtrless 0. \tag{6}$$

Let us consider the case where compensation between generation one and two is impossible. Utilizing the assumptions of symmetry between generations, the assumption of no compensation and $w = 0$ implies that utility in each generation is the same, or $U_2(\overline{Y}_2) = U_1(\overline{Y}_1)$. This implies the marginal utility of generation one (U_1') is equal to marginal utility of generation two (U_2'). Additionally, evaluating the decision at $w = 0$ implies the same risk levels or $\Pi_1^0 = \Pi_2(0)$. Thus, (6) can be rewritten by substituting U_2' for U_1' and $\Pi_2^0(0)$ for Π_1^0 yielding:

$$B'(0) \gtrless \frac{\Pi_2'U_2}{(1 - \Pi_2(0))U_2'}, \quad \text{for} \quad \left.\frac{\partial T}{\partial w}\right|_{w=0} \gtrless 0. \tag{7}$$

(7) states that generation one can evaluate whether or not to build a nuclear facility by determining whether the marginal benefits of nuclear power are greater than, less than, or equal to the incremental risk (Π_2') times the marginal compensation for increased risk of death or value of safety $U_2/(1 - \Pi_2(0))U_2'$ for generation two which, given our assumptions, is the same as the marginal value of safety for generation one. Assuming that compensation is impossible results in no discounting of future damages (the cost of risk to generation two). Thus, in order to pursue nuclear power (so optimally $w > 0$) the marginal benefits to generation one must be greater than the associated incremental risk to generation two times the marginal value of safety of generation two both evaluated at $w = 0$. The discount rate where no compensation is possible under an egalitarian specification of the Utilitarian ethic is thus equal to zero.

Let us now consider the decision for generation one under the Utilitarian criterion where compensation is possible and desirable. In this scenario, condition

(4) holds with equality and the assumption of equal initial income does not hold: $U_1(\overline{Y}_1) \neq U_2(\overline{Y}_2)$. Rearranging condition (4) and solving for U_1' yields:

$$B'(0) \lesseqgtr \left[\frac{1}{1+r}\right][\Pi_2']\left[\frac{U_2}{(1 - \Pi_2)U_2'}\right]. \tag{8}$$

If the marginal benefits of nuclear power are greater than or equal to the discounted value, $[1/(1 + r)]$, of the incremental risk (Π_2') to generation two, times the marginal value of safety $[U_2/(1 - \Pi_2)U_2']$ for generation two, then a policy of nuclear power should be pursued under the Utilitarian criterion. Thus, if compensation is possible under an egalitarian specification of the Utilitarian ethic the discount rate should be equal to the rate of interest.

The Pareto or Libertarian criterion can be stated as follows. If generation one's well-being is improved by using nuclear power and production of nuclear waste, then generation two must be at least as well off as before. The expected utilities for generations one and two defined in (1) and (2) can be used to state the Libertarian criterion:

$$\max_{w,c} \left(1 - \Pi_1^0\right)U_1\left(Y_1 + B(w) - C\right)$$

$$\text{s.t.} \qquad \text{(a)}$$

$$\left(1 - \Pi_2^0(w)\right)U_2\left(Y_2 + (1 + r)C\right) \geq \left(1 - \Pi_2(0)\right)U_2(\overline{Y}_2). \tag{9}$$

$$\text{(b)} \qquad\qquad\qquad\qquad \text{(c)}$$

We maximize the expected utility of generation one [term (a)] subject to the condition that the expected utility of generation two [term (b)] is greater than or equal to the initial utility of generation two [term (c)] where no nuclear waste is produced. Thus, the rights of generation two are defended by the constraint. The first-order conditions are

$$\partial L/\partial C = -\left(1 - \Pi_1^0\right)U_1' + \lambda(1 - \Pi_2)U_2'(1 + r) = 0 \tag{10}$$

and

$$\partial L/\partial w = \left(1 - \Pi_1^0\right)U_1'B' - \lambda\Pi_2'U_2 \leq 0. \tag{11}$$

Again, assuming an egalitarian symmetry between generations, the condition for evaluating the decision to build a nuclear facility from the perspective that initially $w = 0$, is obtained by rearrangement of (11) which yields:

$$B'(0) \gtreqless \frac{\lambda\Pi_2'U_2}{\left(1 - \Pi_1^0\right)U_1'}. \tag{12}$$

Only one situation relating to compensation is available for analysis in the Libertarian case due to the structure of the constraint. That is, if no compensation is possible then the amount of nuclear waste must be zero or the Pareto criterion is violated. This is, the term (b) in eq. (9) would be less than term (c) and generation two would not be at least as well off as before. Thus the only situation of interest for the decision to build a nuclear facility is where compensation for generation two due to the existence of nuclear waste is possible. Solving for λ in condition (10) assuming compensation is possible yields:

$$\lambda = \frac{\left(1 - \Pi_1^0\right)U_1'}{\left(1 - \Pi_2\right)U_2'(1 + r)}. \tag{13}$$

Substituting into (13) yields:

$$B'(0) \gtreqless \frac{1}{1 + r} \frac{U_2}{\left(1 - \Pi_2\right)U_2'}. \tag{14}$$

A policy of nuclear power should be pursued under the Libertarian ethic only when compensation is possible and the marginal benefits to generation one are greater than the discounted marginal value of risk to generation two.

We can summarize our results as follows. The Utilitarian ethic, in the case where identical initial incomes and utility functions are assumed, would require discounting only if compensation can actually be paid. Otherwise a zero discount rate is appropriate. The Libertarian case would reject nuclear waste storage outright if compensation cannot be paid, but accepts the discounting procedure if compensation between generations is possible. Since it is unreasonable to assume that compensation can be paid to generations 10 000 years or more in the future for the storing of nuclear waste, this analysis leads under the assumption of an egalitarian specification of the Utilitarian ethic, to the use of a zero discount rate or, under the assumption of a Libertarian ethic, to the outright rejection of nuclear waste storage. Traditional benefit–cost analysis, on the other hand, would almost certainly lead to the conclusion that nuclear waste storage is unimportant in the nuclear power decision since future damages would, at any usual positive rate of interest, be discounted to near zero.

8. Conclusion: Ethics and a policy debate

In discussing environmental policy, economists have tended to favor approaches that emphasize economic incentives (e.g. effluent charges) in contrast to command and control regulation (e.g. effluent standards). Many environmentalists have also supported economic incentives as part of environmental policy. A large and influential group of environmentalists have, however, been adamantly opposed to the use of charges to help manage environmental quality. This group of environmentalists and economists who advocate charges have not found it possible (or perhaps desirable) to communicate with each others positions and therefore have been unable to understand each other properly. In an important recent book political scientist Kelman (1981) attempts to interpret each group to the other.

We close this chapter with a brief discussion of that book and a statement of our own perspective on ethics and environmental economics.

In the first chapter, Kelman presents the economists' rationale for charges in a highly simplified form. The argument is that charges will be more efficient than uniform emission standards in the sense that a given level of ambient environmental quality can be attained by their use at less cost than by the implementation of standards. Theory and several quantitative case studies support this view, but the issue is a lot more complex than one would gather from this chapter. This is no real complaint, however, because, for the sake of understanding the differences between economists who support effluent charges and those environmentalists who oppose them, the relative efficiency of charges can be taken as given, for the argument is not primarily about that.

The second chapter presents a discussion of ethical theory and the case for concern about charges. This is the chapter that is most salient to our present concerns, and we will dwell mostly upon it in this discussion. We note in passing that if one only read this chapter, one would get the impression that on ethical grounds, *all* environmentalists are opposed to charges. This, as we just noted, is not true. The interviews reported in the third chapter of Kelman's book show that the community of environmentalists is divided on the question. Indeed, for a time in the 1970s, there existed a group of environmental organizations called the "Coalition to Tax Pollution". In particular, they supported a charge on sulfur compounds emitted to the atmosphere. Once again though, for the sake of ethical discussion, this split among the environmentalists does not matter. A large number of environmentalists are opposed to charges. Also, the ethical positions described in Kelman's chapter two do probably fairly characterize the group of environmentalists, both inside and outside of government, who drafted and lobbied through Congress the basic national air and water pollution legislation in the early 1970s. This legislation rejected charges and established effluent standards based on concepts of "best available technology".

The remaining chapters of the book are not of particular pertinence to the present discussion. Let us therefore return to the presentation in Chapter 2 of the ethical ideas that in Kelman's view are held by those hostile to charges. This chapter proved to us, as economists, extremely revealing and insightful. As noted in earlier discussion, in the normal course of things, economists take people's preferences as given. They do not inquire into people's motives except, also as previously discussed, that they assume people are guided mostly by their self-interest, at least in economic matters. This assumption of self-interest is at the heart of the efficiency case for charges.[6] To capture the essence of the idea, if public policy specifies that emissions to the atmosphere be reduced by a certain amount, say in a metropolitan area, this could be accomplished in alternative ways. All discharges could be cut back by a certain fraction by enforcing

---

[6] Charges and standards are discussed in detail in Chapter 10 of this Handbook.

emissions standards. Alternatively, a charge could be levied on each unit of discharge and each emitter could be left to decide how much to control and how much to discharge. Acting in his own best interest, he would reduce discharge until the cost of another unit of discharge reduction is equal to the charge. This is because up to that point, his overall costs will be lower if he curbs the discharge than if he pays the emissions fee. If cost of reducing discharge are different for different dischargers, as in practice they are, much control will be induced at points where control costs are low and little control where costs are high. Thus, if the charge is set at the appropriate level, the combination of the economic incentive provided by it and the self-interest of the dischargers will produce a situation where the same amount of overall discharge reduction can be achieved as with emission standards, but at lower (possibly much lower) overall cost. This means that the real cost to society is lower with charges than with standards to achieve the same social objective.

But according to Kelman's analysis, the environmentalist hostile to charges would not find the results of applying the charges technique acceptable even if he agreed that the outcome just indicated would really happen. He would object that discharging substances to the environment that put others at risk or harm them economically is ethically wrong. As we saw in the discussion above, the Pareto or Libertarian ethical system could provide a foundation for this view of the matter.

The environmentalist in question then *does* care about motives, and he *does not* want to create a situation in which discharges to the environment appear to those doing them to be legitimate. This, apparently, is what is behind the cliche "license to pollute" that some environmentalists have so long used to inveigh against charges and which has so long baffled economists. The economist tends to see emissions standards that do not forbid discharges entirely (and for practical reasons, few do) as the real license to pollute. This is because once the standard is met, remaining discharges to the environmental commons can occur with no penalty at all to the polluter. In other words, they are free gifts to the polluter.

Again, here economists and environmentalists sail past each other in the night. According to Kelman, even though environmentalists are realistic enough to see that zero discharges is, in most cases, an impossible dream, they feel that polluting activity should be stigmatized by making it illegal and by persuading others to share their ethical view of the matter. If the emitter cannot realistically stop entirely, then he should want to "do his best" to do so. This appears to be the ethical foundation, at least in those particular environmentalists' minds, for using discharge permit systems that require "best available technology" somehow defined. If the discharger is within his permit requirements, he is by definition doing his best. Regulatory systems incorporating economic incentives are not acceptable because they do not ensure that everyone will be doing his best, even if they result in lower costs to society, of meeting the same environmental goals, or in meeting higher environmental goals at the same cost.

This environmental policy stance is only apparently oriented to results. In fact, it does not care about the overall efficiency of the system, it neglects opportunities for improving environmental quality other than by discharge reduction (for example, by reservoir operations in a river system), and in its extreme sense, it does not even care about environmental quality as long as everyone is doing his best.

It seems clear to us that the ethical attitude described by Kelman has left us with environmental policies that produce both higher costs and less environmental quality than an approach that would have paid attention to efficiency. That situation in itself presents an interesting ethical dilemma.

As discussed in Chapter 1 the first law of thermodynamics requires that the mass of materials extracted from nature and used in man's production and consumption activities must be returned in some manner to the natural environment because matter is not destroyed in these activities. All that can be altered is the form and location of these residuals discharges or the total throughput can be altered somewhat by recycling of used materials. It strikes us as distinctly odd to regard a socially necessary activity, residuals generation, dictated by natural law, as being *inherently* immoral in the same way that most people, including economists, regard rape or murder as immoral. Much more appropriate, in our opinion, is to regard it as an important societal problem that requires collective choices and public management as part of which a variety of policy instruments may be employed.

In closing, it may be interesting to discuss briefly how the ethical ideas put forth in the preceding parts of this chapter would view polluting activity. A utilitarian would presumably conclude that if the utility to the polluter outweighed the utility to the damaged parties, polluting would be all right. To an egalitarian, presumably whether the activity led to a more or less equal distribution of utilities or opportunities would be the dominant consideration.

In cases where damaged parties cannot be, or are not, compensated, i.e. almost always, two other ethical rules are unequivocal and, in result, agree with the environmental fundamentalism described by Kelman if the status quo point is taken to be a condition of no pollution. A libertarian presumably would reject any polluting activity because it infringes on the rights of others. Interestingly, a rule derived from economic theory, the Pareto principle discussed earlier, also leads to the environmentalists' result. This criterion, as the reader will recall, holds that an action can only be regarded as an unambiguous economic improvement if it makes at least one person better off and no one else worse off. In the absence of compensation, application of this criterion would foreclose any polluting activity. However, if the status quo is taken to be the actual state of pollution, the criterion would counsel us to do nothing or else compensate the polluters. Economists interested in public policy almost always reject the Pareto criterion because it enshrines the status quo and would prevent virtually any public action. This is the trouble with absolutist criteria of any kind. Their application would either hang up any possibility of action or otherwise muck up the functioning of the economic and social system in an unacceptable manner.

A more suitable way to think about ethical aspects of public policy might be to view it in terms of combinations of criteria. An appropriate ethical, as contrasted to political, goal or public policy might be a utilitarian one (since we do care about the good of the whole), but constrained by Libertarian considerations (limits on how much individual interests may be intruded upon) and egalitarian considerations (permit differences of income based primarily on productivity incentive objectives). Should one view the matter in this way, economic theory and method might make some interesting contributions to philosophical discourse, for the stuff of microeconomics is optimization under multiple constraints. Intriguing thought!

References

Bentham, Jeremy (1789) *Introduction to the Principles of Morals and Legislation* (London). Quoted in John Passmore (1974) *Man's Responsibility for Nature* (Charles Scribner's Sons, New York).

Ciriacy-Wantrup, S.V. (1952) *Resource Conservation: Economics and Policies* (University of California Press, Berkeley and Los Angeles).

Committee of the National Academy of Sciences (1974) "Air Quality and Automotive Emissions Control", vol. 4, *The Costs and Benefits of Automotive Emissions Control*, serial no. 19–24 (GPO, Washington, D.C.).

Eckstein, Otto (1958) *Water Resources Development: The Economics of Project Evaluation* (Harvard University Press, Cambridge).

Edgeworth, Francis (1967) *Mathematical Psychics: An Essay on the Application of Mathematics to the Moral Sciences* (A.M. Kelley, New York).

Feinberg, Joel (1974) "The Rights of Animals and Unborn Generations", in: William T. Blackstone (ed.), *Philosophy and the Environmental Crisis* (University of Georgia Press, Athens).

Gray, Elizabeth Dodson (1979) *Why the Green Nigger? Re-Mything Genesis* (Roundtable Press, Wellesley)

Goodpaster, Kenneth E. (1978) "On Being Morally Considerable", *The Journal of Philosophy* 75, 308.

Hirschleifer, Jack, James De Haven and Jerome Milliman (1960) *Water Supply: Economic Technology and Policy* (University of Chicago Press, Chicago).

Hunt, W. Murray (1980) "Are 'Mere Things' Morally Considerable", *Environmental Ethics* 2, no. 1, 59.

Jackson, Clement, et al. (1976) "Benefit-Cost Analysis of Automotive Emissions Reductions", General Motors Research Laboratory GMR 2265.

Kelman, Stephen (1981) *What Price Incentives–Economists and the Environment* (Auburn House Publishing Company, Boston).

Leopold, Aldo (1949) *A Sand County Almanac and Sketches Here and There* (Oxford University Press, New York).

Maass, Arthur, Maynard Hufschmidt, Robert Dorfman, Harold A. Thomas, Jr., Stephen Margin and Gordon Fair (1962) *Design of Water Resource Systems* (Harvard University Press, Cambridge).

MacIntyre, Alasdair (1981) *After Virtue* (University of Notre Dame Press, Notre Dame).

Marietta, Don E., Jr. (1982) "Knowledge and Obligation and Obligation in Environmental Ethics: A Phenomenological Analysis", *Environmental Ethics* 4 no. 2, 155.

Nozick, Robert (1974) *Anarchy, State and Utopia* (Johns Hopkins University Press, Baltimore).

Page, Talbot (1977) *Conservation and Economics Efficiency* (Johns Hopkins Press for Resources for the Future, Inc., Baltimore).

Page, Talbot (1982) "Intergenerational Justice As Opportunity", in: Douglas MacLean and Peter Brown, (eds.), *Energy and the Future* (Rowman and Littlefield, Totowa).

Pigou, A.C. (1920) *The Economics of Welfare* (Macmillan, London).

Rawls, John (1971) *A Theory of Justice* (Harvard University Press, Cambridge).

Robinson, Joan (1963) *Economic Philosophy* (Aldine Publishing, Chicago).

Shute, Sara (1980) *Environmental Ethics* 2 no. 2, 187.

U.S. Atomic Energy Commission, Division of Reactor Development and Technology (1972) *Updated 1970 Cost–Benefit Analysis of the U.S. Breeder Reactor Program* (Washington, D.C.).

Warnock, G.J. (1971) *The Object of Morality* (Methuen, New York).

Watson, Richard A. (1979) "Self-Consciousness and the Rights of Nonhuman Animals and Nature", *Environmental Ethics* 1 no. 2, 99.

[3]

D.2.   The sustainable economy

ROBERT U. AYRES and ALLEN V. KNEESE

Another very important aspect of ecological economics which is receiving more and more attention is the problem of pollution and exhaustion. Economists frequently tend to dismiss this problem with cheerful platitudes.

Kenneth E. Boulding, *Economics as a Science* (McGraw-Hill. New York. 1970) 41.

I have been gradually coming under the conviction, disturbing for a professional theorist, that there is no such thing as economics—there is only social science applied to economic problems. Indeed there may not even be such a thing as social science—there may only be general science applied to the problems of society.

Boulding, from the preface of *A Reconstruction of Economics* (Wiley, New York, 1950).

We cannot escape the proposition that as science moves from pure knowledge toward control, that is, toward creating what it knows, what it creates becomes a problem of ethical choice and will depend upon the common values of the society within which the subculture is embedded, as well as the common values of the scientific subculture.

Boulding, *Economics as a Science*, p. 122.

The origin of this book in my own mind can be traced back to a passionate conviction of my youth that war was the major moral and intellectual problem of our age. If the years have made this conviction less passionate, they have made it no less intense.

Boulding from the preface of *Conflict and Defense—A General Theory* (Harper, New York, 1962).

1. Introduction

While his contributions to it have been many and important, Ken Boulding, as the first two quotations show, has always been somewhat dubious of his chosen profession. His reservations about current doctrine have sometimes been hard to understand at first, because they were subtle and reached out of the near-term context, and when they were understood, sometimes they were hard to take. But they have played no small role in helping to produce healthy and constructive changes in the theory and practice of economics.

One of his main areas of uneasiness has been about economic growth based on ever-increasing "throughputs" in the economy. This reservation far predates the present crop of zero-growth advocates. It is a main theme, for example, in *A Reconstruction of Economics*, his 1950 book in which he tried to persuade economists, without much effect it must be admitted, that they should give attention to assets in their thinking and not focus so single-mindedly on income as conventionally measured. In later years, his concern came to include the environmental pollution and resource depletion which he saw was an integral result of the nature of our contemporary growth processes. He contributed such evocative terms as "cowboy economy" and "spaceship earth" to the lexicon of environmental and natural-resource discourse. His ideas helped stimulate others to work along related lines—including the present authors.[1]

The third quotation illustrates Boulding's concern for the ethical content of science as an influence in human decision making. Such concern often sits uneasily with "scientific" economists who continue to strive manfully for a "wertfrei" discipline. But as one tries to use economics on today's pressing questions of conflicts in human values, unresolvable by the market, and even further on the large issues surrounding humanity's future, it becomes clear that his enduring concern for the moral aspect of this discipline, and of the sciences more generally, was not misplaced.

The fourth quotation displays Boulding's deep concern about the insane level of violence in our contemporary society. In the few years since it was written, the world has seen several more major wars.

In this essay we consider a set of Bouldingian questions, epitomized by the opening quotations, about whether humanity can converge to an indefinitely sustainable economy in a way that is reasonably orderly, peaceful, and safe, or whether it is on a one-way track to disaster. As we contemplated these cosmic issues, we grew increasingly aware of how

[1]See Robert U. Ayres and Allen V. Kneese, 'Production, Consumption, and Externalities', *American Economic Review 59*, No. 3 (June 1969).

complex these matters really are and how foolhardy it is for ordinary mortals to write about them—and yet, the questions won't go away. Recently constructed global models, despite some of the claims made for them, don't answer them. Simple solutions for avoiding the risk of disaster like "stop growth" are not persuasive. Wishing growth away won't make it so and, if it did, clear and present disasters would certainly take the place of more remote and problematical ones.

2. A look at the present context of the growth issue

Contemporary interest in no-growth economics seems to stem from two general causes.

The first is the exponentially soaring rise in world population in the last few hundred years and especially in the post-World War II period.

The second is strongly increasing resource-extraction rates and associated environmental pollution, again at an accelerated pace in the post-World War II period.

Both these phenomena are contributing to large-scale and, many fear, strongly adverse imbalances in ecological systems and irreversible depletion of resources.[2]

Since 1920, the world's population has about doubled, and the gross load of materials and energy residuals returned to the environment has probably more than quadrupled. Because of mass conservation, the mirror image of the extraction of material and energy resources from the earth is the residuals load on the environment. The disposition of the types of residuals now emitted to the environment can probably not grow very much beyond present levels without highly adverse effects on ecological systems and human health, and, clearly, the only imaginable, really long-term sustainable equilibrium involves stationary populations and very low levels of net use of non-renewable resources from earth sources.

These harsh facts have caused some to jump to the conclusion that the world must immediately achieve stable population *and* no-growth economies. But achieving these goals quickly involves complexities and side effects which are coming to be more widely understood—the apparent simplicity of such "solutions" is dissolving in the cold light of reality. For example, population growth is the result of complex interac-

[2]The laws of thermodynamics are often invoked to explain why irreversible depletion of resources in inevitable. Someone has paraphrased them as follows:

    (1) You can't win the game.

    (2) You can't even break even.

    (3) You can't get out of the game.

tions in a system which is excruciatingly slow to adjust into full equilibrium with current changes in birth rates, and stopping economic growth has widespread ramifications—especially in the face of continuing population growth.

2.1. THE GENERAL SITUATION IN DEVELOPING COUNTRIES

Given the huge inertia in population growth, even if active population policies were to come into being soon, a stationary economy for most of the world seems clearly out of the question as a policy objective for some decades to come. This inertia stems from presently high fertility rates and the youthful age structure of the population. Even if fertility rates were to drop drastically, say, to where each family had only two surviving children, the youthful age structure would propel population growth forward for a number of decades. The developing countries, where most of the world's population growth is, have no real choice for the time being but to increase production or face the grim old Malthusian checks on population increase. Furthermore, production must rise fast (5 percent a year or more) if the impoverished state of the masses is to be improved even slightly over the next few decades.

This does not mean that developing countries dare neglect objectives other than growth, such as environmental-quality management. Because of extreme congestion, poor combustion processes, bad local sanitation, and frequently adverse meteorological or hydrological conditions, major cities in developing countries experience some of the most intense pollution in the world. Sao Paulo, Seoul, Taipei, Accra, and Mexico City are only a few examples. Moreover, these problems, unless brought under effective management, will get rapidly worse as industrial production grows and the size of cities continues to grow spectacularly.[3] Whether developing countries will be *able* to grow at rates needed to prevent increasingly grinding poverty and in addition avoid disastrously deteriorating environmental conditions is an open question. But they have no alternative but to try.

We might add that it is the opinion of many ecologists and others, shared by the authors, that *if* the world does finally manage to arrive at some sort of low-birth-rate and low-death-rate equilibrium through non-catastrophic means, it will be at a level of population several times higher—perhaps 15 to 20 billion persons—than would be optimum for the human condition. But there really seems to be nothing that can be done about that—at least not for a very long time to come.

[3]We assume that in the longer time horizon the present "energy crisis" will have been resolved—but presumably at considerably higher prices for energy than have prevailed in recent decades.

To understand why this tremendous inertia in population growth in developing countries exists, it is necessary to look at the reasons for the recent rapid population growth there. It appears to be primarily due to the sudden transfer of a very specialized technology, that of disease control, to the developing countries after World War II.[4] Because of this lopsided technology transfer, death rates dropped much faster than ever happened in the developed countries. Unfortunately, birth rates have remained generally at a high level and even increased — although there are a few cases of decreases as well. Today the world's seven largest nations have about three-fifths of the world's population. These are China, India, USSR, United States, Pakistan, and Indonesia. Only two of these have reached advanced stages of economic development, and the population of poor countries is growing much faster.

One heritage of rapid rates of mortality reduction, centered on infants and children, is an extremely youthful population in the developing countries. On the average, about 41 percent of the population in these countries is below 15 years of age. There are about 76 dependents for every 100 persons of working age (15 to 64 years). That this presents immense difficulties for raising the standard of living needs no elaboration. Moreover, it foreshadows a long period of continued population pressure as these massive numbers move through the childbearing ages, even if birth rates among those in these age brackets should fall. By contrast, in the economically developed world, because both mortality and fertility have been declining for a long time, only around 30 percent of the population is under 15. But even where the situation, as in the United States, is much less extreme, youthful populations will nevertheless drive population growth for a long time. For example, in the United States the net reproduction rate has recently approached unity. Should this situation persist, the nation's population will still increase by about one-third before equilibrium is reached sometime in the next century. This is because the young people move into childbearing age brackets and will be represented there in disproportionate numbers for a period of many years.

Thus, the stage is set not only for continuing difficulties in achieving a high quality of life for vast existing populations but for further unusually rapid population growth in those large areas of the world that are already grindingly poor. The projections displayed in Table 1 show population growth in the developing countries to be five times as great as the growth in the more developed countries during the second half of this century.

[4]This point is, however, controversial. For a conflicting interpretation, see Roy E. Brown and Joe D. Wray, 'The Starving Roots of Population Growth', *Natural History* (Jan. 1974) 46.

TABLE 1

Population estimates according to the UN "medium" variant, 1960–2000, for major areas and regions of the world (population in thousands)

Major areas and regions	1960	1970	1985	2000
World total	2,998,180	3,591,773	4,746,409	6,129,734
More developed regions[a]	976,414	1,082,150	1,256,179	1,441,402
Less developed regions[b]	2,021,766	2,509,623	3,490,230	4,688,332
(A) East Asia	794,144	910,524	1,104,903	1,287,270
(B) South Asia	865,247	1,106,905	1,596,329	2,170,648
(C) Europe	424,657	453,918	491,891	526,968
(D) USSR	214,400	245,700	296,804	353,085
(E) Africa	272,924	345,949	513,026	767,779
(F) Northern America	198,664	226,803	283,105	354,007
(G) Latin America	212,431	283,263	435,558	638,111
(H) Oceania	15,713	18,711	24,793	31,866

[a] Including Europe, the USSR, Northern America, Japan, Temperate South America, Australia and New Zealand.
[b] Including East Asia less Japan, South Asia, Africa, Latin America less Temperate South America, and Oceania less Australia and New Zealand.
Source: World Population Prospects as assessed in 1963 United Nations Population Studies No. 41.

Probably more than three-fourths of the world's population will live in the poor countries by the end of this century as contrasted with about two-thirds at the present time. Furthermore, as population continues to increase after the turn of the century, the balance will weigh even more heavily in the direction of the low-income countries.

In the face of this situation, the income gap between the developed world and the poor countries seems bound to grow inexorably unless some rather spectacular things happen. We indicate some that possibly might in the scenarios we present later.

2.2. THE GENERAL SITUATION IN DEVELOPED COUNTRIES

It is only in the developed countries — which after all use the lion's share of non-renewable resources and produce the bulk of residuals — where one can seriously discuss zero growth as a policy objective in the near-term future. But there are major difficulties and complexities and problems associated with this objective, even in developed nations, especially if they strive to achieve it quickly. Another aspect of the situation is also now becoming more widely recognized. Environmental problems do not have to grow in a one-to-one relationship with either population growth or economic growth. We would, in fact, argue that environmental improvement is compatible with growth in the developed countries, and, because of more rapid replacement of obsolete technology and increased economic capacity to meet various objectives, it may, within limits, even be made easier by it. The urgent question is whether advanced countries will adopt the policies necessary to protect the environment.

A recent careful study of the U.S. situation until around the year 2000 shows that environmental pollution can be reduced by large amounts by the end of the century without large negative effects on economic growth if active abatement policies are followed. Considerable changes in relative prices and life styles may be *on* the cards, however.[5] While the same result would, it seems, be applicable in other developed countries, both economic growth and environmental management are in several cases heavily dependent on their ability to meet energy demands from external sources—a major uncertainty at the moment.

But since they are so much discussed, we proceed to discuss the objectives of zero population growth and zero economic growth in a little detail in the U.S. context. This situation may be considered very roughly typical of the general situation prevailing in many of the more developed countries.

The main source of economic growth in the developed countries has not been rising population and labor force but increases in the productivity of capital and labor. In the United States, for more than a century, the average output per worker-hour has risen at a mean rate of between 2 and 3 percent a year. The figure is lower for the service sector and somewhat larger for the manufacturing, mining, and agricultural sectors (which are exclusively concerned with processing material resources). As we already noted, population growth even in the United States will respond with a very long lag to the reductions in birth rates now occurring. The age structure in a number of other developed countries will lead to a similar result. The labor force for the next couple of decades is already born, and most of these people must work to earn a living unless the world changes its ways quite drastically.

If measured productivity keeps climbing at recent rates, around 3 percent a year, and we continue to have growth in the labor force of around 1 percent a year, and this is likely under any reasonably acceptable population policy, measured national product will grow at about 4 percent a year for at least a few decades. This implies that the

[5]See Ronald G. Ridker (ed.), *Population, Resources, and the Environment*, Vol. III of Research Reports of the Commission on Population Growth and the American Future (U.S. Government Printing Office, Washington, D.C., 1972).

level of measured GNP in 1980 will most likely be something of the order of 50 percent higher (in constant dollars) than it is now. The only way to bring this tendency to a halt quickly would be to reduce labor input either through unemployment or increased leisure. It seems unlikely that there would be large increases in voluntary leisure under circumstances where a major portion of the labor force still lives at comparatively low levels of affluence—median income of American households is still under $10,000. And one does not have to be an environmental Luddite to point out that the enforced leisure (unemployment) alternative also seems very unattractive.

Similarly, and closely related, the ending of population growth presents problems even in developed nations if they have youthful populations, such as the United States and the USSR do, in both cases largely as a result of World War II.[6] Because of this, if the United States, for example, were to attain zero growth rate immediately, it would be necessary to cut the birth rate about in half, beginning instantly. In other words, over the next 15 or 20 years, women would have to bear children at a rate that would produce only a little over one child per completed family. Leaving aside the ways and means of achieving such a situation, at the end of that time we would have a very odd population distribution skewed sharply toward old age.

The more desirable and feasible goal would seem to be to reduce fertility as soon as possible to a level where just enough children are produced to assure that each generation exactly replaces itself and, as we have mentioned, the United States is now at about this point which will nevertheless yield a residual population increase of about one-third. One should be clear that stabilization, even by this process, may have some undesirable features. Assuming that present mortality levels persist, a stationary population achieved in this way would be much older than any that the United States has ever experienced. It would have more people over 60 than under 15, and half of the population would be over 37 rather than over 27, as is the case today.

In this society, the number of people aged, say, 20 would be only slightly larger than the number of people aged 50. This distribution would no longer conform to our traditional social structure—to the distribution of privileges and responsibilities in the society. In the growing population, the diminishing numbers at higher ages and the smaller number of high positions relative to low positions in the economy and the society tend to reduce (though not eliminate) friction between the generations. In

[6]The USSR has been in a state of very low birth rates for some years. They now seem to be rising.

the stationary-population case, there would be a much reduced expectation of advancement as a person moves through life.

Furthermore, the present ratio of units in the net reproduction rate may well be fortuitous since there is no logical reason to believe that in the long run people would voluntarily choose a level of fertility that the society would deem desirable. So it seems important to consider what other policies might be applicable. Certainly a good place to start would be to reexamine the enormous direct and indirect subsidies which public taxation and expenditure policy grants to those who choose to have large families.

3. Some summary thoughts about growth in the next few decades

It seems to us incontrovertible that the world's population will continue to rise inexorably for several more decades, at least. This will be so, even if the effectiveness of birth-control measures is greatly increased and even if the underlying dynamics of population growth is such that it will tend toward an equilibrium combining low birth rates and low death rates. This means that many countries (containing most of the world's population) will have little choice but to strive hard for economic growth, in some cases for a very long time, perhaps a century or more. Also, it will probably not prove desirable for the major developed countries (especially those with youthful populations) to develop policies which will end population or economic growth suddenly. Over this period, however, it will be essential to stringently limit the discharge of harmful by-products of production and consumption activities to the environment. If this is done by policy instruments, such as appropriately high emissions taxes which bring social and private costs into conjunction, it will result in more recycling, increased durability of articles, and a price shift which will tend to favor services over goods. Perhaps most important, technical advances in the handling and reuse of residuals will be induced. It should be possible to reduce the rate of discharge of residuals—except CO_2, heat, and possibly organics—while continuing to achieve economic growth in the developed countries. The effects of CO_2 and heat rejection to the atmosphere are still somewhat problematical, and their occurrence, if any, is some decades off.

If prevailing incentive systems are appropriately revised in developed countries to reflect environmental values, it seems reasonable to expect that industrial skills and technology will evolve toward a situation in which the rate of use of non-renewable material reserves per unit output might be greatly moderated.

But even if materials-saving technologies are introduced, there will

Robert U. Ayres and Allen V. Kneese

continue to be a heavy net draft on non-renewable resources as growth continues over the next few decades (and indeed there would if it stopped, unless the nature and scale of economies changed drastically, and probably catastrophically) with quantities used shifting increasingly toward developing countries if they can sustain a high rate of growth.

In point of fact, the deflated price of most natural-resource commodities has been going down more or less steadily, or been about constant, for several decades. However, for a variety of reasons, some of which we explore on, we believe that this tendency will begin to reverse itself in the next few decades—if not immediately. Nevertheless, in terms of the sheer availability of adequate supplies of resource commodities—food, fuels, metals, water, and the like—the outlook to the end of this century for the more developed countries seems rather favorable—if channels of international trade remain open. But as the energy crisis of 1973–74 showed, the position of several of them is rather precarious, and existing growth policies may be reconsidered. It is also not out of the question that some countries will be motivated to pursue military solutions or push the development of hazardous technologies in their quest of greater self-sufficiency—possibilities to which we return later.

For the densely-populated, high-population-growth, poor countries, the outlook is even much more dubious and uncertain. However, a combination of production increase internally and "rescue operations" on the part of developed countries makes it likely that the levels of population foreseen for the end of this century will actually be achieved. The combined result of population and economic growth, at least for the next few decades, will be greatly increased discharges of harmful residual materials in the developing countries. The developed countries should be able to check pollution of the worst kinds and, indeed, even reverse it, while continuing to grow, if they develop effective and efficient policies for doing so. Accordingly, it is reasonable to suppose that the proportion of environmental pollution contributed by developing countries will shift considerably in their direction by the end of the century.

It seems inevitable too that, at the end of the next few decades, there will be vastly more malnourished and grindingly poor people in the world than there are now. The situation will be one in which many incentives to hostility and violence inhere. Higher-income countries may be increasingly heavily dependent on poor countries for resources inputs. Poor countries with crushingly dense populations will be cheek-by-jowl with relatively thinly populated rich countries. Thermo-nuclear and biological weapons will be readily available to numerous countries. Major issues will arise as to whether it is permissible to use certain high-risk technologies in the interest of continued growth or, in the case of some countries, even survival. Nuclear fission and persistent pesticides are current examples. The poor countries will probably be predisposed, if not forced, to take risks unacceptable to the richer ones—some of which risks may have global implications.

Eventually, banning catastrophe in the interim, the world will have to face the question of whether a sustainable world economic system, one that emits vastly lesser amounts of harmful residuals per unit output than the current one and simultaneously makes a much smaller draft on non-renewable resources—is possible while sustaining a world population of 15–20 billion persons. This is the level at which populations may stabilize late in the next century in the absence of large increases in death rates. And, furthermore, there arises the question as to whether the planet can achieve this stabilization in the face of vast differences in wealth, motivations and imperatives, technological competence, and longevity and effectiveness of public institutions among the world's nations. In the next section we develop some scenarios which, we hope, will illuminate some of the possibilities and problems bearing upon the feasibility of evolving toward a substainable world economy. Whether this goal is attainable at all depends heavily on the paths of development which evolve in the interim period. In the next section we look at these paths in a bit more orderly way than we have so far done.

4. Some paths to the future economy

As we turn more directly to the prospects and prerequisites for a "sustainable" world economic system, a number of caveats are necessary. Among the more important of them seem to be the following.

First, the "future" is not predetermined, but some key driving forces can be projected with a fairly high degree of certainty,[7] whereas others are essentially indeterminate or their relevance is not understood at present. We will try to distinguish between the two (or three) kinds.

Second, some imaginable future scenarios are actually impossible for technical reasons, but there are many futures that are both imaginable and possible. However, no particular future scenario can be regarded as "probable" or even "not unlikely." A so-called "surprise-free" future would, in fact, be extremely surprising! However, the degree of "unlikelihood" of possible future events is tremendously variable. All scenarios are inherently unlikely, but some scenarios are very much

[7]Long-continued population growth is, as we have seen, one of these.

Robert U. Ayres and Allen V. Kneese

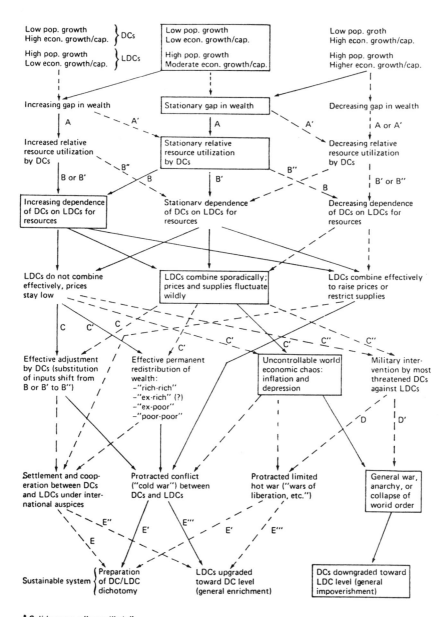

* Solid arrows = "more likely"

Fig. 1. *A*: Developed countries increase consumption of material goods *faster* than material/energy content is reduced by technology and design innovations. *A'*: Converse of above. *B*: Developed countries export resource extraction technology and capital to LDCs

more unlikely than others.[8] Again, we will try to distinguish some of the less and more likely cases and their interrelationships.

Third, not all future world economies are "sustainable". The possibilities of a major war or world-wide economic collapse cannot be ignored. Moreover, it seems inadequate to us to simply mention the possibility and pass on to other topics. In fact, one purpose of this paper is to explore—at least superficially—how some of these unpleasant outcomes might occur, in order to begin to understand what, if anything, can be done to avoid them.

A scenario can be played out by simply connecting any sequence of logical possibilities from the various levels shown in fig. 1. For illustration we have specified a scenario containing the following ingredients:

(1) Low per-capita economic growth by advanced countries and moderate growth by less-developed countries, combined with a higher population growth rate, results in a stationary gap in per-capita wealth.

(2) Resource *utilization* per capita in developed countries remains roughly constant, the increases in population and income per capita being compensated by moderately greater efficiency in the use of raw materials and energy.

(3) Resource *availability* in developed countries decreases relative to less-developed countries (i.e. historical trends continue) and, as a consequence, DCs become increasingly dependent on LDCs for resources. DCs do nothing effective to check this trend.

(4) Because of cultural, economic, political, and geographical differ-

---

[8]One that strikes us as essentially too unlikely to consider is the scenario in which the rich and poor countries of the world voluntarily agree to settle their differences and set aside their sovereignity under the framework of a world government!

---

in order to exploit cheapest available sources of raw materials (free trade policy). B': Developed countries seek to protect domestic resource development activities through tariffs, import quotas or subsidies for domestic producers. B'': As above, but where domestic sources are unavailable, or absolute exhaustion of the resource occurs, substitutes are developed deliberately regardless of cost. C: Developed countries respond to the challenge through rapid technological substitution. C': The challenge is too great, because insufficient time for adjustment is available or institutional rigidity prevents adequate adjustment. C'': Frustration leads to a military response by most threatened DC. D: "Rich rich" (less threatened) remain passive or help to end the conflict. D': "Rich rich" countries enter the conflict on opposite sides. E: Despite assistance (or because of it), "poor poor" countries cannot close the gap. E': Without assistance, "poor poor" countries cannot (or do not) close the gap. E'': Because of assistance, "poor poor" countries are able to develop. E''': *Because of* external pressures (cold or hot), "poor poor" countries achieve necessary internal cohesion and sense of direction to overcome obstacles.

ences, LDCs do not respond to the opportunity (as they might) by creating a worldwide cartel to raise prices and restrict supplies. However, there are sporadic attempts to do so, with varying degrees and duration of impact. The net result is increasing instability in raw-material markets, wildly fluctuating supplies and prices, increasing amounts of speculation and hoarding both by private producers and by nations (including some countries with large cash surpluses).

(5) This syndrome leads to rapid inflation of major currencies, and a breakdown of confidence in the economic system, finally resulting in a "crash" of worldwide dimensions.

(6) The postulated economic crash produces intolerable strains on some of the more fragile parliamentary democracies of the world, both among DCs and LDCs. Totalitarian regimes of the extreme left and extreme right come into being, and there is a reprise of the 1920s and '30s with a high level of violence, disorder, and conflict.

(7) Even if there is no major nuclear war, the likely outcome of this scenario would be general impoverishment.

Of course the reader is free to disagree with our subjective assessment of what might follow from what. Fig. 1 is, essentially, a "do-it-yourself" scenario kit.

Letters $(A, A', B, B', \ldots)$ represent apparent alternatives, many of which seem to us to be either indeterminate or unknowable at present. These alternatives are defined in the attached set of notes. For instance, it is by no means clear to us whether a large international program of foreign development assistance would be effective in closing the "gap" between developed and less-developed countries. On the contrary, it seems possible that a moderate degree of xenophobia and self-reliance induced by real (or apparent) external pressure would be more effective in many cases. The recent examples of China and India may be relevant: China appears to have accomplished far more by turning its back on the outside world than India has by actively seeking assistance from the developed countries.

1. DEVELOPING COUNTRIES

One striking feature of figure 1 which deserves comment is that there is no path leading to an automatic favorable outcome for LDCs simply by raising prices for raw materials exported to developed countries. The outcome of recent price increases for petroleum will materially improve the relative economic position of the Arab countries (except Egypt and Syria), Iran, Venezuela, and Nigeria. These may be described as "ex-poor". On the other hand, India, Pakistan, and the rest of Africa and

South America will become poorer even than they were before. It is less likely, but not altogether inconceivable, that Europe and Japan will be hurt badly enough to fit the term "ex-rich".

A major predictable impact of the sharp increase in resource prices, if it is sustained, and it seems likely to us that it will (not ruling out some cyclical behavior),[9] will be large-scale substitution. In North America the development of oil shale, tar sands, and geothermal energy will proceed rapidly—along with other, less immediate, technological possibilities. In India, Japan, and elsewhere, it can be presumed that efforts to develop nuclear power will be redoubled. The case of India is particularly pertinent, in this regard, since the uranium-bearing sands of Kerala constitute one of the major energy resources of that country. Large-scale hydroelectric developments in the Himalayas are another obvious possibility. It would be understandable if these technological alternatives were pursued with rather less concern for safety or care for the environment than might be the case in the United States. It would also not be surprising if border conflicts between India, Pakistan, Bangladesh, Burma, or China should be exacerbated as a result of this situation. In short, many parts of the world may become more turbulent and dangerous as more and more LDCs become dependent on others for basic resources and correspondingly vulnerable.

[9]To see the significance of this statement, one must understand that the long-term trend of real prices for resources commodities has been down. The reasons we think this tendency will not persist indefinitely—while recognizing that considerable fluctuations will probably occur—are as follows:

(1) Lower-quality ores in some important materials do not necessarily exist in exploitable quantities. This appears to be the case for lead and zinc. The same is probably true for practical purposes with regard to hydrocarbons as such (i.e. for non-fuel purposes) since hydrocarbons are not simply dispersed by consumption but are actually used up—that is, chemically transformed into CO_2 and H_2O.

(2) The increased output of the extractive industries in the last century can be attributed in part to the opening up of previously un-explored areas (e.g. Canada, Siberia, Africa, Brazil, Australia). Except for the ocean bottom—which is not easily accessible or easy to exploit—"new" sources will become rarer and rarer in the future.

(3) The prices of mineral commodities historically did not—but in the future must—reflect social costs arising from pollution and waste disposal. But these costs evidently increase non-linearly as the amount of processing increases (requiring more energy and more technological inputs), and as human settlement becomes more dense.

(4) The increased productivity of the extractive industries in the last century is also partly due to economies of scale and the application of mechanical technology. Both are probably subject to the law of diminishing returns.

(5) The developed countries (except for the Soviet Union) are rapidly using up their domestic high-grade sources of minerals and fossil fuels and becoming dependent on the less-developed nations. It seems likely that raw-material exporters will increasingly band together to multiply their bargaining power and increase their revenues from this source.

Indeed, it is very difficult to see how the "poor poor" countries—
LDCs with large and growing populations in relation to arable land and
other basic resources—can ever catch up to the developed world, or
even become much better off than they are, except by undertaking very
harsh universal programs to control population growth, reduce consumption, and increase labor productivity and investment. Whether this is
possible at all for a country like India is doubtful, but it certainly cannot
be imposed successfully from outside. External pressure in favor of birth
control, for instance, is very likely to generate internal opposition to it.
Yet, external aid *without* such measures can only postpone the day of
reckoning, and then probably not much, and consequently increase its
severity.

A rich-poor dichotomy between nations may be economically sustainable if the poor countries are, at least, self-supporting. Whether it is
politically (or ethically) sustainable is another matter, of course. We
cannot throw light on this question here.

4.2. DEVELOPED COUNTRIES

We return now to a consideration of some of the implications of "zero
growth" within an advanced country such as the United States. We
assume, for purposes of discussion, that this state occurs as a result of
evolutionary (rather than revolutionary) changes. In other words, for the
present discussion we assume that the transitional problems (which will
reach at least into early the next century) considered in an earlier section
are successfully resolved.

Some of the more interesting and salient issues emerge when one asks
the question: is it possible to combine sustained *economic* growth without
a stationary (or declining) population, and do so in the presence of a much
more limited supply of non-renewable resources? A number of salient
interactions are illustrated schematically in fig. 2.

To illuminate these issues, it is necessary to survey briefly the relative
roles in the past of raw materials, labor, and technological change in
increasing productivity.

One of the classic boosters of productivity in the past—especially in
the United States—has been the opening up, at intervals, of access to
large, cheap new sources of raw materials. The settlement of the rich
agricultural land of the Midwest had a dramatic impact on grain and beef
prices, for instance. Similarly, the immense timber resources of the
West—especially redwood and Douglas fir—brought lumber prices
down to very low levels. These, along with the great discoveries of coal
(Pennsylvania, Kentucky, etc.), oil (Pennsylvania, Texas, Oklahoma,
etc.), iron ore (Minnesota), gold (California, S. Dakota), silver (Nevada),

Natural Resource Economics

The sustainable economy

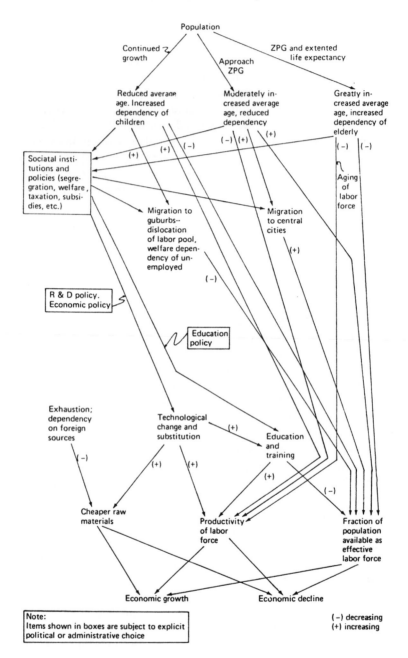

Fig. 2.

copper (Montana, Utah, Arizona), lead (Missouri), and natural gas (Louisiana) had a tremendous cumulative impact on the rate of U.S. industrial development in the 19th and 20th centuries vis-à-vis European countries lacking in comparable sources of wealth.

Evidently, this "cream-skimming" phase of U.S. development is clearly over, and unexploited resources (such as oil shale)—though still vast in quantity—will, especially including environmental costs, not be nearly so cheap to extract. The same is true of coal resources in other developed countries. For the moment, cheap resources reside mainly in the less-developed countries. Judging by recent experience with oil, we would be unreasonable to expect these countries not to "skim the cream" for themselves and sell raw materials to the more advanced countries at prices more nearly reflecting the cost of finding suitable substitutes. Clearly, the level of technological capability is critical in determining the marginal cost of substitution. In any case, however, cheap raw materials do not appear likely to contribute to economic growth of the developed countries from now on. In the much longer term—which is our main concern here—there will be no cheap non-renewable resources any-where. A scenario of more or less continuing increases in the real prices of virgin raw materials into the indefinite future seems quite probable.

Clearly, the *size* of the labor force has also in the past been an important contributor to growing production, and extended schooling has contributed to this effect. Moreover, other demographic and sociological factors have contributed to increased real productivity in the past few decades:

• Urbanization and the end of the self-sufficient (non-cash) family farm.

• Smaller families releasing some women to the work force, both before and after having children.

• Better health and longer life, extending the ratio of productive to non-working periods.

These trends have been counteracted to some extent, however, by trends toward longer schooling, earlier retirement, and shorter work-weeks.

In a stable state of ZPG, as noted previously, the number of younger vis-à-vis older persons will shift markedly toward the latter. If length of schooling, length of work week, and age of retirement remain constant, the number of dependents will decrease—relative to the work force, with a favorable impact on per capita income. This would be reflected by apparent economic growth between now and the time when a stable population is achieved, but most of the impact would occur in the first two decades. Eventually the increased availability of women to the work force resulting from demographic shifts will also work itself out, and there is not much further room for shifting workers out of agriculture into urban pursuits—even if technology continues to permit it.

In the very long term (ZPG—no vast new discoveries of resources to be exploited—this is what we will henceforth mean when we speak of a stationary economy), technological improvement can be the only source of economic growth in developed countries. Indeed, if one considers the dispersion of materials and the necessary resort to lower-grade sources, which even a stationary economy implies, it can be the only possible source of a sustainable economy whether growing or not.

In this connection, it seems important to emphasize the complex relationship between societal institutions in general, the education/training institutions more particularly, and the "process" of technological innovation. A high rate of technological change and innovation certainly requires a willingness to take risks on the part of industry and financial institutions, a flexible educational system, and an adaptable and retrainable labor force. It also requires a flexible legal and institutional framework to cope with change. All of these are much more compatible with a youthful population than with the older and stationary one which must characterize the zero-growth situation. (The correlation between voter age and conservation is well documented, for instance.) We shall return to this point later.

Apart from sociological factors, there is—at first sight—no inherent reason why technology should not continue to improve, nor does there seem to be any basic reason why wealth should not increase, even in the extreme case where total inventory of physical materials (except energy) remains unchanged. Material goods may increase in value (i.e. by offering more services to the user) without increasing their basic re-source inputs. A good example of this evolution is the history of radio and TV; thirty years ago even a crude AM radio was both expensive and bulky. Today, the same or better services (i.e. quality of sound reproduction and accessibility to programs) are available in a miniature transistor-ized radio at a far lower price requiring only a tiny fraction of the physical resources.

Clearly, if wealth is to grow without increasing the requirements for resources, it will be necessary to find ways of greatly reducing the physical resources "frozen" in material objects. That is to say, the material component of physical wealth must decline sharply. What is embodied must be carefully maintained and extensively reused, both to reduce the use of resource inputs and to control the discharge of residuals.

The use of energy in the postulated stationary economy would also have to be far more conservative than is now the case in so-called "developed" countries. This is true not only because of rising prices but also, among other things, because the residual energy "rejected" to the atmosphere might become a severe problem. Present emission of energy is about 1/15,000 of the absorbed solar flux. But if the present rate of growth continued for 250 years, emissions would reach 100 percent of the absorbed solar flux. The resulting increase in the earth's temperatures would be about 50°C—a condition totally unsuitable for human habitation.[10]

It is almost axiomatic in the conventional wisdom that energy consumption per capita is an index of wealth. It is perfectly true, of course, that rising GNP and rising energy consumption have been historically correlated. It is true, also, that the current pattern of increased output of fabricated goods derived from extractive industries tends to result in a non-linear increase in demand for energy, since the declining quality of raw materials necessitates greater expenditures of energy for processing. In a very real sense, however, energy has been utilized in the development of our industrial society as though it were (nearly) a free resource. One recent estimate puts the average efficiency with which energy is utilized in producing "final" (household) services at 4.5 percent for the United States. The figure is higher—but not much higher—for Europe, where energy has been historically more expensive. To double or even quadruple, this efficiency figure should not be beyond the realm of possibility during the next half century or so.

Thus, processing of virgin materials (e.g. metals) is a major use of energy. In an economy based on nearly total recycle of non-replaceable materials, the energy expanded on raw-materials processing could and would be cut drastically—depending upon the specific manufacturing and fabricating technology in use. The details of the technology, in turn, would presumably evolve (given the appropriate incentive structure) in such a way as to reduce both the energy and dollar cost of reprocessing. To give one example of the likely direction of technological evolution, most tasks currently carried out by complete machines built for the purpose, could equally well be accomplished by programmed modular assemblies of flexible multi-purpose components. These modules would be, increasingly, electronic or fluidic rather than mechanical in mode of operation. These modules would be replaceable and repairable individually. Since the most efficient form of recycling (from a materials and energy point of view) is that which involves the least change in form or

[10]William R. Frisken, *The Atmospheric Environment* (The Johns Hopkins University Press for Resources for the Future, Inc., Baltimore, 1974).

composition, it is apparent that repair or rebuilding of modules would be highly favored over replacement by new or different types, since the latter would involve the use of virgin materials. Thus, conservation of energy and materials, also would seem to be incompatible with a rapid rate of technological change.

For several reasons, then, there are grounds for believing that technological change is likely to slow down, rather than speed up, in a society where the level of population is constant, and where most physical resources are non-renewable and must therefore be conserved and recycled.

It appears, then, that one cannot expect a continued increase in wealth, and that decline is quite possible, in a stationary society (stationary in the sense defined earlier) unless special incentives are created to "institutionalize" technological innovation. The usual notion is that technological change is a consequence of research and invention. If this were so, it would be simple enough to institutionalize technological change by diverting a significant amount of economic resources into research and development. Historically, one observes a strong correlation between periods of rapid technological change and periods of great fertility of invention as measured, for instance, by numbers of patents filed. However, examination of the historical evidence does indeed suggest that invention may be stimulated by rapid change, rather than the reverse.[11] In any case, there is no guarantee that inventions and discoveries will be implemented, simply because they exist. Innovation is often a fairly painful process which corporations and institutions embrace reluctantly, if at all.

Under the present "rules of the game", technological progress is one of several mechanisms for gaining a competitive advantage, or an increased return on investment. Technological progress often stagnates, however, when the market is not competitive (i.e. in a monopoly or oligopoly), or when other competitive strategies, such as heavy advertising, are more effective. On the other hand, even a natural monopoly may be quite innovative if it is constrained for some reason against raising prices for the same product, and can only increase its earnings by cutting operating costs or providing new services which can be sold at a higher price. The telephone company seems to be an example of this. "Japan Incorporated" is, perhaps, a better illustration, since Japan has maintained a high rate of economic growth for more than two decades, with a rather rigid social structure, a nearly stationary population, a centrally-

[11] J. Schmookler, *Invention and Economic Growth* (Harvard University Press, Cambridge, Mass., 1966).

guided oligopolistic economy, and an elderly leadership echelon. This pattern may be generalizable. A more reliable guarantee of institutionalizing technological change, at least in a regulated industry, would be to depreciate the rate base, as the "embodied" technology ages. Various revisions of the incentive system might be devised to induce innovation even in a relatively static system, and no doubt human ingenuity will turn in this direction as the stationary society approaches.

5. *The minimum imperatives — energy and food*

Even assuming that the world economy is capable of operating on much reduced quantities of non-renewable natural-resource commodities, and that the rich-poor gap turns out to be maintainable without catastrophe, if it is to have any hope of achieving a sustainable economy at a population level of 15–20 billion persons—must be able to produce energy and food in huge amounts—even if much more conservative ways of using the former are found.

We do not believe that energy as such will prove to be an ultimate constraining factor. Although available reserves of petroleum and natural gas must inevitably begin to run out—probably by the end of the century—there are very large reserves of low-quality coal, lignite, and oil shale, which could supply large amounts of energy for a number of decades, probably at something like present (1974) prices, provided that society is willing to tolerate what is sure to be a substantive amount of unavoidable environmental degradation accompanying their use.

The developed countries have put their very-long-run hopes primarily in nuclear power, and this may become a major source for developing countries, too. High-quality uranium sources are limited, also, but plutonium breeder reactors could make it possible to vastly extend the availability of nuclear fuel. Thorium, also, is a potential source of nuclear power, and vast quantities exist in recoverable quantities in granite. Fusion power may be limited by the availability of lithium-6 (to produce tritium), rather than deuterium, but lithium is not a rare element on the earth's surface. Both solar and geothermal power can also be tapped in large quantities—though their cost is uncertain. Technologically speaking, it is probably feasible to capture solar power outside the earth's atmosphere and ship it back to earth either in the form of a high-intensity coherent electromagnetic beam or as synthetic chemical fuels. (It must be remembered that we are speaking of a very long-run scenario in which space technology is highly developed and by no means exotic.)

Also, we do not believe that food availability as such will necessarily be limiting in the very long run if population stabilizes—leaving aside the question of whether the needed technology can be developed rapidly enough. Food is, basically, biologically available energy—in the form of carbohydrate, protein, or fat—plus some needed chemical building blocks which the human organism cannot synthesize from basic elements. These essential components of food include some twenty amino acids. Food must also include a number of minerals such as sodium, potassium, calcium, phosphorus, and iron, of course.

Much remains to be learned about the chemical synthesis of amino acids and vitamins, but most of the basic steps have already been duplicated in the laboratory. In the long-run future, there is absolutely no reason to doubt that food could be manufactured in a chemical plant, given the availability of sufficient energy, capital equipment, and knowledge. This is not to imply that synthetic food would necessarily replace food derived from biological origins. Certainly as far ahead as one can foresee, the latter is likely to be both more palatable and more economical to produce. Ultimately, however, chemical synthesis of food may have to be introduced, too.

Food production, whether based on photosynthesis or chemical synthesis, is evidently energy-limited. We are confronted with an apparent paradox here. World food production, based on photosynthesis, is apparently quite limited. Some experts have predicted world-wide famine within a decade or two. Others, citing the "green revolution", are much more optimistic. But it is painfully clear that conventional agriculture is beginning to approach its limits, and that even though the present world population could probably be fed adequately (though two out of three people on the globe are now receiving inadequate diets), and conceivably even the year 2000 population and beyond could be supported if new strains of grain and the use of fertilizers spread rapidly enough through Asia and Latin America, it is almost impossible to see how conventional agriculture could support 15–20 billion people at the present U.S. or European dietary standard, with 40 percent (or more) of dietary calories derived from animal sources. But unconventional agriculture perhaps could.

By unconventional agriculture, we mean a system based mainly on harvested or recycled cellulose—rather than carbohydrates—which is converted by bacterial action into feed for cattle, hogs, poultry, or fish. All solid organic wastes, whether cornstalks and cobs, brush, grass clippings and leaves, food-processing wastes, waste paper, animal manure, and even sewage, can be converted into animal feed and thus recycled without benefit of additional photosynthesis. The overall efficiency of conversion of solar energy to food can thus be increased manyfold—probably by an order of magnitude—without increasing the intensity of cultivation or altering the primary ecology. Whatever agricultural processes might be found compatible with the indefinite high-level maintenance of a population of 15–20 billion, one thing is clear—they must be arranged so that much less pesticide and plant nutrient is lost to the environment relative to output than is true of present "developed" agriculture. The results of not achieving this would be profoundly destructive effects on ecological systems.

6. Two more big questions

Without commenting further about how mankind got itself into an idiotic race between population growth and technological development, if technical progress can be sustained or accelerated—despite the incentives to slow it down which seem inherent in stationary societies, it is not ridiculous on the face of it to suppose that an ultimate world population of 15–20 billion people could be maintained at a reasonable standard of living. This would necessarily be in an economy using very large amounts of energy, but not so large as to greatly damage the livability of the planet, yet having drastically lower material throughput per unit product than the developed countries of today.

But we cannot conclude on this even vaguely optimistic note without calling attention to two more truly major reservations that we have about the ability of mankind to achieve this relatively favorable outcome.[12] The first is a question of whether the potential for technological progress is truly limitless for practical purposes. The second is whether coping with the increased human interdependence and the risks of some of the more promising new technologies is not beyond the capacity of human institutions.

6.1. IS TECHNOLOGICAL PROGRESS LIMITLESS?

One may suspect that scientific R & D is ultimately subject to diminishing returns. The classical economists of the 18th and 19th centuries felt that economic growth would be brought to an end as an increasing amount of labor was applied to a fixed resource stock so that, eventually, further increments of labor would not yield any additional output. Actually, technology turned out to be the main factor which permitted this dismal result to be avoided—or at least put off for a long time. Labor productivity has been rising almost steadily and fast since the beginning

---

[12]This means relative to perfectly disastrous ones. It puts us in mind of a remark once attributed to Maurice Chevalier. When asked how he felt about getting old, he said, "it's not so great, but much better than the alternative".

of the industrial revolution. In fact, as we have seen, increased productivity has been the main element in economic growth. To get this result, the developed economies have been increasing technology as a production factor faster than the other inputs for a long period of time. Most projections of economic activity and resource use implicitly assume that we will continue to achieve at least constant returns from scientific and technological input. In other words, labor productivity will continue to rise as it has in the past few decades. In the United States this means at about 3 percent per year. This may be quite justifiable if one is looking a relatively few decades into the future. But on the longer-time scale, doubts may well arise, even if institutional arrangements can successfully sustain a higher level of scientific enterprise and innovative behavior.

The noted classical economists, Malthus and Ricardo, were products of the enlightenment which restored Western man's confidence in his ability to understand the workings of the world through reason. And their works are strong testimonials to the power of this confidence. But the Enlightenment's systematic, analytic engine, the scientific method, was just starting to evolve. A method of discovery was being discovered. It is not hard to understand why the classical economists could not grasp fully the implications of this other product of the Enlightenment. The industrial revolution at first produced enormous productivity gains through the application of reason and ingenuity to mechanical devices without the benefits of systematic science. For example, Cartwright, who made the first power loom and other important textile equipment, was not a scientist, but a clergyman who wrote verses, and Benjamin Huntsman, who first made cast steel, was a clockmaker. It was only gradually that industrial innovation moved beyond the basically mechanical and began to incorporate more esoteric accomplishments of formal science, such as chemistry.[13] But science, once it took hold, continued to propel productivity forward despite the fact that some of the more obvious improvements permitted by the spirit of the Enlightenment had been made. As Sir John Hicks, the eminent British economist, has stated in his recent commentary on economic history, "There might have been no Crompton and Arkwright, and still there could have been an industrial revolution; in its later stages it would have been much the same. The impact of science, stimulating the technicians, developing new sources of power, using power to create more than human accuracy, reducing the cost of

[13]A fascinating account of this process is found in 'Machines and Men', Ch. XI, in: G. D. H. Cole, *Introduction to Economic History*, 1750–1950 (MacMillan, London, 1952).

machines until they were available for a multitude of purposes; this surely is the essential novelty, . . . ".[14]

The application of science to industry has continued to increase the productivity of labor and more or less steadily to push back resources scarcity, despite huge increases in labor and capital inputs. Perhaps it will continue to do so for a long time to come. But it would seem strange if the application of effort to science and technology were entirely immune from diminishing returns. One may speculate that the return from the applications of resources to scientific discovery and technological development in certain important instances has already begun to diminish. For example, most of the basic mathematical concepts which are used in today's applied science were well known by the beginning of this century. In this connection, it is worth noting that a former president of the American Association for the Advancement of Science (Bentley Glass) has forecast, in a speech before the 1970 AAAS meetings, that we cannot expect continued basic scientific discoveries on the scale of the last 100 years.

While new discoveries always do remain to be made, although not necessarily at an undiminished pace, there are some basic reasons why quantitative technological improvements may require greater efforts to bring about, and why the percentage rate of improvement in many fields, as measured in terms of functional indices, will inevitably begin to decline. The efficiency of energy conversion is a good illustration of the point. Power plants have increased in efficiency from 1 or 2 percent to over 40 percent in the most advanced power plants today. Thus we have already experienced a 40-fold improvement in two centuries. The next 30 years may conceivably see a further increase to 60-percent overall efficiency, but this only represents a 50-percent improvement over the present level. Obviously the rate of advance thereafter must slow down markedly if only because 100-percent efficiency is the absolute upper limit, and it can never be actually reached. In many other areas, also, this same phenomenology holds true.[15]

Should we encounter strongly diminishing returns to scientific technological development, it may well prove to be impossible to converge to a stable, sustainable economy of 15–20 billion persons in which labor productivity is relatively high. Indeed it may not be possible to indefinitely sustain that level of population at any level of living. Thus, as far as we can see, science and technology is not the villain but rather the

[14]Sir John Hicks, *A Theory of Economic History* (Oxford University Press, London, 1969) 147.
[15]For a more detailed discussion, see Robert U. Ayres, *Technological Forecasting and Long Range Planning* (McGraw-Hill, New York, 1969).

potential hero of the piece, if it can be properly developed and directed
and if it continues to be highly productive of improved ways of doing
things. But we cannot have high confidence that it will do so indefinitely.

6.2. CAN HUMAN INSTITUTIONS COPE WITH NEW TECHNOLOGY?

A second nagging doubt has its basis in the imperfections of social
organization and social institutions. We have already hinted at this
before but it seems useful to spell it out a little. It is a commonplace that
the industrialization has increased interdependence. So although it can
produce high levels of material welfare, it can do so only if a high degree
of social order is maintained. The system becomes not only vulnerable to
breakdowns in the technological chain, but also to human error and
malevolence. Some of the technologies which can be foreseen for
simultaneously increasing productivity over the long-run future and
reducing dependence on non-renewable resources, seem to carry with
them huge extensions of interdependency in both space and time. Even
without an all-out catastrophic war, which we cannot, unfortunately, rule
out as entirely unlikely, such interdependencies may come to be viewed
as intolerable and may severely limit the application of certain technologies.

Another possibility is that presumed necessity may dictate their
applications anyway—with possibly disastrous results. This may be
particularly a possibility in the less-developed countries. The large-scale
and continued use of persistent pesticides could be an example here.
Other examples of technologies which might be vastly productive of
useful work serving great numbers of people but vulnerable to catastrophic failures are tapping energy from extraterrestrial sources, trans-
mitting vast amounts of energy in a limited number of superconductors,
and nuclear fission.

That these problems are not remote and hypothetical is amply demonstrated by the debate going on even now over whether the world should
become dependent upon a large-scale nuclear-fission energy economy.
This debate illustrates very nicely the interrelation of the moral and
economic questions and the limits of conventional economic analysis,
both of which have so occupied Kenneth Boulding. Therefore we discuss
the matter in a little detail.

The Atomic Energy Commission has suggested that the problem of
whether to develop such a large-scale fission economy can be solved by
benefit-cost analysis.[16] It is our belief that this, frequently very valuable,

[16] *Environmental Survey of Nuclear Fuel Cycle: Power Reactor Licensing and Rule Making*,
U.S. Atomic Energy Commission (Nov. 1972).

mode of analysis cannot answer the most important policy questions surrounding this issue. To expect it to do so is to ask it to bear a burden it cannot sustain. This is so because these questions are of a deep ethical character. Benefit-cost analyses certainly cannot solve such questions and may well obscure them.

These questions have to do with whether society should strike the Faustian Bargain, as Alvin Weinberg describes it in evocative terms, with the atomic scientists and engineers.[17] If so unforgiving a technology as large-scale nuclear-fission energy production is adopted, it will impose a burden of continuous monitoring and sophisticated management of a dangerous material, essentially forever. The penalty of not bearing this burden may be unparalleled disaster. This irreversible burden would be imposed even if nuclear fission were to be used only for a few decades, a mere instant in the pertinent time scales.

Clearly, there are some major advantages from using nuclear fission technology, else it would not have so many well-intentioned and intelligent advocates. Residual heat is produced to a greater extent by current nuclear-generating plants than by fossil-fuel-fired ones. But otherwise the environmental impact of routine operation of the nuclear fuel cycle, including burning the fuel in the reactor, can very likely be brought to a lower level than will be possible with fossil-fuel-fired plants. In general, the costs of nuclear and fossil-fuel energy, with the latter having a fuel cycle in which residuals generation is controlled to a high degree, do not seem to be so greatly different.

Unfortunately, the advantages of fission are much more readily quantified in the format of a benefit-cost analysis than are the associated hazards. Therefore there exists the danger that the benefits may seem more real. Furthermore, the conceptual basis of benefit-cost analysis requires that the redistributional effects of the action be, for one or another reason, inconsequential. Here we are speaking of hazards which may afflict humanity many generations hence and distributional questions which can neither be neglected as inconsequential nor evaluated on any known theoretical or empirical basis. This means that technical people, be they physicists or economists, cannot legitimately make the decision to generate such hazards based on technical analysis. The society confronts a moral problem of a great profundity. In a democratic society the only legitimate means for making such a choice is through the mechanisms of representative government.

In his excellent article referred to above, Weinberg emphasized that part of the Faustian Bargain is that to use fission technology safely,

[17]Alvin M. Weinberg, 'Social Institutions and Nuclear Energy', *Science* (July 7, 1972).

society must exercise great vigilance and the highest levels of quality control, continuously and indefinitely. In part this is because of the great hazards involved in imperfect operation of reactors and the nuclear fuel cycle. Especially the breeder reactor involves large quantities of plutonium which is one of the most toxic substances known to man and which could be used to fabricate nuclear weapons. As the fission energy economy grows, many plants will be built and operated in countries with comparatively low levels of technological competence and a greater propensity to take risks. A much larger amount of transportation of hazardous materials will probably occur, and safety will become the province of the sea captain as well as the scientist. Moreover, even in countries with higher levels of technological competence, continued success can lead to reduced vigilance. We should recall that we managed to incinerate astronauts owing to a very straightforward accident in an extremely high-technology operation where the utmost of precautions were allegedly being taken.

But even deeper moral questions surround the storage of high-level radioactive wastes. Estimates of how long these waste materials must be isolated from the biosphere apparently contain major elements of uncertainty, but current ones seem to agree on "at least two hundred thousand years."

In the United States, heavy emphasis has been given to the storage of these wastes in salt formations, and a site for experimental storage was selected at Lyons, Kansas. This particular site proved to be defective. Oil companies had drilled the area full of holes, and there had also been solution mining in the area which left behind an unknown residue of water. But comments of the Kansas Geological Survey raised far deeper and more general questions about the behavior of the pertinent formations under stress and about the operations of geological forces on them. The ability of solid-earth geophysics proves very limited to predict for the time scales required. Furthermore, there is the political factor. An increasingly informed and environmentally aware public is likely to resist the location of a permanent storage facility anywhere.

Because the site selected proved defective, and possibly in anticipation of political problems, emphasis is now being placed upon the design of surface storage facilities intended to last a hundred years or so, while the search for a permanent site continues. These surface storage sites would require continuous monitoring and management of a most sophisticated kind. A complete cooling-system breakdown would soon prove disastrous, and even greater tragedies can be imagined.

Just to get an idea of the scale of disaster that could be imagined, consider the following scenario. Political factors force the federal government to rely on a single above-ground storage site for all high-level radioactive waste accumulated through the year 2000. Some of the more obvious possibilities would be existing storage sites like Hanford or Savannah, which would seem to be likely military targets. A tactical nuclear weapon hits the site and vaporizes a large fraction of the contents of this storage area. The weapon could come from one of the principal nuclear powers or a lesser-developed country with one or more nuclear power plants, or it might be crudely fabricated by a terrorist organization from black-market plutonium. The radiation fallout from such an event would exceed that from all past nuclear testing by a factor of 500 or so, with radiation doses exceeding the annual dose from natural background radiation by an order of magnitude. This would be a drastically unfavorable, and long-lasting, change in the environment of the majority of mankind. That massive numbers of deaths might result seems clear, but the exact magnitude of the disaster is apparently quite uncertain.

Furthermore, by the year 2000, high-level wastes would have just begun to accumulate. Estimates for 2020 put them at about three times the 2000 figure.

Sometimes, analogies are used to suggest that the burden placed upon future generations by the "immortal" wastes is really nothing so very unusual. The Pyramids are cited as an instance where a very long-term commitment was made to the future, and the dikes of Holland as one where continuous monitoring and maintenance is required indefinitely. These examples do not seem at all apt. They do not have the same quality of irreversibility as the problem at hand, and no major portions of humanity are dependent on them for their very existence. With sufficient effort, the Pyramids could have been dismantled and the Pharaohs cremated if a changed doctrine so demanded—also, it is worth recalling that most of the tombs were looted already in ancient times. After World War II the Dutch dikes were in fact opened. Tragic property losses, but no destruction of human life, ensued. Perhaps a more apt example of the scale of the Faustian Bargain would be the irrigation system of ancient Persia. When Tamerlane destroyed it in the 14th century, a civilization ended.

But none of these historical examples tell us much about the time scales pertinent here—one speaks of two hundred thousand years. Only a little more than one-hundredth of that time span has passed since the Parthenon was built. No government has ever existed whose life was more than an instant by comparison with the half-life of plutonium. There also seems to be a noticeable upward trend not only in the capacity for, but in the frequency of, large-scale violence. Much of this has happened in our lifetime and several notable "incidents" have happened quite recently or are still in progress. As we have seen, the occasions for hostility are very likely to increase further in the future.

It seems clear that there are many factors here which a benefit-cost analysis can never capture in quantitative, commensurable terms. It also seems hard to claim that the nuclear fuel cycle will not sometime, somewhere experience major unscheduled events. These could range in magnitude from local events. like the fire at the Rocky Mountain Arsenal, to an extreme disaster affecting most of mankind if a large part of the high-level wastes in storage were released. Whether these hazards are worth incurring in view of the benefits achieved is what Alvin Weinberg has referred to as a trans-scientific question. As professional specialists, we can try to provide pertinent information, but we cannot legitimately make the decision, and it should not be left in our hands.

Whether the benefits exceed the risks is partly a scientific and economic question and partly. even mostly, a value-judgment question which, as we have said, can only be legitimately answered through our system of representative government. But the committee structure of the Congress, dominated as it is by jurisdictional problems and the special interest orientation of committee memberships, is not a suitable arrangement. The Congress has unfortunately had great difficulty in reforming itself even on issues of much less moment. This is another facet of the institutional challenge that we face.

7. Concluding comment

Can mankind converge monotonically toward a state in which human life is both pleasant and more or less indefinitely viable? This is a very open question, it seems to us. It is one on which, despite our congenital optimism, we are rather pessimistic. But the uncertainties are so great that it is difficult to see how we could rationally influence present policies to take account of possibilities on the pertinent time scale. The only clear signal seems to be that if we fail to bring world population under control soon — very soon — humanity's future problems may be totally insoluble. If we do succeed, there is a chance.

The dangers that perhaps impress us most are subtle ones. They revolve around the probability that, as human society makes greater and greater demands on available resources, margin for error decreases. As it decreases, a more and more interdependent, elaborate, and fail-safe organization is required simply to prevent the system from collapsing at the first perturbation. Recent unhappy experiences with massive breakdowns or tie-ups of essential public services—electric power, telephones, sanitation, transportation, international distribution of petroleum—suggest very clearly the magnitude of potential instabilities inherent in a system which depends, for example, on maintaining regular communications in space or beneath the ocean, or the timeless "fail-safe" monitoring and management of certain materials. The elemental need to prevent catastrophic breakdowns or hold-ups may conceivably result in the development of a rigidly structured, rather inhuman "1984" type of social system which subordinates individual talents, needs, or desires to the survival of the social organism as a whole. Or else, the world may "solve" its otherwise insoluble problems of war, famine, or anarchy. We hesitate to dwell on this possibility, and it is distasteful to us to end on such a note. We cannot help but hope that others will soon begin to find positive answers where we have uncovered grounds for pessimism. What does seem clear is that humanity faces a future full of stresses and strains, and that life will not be comfortable for any persistent periods for a long, long time to come—if ever. Analyses, of which there have been many, that address the question of the long-term viability of a very numerous humanity solely in terms of potential technological, or even economic, capabilities miss some of the most central questions. The large Boulding-ian questions of man and nature, war and peace, and private and international morality cannot but come more and more into the forefront of civilized man's preoccupations.

CHAPTER

33

ENVIRONMENTAL QUALITY
AND THE OPTIMAL JURISDICTION

Allen V. Kneese
Edwin T. Haefele

ECONOMIC RESEARCH ON RESIDUALS
MANAGEMENT: A SUMMARY

Our starting point is with the results of about a decade of theoretical and empirical research on residuals management, based primarily on economic concepts. We summarize these results only very briefly here, since they are well documented in other publications and since our main objective is to consider some political-institutional aspects of the environmental problem.

By residuals we mean all the nonmarketable material and energy outputs of the production and consumption activities of an economy. Disposal of these residuals usually influences the quality of common property resources—the air mantle, hydrologic systems, and large ecological systems. Since the latter are difficult or impossible to reduce to unambiguous private ownership, they are, in a market system, subject to a rule of physical capture rather than to allocation through voluntary exchange of property rights. Consequently, activities with superior physical access to them, such as residuals discharge, overwhelm other and conflicting valuable uses such as life support and recreation unless an appropriate intervention is made through collective choice. The common property characteristic of these resources (which in turn is related to the public good or joint supply character of many of their uses) is the source of Pareto-relevant external costs of production and consumption. [1]

One insight from recent research is that residuals-associated externalities are not unusual or freakish phenomena, as much of the

---

Note: The authors wish to acknowledge the helpful comments of Martin McGuire, Irving Hoch, Mark Reinsberg, Clifford Russell, and Paul Portney.

earlier economics literature suggests (it happens that a factory chimney emits smoke), but rather inherent in a market-type economic system once a certain stage of development has been reached.[2] Mass and energy conservation requires that all materials and energy used as basic inputs to the economy must again appear as residuals. So long as the sinks are open-access common property resources, the growth of the economy means the progressive degradation of these resources.

Moreover, the first law of thermodynamics tells us that unless the total throughput of mass-energy can be reduced by recycling or other measures leading to more technically efficient use, reduction of discharges to one environmental medium must necessarily mean an increased residuals flow to another. All things being equal, waste treatment processes, for example, actually increase the amount of material and energy flow, although if they are well designed in view of their environmental systems context, their residuals will be less noxious than the ones they operate on. But the point is that physical conservation forces an interdependency among solid, liquid, and gaseous residuals streams. These are direct nonmarket linkages whose existence means that an effective and efficient collective management strategy in a highly developed area must consider all significant residuals streams simultaneously.

Since collective action is needed to control overuse of common property resources for residuals disposal, the question naturally arises as to what would be the best policy instruments for accomplishing this purpose. The conclusion of most economists (based on considerable empirical as well as theoretical research) is that the preferred approach, in view of the difficulty of measuring specific damages in monetary terms (as well as various conceptual difficulties), is for society to first set ambient standards (which pertain to the quality of the environment itself, that is, parts per million of sulfur oxides in the atmosphere, as contrasted with effluent standards, that is, pounds of sulfur in stack emissions). Then society should use taxes or effluent charges to provide an economic incentive to attain these ambient standards. This procedure is generally regarded among economists as being better (on efficiency and informational grounds) than direct controls on discharges (effluent standards).[3] The expected response to a well-designed set of charges would be to control residuals discharges at individual sources by whatever means are least costly (recycle, residuals transformation processes, byproduct recovery, and so forth) and to concentrate reductions of specific residuals discharges at those sources where control is least costly.

But this body of research has further shown that sometimes it is possible to alter the environmental medium itself in such a way as to improve its service flow to other users for a given level of residuals discharge. For example, low river flows (usually corresponding to low water quality) can be raised by the use of flow-regulating reservoirs, and oxygen can be added to water courses by artificial means. Sometimes a more adaptable species (such as the Coho salmon introduced into Lake Michigan) can be substituted for naturally occurring ones. The practical importance of these regional scale measures has been amply demonstrated.[4] Accordingly, it can be concluded that a management agency seeking efficient solutions would have to explore the full range of technological options in the environmental quality production function and then develop a program of collectively provided facilities and effluent and user charges that meets ambient standards at least cost. The areal scope of both possible controls and external costs usually corresponds more or less to physical problem shed regions such as watersheds and meteorological regions. Accordingly it is concluded that a regional agency that internalizes the external costs and incorporates possible control technologies within its geographical scope is needed to execute a systematic and efficient continuing management program. It is recognized that the various regions most closely corresponding to different problem sheds and control options are usually not coterminous—but this fact has so far not been dealt with very well in the pertinent economics literature.

What are the main conclusions of the economic-technological research just discussed?

1. External costs associated with residuals discharge are inherent in our economic system and must be continuously managed through collective action if we are not to experience severe (and eventually fatal) environmental degradation.

2. Liquid, gaseous, and solid residuals are interdependent (through nonmarket physical linkages), and effective and efficient management requires that they be analyzed and managed simultaneously.

3. Residuals management problems and control options are regional, but the economic-technological research conducted so far does not provide much guidance as to how the disparate problem sheds and spatial range of physical control options could be handled institutionally.

4. "Society" must set ambient standards to which to key its control programs. But the economic-technological research so far completed does not provide much guidance as to how this might best be done via political institutions and what the normative properties of results would be under different institutional arrangements for making these choices.

In connection with the last point it should again be noted that environmental improvement has the characteristics of a public good in the technical economic sense (in the pure case, this is a good which displays strict jointness in supply for multiple parties). The literature on public-goods economics contains the general prescription that the marginal rate of transformation in production between private goods and public goods should be equated with the sum of the marginal rates of substitution of the public good for private goods for all parties to whom the public good is jointly supplied (MRT = Σ MRS). But this rule suffers a little in practical application, and its normative base is destroyed (or at least badly dented) when lump-sum transfers of income or equivalent taxing arrangements are not possible (that is, nearly always).* This is because income distribution is directly affected by the provisions of the public good.

But one line of discussion of public goods problems stresses mobility of households as permitting market exchanges to move in the direction of meeting the efficiency criterion and making the mitigation of distributional effects relatively simple. We will discuss this approach at some length below, but first we wish to state the political (collective choice) problems that occur in environmental quality (residuals) management a little more specifically. We find three:

---

*The conditions for efficient non-redistributive provision of public goods have been developed most clearly by Martin C. McGuire and Henry Aaron in "Efficiency and Equity in the Optimal Supply of a Public Good," The Review of Economics and Statistics (February 1969), pp. 31-39. A somewhat terse statement of their most salient conclusions is as follows: Assume $\Sigma\ MRS^i = MC$, where i indicates households. Let t^i be the amount each household pays per unit of public good. If $t^i = MRS^i$ for every household, the solution is called a "Lindahl" solution. The income value of the public good to each household equals its MRS^i times the amount of the public good supplied. If t^i is set to equal MRS^i, the income value of the public (evaluated at its marginal utility) is exactly offset by the tax (although there may be consumer surplus associated with inframarginal units of the public good). This result is analogous to marginal cost pricing for private goods. Any difference between the household's MRS and the tax it actually pays represents the entire income redistribution effect of the public goods supply. If public goods are produced at increasing (decreasing) average cost and the efficiency condition $\Sigma\ MRS = MC$ holds, total taxes collected exceed (fall short of) total production cost. The deficit or surplus must then be compensated from the "general redistribution" accounts. The tax scheme just described, of course, requires that the taxing authority know the individual MRS of every household. Furthermore, even if it does, if fixed tax laws, customs, and so forth, determine tax shares and no direct income transfers are allowed among individuals, the efficiency rule $\Sigma\ MRS = MC$, while still Pareto-optimal, is of no help in deciding how much of the public good to supply, since this becomes as much a matter of distributional ethics as of allocative efficiency.

1. The choice of what levels of environmental quality the area is to have. In particular, the collective choice problem involves setting a level(s) of air quality with regard to, say, sulfur dioxide, particulates, and carbon monoxide. It involves setting levels of water quality in terms of allowable heat and BOD loadings. It involves decisions about aesthetic aspects of solid waste handling (dumps, and so on) and thus raises issues of land use. Clearly these issues present a collective choice problem because, as we have pointed out, they involve common property resources, have public goods characteristics, and even if preferences could be perfectly known, no optimal levels could be unambiguously specified aside from highly exceptional cases. [5]

2. Choices must be made about the income distribution issue as it relates both to benefits and to costs. There will be several ways of achieving any specified level of quality. Each may have a different distribution of benefits and costs. (Indeed, in models prepared at Resources for the Future, the variations of both costs and benefits are wide even over very small changes in levels of ambient concentrations. [6]) As we have stated, urban economists have generally been content to assume a reshuffling of people (voting with the feet) as a way whereby individuals try to choose the best available mix of public services, including environmental amenities, within their budget constraints. Such movements, while they occur regularly, are of limited help for several reasons that will be discussed in more detail later. We will conclude in the next section that the collective choice issue cannot be avoided by ambulatory elections.

3. Management instruments must be chosen collectively. While this choice is closely connected to the distributional issue, it is a distinct problem, for it simultaneously includes the efficiency issue. In the residuals management area, one can achieve a given ambient concentration of, say, sulfur dioxide either by setting emission controls (each source restricted to some quantity of sulfur dioxide emission, not necessarily the same for all) or by setting effluent charges on each source. Clearly these will have different distributional effects depending on which course is taken. But there will also be efficiency differences in the aggregate between the two methods of control. As we have indicated, opting for effluent charges may well bring large efficiency gains for the overall residuals management systems. Moreover, there is the matter of providing collective facilities such as reservoir systems, reaeration equipment and regional treatment facilities.

With these three main types of collective choices to be made, how do we decide which collectivity makes them? The simple answer, "everyone who is affected by them," does not help us much. The airshed and watershed will not usually be coterminous. Solid waste disposal may affect land use miles away. The whole residuals management problem is but one public service problem, and it must compete for a share of a limited public purse. The question of the optimal jurisdiction is upon us.

THE RECEIVED THEORY OF
OPTIMAL JURISDICTION

For several years a few economists have studied the question of optimal jurisdiction for the provision of public goods. We do not wish to go as far as H. L. Mencken, who is said to have remarked, "For every problem economists have an answer—simple, neat, and wrong." But the results of this research do appear to be leading down a rather narrow path.

A classification of criteria suggested by Rothenberg provides a useful starting point for our summary discussion of this literature. He suggests four (which often conflict): (1) minimize political externalities; (2) minimize cross-jurisdictional externalities; (3) minimize the resource cost of providing public goods; and (4) maximize achievement of redistributive goals.[7] The last three are straightforward in concept; the second and third will be considered in some detail in the last section. The last point, as a general matter, seems to us largely inapplicable to our topic, which surrounds the regional scale and structure of government. As others have argued, this scale of government is not suitable for undertaking general redistributions of income.*

But we hasten to point out that this conclusion does not extend to redistributions of income that are inherent (except under unusual circumstances) in the provision of public goods to nonhomogenous populations. Since a public good is supplied in bulk, so to speak, to a large number of persons, and the amount the individual gets is not under his individual control, redistribution occurs simultaneously and inevitably with the provision of the good unless canceling lump-sum transfers (or equivalent tax arrangements) can be made. The concept of lump-sum transfers has been an immensely useful device in the elaboration of public goods theory, but it is entirely inapplicable in practical situations. Accordingly, criteria based strictly on efficiency tend to be unacceptable, and the redistribution issue becomes a central one that the political process must somehow resolve. We examine the functioning of a representative government process in this connection in some detail in the next section.

---

*We must note, however, that to the extent that general income distribution is regarded as a problem for this level of government, its solution requires nonhomogenous jurisdictions. (For a discussion of this issue see Paul V. Pauly, "Income Redistribution as a Local Public Good," paper given at Public Choice Society Annual Meeting, Pittsburgh, 1972.)

Here we wish to come to a focus on what Rothenberg, in his listing of criteria, has termed "political externalities." Consideration of this matter is important, since the "voting with the feet" line of theoretical development, so prominent in the recent literature, is focused mainly on it. Most simply, political externalities means imposing the majority will on minorities—if 51 percent of the people vote for something in a majority-win election, 49 percent are not represented no matter how unhappy they may be with the outcome. This is "tyranny of the majority." For reasons we develop shortly, we believe this argument either betrays a profound misunderstanding of the representative government process or an unwarranted emphasis upon an issue-by-issue referendum approach to collective choice. Of course, if one believes that the concept of political externalities provides insight into the question of optimum jurisdictions, then (aside from conflicts with the other criteria) the clear implication of the political externalities argument is that people with homogenous preferences should be grouped into separate jurisdictions.

Before considering this argument further, it may be useful to present it a bit more fully. A recent paper by McGuire—which is by far the best of this genre—provides a suitable basis. [8]

Actually, though, the "voting with the feet" viewpoint stems back to a seminal article published more than 15 years ago by Charles M. Tiebout. [9] In it he assumed mobile consumer-voters and flexibly redefinable local jurisdictions which can be independent of each other in the sense that there are no interjurisdictional externalities. He concluded, among other things, that for a given configuration of jurisdictions (group size, collective output, tax rates, and expenditures), each consumer-voter "moves to that community whose local government best satisfies his set of preferences." And, further, that "the greater the number of communities and the greater the variance among them, the closer the consumer will come to fully realizing his preference position."

McGuire has provided a proof of this proposition under the following assumptions:

1. Population heterogeneity is taken to mean that there are multiple subpopulations, each homogenous unto itself and discreetly (in the mathematical sense) separated from every other homogenous subpopulation—every member of a homogenous subpopulation has the same demand curve for the public good.

2. Each homogenous subpopulation is large enough to form many efficient jurisdictions in the sense of being able to provide any particular public good at issue at minimum average cost.

3. A separate and distinct jurisdiction can be formed for each local public good.

The implication of these assumptions is that "it is [aside from transactions costs] Pareto-optimal to allow homogenous (with respect to marginal rates of substitution) groups to form their own

collectives." This conclusion is derived by means of an elegant
mathematical analysis. We will not repeat it here because the central reason for the result is intuitively very plausible. First, we
should note that the problems of cross-jurisdictional externalities
and minimizing the cost of public service are, as is readily seen,
either ruled out by or very straightforwardly follow from the assumptions.

Given the assumptions, the reason for the stated result is that
when persons have arranged themselves in homogenous groups (with
respect to MRS for the public versus the private good), the criterion
that $MRT = \Sigma MRS$ implies that $MRS^1 = \ldots MRS^i = \ldots MRS^n = MRT/n$. In other words, the marginal rates of substitution of all
individuals are identical and are all in the same proportion to the
MRT. If the groups were integrated, this result would be violated
and preferences could not be met to as high a degree, given available
resources for the production of public and private goods. Since movement could increase the welfare of each person voluntarily changing
his location, the integrated result cannot be Pareto-optimal.

Furthermore, since the public good is being produced efficiently
(at lowest average total cost), a simple pricing scheme (average cost
pricing) that can, in this case, be implemented by a simple tax system (everyone pays an equal share) prevents any income distributional
effects (in the $MRS^i \times Q$ sense) from the provision of the public good.
Another way of putting the result is that absolutely no political externalities (majority effects on minorities) are imposed, that is, the
result would be determined by a unanimous vote if the issue were the
amount of public good provided given the above cost-sharing scheme.
A compulsory cost-sharing scheme must be specified to avoid the
so-called "free-rider" problem. Since the jointness-in-supply characteristic means that no one in the relevant area can be excluded
from receiving the public good, its provision cannot be arranged via
voluntary individual payments.

McGuire's particularly clear and precise analysis provides an
excellent frame for further discussion of the "voting with the feet"
solution to the jurisdictional problem with respect to the public good
and externality aspects of residuals management problems. To this
we now turn.

A CRITIQUE OF THE RECEIVED THEORY

The severity of the strict homogeneity assumption is, perhaps,
self-evident. But not so much as to keep a generation of urban economists from relating Tiebout's theory to the widely observed phenomenon of persons moving around in a metropolitan area and then
drawing the conclusion that this results in homogenous jurisdictions.
Clearly they are more homogeneous than they would be without such
moves, but far from the degree needed for the Tieboutian models to

have much real world significance. Without belaboring the point, simply reflect on (1) the history of self-selected communes, where homogeneity of preferences is vastly greater than in most other communities, and (2) the last PTA meeting you attended in your homogeneous suburb.

That we do not regard voting with the feet as a general solution to the public goods problem does not mean that we fail to recognize a role for it. It is useful to think of two categories of public good (bad) situations.

In the first are those that can be obtained (avoided) only by locating in particular places. For example, if one feels strongly about either living with or not living with a certain ethnic group (we pass no moral judgments here), there is no way of meeting one's desire except by location decisions. The same is true of having access to landscape or other fixed locational aspects of an area. Of course, moves to meet preferences of this type will not fully solve the public goods problems since, contrary to McGuire's simplifying assumption, multiple public goods are always supplied by every jurisdiction or by multiple jurisdictions overlapping the same space. Nevertheless, if a person feels strongly about some fixed locational feature of the area, he may well move, and thereby improve his welfare, even though this does not permit him to equate his MRS with that of all others in the area for all public goods provided. That is to say, he might prefer more or less of some public good, given the cost of providing it and the share he would bear even under a nondistributive, cost-bearing scheme. 10

The other class of public goods consists of those whose supply can be altered, at thinkable cost, by collective action. There are many such—quantity and quality of education, transport facilities, police and fire protection are all examples, as is, of course, the quality of environmental media as affected by residuals generation and disposal practices. Public investment, regulations, and prices can, and do, alter all of these. In these instances, locational choice is not the only adjustment and, in view of the multiple public good characteristic of each location, is often not an efficient adjustment. This does not gainsay that in the absence of government institutions of appropriate scale and capability for making collective choices it may not be second best. It is at least arguable that mobility has been a substitute for, and perhaps even hindered the development of, political institutions that could have been the vehicle for attaining greater aggregate welfare. Private costs (for example, commuting) may have been substituted for public goods (better air quality in central cities) in part because no appropriate institutional vehicle for collective action was available. This suggests that there is an important role for higher units of government to assist in organizing institutions for collective action at the local and regional scale. Indeed we regard the question of political institution building through public policies at the federal governmental level as being one of the most important and least recognized problems facing the national government. We return to this matter in the final section.

Before going on to consider other matters, however, we should note once more that management of the natural environment can only be done efficiently by rather large problem-shed authorities. Within such a geographical scope, numerous quite diverse public goods will have to be provided. The population simply cannot be very homogenous within these spaces.

The more fundamental point, however, is that homogeneity is not needed to deal with political externalities. To oversimplify somewhat, the <u>raison d'etre</u> of any body politic is to handle political externalities. Were any group of people totally homogeneous with respect to MRS for the public vis-à-vis the private good, then the only reason for government would be to avoid free riders. Any one individual could be designated to make the choices, since all choices would be the same. Government is necessary in part because no two men (not to speak of large groups) ever agree completely about public goods. In democratic regimes, where individual preferences form the basis for social choices, the heterogeneity of the community is the engine that resolves social conflicts, that is, makes social choices. A famous case may illuminate this assertion.

In the first Congress following the adoption of the Constitution there were two large issues, neither of which could at first be resolved. One was the question whether the United States would assume the wartime debts of the states—the South said no, the North yes. The other issue was where to locate the U.S. capital—the South said on the Potomac, the North said no. Hamilton was in despair. However, when Jefferson returned from Paris he called the leaders of the two sides together and uncovered an additional fact that had escaped Hamilton's attention. He found how each side ranked the two issues. Using subscripts for ranking, the situation was as follows:

	North	South
Potomac site	N_2	Y_1
Assume debts	Y_1	N_2

He quickly saw the possibilities for a political transaction. Accordingly, he arranged a vote-trade with the North agreeing to the Potomac site in exchange for the South's agreeing to assume the states' debts.

Any representative assembly deals similarly with intense minority opinion, so well in fact that many complain of the undue strength of minorities under our system. It is worth noting that what usually passes for homogeneity in "voting with the feet" arguments is agreement of ordinal ranking of issues, for example, "good schools are most important." What happens in this situation is that people disagree on the means to achieve them, resulting in a vote as follows:

Voters	1	2	3	4	5	...
Specific School Issue A	Y_1	N_1	Y_1	Y_1	N_1	...

No trades are possible on this issue, since everyone ranks it first. The initial majority prevails and the minority suffers without any compensating gain. Thus homogeneity in an ordinal sense may well bring on a majority tyranny. The theory underlying the preceding points is elaborated elsewhere. [11]

While vote-trading permits dealing with heterogeneity in a single political jurisdiction, it does not directly address the question of appropriate jurisdictional boundaries. Madison's implied definition for a political jurisdiction was a heterogeneous population having common problems. This probably had much to do with giving us territorial representation, as opposed to "interest" representation, but it says little about how to carve up the territory.

As we have seen, environmental issues illustrate the boundary problem effectively. The water, air, and solid waste disposal problem sheds of an area will rarely coincide. Shall we have three separate governments while the technology and economics of residuals management demand that we have one integrated system? Whose views should be represented in such an integrated system—for example, the largest set (probably the watershed)? To do so will bring into the decision some people who are remote from the area, who care little about its problems, who will propose solutions that force the costs on other people. How different is that from a situation in which a metropolitan area, with the help of a corps of engineers, forces costs (dams with flooded farmlands) on upstream users?

These questions are sufficient to tell us that the optimal boundary question is a real one, but its resolution will require a broader framework than we have so far given it. We cannot be content with the solution of the Master of University College, Oxford, who, it is said, when confronted with the task of refusing admission to the son of a rich alumnus, wrote the latter, "We think your son would be much better off in a smaller college, or perhaps in a larger college, but in any case in a college of different size."

We now turn directly to the boundary question and first look at it in the context of a population of fixed location. We start by providing a little background on current social choice theory.

REPRESENTATIVE GOVERNMENT WITH
A FIXED-LOCATION POPULATION

Following Kenneth Arrow's landmark book, [12] there has been a substantial development of social choice theory. Though most of it has concerned problems rather remote from the problem at hand, it has refocused the problem of government on lines more consonant with thinking in the eighteenth century, namely, personal utility as the basis for values.*

The framers of the Constitution were concerned with a system of making social choices from individual preferences. So are those who now labor in social choice theory. The Arrow conditions for proper social choice—collective rationality, Pareto principle, independence of irrelevant alternatives, and nondictatorship—provide a good starting point for considering some recent developments in collective choice theory. Given these conditions, Arrow showed in his Restricted Theorem for Two Alternatives that majority vote under a two-party system could always lead to a social choice that correctly aggregated any set of individual preferences vis-à-vis the two alternatives presented by the respective parties. Following this line of Arrow's work, one of the authors examined ways of choosing the two alternatives to see if there existed a way that met all of Arrow's conditions.[13] It is worth noting that this effort was not an attack on Arrow's general theorem (as it has sometimes been interpreted to be) but an attempt to shift the focus of analysis from working out the implications of a social welfare function (a highly artificial artifact from a political point of view) to social choice per se. The attempt succeeded by constructing a set of rules for voting that correspond roughly to real world two-party electoral politics, particularly to the temporal dimension of election campaigns.

Close on the heels of this re-invention of the traditional Anglo-American system of representative government came some doubts as to whether individual preferences could be "trusted" to give us solutions "in the public interest." Most people do not vote. Won't greed, particularly with vote-trading, result in "worse" decisions than we have now? Didn't we invent benefit-cost and other "objective" ways of making social choices as a way of insulating such decisions from political wheeling and dealing?

We indicate the normative bias in the preceding questions by quotation marks. We suggest that the counterthrust to these questions is provided by the movement toward "participatory democracy," "adversary planning," and "citizen involvement," leaving the issue there except to note that the country is clearly readjusting itself in an effort to cope simultaneously with economic growth and environmental quality. The optimist may believe that in this process of readjustment the country will rediscover the strength and sophistica-

---

*This base should not be confused with the later flowering of "utilitarianism." Macaulay's criticism of James Mill and the other utilitarians of the nineteenth century is still a good remedy for this possible confusion.

tion of the government as conceived (and will throw out those procedures not consonant with it). The pessimist may think that humans
are destined to travel the same road again and again, forgetting their
past and learning nothing from their present.

If one is willing to accept, as we are, individual preferences as
the source of values, we can proceed to analyze the boundary question under a fixed population location assumption.

In another paper, one of the authors has suggested that one component of the boundary question could be resolved by electing a
general-purpose representative at a district level (the districts being
smaller than any general government). [14] Such representatives
would sit in all local and regional governmental bodies having jurisdiction over the district (as measured, say, by taxing authority or
control over land use). The purpose of this building-block approach
would be twofold: (1) to enable the representative to have control
over the whole range of local issues so that he could use his vote in
one assembly as a lever in another, thus providing an opportunity
for registering intensity of preferences, and (2) so that governments
of varying territorial reach could be assembled (and perhaps more
important, disassembled) easily and conveniently with no upheaval
in the basic political fabric of the area. (For example, a district
could opt into any local governmental body by being willing to be taxed
by that body. It could not opt out without the permission of the governmental body concerned.) The suggestion has the added advantage
of focusing local politics so that citizen participation in the party
structure and electioneering have more potential payoff. The representative is less vulnerable to special-interest groups if he sits on
the sewer board, zoning board, and the school board, as well as on
a local government council, than he would if he sits on only one
board. It seems reasonable to assume that the general-purpose
representative system could go a long way toward overcoming voter
apathy in local elections, since all issues would be focused in the
election of one man, much as they are in the election of a governor,
a senator or representative, or the President. Moreover, by focusing
all issues in one election, the tendency for majority tyranny to emerge
(in small populations such as the district) is mitigated. Intense preferences of minorities on one issue can be used to advantage in
electoral politics as well as in legislative politics. [15]

Moreover, in the context of our present concern with environmental management in a metropolitan area or region, the general-
purpose representative (GPR) provides, perhaps, a way out of the
dilemma posed by the mismatch of jurisdictions to problems. If we
have a management agency whose reach encompasses the problem
(an expanded river basin commission, for example), we have only
to put such an agency under the policy control of a representative
body composed of the GPRs covering that region. While at first
blush such a move seems to make the agency answerable to too

many bosses, in fact it gives the agency clear policy direction from
one source.

It will be apparent that how the district lines are drawn will influence the outcome of any preference aggregation procedure. [16]
Equal population districts will be necessary to meet Supreme Court
tests, and the gerrymandering is ever present in the drawing of any
political line. This question will, however, be begged, as it is a
universal one and not unique to local districts. Moreover, the
present political party structure provides an adversary procedure
to cope with the problem.

RELAXING THE FIXED-POPULATION ASSUMPTION

In a recent paper, John M. Orbell and Toru Uno provide some
empirical evidence of who leaves and who stays and why. [17] In brief,
they suggest that when neighborhood problems arise, higher-status
whites are more apt to stay and fight and lower-status whites are
more apt to move. Blacks of similar status are more apt to stay
than whites, having fewer opportunities to move. For whites, once
a move has been made there is a tendency to stay, for 3 to 6 years,
during which political action efforts are greatest. Beyond 6 years,
moving increases again as a political solution. Among blacks,
political action increases monotonically with length of residence.

Such evidence, scanty though it may be, is an indication that
people do make an effort to change their neighborhoods in ways other
than by moving. That fact, coupled with recent Supreme Court rulings granting instant voting privileges (no more year-long wait to
participate in local elections) and other Court rulings demanding
equal public services in all areas of any political jurisdiction (if one
street in Suburb A gets street lighting, then all streets in Suburb A
should get street lighting) leads to the following speculation: General-
purpose governments will be getting smaller and their representatives
will be elected more frequently.

Not a shred of empirical evidence exists to support the speculation. We simply find it unlikely that equal services can be supported
across large jurisdictions; hence we feel that smaller jurisdictions
will provide a way out of that problem. Similarly, if local pressures
for participatory democracy grow, we may find ourselves back to
the days of the early Republic, when annual elections were considered
de rigueur—that is, when semiannual ones were not required.

It will be noted that both suggestions run counter to the orthodoxy
of large, consolidated governments required on efficiency grounds and
long intervals between elections sought for "stability" reasons, so
that long-range planning can be effected. We suggest that the orthodoxy confuses the needs of executive management with those of representative government. Were we to couple our district GPRs (with
frequent elections) with large area management agencies (metropol-

itan transport commissions, environmental management agencies,
planning commissions), then it might be possible to achieve efficiency
in planning and execution with responsiveness to shifts in population.

Since the preceding statement is anything but intuitively obvious,
a sketch in terms of environmental management is needed.

AN INSTITUTIONAL STRUCTURE FOR
ENVIRONMENTAL MANAGEMENT

The institutional structure for environmental management will
logically consist of legislative, executive, and judicial elements,
but we shall be concerned mostly with the first two. The judiciary's
entrance into the environmental field is already well advanced. In
some ways the judiciary is providing a useful transitional instrument
for questioning the traditional executive agency handling of environmental issues. Under the leadership of such lawyers as Joseph Sax,
groups have been able to call public agencies to account and individuals whose rights have been violated have been able to seek and obtain
relief.[18] There are indications, however (for example, the Supreme
Court's refusal to give standing to the Sierra Club in the Mineral
King case) that the courts are near the end of their capacity to assist
in the resolution of social choice questions. By its very nature the
judiciary must focus on the procedures followed rather than on the
substantive aspects of decisionmaking. We can take issue, in the
courts, with the executive agencies' handling of environmental matters, but we must, finally, face up to making the choices, and that
involves both the legislative and executive sides of government.

It will be easier to sketch out the executive side of a metropolitan
or regional environmental management structure first. We have already indicated that the technical tradeoffs among residual physical
forms and the economics of the regional system are such as to demand one integrated executive agency capable of capturing these
effects and economies. No particular problem arises in any such
environmental management agency (EMA) beyond the following questions: Should it be a public corporation chartered by the state or
should it be a governmental agency, either state or locally created?
Should it try to manage a whole watershed? Who should control the
agency?

The answer to the first question seems to be indeterminate.
Either agency could run a monitoring service, make economic and
technical calculations of alternative ways of meeting given ambient
standards, draw up schedules of effluent charges, initiate punitive
action against violators, and advise the policymakers of potential
gains and losses and their distributional effects. How to set up the
EMA seems to depend on the peculiarities of the local or state situation and not on any conceptual differences between the two methods.

The second question may similarly be begged, that is, how big is the "whole" watershed? It is worth noting, however, that an EMA could work either way. If it has an entire watershed, its options concerning the use of the waterway for disposal of residuals may be expanded, for example, low-flow augmentation. If the EMA does not control the whole watershed, then it should have to meet exogenously determined water quality standards, either at its regional boundary or throughout its reach of the river. The former is preferable, since the EMA may want to use the river for disposal and meet its downstream standards by instream aeration or other means. Exogenous standards that close out such uses will unnecessarily restrict the range of management options.

The third question raises the social choice issue. It is abundantly clear that the technical officials, the professionals who run the EMA, will take an overall efficiency point of view. They can prepare long-range plans under different sets of assumptions. What they lack is a policy body that can choose among the plans and can ask that other sets of assumptions be used. This is where the legislative body composed of district general-purpose representatives can be useful. It will quickly be seen that using the GPR approach might result in a legislative body of several hundred people for a major metropolitan area. This prospect frightens many, though the reasons given for the fear do not appear substantial. The main fear is that the body would be "unmanageable." There are some normative overtones to that fear, epitomized by asking, "Unmanageable for whom?" Legislative bodies of such size manage themselves very well. (Moreover, if the area becomes very large, obviously the GPRs needed are not the district ones, but the state representatives from the affected area.) A more reasonable way to address the issue is to ask, "Who controls the agenda?" The answer is clear: the EMA, in large measure, by the options it generates for consideration. Indeed, the emphasis should be put on how the process of option generation can be opened up in a nonfrivolous sense. We are currently exploring the ways in which an optimizing model of residuals management can be used in a legislative setting. The essence of the idea is to break out of the model the distributional consequences (good and bad) of particular management options and then allow legislators to build up coalitions as a result of mutual acceptance of constraint sets. [19] Legislative use of such management models may provide one way by which optimal solutions of determinate problems may be evaluated in a social choice sense.

The district representatives will, of course, be interested in the environmental implications of each proposed solution for their districts. They will also note the financial implication of each solution and weigh it against the overall tax situation in their district. Some representatives will opt for high environmental quality, even at the expense of higher taxes. Others will accept a deteriorating

environment, if necessary, to hold tax rates down. Both will be reflecting constituent preferences. A plan is adopted. People move.
Is it likely that persons holding contrary preferences, assuming they
move, will move into, or out of any district? Both the Tiebout
model and the present authors suggest they will move out. Hence
this population shift will not affect our solution.

What if one GPR has misjudged his constituency? If he has, and
if elections are frequent, he will be defeated and his successor will
want to undo what he has done. What does this do to the continuity
of planning? It will clearly upset it unless an additional rule is
made—no execution of a plan until it has been passed in two (or
three?) legislative sessions. Such rules were once usual in legislative bodies, and were used for just such purposes, to ensure that
preferences were correctly interpreted on controversial issues.
(For example, the British Parliament Act of 1911 (1 & 2 Geo. V,
c13) which provides for passage by Commons in three successive
sessions, extending over at least 2 years, of any bill voted down in
Lords.)

If elections are not frequent and/or if one vote can put an area
on an irreversible course, then there is no alternative for people who
disapprove of the decision except to move. Even under these conditions, which are the ones that obtain in most instances, the extent of
political protest, court suits, and civil disobedience suggests that
many would rather fight than switch even in such a hopeless case.

Frequent elections might, in particular instances, be an inducement for moving into an area rather than out.* An historic, pictur-
esque, but soon-to-be-destroyed area might be saved by a movement
in by those determined to save it, encouraged by the fact that their
votes could swing the balance. Political action and moving could be
teamed in such cases (remembering, however, the assumption that
all issues are encompassed by one GPR) so that one election can turn
a district around on many issues.

The operation of such an institutional scheme raises some
worries, however. Perhaps a "residuals sink" will be created in
one area, either because the economics and technology favor it or
because a majority coalition is built up that finds it to their mutual
advantage to create it, or perhaps both. How are the minority districts in this situation to be protected? While such an event may not
be likely, it is possible that it could occur. If it does, then by definition the minority could not "trade out" of the situation, since the
situation results from there being a majority-sized "core" in a game-

---

*We acknowledge that the strength of Olsen's "logic of collective
action" could operate against such moves. Since the total economic
gain would accrue only to those who made the move (and not to all
persons desiring to save the area), the idea is still reasonable.

theory sense, that is, a majority coalition no member of which can
be made better off by getting out of the coalition.

One defense against this occurring is to accompany the creation
of the new structure with certain minimum environmental standards
that are inviolable. Residuals sinks would simply be prohibited,
probably by a higher-level government. Another defense would be
to assess costs in relation to levels of relative quality, so that people
at the lowest quality levels pay nothing or are paid while those at the
higher quality levels pay progressively more.

A second problem might occur if the combination of frequent
elections and the rule that some plans must be passed twice result
in an impasse or oscillation. Nothing could be passed. While the
authors do not regard this problem as significant in a practical
sense, it is possible.* Safeguards could be provided against such
contingencies by allowing the agency head to go to the next highest
level of general government (usually the state) for approval of a
plan if no plan can be adopted locally. This is routinely done in
certain cases now.

Another problem that will remain is what happens at the boundary line. We have already alluded to the issue in the water area,
but it also occurs in air and in solid-waste disposal. Having an
EMA will not preclude the necessity for exogenously determined
ambient standards at the boundaries; it simply greatly reduces the
number of boundaries and simplifies the problem of setting the standards. We may go further and say that the concept of an EMA is in-
structive to the issue of levels of government in environmental
management. Since the rationale of an EMA is to take advantage of
technical and economic efficiencies inside a given boundary, it follows that no higher level of government should specify means, only
ends. In other words, it may make sense for state or federal
agencies to specify an ambient standard (for example, minimum
national levels, ban on heavy metals), but it will not make sense for
those governments to prescribe how the ambient standards are to
be met (for example, secondary treatment everywhere). The point
is well worth making, since it is opposite to the prevailing trend of
policy at the federal level, which is increasingly concentrated on
enforcing certain methods of treatment on a national basis rather
than on emphasizing the result wanted. This procedure is not only
grossly inefficient, ignoring the preferences of the people affected,
but probably will not work.

---

*Note, on the other hand, the present impasse in both transport
and power projects under a governmental structure are heavily protected from voter preference.

NOTES

1. For a discussion of the concept of Pareto relevancy see J. M. Buchanan and W. C. Stubblebine, "Externality," Economica (November 1962), pp. 371-84.

2. See Allen V. Kneese, Robert U. Ayres, and Ralph C. d'Arge, Environmental Economics: A Materials Balance Approach (Washington, D.C.: Resources for the Future, Inc., 1971).

3. For a recent discussion of this two-step procedure, see W. J. Baumol, "On Taxation and the Control of Externalities," American Economic Review (June 1972), pp. 307-22.

4. See Allen V. Kneese and Blair T. Bower, Managing Water Quality—Economics, Technology, Institutions (Baltimore: The Johns Hopkins Press, 1968).

5. This point is developed in more detail in Edwin T. Haefele and Allen V. Kneese, "Residuals Management and Metropolitan Governance," in Lowdon Wingo, ed., The Governance of Metropolitan Areas (Washington, D.C.: Resources for the Future, Inc., 1972).

6. See Clifford S. Russell, Walter O. Spofford, Jr., and Edwin T. Haefele, Environmental Quality Management in Metropolitan Areas, Presented at the International Economics Association Meeting, Copenhagen, Denmark, June 19-24, 1972.

7. J. Rothenberg, "Local Decentralization and the Theory of Optimal Government," in J. Margolis, ed., The Analysis of Public Output (New York: Columbia University Press, 1970).

8. Martin McGuire, "Group Segregation and Optimal Jurisdiction," unpublished.

9. Charles M. Tiebout, "A Pure Theory of Local Expenditures," Journal of Political Economy (October 1956), pp. 416-24.

10. For discussion of the nondistributive so-called Lindahl solution, see McGuire and Aaron, op. cit.

11. Edwin T. Haefele, "Coalitions, Minority Representations, and Vote Trading Possibilities," Public Choice (Spring 1970).

12. Kenneth J. Arrow, Social Choice and Individual Values (New York: John Wiley & Sons, Inc., 1963).

13. Edwin T. Haefele, "A Utility Theory of Representative Government," American Economic Review (June 1971), pp. 350-67.

14. Edwin T. Haefele, "General Purpose Representatives at the Local Level: A New Approach to the Problem of Governmental Boundaries," Public Administration Review, forthcoming.

15. For a clear presentation of the case, see John E. Jackson, "Intensities, Preferences and Electoral Politics," The Urban Institute, Working Paper 705-72, March 1972.

16. See Russell, Spofford and Haefele, op. cit., p. 55 passim.

17. John M. Orbell and Toru Uno, "A Theory of Neighborhood Problem-Solving: Political Action vs. Residential Mobility," Americal Political Science Review 66 (June 1972), pp. 471-89.

18. Joseph L. Sax, Defending the Environment (New York: Alfred A. Knopf, 1970).

19. See Russell, Spofford, and Haefele, op. cit.

[5]

The Faustian Bargain

In its original form, this statement bore the somewhat abstract title, "Benefit-Cost Analysis and Unscheduled Events in the Nuclear Fuel Cycle." The Atomic Energy Commission had asked for comments on one of its documents, noting that environmental statements for a power reactor should contain a cost-benefit analysis which, among other things, "considers and balances the adverse environmental effects and the environmental, economic, technical and other benefits of the facility." In response to the invitation, Allen V. Kneese, director of RFF's program of studies in the quality of the environment, submitted the following remarks.

I AM SUBMITTING this statement as a long-time student and practitioner of benefit-cost analysis, not as a specialist in nuclear energy. It is my belief that benefit-cost analysis cannot answer the most important policy questions associated with the desirability of developing a large-scale, fission-based economy. To expect it to do so is to ask it to bear a burden it cannot sustain. This is so because these questions are of a deep *ethical* character. Benefit-cost analyses certainly cannot solve such questions and may well obscure them.

These questions have to do with whether society should strike the Faustian bargain with atomic scientists and engineers, described by Alvin M. Weinberg in *Science.* If so unforgiving a technology as large-scale nuclear fission energy production is adopted, it will impose a burden of continuous monitoring and sophisticated management of a dangerous material, essentially forever. The penalty of not bearing this burden may be unparalleled disaster. This irreversible burden would be imposed even if nuclear fission were to be used only for a few decades, a mere instant in the pertinent time scales.

Clearly, there are some major advantages in using nuclear fission technology, else it would not have so many well-intentioned and intelligent advocates. Residual heat is produced to a greater extent by current nuclear generating plants than by fossil fuel-fired ones. But, otherwise, the environmental impact of routine operation of the nuclear fuel cycle, including burning the fuel in the reactor, can very likely be brought to a lower level than will be possible with fossil fuel-fired plants. This superiority may not, however, extend to some forms of other alternatives, such as solar and geothermal energy, which have received [1]

comparatively little research and development effort. Insofar as the usual market costs are concerned, there are few published estimates of the costs of various alternatives, and those which are available are afflicted with much uncertainty. In general, however, the costs of nuclear and fossil fuel energy (when residuals generation in the latter is controlled to a high degree) do not seem to be so greatly different. Early evidence suggests that other as yet undeveloped alternatives (such as hot rock geothermal energy) might be economically attractive.

Unfortunately, the advantages of fission are much more readily quantified in the format of a benefit-cost analysis than are the associated hazards. Therefore, there exists the danger that the benefits may seem more real. Furthermore, the conceptual basis of benefit-cost analysis requires that the redistributional effects of the action be, for one or another reason, inconsequential.

Here we are speaking of hazards that may affect humanity many generations hence and equity questions that can neither be neglected as inconsequential nor evaluated on any known theoretical or empirical basis. This means that technical people, be they physicists or economists, cannot legitimately make the decision to generate such hazards. Our society confronts a moral problem of a great profundity; in my opinion, it is one of the most consequential that has ever faced mankind. In a democratic society the only legitimate means for making such a choice is through the mechanisms of representative government.

For this reason, during the short interval ahead while dependence on fission energy could still be kept within some bounds, I believe the Congress should make an open and explicit decision about this Faustian bargain. This would best be done after full national discussion at a level of seriousness and detail that the nature of the issue demands. An appropriate starting point could be hearings before a committee of Congress with a broad national policy responsibility. Technically oriented or specialized committees would not be suitable to this task. The Joint Economic Committee might be appropriate. Another possibility would be for the Congress to appoint a select committee to consider this and other large ethical questions associated with developing technology. The newly established Office of Technology Assessment could be very useful to such a committee.

MUCH HAS been written about hazards associated with the production of fission energy. Until recently, most statements emanating from the scientific community were very reassuring on this matter. But several events in the past year or two have reopened the issue of hazards and revealed it as a real one. I think the pertinent hazards can usefully be divided into two categories—those associated with the actual operation of the fuel cycle for power production and those associated with the long-term storage of radioactive waste. I will discuss both briefly.

The recent failure of a small physical test of emergency core cooling equipment for the present generation of light-water reactors was an alarming event. This is in part because the failure casts doubt upon whether the system would function in the unlikely, but not impossible, event it would be called upon in an actual energy reactor. But it also illustrates the great difficulty of forecasting behavior of components in this complex technology where pertinent experimentation is always difficult and may sometimes be impossible. Other recent unscheduled events were the partial collapse of fuel rods in some reactors.

There have long been deep but suppressed doubts within the scientific community about the adequacy of reactor safety research vis-à-vis the strong emphasis on developing the technology and getting plants on the line. In recent months the Union of Concerned Scientists has called public attention to the hazards of nuclear fission and asked for a moratorium on the construction of new plants and stringent operating controls on existing ones. The division of opinion in the scientific community about a matter of such moment is deeply disturbing to an outsider.

No doubt there are some additional surprises ahead when other parts of the fuel cycle become more active, particularly in transportation of spent fuel elements and in fuel reprocessing facilities. As yet, there has been essentially no commercial experience in recycling the plutonium produced in nuclear reactors. Furthermore, it is my understanding that the inventory of plutonium in the breeder reactor fuel cycle will be several times greater than the inventory in the light-water reactor fuel cycle with plutonium recycle. Plutonium is one of the deadliest substances known to man. The inhalation of a millionth of a gram—the size of a grain of pollen—appears to be sufficient to cause lung cancer.

Although it is well known in the nuclear community, perhaps the general public is unaware of the magnitude of the disaster which would occur in the event of a severe accident at a nuclear facility. I am told that if an accident occurred at one of today's nuclear plants, resulting in the release of only five percent of only the more volatile fission products, the number of casualties could total between 1,000 and 10,000. The estimated range apparently could shift up or down by a factor of ten or so, depending on assumptions of population density and meteorological conditions.

With breeder reactors, the accidental release of plutonium may be of greater consequence than the release of the more volatile fission products. Plutonium is one of the most potent respiratory carcinogens in existence. In addition to a great variety of other radioactive substances, breeders will contain one, or more, tons of plutonium. While the fraction that could be released following a credible accident is extremely uncertain, it is clear that the release of only a small percentage of this inventory would be equivalent to the release of *all* the volatile fission products in one of today's nuclear plants. Once lost to [2] the environment, the plutonium not ingested by people in the first few hours following an accident would be around to take its toll for generations to come—for tens of thousands of years. When one factors in the possibility of sabotage and warfare, where power plants are prime targets not just in the United States but also in less developed countries now striving to establish a nuclear industry, then there is almost no limit to the size of the catastrophe one can envisage.

It is argued that the probabilities of such disastrous events are so low that these events fall into the negligible risk category. Perhaps so, but do we really know this? Recent unexpected events raise doubts. How, for example, does one calculate the actions of a fanatical terrorist?

The use of plutonium as an article of commerce and the presence of large quantities of plutonium in the nuclear fuel cycles also worries a number of informed persons in another connection. Plutonium is readily used in the production of nuclear weapons, and governments, possibly even private parties, not now having access to such weapons might value it highly for this purpose. Although an illicit market has not yet been established, its value

has been estimated to be comparable to that of heroin (around $5,000 per pound). A certain number of people may be tempted to take great risks to obtain it. AEC Commissioner Larsen, among others, has called attention to this possibility. Thus, a large-scale fission energy economy could inadvertently contribute to the proliferation of nuclear weapons. These might fall into the hands of countries with little to lose, or of madmen, of whom we have seen several in high places within recent memory.

In his excellent article referred to above, Weinberg emphasized that part of the Faustian bargain is that to use fission technology safely, society must exercise great vigilance and the highest levels of quality control, continuously and *indefinitely*. As the fission energy economy grows, many plants will be built and operated in countries with comparatively low levels of technological competence and a greater propensity to take risks. A much larger amount of transportation of

hazardous materials will probably occur, and safety will become the province of the sea captain as well as the scientist. Moreover, even in countries with higher levels of technological competence, continued success can lead to reduced vigilance. We should recall that we managed to incinerate three astronauts in a very straightforward accident in an extremely high technology operation where the utmost precautions were allegedly being taken.

DEEPER MORAL questions also surround the storage of high-level radioactive wastes. Estimates of how long these waste materials must be isolated from the biosphere apparently contain major elements of uncertainty, but current ones seem to agree on "at least two hundred thousand years."

Favorable consideration has been given to the storage of these wastes in salt formations, and a site for experimental storage was selected at Lyons, Kansas. This particular site proved to be defective. Oil companies had drilled the area full of holes, and there had also been solution mining in the area which left behind an unknown residue of water. But comments of the Kansas Geological Survey raised far deeper and more general questions about the behavior of the pertinent formations under stress and the operations of geological forces on them. The ability of solid earth geophysics to predict for the time scales required proves very limited. Only now are geologists beginning to unravel the plate tectonic theory. Furthermore, there is the political factor. An increasingly informed and environmentally aware public is likely to resist the location of a permanent storage facility anywhere.

Because the site selected proved defective, and possibly in anticipation of political problems, primary emphasis is now being placed upon the design of surface storage facilities intended to last a hundred years or so, while the search for a permanent site continues. These surface storage sites would require continuous monitoring and management of a most sophisticated kind. A complete cooling system breakdown would soon prove disastrous and even greater tragedies can be imagined.

Just to get an idea of the scale of disaster that could take place, consider the following scenario. Political factors force the federal government to rely on a single aboveground storage site for all high-level radioactive waste accumulated through the year 2000. Some of the more obvious possibilities would be existing storage sites like Hanford or Savannah, which would seem to be likely military targets. A tactical nuclear weapon hits the site and vaporizes a large fraction of the contents of this storage area. The weapon could come from one of the principal nuclear powers, a lesser developed country with one or more nuclear power plants, or it might be crudely fabricated by a terrorist organization from black-market plutonium. I am told that the radiation fallout from such an event could exceed that from all past nuclear testing by a factor of 500 or so, with radiation doses exceeding the annual dose from natural background radiation by an order of magnitude. This would bring about a drastically unfavorable, and long-lasting change in the environment of the majority of mankind. The exact magnitude of the disaster is uncertain. That massive numbers of deaths might result seems clear. Furthermore, by the year 2000, high-level wastes would have just begun to accumulate. Estimates for 2020 put them at about three times the 2000 figure.

SOMETIMES, analogies are used to suggest that the burden placed upon future generations by [3] the "immortal" wastes is really nothing so very unusual. The Pyramids are cited as an instance where a very long-term commitment was made to the future and the dikes of Holland as one where continuous monitoring and maintenance are required indefinitely. These examples do not seem at all apt. They do not have the same quality of irreversibility as the problem at hand and no major portions of humanity are dependent on them for their very

existence. With sufficient effort the Pyramids could have been dismantled and the Pharaohs cremated if a changed doctrine so demanded. It is also worth recalling that most of the tombs were looted already in ancient times. In the 1950s the Dutch dikes were in fact breached by the North Sea. Tragic property losses, but no destruction of human life, ensued. Perhaps a more apt example of the scale of the Faustian bargain would be the irrigation system of ancient Persia. When Tamerlane destroyed it in the 14th century, a civilization ended.

None of these historical examples tell us much about the time scales pertinent here. One speaks of two hundred thousand years. Only a little more than one-hundredth of that time span has passed since the Parthenon was built. We know of no government whose life was more than an instant by comparison with the half-life of plutonium.

It seems clear that there are many factors here which a benefit-cost analysis can never capture in quantitative, commensurable terms. It also seems unrealistic to claim that the nuclear fuel cycle will not sometime, somewhere experience major unscheduled events. These could range in magnitude from local events, like the fire at the Rocky Mountain Arsenal, to an extreme disaster affecting most of mankind. Whether these hazards are worth incurring in view of the benefits achieved is what Alvin Weinberg has referred to as a trans-scientific question. As professional specialists we can try to provide pertinent information, but we cannot legitimately make the decision, and it should not be left in our hands.

One question I have not yet addressed is whether it is in fact not already too late. Have we already accumulated such a store of high-level waste that further additions would only increase the risks marginally? While the present waste (primarily from the military program plus the plutonium and highly enriched uranium contained in bombs and military stockpiles) is by no means insignificant, the answer to the question appears to be no. I am informed that the projected high-level waste to be accumulated from the civilian nuclear power program will contain more radioactivity than the military waste by 1980 or shortly thereafter. By 2020 the radioactivity in the mili-tary waste would represent only a small percentage of the total. Nevertheless, we are already faced with a substantial long-term waste storage problem. Development of a full-scale fission energy economy would add overwhelmingly to it. In any case, it is never too late to make a decision, only later.

WHAT ARE THE benefits? The main benefit from near-term development of fission power is the avoidance of certain environmental impacts that would result from alternative energy sources. In addition, fission energy may have a slight cost edge, although this is somewhat controversial, especially in view of the low plant factors of the reactors actually in use. Far-reaching clean-up of the fuel cycle in the coal energy industry, including land reclamation, would require about a 20 percent cost increase over uncontrolled conditions for the large, new coal-fired plants. If this is done, fission plants would appear to have a clear cost edge, although by no means a spectacular one. The cost characteristics of the breeder that would follow the light-water reactors are very uncertain at this point. They appear, among other things, to still be quite contingent on design decisions having to do with safety. The dream of "power too cheap to meter" was exactly that.

Another near-term benefit is that fission plants will contribute to our supply during the energy "crisis" that lies ahead for the next decade or so. One should take note that this crisis was in part caused by delays in getting fission plants on the line. Also, there seems to be a severe limitation in using nuclear plants to deal with short-term phenomena. Their lead time is half again as long as fossil fuel plants—on the order of a decade.

The long-term advantage of fission is that once the breeder is developed we will have a nearly limitless, although not necessarily cheap, supply of energy. This is very important but it does not necessarily argue for a near-term introduction of a full-scale fission economy. Coal supplies are vast, at least adequate for a few hundred years, and we are beginning to learn more about how to cope with the "known devils" of coal. Oil shales and tar sands also are potentially very large sources of energy, although their exploitation will present problems. Geothermal and solar sources have hardly been considered but look promising. Scientists at the AEC's Los Alamos laboratory are optimistic that large geothermal sources can be developed at low cost from deep hot rocks—which are almost limitless in supply. This of course is very uncertain since the necessary technology has been only visualized. One of the potential benefits of solar energy is that its use does not heat the planet. In the long term this may be very important.

Fusion, of course, is the greatest long-term hope. Recently, leaders of the U.S. fusion research effort announced that a fusion demonstration reactor by the mid-1990s is now considered possible. Although there is a risk that the fusion option may never be achieved, its promise is so great that it merits a truly national research and development commitment.

A strategy that I feel merits sober, if not prayerful, consideration is to phase out the present set of fission reactors, put large [4] amounts of resources into dealing with the environmental problems of fossil fuels, and price energy at its full social cost, which will help to limit demand growth. Possibly it would also turn out to be desirable to use a limited number of fission reactors to burn the present stocks of plutonium and thereby transform them into less hazardous substances. At the same time, the vast scientific resources that have developed around our fission program could be turned to work on fusion, deep geothermal, solar, and other large energy supply sources while continuing research on various types of breeders. It seems quite possible that this program would result in the displacement of fission as the preferred technology for electricity production within a few decades. Despite the extra costs we might have incurred, we would then have reduced the possibility of large-scale energy-associated nuclear disaster in our time and would be leaving a much smaller legacy of "permanent" hazard. On the other hand, we would probably have to suffer the presence of more short-lived undesirable substances in the environment in the near term.

This strategy might fail to turn up an abundant clean source of energy in the long term. In that event, we would still have fission at hand as a developed technological standby, and the ethical validity of using it would then perhaps appear in quite a different light.

We are concerned with issues of great moment. Benefit-cost analysis can supply useful inputs to the political process for making policy decisions, but it cannot begin to provide a complete answer, especially to questions with such far-reaching implications for society. The issues should be aired fully and completely before a committee of Congress having broad policy responsibilities. An explicit decision should then be made by the entire Congress as to whether the risks are worth the benefits. [5]

PART II

Water Resources and Benefit–Cost Analysis

[6]

Economics and Water Resources

Allen V. Kneese

Introduction

My assignment is to describe and assess the contribution of economics to water management. This is a very large topic so, to meet space limitations, I will confine my discussion to water issues in the western United States and limit the topic further to mostly water quantity rather than quality matters. I should note, however, that the economics of water quality has been a large and influential area of research.

Water allocation institutions in the West were built up during a period of rapid water development and were designed to foster and aid that development. Prior appropriation law helped to provide a degree of security of supply so that private developers of irrigation had the incentive to commit capital and labor to the construction of diversion and distribution systems. Yet, the relationships between law, institutions, and development did not stop there.

Even after water sources were fully appropriated, agriculture continued to expand by developing supplies through the federal program to reclaim the arid West. The era of reclaiming arid lands began in the late nineteenth century, and the 1902 Reclamation Act established this objective as a national goal. The period following the Reclamation Act was one of heavily subsidized and increasingly centralized, large-scale irrigation projects. Long-term, interest-free financing based on "ability to pay" further institutionalized the notion that unappropriated and undeveloped water was itself free, with its only cost being the capital cost of constructing works and the subsequent operations and maintenance cost. The Bureau of Reclamation provided dams and diversion works on most major waterways in the West. Transbasin diversion projects were also commonplace. Special water districts were created to repay the federal government and to operate and maintain reclamation works. If projects experienced hardships, contract obligations were deferred. Regions that had political clout

23

Multidisciplinary Perspectives on Water Resources Policy

in Congress were usually treated most generously. Frequently, hydroelectric power production was part of these projects and was used as the "cash register" to subsidize irrigation water development.

The West is rapidly undergoing a major transformation with respect to water. Increasing water scarcity already has brought changes in western development and water-use patterns, and much greater changes are likely to occur in the future. In particular, the expansion of irrigated agriculture based on the availability of inexpensive water is ending.

Just a few decades ago supplies were sufficient to satisfy a rapid growth of water use throughout virtually all of the West. More recently, however, high costs and limited opportunities for developing new supplies have severely constrained the growth of offstream water use in many areas, especially where users are heavily dependent on diminishing supplies of groundwater. Total water withdrawals for all but hydroelectric generation rose 4.6 percent per annum from 1950 to 1960, compared to only 1.4 percent per annum from 1970 to 1980. Excluding the northern plains states of Kansas, Nebraska, and North and South Dakota, where water withdrawals nearly doubled over the last decade, water withdrawals rose only 0.9 percent per annum from 1970 to 1980.

Rights to most of the surface waters have been allocated, and with rising frequency, potential users are forced to compete for the same water. This competition has been intensified by the rising value that society is placing on instream water uses. In nearly half of the West's water resource subregions, the sum of instream use (defined as the flow at the discharge point of the subregion required to satisfy the higher of minimum needs to maintain fish and wildlife populations or navigational needs) and offstream consumption exceeds average yearly streamflow. Furthermore, since current levels of water consumption result in the groundwater mining of about 22.4 million acre-feet per year, future competition over supplies likely will intensify even in the absence of further growth in demand.

Approximately 90 percent of western water consumption is for the irrigation of about fifty million acres. As both the largest and a relatively low-value user, irrigation is the sector most directly affected by the changing water situation. Nonagricultural water consumption grew twice as fast as irrigation use from 1960 to 1980. Where water has become particularly scarce and expensive, water for irrigation has started to level off or even decline. In Arizona, for example, total irrigation water consumption declined by about 6 percent from 1970 to 1980, while consumption for other uses rose by 67 percent. Only in the northern plains did the growth of water consumption for irrigation exceed the growth for other uses during the last decade.[1]

My discussion will proceed in two parts. The first will focus on benefit-cost analysis, which was concerned with the economics of the allocation of public capital during the rapid development phase of water resources. While benefit-cost analysis is of historical interest and was first applied to the economic evaluation of water projects, it is now finding applications in many other areas of public decision making as well. The second part addresses the theory and practice of markets and pricing, a field that concentrates on the allocation of the water resource itself now that the era of massive water development is about over.

Benefit-Cost Analysis: The Historical Context

Introduction

Benefit-cost analysis, an applied welfare economics technique, has played a very large role historically in water resource economics and, more recently, in environmental economics. This mode of analysis initially was developed to evaluate water resources investments made by federal water agencies in the United States, principally the U.S. Bureau of Reclamation and the U.S. Army Corps of Engineers. The general objective of benefit-cost analysis in this application was to provide a useful picture of the costs and gains from making investments in water development. Here I briefly consider the history of this mode of analysis and show how its applications have evolved over time.

The intellectual father of the technique is often said to be Jules Dupuit, who in 1844 wrote a frequently cited study, "On the Measure of the Utility of Public Works."[2] In this remarkable article, Dupuit recognized the concept of consumer's surplus (a central concept in the modern application of benefit-cost analysis) and saw that consequently the benefits of public works are not necessarily equal to the direct revenues that the public works projects will generate.

Benefit-Cost Analysis and Water Resource Development

Early contributions to benefit-cost analysis generally came from the federal agencies responsible for water development. In fact, such agencies have long been aware of the need for economic evaluation of projects, and the benefit-cost procedure is now embodied in agency policy and in government legislation. As examples, in 1808 Albert Gallatin, President Jefferson's secretary of the treasury, issued a report on transportation programs for the new nation in which he stressed the need to compare the benefits and the costs of proposed waterway improvements. The Federal Reclamation Act of 1902, which created the Bureau of Reclamation (first called the Reclamation Service) and was aimed at opening the American West to irrigation, required analysis to establish the repayment capacity of projects.

In more recent times the Flood Control Act of 1936 has a special significance for the development of benefit-cost analysis. This statute declared the constitutional powers of the federal government to improve rivers in general and their watersheds for flood control purposes. It thus extended Corps of

Multidisciplinary Perspectives on Water Resources Policy

Engineers operations to the many unnavigable streams along with navigable streams and their tributaries. The same flood control act provided that federal improvements for flood control could be undertaken "if the benefits to whomsoever they may accrue are in excess of the estimated costs. . . ." This provision effectively subjected all flood control projects of the Corps to a benefit-cost test, and made an excess of benefits over costs a requirement for authorization of a project. Whether the legislators who framed and enacted this statute knew it or not, with this provision they enshrined the "Kaldor-Hicks" potential compensation criterion in federal law. This criterion says that a project is economically justified if the beneficiaries could compensate the losers, whether they do so or not.

Although the statutory directive applied specifically only to flood control improvements by the Corps of Engineers and the Department of Agriculture, all water planning agencies soon adopted it for all water resources purposes. Each agency, however, adopted different and often inconsistent criteria for estimating benefits and costs.

A few years after the passage of the Flood Control Act of 1936, Congress provided a statutory basis for benefit-cost analysis by the Bureau of Reclamation. The Reclamation Project Act of 1939 authorized the secretary of the interior to take into account a variety of joint and alternative uses in the development of any reclamation project, including irrigation, power production, urban water supplies, flood control, navigation, and other miscellaneous purposes. It required that he consult with the Corps of Engineers on flood control and navigation features of projects and secure special congressional appropriations for such features.

Most significantly for our purposes, the 1939 act required the secretary of the interior to estimate the total benefits and costs of every multipurpose project, and required that the sum of benefits from a project at least cover the total project costs if congressional authorization for a project is to be secured. This law subjected Bureau projects, like those of the Corps of Engineers, to trial by benefit-cost analysis.

In 1946, the U.S. Federal Interagency River Basin Committee (a group composed of representatives of federal agencies with water resource responsibilities) appointed a subcommittee on benefits and costs to reconcile the practices of federal agencies in making benefit-cost analyses. This reflected the concern over the diverse practices of several agencies. In 1950, the subcommittee issued a landmark report entitled *Proposed Practices for Economic Analysis of River Basin Projects.* This volume was known affectionately to a generation of resource economists as the Green Book because of the color of its cover.[3] While never fully accepted either by the parent committee or the federal agencies, this report was remarkably sophisticated in its use of economic analysis and laid such an intellectual foundation for research and debate as to set it apart from other major reports in the realm of public expenditures.

Economics and Water Resources

This document also provided general guidance for the routine development of benefit-cost analysis of water projects that persists to the present day, a theme I will pick up again shortly.

Following this report came some outstanding publications from the research and academic communities. Several books appearing since the late 1950s have clarified the welfare economics concepts applicable to water resources development and use and have explored the fundamental rationale for government activity in the area. For example, Otto Eckstein's 1958 book, *Water Resources Development: The Economics of Project Evaluation*,[4] is outstanding for its careful review and critique of federal agency practice with respect to benefit-cost analysis. While naturally somewhat dated it remains a valuable reference.

In 1960, Jack Hirschleifer and collaborators prepared a clear exposition of principles together with applications to several important cases.[5] Other reports appeared during the early 1960s. In 1962, a group of economists, engineers, and hydrologists at Harvard University published an especially notable study which probed into applications of systems analysis and computer technology within the framework of benefit-cost analysis.[6] The intervening years have seen considerable additional work on the technique and its gradual expansion to areas outside the field of water resources.

Further Developments in the Federal Government

Meanwhile, back in Washington efforts to standardize benefit-cost practices in water projects continued. From the early 1950s to the early 1960s, the federal government issued two major documents of relevance. The first was Bureau of the Budget Circular A-47, developed in 1952 during the Truman administration and adopted by the Eisenhower administration the following year.[7] The second was Senate Document No. 97 which the Kennedy administration issued in 1962.[8] Neither differed substantially from the principles for national economic efficiency analysis set out in the Green Book, but they did reflect political differences between the two administrations. The Eisenhower administration wanted rules that would justify fewer projects, and the Kennedy administration wanted rules that would justify more projects. Thus the documents concerned themselves with such matters as appropriate discount rates and what types of benefits would be permissible for inclusion. This is one illustration of the fact that, as Mr. Dooley said of the Supreme Court, benefit-cost analysis "follows the election returns." More broadly, over the years economists have complained loudly that benefit-cost analysis is influenced by the self-interest of the agencies conducting it and their clientele groups. On the other hand, benefit-cost analysis has probably served to weed out the very worst water projects, and by presenting assumptions and data in an organized way it provides an opportunity for critics to question

27

assumptions and data and to test the sensitivity of results to them. Such reanalysis has influenced decisions on public projects.

Also Senate Document 97 moved toward introducing multiobjective planning concepts into the evaluation process. It specified that three objectives should be included in water resource planning (1) national economic development, (2) resources conservation, and (3) the "well-being" of the people. The first (Green Book) objective came, in later discussions and documents, to be known as the NED objective. This thrust toward multiobjective planning was in practice a failure. The other objectives were given lip service; only NED was quantified in project evaluation.[9]

National interest in water resources planing peaked in the 1960s. This decade saw the great dam-building era in the Columbia, Missouri, and Colorado Basins, and enormous water works construction in California. In 1965 Congress passed the Water Resources Planning Act. Under the act, a Water Resources Council (WRC) was formed to report to the President and was charged with establishing principles, standards, and procedures for water resource and related land use planning. To guide this effort, the Council established four different objectives for water resource planning: (1) regional economic development, (2) the quality of the total environment, (3) the well-being of the people, and (4) NED. One assumes NED was put at the end to deemphasize it. However, of these stated objectives NED and environmental quality (EQ) were the only ones for which an actual planning procedure was outlined in the published document resulting from the Councils deliberations, *Principles and Standards for Planning Water and Related Land Resources* (P&S).[10] A.B. Jaffe described the new procedures in this way:

> To guide the water resource planing effort towards these dual objectives of National Economic Development (NED) and Environmental Quality (EQ), the P&S also establish for the first time a detailed planning process. Two of the required steps in the planning process, formulation of alternative plans and analysis of tradeoffs among these alternatives, deserve special attention. The required formulation of alternative plans must be conducted to ensure that at least one alternative designed to achieve the objectives of NED and one alternative designed to achieve the objectives of EQ be prepared. The impact of all plans on the NED objectives and the EQ objectives are to be evaluated by a "system of accounts." For each alternative project or program, the agency is to evaluate the beneficial and adverse effects on the NED objective and tabulate these in the NED "account" for that objective. The NED account is the B-C analysis presented in a disaggregated form so that the particular categories of costs and benefits can be seen. Similarly, the beneficial and adverse effects of each alternative on the EQ objective are tabulated in the EQ account. The EQ account should display effects on the environment, quantified as much as possible and described qualitatively where necessary.

Economics and Water Resources

Effects on Regional Development and Social Well-Being are also to be displayed, but are not to be primary objectives.[11]

Actually, P&S procedures had little effect on agency practice which continued to emphasize NED benefits in project evaluation. Efforts were made under the Carter administration to tighten evaluation procedures and require more cost sharing in federal projects by state and local entities. These points were somewhat moot however, since by then the great dam-building era was drawing to a close and few major new federal projects were being proposed. In September 1981, President Reagan terminated the WRC.

At least he thought he had. Actually, the Council exists in law. However, since the early days of the Reagan administration the Council has not met and has no staff. Nevertheless it endorsed, by mail, the most recent guidance document from an interagency committee. The new document is entitled *Principles and Guidelines*, as opposed to the previous *Principles and Standards*, but it is still held to be binding on federal water resources agencies. For present purposes the main feature of this new document is its elevation of NED as the sole object of the evaluation process while relegating the environment once again to being an account.[12] It should be noted, however, that under the National Environmental Policy Act of 1969 all major federal actions require an "environmental impact statement." This is the primary way in which environmental considerations enter into the planning of new, and now rare, federal water resource projects.

The most striking development in benefit-cost analysis in recent years has been its increasing application to the environmental consequences of new technologies and scientific and regulatory programs. For instance, the Atomic Energy Commission used the technique to evaluate the fast breeder reactor research and development program. The technique has also been applied to other potential sources of hazard and environmental pollution. Its development and application to environmental issues were accelerated by a Reagan administration directive requiring the benefit-cost analysis of "major" federal regulations. This directive remains in effect.

However, while benefit-cost analysis was limited largely to the relatively straightforward problem of evaluating investment in water resources, economists actively debated the proper way of handling both empirical and conceptual difficulties with the technique. Some of the discussion centered on technical issues such as ways to compute consumer surplus and estimate demand functions for various outputs. For water projects these functions included flood control, irrigation, navigations, municipal and industrial water supply, and, later, recreation. Other issues more clearly related to questions of value and equity, including whether the distribution of benefits and costs among individuals needed to be addressed or whether it was adequate to consider only aggregates, as the 1936 Flood Control Act and the 1939 Federal

Multidisciplinary Perspectives on Water Resources Policy

Reclamation Project Act directed. Another question focused on the appropriate discount rate to use on water projects.

Application of the technique to issues like the development of nuclear energy, the storage of atomic waste, man-induced climate change, and the regulation of toxic substances complicates both the empirical and value (ethical) issues found in water resource applications.[13]

Allocating Existing Supplies

As noted earlier, there are basically no more unallocated supplies of water in the arid West. This means attention is shifting away from development projects and associated economic evaluation problems to the efficient and equitable allocation and reallocation of existing supplies. Western water allocation institutions need to evolve toward greater reliance on economic incentives through the formation of markets and the improvement of pricing policies for publicly supplied wastes. Evidence shows that water use is sensitive to price, and demand-side management is increasingly important for balancing demand with supplies.

Water Marketing[14]

Economic theory says that competitive markets can efficiently allocate resources among competing uses over time, but the nature of the resource presents problems for establishing and relying on unfettered water markets. Thus, the manner and ease with which a region deals with increasing water scarcity depend largely on the institutions, that is, the policies, laws, organizations, and norms, governing the allocation and use of water.

State institutions, except where water is specifically in the purview of the federal government, establish the framework and determine an individual's rights to use and transfer water. Traditionally, however, state governments have not created conditions conducive to water marketing, but have often limited the role of economic incentives in the allocation of water use.

All state water law was initially based on the common law doctrine of riparian rights. This doctrine granted landowners the right to make "reasonable" use of water that bordered on or passed through their land as long as the use did not unduly inconvenience other riparian owners. By tying water rights to the land, the doctrine precludes markets. Water scarcity and the need to supply water to nonriparian lands caused the western states largely to abandon the doctrine of riparian rights in favor of the doctrine of prior appropriation— "first-in-time, first-in-right."

Although the appropriation doctrine was potentially an important step for creating clear, transferable property rights to water, the potential has yet to be fully realized because legal and administrative factors have obscured the nature and transferability of the rights. Among these factors are the beneficial-use

Economics and Water Resources

provisions of the states' water laws. Rather than grant absolute ownership, the states granted rights to use water for "beneficial" purposes. Consequently, water rights that are not put to a beneficial use may be forfeited. Moreover, in some instances, sale of a right has been interpreted as evidence that the original user could no longer put the water to beneficial use. These provisions of western water law underlie the "use-it-or-lose it" attitude that characterizes many water users and discourages marketing and conservation.

Despite the institutional obstacles, which may be greatly exacerbated in the future by efforts to implement the Endangered Species Act, water rights do get transferred among users, and water marketing has become fairly common in many western states. Most western states permit water transfers if third parties are protected. Providing for these interests, however, can be time-consuming, costly and uncertain. Because the requisite legal and administrative hurdles add to the costs of a water transfer, the potential benefits generally have to be large to justify the effort and risk to the buyer and seller.

Recently, water marketing has increased, reflecting both the growing potential benefits of transfers and a more receptive posture toward water transfers. Laws to facilitate marketing of privately held water rights have been passed or are being considered. California now classifies water sales as a beneficial use. In 1988, Oregon's legislature passed a law that would permit any water right holder to implement conservation and apply to the Oregon Water Resources Commission for the right to sell the conserved water.[15] At the same time a bill to facilitate the transfer of water from irrigation to urban uses wended its way through the Texas legislature.[16]

Though increased marketing should be encouraged, free markets are not a panacea for efficient allocation of water over time. Two problems illustrate the limitations of markets and the challenges facing policymakers. First, third-party impacts associated with transfers need to be taken into account without unduly restricting marketing. Second, provision must be made for instream uses. Historically, instream uses were overlooked; appropriate water rights were established only by diverting water from its source. Streamflow depletion has directed attention to such values as hydroelectricity, recreation, and fish and wildlife habitat. Most western states have recently adopted measures to protect streamflows. These measures include reserving flows or granting rights for particular instream uses and directing agencies to review impacts before granting new rights. Still, the task of efficiently allocating water among instream and other uses is particularly complicated because instream uses such as fish and wildlife habitat are not marketed and thus, not easily valued. The values society attaches to these and other water uses change with population and income levels. The Endangered Species Act may be of particular significance in this connection.

Federally Supplied Water

As explained earlier, Congress established the Bureau of Reclamation early in this century to promote the development of irrigation in the arid and semi-arid West. The Bureau provides full or supplemental irrigation for about 11 million acres, more than one-fifth of the total irrigated acreage. In 1975 it supplied 28.1 million acre-ft of water, 93 percent for irrigation.[17] Since the bureau accounts for nearly one-third of all surface and about one-fifth of total water deliveries in the 17 western states, improved efficiency in the use of this water could be important.

Although reclamation law originally intended for irrigators to pay for operation and maintenance plus construction, exclusive of interest charges, more than 90 percent of the capital costs of the Bureau's irrigation projects have been subsidized. With long-term contracts making no adjustment for inflation, payments on some projects no longer pay even for operation and maintenance.[18]

Irrigators fortunate enough to receive such inexpensive water have little or no incentive to conserve. Not only is water cheap, farmers who attempt to conserve risk losing their rights to the water. Federally subsidized water generally cannot be sold by a farmer or irrigation district at a profit. Under these conditions it is not surprising that the demand for Bureau of Reclamation water has been almost completely unresponsive to price changes.

The obstacles to moving toward marginal-cost pricing of federal water are large. For one thing, long-term supply contracts reduce the possibilities of flexible pricing. Another obstacle is that many reclamation projects are so inefficient from an economic point of view that many farmers could not survive a large price increase. Pricing policies that would shut down Bureau projects would probably not pass political muster.

Perhaps more likely than achieving higher prices for Bureau water is increased voluntary transfers of federal water both within and outside the conservation districts established to distribute the water. While such transfers are not common, Richard Wahl identified several transactions ranging from short-term rental or lease arrangements to permanent transfers.[19] There is even precedent for federal legislation to facilitate such transfers: during the 1976-1977 drought, Congress authorized temporary transfers of water from the Central Valley Project.

Although transfers do occur, their high transaction costs undoubtedly stymie many potentially beneficial ones. In Wahl's judgment, these costs stem mainly from lack of a clear Bureau policy about procedures for making transfers and its unwillingness to approve them. Wahl maintains that there is a considerable latitude for voluntary transfers within existing law if the Bureau were only willing to cooperate with interested trading parties and modify existing contracts that inhibit transfers. Such a policy shift would be consistent

Economics and Water Resources

with the Bureau's *Assessment '87,* which concludes that "the Bureau's mission must change from one based on federally supported construction to one based on effective and environmentally sensitive resource management." Nevertheless, legislation extending the area and uses for federal water may be required to enable some of the most potentially beneficial exchanges.

Conclusions

The organizers of this session asked the authors to reply to two questions:
• What does your discipline bring to water resources management?
• How can we increase the application of your discipline to the management of water resources.

Given the context of my paper, I will address these questions with respect to water development and use in the West. Economics brings to the management of western water resources the constant reminder to planners, managers and legislators that water use presents a problem in the allocation of scarce resources. Early the emphasis was on scare capital. In this context benefit-cost analysis developed. Although economists often intensely criticized benefit-cost analysis as it was actually practiced, the approach probably did serve to eliminate some of the most inefficient potential projects. One vehicle for this is that it provides a framework and data that critics use to debate a project.

More recently the problem has become one of allocating existing, or even shrinking supplies of water. In this connection western water allocation institutions appear to be evolving in the desired direction. Several states either have passed or are considering legislation to encourage conservation and facilitate marketing of water rights. Further changes in state law and policy could help, and federal initiatives are needed to make federally supplied and controlled water responsive to both existing and changing supply and demand.

The hardest remaining problem in the economics of water allocation is how and to what extent to protect third parties affected by water transactions, including instream uses. A recent report from the National Research Council, *Water Transfers in the West: Efficiency, Equity, and the Environment,*[20] attempts to address this problem. The report suggests ways of providing third party participation in the transaction process.

Efforts to implement the requirements of the Endangered Species Act bring a new, large uncertainty into the water marketing picture. The federal act was passed in 1973, but it has made major waves in western water only within the last few years. Nearly all western water courses contain species that could be, and in some cases have been, declared threatened or endangered, and therefore require mandatory protection. Examples are several species of Columbia River salmon, snails in the Snake River, salmon in the Sacramento River, smelt in the San Francisco Delta, and Sqawfish in the Colorado River. In many cases proposed protective measures require provision of additional instream flows

Multidisciplinary Perspectives on Water Resources Policy

and/or major changes in the way reservoir systems are operated. Water rights, as noted earlier, are granted under state law, primarily under the prior appropriations system. These rights may be, in some cases, greatly threatened by efforts to implement the Endangered Species Act.

For example, *The Wall Street Journal* reports on efforts on the part of the Bureau of Reclamation to save the fast-disappearing winter run of Chinook salmon up the Sacramento River. These salmon are listed as threatened species under the Endangered Species Act.

> Moreover, the bureau is contemplating reducing deliveries to so-called "water rights holders"—farmers who owned water rights on the system's rivers before the Central Valley Project was constructed in the 1920s—by about half. That is a potentially explosive move, because water right holders, many of whom are among the biggest and most politically well-connected agricultural barons in the state have always maintained that water rights laws and guarantees made by the bureau assure that they can't receive less than 75 percent of their allotments in a given year, no matter how severe a drought is. The matter likely would end up in court.[21]

Uncertainty about impacts on right holders may persist for many years as litigation proceeds. This introduces a wild card into the water rights game. Since secure rights are essential to well functioning markets, efforts to implement the act may well put a damper on further development of the fledgling water markets.

Indeed efforts to protect endangered species and/or threatened ecosystems is likely to be *the* premier natural resources issue of the 1990s for economists and other pertinent disciplines.

Notes

1. Kenneth D. Frederick and Allen V. Kneese, "Reallocation by Markets and Prices" in *Climate Change and U.S. Water Resources,* ed. Paul E. Wagoner (New York, 1990).
2. Jules Dupuit, "On the Measurement of the Utility of Public Works," *International Economic Papers* 2 (nd). Translated from the French.
3. U.S. Federal Interagency River Basin Committee, Subcommittee on Benefits and Costs, *Proposed Practices for Economic Analysis of River Basin Projects*, (Washington, D.C., 1950).
4. Otto Eckstein, *Water Resource Development: The Economics of Project Evaluation* (Cambridge, MA, 1958).
5. Jack Hirshleifer, Jerome W. Milliam, and James C. De Haven, *Water Supply: Economics, Technology and Policy* (Chicago, 1960).
6. Arthur Maass, Maynard M. Hufschmidt, Robert Dorfman, Harold A. Thomas, Jr., Stephen A. Marglin, and Gordon Maskew Fair, *Design of Water-Resource Systems* (Cambridge, MA, 1962).

Economics and Water Resources

7. U.S. Bureau of the Budget, "Reports and Budget Estimates Relating to Federal Programs and Projects for Conservation, Development, or Use of Water and Related Land Resources," Circular A-47 (December 1952).

8. The President's Water Resources Council, *Policies, Standards, and Procedures in the Formulation, Evaluation, and Review of the Plans for Use and Development of Water and Related Land Resources* S. Doc. 97, 87th Cong., 2d sess. (1962).

9. For a more detailed discussion, see A. B. Jaffe, "Benefit-Cost Analysis and Multi-Objective Evaluation of Federal Water Projects," *Harvard Environmental Law Review*, 4, no. 58 (1980): 58-85.

10. 38 *Federal Register* 24.778 (1973).

11. Jaffe, "Benefit-Cost Analysis," 70.

12. Richard W. Wahl, "Water Marketing, Efficient Water Use, and the Bureau of Reclamation," paper presented at the Program on Comprehensive River Basin Management at the Annual Research Conference of the Association for Public Policy Analysis and Management, Austin, TX, 31 October 1986.

13. See Allen V. Kneese and Wiliam Schulze, "Ethics and Environmental Economics" in *Handbook of Natural Resources and Energy Economics,* eds. Allen V. Kneese and James L. Sweeney (Amsterdam, 1985).

14. The next two sections are based heavily on Frederick and Kneese, "Reallocation by Markets and Prices."

15. Joseph L. Sax, "The Constitution, Property Rights and the Future of Water Law" Western Water Policy Project, Disc. Ser. Paper 2, Natural Resources Law Center, University of Colorado School of Law (1990).

16. *Water Market Update* 1, no. 4 (1987).

17. U.S. Bureau of Reclamation, *Federal Reclamation Projects: Water and Land Resource Accomplishments, 1975, Summary Report* (Washington, D.C., 1976), 2.

18. Kenneth D. Frederick and J. C. Hanson, *Water for Western Agriculture* (Washington, D.C., 1982), 66-71.

19. Richard W. Wahl, *Promoting Increased Efficiency of Federal Water Use Through Voluntary Water Transfers,* National Center for Food and Agricultural Policy, Resources for the Future, Discussion Paper Series No. FAP87-02 (September 1987).

20. Committee on Western Water Management, *Water Transfers in the West: Efficiency Equity and the Environment* (Washington, D.C., 1992).

21. *The Wall Street Journal,* 14 February 1992.

[7]

Chapter 17

Reallocation by Markets and Prices

Kenneth D. Fredrick and Allen V. Kneese

While there is now a near-consensus that human-induced changes will produce a global warming, there is no such agreement as to how temperature and precipitation in specific areas will be affected. Some models show substantial decreases in precipitation and others increases, but with changed seasonal patterns. But even if precipitation does increase in an area, water supplies may still decline as evapotranspiration rises with temperature levels and seasonal changes reduce available supplies during critical periods.

Water can be and often is transported among regions. But relative to its value for most uses, the costs of moving water long distances out of natural channels are high. Moreover, political resistance to interbasin transfers is strong and appears to be growing. Thus, water problems as well as their solutions tend to be regional. And in view of the uncertainty of the regional changes that may be induced by climate change, planning institutional development on zero or negative impacts to water resources from human-induced climate change would be prudent.

EMERGING SCARCITY IN THE SEVENTEEN WESTERN STATES

In the western states, water allocation institutions were built during a period of rapid water development and were designed to foster it. Unappropriated water was free to anyone who could put it to a "beneficial" use, and prior appropriation law helped to provide a degree of security of supply to encourage private developers of irrigation to commit capital and labor to construct diversion and distribution systems. When the projects became too big and the costs too high for the private sector, the federal government provided the skills and subsidized funding to continue reclamation of the West.

Until a few decades ago supplies were sufficient to satisfy a rapid growth of

395

water use, even in the arid and semiarid West. More recently, high costs and limited opportunities for developing new supplies have constrained the growth of off-stream water use. Total water withdrawals in the West for all but hydro-electric generation rose only 1.4% per annum from 1970 to 1980 compared to the 4.6% per annum growth from 1950 to 1960. Outside the Northern Plains states of Kansas, Nebraska, and North and South Dakota, where withdrawals nearly doubled, extraction of water from western streams rose less than 1% per annum during the 1970s (MacKichan, 1951; MacKichan, and Kammerer 1961; Murray and Reeves, 1974; Solley et al., 1983).

As both the largest and a relatively low-value user, irrigation is the sector most directly affected by the changing situation. The expansion of irrigated agriculture based on the availability of inexpensive water has ended. Nonagricultural water consumption grew twice as fast as irrigation use from 1960 to 1980. Where water has become particularly scarce and expensive, its use for irrigation has started to level off or even decline (MacKichan, 1951; MacKichan and Kammerer, 1961; Murray and Reeves, 1974; Solley et al., 1983).

Since passage of the 1902 Reclamation Act, the West has undergone a major transformation with respect to water. Even in the absence of man-made climate change, there are pressing reasons to examine existing allocative institutions that are still suited to fostering rapid water development rather than efficiently allocating scarce supplies. In the past, natural climate variability has placed the West's water institutions under serious stresses, and even with average precipitation, water is scarce in much of the West. In many areas, existing supplies are overappropriated, and "free" water for appropriation is rare and no longer available in the areas of greatest demand. In the mid-1970s, total water use, which is defined as the sum of in-stream needs and off-stream consumption, exceeded average streamflow in 24 of the 53 water-resource subregions in the 17 western states (Water Resources Council, 1978). In a dry year with a precipitation level exceeded by 80% of the years, total use exceeded streamflow in 48 of 53 subregions. Moreover, with current levels of consumption depending on groundwater mining of over 20 million acre-ft/yr, future competition over supplies will intensify even in the absence of further growth in demand or adverse climate change.

WATER DEVELOPMENT AND ALLOCATION IN THE COLORADO BASIN

Throughout the arid West, the era of rapid water development is ending, and the challenge is shifting to managing and allocating increasingly scarce supplies. In the Colorado River Basin the challenge is particularly striking because expectations already appear to exceed the river's ability to meet them.[1]

The problems of the Colorado Basin rise, at least in part, from the Colorado River Compact which anticipated more water than the river can deliver long-

[1] This section draws extensively from Kneese and Bonem (1986).

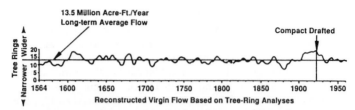

FIGURE 17.1. Reconstructed virgin flow of the Colorado River at Lee Ferry, Arizona, based on tree-ring analyses, 1564–1960. *Source:* Stockton and Jacoby (1976). Stockton, W. C. and Jacoby, G. C. Jr. 1976. *Long-term Surface Water Supply and Streamflow Trends in the Upper Colorado River Basin,* Lake Powell Research Project Bulletin No. 18, March.

term. Apparently the framers of the compact assumed the dependable yield of the river would exceed 16 million acre-ft/yr by a comfortable margin. Thus, they felt comfortable dividing 15 million acre-ft/yr evenly between the Upper and Lower Basins. And if their assumption had been correct, the subsequent allocation by international treaty of 1.5 million acre-ft to Mexico would have posed no problem.

Studies of long-term historical flows suggest that the information available to the framers was gathered during unusually, actually uniquely, persistent high streamflow. A dendrohydrograph constructed by the application of complex statistical methods to tree-ring observations in the basin and reproduced in Figure 17.1 estimates the average annual virgin flow at Lee Ferry, Arizona at about 13.5 million acre-ft for the years 1564 to 1960. It also shows that in 1922, when the Colorado River Compact was signed, the basin was in the midst of the wettest period in several centuries.

Although the Upper Colorado River Commission's estimates of river flows presented in Figure 17.2 are more encouraging, they still indicate the river has

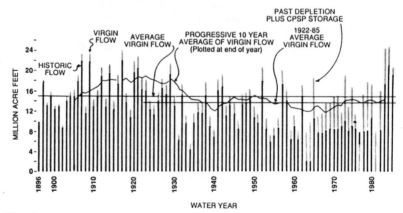

FIGURE 17.2. Colorado River flow at Lee Ferry, Arizona, 1896–1985. *Source*: Upper Colorado River Commission (1983).

been overallocated. The commission's estimates suggest the virgin flow at Lee Ferry averaged 15 million acre-ft from 1896 to 1985 (Upper Colorado River Commission, 1985). A vast majority of the high flows over this period, however, occurred before 1930.

From 1896 to 1929 flows averaged 16.8 million acre-ft, but since 1930 they have averaged only 13.9 million acre-ft. For the 1934 water-year of October 1933 to September 1934 the estimated virgin flow was only 5.6 million acre-ft, and during the 1976-1977 drought it was 5.8 million acre-ft.

The lowest flow averaged over a decade may be more relevant than single years for evaluating the Colorado River Compact. It requires the Upper Basin to deliver 75 million acre-ft at Lee Ferry in any decade. With the addition of the Upper Basin's share of the nation's commitment to Mexico, a minimum of 82.5 million acre-ft must be delivered to Lee Ferry in any decade. Although we assume the Upper Basin's share of the treaty obligation to Mexico is 7.5 million acre-ft over a 10-yr period (or half of the total obligation), this is likely to become a matter of considerable controversy if total supplies are insufficient to meet all legal obligations. The commission's data indicate, that the lowest decadal estimated virgin flows were about 118 million acre-ft during 1954–1963 and 1931–1940. The Arizona Tree Ring Laboratory's reconstructed hydrograph indicates the lowest decadal flow was 97 million acre-ft from 1584 to 1593. Consequently, without any climate change, history suggests a range of expected 10-yr drought flows of 97 to 118 million acre-ft. At the higher end of this range, after delivering 82.5 million acre-ft for downstream use, the Upper Basin would have 35.5 million acre-ft plus whatever water could be withdrawn from storage to meet its needs and commitments to supply water outside the basin to such places as the Front Range.

The inconsistency between the 16.5 million acre-ft that have seen allocated by the compact and treaty and the long-term average flow of the river has not been a problem so far because use in the Upper Basin has been well below its quota. From 1972 to 1981 consumptive use in the Upper Basin, including transbasin diversions and reservoir evaporation, was about 36.8 million acre-ft (Table 17.1). If the 10-yr low flow of this century were repeated, this level of use by the Upper Basin could be met with only modest depletions of storage.

However, assuming its use continues to grow at about 3% annually, which is the actual average growth rate from 1952 to 1981, by 2000 A.D. annual water use in the Upper Basin will be approximately 7.5 million acre-ft, equivalent to their allocation under the compact. Considerable uncertainty exists as to how the waters would be allocated if use in the Upper Basin approaches its allocation of 7.5 million acre-ft, a prolonged drought occurs, or supplies decline in a changed climate.

Supplying the Upper and Lower Basins an annual average of 7.5 million acre-ft each and Mexico with 1.5 million acre-ft when the 10-yr flow is only 118 million acre-ft could only be achieved by depleting the reservoirs to unacceptable levels. Despite the storage on the Colorado of nearly five times its average annual flow, meeting the "entitlements" of all three areas would require depleting the reservoirs to less than one-fourth capacity even if they were 90% full at the beginning of the drought.

How could the region respond and how would water be allocated under conditions of severe water scarcity? Early on in an extended drought, spot shortages would emerge throughout the basin, residential use would be restricted, and as crop yields fell, irrigators would scramble to install sprinklers, line canals, and drill new wells. The ski industry would be affected.

As the drought continued, the reservoirs would be subjected to enormous pressures. Assuming that the drought starts with the reservoirs nearly full and that policymakers are willing to empty the reservoirs, the legal "entitlements" of the Upper and Lower Basins and Mexico might be maintained for about a decade. Continuing to slavishly draw down reservoirs without any prior knowledge about when the drought would end would be extremely imprudent. Moreover, given the recreational value of these reservoirs, pressure to keep water levels high would be strong. The loss of head would also affect power generation, power revenues used by the bureau to subsidize irrigation, and power for pumping on the bureau's projects themselves. Thus, the simple statistics do not reveal the conflicts that would occur among interests and the stresses and strains on the region's water allocation institutions.

The foregoing assumptions illustrate water supply problems that could emerge within two to three decades even without climate change. Yet, as the first two sections of this volume suggest, a greenhouse-induced climate change could adversely affect the region's water supplies. For instance, even with no change in precipitation, a 2°C warming might reduce runoff as much as 20 to 30% within the basin. A 20% decline would reduce average annual flows to the levels of the two severe 10-yr droughts of this century. If precipitation were also to decline, and reductions of 10 to 20% are not out of the question, the impacts could be catastrophic. Just the prospect that climate change could reduce runoff below the historical experience makes a policy of rapidly drawing down stocks to maintain "entitlement" levels during times of shortage more reckless.

Considerable uncertainty exists as to how the waters of the entire Colorado Basin would be allocated as use in the Upper Basin approaches its legal allotment, a prolonged drought occurs, or a secular decline in water begins. One thing is clear, however. The current institutions—including the international treaty, the interstate compacts, and water laws of the various basin states—were not designed to deal with such a situation. A severe drought or secular drying of the area would stress the basin's legal and economic institutions and invite greater attention to economic efficiency in use and flexibility in allocation than now exists.

Such stresses would not be unique to the Colorado Basin. Water is becoming increasingly scarce even in the nation's more humid regions, and the prospect of a changing climate adds to the uncertainties surrounding the water supplies of all regions. Efficient management and use of these resources and the ability to reallocate scarce supplies in response to changing supply and demand are assuming greater significance throughout the United States.

TABLE 17.1   Average Annual Depletions in the Upper Colorado River (in Thousands of acre-ft)

	1952–1961	1962–1971	1972–1981
Within basin depletions			
Quantity	1614	1986	2366
Percentage change from			
· previous decade		23	19
Transbasin diversions	463	508	704
Net Reservoir evaporation loss	0	257	609
Total quantity	2050	2751	3679
Percentage change from			
previous decade		34	34

Source: Kneese and Bonem (1986).

Before examining how water is allocated and what changes might enable a region to cope with scarcity, the next section briefly discusses the concept of economic efficiency in water use.

CONCEPTS OF EFFICIENCY IN RESOURCE USE

Competition for nature's scarce resources is a fundamental fact of economic life. The primary purpose of an economic system is allocating these resources among competing uses and distributing the final products efficiently, that is, in a manner that tends to maximize net economic benefits to society. In our economy, prices and markets are the primary mechanisms for allocating resources. Producers decide how much of a commodity to supply on the basis of the prices of productive resources and the price of the commodity. Consumers decide how much to purchase based on their preferences and incomes and the commodity's price. Thus, in a competitive market economy, prices provide the signals and incentives encouraging conservation and development of new supplies and directing scarce resources to their most valued uses.

Two fundamental concepts underlie the economically efficient use of resources: free market exchange of well-defined property rights in open competitive markets and marginal-cost pricing of goods and services produced by public agencies. Efficiency of production and consumption depends on a comparison of marginal value in use with the marginal cost of the last unit produced. The marginal cost is the increment to total cost associated with producing the last unit. As long as the amount consumers are willing to pay (i.e., their value in use) exceeds the marginal cost, production should be expanded. Production should be stabilized when the marginal cost equals the price consumers are willing to pay. At this point, the marginal value in use of the product is equal for all consumers who purchase the product, and it is also equal to the marginal opportunity cost of the resources to produce it. If these conditions are not met, economic theory suggests that resources could be reallocated to increase net economic benefits to society. The same principles apply to investments for conserving resources. Conservation is profitable whenever the marginal costs of conserving a unit of a resource are less than the marginal value of that unit as determined by its market price.

In practice, the marginal cost of providing a product at any time may vary for different classes of consumers. Moreover, within a consumer class, marginal cost may vary cyclically. Although these situations make setting prices more complex, the basic principles endure. Consumers serviced at the same cost should be charged the same price, and the product should be supplied and priced so that the price for each class of service equals the marginal cost of serving that class. In other words, where marginal costs differ, prices should differ.

In a competitive economy, prices are set by a market mechanism that automatically takes account of changes in consumer demands and producer costs so that the quantity supplied always equals the quantity demanded. If the producers and consumers and the buyers and sellers bear the full social costs and benefits of producing, using, or exchanging the resource, the quantities produced as well as their allocation tend to be socially efficient.

Although the market mechanism works reasonably well for most resources, well-functioning water markets are rare. Even where water is marketed, the prices often fail to reflect full costs of using or transferring the resource. The reasons for the scarcity of water markets involve (a) the nature of the resource, (b) a belief that use does not respond to price, and (c) institutions replacing or obstructing the operation of markets in allocating and managing water. These factors are addressed in subsequent sections.

NATURE OF THE RESOURCE DISCOURAGES MARKETING

Four characteristics of water pose obstacles to establishing well-defined, transferable property rights essential to efficient markets. First, water may be a common rather than a private property resource.

The hydrological cycle makes water fugitive in time and space. Streams and groundwater flowing from one property to another have characteristics of common property resources, making clear property rights elusive. When a resource is owned only if captured by a riparian user or groundwater pumper, property rights are not transferable and the individual's incentive is to use the resource before another captures it.

Second, use and transfer often affect people other than the user, buyer, or seller. Since use is rarely fully consumptive, a unit of water often gets reused many times. Each use, however, likely alters its quality, quantity, location, or availability for others. Consequently, when water is marketed, parties other than the buyer and the seller are probably affected. These externalities, or third-party effects, become particularly important when a transaction alters the point of diversion or return or important social values of water such as wildlife habitat are affected. To ensure that a water exchange does indeed produce net social benefits, third-party impacts must be taken into account. Since the buyer and the seller cannot be expected to represent the third parties, government oversight of water transfers may be in the social interest. Third, water resources produce public as well as private goods. Such products of natural water bodies as scenic amenities or wildlife habitat are generally public goods. Private owners find free-riders are able to enjoy public goods, and investment in them falls below the social optimum when left entirely to the free market.

Finally, the large capital costs and economies of scale characteristic of the water supply industry generally make more than one supplier impractical. To prevent monopolistic pricing, water service is usually government owned or regulated. Thus, prices are not set by a market but by utility managers or regulatory agencies.

USE RESPONDS TO PRICE

Natural market failures provide a rationale for the prominence of federal, state, and local governments in supplying, managing, and allocating the nation's water resources. The characteristics of the resource make it difficult, and in some situations perhaps impossible, to establish unbridled marketing in water. Nevertheless, these characteristics do not rule out either the possibility or the desirability of using prices and regulated markets to introduce economic incentives to restrain use, encourage conservation, and facilitate reallocation of supplies. Until recently at least, this has seldom happened. Many government policies limit rather than encourage the use of economic incentives to balance supply with demand.

Traditionally water planning and management have taken a supply-side approach, concentrating on off-stream and neglecting in-stream uses. Off-stream uses have been treated as virtual requirements growing in step with population and income that should be met regardless of cost. Concerns about future supply invariably led to new dams, reservoirs, and canals to increase supplies for irrigators, households, and industries. The impacts of the structures and withdrawals on the amenities provided by natural streamflows were usually ignored.

Two assumptions underlie the traditional, supply-side approach: the in-stream value of the water is essentially zero and can be ignored; its use does not respond to price. In the West 50 or so years ago, both assumptions may have been reasonably accurate. When streamflows far exceeded demand, diverting water for one use did not affect its availability for others. And when the costs of supplying the water and the prices charged for it were very low, the quantity demanded changed imperceptibly when prices inched up.

But conditions have changed. Water resources are now scarce and additions to reliable supplies are expensive. Furthermore, prospects of economic and population growth and a climate change induced by a greenhouse warming make planning for increasing scarcity and rising water costs prudent. Indeed, rising water costs are inevitable. First, the least-expensive supplies, which required simply diverting a stream's natural flow, were developed first. Second, additions to reliable supply require storage, and the costs of additional capacity rise as less desirable sites are developed. Third, the amount of water that a stream can supply with a high degree of probability increases at a diminishing rate as storage increases (U.S. Geological Survey, 1984). And fourth, the opportunity costs of storing and diverting water rise as the amount left for in-stream use declines.

Adding to water supplies is now generally costly in comparison to current water prices. In southern California, for instance, the costs of water from the State Water Project (SWP) rose from $122/acre-ft in 1982 to $221 in 1985, and projects to increase SWP supplies are likely to add $100 or more to these costs (Wahl and Davis, 1986, pp. 114–118). Even though these proposals call for exporting more water from northern California, the estimates do not include the opportunity costs of the water in the basin of origin. In view of northern California's strong, and so far successful, opposition to recent proposals to export more of its water south, the value of leaving the water in the basin of origin is evidently substantial.

The water supply industry has generally rejected marginal-cost pricing because of a belief that use is insensitive to anything less than unacceptably high price increases. But the growing scarcity of water is forcing reexamination of that conventional wisdom. The following section examines the opportunities for applying the principles of marginal-cost pricing to municipal water pricing, making specific reference to the situation in southern California. This is followed by consideration of the implications of price on agricultural water use.

MUNICIPAL WATER PRICING

Since municipal use accounts for less than 10% of total consumptive water use in the West, conservation and improved efficiency in this sector provides only limited opportunities for reducing overall demand. Yet, throughout the country cities are finding it difficult and expensive to augment supplies to meet the demands of population and economic growth and are increasingly concerned about efficient use of existing supplies.

Since the early 1900s, the urban water industry has emphasized increasing supplies rather than decreasing demand via price. Underlying this approach is the assumption that water is a unique commodity, a necessity for life that must be provided almost without regard for cost. Demand for municipal water is regarded as essentially perfectly inelastic—that is, not responding to price changes. Water demand has been viewed as an immutable requirement that increases with economic and population growth and requires larger and more complex supply facilities (Hanke and Davis, 1971).

The basic economic problem in the view of the water utilities is finding the least-cost and most technologically efficient methods of providing what is considered the necessary water supply. Thus, their prices are geared to recovering the costs of providing water to different customer classes, accumulating capital for future expansion, and generating a "fair rate of return" for capital invested in privately owned but publicly regulated utilities. Indeed, the guidelines of the American Water Works Association, set forth in the early 1950s and widely used, clearly reflect this view.

> Every water work should receive a gross revenue in an amount that will suffice to provide adequate service and assure the maintenance, development and perpetuation of the system.... An attempt is made to present definite rules for the formulation of rates which will distribute normal expense among all customers, as nearly as possible in proportion to the cost of supplying the commodity (American Water Works Association, 1954).

In economic terms, the American Water Works Association was advocating average-cost pricing. This is an accounting rather than an economic approach to setting rates. Residential, commercial, and industrial customers generally pay different rates. The typical rate structure for a customer class includes a fixed service charge per billing period plus a per volume fee that decreases as consumption increases.

Many studies belie the common assumption of the utilities that the demand for municipal water is not sensitive to price (see Gibbons, 1986). Although the Metropolitan Water District (MWD), a large water wholesaler servicing southern California, rejects so-called demand-side solutions,[2] raising water prices to reflect the marginal-cost of supplies may offer the least expensive means of closing the gap between MWD's estimates of supply and demand in the year 2000. Several studies suggest the elasticity of urban water demand in southern California falls within a range of − 0.26 and − 1.09. Even with the lowest of these elasticitites, Wahl and Davis conclude that an increase of $99/acre-ft could reduce the quantity of water demanded in MWD's service area by 300,000 acre-ft annually, which is more than 70% of MWD's predicted increase between 1985 and 2000 (Wahl and Davis, 1986, pp. 116–117). A price increase of $150/acre-ft at a constant elasticity of − 0.26 would reduce use sufficiently to offset MWD's projected increase. A 1967 pathbreaking study by Howe and Linaweaver first documented that the elasticity of demand for municipal water varies among regions and seasons. Although the demand for winter or indoor use is not especially sensitive to price (elasticity of − 0.23), the demand for summer sprinkling, which contributes to peak use and largely determines the capacity of the supply system, is sensitive to changes in price (elasticities of − 1.6 in the East and − 0.7 in the West) (Howe and Linaweaver, 1967).

Other studies tend to support Howe and Linaweaver. Hanke (1970) studied the effect of meters on residential consumption in Boulder, Colorado. Before the installation of meters, customers paid a fixed fee for water service regardless of

[2] A 1984 memorandum from the general manager to the board of directors of the Metropolitan Water District concluded that the elasticity of demand for urban water use is so low that it is not even worthwhile incorporating price into their demand projections (Wahl and Davis, 1986, p. 116).

use. The marginal cost of water was zero until metering permitted levying a charge on actual consumption. Initially both indoor and sprinkling uses decreased in response to the price rise. Over time, the decreased domestic use became permanent while sprinkling continued to decrease, but at a slower rate than initially. Evidently, consumers place different values on different uses and adjust water use in the light of price.

The industry's supply-side approach and its reliance on average-cost pricing have produced several results. First, the role of price in determining demand is largely ignored in forecasts and planning begins with an inadequate estimate of demand.

Second, the price is incorrect for efficient allocation when historical average costs rather than current marginal costs are used. As noted earlier, efficient resource allocation requires that prices reflect the current marginal cost of resources used or saved by changes in consumption. Historical or sunk costs create the impression that the cost of resources is virtually unchanging. Since marginal costs are higher than historical average costs in almost all the nation's larger cities, this causes overinvestment in system capacity or overuse of present capacity.

Third, current pricing policies rarely take account of variations in cost within customer classes caused by different locations and timing of consumption. A constant average-cost price within a customer class creates the illusion that costs of service are constant and identical at different locations, times of day, or seasons. Thus, the output of municipal water utilities is inefficiently allocated and undesirable patterns of urban development may be encouraged.

Constructing a rate structure to perfectly reflect changes over time in marginal costs would be neither feasible nor politically acceptable. Nevertheless, if the gains of reflecting such changes in the cost structure outweigh the costs of imposing them, adjustments in rate structures seem wise. Varying prices among seasons and locations are practical ways to introduce marginal-cost-pricing principles (Hanke, 1972, 1975).

As noted, the criterion for efficient pricing is: price equals the marginal cost of increased usage. Marginal costs are usefully divided into customer costs incurred simply by being connected to the system and usage costs for the water actually taken. Usage costs can be further broken down into operating costs, which vary immediately with changes in water use (energy costs, pumping, etc.), and capacity costs, which include costs of wells, pumps, reservoirs, and pipes. Systems are designed to meet peak demands and a large proportion of system capacity is idle most of the year.

Increases in usage during the off-peak season result only in changes in operating costs. In contrast, increases in consumption during the peak season press against a system's capacity and result in marginal capacity costs as well as operating costs. In all areas of the country but especially in the arid Southwest, sprinkling lawns and gardens causes large differences between summer and winter usage. The ratio of use during the peak to the average hour is as high as 5:1 in some areas, although a range of 2 to 4:1 is more typical. Thus, rate structures should vary with the season of the year. Higher prices during the summer peak season help reduce the growth and level of peak usage. On the other hand, winter prices would be lower than an average-cost rate, promoting greater consumption while capacity is idle. Overall, the efficiency of water production and use throughout the year would be improved, making better use of existing capacity and permitting more effective planning of expansion.

Where water as well as the capacity of the system are scarce, seasonal price differences should also encourage lower annual water use.

Constant average-cost prices also disguise the extra cost of serving customers far from the storage facilities, in sparsely populated areas, or on hills requiring additional pumping. Each of these situations increases marginal costs. In effect, constant average-cost pricing taxes customers in high-density areas near the load center and subsidizes customers in low-density outlying areas. Thus, the poor in the ghetto subsidize the rich in the suburbs. Further, constant prices encourage overinvestment in supply and distribution facilities and promote population diffusion and urban sprawl. These inefficiencies can be reduced by dividing the area into distance and elevation zones and basing rates on the marginal costs for serving customers within those zones.

Where long-run marginal greatly exceed average costs, pricing all water at marginal cost produces revenues in excess of full costs. To avoid such a "windfall," economic theory suggests that the price of water should be reduced somewhat below marginal cost for such uses as indoor-domestic that are most unresponsive to price. Customer charges unrelated to consumption should be reduced first, followed by the price of the early blocks of winter usage, and then the early blocks of summer usage, until revenues no longer exceed costs. These economic principles would usually invert the rate structure, making it progressive unlike the declining-block rates that are now typical. Under this new structure, customers using more would be charged more per unit than lower volume users. The summer and winter "tail blocks" would be priced at their long-run incremental cost.

This workable and practical application of marginal-cost pricing theory would greatly increase economic efficiency over the typical declining-block rate structure based on average cost.

Economists have long maintained that the pricing policies of water utilities inefficiently allocate productive resources and final output, and encourage excessive water use. Until recently, these recommendations have been largely ignored. But the rising costs associated with past policies are beginning to prompt a reconsideration of the role of pricing in overall water management and planning.[3]

---

[3] The experience of instituting a modified marginal cost pricing system in Tucson, Arizona is especially interesting. See, for example, Zamora, et al. (1981). Also see Martin et al. (1984).

AGRICULTURAL WATER USE

In 1980 irrigators withdrew an estimated 170 million acre-ft, fully one-third of all withdrawals from the nation's streams, lakes, and groundwater aquifers. Moreover, irrigation accounted for 5 of every 6 gal of the nation's consumptive use of water. In the 17 western states, irrigation accounted for 83% of the withdrawals and 90% of the consumptive use of water (Solley et al., 1983). Consequently, relatively small percentage changes in irrigation can have a major impact on total use.

Inexpensive water was a key factor in expanding the acreage under as well as in selecting the method of irrigation. Where water is virtually free, investments in conservation have no appeal unless they also offer such advantages as more acreage irrigated or higher yields. Relatively inefficient irrigation systems are still common among irrigators sheltered from increasing water costs. During the past decade or two, however, water-saving technologies and management practices have become important.

Two considerations suggest that water use for irrigation is likely to be particularly sensitive to water costs. First, water costs are likely to be a higher proportion of total production costs for irrigators than for others.[4] This is especially true for relatively low-value crops such as hay and pasture, which occupied a quarter of the nation's irrigated acreage in 1982. It is also true for most grains, which accounted for 44% of the irrigated acreage in that year. And even for such higher-value crops as vegetables, orchards, and cotton that combined accounted for 18% of the 1982 acreage (Day and Horner, 1987), water costs are likely more important to a farmer's "bottom line" than for industrial firms.

Second, irrigators have several ways of saving water as costs rise. These include lining canals or installing pipes to reduce conveyance losses; leveling fields, recycling tailwater, and irrigating alternate furrows to improve water-use efficiencies of gravity systems; scheduling irrigations only for the periods most critical to plant growth; and installing sprinkler irrigation systems.

Sprinklers provide more control over water than gravity systems and, thus, more opportunities for increased efficiency in its application. Sprinkler systems vary widely in efficiency in delivering water to the plants. They also differ in cost, use of energy, and suitability for particular crops, soils, and terrain; these factors are likely to be more important than water-use efficiency in selecting a technology. For example, center pivots are suitable for undulating terrain, but they use much energy and seldom produce water efficiencies above 80%. In contrast, drip systems essentially eliminate losses by evaporation and require little energy, but they are expensive and not suitable for field crops.

Other opportunities for reducing water use include cutting back the quantity

---

[4]The impacts of water costs on the profitability of alternative irrigation systems and irrigated agriculture in general are examined in Frederick and Hanson (1982, Chap. 5). A more recent examination of how farmers might respond to higher water costs is found in Sloggett and Dickason (1986, pp. 5–10).

of water per irrigation, reducing the number of irrigations, and switching to crops that use less water. Technological developments should continue to provide new options such as improved water management techniques and varieties of crops offering higher returns per unit of water. Moreover, research should broaden the opportunities for irrigating with poor quality water for which there is less competition from other users. The ultimate water-saving option, of course, is to stop irrigating and grow food where precipitation is sufficient to support dryland farming.

Many western farmers have taken one of these options in recent years. In Arizona, for example, the consumptive use of water for irrigation declined about 6% during the 1970s while consumption for other uses rose 67%. In the 1970s rising energy prices combined with declining groundwater tables to make pumping from the Ogallala Aquifer more expensive and forced irrigators in the High Plains to adjust. From 1977 to 1983 the area irrigated with groundwater in Texas declined by 1.2 million acres on 15% (Sloggett and Dickason, 1986, p. 3). And where irrigation continued, measures were adopted to improve the returns to water.[5]

To summarize, irrigators have ways of adjusting to higher prices, but incentives to abandon traditional, water-intensive practices are often lacking. Where water costs have risen sharply, water use was reduced. For reasons explained below, however, many irrigators remain isolated from increasing water scarcity. Where there is no opportunity to transfer water to other uses, irrigators with high-priority surface water rights or access to subsidized, federally supplied water continue to view water as essentially free, and they act accordingly.

WATER MARKETING

For reasons discussed earlier in this chapter, competitive markets can efficiently allocate resources among competing uses over time. But the nature of the resource presents problems for establishing and relying on unfettered water markets. Thus, the manner and ease with which a region deals with increasing water scarcity depend largely on the institutions, that is, the policies, laws, organizations, and norms, governing the allocation and use of water.

State institutions, except where water is specifically in the purview of the federal government, establish the framework and determine an individual's rights to use and transfer water. Traditionally, however, state governments have not created conditions conducive to water marketing, but have often limited the role of economic incentives to curb water use.

---

[5] Water-saving measures adopted by farmers in the Texas High Plains are described in various issues of *The Cross Section*, a monthly publication of the High Plains Underground Water Conservation District No. 1 (Lubbock, Texas). See for example the issue (volume 32, no. 11, November 1986) describing the water saving likely from recent purchases by the district's farmers of center pivot systems, surge valves to improve the efficiency of furrow irrigation systems, and laser leveling equipment.

All state water law was initially based on the common law doctrine of riparian rights which granted landowners the right to make "reasonable" use of water that bordered on or passed through their land as long as the use did not unduly inconvenience other riparian owners. By tying water rights to the land, this doctrine precludes markets. Water scarcity and the need to supply water to nonriparian lands caused the western states to abandon the doctrine of riparian rights in favor of the doctrine of prior appropriation or "first-in-time, first-in-right."

Although the appropriation doctrine was potentially an important step for creating clear, transferable property rights to water, the potential has yet to be realized because the nature and transferability of the rights have been obscured by legal and administrative factors. Among the factors are the beneficial-use provisions of the states' water laws. Rather than grant absolute ownership, the states granted rights to use water for "beneficial" purposes. Consequently, water rights that are not put to a beneficial use may be forfeited. Moreover, in some instances, sale of a right has been interpreted as evidence that the original user could no longer put the water to beneficial use. These provisions of western water law underlie the "use-it-or-lose-it" attitude that characterizes many water users and discourages marketing and conservation.[6]

Despite the institutional obstacles, water rights do get transferred among users, and water marketing is becoming common in many western states. Most western states permit water transfers if third parties are protected. Providing for these interests, however, can be time consuming, costly, and uncertain. Because the requisite legal and administrative hurdles add to the costs of a water transfer, the potential benefits generally have to be large to justify the effort and risk to the buyer and seller.

Recently water marketing has increased, reflecting both the growing potential benefits of transfers and a more receptive posture toward water transfers.[7] Laws to facilitate marketing of privately held water rights have been passed or are being considered. California now classifies water sales as a beneficial use. In 1987 Oregon's legislature considered a bill that would permit any water right holder to implement conservation and apply to the Oregon Water Resources Commission for the right to sell the conserved water. At the same time a bill to facilitate the transfer of water from irrigation to urban uses was making its way through the Texas legislature (*Water Market Update*, 1987).

The federal role in the use of the nation's water resources is considered in the next four sections.

---

[6]An extensive discussion of the institutional arrangements and their impacts on water marketing in six southwestern states is available in Saliba and Bush (1987), chapter 4.

[7]The following publications and activities attest to the recent growth in water marketing: Saliba and Bush (1987); Shupe (1986); a new monthly newsletter, *Water Market Update* (Western Network, Santa Fe, New Mexico); and the formation in 1987 of The Water Exchange Information Service (1099 18th Street, Suite 2950, Denver, Colorado 80202) to provide timely information on Colorado water rights for sale and recent sales activities.

FEDERALLY SUPPLIED WATER

The Bureau of Reclamation was established early in this century to promote the development of irrigation in the arid and semiarid West. The bureau provides full or supplemental irrigation for about 11 million acres, more than one-fifth of the total irrigated acreage. In 1975 it supplied 28.1 million acre-ft of water, 93% for irrigation (Bureau of Reclamation, 1976, p. 2). Since the bureau accounts for nearly one-third of all surface and about one-fifth of total water deliveries in the 17 western states, improved efficiency in the use of this water could be important.

Although reclamation law originally intended for irrigators to pay for operation and maintenance plus construction, exclusive of interest charges, more than 90% of the capital costs of the bureau's irrigation projects have been subsidized. With long-term contracts making no adjustment for inflation, payments on some projects no longer even pay for operation and maintenance (Frederick and Hanson, 1982, pp. 66–71).

Irrigators fortunate enough to receive such inexpensive water have little or no incentive to conserve. Not only is water cheap, farmers who attempt to conserve risk losing their rights to the water. Federally subsidized water generally cannot be sold by a farmer or irrigation district at a profit. Under these conditions it is not surprising that the demand for Bureau of Reclamation water has been almost completely unresponsive to price changes.

The obstacles to moving toward marginal-cost pricing of federal water are large. For one thing, long-term supply contracts reduce the possibilities of flexible pricing. Another obstacle is that many reclamation projects are so inefficient from an economic point of view that many farmers could not survive a large price increase. Pricing policies that would shut down bureau projects would probably not pass political muster.

Perhaps more likely than achieving higher prices for bureau water is increased voluntary transfers of federal water both within and outside the conservation districts established to distribute the water. While such transfers are not common, Wahl (1987) identified several transactions ranging from short-term rental or lease arrangements to permanent transfers. There is even precedent for federal legislation to facilitate such transfers: during the 1976–1977 drought Congress authorized temporary transfers of water from the Central Valley Project.

Although transfers do occur, their high transactions costs undoubtedly stymie many potentially beneficial ones. In Wahl's judgement, these costs stem mainly from lack of a clear bureau policy about procedures for making transfers and its willingness to approve them. Wahl maintains that there is a considerable latitude for voluntary transfers within existing law if the bureau were only willing to cooperate with interested trading parties and modify existing contracts that inhibit transfers. Such a policy shift would be consistent with the Bureau's Assessment '87, which concludes that "the Bureau's mission must change from one based on federally supported construction to one based on effective and environmentally sensitive resource management" (Bureau of Reclamation, 1987). Nevertheless, legislation extending the area and uses for federal water may be required to enable some of the most potentially beneficial exchanges (Wahl, 1987, p. 34).

The following discussion of the Westlands Water District in California illustrates both the pricing and transfer issues with respect to federal water while introducing another dimension of western water supply—mineral contamination management.

FEDERAL WATER—THE WESTLANDS WATER DISTRICT

In the 1950s declining groundwater tables threatened farming on the west side of California's San Joaquin Valley, and the area's farmers turned to the Bureau of Reclamation for a secure and renewable water supply. In 1960 Congress authorized the San Luis Unit as part of the federal Central Valley Project. Eight years later the San Luis Canal and related pumping facilities began taking water from the Sacramento–San Joaquin Delta and delivering it to irrigators 150 miles south.

The primary beneficiary of the San Luis Unit is the Westlands Water District, which irrigates more than 500,000 acres in the center of one of California's richest agricultural areas. Annually Westlands receives about 1.12 million acre-ft of highly subsidized water from the Delta.

According to one study, the Westlands Water District is paying less than 10% of the delivery cost of this water. The annual subsidy amounts to $217 per irrigated acre or almost $500,000 for the average farm (Le Veen and King, 1985, pp. 3–4). As noted earlier, federal reclamation law intended to subsidize irrigation by establishing long repayment periods without interest. The interest subsidy, however, accounts for only part of the actual subsidy enjoyed by Westlands. Depending on the assumptions about future repayments, 34 to 56% of the total subsidy was not authorized by Congress and is attributable to the practices and decisions of the Bureau (Le Veen and King, 1985, pp. 2 and 99).

Subsidies account for only part of the distortions in the incentives for managing and allocating water from the San Luis Unit. The project implicitly assumes that the water pumped from the Delta has no value at its source. But the concerns over the impacts of diversions on water quality and wildlife in the Delta and southern California's efforts to secure more water from the north belie this assumption. Furthermore, drainage from the Westlands has produced an environmental disaster while adding to the nation's agricultural surpluses.

Salt management is a common problem on irrigated lands, particularly on the naturally saline and poorly drained soils of the Westlands. To prevent salts from accumulating and stunting crops, they must be periodically flushed ("leached") from the root zone by applying more water than the plants utilize. Where drainage is naturally poor, subsurface drains are required to remove the excess water.

Leaching and good drainage can solve an individual farmer's and even an irrigation district's salt problems. Lacking an ultimate outlet for the salt-laden drainage, however, the salinity problem just gets passed on in a concentrated form to those lower in the drainage basin.

In recognition of the area's salt and drainage problems, authorization of the San Luis Unit provided for a drain. The bureau first attempted to work with the state to provide a master drain for the San Joaquin Valley. When this failed, the bureau started construction in 1968 of a drain from the San Luis Unit to the Delta. A decade later, a section of this drain extending from Westlands to Kesterson Reservoir 82 miles north was opened. Lack of money and growing opposition to dumping the effluent in the Delta halted the project.

Kesterson Reservoir was intended to be a regulating reservoir and a wildlife refuge along the drainage route. It was not intended to serve as the permanent repository for Westlands' drainage. Yet it served this purpose until 1983 when the U.S. Fish and Wildlife Service noticed gross deformities and death among the reservoir's wildlife caused by selenium, a natural trace element beneficial to humans at low concentrations but toxic at higher concentrations. The unusually high selenium levels of the Westlands' drainage was picked up in the vegetation and small animal life and passed on in increasing and eventually toxic concentrations as it moved up the food chain.

Under threat of losing its water, Westlands was forced to terminate use of the drain in June 1986. No longer able to just drain the effluent onto others, the district now. had an incentive to develop economical ways to reduce the quantity and toxicity of its drainage. Alternatives under consideration include deep-well injection of drainage, concentration and removal of selenium from the drainage, and incentives for farmers to reduce drainage. Preliminary evidence suggests deep-well injection below 5000 ft would cost $164 to $189/acre-ft (San Joaquin Valley Drainage Program, 1987, p. 1). Microbes that eat selenium are being studied to isolate the selenium for eventual removal (San Joaquin Valley Drainage Program, 1986b). The district even started paying irrigators $25/acre-ft of subsurface tailwater recycled in an attempt to reduce the magnitude of the drainage. In its first year, these payments encouraged recycling on about one-third of the 42,000 acres that had drained into the Kesterson reservoir (San Joaquin Valley Drainage Program, 1987, p. 3).

A long-term solution to Westlands' drainage problems is still sought. The district has not abandoned hope that a drain will eventually permit it to unload salt-laden discharges into the Delta or elsewhere. In the summer of 1986 the bureau kept these hopes alive by accepting a good-faith obligation to secure authorization and funding for a drain. Under the agreement Westlands would contribute operation and maintenance costs plus $5 million a year (not to exceed $100 million or 35%) toward capital costs. Despite the bureau's generosity with public funds and disregard of incentives to encourage alternative solutions, the Westlands is likely to be left to deal with their own effluent. Cost and environmental concerns brought the initial drainage project to a halt more than a decade ago. Since then, record federal budget deficits, awareness of the toxicity of Westlands' effluent, and growing reluctance to accept waste from other areas have arisen. All these factors make exporting Westlands' drainage increasingly difficult.

The Environmental Defense Fund (EDF) proposal for dealing with West-lands' drainage has three principal components: reducing the drainage through incentives for more efficient irrigation, removing salts and selenium from the drainage, and marketing water recovered through conservation and desaliniz-ation (EDF, 1985). With desalinization costing in excess of $1100/acre-ft and problems in producing electricity from the salty-brine residue from the desaliniz-ation process, the overall EDF plan is probably not feasible (San Joaquin Valley Drainage Program, 1986a). However, two elements of the proposal—incentives for improved on-farm water use and marketing of conserved water—are likely components of successfully dealing with the Westlands' drainwater without new government funding.

INTERSTATE TRANSFERS OF WATER

For many years, western states assumed that their power to regulate ground-water was complete, their compacts dividing surface waters among states unquestionably governed the interstate allocation of supplies, and all water transfers would be within their boundaries. Several recent court cases—especially the Sporhase case decided by the Supreme Court in 1982 and the El Paso case decided by the Federal District Court of New Mexico in 1983—have called these suppositions into question. In both cases, the courts have for the first time unequivocally proclaimed that water is an article of interstate commerce. These rulings, especially if the El Paso ruling is affirmed in the higher courts, may have substantial implications for the states' ability to control the interstate transfer of water.

In the Sporhase case (Laney, 1982) the appellants owned property extending across the Colorado–Nebraska boundary. From a well on the Nebraska side, they transported water to a sprinkler system in Colorado. To do this legally, the owners would have had to, but did not, obtain a permit from the Nebraska Department of Water Resources. Such a permit can be granted under Nebraska law for interstate transport of water, but only if, among other things, the state to which it is transported has granted reciprocal rights to Nebraska. Colorado law flatly prohibits interstate transportation of groundwater. Thus, had the appel-lants requested a permit, which they did not, it would have been denied.

The attorney general of Nebraska sued Sporhase and Moss, et al., owners of the land, to end further transportation to Colorado. The district court issued an injunction prohibiting such exports, and the Nebraska Supreme Court affirmed this action on grounds that groundwater is not an article of interstate commerce in Nebraska.

The state's position was rejected on appeal to the Supreme Court of the United States. The Court held that water is an article of commerce and, therefore, subject to congressional regulation. The state's claim to ownership of the water was ruled to be a legal fiction. It held further that agricultural markets supplied by irrigated farms provide an archetypal example of commerce among the states for which the farmers of the Constitution intended to authorize federal regulation. The reciprocity provision of the Nebraska statue was specifically ruled in violation of the Commerce Clause.

The Supreme Court recognized a state's legitimate interest in water conservation to protect the health and welfare of its population, but held that the de facto prohibition of the reciprocity provision was not tightly related to such purposes. Essentially, the Court forbade restrictions on water exports for the purpose of permitting or promoting economic development in the originating state. The Court conceded, however, that "a demonstrably arid state conceivably might be able to marshall evidence to establish a close means-end relationship between even a total ban on the exportation of water and a purpose to conserve and preserve water."[8]

The district court's ruling in the El Paso case extended the view that mere aridity is insufficient cause for restricting water exports. Like Colorado and a number of other states, New Mexico had a statute flatly forbidding export of groundwater. After preparing in secret, the city of El Paso, Texas applied in 1981 to the New Mexico state engineer for the right to develop a large amount of unappropriated groundwater in southern New Mexico. El Paso claimed that it needed this water to meet the needs of its future population and economic development. The district court held that the New Mexico statute was an illegal barrier to interstate commerce and affirmed that water is indeed an article of such commerce.

Specifically, the court said: "The Court recognizes that the conservation and preservation of water is of the utmost importance to the citizens of New Mexico... Nevertheless the New Mexico groundwater embargo violates the Commerce Clause of the United States Constitution, and an order will be entered herein enjoining the defendants from enforcing it."[9] New Mexico responded with a new statute permitting exports but only under tight restrictions. The disposition of El Paso's export application is still being debated in the courts.

To regain control of "their" water supplies, it appears that states will either have to make more persuasive "conservation" and "health and welfare" arguments, ask Congress to grant them power to forbid exports, or assume actual state ownership by purchasing or condemning private water rights.

The implications of the Sporhase and El Paso cases for possible interstate transfers of surface water that are not provided for by compacts are unclear. A recent proposal to transfer some of Colorado's share of the Colorado River water to San Diego has raised the issue, and its legality is hotly debated.[10] In the

---

[8] *Sporhase et al.* v. *Nebraska*, appeal from Supreme Court of Nebraska no. 81-613, argued March 30, 1982, decided July 2, 1982. Syllabus, p. 2.

[9] The United State District Court for the District of New Mexico, Memorandum Opinion, *the City of El Paso* v. *S. E. Reynolds*, Civ. No. 80-730 HB, January 17, 1983.

[10] The issue centers around a proposal by the Galloway Group Limited to lease 300,000 to 500,000 acre-ft of water developed in Colorado to San Diego. This proposal is discussed in an unpublished paper by Richard Wahl, "The Prospects for a Market for Leasing Compact Rights on the Colorado River," May 7, 1986.

absence of a federal law or Supreme Court ruling to the contrary, proposals for interstate water transfers are likely to become more common as the potential benefits of transfers increase with the scarcity of the resource. Moreover, because climate changes would likely affect the water resources of states differently, the economic benefits of interstate water transfers may rise substantially in the coming decades.

IMPLICATIONS OF INDIAN CLAIMS

As this chapter has emphasized several times, markets for lease or sale of water require well-defined property rights. But in 1908 a sword of Damocles was hung over future arrangements for water allocation in the West when the case of *Winters* v. *United States* was decided. The Supreme Court ruled that in land reserved for Indians, water was implicitly reserved as well. The 1963 Supreme Court decision in *Arizona* v. *California* upheld the "Winters-doctrine" water rights attached to Indian reservations and extended the principle of reserved rights to reserved federal lands.

Although many of these reserved rights have not been quantified, they are potentially large and outside state water law. The reserved rights also have high priority under the prior appropriation system since Indian and federally reserved claims date back to the time lands were set aside by Congress.

The 1963 decision provided guidelines for quantifying Indian rights based on a reservation's "practicably irrigable acreage." Subsequent court decisions have held that, while the measurement of the right is irrigable acreage, the tribes are not limited to agriculture in putting their water to use.

Determining the amount of irrigable land available and, therefore, the actual extent of the Indian water rights is still contested (Hundley, 1986). In 1983, the Court rejected recommendations of a special master assigned to deal with claims of the Colorado River tribes and assigned the River tribes approximately 900,000 acre-ft of water rather than the 1.2 million they wanted. The issue is still open, however, as the Indians claim larger boundaries for their reservations than considered by the Court and the Metropolitan Water District of southern California is protesting any extension of the Indian rights (*Aqueduct*, 1987).

The water right of the Colorado River tribes is large from the Colorado River perspective. Although they are less clear-cut, the claims of the Navajo are potentially much larger. The Navajo reservation is huge—25,000 square miles—and entirely in the Colorado River Basin. Despite the large size of the reservation, and its potentially huge Winters-doctrine rights, the Navajos were essentially ignored in the agreements dividing up the water of the river[11]. In the 1920s the complex negotiations over the Colorado River Compact proceeded entirely without Indian participation. To head off the issue of Indian rights in Congress, a brief passage stated that nothing in the compact should be construed as affecting

[11]The following discussion is based on Back and Taylor (1980).

the obligation of the government to Indian tribes. Similar language was inserted in the Upper Colorado River Basin Compact (1948) dividing the Upper Basin allotment among the states above Lee Ferry. While it considered the question, the Upper Colorado River Storage Project Act of 1956 that authorized construction of Glen Canyon Dam and the creation of Lake Powell avoided the issue of Navajo rights.

The Navajo Indian Irrigation Project Act of 1962 could not entirely avoid the issue of water rights. The Navajo Indian Irrigation Project (NIIP) for irrigating 110,000 acres in the northeastern portion of the Navajo reservation is in the San Juan tributary of the Colorado. In exchange for congressional approval of NIIP, the Navajo Nation agreed in 1957 to waive its priority on the San Juan River and to share water shortages proportionately with non-Indians. The issues raised by this agreement are complex and its meaning in terms of Winters-doctrine rights unsettled. However, the NIIP water-delivery contract states that the Navajo do not waive any reserved Winters-doctrine rights, and the Navajo Tribal Council contends that the tribe did not do so.

How large is the Navajo claim to Colorado River water rights? As noted, *Arizona v. California* applies the irrigability test. If this test is valid for the Navajo and only 500,000 acres, or 4% of the 13 million irrigable acres within the reservation, are practically irrigable, the tribal entitlement would be about 2 million acre-ft/yr. Under *Arizona v. California*, Arizona's entire Lower Basin entitlement is only 2.8 million acre-ft. The Navajos have employed engineers and attorneys to prepare a water-rights case against the Basin states and the federal government. Some observers believe that the suit, when and if it is filed, will be for 5 million acre-ft or more (Price and Weatherford, 1976).

Unquantified water rights challenge the water institutions of several states. Not only are these rights outside state law, they can usually only be met by terminating or reducing the rights of existing users.

Resolution of these potential conflicts is a prerequisite for establishing well-defined, transferable property rights in water. To respond to changing supply and demand, these claims must be settled without locking large quantities of Indian water into specific uses or locations. Reducing the transferability of water would limit the options for adjusting to changes in supplies accompanying a greenhouse warming.

CONCLUSIONS

Even without climate change western water-allocation institutions need to evolve toward greater reliance on economic incentives both in the form of markets and improved pricing policies for publicly supplied water. Evidence shows water use is sensitive to price and demand-side management is increasingly important for balancing demand with supplies.

The prospect of climate change strengthens the case for transferability of water. Just the uncertainties associated with the possibility of global warming argue for fostering flexibility. In addition, since the impacts on water supplies will vary among regions, the economic advantages of interregional transfers may increase. Institutional arrangements directing water into uses irrespective of supply and demand will likely become increasingly costly and difficult to maintain as conditions deviate from those assumed when the arrangements were made.

Although climate change could push regional water values either up or down, prudence requires that planning, especially in arid areas, not depend on increased precipitation and runoff. Reduced supplies would probably present the greatest problems for managers and planners. But even if precipitation increases, it will likely be in the form of more rain and less snow, decreasing the natural storage in snowpacks and altering the seasonal pattern of streamflows. Although storage is probably not a problem in the Colorado Basin because of its large reservoirs, it could be a problem elsewhere. Seasonality of streamflow now matches fairly well to agricultural water demand, reducing the need for intra-annual storage. Climate change could throw off this match and place greater demands on storage.

Western water allocation institutions appear to be evolving in the desired direction. Several states either have passed or are considering legislation to encourage conservation and facilitate marketing of water rights. Further changes in state law and policy could help, and federal initiatives are needed to make federally supplied and controlled water responsive to both existing and changing supply and demand.

Quantification of Indian and other federally reserved water rights is needed to establish clear property rights essential to well-functioning markets. If such markets are to develop, it is important not to restrict where and how the water can be used. Requiring that Indian water must be used on the reservation limits the value of the water right and increases the scarcity of water elsewhere.

Although increased marketing should be encouraged, free markets are not a panacea for efficient allocation of water over time. Two problems illustrate the limitations of markets and the challenges facing policymakers. First, third-party impacts associated with transfers need to be taken into account without unduly restricting marketing. Second, provision must be made for in-stream uses. Historically, in-stream uses were overlooked as appropriative water rights were established only by diverting water from its source. Streamflow depletion has directed attention to such values as hydroelectricity, recreation, and fish and wildlife habitat. Most western states have recently adopted measures to protect streamflows. These measures include reserving flows or granting rights for particular in-stream uses and directing agencies to review impacts before granting new rights (Lamb and Meshorev, 1983). But the task of efficiently allocating water among in-stream and other uses is particularly complicated because in-stream uses such as fish and wildlife habitat are not marketed and, thus, not easily valued. The values society attaches to these and other water uses change with population and income levels. They are also likely to be affected by changes in precipitation and temperature levels resulting from a greenhouse warming.

418 KENNETH D. FREDERICK AND ALLEN V. KNEESE

REFERENCES

American Water Works Association. 1954. Determination of Water Rate Schedules. *J. Am. Water Assn.* **46**(3).

Aqueduct. 1987. **1**(1), 8.

Back, W. D., and Taylor, J. S. 1980. Navajo Water Rights: Pulling the Plug on the Colorado River. *Natural Res. J.* January, pp. 70–90.

Barr, J. L., and Pingry, D. E. 1976. Rational Water Pricing in the Tucson Basin, *Arizona Rev.* **25**(10).

Bureau of Reclamation. 1976. Federal Reclamation Projects: Water and Land Resource Accomplishments, 1975, Summary Report. Washington, DC.

Bureau of Reclamation. 1987. Assessment '87:..A New Direction for the Bureau of Reclamation. September, p. 1.

Burr, J. K. 1978. Water Demand Study, Load Research Section, System Planning Department, Public Service Company of New Mexico, Albuquerque.

Day, J. C., and Horner, G. L. 1987. U.S. Irrigation: Extent and Economic Importance. U.S. Department of Agriculture, Economic Research Service, Agricultural Economic Report No. 523.

Environmental Defense Fund. 1985. *EDF Letter.* New York, November.

Frederick, K. D., and Hanson, J. C. 1982. *Water for Western Agriculture.* Resources for the Future, Washington, DC.

Gibbons, D. C. 1986. *The Economic Value of Water.* Resources for the Future, Washington, DC, pp. 9–14.

Hanke, S. H. 1970. Demand for Water Under Dynamic Conditions. *Water Res.* **6**(3).

Hanke, S. H. 1972. Pricing Urban Water, in S. J. Mushkin (Ed.) *Public Prices for Public Products.* The Urban Institute, Washington, DC.

Hanke, S. H. 1975. Water Rates: An Assessment of Current Issues. *J. Am. Water Works Assn.* **63**(9).

Hanke, S. H., and Davis, R. K. 1971. Demand Management Through Responsive Pricing. *J. Am. Water Works Assn.* **63**(9).

Hirschleifer, J., C. DeHaven, and J. W. Milliman. 1960. *Water Supply: Economics, Technology, and Policy,* University of Chicago Press, Chicago.

Howe, C. W., and Linaweaver, F. P., Jr. 1967. The Impact of Price on Residential Water Demand. *Water Res. Res.* **3**(1).

Hundley, N., Jr. 1986. The West Against Itself: The Colorado River–An Institutional History, in G. Weatherford and F. L. Brown (Eds.) *New Courses for the Colorado River.* University of New Mexico Press, Albuquerque, Chapter 2.

Kneese, A. V., and Bonem, G. 1986. Hypothetical Shocks to Water Allocation Institutions in the Colorado Basin, in G. Weatherford and F. L. Brown (Eds.) *New Courses for the Colorado River.* University of New Mexico Press, Albuquerque, pp. 87–108.

Lamb, B. L., and Meshorer, H. 1983. Comparing In-stream Flow Programs: A Report on Current Status, in *Proceedings of the Speciality Conference on Advances in Irrigation and Drainage: Surviving External Pressures, July 20–22, 1983.* American Society of Civil Engineers, New York, pp. 435–443.

Laney, N. 1982. Does Arizona's 1980 Groundwater Management Act Violate the Commerce Clause? *Arizona Law Rev.* **24**, 202.

LeVeen, E. P., and King, L. B. 1985. *Turning off the Tap on Federal Water Subsidies: Vol. 1, The Central Valley Project: The $3.5 Billion Giveaway.* Natural Resources Defense Council, San Francisco.

MacKichan, K. A. 1951. Estimated Use of Water in the United States in 1950, circular 115. U.S. Geological Survey, Washington, DC.

MacKichan, K. A., and Kammerer, J. C. 1961. Estimated Use of Water in the United States in 1960, circular 456. U.S. Geological Survey, Washington, DC.

Martin, W. E., Ingram, H. M., Laney, N. K., and Griffen, A. H. 1984. *Saving Water in a Desert City.* Resources for the Future, Washington, DC.

Murray, C. R., and Reeves, E. B. 1974. Estimated Use of Water in the United States in 1970, circular 676. U.S. Geological Survey, Washington, DC.

Price, M., and Weatherford, G. D. 1976. Indian Water Rights in Theory and Practice: Navajo Experience in the Colorado River Basin. *Law and Contemporary Problems.* **40**, 108–131.

Saliba, B., and Bush, D. 1987. *Water Markets in Theory and Practice: Market Transfers, Water Values, and Public Policy.* Westview Press, Boulder, CO.

San Joaquin Valley Drainage Program. 1987. Status Report 6, January, p. 1.

San Joaquin Valley Drainage Program. 1986b. Status Report 4, July, p. 2.

San Joaquin Valley Drainage Program. 1986a. Status Report 3, March, p. 1.

Shupe, S. J. (Ed.). 1986. *Water Marketing: Opportunities and Challenges of a New Era.* Watershed West.

Sloggett, G., and Dickason, C. 1986. Ground-Water Mining in the United States. U.S. Department of Agriculture, Economic Research Service, Agricultural Economic Report No. 555.

Solley, W. B., Chase, E. B., and Mann, W. B. IV. 1983. Estimated Use of Water in the United States in 1980, circular 1001. U.S. Geological Survey, Washington, DC.

U.S. Geological Survey. 1984. National Water Summary 1983—Hydrologic Events and Issues, Supply Paper 2250. Government Printing Office, Washington, DC, pp. 30–36.

U.S. Water Resources Council. 1978. *The Nation's Water Resources, the Second National Water Assessment,* Vol. 3, App. II and III. Washington, D.C.

Upper Colorado River Commission. 1985. Thirty-Seventh Annual Report. Salt Lake City, September 30, pp. 20–27.

Wahl, R. W. 1987. Promoting Increased Efficiency of Federal Water Use Through Voluntary Water Transfers. National Center for Food and Agricultural Policy, Resources for the Future. Discussion Paper Series, No. FAP87-02, September.

Wahl, R. W., and Davis, R. K. 1986. Satisfying California's Thirst for Water: Efficient Alternatives, in K. D. Frederick (Ed.) *Scarce Water and Institutional Change.* Resources for the Future, Washington, DC, pp. 114–118.

Water Market Update. 1987a. 1(4)

Water Market Update. 1987b. 1(5)

Zamora, J., Kneese, A. V., and Erickson, E. 1981. Pricing Urban Water: Theory and Practice in Three Southwestern Cities. *Southwestern Review of Management and Economics* 1(1), 89–113.

8

4 Hypothetical Shocks to Water Allocation Institutions in the Colorado Basin

Allen V. Kneese and Gilbert Bonem

Water allocation institutions in the Colorado River Basin were built up during a period of rapid water development and were designed to foster and aid that development. This is also the case for the West more broadly. Prior appropriation law helped to provide a degree of security of supply so that private developers of irrigation had the incentive to commit capital and labor to the construction of diversion and distribution systems. But the relationships between law, institutions, and development did not stop there.

Even after water courses were fully appropriated, agriculture continued to expand by developing supplies through the federal program to reclaim the arid West. The era of reclaiming arid lands began in the late nineteenth century, and the 1902 Reclamation Act established this objective as a national goal. The period following the Reclamation Act was one of heavily subsidized and increasingly centralized, large-scale irrigation projects. Long-term, interest-free financing based on "ability to pay" further institutionalized the notion that unappropriated and undeveloped water was itself free, with its only cost being the capital cost of constructing works and the subsequent operation and maintenance cost. The Bureau of Reclamation provided dams and diversion works on most major waterways in the West. Transbasin diversion projects were also commonplace. Accompanying the reclamation program was the creation of special water districts as entities responsible for repayment, operation, and maintenance functions with

87

respect to these public works. If projects experienced hardships, contract obligations were deferred. Regions that had political clout in
Congress were usually treated most generously. Frequently, hydroelectric power production was part of these projects and was used as
the "cash register" to subsidize irrigation water development.[1]

But the West is rapidly undergoing a major transformation with
respect to water. Increasing water scarcity already has brought changes
in western development and water-use patterns, and much greater
changes are likely to occur in the future. In particular, the expansion
of irrigated agriculture based on the availability of inexpensive water
is ending.

Just a few decades ago supplies were sufficient to satisfy a rapid
growth of water use throughout virtually all of the West. More recently,
however, high costs and limited opportunities for developing new
supplies have severely constrained the growth of offstream water use
in many areas, especially where users are heavily dependent on diminishing supplies of groundwater. Total water withdrawals for all but
hydroelectric generation rose 4.6 percent per annum from 1950 to
1960, compared to only 1.4 percent per annum from 1970 to 1980.
Excluding the northern plains states of Kansas, Nebraska, and North
and South Dakota, where water withdrawals nearly doubled over the
last decade, water withdrawals rose only 0.9 percent per annum from
1970 to 1980.[2]

Rights to most of the surface waters have been allocated, and
with rising frequency, potential users are forced to compete for the
same water. This competition has been intensified by the rising value
that society is placing on instream water uses. In nearly half of the
West's water resource subregions, the sum of instream use (defined as
the flow at the discharge point of the subregion required to satisfy the
higher of minimum needs to maintain fish and wildlife populations or
navigational needs) and offstream consumption exceeds average yearly
streamflow.[3] And since current levels of water consumption result in
the groundwater mining of about 22.4 million acre-feet per year,[4]
future competition over supplies likely will intensify even in the absence of further growth in demand.

Approximately 90 percent of western water consumption is for
the irrigation of about fifty million acres.[5] As both the largest and a
relatively low-value user, irrigation is the sector most directly affected

by the changing water situtation. Nonagricultural water consumption grew twice as fast as irrigation use from 1960 to 1980. Where water has become particularly scarce and expensive, water for irrigation has started to level off or even decline. In Arizona, for example, total irrigation water consumption declined by about 6 percent from 1970 to 1980, while consumption for other uses rose by 67 percent. Only in the northern plains did the growth of water consumption for irrigation exceed the growth for other uses during the last decade.[6]

Thus, while the era of rapid water development is ending in most of the arid West, and the problem of allocating and managing a fixed supply is becoming the dominant one, the situation appears to be particularly striking in the Colorado River Basin. Expectations from the river already appear to exceed its ability to meet them. This results, at least in part, from the fact that the Colorado River Compact anticipated more water than the river can deliver on a long-term basis. As Professor Hundley has pointed out, the framers of the compact assumed the dependable yield of the river to exceed sixteen million acre-feet per year; the framers apparently believed the average flow to be close to seventeen or eighteen million acre-feet. It is now widely believed by students of the matter that the average annual yield is less, possibly considerably less, than the fifteen million acre-feet actually divided up by the compact.

The Second National Water Assessment estimated the total streamflow of the Upper Basin to be nearly fifteen million acre-feet, considerably below the amount assumed in the compact negotiations.[7] Other evidence, however, suggests that the actual flow is even lower. A particularly interesting effort to construct a very long-term hydrograph for the Colorado River was done by the staff of the Tree Ring Laboratory at the University of Arizona. Figure 1 shows a dendrohydrograph of estimated virgin flow at Lee Ferry. This hydrograph was constructed by the application of complex statistical methods to tree-ring observations in the basin and traces the estimated flow from the year 1564 to 1960. This is shown in the bottom graph. The top graph shows estimated virgin flows since 1915 past the same point based on actual streamflow observations.

Both graphs strongly suggest that streamflow information available to the framers of the compact was gathered during a period of unusually, actually uniquely, persistent high streamflow. The den-

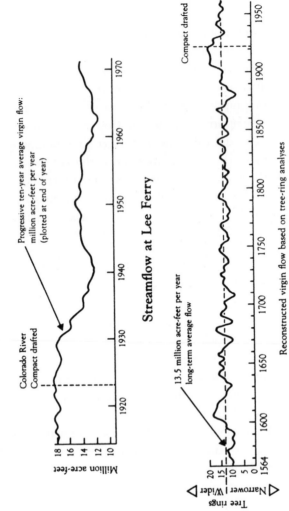

Source: Charles W. Stockton and Gordon C. Jacoby Jr., *Long-term Surface-Water Supply and Streamflow Trends in the Upper Colorado River Basin*, Lake Powell Research Project Bulletin No. 18, March 1976.

Figure 1.   Flow of the Colorado River

drohydrograph indicates an average long-term flow of about 13.5 million acre-feet. It also shows several periods of persistently low streamflow. We will return to those periods later when we consider the possible implications of extended drought in the Upper Basin.

Another way of looking at streamflow data is through probability analysis. Prior to the passage of the Colorado River Basin Project Act in 1968 the Lower Basin states of California, Arizona, and Nevada decided to agree on a water-supply study and make a joint presentation on water supply to the House Subcommittee on Irrigation and Reclamation. Engineers making the study agreed to do a probability study based on methods developed by Luna Leopold, formerly chief hydraulic engineer of the United States Geological Survey. In their testimony,[8] they concluded that there is a fifty-fifty chance that the supply available in the main stream will equal or be greater than the amount needed to provide: (1) 4.4 million acre-feet a year for California (this is the amount awarded California in 1963 by the decision of the Supreme Court in *Arizona v. California*); (2) water for decreed rights and existing mainstream projects in Arizona and Nevada and the southern Nevada water-supply project; (3) water for increasing demands on the Upper Basin; and (4) a full supply of 1.2 million acre-feet for the prroposed Central Arizona Project until about the end of the century, with a gradually reduced supply afterwards.

Myron Holburt, chief engineer of the Colorado River Board of California, later commented on these results. Since Mr. Holburt has been one of the chief figures in Colorado River affairs for many years, his statement is worth quoting at some length:

> Under normal circumstances, it would not be prudent to
> construct an elaborate and expensive water conveyance system
> that would serve a growing agricultural-urban civilization based
> upon anticipation of a water supply having only a 50 percent
> probability of occurrence. The special circumstances which
> made feasible the authorization of the Central Arizona Project,
> even though it was recognized that there was an inadequate
> long-term supply, are:
>
> 1. A pending program to bring new water into the river; the
> bill directed the Secretary of the Interior to develop a regional
> plan to supply the water needs of the region.
>
> 2. The bill gave priority to existing contractors in the Lower

Basin against the Central Arizona Project with California's protection limited to 4.4 million acre-feet per year (California now uses 5 million acre-feet per year).

3. Water from the project cannot be used to serve new lands. Service is limited to existing agricultural users in central Arizona and the expanding urban areas of Phoenix and Tucson. In the event of shortages, these users can fall back upon the alternative source of local groundwater supplies.

Thus, it is expected that any insufficient project water supplies can be overcome on a short-term basis by additional ground water pumping and can be overcome on a long-term basis by river augmentation. The interval between the completion of the Central Arizona Project and the completion of works to augment the flow of the Colorado River is the period during which there is the greatest risk of water shortage.[9]

Since the Central Arizona Project is nearly complete and since the interval between its completion and augmentation of the Colorado, at least by interbasin transfers, may well be infinitely long, we are, on this analysis, likely to have shortages. Thus, even with "normal" development there will probably be periods of more or less stress on the basin's water allocation institutions.

However, the chief purpose of this chapter is to imagine some "events" that might occur that could greatly exacerbate such stresses. We do not argue that any of them except the last (prolonged deep drought) will occur, or is necessarily likely. But it certainly is not incredible that shocks will occur even if we look only at what has already happened. For example, after the Arab oil boycott there was what seemed for a time to be a brute-force effort on the part of energy companies and the government to develop the region's energy resources. Furthermore, recent rulings in the *Sporhase* and *El Paso* cases call into question the states' previously unquestioned jurisdiction over "their" water supplies and so have already produced some cracks in the institutional structure. The hypothetical situations discussed in the following sections can serve to assist in conducting "thought experiments" to test the strength and resiliency of the Colorado's water institutions. Four situations are considered. The first three situations are discussed quite briefly but comprehensively enough that we hope to stimulate thought about them. The last situation, deep and prolonged drought in the Upper Colorado Basin, is discussed more fully because we believe it to be the most credible situation and one which could, in the foreseeable future, produce a genuine crisis for the Colorado's water allocation institutions, the current relative abundance of water supplies in the basin notwithstanding.

First Hypothetical: Renewed Disruption in International Trade and an Urgent National Need to Find and Develop Energy Resources in the Western Hemisphere

Presently there is a glut of oil in international markets. But imagine a situation in which a complete cutoff of oil from the Middle East (because of, say, an international, but contained, war in the region) damages our economy severely, both because we are still partly dependent on that region for supplies and because we have commitments to share with our allies during times of shortages. This situation would set up intense and serious pressure both to develop domestic energy supplies quickly and to help develop more secure foreign sources, most logically in Mexico. With respect to the former, as part of the Southwest Region under Stress Project we examined the water-use implications of several energy development scenarios. Scenario D was specifically designed to be a brute-force crash development scenario. The scale of development is massive but consistent with the energy resources of the region. It projects an additional 36,000 megawatts of electrical generating capacity, 10,000 million cubic feet per day of coal gasification, and 1 1/2 million barrels per day of oil-shale production. Such growth might be possible over the course of about two decades. This scenario, assuming some investment in water-saving technology, might require consumption in the neighborhood of one million acre-feet of water a year.[10]

Imagine further that, at the same time, as a reward for developing its petroleum reserves at a faster rate than it deems to be in its own national interest, Mexico demands the reopening of negotiations about its share of the Colorado River. Assume it obtains agreement from the United States to gradually increase its release of water to the Mexicali Valley, until after twenty years it receives an additional two million acre-feet per year.

Taking these circumstances in combination would mean that over a period of twenty years there occurs an increase in requirements for water for three million acre-feet per year over and above what would otherwise have happened. Clearly, these requirements could not be met from basin sources without disastrous effects on the region's agriculture. In this circumstance, the states in the region once more marshal all their political forces around water issues and form a coalition with northeastern states, who badly need the Mexican oil, to pressure the federal government to provide and pay for interbasin transfers to protect the region's agricultural water and to possibly increase it. In drafting the Colorado River Basin Act (which, as noted, contemplated interbasin transfers), the political representatives of the region were careful to include a provision stating that under the act the United States (not just the basin states) assumes the Mexican water treaty obligation. The international dimension, which also played a considerable role in the assumption of the cost of the Colorado Salinity Control Program by the United States,[11] plus the powerful internal political coalition provides the key to putting together the last and greatest "Christmas tree" for the traditional distributive water politics of the region, which results in a massive transfer of water from the Pacific Northwest.

Second Hypothetical: Indian Water Claims Are Quantified and the Quantities Are Large

A sword of Damocles was hung over future institutional arrangements for water allocation in the Colorado Basin in 1908 when the case of *Winters* v. *United States* was decided. The Supreme Court ruled that in land reserved for Indians water was implicitly reserved as well. These reserved, or "Winters' doctrine," rights have, for the most part, never been quantified but are potentially very large, and they, as well as other reserved rights, lie entirely outside of the prior appropriation system. As pointed out by Professor Hundley, in Chapter 2, the decision in *Arizona* v. *California* has far-reaching implications for Indian water rights; for the Colorado River tribes most directly, but by implication, for other tribes as well. As Professor Hundley observes, the Court supported the position of the federal lawyers and invoked the principle laid down in *Winters* v. *United States* that in an arid climate the reservation of land for Indians implies the reservation of water. The Court further adopted the government's position that the only feasible and fair way to determine the extent of that right is in irrigable acreage. But in a later decree, the Court held that, while the measurement of the right is irrigable acreage, the Colorado River tribes were not limited to agriculture in putting their water to use. That Indian water rights are not limited to irrigation water was recently affirmed in a state court ruling in Wyoming granting water rights to Indians (Shoshone and Arapaho) in the Big Horn River Basin.[12]

But the amount of irrigable land available is, under both the Winters' doctrine and *Arizona* v. *California,* a critical factor in determining the actual extent of the Indian water rights, and this was the subject of contention among the Colorado River Indians and interested non-Indian parties in Arizona.[13] In 1983, the Court rejected recommendations of a special master who had dealt with claims of the Colorado River tribes. This decision left the river tribes with approximately 900,000 acre-feet of water rather than the 1.2 million they wanted.

But the Colorado River tribes' water is still a large quantity from the Colorado River perspective. The claims of the Navajo, whose situation is much less clear-cut, are potentially much larger since their reservation is relatively huge—25,000 square miles—and lies entirely in the Colorado River Basin. It straddles the divide between two major tributaries, the San Juan and the Little Colorado, and its western boundary is the main stem of the Colorado. The Colorado River Basin and the Navajo reservation are shown in Figure 2.

Despite the large size of the reservation, and its potentially huge Winters' doctrine rights, it received little notice in the various agreements that have divided up the river over the last several generations.[14] The complex negotiations, described by Professor Hundley, leading to the Colorado River Compact—signed by representatives of the basin states in 1922 (except Arizona, which signed later), ratified by Congress in 1928, and proclaimed by the president in 1929—proceeded entirely without Indian participation. During the negotiations, however, Secretary of Commerce Herbert Hoover, federal delegate to the Compact Commission, requested wording designed to head off the issue of Indian rights from being raised in Congress. The resulting

96

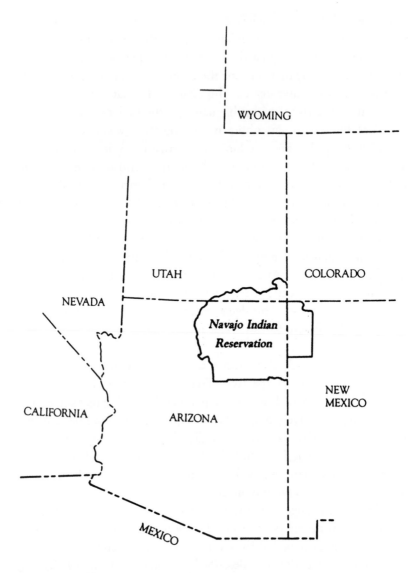

Figure 2.   The Colorado River Basin and the Navajo Indian Reservation

brief passage simply says that nothing in the compact should be con-
strued as affecting the obligation of the government to Indian tribes.
Similar language was inserted in the Upper Colorado River Basin
Compact (1948) that divided the Upper Basin allotment among the
states above Lee Ferry. While it considered the question, the Upper
Colorado Compact Commission decided not to attempt to quantify
Navajo rights. Again, the Colorado River Storage Project Act of 1956,
which was the basis for the construction of Glen Canyon Dam (Lake
Powell), the main river regulation structure in the Upper Basin, avoided
the issue of Navajo water rights.

The Navajo Indian Irrigation Project Act, which in 1962 authorized the Secretary of the Interior to construct the Navajo Indian
Irrigation Project, obviously could not avoid the issue of water rights
entirely. The Navajo Indian Irrigation Project (NIIP), which plans to
irrigate 110,000 acres of Navajo land, is located in the San Juan Basin
(tributary to the Colorado) in the northeastern part of the reservation.
In 1957, in exchange for congressional approval of NIIP, the Navajo
Nation agreed to waive its priority on the San Juan River and to share
water shortages proportionately with non-Indians.' The issues raised
by this agreement are very complex, and its meaning in terms of
Winters' doctrine rights remains unsettled. However, wording in the
NIIP water delivery contract states that the tribe does not waive any
reserved Winters' doctrine rights, and it is also the position of the
Navajo Tribal Council that the tribe did not do so.

How large might a Navajo claim to Colorado River water rights
be? As noted, *Arizona v. California* applies the irrigability test. Assuming this same test is valid for the Navajo, and assuming that only
500,000 acres or 4 percent of the total land area is *practicably* irrigable
(the total Navajo irrigable land is 13 million acres), the tribal entitlement would be about 2 million acre-feet per year. Arizona's entire
Lower Basin entitlement under *Arizona v. California* is only 2.8 million
acre-feet. In recent years, the Navajos have employed engineers and
attorneys to prepare a water rights case against the basin states and
the federal government. Some outside observers of the matter believe
that the suit, when and if it is filed, will be for five million acre-feet
or more.[16]

Given the extent of Colorado River tribes' water rights; if such
a Navajo suit were to be successful these two groups of Indians would

be entitled to almost half of the total long-run yield of the river. Since such an entitlement would be quite outside the prior appropriation system, it would not, unlike rights under that system, be contingent on beneficial use. It might therefore be possible for Indians to charge non-Indian users a fee for the continued use of Indian water. Back and Taylor quote Northcutt Ely, chief counsel for California during congressional hearings on the Colorado River Storage Project in 1955, on the matter of whether Indian rights are inside or outside the compact apportionments. "If inside, and as large as claimed," Ely says, "the compact is splitting at the seams, and if outside, busted."

Third Hypothetical:
A Large-Scale Interstate Market
in Water Rights Develops

For many years, states in the Colorado Basin and elsewhere in the West have operated under the assumption that their power to regulate groundwater was complete and that their compacts dividing surface waters with other states unquestionably governed the allocation of supplies. Several recent court cases have called both of these suppositions into question. The two leading ones are the *Sporhase* case decided by the Supreme Court on July 2, 1982, and the *El Paso* case decided by the Federal District Court of New Mexico on January 17, 1983. The *El Paso* case is being appealed and may also finally go to the Supreme Court. In both cases, the courts have for the first time unequivocally proclaimed that water is an article of interstate commerce. These rulings, especially if the *El Paso* ruling is affirmed in the higher courts, may have substantial implications for the states' ability to control the interstate transfer of water. In the *Sporhase* case,[17] the appellants owned property extending across the Colorado-Nebraska boundary. From a well on the Nebraska side, they transported water to a sprinkler system in Colorado. To do this legally, the owners would have had to, but did not, obtain a permit from the Nebraska Department of Water Resources. Such a permit can be granted under Nebraska law for interstate transport of water, but only if, among other things, the state to which it is transported has granted reciprocal rights to Nebraska. Colorado law flatly prohibits interstate transportation of groundwater. Thus, had the appellants requested a permit, it would have been denied.

The attorney general of Nebraska brought suit against Sporhase and Moss et al., owners of the land, to end further transportation of water to Colorado. The district court issued an injunction prohibiting such transportation, and the Nebraska Supreme Court affirmed on the basis that groundwater is not an article of interstate commerce in Nebraska. The case was appealed to the Supreme Court of the United States.

The Court held that water is an article of commerce and therefore subject to congressional regulation. It held that the state's claim that it owned the water is a legal fiction. It held further that agricultural markets supplied by irrigated farms provide an archetypal example of commerce among the states for which the framers of the Constitution intended to authorize federal regulation. The Court held that it is specifically the reciprocity provision of the Nebraska statute that violates the Commerce Clause.

> The reciprocity requirement of the Nebraska statute violates the Commerce Clause as imposing an impermissible burden on interstate commerce. While the first three conditions set forth in the statute for granting a permit—that the withdrawal of the groundwater be reasonable, not contrary to the ' conservation and use of groundwater, and not otherwise detrimental to the public welfare—do not on their faces impermissibly burden interstate commerce, the reciprocity provision operates as an explicit barrier to commerce between Nebraska and its adjoining States. Nebraska therefore has the initial burden of demonstrating a close fit between the reciprocity requirement and its asserted local purpose. Such requirement, when superimposed on the first three restrictions, fails to clear this initial hurdle, since there is no evidence that it is narrowly tailored to the conservation and preservation rationale. Thus, it does not survive the "strictest scrutiny" reserved for facially discriminatory legislation.[18]

Thus, the Court recognized a state's legitimate interest in water conservation to protect the health and welfare of its population, but held that the de facto prohibition resulting from the reciprocity provision was not tightly related to such purposes. Essentially, what the

Court forbade was restrictions on water exports for the purpose of permitting or promoting economic development in the originating state.

The Court conceded, however, that "a demonstrably arid state conceivably might be able to marshall evidence to establish a close means–end relationship between even a total ban on the exportation of water and a purpose to conserve and preserve water."

That the mere fact of aridity is, however, not sufficient is underlined by the district court's ruling in the *El Paso* case. New Mexico, like Colorado and a number of other states, has a statute flatly forbidding the export of groundwater. After making its preparation to do so in secret, the city of El Paso, Texas, applied in 1981 to the New Mexico state engineer for the right to develop a large amount of unappropriated groundwater in southern New Mexico. El Paso claimed that it needed this water to meet the needs of its future population growth and economic development. Following litigation, the court held that the New Mexico statute was an illegal barrier to interstate commerce and affirmed that water is indeed an article of such commerce. Specifically, the court said: "The Court recognizes that the conservation and preservation of water is of the utmost importance to the citizens of New Mexico. . . . Nevertheless the New Mexico groundwater embargo violates the Commerce Clause of the United States Constitution, and an order will be entered herein enjoining the defendants from enforcing it."[19]

It appears that in order for states to regain control of "their" water supplies they will either have to make more persuasive "conservation" and "health and welfare" arguments, seek an act of Congress granting them power to forbid export of water, or assume actual state ownership (by purchase or condemnation) of water rights to prevent uncontrolled operation of the private market.

In this third hypothetical situation, we assume that none of these possibilities occur and that there is a rapid rise in the interstate movement of water. Water comes to be treated like any other commodity, becomes more overtly commercialized; many private water rights become transferable to the highest bidder across state lines; and interstate compacts are undercut. For example, water rights in Wyoming may become interesting to rural and urban interests in southern California as reduced deliveries under the Colorado Compact occur and ground-water is further depleted. The physical facilities to deliver Wyoming water to southern California already exist.

Fourth Hypothetical: Deep Sustained Drought in the Upper Colorado Basin

Unlike the other hypothetical situations, this one is hypothetical only in the sense that we do not know when it will occur; but we can expect with high confidence that it will. The probability analysis reported earlier suggested that water-supply shortfalls are likely to happen in the future. Also, the dendrohydrograph displayed earlier indicates that the data available to the framers of the compact reflected the wettest period to occur in the Upper Colorado in at least several centuries. In this hypothetical situation, we become more specific and postulate an actual and very severe drought, but one that is consistent with what has already occurred in history. We then try to show some of the consequences. We focus primarily upon the ability of the Upper Basin to meet its compact commitment in such a situation. To accomplish this, we must be more quantitative than in earlier sections; therefore, it is necessary to burden the reader with a little arithmetic.

Let us look first at some low-flow episodes that have actually been measured or that have been estimated from tree-ring studies. Hydrological records kept by the Bureau of Reclamation can be used to look at some low-flow episodes that have actually been recorded. The lowest undepleted flow (that is, reconstructed virgin flow) in the Bureau's series is for the 1934 water year (from October 1933 to September 1934) with 5.64 million acre-feet. The 1976 water year flow was near this with 5.78 million acre-feet. But comparing annual minimum flows to compact requirements would be misleading, of course, because the Colorado River Compact, as already indicated, provides that the states of the Upper Basin must deliver 75 million acre-feet at Lee's Ferry in each successive ten-year period. Thus, deliveries do not have to equal 7.5 million acre-feet in one year. (We temporarily ignore deliveries related to the Mexican water treaty.) More pertinent, then, are the lowest flow intervals averaged over ten years. One of these was during the interval from 1954 to 1963, with 11.826 million acre-feet average

102

Table 1.   Selected Colorado River Reservoir Data

Reservoir	Useable Capacity (thousand acre-feet)	Useable Storage (thousands of acre-feet)			Change in Storage	
		October 1976	May 1977	October 1977	October to May	October to October
Flaming Gorge	3,749	3,364	2,496	2,055	868	1,309
Blue Moon	829	583	337	208	246	375
Navajo	1,696	1,279	1,094	1,033	185	246
Glen Canyon	25,000	19,266	18,343	16,030	923	3,236
			Net Releases, Total		2,222	5,166

Source: U.S. Bureau of Reclamation

annual flow. In the ten-year period from 1931 to 1940, average annual flow was 11.833 million acre-feet.

The Arizona Tree Ring Laboratory's reconstructed hydrograph indicates the lowest ten-year flow occurring from 1584 to 1593, with 9.7 million acre-feet per year. Consequently, we might establish a range of expected ten-year drought flows extending from a 97-million acre-feet total to a 118-million acre-feet total for the driest ten-year periods observed or estimated. Of course, any assumed drought flows are subject to considerable uncertainty, but this range is consistent with available data.

A way to obtain an initial perspective on the potential effect of drought in the Upper Colorado Basin on its ability to deliver water to the Lower Basin is to look at reservoir release data during a previous drought. Table 1 indicates releases from four Upper Colorado River Basin reservoirs during the 1976–1977 drought, a drought which some observers labeled the "wettest drought in history" because a very dry fall and winter (1976–1977) was followed by relatively heavy precipitation in the summer of 1977. In other words, the drought was very severe, but also very short by historical standards. Table 1, which was compiled from Bureau records, shows that the net reservoir drawdown at the four largest reservoirs in the Upper Basin from October 1976 to October 1977 was over 5 million acre-feet. In comparison, initial usable storage at these four reservoirs was almost 25 million acre-feet.

Thus, the 1976–1977 drought used about 20 percent of the storage existing. Stating things mildly, we may say that if a drought of this intensity had lasted for three or four years, instead of less than one, the ability of reservoirs to sustain the river's yield would have been seriously impaired.

We now define a specific hypothetical drought of less severity but of greater duration. Our earlier discussion suggests that ten-year undepleted flows at Lee's Ferry, in a severe prolonged drought, would be perhaps 97 to 118 million acre-feet, with some individual years dipping toward the 6 to 7 million acre-feet mark. In such a situation, spot water shortages throughout the basin would be enormous; restrictions on residential water use, reduced crop yields, scrambles for sprinkler irrigation, canal lining, and drilling of new wells would all occur. As a sidelight, we may mention that a real drought would severely affect the region's ski industry; one study showed this to be Utah's most severely affected industry in the 1977 drought. Finally, as a hypothetical drought continued, reservoir storage in the Upper Colorado Basin would begin to be depleted. How serious might this depletion be and how would it affect the Upper Basin's ability to deliver water?

We will try to answer this question in four steps.

1. The Upper Basin must deliver 75 million acre-feet over a ten-year period, plus 750,000 acre-feet per year as its share of the Mexican water treaty. Another 150,000 acre-feet per year of Mexican treaty water is debatable; indeed, the 750,000 is, perhaps, debatable. But we assume the Upper Basin's obligation is 82½ million acre-feet over a ten-year period.

2. The ten-year flow will be in the range of 97 to 118 million acre-feet; we shall assume it to be 100 million acre-feet, not far below the recorded low of 118 million acre-feet in the decade from 1954 to 1963 and slightly above the lowest estimated ten-year flow.

3. To the ten-year virgin flow at Lee's Ferry, we must add water available from storage in reservoirs in the Upper Basin. The four reservoirs listed in Table 1 have usable capacity of 31.27 million acre-feet. Dracup gives an estimate of 33.8 million acre-feet of storage capacity available in the Upper Basin.[20] We assume that at the start of a ten-year drought there are 30 million acre-feet in storage in the

104

Table 2. Depletions in the Upper Colorado River

	1972–1981	1962–1971	1952–1961
Within Basin Depletions			
Quantity	2,366	1,986	1,614
% change from previous decade	19%	23%	
Transbasin Diversions	704	508	436
Net Reservoir Evaporation Loss	609	257	0
Total			
Quantity	3,679	2,751	2,050
% change from previous decade	34%	34%	

Source: U.S. Bureau of Reclamation

Upper Basin. Thus, the undepleted ten-year runoff at Lee's Ferry would be 130 million acre-feet if all the upstream water were available for this purpose.

4. From the undepleted runoff, however, we must subtract Upper Basin depletions. Table 2 shows some compilations that we made of present Upper Basin depletions from Bureau of Reclamation data. In the last ten years, Upper Basin depletions from the Colorado River system have averaged 3.7 million acre-feet per year, including diversions to other basin and reservoir evaporation losses.

We are now ready to conclude the calculations. The hypothetical ten-year drought would leave the Upper Basin with about 130 million acre-feet of water to deliver, of which 82.5 million acre-feet are owed by compact and 37.0 million acre-feet would be depleted by present uses. Thus, the Upper Basin would have excess water of 11.5 million acre-feet over the ten-year period (130—82.5—37.0). This is about 1.1 million acre-feet per year; and we must increase this to about 1½ million acre-feet because evaporation from reservoirs will decline, since we have assumed that all the reservoirs are emptied during the drought. If, then, the reservoirs are almost full at the start of the drought and are emptied, the Upper Basin could, at present, meet its obligations and maintain its water use, with about 1½ million acre-feet per year to spare at Lee's Ferry.

But note that during the twenty-year period shown in Table 2 the Upper Basin depletions increased 80 percent (from 2.05 million acre-feet to 3.68 million acre-feet). We assume that no new transbasin diversions occur and that no new reservoirs are built. Thus, we consider only future increase in depletions from inbasin use. For the twenty-year period shown in Table 2, the increase in these depletions was 47 percent (from 1.61 million acre-feet to 2.37 million acre-feet). Arbitrarily, extrapolating this rate of increase for the next twenty years implies that depletions would increase by 1.1 million acre-feet; such increase would effectively use up all the water remaining during a drought. We emphasize that future water demands in the Upper Colorado could be much larger than the increase obtained by this extrapolation of past trends. See, for example, the first hypothetical situation.

Given our assumptions, we conclude that the Upper Basin could probably make good its compact commitments if a ten-year drought started tomorrow. Of course, this assumes that Upper Basin reservoirs are almost full—as indeed they presently are—when the drought starts and that authorities are willing to empty the reservoirs. If a ten-year drought begins fifteen to twenty years from now, it is unlikely that the Upper Basin can make good its compact commitments even under these extremely favorable assumptions.

In conclusion, we must reemphasize that these results are based on *very* favorable assumptions concerning the delivery of water. If the reservoir system were not to be full when the drought began, shortfalls could easily become large. The assumption that the upstream reservoirs would indeed be emptied is also a very strong one. In working out our example, we have the advantage of knowing ahead of time the length and severity of the drought. In a real situation, reservoir managers and policymakers would never have that information because the future can never be known with certainty. Thus, it might be considered extremely imprudent to continue slavishly drawing down reservoirs virtually to the last drop without any prior knowledge about when the drought will end. Moreover, public pressure not to do so would presumably be enormous, given the vast recreational value of these reservoirs. Furthermore, the extreme loss of head would have large implications for power generation, for power revenues used by the Bureau to subsidize irrigation, and for power used for pumping operations on the Bureau's projects themselves. Thus, the simple statistics we have presented about quantities of water do not reveal the tremendous conflicts that would occur among various interests and the stresses and strains that would be put on the region's water allocation institutions.

We may also add that our calculation may not include the absolute "worst case" drought. Tree-ring research completed in 1979 at Chaco Canyon in northwestern New Mexico indicates that there was an extreme drought in the area from A.D. 1130 to 1180. It was probably this drought that caused the prehistoric Anasazi people to abandon the Colorado plateau. A fifty-year drought featuring annual undepleted flows at Lee's Ferry, which are rarely above ten million acre-feet, would place incredible stress on the basin's legal and economic institutions.[21]

It is possible that a drought of the type we describe could happen in conjunction with any combination of any of the other hypothetical situations we have posited. Almost needless to say, this could greatly aggravate the stresses and strains resulting from the drought itself.

Notes

1. For further discussion of this developmental era in water development, see Gary Weatherford and Helen Ingram, "Legal-Institutional Limitations on Water for Agriculture," in Ernest A. Engelbert and Ann Foley Scheuring, eds., *Water Scarcity: Impacts on Western Agriculture* (Berkeley, 1984).

2. Calculated by Kenneth Frederick from data in the following U.S. Geological Survey circulars: 1950 data—Kenneth A. MacKichan, *Estimated Use of Water in the United States in 1950*, Circular 115 (Washington, D.C., May 1951); 1960 data—Kenneth A. MacKichan and J. C. Kammerer, *Estimated Use of Water in the United States in 1960*, Circular 456 (Washington, D.C., 1961); 1970 data—C. Richard Murray and E. Bodette Reeves, *Estimated Use of Water in the United States in 1970*, Circular 676 (Washington, D.C., 1974). The 1980 data are based on preliminary copies (provided by Ken Reid, USGS hydrologist) of tables 7 and 10 of the forthcoming U.S. Geological Survey Circular on "Estimated Use of Water in the United States in 1980." The references are to water withdrawals (the amount of water taken from a surface or groundwater source for offstream use) rather than to consumption (the portion of the water withdrawn which is not returned to a surface or groundwater source), since consumption data are not available for

1950. Subsequent references to water use will be limited to periods since 1960 and will focus on water consumption.

3. U.S. Water Resources Council, *The Nation's Water Resources, The Second National Water Assessment*, vol. 3, appx. II (Washington, D.C., 1978), table II–4.

4. Ibid., vol. 1, p. 18.

5. The range of estimates of irrigated acreage is wide. The data are examined critically in Kenneth D. Frederick, *Water for Western Agriculture* (Washington, D.C., 1982) appx. II–A. Fifty million acres is a reasonable estimate of irrigated acreage in the seventeen western states in the late 1970s.

6. Calculated from data in the U.S. Geological Survey circulars on the estimated use of water in the United States.

7. U.S. Water Resources Council, *The Nation's Water Resources: The Second National Water Assessment*, vol. 3, appx. V, p. 201.

8. Hearings before the House Subcommittee on Irrigation and Reclamation, 89th Congress, session on HR 4671 and similar bills to authorize construction, operations, and maintenance of the Lower Colorado River Basin Project, p. 532.

9. Myron B. Holburt, "What Are the Odds in Future Colorado River Flows?," meeting preprint ASCE annual meeting and national meeting on Water Resources Engineering, New Orleans, February 1969.

10. The reader interested in a fuller explanation should consult chap. 3 in Allen V. Kneese and F. Lee Brown, *The Southwest Under Stress* (Baltimore, 1981).

11. For a discussion of the politics surrounding the Salinity Control Program, see Allen V. Kneese, "Typical Cases Involving Natural Resources," in Kent Price, ed., *Regional Conflict and National Policy* (Washington, D.C., 1982).

12. "Ruling May Change Wind River Tribes," *The Denver Post*, 13 February 1983, p. 7B.

13. Norris Hundley, jr., Chapter 2 herein, pp. ••–••.

14. The following discussion is based on William Douglas Back and Jeffrey S. Taylor, "Navajo Water Rights: Pulling the Plug on the Colorado River," *Natural Resources Journal* (January 1980), pp. 70–90.

15. Figures are taken from Back and Taylor.

16. Monroe Price and Gary D. Weatherford, "Indian Water Rights in Theory and Practice: Navajo Experience in the Colorado River Basin," *Law and Contemporary Problems* 40 (1976), pp. 108–31.

17. A useful discussion of the case is found in Nancy Laney, "Does

108   *Allen V. Kneese and Gilbert Bonem*

Arizona's 1980 Groundwater Management Act Violate the Commerce Clause?,"
Arizona Law Review 24 (1982), p. 202.

18. *Sporhase, et al.* v. *Nebraska*, appeal from Supreme Court of Nebraska
no. 81–613, argued 30 March 1982, decided 2 July 1982. Syllabus, p. 2.

19. The United States District Court for the District of New Mexico,
Memorandum Opinion, *The City of El Paso* v. *S.E. Reynolds*, Civ. No. 80–
730 HB, 17 January 1983.

20. John A. Dracup, "Impact on the Colorado River Basin and Southwest Water Supply," in National Research Council, *Climate Change and Water
Impact* (1977), p. 130.

21. Robert Powers, William Gillespie, and Stephen Lekson, *The Outlier
Survey, A Regional View of Settlement in the San Juan Basin*, Report no. 3
(Albuquerque, 1983).

9

Establishing the Scientific, Technical, and Economic Basis for Coastal Zone Management

CLIFFORD S. RUSSELL and ALLEN V. KNEESE*

Abstract   This paper has three major aims: first, to put the problems lumped under the rubric "Coastal Zone Management," in perspective; second, to set out a general framework for the construction of coastal zone management models; and third, to discuss institutional problems, particularly those involved in organizing coastal zone research and in transferring the results of that research to the managers and social decision-makers. A fundamental point is that many of the problems commonly discussed in the context of the coastal zone are conceptually the same as "inland" problems with a long history of research and applied management. While there are complications introduced by the peculiarities of the marine and estuarial environment, it is hardly necessary to begin as though nothing were known. Those problems involving large-scale natural systems such as ocean currents, marine fisheries and tropical storms, are, however, unique in the coastal zone. These problems also are properly managed at the national level, and a sensible organization for research probably should involve expansion of NOAA's facilities, particularly in the direction of the social sciences.

Coastal zone management as a phrase and a concept has been around for a number of years. Over time it has received steadily, if slowly, growing attention from public policy makers and the academic field. This increasing interest may be seen as testimony that the phrase has struck a responsive chord in society. But perhaps more accurately, we can guess that the broad support for research and action under this rubric indicates that it covers a multitude of sins, and that nearly everybody's favorite can be fitted in somehow. Thus, problems, as diverse as the zoning of vacation communities, the protection and nourishment of ocean

*Resources for the Future, Inc., Washington, D.C.
Coastal Zone Management Journal 1973, Volume 1, Number 1
Copyright © 1973 by Crane, Russak, & Company, Inc.

47

beaches, the quality of water in tidal estuaries, the regulation of off-shore oil drilling and the fate of the domestic fishing fleet can all be regarded as coastal zone management problems.

But as convenient as it is to have a concept in which there is something for nearly everyone, there are also disadvantages to working under such a large umbrella, and we would like to court unpopularity by pointing some of them out. The first is that not everything which gets lumped in ought to be publicly managed—that is, not every difficulty is properly resolved by government intervention. In the coastal zone, the major justification for "management" is the common-property nature of many of the major resources. Since these resources are, for legal or technical reasons, the property of all, they are the concern of none (save the inevitable few who are philanthropically inclined). The result, in the absence of government intervention, tends to be over-use, misuse and ultimate destruction of the resources. Important examples of common property resources are water bodies, the air mantle, large landscapes, and extensive ecological systems. All of these are, of course, particularly abundant in coastal areas. But it is also important to realize that not everything that appears to be going wrong in the coastal zone is due to the presence of common property resources. Thus, for example, it is difficult (though some would probably find it possible) to argue that "management," i.e. government investment and control, is called for by the demise of the American flag transatlantic luxury liner.[1]

A second disadvantage of trying to work with a program as broad as that seemingly justified by the current reading of coastal zone management is that it encourages duplication of effort by artificially labelling as intrinsically dissimilar the same problem occurring in different places. Difficulties of local zoning and land-use controls, of air and water quality, of preservation and development, and of provision of recreational facilities, occur both in the coastal zone and "inland." And wherever they occur, they are in principle the same.

Admittedly, circumstances in the coastal zone exacerbate some of these universal management problems and make scientific understanding and modeling of others much more difficult. For one thing, the coastal zone is relatively heavily populated and getting more so. Table 1 shows the percentage of the U.S. (excluding Alaska and Hawaii) industrial work force employed in the coastal zone (defined for this purpose as the set of counties actually fronting on the ocean, or the Great Lakes, and their estuarial arms), and the land area of that zone as a percentage of the land area of the "lower 48." From 39 per cent of the work force in 1940, the coastal zone increased its overall share to 43 per cent in 1960. Apparently, during the '60s, this trend, for the U.S. as a whole, came to a

---

[1]The issue of the merchant marine subsidies is similar, and the present program appears to rest on national security considerations. As we have recently seen, this is the broadest of justifications for all manner of "management" activities.

Table 1

Percentage of total U.S. industrial employment in the coastal zone*

Portion of coastal zone	Percentage of U.S. land area	Percentage of total U. S. industrial employment			
		1940	1950	1960	1970
New England	0.50	4.00	3.78	3.68	3.60
Mid-Atlantic	0.85	15.45	15.29	15.18	14.29
South-Atlantic	0.94	1.15	1.39	1.94	2.15
Eastern Gulf Coast	0.77	0.62	0.76	1.03	1.08
Western Gulf Coast	0.88	1.54	1.72	1.91	2.11
Southern California	0.57	2.75	3.54	4.89	5.29
San Francisco Area	0.39	1.73	2.21	2.62	2.83
Northern California-Oregon	0.80	0.20	0.27	0.28	0.27
Washington	0.63	0.84	1.00	1.03	1.09
Great Lakes	2.24	10.77	10.88	10.31	9.85
Total Coastal Zone	8.58	39.05	40.84	42.88	42.57
Total Coastal Zone (less Great Lakes)	6.34	28.28	29.96	32.57	32.72

*Defined as the set of countries contiguous to the oceans or the Great Lakes or their estuarial arms. Alaska and Hawaii are not included.

stop, though a small increase was recorded for the marine portion of the zone. This aggregate movement conceals changes in regional patterns which have been more dramatic. While New England, the Great Lakes and even the Mid-Atlantic zones were declining in importance (at an accelerating rate in the latter two cases), very rapid growth was occurring in the South Atlantic and Gulf Regions and in California, both north and south. In addition, of course, even where the coastal zone is not heavily populated year round, it is subject to the rising pressure of vacation community development. And more people, even for part of the year, mean greater burdens on management—which, up to now, have seldom been successfully sustained. This unusual concentration of population and problems implies that a large share of whatever resources society is willing to devote to understanding and managing common property resources would appropriately go to coastal areas.

Nevertheless, pollution is pollution whether it be found in a bay or a river, and the problems of choosing a desired quality level and setting up an organization and procedure for attaining it are similar in both settings. But the bay does present some obstacles, not present in the river, to constructing models which will tell us what level of ambient quality we shall get out of a certain amount and pattern of discharge control. The most obvious of these difficulties are the tides and the transition zone between salt and fresh or brackish waters. Others include the fact that an important aspect of water quality in a bay is its unique ability to shelter, sustain and nourish certain species of migratory ocean fish (e.g. striped bass) during parts of their life cycle.

We have argued that the broad, umbrella approach to the concept of coastal zone management has the disadvantages of covering things which are not actually public management problems, and of treating similar problems as dissimilar. A further difficulty has arisen because most of the research and actual planning so far done in the area has been fostered by Federal money. This has, inevitably, resulted in a bias in favor of management schemes based on Federal laws and funding. And while we are not necessarily supporters of "the new federalism," we do feel it is obvious that the Federal level is not always the best jurisdiction at which to try to solve coastal zone problems.

There are political as well as technical justifications for doubting the desirability of highly centralized management, and of these the political ones are the more compelling. One can perhaps envisage a Federal bureaucracy of sufficient size and with enough data and financial resources to implement programs and policies of management once decided upon. But the most difficult problem, and the one furthest from solution, in the management of common property resources is how to make the value choices involved in their use. How much pollution? How much public land? How many marinas? How much dredging and filling? Technical benefit-cost analysis can be helpful in making such decisions but in the final analysis they can only be made politically. How to structure a political process which faithfully reflects the informed preferences of the population, in view of the vastly increased pressure on common property resources, is surely one of the most challenging problems facing social scientists and, of course, society generally. Clearly the U.S. Congress cannot, and certainly should not, make all the detailed value choices. We must try to distinguish the choices which are appropriately made at that level (e.g. how many deepwater ports?) from those that are not; and then learn to use, or create, governments of broad jurisdiction at the state or regional (including local) level for the latter. In a few cases there has been encouraging progress on this front (e.g. California) but in most cases the problem has not even been addressed.

The central position of this paper is based on the above general observations. That is, we feel that:

1. Problems which are, in principle, common to many physical environments should be explicitly recognized as such, and research cn them as they occur in

the coastal zone should not start *de novo* or be artificially isolated from similar efforts in other geographic regions. Coastal zone research as such should concentrate on problems unique to the zone. We shall have more to say on this later.

2. Management problems which involve small-scale physical systems, or those that can be isolated from larger systems by setting boundary conditions or constraints, are probably best handled at a jurisdictional level roughly coterminal with the "free body" systems.[2]

3. Coastal zone management at the Federal level should center on the large-scale systems involving several states, for example, through the waters and biota of the territorial sea. The relation between the Federal and local levels can best be expressed in standards set by the former on the actual performance of the management schemes chosen by the latter—the constraints mentioned just above. Thus, for example, we have in mind standards on minimal acceptable survival rates for anadromous fish spawning runs (and for returning fry); maximum allowable discharges of pesticides and heavy metals from estuaries; and minimum building standards and setbacks for hurricane-prone beach areas.

In short, our view is that Federal-level coastal zone management should be conducted in the context of large-scale physical and biological systems. Since it is the smaller systems which generally produce the problems more obviously like those studied in other contexts, this distinction is useful in establishing the scientific, technical and economic basis for coastal zone management.

In the remainder of this paper we address problems which are distinctively those of coastal zone management. Since they are the large system problems, they would tend to fall primarily under the purview of the Federal government.

A Framework for Discussing the Requirements of Coastal Zone Management

In Figure 1 we outline schematically a framework for the information requirements of coastal zone management which we, at RFF, have found useful in connection with other common property resource problems. This simplified view of the actual world emphasizes the dual position of human society as both the creator of detrimental (and beneficial) effects on natural systems and the evaluator and manager of those effects. Thus people, in their roles as producers and consumers, inevitably have direct physical and aesthetic impact on the natural world. These result from the discharge of residuals (the left-overs from production and consumption activities); from fishing, farming, lumbering, and

---

[2]This comment is not meant to minimize the problem of determining or creating the proper jurisdiction for the "problem shed." This is enormously difficult, and there is no technically correct way of doing it. For a discussion laying out some principles to guide the necessarily *ad hoc* process, see Haefele and Kneese, "Environmental Quality and the Optimal Jurisdiction," a paper presented at the Conference on Comparative Urban and Grants Economics, University of Windsor, Canada, November 1972.

other forms of exploitation of natural processes; and from actions designed to modify the environment itself to make it more useful in production processes and to reduce the hazards associated with certain natural events.

These impacts become exogenous inputs to the complex natural processes—physical, chemical, and biological—which occur naturally. Such interlinked processes—or ecological systems, if you prefer—in turn determine what the natural world is to be like, perhaps at other times and places as well as at the point and occasion of direct impact. The third box in our framework refers to the evaluation of alternative states of the world, in relation either to some measure of general social benefit, or to chosen target or constraint levels.

Our problem, then, is to choose among the sets of "environmental quality" and economic activity (material prosperity) levels, those which are most desirable. Such choices and how to implement them, we emphasize, become public management problems when our market institutions fail to take account of all valuable resources affected by an activity, i.e. when activities fall on common property (non-market) resources. In other situations the private market system works tolerably well as a device for choosing.

Once the management objectives are defined, ways must be devised for attaining them—effluent limitations, for example. That is, institutions and incentives must be designed to force private behavior along socially desired lines. Furthermore, the management agency must devise means for instituting those modifications of the environment which must be carried out directly by an agency of government—fresh water flow regulations into estuaries, for pollution dilution, for example.

Since it would be socially and economically far too costly to try out more than a very few alternative policies in order to observe their effects on the natural world, it becomes useful and even, as far as we can see, essential to construct models of the systems represented in the framework. These models can then be manipulated relatively cheaply, and their predictions used as input to either (or both) the choice or implementation phases of the management process. They also provide a framework for structuring data collection programs, designing component studies, and often for testing the relative importance of information of different kinds. Models are intellectual idealizations which range from general conceptualization, usually in the early stages of their development, to ones that define precise quantitative relationships.

The building of models of the processes sketched in Figure 1 is a convenient hook on which to hang the rest of our discussion of the establishment of the bases for coastal zone management. We should emphasize at the outset, however, that even successful models are by no means sufficient to support the weight of that management by themselves. In particular, two other serious problems must be addressed: the design of institutions for making the collective choices and for

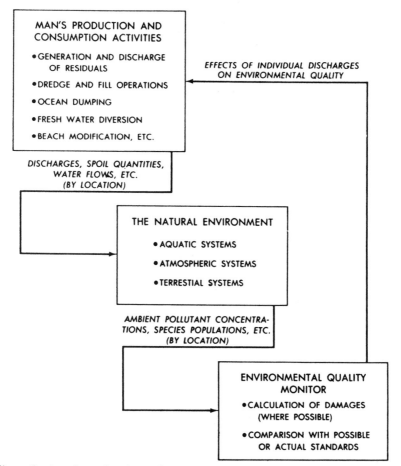

Figure 1. A schematic view of the common property resource management problem.

carrying out the executive management functions; and the transfer of information in useful ways from the scientific, technical and economic side (the models) to the choice and execution side (the instituticns). We shall have more to say on these matters below.

Three Examples of Large Coastal System Management Problems

To illustrate the kinds of knowledge and modeling efforts necessary to put flesh on the bare bones of Figure 1, let us consider three examples of management problems involving large coastal systems: (a) oil spills, ocean dumping, and the outflow of residuals from major estuaries (or what we refer to generally as

54   CLIFFORD S. RUSSELL AND ALLEN V. KNEESE

"ocean quality management"); (b) fisheries in the territorial sea; and (c) threatening tropical storms. For each of these we shall sketch a framework within which information and understanding might be organized to help inform management. This will imply a set of research needs and will suggest the mix of disciplines necessary for policy-relevant research on common property resources management. We shall also mention, in passing, some of the more ambitious existing research aimed at the area in question and using the general approach we advocate. Finally, we also indicate, wherever we are aware of it, the extent to which applicable research has been done in quite different problem settings.

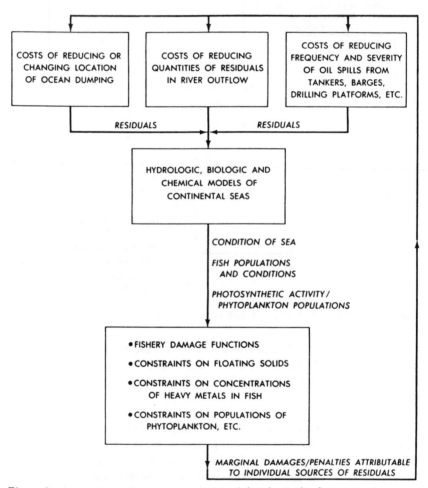

Figure 2. An ocean quality management model: schematic view.

Ocean Quality Management

Figure 2 displays a framework for dealing with problems of pollution from oil spills, ocean dumping and river outflow. This is basically the familiar water-pollution problem writ large, and much of the work done in the context of river pollution is applicable.[3] The major difference is in the scale and dimensionality of the aquatic system involved. Thus, instead of having the orderly flow of a river in one direction between its banks (in the felicitous phrase of an Old Testament writer "water floweth whither it listeth"); or even an estuary with the more complex tidal currents, we have an unbounded body of water, free to flow in any direction.[4] In addition, changes in currents, temperature, and biological communities with depth become more significant in the open ocean, so that the hydraulic part of the natural system model will almost certainly have to be far more complex than the corresponding module in the riverine problem. The chemical and biological systems of the oceans have not been so extensively studied as those of rivers and estuaries, but may not be any more difficult to understand and model (not that the others are easy!).[5] A small but significant start in this direction is being made by NOAA's New York Bight study under the Marine Eco-systems Analysis program (MESA). The MESA approach should be systematically extended to all other important sections of the nation's coastal waters and adjacent oceans.

On the economic side, gaps in our knowledge and techniques for dealing with ocean quality management also exist. True, we do have a general framework

---

[3] A basic source in this area is A. V. Kneese and B. T. Bower, *Managing Water Quality: Economics, Technology, Institutions* (Baltimore: Johns Hopkins Press, 1968). A recent work dealing with a number of technical, economic and political questions is: R. Dorfman, H. Jacoby and H. A. Thomas, *Models for Managing Regional Water Quality* (Cambridge: Harvard University Press, 1973). Other papers which could serve as an introduction to particular technical topics are: D. J. O'Connor and R. V. Thomann, "Water Quality Models: Chemical, Physical, and Biological Constituents," in *Estuarine Modeling: An Assessment*, EPA (Washington, D.C.: USGPO, February 1971), Chapter III; R. A. Kelly, "Conceptual Ecological Model of Delaware Estuary," to be published in B. C. Patten, ed., *Systems Analysis and Simulation in Ecology*, Vol. III (New York: Academic Press, forthcoming 1974); and E. Johnson, "A Study in the Economics of Water Quality Management," *Water Resources Research*, Vol. 3, No. 2 (1967), pp. 291-305.

[4] We do not mean to indicate here that there are no predictable forces operating on water in the oceans, or that there are no well-defined current regimes on various scales. We merely wish to emphasize the contrast between say, the Connecticut River which cannot flow from Springfield to Boston and the open ocean in which very large changes in currect direction are possible under seasonal and shorter term influences.

[5] A large model of the southern section of the North Sea is being constructed by a team at University of Liége in Belgium. See "Mathematical Model of Continental Seas: Preliminary Results Concerning the Southern Bight" (of the North Sea), by Math Modelsea (name of the research group at University of Liége under the direction of Professor C. J. Nihoul), 1973. It is intended that this will eventually be linked to an economic model including the costs of changing levels of ocean dumping and river pollution outflow.

from the benefit-cost analysis developed in connection with water resource planning and "inland" pollution problems. But this framework needs refinement and elaboration in order to deal effectively with long time horizons and potential irreversibilities,[6] as well as random events. Perhaps just as important, we currently lack the information from which to put together cost functions for reducing or moving ocean dumping, and for reducing the quantities of various residuals in river outflows. The costs of reducing the probabilities of tanker collisions and groundings, and of reducing oil spillage in an event of given severity are not, to our knowledge, available either.[7]

The matter of residual discharges to the oceans, particularly ocean dumping, has of course been the object of considerable recent activity both domestically and internationally. But the problems are far from solved. At best we can consider that the dumping of substances generally agreed to be highly dangerous has been deemed a bad thing, and probably prohibited to persons and firms using U.S. ports. But there is an enormous range of other substances for which the socially desirable dumping rate may not be zero. We need some basis for understanding what effects follow from what limits. In particular, how does dumping of various residuals at different distances from shore, in varying water depths and current regimes, affect near and distant coasts; the quality of the ocean itself, and the fishing available over the continental shelf and slope?[8] Similarly, we need to understand how river pollution affects the oceans and coasts in both the short and long runs. Such knowledge can only be the product of systematic data collection and analysis within the framework of the best models of the salient systems which can be devised. In practice, modelling and data collection must be an iterative process reaching successively higher levels of insight and quantitative accuracy.

---

[6]On this point there has been considerable innovative work done by John Krutilla and his colleagues. See, for example, A. C. Fisher, J. V. Krutilla and C. J. Cicchetti, "The Economics of Environmental Preservation: A Theoretical and Empirical Analysis," *American Economic Review*, September 1972, Vol. LXII, No. 4, pp. 605-19; and J. V. Krutilla and C. J. Cicchetti, "Benefit-Cost Analysis and Technologically Induced Relative Price Changes: The Case of Environmental Irreversibilities," in *Benefit-Cost Analyses of Federal Programs*, Joint Economic Committee, 92nd Cong., 2nd Session (Washington: USGPO, 1973).

[7]But the questions are receiving increasing attention. See, for example, K. Nair *et al.*, *Cargo Spill Probability Analysis for the Deep Water Port Project* (Oakland, Cal.: Woodward-Lundgren & Associates, Feb. 1973), available from NTIS as AD-758-330; *The Georges-Bank Petroleum Study*, Offshore Oil Task Group, MIT, Report MITSG 73-5, 1 Feb. 1973, Vol. II; and W. J. Mead and P. E. Sorensen, "The Economic Cost of the Santa Barbara Oil Spill," a paper presented at the Santa Barbara Oil Symposium, University of California, Santa Barbara, Dec. 1970.

[8]See, for an example of such a study, R. T. Dewling, K. H. Walker and F. R. Brozenski, "Effects of Pollution: Loss of an $18-million/year Shellfishery," a paper presented at the FAO Conference on Marine Pollution and its Effects on Living Resources and Fishing, Rome, Dec. 1970.

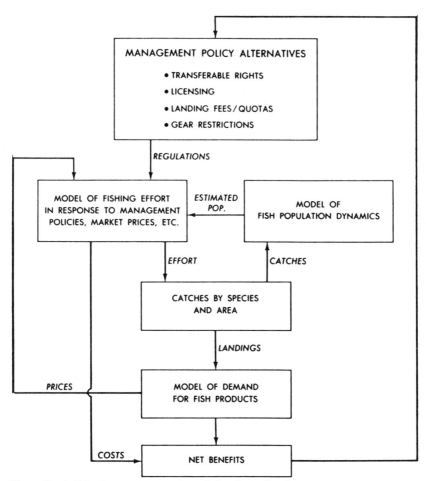

Figure 3. A fisheries management model: schematic view.

Fisheries Management in the Territorial Sea

To judge by the reports from Iceland, Peru, and Georges Bank, fisheries management in territorial seas is a problem of worldwide importance and one on which critical decisions are being made nearly every day. It is also true that models of specific fisheries have been around for some time and that they have been used in guiding policies.[9] For the most part, however, these models have been extremely rough affairs, and it has been rare for economic and biological models to be linked in the manner shown schematically in Figure 3.

---

[9]The father of this field is generally acknowledged to be the late M. B. Schaefer. See, for example, his paper, "Fishery Dynamics and Present Status of the Yellowfin Tuna Popula-

58   CLIFFORD S. RUSSELL AND ALLEN V. KNEESE

The concern (if not necessarily the accomplishment) of management agencies has generally been to find the maximum sustainable biological yield and to regulate catches, usually by quotas, to stay close to that level. There has, at the same time, been considerable work by economists in the area of regulatory mechanisms (quotas, taxes, license fees, etc.) and on theoretical models of fisheries regulation using hypothetical "fish production functions."[10] Some research has also been done on demand for fisheries products.[11]

What is needed now is a series of large-scale applications of what is already known, along with an effort to improve the central biological models and our information on costs as related to catching power. One attempt at such a synthesis and improvement is being made in the NORFISH project at the University of Washington in Seattle.

Predicting and Altering Tropical Storm Tracks

NOAA and its predecessors have been interested for some time in the prediction of tropical storm tracks and the reduction of storm intensity. The immense property damages and often substantial toll in human lives associated with these great cyclones have made such activities highly attractive. Accordingly, research has been conducted on possibilities for "protecting" shore areas from damage and loss of life, and currently track prediction is undertaken more or less routinely.[12] Modification is still in the research phase, with some success having

---

tion of the Eastern Pacific Ocean," *Inter-American Tropical Tuna Commission Bulletin,* 12(3), pp. 87-136.

[10]Examples of such abstract model-building include: H.S. Gordan, "The Economic Theory of a Common Property Resource: The Fishery," *Journal of Political Economy,* April, 1954, pp. 124-42; A. Scott, "The Fishery: The Objectives of Sole Ownership," *Journal of Political Economy,* April 1955, pp. 116-24; V. L. Smith, "Economics of Production from Natural Resources," *American Economic Review,* June 1968, pp. 409-32; V.L. Smith, "On Models of Commercial Fishing," *Journal of Political Economy,* June 1969, pp. 181-98; R. Turvey, "Optimization in Fishery Regulation," *American Economic Review,* March 1964; J. P. Quirk and V. L. Smith, "Dynamic Economic Models of Fishing," unpublished mimeo; T. Hansen, "An Analysis of the Factors Determining the Economic Yield of the Winter Capelin Fishery by Means of a Mathematical Model," paper presented at the OECD International Symposium on Fisheries Economics, Paris, 29 November-3rd December 1971.

[11]For example, F. W. Bell, "The Pope and the Demand for Fish," *American Economic Review,* Dec. 1968, 1346-50; W. C. Gillespie, J. C. Hite and J. S. Lytle, "An Econometric Analysis of the U.S. Shrimp Industry," *Economics of Marine Resources No. 2,* Department of Agricultural Economics & Rural Sociology, Clemson University, Clemson, S.C., December 1969; and L. M. Pickles, "An Economic Analysis of the U.K. Humber Distant Water Cod Price," a paper presented at the OECD International Symposium on Fisheries Economics, Paris, December 1971.

[12]For example, the *NOAA Week,* Vol. 4, No. 23, for 1 June 1973, contains the following description of activities planned for the 1973 hurricane season: "In 1973, as before, surveillance of tropical storms will be conducted by satellites, including NOAA's ESSA-8 and NOAA-2 satellites; aircraft of the Air Force, Navy, and the Environmental Research

been reported, but with suitable experimental opportunities few and far between.[13]

At this point it seems logical, and indeed even urgent, to set up research in
the framework of the broader systems and to begin to look at the coastal and
other land-based management problems implied by present and anticipated
capabilities. A possible framework for such a study is shown in Figure 4. Most of
the modules in this framework, while difficult to construct quantitatively and to
verify, are at least conceptually similar to others we have seen above. Thus, the
cost functions for modifying or predicting the tracks of tropical storms, expressed in whatever probabilistic terms seem appropriate, are not now known,
but their estimation is conceptually similar to that for reducing, say, oil spills.
Similarly, the model of storm tracks and intensities is probably on the edge of or
beyond current knowledge, and will be a complicated probabilistic monster
when constructed, but such a model can probably grow logically out of the
research now being done.[14]

The "adjustment" module in Figure 4 is, however, quite a different matter.
While it is at the heart of the management problem, it has hardly been
researched at all, to our knowledge, though some of the work done by Gilbert
White and his students on other natural hazards is certainly germane.[15] What is

---

Laboratories' Research Flight Facility, . . . and by radar. The goal of the forecasters is to
provide at least 12 daylight hours of warning time for people to evacuate before a hurricane
strikes. Computerized predictions of the expected height of storm surges again will be issued
this year. . . . Refinements under investigation include more precise forecasts for surges
moving into estuaries—a particularly difficult problem. The computerized storm-surge program is an outgrowth of work done by Dr. Chester Jelesnianski, of the NWS Techniques
Development Laboratory. The series of storm-evacuation route maps being prepared by the
National Ocean Survey now includes published maps for Galveston, Texas; the Mobile,
Ala./New Orleans, La., strip; and Corpus Christi, Tex. Under preparation are maps for the
Charleston, S.C./Savannah, Ga., area; Norfolk, Va., and vicinity; and the New York City/
Long Island/northern New Jersey area. These maps show areas that would be inundated by
various levels of tidal storm surge, and indicate preferred evacuation routes. A limited
number of the maps are available to local officials in areas involved, from the nearest
Weather Service office."

[13]For a description of the 1972 program see *NOAA Week*, 28 July 1972, Vol. 3, No. 30,
p. 1, "Project Stormfury Ready for 1972 Seedings," and for a larger perspective, *Summary
Report: Weather Modification*, U.S. Dept. of Commerce, NOAA, Rockville, May 1973, esp.
pp. 41-43.

[14]This is not to say that the linkage between the cost and stormtrack models would be easy,
or even straightforward in principle.

[15]An introduction to this work is provided by Gilbert F. White, *Papers on Flood Problems*,
Gilbert F. White (ed.), Department of Geography Research Paper No. 70, University of
Chicago, 1961, and *Choice of Adjustment to Floods*, Department of Geography Research
Paper No. 93, University of Chicago, 1964. This work has been extended to other hazards
by members of White's "school." See, for example, Ian Burton, Robert W. Kates, and
Rodman Snead, *The Human Ecology of Coast-Flood Hazard in Megalopolis*, Department of

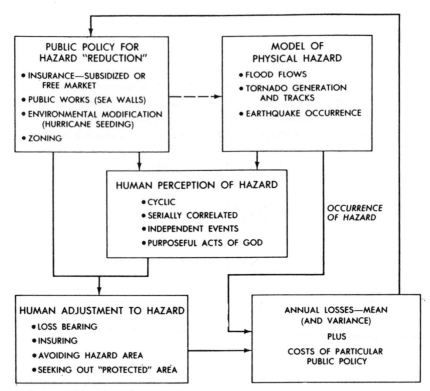

Figure 4. Natural hazard protection and modification.

involved here is the reaction of people to the knowledge that they are now being "protected" but are not being asked to share in the cost in relation to the expected benefits. In river basins this reaction takes the form of intensive utilization of flood plains "protected" by levees, upstream dams, etc. The net result of the common property approach to protection and the public adjustment to it may very well be an *increase* in average annual damages, and a very large increase in the potential for catastrophe when the protection system fails under the stress of an event far out in the tail of the distribution.

Something along these lines may very well happen if and when NOAA goes into the business of routinely seeding hurricanes to reduce wind intensities or to alter predicted tracks. But considerable work will be necessary to replace this imprecise, qualitative prediction with something approaching the quantitative "hardness" necessary to inform management decisions.

Geography Research Paper No. 115, University of Chicago, 1969; and Duane Bauman and John H. Sims, "Tornado Threat; Coping Styles of the North and South," *Science*, Vol. 176, June 30, 1972, pp. 1386-92.

Another aspect of the cost of severe storm modification is much more indirect. These storms frequently induce rainfall over vast areas, oftentimes areas that normally have low rainfall or are semi-arid. To our knowledge the effect of modification activities on rainfall at points remote from the coastal zone is not well understood and little studied. It is possible that economic losses from reduced rainfall in some areas could offset, in whole or in part, the gains from hazard reductions in other areas. This is another reason why this coastal zone management problem must be examined in a wide context.

Institutions Again

Having discussed several specific problems in coastal zone management, let us now return to institutional questions raised in the opening section of the paper. We shall concentrate here, however, on approaches to transferring to such institutions information on the economic, technical and scientific aspects of the problems they face. Finally, we shall go into the matter of appropriate institutions for doing research in coastal zone management.

Institutions and Information Transfer

As we have already noted, the matter of institutions is especially important—and especially difficult—at the level of the regional problems often discussed under the heading of coastal zone management problems, e.g. pollution of a large estuary such as Delaware Bay or Chesapeake Bay. But again we must note that the institutional problems are not unique to coastal zone problems, and while work in the area of institutional design for common property resource management is not far advanced, it has gotten off to a useful start.[16] Fortunately, at the level of large systems, those of national importance, the institutional design problem hardly exists. We have the necessary collective choice mechanism in the Congress and the potential, at least, for the executive management agency in NOAA. Since we are concentrating on the large-system problems, we shall not discuss institutional design further.

Information transfer is a serious matter at all jurisdictional levels in the coastal zone. Research may produce an accurate model on the lines of Figure 1 for some particular management problem, but unless that model is structured in such a way as to speak to the concerns of the legislators and executives involved, it will probably not make a significant contribution to informing the collective decisions or the management actions. This is widely understood, and many efforts have been and are being made to find model structures which facilitate communication. One group is exploring the use of computerized games to

---

[16]For example, see Martin McGuire, "Group Segregation and Optimal Jurisdictions," unpublished paper, University of Maryland; and Kneese and Haefele, "Environmental Quality and the Optimal Jurisdiction," *op. cit.*

62   CLIFFORD S. RUSSELL AND ALLEN V. KNEESE

inform concerned public figures on the nature of the problem, the roles of other participants, and the possibilities for solutions. In this approach the players may adopt roles other than the one they actually play and may choose policies and strategies which are played out against the policies of the other participants within the computer.[17] Another approach rests on a mapping of the "politically feasible" solution space through the use of a model which contains in its objective function weights on the outcomes accruing to various groups in the region (e.g. heavy industry, fishermen, recreational boaters). The intention is that politicians or executive agency people can, either by observing a previously prepared "map" or by varying the weights (on a confidential basis) themselves, begin to understand what is both physically and politically feasible.[18] A third effort to improve communication between model and politician has been undertaken at RFF. Here the idea is to build into models constraints on the distribution across legislative districts of the costs and benefits arising from a collective decision. It is intended that the model be available for use by legislators themselves or by their staff members (again, on a confidential basis) and that by playing with the constraints, these participants can more efficiently go about the business of compromise and vote trading which is at the heart of the collective decision process.[19]

Institutions for Doing Research and Providing Information

Understanding and providing useful information about large coastal zone systems such as the ones discussed in this paper will require sustained multidisciplinary research and data collection. This can almost certainly not be done successfully in a university environment except under unusual circumstances. This is because of the limitation imposed by departmental boundaries, the time constraints set by the needs of students, and a reward structure which puts a premium on small, short-term projects concentrating on "respectable" (often theoretical) problems.[20] It appears to us that regional laboratories of some form are needed. These might be strengthened versions of existing oceanographic institutions, or entirely new institutions. The NOAA Research Institutes may

---

[17]A leading center of this approach is the Sea Grant Program at the University of Michigan.

[18]An important discussion of this approach is to be found in Robert Dorfman, Henry Jacoby, and Harold Thomas, *Models for Managing Regional Water Quality* (Cambridge: Harvard University Press, 1973), especially chapters 2 and 3.

[19]For a discussion of this approach see C. S. Russell, W. O. Spofford, Jr. and E. T. Haefele, "Environmental Quality Management in Metropolitan Areas," prepared for delivery at the International Economic Association Conference on Urbanization and the Environment, Copenhagen, Denmark, June 19-24, 1972. Also E. T. Haefele, "A Utility Theory of Representative Government," *The American Economics Review,* Vol. LXI, June 1971.

[20]For a possible counter example, however, see the work by MIT on off-shore oil referred to above.

provide a pattern, although it is clear that a large social science component would have to be added to equip such institutes for research of the sort we see as informing the coastal zone management process. Whatever their genesis, the laboratories should have not only strong in-house capabilities but also contract money available so that they can use, as necessary, the specialized skills, knowledge and equipment found in other institutions, including universities.

Even in a special research institution there will, of course, be conflicting pressures—particularly the tension between applied-research needs and basic-research professional rewards—which will make the hiring and retention of good people no easy chore. We are not prepared to suggest any single solution to this difficulty, but it does seem that there are and have been models around, the study of which might give us both a list of do's and a list of don'ts.[21] The most important feature on the positive side is probably that the facility enjoy the enthusiastic support of the over-all agency head: the man who must fight with the Secretary and the Congress.

University programs, such as Sea Grant, are much more promising in the context of the detailed problems of local areas, and of extension-type work designed to assist private, rather than public, decision makers. Even in the local context, however, it would be an unusual university which could provide the whole range of needed research services. Public management agencies at the state level especially will have needs which can probably best be met by developing internal capacity and through contracts with private research firms.

There is also an important role for institutions that are not directly responsible to any governmental agency. This role is particularly vital in the areas of institutional design and policy studies, since these independent groups are able to cast a critical eye on established institutions and existing agency missions. They can also undertake high-risk research on new methods which a government lab might fear would endanger its appropriations. Private foundation funding of coastal zone research can play a particularly significant role here. Indeed, the importance of privately funded research in establishing strategic policy and institutional alternatives has been richly demonstrated, for example, in the area of water quality management.

---

[21]Without making invidious comparisons among domestic agencies, let us simply point to the Water Resources Board in Great Britain as an example of an institution in which the tension was recognized and apparently used constructively. Its history might be worth studying.

10

15 Israel's Water Policy*

Allen Kneese

INTRODUCTION

This chapter is a broad examination of Israeli water policy and of decision making processes and administrative practices with respect to water resources development, use, and management in Israel. This examination was made from the perspective of an economist, but also with recognition

---

* This study of Israeli water policy was carried out by means of extensive reading of documents about the Israeli experience, policies, and future plans, and two study trips to Israel. The first trip was in January 1976, and the second in May and June 1976. In the interim, staffs of the Water Commission and Tahal prepared material which I had requested for use during the second visit. During both visits, field trips were made which eventually covered each of the main water sources and water-using regions of Israel. Also, interviews were conducted with many of the leading figures involved in Israeli water development and use. As two years have passed since the report was written, some comments which are no longer relevant have been deleted. Some of the material has been updated in line with information provided by the Water Commission, but no attempt has been made to rewrite the report in the light of the changes which have taken place in the interim. Sponsorship of the study was by the Water Commission and the Ministry of Health. Funding was provided by the World Health Organization. This chapter is published with the permission of the Israeli Water Commissioner. However, it must be stressed that the views expressed are entirely my own; his granting permission to publish does not imply agreement with any or all of these views.

357

of the broader social, ideological, and security goals which have been major forces in the way water development and allocation occurred in the State of Israel.

There is no lack of expertise in Israel for making such an assessment and developing recommended changes. I must infer that I was asked to do the study because, while rather broadly experienced in many aspects of water policy and management, my prior knowledge of the Israeli situation was only of a very general character. Indeed, I now find that I had a number of major misconceptions about it. This innocence permitted me, or even required me, to take a fresh, and I hope relatively unbiased, look at the situation.

A first task, therefore, was to develop information and perspectives of a rather general nature about the situation. While these generalities will not be new to Israeli readers of this chapter, some might see them in quite a different context than I do. Therefore, I feel that it is important to set these perspectives out explicitly because they influence quite fundamentally what is said about policy, administrative and institutional matters later in the chapter.

FINDINGS PERTAINING TO MATTERS OF PERSPECTIVE

Urbanization versus Agriculture

Israel is a highly urbanized society and becoming more so. In his statement to the International Meeting on Water Managing Institutions, the Water Commissioner, Menahem Kantor, put the early situation in Israel succinctly:

> When the state was established in 1948 the total population was some 800,000. The following years were characterized by very rapid population growth as a result of large scale immigration. In a country with hardly any industrial base and little in the way of local raw materials, agriculture had to play a central role in the absorption of immigrants into the productive life of the economy and in the settlement of the sparsely populated regions of the south. (1)

The need, and desire, to absorb immigrants in agriculture led to rapid water development with many interesting technological and hydrological aspects, especially in regard to interregional transfers. Water development and allocation laws and institutions appropriate to the situation were also devised.

Agriculture still carries great weight in Israeli ideology and social concepts. Also one cannot come away from a field examination of Israeli agriculture without tremendous regard for what it has achieved. But contemporary Israel is an urban society, perhaps one of the most urbanized societies
in the world. Among the Jewish population in 1970, 7.4 percent of the employed labor force worked in agriculture. Now it is about 6 percent, and by
1990 it may be expected to be below 5 percent (Table 15.1). Even within the
rural settlements, the kibbutzim and moshavim, often less than half the working population is actually engaged in full-time farming (Table 15.2).

TABLE 15.1. Employed Persons by Economic Branch (Jews)
(In Percentages)

	1960	1970	1974	1976
Agriculture	15.0	7.4	5.8	5.5
Industry	23.8	25.1	26.3	25.1
Construction	8.9	7.1	6.6	6.2
Commerce services and Others	52.3	60.4	61.3	63.2
Total	100.0	100.0	100.0	100.0

Source: Statistical Abstracts of Israel, Central Bureau of Statistics,
1977.

The absolute numbers employed in agriculture will probably change
little in the foreseeable future with some limited settlement in the Arava
and B'sor Regions and in Samaria, Judea, and in the Sinai. Nearly one-
third of Israel's population lives in the Tel Aviv district, and more than one-
half lives in the Tel Aviv, Jerusalem, and Haifa districts. As in many countries, the larger cities and towns are the magnets which attract population
(Table 15.3). It seems unlikely that the settlement plan will affect this very
much except possibly in the south, which appears to have powers of attraction of its own in any case.

TABLE 15.2. Employment by Economic Branch, Residents of
Kibbutzim and Moshavim, 1974
(In Percentages)

	Kibbutzim		Moshavim	
	1974	1976	1974	1976
Agriculture	29.2	27.6	55.6	55.6
Industry	19.4	20.0	11.7	11.5
Commerce, restaurants and hotel	10.5	10.2	4.4	4.1
Personal and public services	34.1	32.3	19.2	21.3
Others	6.8	9.9	9.1	7.5
Total	100.0	100.0	100.0	100.0

Source: Statistical Abstracts of Israel, Central Bureau of Statistics,
1977.

TABLE 15.3. Distribution of Population by Type of Settlement, 1975
(In Percentages)

	Jews	Non-Jews	Total
Towns	75.3	35.5	68.6
Smaller urban settlements	15.2	33.9	17.2
Villages	0.8	31.8	5.6
Moshavim	4.7	--	4.0
Kibbutzim	3.3	--	2.8
Other	0.7	9.8	1.8
Total	100.0	100.0	100.0

Source: Statistical Abstracts of Israel, Central Bureau of Statistics,
1976.

Agriculture's role in the macroeconomy has diminished rapidly. While
output per hour of labor and output per m^3 of water has risen rapidly in the
agriculture branch, the weight of this branch in aggregate economic indicators has dropped sharply. Agricultural production per capita nearly doubled
between 1953 and 1970, but other economic sectors grew even faster. In
the last few years agriculture has accounted for about 6 percent of total
gross investment, while about 16 percent of the gross capital stock was in
that branch. The greater weight in the latter category results from the
heavy investments made in agriculture in earlier years (Table 15.4). Since
1959, agricultural exports have dropped to about one-third of the weight in
total exports they carried in that year. In the last few years farm exports
have accounted for about 7 percent of total exports and industrial exports
for about 40 percent. Agriculture weighed slightly more heavily on a value-
added basis. It is officially expected that agricultural exports will retain
about their present share of the total over the next two decades (Table 15.5).
It should be noted, however, that this would require a change in the downward trend.

Population growth in the foreseeable future will probably be mostly the
natural increase of the present population. Forecasting net immigration is
a problematic task in Israel. My examination of the situation suggests immigration will play a relatively minor role in population growth in the foreseeable future. Since 1948, net immigration as a proportion of population
increase has shown a sporadic, but reasonably consistent, downward tendency. The effects of wars on population movement are clearly visible, but
since 1965 net immigration has never accounted for as much as half the population increase. Furthermore, several large immigrations have recently
come to a close (Table 15.6). Future population growth is likely, therefore,
to be mostly natural increase; for Jews, that would be about 1.7 percent annually and for non-Jews, about 4 percent. If the experience of other countries is any indication, those rates will probably drop if the standard of living continues to increase.

Water

Prices

Water pricing is not a principal policy instrument for inducing efficient
use of water or in meeting water costs in the history of Israeli water development; the allocation system, with its rather rigid structure, has failed to
keep pace with the rapid rate of agrotechnical, economic and social change.
A principle for efficient use of an economic resource is that it must carry a

TABLE 15.4. Investments in Water Projects and Agriculture
as a Percentage of Gross Domestic Capital Formation
(Excluding Housihg) 1952–1975
(In Percentages)

Years	Water Projects	Agriculture and Forestry
1952	15. 4	14. 0
1953	20. 2	20. 1
1954	18. 6	17. 6
1955	7. 8	24. 7
1956	5. 8	23. 8
1957	5. 8	21. 9
1958	5. 5	23. 1
1959	5. 9	20. 0
1960	7. 3	16. 5
1961	7. 2	13. 1
1962	8. 9	11. 4
1963	8. 7	9. 4
1964	5. 0	8. 5
1965	3. 7	8. 1
1966	4. 1	8. 6
1967	4. 5	10. 9
1968	2. 6	7. 6
1969	1. 5	6. 6
1970	1. 6	7. 3
1971	1. 4	5. 8
1972	1. 6	6. 7
1973	1. 2	5. 8
1974	1. 0	6. 4

Source: Statistical Abstracts of Israel, Central Bureau of Statistics,
1976.

TABLE 15.5. Total Exports and Exports of Agricultural Produce 1971–1975; Forecast for 1976–1980

Year	Total Exports ($ million)*	Services (% of total)	Commodities		
			Total (% of)	Agricultural Produce (% of total)	Citrus (% of total)
1971	1,814	50.3	49.7	8.5	6.3
1972	2,129	49.2	50.8	7.5	5.1
1973	2,654	48.5	51.5	6.5	4.1
1974	2,732	48.0	52.0	7.0	4.4
1975	3,454	49.7	50.3	7.8	4.9
Forecast					
1976	3,837	47.4	52.6	7.8	4.7
1977	4,340	46.0	54.0	7.6	4.4
1978	4,855	44.7	55.3	7.5	4.2
1979	5,525	42.8	57.2	7.6	4.0
1980	6,310	40.9	59.1	7.4	3.7

* Current prices, 1971–1975; 1975 prices 1976–1980

Source: 1971–1975, 1975 Bank of Israel Report.

TABLE 15.6. Immigration to Israel by Continent of Birth, 1948-1974

		Gross Immigration			Net Immigration		
Year	Total	Asia-Africa	Europe-American	Emigration	(1)-(4)		(5) as % of Population Increase
	000	(%)	(%)	000	000		
Year	(1)	(2)	(3)	(4)	(5)	(5a)	(6)
1948	101.8	14.4	85.6	1.0	100.8	22.9	
1949	239.6	47.3	52.7	7.2	232.4	26.6	91.1
1950	170.1	49.6	50.4	9.5	160.8	15.4	82.4
1951	175.1	71.1	28.9	10.1	165.0	13.2	80.6
1952	24.4	71.6	28.4	13.0	11.4	1.7	21.3
1953	11.3	75.1	24.9	12.5	-1.2	0.8	-3.8
1954	18.4	88.7	11.3	7.0	11.4	1.2	22.6
1955	37.5	92.9	7.1	6.0	31.5	2.4	43.7
1956	56.2	86.7	13.3	11.0	45.2	3.5	51.7
1957	71.2	42.5	57.5	11.0	60.2	4.1	59.9
1958	27.1	44.3	55.5	11.5	15.6	1.5	26.4
1959	23.9	33.2	66.8	9.5	14.4	1.3	25.4
1960	24.5	29.0	71.0	8.5	16.0	1.3	27.9
1961	47.6	47.3	52.7	9.1*	38.5	2.5	53.6
1962	61.3	78.5	21.5	12.1	49.2	3.0	63.1
1963	64.4	69.3	30.7	10.8	53.6	3.0	61.1
1964	54.7	41.6	58.4	9.7	45.0	2.5	57.4
1965	30.7	46.4	54.6	8.5	22.0	1.9	38.2
1966	15.7	42.3	52.7	11.6	4.1	0.7	18.1
1967	14.3	61.8	38.2	12.0	2.3	0.6	11.1
1968	20.5	68.4	31.6	5.7	14.8	0.8	24.8
1969	37.8	44.0	56.0	5.0	32.8	1.5	44.2
1970	36.7	37.2	62.8	4.1	32.6	1.4	42.8
1971	41.9	24.6	75.4	5.2	36.7	1.6	41.3
1972	55.9	13.6	86.4	9.8	46.1	2.1	48.6
1973	54.9	10.5	89.5	15.2	39.7	2.0	42.9
1974	32.0	10.0	90.0	22.1	9.9	1.1	12.1

Column (5a) gives population growth as a percentage of average population during the year.

* Calculated emigration - residents abroad for at least two years less residents returning after at least two years abroad.

Source: Statistical Yearbook, 1976.

price equal to its marginal cost of production. While water has carried a
price in Israel, in many regions and for many consumers, that price has been
far below the marginal cost of developing additional supplies and even far below its average cost of production and delivery. In recent years, the water
price has even been below the operating cost of the delivery system in some
regions. Norms and allocations have been used instead of prices to try to
induce frugal use of water, as well as to distribute water among settlements.

Allotment of water is made to the settlement as a whole. Irrigation and
other agricultural technology has changed very rapidly, and industrialization
of the settlements has taken place, especially in the collective settlements
(Table 15.2). In addition, the forecast population of many settlements on
which the water allocations were based, has, in some cases, not been reached
and in others exceeded. The allocations, therefore, have no direct meaning
at all in terms of conservation practices. It is rather the limitation of the
total water available plus various kinds of help from the government that has
induced the use of conservation measures.

Allocation of water to existing settlements at present functions, in fact,
as a nontransferable water right for the settlement. It is not in any meaningful sense an administrative device for achieving national goals, water use efficiency, or economic efficiency. In view of changes in population within settlements, changes in crop patterns, development of industry, and changes in
agricultural technology, the present distribution of water among established
settlements (although perhaps not among regions) must be regarded as arbitrary on any criterion. In addition, some regions, especially those where
water is relatively abundant and where water flows in open channels, are not
effectively in the allocation system at all.

Furthermore, the allocation system probably cannot be effectively improved as an instrument of national policy. The matter of reallocations is
a delicate one with social, political and economic implications. In my view,
the situation implies a need to rely much more heavily on economic approaches to the question of water allocation and water use efficiency than has been
true in the past.

For industrial users, the administrative system appears to have worked
more successfully since water use practices in each establishment are carefully reviewed. But economic approaches could play an important role here,
too, especially as broad questions of water quality management come to the
forefront.

Sources

Conventional water sources in Israel are nearly depleted, and the only
substantial, near term increment to total supply would have to come from
reclaimed sewage. In view of the need at some, as yet undetermined, time

to stop seawater intrusion, conventional water sources in Israel are fully developed or perhaps somewhat overdeveloped. (See Table 15.7 for an overall picture of Israel's water balance.) Some government reports still look to desalination to provide a large increment to Israel's water supply after 1985. But a consensus seems to be developing among water specialists that this is unrealistic. With costs in the range of 6 to 10 IE/m^3 for the water factor at sea level, there are no agricultural uses that could come close to paying the cost, except possibly the highly capital-intensive drip systems used for some winter crops. Recent energy cost increases are highly adverse to desalting, and scale economics are such in seawater desalting that there would be a serious mismatch of supply and demand. Unless very heavy government subsidies are provided, in my view mistakenly, desalting will not be a factor in the Israeli water balance in this century, if it ever is.

Reclaimed sewage should be much less costly than desalted water, but still high relative to most existing sources. Moreover, the production, allocation, and use of reclaimed water presents complex problems of policy and administration unprecedented in Israel's water history.

It is possible that mined brackish water could provide the basis for expanding agriculture in the south by the use of capital-intensive methods, including drip irrigation. Depending on supplies available, and given the fact that drip systems use water parsimoniously, such development could be on a rather long-term basis, despite the fact that this system is founded on a depleting resource. Because of incomplete hydrological information, this possibility is speculative. The estimates in Table 15.7 should be taken as only the most preliminary of estimates. Yet studies to clarify the situation still seem well worth pursuing.

Efficient Use

Despite impressive gains in efficiency of agricultural water use, there are still major advances possible; making them is probably a very good investment vis-à-vis the development of new supplies, where these alternatives can be meaningfully compared. Israeli agriculture has shown a very impressive ability to reduce water consumption per unit of output. Major gains in economic and technological efficiencies in agricultural water use appear still possible. One study by the Ministry of Agriculture has concluded that in regions where water is relatively abundant, water use could be cut by 30 percent with little or no loss in farm income. (2) Drip irrigation has been spreading rapidly, but the gains from it are by no means exhausted. Only about 5 percent of Israel's irrigated land is now under drip irrigation. Of course, not all of that land could ever be drip irrigated economically. But orchards, which use about half of the agricultural water supply, are less than 10 percent under drip irrigation. If only those on which dripping is now

TABLE 15.7. Water Balance of Israel - 1977, 1985, 1990

	1977	1985	1990
	(million cubic meters, Mm^3)		
Freshwater potential without further development	1565	1525	1495
Freshwater potential with full development	1565	1620	1620
Sewage reclamation	30	240	290
Total available resources	1595	1860	1910
Domestic and industrial demand	400	500	510
Losses in system (including diversion of salt springs)	60	50	50
Total available for agriculture and adjacent territories	1135	1310	1280
Total for agriculture	1110	1250	1200

Note: Actual agricultural use in 1977 was somewhat higher because of exploitation of reserves.

Sources: Tahal and Water Commission

economical were so watered, roughly 75 million cubic meters (75 Mm^3) could be saved while increasing the yield and quality of the fruit. If all orchards were under the drip system, perhaps 165 million m^3 could be saved (see Table 15.8). Apparently, with further development, the drip system holds enormous potential for other crops as well.

The general point is that technological change has made it possible to substitute capital for water to quite a far-reaching extent. In that sense there

TABLE 15. 8. Drip Irrigation Use

1. Areas irrigated and water use
Crop	dunams (10^3)	Water use ($10^6 m^3$)
Total	1,800	1,100
Orchards	700	530

2. Drip irrigation[*]
Crop	dunams (10^3)
Total	121
Orchards	66

3. One Water Commission staff estimates it is now economical to irrigate one-half of the orchards by the drip method and that this will save one-third of the water while improving yields.

4. Normative water consumption per dunam in orchards is = 780 m^3.

5. One-half of 700 (10^3 dunams) is 350 (10^3 dunams). Since approximately 66 (10^3 dunams) are dripped, this leaves (350 - 66) (10^3 dunams) or = 285 (10^3 dunams) on which the drip system could now be economical.

6. If these dunams use water at the normative rate, they should use 285 (10^3 dunams) x 780 m^3 of water. This is = 220 ($10^6 m^3$).

7. One-third of 220 ($10^6 m^3$) is = 75 ($10^6 m^3$).

8. For total orchards (700 - 66) (10^3 dunams) would be available for application of the drip system. This is = 645 (10^3 dunams) which, on the same assumption used previously, would represent a water use of = 500 ($10^6 m^3$).

9. One-third of 500 ($10^6 m^3$) is = 165 ($10^6 m^3$).

---

[*]   Based on data supplied by Netafim. The numbers include the equipment for the dunams supplied by this company plus an estimated 10 percent supplied by other companies. A dunam = 1000m^2.

is no water "requirement. " The idea of requirements has underlaid the
"water balance" approach to planning. In Israel this approach has been reinforced by the belief that it is politically impossible to reduce the overall allocation of water to agriculture. But as Wiener, former Managing Director
of Tahal, has said, it now is appropriate to bring consumers into the "planning space. " This means that, instead of taking requirements as exogenously
given, planning must now take into account economic and other variables affecting the amount of water consumption.

It appears that over the next one or two decades, further conservation
measures could make a greater contribution to Israel's water supply picture
than any other source, other than possibly sewage reclamation, and do so
economically. This in itself, of course, does not mean that sewage reclamation schemes should not be pursued; but it does mean that policy making must
give full and, at least, equal attention to conservation, the "hidden" resource.

The main problem in Israeli water policy over the next decade or two is
how to make effective and efficient use of existing water supplies (including
sewage), rather than the traditional one of developing further sources and
supplying new settlements. Except for some possibilities of using brackish
water, the era of development of water resources is over in Israel, at least
for the time being. Inside the "Green Line" separating areas of some vegetation from arid desert areas, even new settlements in areas where settlement is to be encouraged will be based on irrigated agriculture only in instances where capital is substituted for water to an extremely high degree.

The problem is how to make the best use of existing sources and facilities, to expand reclamation and reuse of water, and to develop a stringently
limited amount of additional storm water where economically feasible. In
such a context, questions of water rights, water allocation, rural-urban conflicts over water, use of water for environmental and aesthetic purposes,
operation of systems with differing qualities of water flowing in them, the efficient operation of systems, and, especially, who gets to play what role in
decision making become much more intricate and contentious than in an expanding system where all user groups are enjoying increases in supplies of
relatively uniform quality water. The details of decision making and implementation of programs are best done by some combination of national and regional institutions in this context, rather than exclusively at the national level. The matter of forming the appropriate institutions at both levels consists
of two parts: 1) a technical one of designing systems, and 2) the matter
of how value choices are to be made and conflicting goals are to be reconciled.
The first has been getting significant attention from water experts in Israel.
The second has hardly been raised with respect to the projected development
of new water institutions, insofar as I know. These perspectives may be regarded as parameters or points of departure, for the more explicit discussion
of particular issues to which I now turn.

FINDINGS PERTAINING TO POLICY, ADMINISTRATIVE
PRACTICE, AND INSTITUTIONAL REFORM

Mekorot

Mekorot is the public company which has executed the major national
and regional water projects of the country. Both as developer and water
supplier, Mekorot has functioned as a monopoly in most regions of the country. This was not a matter of deliberate policy. It was the unavoidable consequence of the fact that there were no other firms capable of or interested
in competing for work in difficult and high-cost development areas. Nor
were there any prospects of high returns from the sale of water to novice
farmers who settled these areas on government directives.

Monopoly, however justified by specific conditions at the time of its birth,
has a dynamic of its own. During the period of construction of the national water system, Mekorot grew larger than could subsequently be justified by new
water projects. Its attempts to diversify into other fields were not successful, and the general consensus seems to be that the construction subsidiaries
remain considerably overstaffed. While the major inefficiencies appear to be
in the construction division of Mekorot, it seems unlikely that the high cost
and overhead problems do not spill over to the water supply division as well.
The efficiency of the delivery system is a matter for urgent concern since
real costs are rising rapidly and any effort to get prices in line with them
will mean rapidly increasing prices to water consumers.

Changes in Mekorot

Based on the above, in my original report I made the following suggestion on
changing the structure of Mekorot:

> The portions of Mekorot dealing with the provision of water supplies
> through the existing system should be completely severed from the
> Mekorot's construction division.

This would enable the pinpointing of sources of inefficiencies as well as preventing inefficiencies in one branch from spilling over into another.

> Any new projects needed by the water supply company should be construct-
> ed under contracts awarded on the basis of tender. Mekorot's construc-
> tion company would be entitled to bid on them but only on the same basis
> as other qualified companies. (3)

Some steps have been taken in this direction in the interim. For the
budget year 1978-1979 at least 15 percent of the works financed from the
government development budget will be awarded on the basis of tenders (bids).
Those construction works carried out by Mekorot subsidiaries without tender
will be subject to much tighter supervision and price control than previously.

Design and Operation of the System

A careful reevaluation of the design and operation of the existing system
should be conducted in light of the radical increase in energy costs that has
occurred over the past few years. The real cost is even larger than it may
appear because the electric company rates do not reflect depreciation adequate to recover capital at present prices. In addition to inflation, the real
cost of constructing electrical plants has risen greatly in recent years. Furthermore, the electric company gets other subsidies. In the past, an important factor in costs of electricity over time was the increasing thermal efficiency of new generating plants. But thermal efficiency is no longer increasing.

The present intake point of the National Water Carrier is located at
Lake Tiberias (also known as the Sea of Galilee or Lake Kinneret). The water from the lake, which is 212 meters below sea level, must be pumped up
to the intake point above it. The water system now uses approximately 20
percent of the electricity generated in Israel. This is a striking indication
of the energy intensiveness of the Israeli water system. In light of this picture, it may be worth reconsidering Lake Tiberias as the intake for the national carrier. Also it may be worth shutting down some of the deepest wells.
Since a reconsideration of the design and operation of the water system may
have major policy implications, the Water Commission should review this
matter in depth and detail. Special care should be taken to use the full social
costs of electricity in making this review.

Efficient Use of Existing Supplies

Agriculture

According to economic theory, efficient use of a resource requires that
it be priced at marginal cost. However, not only water pricing but the whole
pattern of agricultural settlement in Israel has not been dictated by economic
considerations. For most farmers in the country, the region in which they
are settled, the amount of agricultural land and irrigation water at their disposal, the terms on which they obtain credit, the crops they grow and the

prices which they receive for part of their produce are all determined or affected by government policy. Farmers subjected to restrictions on their
freedom of decision (and benefits are also effectively restrictions) do not
take kindly, with justification, to the application of economic theory to one
part of the whole system.

This explains the search for the partial solutions described below - solutions which make the farmer face a decision making framework serving
the general economic interest without affecting the subsidy he receives
through water. The first attempt in this direction was the introduction of
graduated prices as recommended in the Jacobi Report. The Jacobi Committee recommendations which suggested three levels of price, depending
upon the portion of the allocation used or whether the allocation is exceeded,
was an effort to implement the marginal cost principle in a limited way. (4)
They did not, however, entirely come to grips with the macroeconomic aspect of continued subsidies to agricultural water use. Furthermore, they
may have encouraged relatively inefficient use of water by part-time farmers
in the moshavim because the first 85 percent of the water is so relatively inexpensive. The system of graduated prices was abolished in July 1977. Opin-
ions differ on the effectiveness of the pricing system. The limited statistical
studies were inconclusive. What is clear is that it imposed an unacceptable
burden on the administration and that exasperation with bureaucratic frustra-
tions not counterbalanced by clear gains made its end inevitable.

Therefore, for the year 1978-1979 the Water Commission has proposed
a new system of graduated prices which will avoid the administrative pitfalls
of the previous system. This is a system of peak pricing for agricultural water. Administratively, its major advantage is that price is not based on what
use each individual consumer makes of his allocation of water, but rather is
related unambiguously to each unit of water according to the period and region of its supply.

The explanatory notes, presented to the committee of the Knesset responsible for approving the regulations, explain the reasons for the proposals as follows:

The logic of the proposal to introduce differential prices for the peak
season (June, July and August) and the remainder of the year flows from
the following facts:

(1) The supply of a given quantity of water over a short period costs
more than the supply of the same quantity over a long period. It requires
heavy investments and under some conditions a larger input of energy
per unit of water. In existing projects increasing peak supply above
what was originally planned is not costless either. It is achieved at the
expense of the engineering reserve needed to assure reliability of supply
to all consumers and is possible without additional investment only for a

limited period. A preliminary estimate of the costs of increasing peak supplies by 1% is Ib 1. 7 per m^3 (at January 1978 prices). The proposed system gives very partial expression to this additional cost.

(2) Consumers distribute their consumption in different ways during the year. Cotton growers use practically all their water during the three peak months, citrus and orchard growers less, and vegetable growers less still. It is desirable that payment for water in the different seasons should reflect the costs of supplying water in those seasons.

(3) The transfer of water use from the off-peak to the peak season is widespread. There is a clear trend in this direction. The effect of this trend on the water supply systems of Mekorot and even more on the demands on the development budget cannot be ignored. (5)

The first major change in water policy directed toward agricultural use which I recommend is in the area of water pricing. The Jacobi system should be modified so that the first 85 percent of the water allocation would be priced at the real average cost of delivering water to the settlement. This should include the real costs of capital recovery for all elements of the water system except, perhaps, the most durable ones. The argument is sometimes made that this is not necessary because technological improvement will reduce the cost of replacing the system. There are two difficulties with this argument.

First, inflation is presently proceeding at a much more rapid rate than could possibly be cancelled out by technological advancements, and the capital assets in the system have not been revalued to take inflation into account. Secondly, I do not think that it is realistic to suppose that technological advancement will reduce costs valued in constant dollars enough to overcome the effects of rising energy costs. The overall cost of pumps, pipes, and electrical facilities all have large energy cost components in their production chains. Furthermore, these are well-established technological components whose efficiency of performance does not seem likely to advance much further. Therefore, it is prudent to assume that the system will cost at least as much, in real terms, to replace as it did to build initially.

The remaining 15 percent of water allocation and water use exceeding the quota should be priced at real marginal cost. Marginal cost is here intended to mean the cost of the most expensive elements in the pertinent regional water system - the cost of water from the deepest wells, the cost of sewage reclamation, and the cost of capturing storm water runoff might be examples. The objective is to assure that this expensive water is not put to uses whose marginal value product is less than marginal cost, but is instead directed toward the highest value uses. This should foster some mobility of water within the agricultural sector. Such movement, an objective of the Jacobi Committee, apparently has not been achieved. In addition, this pricing system should release some increments of supply for possible use in reducing overdraft and for municipal and industrial demands. These demands will surely grow to some extent in the future, but probably much less than projected by the Water Commission. (6) Municipal and industrial water use projections are discussed further in this chapter.

The proposed pricing system might yield some revenues above real average cost, but they probably would not exceed the actual social costs of supplying the water because the operating costs of the system are indirectly subsidized through electrical rates. Since electricity accounts for about half of Mekorot's calculated, but not real, cost of supplying water, this subsidy might be large. To the extent that they are produced, however, the question arises about to what use excess revenues should be put. Since other suggestions I have for pricing reform might also produce modest amounts of net revenue, I will discuss this issue separately later. Data provided by the Water Commission staff suggest that, overall, the returns to water in the agricultural branch are such that the full costs of water can be paid by that sector with some adjustments, but without massive dislocations (Table 15.9).

There seems to be general agreement among Israeli water experts and others that agricultural settlements in some regions were established for national strategic purposes and not for economic reasons. Agricultural interests claim that if these settlements cannot pay for water, it is unfair to load the costs of sustaining them upon the farming sector alone by raising prices in areas where water is cheap. I find some force in this argument, but it cannot then be used to justify heavily subsidized water prices to all users. In those instances where the national interest demands support of a settlement unable to pay its costs, the settlement should be directly subsidized, over and above other normal land and capital subsidies but not through water prices. The subsidy might be in the form of a payment in proportion to the value of agricultural production from the settlement, not a general price support. Direct subsidies are to be preferred to a system which underprices water and creates distortions in input and output decisions throughout the agricultural sector.

Because of limited storage in the water system and because the capacity of the system has to be determined by the peak demand put on it, consideration should be given to the development of a system of peak-load pricing (as indicated, the Water Commissioner has now approved this). One possible way of instituting such a system would be to differentiate prices on a seasonal basis. The purpose would be to provide a special incentive to use water conservatively when there are the most demands being made on the limited

TABLE 15.9. The Return to Water by Region, 1975 Prices (midyear)

1971 Data Adjusted for 1975 by Estimate of Technological Progress (I£/m³)

Region	Cost of Water 1975 (I£/m³)	Average Gross Return to Water* (I£/m³)	Gross Return to Water by Agricultural Branch					
			Dairy Cattle	Fish Ponds	Citrus	Orchards	Field Crops	Vegetables and Potatoes
Huleh	0.46	1.13 (78.6)	2.08 (5.0)	0.69 (14.8)	1.53 (3.7)	1.23 (21.0)	1.09 (32.1)	0.70 (2.0)
Marom Hagalil	1.94	1.02 (23.2)	1.25 (3.0)	0.72 (6.9)	1.55 (1.0)	1.18 (7.5)	1.06 (4.5)	-0.78 (0.3)
Maale Hagalil	2.67	-0.07 (2.6)	-	-	-0.55 (0.1)	0.01 (2.4)	-	-1.60 (0.1)
Akko	0.78	1.67 (53.4)	3.48 (7.0)	0.56 (10.5)	2.02 (8.4)	0.93 (12.5)	2.56 (11.0)	0.60 (4.0)
Kinorot	0.29	0.84 (76.9)	1.63 (10.2)	0.40 (20.5)	1.20 (5.2)	0.81 (30.5)	0.87 (7.4)	0.71 (3.1)
Bet Shean	0.25	0.79 (83.8)	2.20 (3.6)	0.46 (38.6)	1.22 (6.1)	0.71 (4.1)	0.78 (26.6)	1.96 (4.8)
Gilboa	1.35	1.42 (23.8)	3.95 (2.9)	0.71 (5.9)	1.81 (3.2)	0.86 (1.4)	1.05 (10.2)	2.69 (0.2)
Lower Galilee	1.23	1.32 (12.8)	3.28 (3.2)	-	1.16 (2.8)	-0.51 (1.8)	1.17 (2.9)	0.37 (2.1)
Yuzrael Valley	0.88	2.11 (46.3)	4.50 (7.6)	-	1.42 (9.2)	1.93 (8.1)	1.86 (16.7)	0.92 (4.7)
Iladera	0.54	0.96 (163.3)	3.08 (12.8)	0.30 (32.7)	0.70 (59.6)	0.93 (19.8)	1.87 (22.9)	0.31 (15.5)
Rahanana	0.57	0.98 (145.2)	2.26 (6.7)	-	0.84 (98.5)	1.00 (8.6)	1.97 (15.4)	0.47 (16.0)
Rehovot	0.81	0.85 (169.7)	1.55 (26.7)	-	0.60 (93.9)	0.18 (14.6)	2.08 (19.7)	0.21 (14.8)
Jerusalem	2.81	0.83 (21.5)	0.38 (1.7)	-	0.32 (1.3)	0.48 (8.2)	1.85 (6.7)	0.10 (3.6)
Lachish	1.31	1.03 (78.7)	2.18 (7.5)	-	0.56 (28.1)	0.30 (7.4)	1.68 (22.8)	0.65 (12.9)
Negev	2.04	1.03 (110.7)	3.99 (5.7)	-	0.47 (22.3)	0.59 (8.4)	1.18 (44.3)	0.78 (30.0)
Arava	1.13	0.90 (4.1)	2.27 (0.5)	-	-	-0.05 (1.7)	1.23 (0.4)	1.68 (1.5)
National Average	0.88	1.04 (1094.6)	2.52 (104.1)	0.47 (129.9)	0.78 (343.4)	0.82 (158.0)	1.47 (243.6)	0.56 (115.6)

Notes: 1. The Nazareth region is not included.
       2. The figures in brackets are quantities of water (Mm²)

Source: Economic Bureau, Water Commission, unpublished material. July 1976.

---

* Average gross return to water in all branches weighted by quantities of water. Land rent is not charged as a cost in these calculations so that the return figure given is actually returns to land and water. But since farmers pay virtually no rent, the return figure may be taken as an estimate of the ability to pay for water.

supply and at the time when the capacity of the system is stressed. Peak-load pricing might also result in a shifting of crop patterns so that more water is used in seasons when water is more abundant. The peak problem is due, to a considerable extent, to irrigating cotton, the importance of which has increased sharply in recent years. Unlike most other crops grown in Israel, which have a relatively long peak season of about six months, cotton needs intensive irrigation for a relatively short time, 60 to 70 days between June and the end of August when water demand for other purposes is also high.

Studies suggest that implementation of the type of pricing system suggested above might result in a tendency to move water use to the lower-cost regions which would be counter to national policy. (7) The extent to which it might happen is uncertain because the returns to water in some agricultural activities, due to heavy capital investments, appear to be quite high in the hill regions and in the south. There are also other rigidities in the system, primarily resulting from the structure of the delivery system. Additionally, any such tendency could be countered by imposing levies on inexpensive water. Note that these would not be the levies which now go into the equalization fund; for, if my earlier suggestion on pricing were adopted, the fund would be eliminated.

There are further reasons to make such levies on inexpensive water. First, water use is effectively outside the allocation system in some of the low-cost areas and, therefore, not controlled by it; secondly, water is put to some low-value uses. Making the water more expensive seems to be the most effective and efficient way to release it from inefficient uses. The levies should not be so high as to eliminate regional differences in water prices, however, because water costs are an element of regional comparative advantage in production.

At least in the most established regions, it seems time to take a new look at the whole idea of using an administrative allocative system for water distribution. As indicated in the first section of this chapter, there is a large element of arbitrariness in the present distribution of water among users due to the inflexibility of the system. The system seems to have become more of a restraining device than an allocative system. I suggest that consideration be given, at least in the most established farming areas, to replacing the present system of allocation with a limited type of water market. One possibility would be to permit holders of present allocations to make long-term contracts, say for 20 years, for their allocations with payments based on the two-price system suggested earlier. The contract could be of the annually renewable roll-forward type so that, at any given time, users would have a long time horizon which would permit them to contemplate long-term investments without fear of losing water. A user would also have the annual option of changing the amount of water contracted for, but he would have to pay for the contracted amount each year whether he used it or not. Since the price on the last 15 percent of the allocation would be high - equal to marginal cost - it is likely that some allocation holders would not wish to contract for, and therefore pay for, their full allocation. If in this way some water were released, it could be available for contract to other allocation holders at a price equal to marginal cost, but otherwise on the same basis as described above. If there were an excess demand for this water at the marginal cost price, it could be contracted for on a highest-bid price basis. Under this system, a process of limited reallocation of water based on economic demand could be started.

While many examples of highly efficient farming can be found among both the kibbutzim and the moshavim, some moshavim have special problems. The kibbutz has proven itself more adaptable to technological change in agriculture and to industrialization. The moshav, founded on the concept of a small family farm, and, in the past, often established on the basis of norms for land and water which have become outdated, has had more difficulty in developing economically viable operations. The result is that many "farmers" are employed off the farm, and many farms have become inactive. In one moshav in western Galilee studied by the Ministry of Agriculture, only 23 out of 60 farms were active. (8) In some cases moshavim have established collective operations to which land and water quotas are transferred. The water may simply be wasted in order to not lose the allocation, or sometimes it is informally and extra-legally transferred to other farmers on an ad hoc basis. Uncertainty of supply reduces the receiving farmers' incentive to make investments in large-scale production units. The situation in these moshavim is not conducive to economic success, and it seems doubtful that a farming operation which is an economic failure would be a social success. (See Chapter 14 for further economic considerations.) How to deal with the situation is a delicate matter involving conflicting national goals, none of which are achieved in full. It would seem that a procedure must be found formally and legally to transfer water and land quotas to the more efficient farmers who can be economically successful or to collective operations within the moshav, and to recognize the fact that there will be many part-time farmers and nonfarming residents in the moshavim.

Industry

In general, the water allocation system has been much more successful in reaching down to the individual industrial consumer and shaping his behavior than in the case of agriculture. As a result, water use per unit of output has fallen rather dramatically over a period of time. Nevertheless, the allocation system based on norms has its weaknesses. First, the norm must be achievable by an average establishment and, therefore, must not be too rigorous. Secondly, technologies change, and it is a large and difficult technical task to keep norms up to date.

If water is priced below real cost, as it is for industrial users, there is then no adequate incentive to weigh real water costs against further conservation measures or to use lower quality supplies which may be less costly socially. The quantities of water involved are not large compared with those in agriculture, but efficiency and equity with other users implies pricing water at its real cost in the industrial sector, also. In addition, the ratio of water costs to total costs in the non-water-intensive industries which one might consider locating in high water cost regions is usually so small that these water costs should have but little effect on industrial location decisions.

With this in mind, I suggest pricing industrial water on the same basis as agricultural water, that is, 85 percent of the allocation at average cost and the remainder, or above the allocation, at marginal cost. The pricing should be arranged so that the graduation is not on the portion of the total allocation used, but on the water used per unit of production, that is, the portion of the allocation per unit of production which is used. This will avoid the incentive to push for large total allocations - by exaggeration of production, for example - in order to avoid paying the high price. If this pricing system is adopted, continuation of subsidies to water conservation practice by industrial firms then should no longer be needed because conservation costs will be properly weighed against water cost by the firm. The elimination of such subsidies would beneficially simplify the administrative system and reduce demands on the budget. If it is deemed in the national interest to influence industrial locations in the direction of certain regions, any subsidies needed for this purpose should be granted by means other than low-price water since water is, perhaps, Israel's most limiting resource.

Municipalities

Under the present system, there are generally two systems of operation and administration in the production and delivery of municipal water from the water source to the final user. Mekorot supplies the water to the municipality, and the local authorities, under the general administration of the Ministry of the Interior, own and operate the distribution networks. Some of the municipalities also have their own supply sources. Until recently, prices to consumers were determined by local bylaws which are slow and cumbersome to change. Because of inflation, prices became far out of line with costs. At the request of the Ministry of the Interior, the Minister of Agriculture used his power to fix prices to the final consumer (the only time this authority has been used). He set prices at a uniform rate, graduated by amount of use, across the country. Deficits which occur in this system are subsidized by the Ministry of the Interior.

In addition, most municipal distribution systems contain steel pipes which are subject to corrosion, resulting in a 15 to 30 percent loss of the water delivered to them. A central "pipeline fund" which provides financing

for the replacement of pipes in municipal water systems has been operating
for some years and has brought about a sharp reduction in water losses.
The sources of income of the fund are charges on municipal water supply
(calculated per m^3 of water supplied)˙ and matching government grants. Participation is optional; but after a slow start, the large majority of municipalities now take advantage of this facility.

I concur with the Jacobi Committee which, after considering the possibility of a policy of uniform prices across the country, concluded that there
should be a link between costs and prices on a regional basis. Studies have
found that there is some price elasticity in the demand for municipal water.
If water is highly subsidized, the municipality does not have a proper incentive to control leaks (for which there is now a loan fund available); for macroeconomic reasons the subsidy to overall municipal use is undesirable. A
problem closely related to pricing is that, in principle, meters are to be read
every two months and consumers are to be billed promptly so that they may
adjust their behavior accordingly. In practice, the whole process may take
months and is, therefore, of only limited informational value.

In the case of municipalities, there is also a two-part question about the
rate at which water use will rise. First, what will happen to per capita demand; and second, what will be the rate of population growth? Both are speculative matters, but systematic study can at least reduce the uncertainty
about the former. As to the latter, material discussed earlier suggests that
existing water use projection may be based on too high a projected rate of
population growth. With respect to per capita usage, a study of time series
data for different parts of Israel reveals that per capita growth is slow in the
older areas of the country and that water use is lower, but growing more
rapidly, in the newer parts of the country. This suggests that a catching-
up phenomenon is taking place and that water use may saturate at about the
level of use of the older towns. There is also the recurring question of what
effect the pricing policies proposed earlier would have on per capita demand.

A study is needed that will look, in detail, at the probable future structure of industry in Israel, the extent to which further conservation possibilities exist, and the probable effect of pricing policies on industrial use. Existing projections should be revised if indicated. In addition, the availability of data on water use, water prices, demographic characteristics, climate, etc., should make possible a thorough econometric study of the factors
determining per capita water demand in Israel. Such a study is needed, for
it would enable the reconsideration of the projections of municipal water demand.

Effluent Charges

Since Israeli agriculture appears not to discharge much in the way of
waste water effluents to the environment, the matter of projecting the quality of the water environment pertains largely to the effluents of municipalities
and industries (except, of course, for the very important matter of degradation of water quality in aquifers through irrigation water percolation). Broadly, two policy-administrative approaches to controlling waste water discharges are used in various parts of the world. One is much like the Israeli water allocation system in reverse. Permits are issued for quantities and qualities of discharge from point sources, and efforts are made to enforce them.
This is often called the "effluent standards" approach and, indeed, has many
problems parallel to those of the Israeli water allocation system. The other
approach exacts a payment for the discharge of waste water to provide an
economic incentive for establishing effluent control apparatus and operating
it efficiently. This is known as the "effluent charges" approach and is sometimes used in combination with an effluent standards approach.

Even though their intent is partially the same and they are often referred
to collectively as effluent charges, a clear distinction should be made between an effluent charge and a waste water handling charge. A real effluent
charge is a fee levied for the privilege of discharging waste water into the
environment. The waste handling type of effluent charge is a fee levied for
handling waste waters in a treatment plant or, perhaps, in a larger regional water quality management system. In the latter case, as I shall explain
in more detail further on, the distinction is largely lost.

Waste water handling charges arise as an issue in Israel in connection
with the many waste water treatment plants now being constructed under the
auspices of the National Sewage Project, and the matter of charges arises
especially in regard to industrial connections to these plants. There is no
doubt in my mind that a system of special charges for handling industrial
waste waters in these plants is justified. Where such charges are used, the
generation of industrial wastes is greatly reduced, with considerable implications for the effectiveness of waste water treatment plants, especially
those which depend on biological processes for their effectiveness, as those
constructed in Israel generally will. I have seen a copy of the December
1975 recommendations of the committee working on effluent charges. I am
broadly in accord with their recommendations and have only one item for
comment. The committee states:

In order that industrial dischargers of sewage should not receive subsidies which will encourage the generation of sewage and its discharge
to public sewers, the capital costs included in the effluent charge should
be calculated at that rate of interest which is used by the Treasury for

assessing all projects (15% fixed prices) and not the subsidized rate of interest paid by the sewage works. (9)

I strongly concur with this recommendation and its underlying reasoning.

The effluent charges approach proper has stirred much interest around the world and has been implemented or partially implemented in a number of countries. Czechoslovakia, Hungary, Holland, and France have effluent charges systems in operation. Such charges are under strong consideration in Britain and Germany. In the latter country, a bill is before the parliament which would institute a relatively pure system of effluent charges throughout the country. In the Ruhr area of Germany is a highly developed system of charges in operation in conjunction with a sophisticated regional water quality and quantity management system, about which I will say more later. In the United States, effluent charges schemes are being considered with increasing seriousness.

In most cases, the interest in charges arose because of very disappointing experiences with effluent standards systems. The effluent standards approach has shown itself to be both excessively costly, because of neglect of cost considerations in issuing permits and lack of success in achieving its water quality improvement goals as well. Effluent charges permit some flexibility of response by dischargers and induce most response at those points where costs are lowest, thereby holding down total costs of the whole quality management system. But they do not permit any discharge to the environment, a common property resource, free of charge, as effluent standards do.

Charges on effluents are also an inducement on those plants already built to operate effectively. Poor operation of existing plants is a very serious problem in many countries, including the United States. Plants are built, but their treatment results are poor due to overloading or poor operation. Economic theory dictates that charges should be equal to the marginal damages imposed by the discharge. Economists usually call such damages external costs because they occur external to the activity causing them and are, therefore, ignored by the activity. If damages are not priced by a collective body, environmental resources will be overused and degraded in quality.

In practice, it is not usually practical to obtain a sufficiently accurate estimate of external costs on which to base effluent charges. Consequently, actual charges are usually based on some estimate of average costs for implementing minimal environmental protection measures at point sources plus perhaps some extra to provide a strong incentive to control discharge. In Israel, at least until the regional agencies can be established, a simple system of charges based on the application of uniform criteria and applied to all waste waters across the nation could be implemented as a first step toward more sophisticated systems which are better developed in the regional context.

In the Ruhr system, which merits a careful examination because of the interest in regionalization in water management in Israel, the entire treatment and water quality management system is operated by the river basin authority, the <u>Genossenschaft</u>. Measures in addition to treatment for water quality improvement (which is really not for agriculture, as in the case of Israel, but for reclamation for municipal, industrial, and recreational use) are low flow regulation, large oxidation pools in the river itself, mechanical aeration, and others. Effluent charges are levied on the basis of a uniform formula on all industries and municipalities, whether they discharge to the <u>Genossenschaft</u> treatment plants or to the river. The rationale is that somewhere in the system something is being done to maintain water quality standards in the watercourse. The collective association takes responsibility for meeting the environmental standard and covers its costs by levying water use charges and effluent charges on its members.

In Israel, levying an effluent charge would be an additional step toward the implementation of a total water utilization charge which, in my view, should be the ultimate goal. The user would be charged for the water delivered to him, and he would be charged for discharging his effluent. If the effluent is recovered for reuse, the effluent charge would be forgiven; but he would still have to pay the cost of the treatment which was instituted for purposes of environmental protection. If the effluent is sufficiently valuable, he would be reimbursed for it, because his purchase of the water and failure to use it up completely will have created a valuable resource in the region. In this way the quantity of water brought to him, the quality of his effluents, and the amount he depletes from the system all determine how much he pays on balance - a total water utilization charge.

Various modifications I have suggested in the Israeli water pricing scheme would result in some revenues in excess of average costs of operating and recovery of the water system's capital. These include the charge for effluent discharges, the charge for discharging industrial waste water to municipal treatment plants on a real cost basis, pricing some of the water delivered to users at marginal rather than average cost, and levies on inexpensive water. I suggest that such excess revenues be put into a fund to help finance the future development of water resources in Israel.

DEVELOPMENT OF NEW SUPPLIES

During the early history of the State of Israel, there was an urgent need to support rapid population growth and to do so mostly on the basis of agriculture. It was necessary to quickly outline a general plan for supplying the needed water and then concentrate on the details of engineering such an encompassing system. The whole process was propelled by comparatively lavish assistance from outside sources of funds. In such a situation careful economic calculations could not, and perhaps should not, have played any major role.

But the situation has since changed fundamentally. There are now severely limited opportunities for further development of water resources on a large scale. Accordingly, the use of these additional supplies is a very important matter. Furthermore, the costs of additional water development are very high relative to historic costs, and such development must compete with other strong demands on the overstrained public purse. Finally, questions of water quality are involved in the present situation in a more central way than they ever were before, thus greatly extending the range of considerations in water use and water allocation. These changed circumstances call for reconsideration of institutional arrangements and planning and decision making procedures for water management in Israel. This process of reconsideration has begun in a limited way.

My discussion of the main need for changes in planning procedures and in the generation of information for decision making will center on the Dan Region Project because it is, in my view, both an excellent example of the deficiencies of the present procedures as well as the largest water project on the immediate horizon.

The Dan Project

The Dan Project has been under discussion for at least a decade and is partially started. (10) There is presently in operation in the south of Tel Aviv a plant using oxidation ponds, lime ammonia stripping to reduce nitrates and remove other pollutants, and stabilization ponds. The plant treats about 15 Mm^3 of waste water. It had serious problems of odors and infiltration of sewage in the beginning; but it now appears to be operating properly, except that infiltration rates are still high. The intent is to recharge the reclaimed water and to recover it with a well field which would, at the same time, contain the recharged water in a limited part of the aquifer. The extracted water is then intended for nearly unlimited irrigation at an undetermined location. At present, purposeful recharge is not taking place because a permit has not been issued for this activity.

There are advocates of a variety of schemes for using the reclaimed water, each of whom argues his case strongly, but I believe, with very limited information. Since budgeting problems may well require a slow start on any scheme, the debate will, no doubt, continue despite the decision of the Sewage Committee. In this environment, there are those who are close to being willing to argue that any decision is better than no decision.

The extraordinary thing about the whole debate is that not a single one of the potential alternatives has ever had a proper feasibility study. There have been no benefit studies at all. There have been studies of the costs of alternative treatment systems, but apparently even these have been less than totally convincing. In their <u>Report on the Dan Region Soreq Project to the General Directors of the Ministries</u>, consultants Martin Lang, Wilbur N. Torpey, and G. J. Stander stated:

> In their view, Torpey and Lang found the Consultants' report indecisive on the ultimate use or disposal of the effluent. Although the Consultant did cite alternative modes of treatment, these appeared to be just for the purpose of contrast with their obvious choice, so-called "MBT," Modified Biological Treatment. (11)

On the basis of the information now available, it would seem impossible to make an informed decision about the appropriate treatment and disposition of Dan region sewage. The absence of systematic studies is particularly odd because Tahal apparently performs feasibility studies abroad on a routine basis.

Suitable studies in an extended cost-benefit format could be an enormous aid to decision making. This is not at all to say that the final choice would have to be the one that maximizes quantifiable net benefits, but only that information on costs and benefits is essential to informed decision making. Such an analysis can help to quantify the cost of pursuing noneconomic goals and could also be helpful in explicitly identifying areas of uncertainty about the beneficial and adverse aspects of a candidate plan.

The research group in Tahal used a dynamic optimization model to run with the Dan Project activated and with the project not in force. The objective function is significantly higher when the project is ongoing. (12) The Tahal group is the first to point out that the data used in the runs is so general and at such an aggregative level that not very much weight should be put on this result. It certainly says nothing about the appropriate design of any specific system, but it does suggest that some form of reclamation will probably turn out to be economically justified.

I have referred primarily to the Dan Region Project because that is the one which looms largest on the immediate horizon, but the Water Commission has projected other large investments over the period of 1975 to 1985. (13) These include investments for the development of 185 million m^3 of natural water, desalting plants for 100 million m^3 per annum, additional conveyance facilities, underground storage, and general improvement of supply conditions. The comments I have made about the need for evaluation analysis of the Dan Project apply equally to other major investments also.

Cost-Benefit Analyses of Water Proposals

One general comment about cost-benefit analysis is appropriate before proceeding to specific suggestions. In the past, less so now, cost-benefit analysis was used by the chief water agencies in the United States, who pioneered in its applications, in a manner which made very limited use of its potential powers. The usual process was to design a particular project from an engineering point of view and then to tack on a cost-benefit analysis at the end to see if the project was economically justified. The more appropriate way to proceed is to conduct the engineering analysis at a general level simultaneously with economic analysis and thereby to generate a set of, necessarily, partially evaluated alternatives for the decision making process to consider along with aspects which have not been successfully quantified.

A range of realistic alternatives for treating and for using the Dan Region Project, or any other major water project, requires that sewage be explicitly identified and that the incremental cost of each alternative above the minimal system for protection of the environment be calculated. The minimum environmental protection alternative would probably be primary treatment with one or two long outfalls to the sea. Insofar as possible, the benefits of each alternative system should also be calculated. These would depend on crop patterns, irrigation efficiencies, prices, etc. In some cases there may be great uncertainty about an element entering into benefits (prices for example), in which case a realistic range of benefits should be calculated.

As additional information, a statement about the environmental impact of each alternative should be prepared. This should concern itself with matters of health, impact on the ecological system, landscape disruption, etc. Finally, other considerations with respect to the project alternative should be indicated. Examples might be the impact of each alternative on the foreign trade balance, and how well or poorly it fits with existing social institutions like the moshav and the kibbutz.

A study such as that just suggested would require a team composed primarily of engineers and economists, but with some input from ecologists and other social scientists. Although the necessary staff competence is available in existing water institutions in Israel, it does not appear that the present institutional structure with respect to water in Israel could readily produce such an effort. Consequently, the type of analysis which I suggest has implications for institutional reform and reorganization.

REORGANIZATION

As indicated earlier, I think Israel has reached a point where the primary need is for improved management of existing supplies rather than large-scale new development. The details of such managment involve many local and regional considerations. The reclamation of waste waters and their integration into the overall water supply as well as the development of small local sources is better accomplished at the regional level than at the national level.

The Water Commissioner has proposed that the entire water system, including waste water handling and delivery of water to final consumers, should be under one integrated management and operation. (14) I strongly concur since one of the main water problems in many countries, including the United States, is poor operation of facilities by local authorities, especially poor operation of waste water treatment plants. The Genossenschaften, referred to earlier, have demonstrated with great clarity what improvements are possible by centralized operation of treatment plants.

While the details of the structure of the administrative and operational functions are not yet complete, a number of generalizations are possible. First, the regional authorities must be seen as an instrument for carrying out national water policy and must operate under strong national control. Even though Israel has several natural hydrological regions, it is a small country with a highly integrated water system. The national operation of that system should not be disrupted by regionalization, and main elements of it should be operated by, or under the close supervision of, the national authority. Second, the national water authority should have a strong economic systems analysis capability so that it can develop information for decision making of the type described in the previous section. This will require a high-quality unit composed primarily of economists and system engineers with some capacity in ecology and the other social sciences as well. Third, certain services, because of economies of scale, should be provided centrally. Good laboratory services, for example, are needed for the water quality management activities of the regional bodies, while not each region needs a sophisticated laboratory of its own. Some engineering services would best be provided centrally as well.

The Commissioner has also suggested a number of other elements for the administrative and operational structure of the reorganized water system. They seem to be logical and reasonable, and I have no quarrel with them. The deficiency I see in the Commissioner's statement is that it deals only with administrative and operational matters. It is a design for executive agencies. That is important and needs to be done well. It is not, however, the most difficult problem that reorganization raises. That problem is the governance of the water system, that is, how the policy decisions and value trade offs will be made.

This problem exists at both the national and regional levels and is equally important at both levels. Turning first to the regional questions, it seems clear that urban people should be represented in the decision making processes of the regional agencies. This is because the nation is so heavily urbanized and because rural-urban value issues will occur increasingly as water management steps into the arena of water quality. Matters of aesthetics, public health, location of facilities, and uses of reclaimed water will arise frequently. An example is the use of sewage from the settlement of Dimona. Dimona wants to use it to grow trees for aesthetic and recreational purposes, and nearby industries want it for process water. Another example is the dispute between Elat and Kibbutz Elot over the use of that city's sewage.

How to arrange for the representation of all affected parties seems a difficult and important question. Most American political scientists feel that democratic government is best served when public decisions involving conflicting values and preferences are made by popularly elected governments of general jurisdiction. This is because such governments consider simultaneously the whole range of public demands for an always limited budget and because vote trading permits the intensity of preferences to be expressed by representatives in behalf of their constituencies. An exceedingly simplified example can illustrate this point.

Imagine a situation in which there are only two voters and two issues

	Issue 1	Issue 2
Voter 1	N	Y_1
Voter 2	Y_1	N

The Ns and Ys stand for yes and no votes, and the subscript 1 indicates the issue about which the voter has the strongest preferences. Thus, voter 1 wants very much to win on the second issue, and the second voter wants to win on the first. If no vote trading is possible - say because the two issues are being considered by different units of government - there is a deadlock on both issues, neither wins. But if the voters are allowed to trade, each will be willing to change his vote on the issue about which he feels least strongly in exchange for the other voter's changed vote on the issue about which he, in turn, feels less strongly.

The outcome then will be:

	Issue 1	Issue 2
Voter 1	Y	Y
Voter 2	Y	Y

Both issues pass, and both voters win on the issue about which they feel strongly. It has been demonstrated in much more complex situations that if members of a legislature represent their constituencies, vote trading in such an assembly leads to higher levels of preference satisfaction than when vote trading is not possible. Considering a wide range of issues in the same forum along with vote trading also tends to avoid block voting in which competing groups either tend always to be at loggerheads or one of them always loses. It is a way of reflecting strongly held preferences of minorities in the political decision making process.

These abstract considerations have found practical expression in the formation of several democratic governments, but they have seldom been the basis for government institutions to deal with regional problems. There are exceptions, however. In both the greater Vancouver region in Canada and in the Minneapolis-St. Paul region in the United States regional governments of general jurisdiction exist which appear to be functioning very well. They concern themselves with water supply, waste water handling, solid wastes, airports, roads and other public issues which occur on a regional scale. But the idea may be sufficiently novel and far-reaching that it would be difficult for it to be given much attention in the Israeli context. If so, other devices must be found to represent the preferences and interests of all affected persons in the governance of the proposed regional water agencies.

In other regions in other parts of the world where regional management agencies have been established, the approach to the governance has taken varied forms. In the <u>Genossenschaften,</u> government is strictly of the interest group and is based primarily on the proportion of total fees paid to the cooperative by each group. In France, the regional agencies are essentially departments of the central government with regional interest group committees having some policy powers. In the Delaware River Basin Commission, which is an interstate-federal compact, government is by the governors of the state involved and a federal representative. The British authorities use a hybrid form based partly on elected officials in the region and partly on appointments from the central government. Working out a form of governance for the regional authorities which adequately represents affected parties and is, at the same time, fitted to Israel's history, tradition, and other institutions will, I believe, be among the most challenging tasks in bringing about a successful reorganization.

There are equally important questions of how decision making will operate at the national level. The present de facto division of authority among the Water Commission, Tahal, and Mekorot will present fairly obvious difficulties, since the national authority should clearly be a government agency and should absorb and further develop some of the functions of both Tahal and Mekorot. Matters of jurisdiction, prerogatives, and even ownership of property will probably pose complex and difficult problems. I have suggested earlier that Mekorot's water supply function be separated from the construction division. The operation of the existing supply systems could be taken over by the new national authorities and the regional authorities. Issues arise also with respect to Tahal's operations. General planning and associated economic systems analysis should be conducted by the national authority directly for the country as a whole and as a service to the regional authorities. Thus, the national authority would itself conduct the general planning and evaluation functions.

The question remains of the actual engineering design of proposed physical units. The reasons for Tahal's present monopoly in this regard are historical. There was no pre-existing capacity in Israel to design these units, but a number of companies have the capability. Efficiency might be served by contracting this work, as well as the construction on the basis of tender, as was suggested earlier.

Even more fundamentally, it is not at all clear that the reorganized water institution should stay under the administration of the Ministry of Agriculture. The range of considerations in water management still include, but have moved substantially beyond, agriculture. Moreover, there is no obvious home for the water management authority in any other present ministry. Perhaps it is time to consider seriously pooling a number of related activities into a Ministry of Natural Resources, or a Ministry of Natural Resources, Development, and Environment. If so, this would be a fundamental change of structure calling for the most careful study and design.

Another issue is the proper division of authority between the national and regional levels. Should, for example, the system of central allocations of water to users be abandoned or modified to permit some discretion over allocation at the regional level? Is the relationship between the central authority to be uniform for all regions, or must it be adapted to each region, depending upon such things as level of development, degree of pre-existence of regional institution, and availability, or lack thereof, of local sources of supply?

I believe that these political/institutional questions are going to be much more difficult to answer than the administrative operational questions which have been addressed thus far. Yet, they are so fundamental, raising as they do questions of relationships among interest groups - some of which are well established and some of which are not - relationships among powerful institutions, possible reorganization of the government, and even matters of basic political philosophy, that confronting them is a matter of high national priority.

SUMMARY

In a real sense, the rapid and highly successful development of irrigated agriculture is what made the State of Israel possible. Agricultural settlements continue to play a significant role in the economic life of the country and an important role in its political and military affairs. But in the course of time, Israel has become a highly urbanized country. Only about 6 percent of the country's employment and macroeconomic activities are now found in the agricultural branch. It is no longer the leading force in Israel's economic development.

Israel's economic problems are critical. Rapidly increasing dependence on unilateral transfers, in general, and United States aid in particular, heavy foreign borrowing to meet short-term demands and a severe balance of payments deficit all require action at both the macro- and microeconomic levels. Demands on the public budget must be reduced. There is an urgent need to make the economy run as efficiently as possible. Economic efficiency must move up on the scale of national priorities vis-à-vis sociological and ideological goals.

Conventional sources of water are almost fully developed in Israel. The main problem in the next two decades will be the efficient use of existing supplies. New sources and reclaimed water will be expensive and present much more complex problems of planning, management, execution of programs, and allocation of water than have been encountered previously. Institutional reforms and increased reliance on economic approaches are needed.

Despite impressive improvements in the efficiency of water use, there are still very significant gains possible, particularly in regions where water is relatively abundant. The increased use of drip irrigation and other advanced irrigation techniques are some areas of improvement.

The water allocation system can no longer be regarded as an instrument of national policy that has meaning in terms of efficiency or allocation goals. It has produced an arbitrary distribution of water among users. Economic incentives must become a larger factor in water use in Israel, and the institutional structure for water development and allocation must be reconsidered in view of the new realities.

NOTES

(1) Menahem Kantor, Israeli Water Commissioner, statement to Interna-
     tional Meeting on Water Managing Institutions, Mexico City, June 1976.

(2) Samuel Pohoryles et al., Agricultural Adjustment in Semi-Arid Areas,
     Case Study - Israel (Tel Aviv: Tel Aviv University and Ministry of Ag-
     riculture, 1975).

(3) Allen Kneese, Consultant's Report on Israel's Water Policy, Submitted
     to the World Health Organization, (Albuquerque, N. M.: The University
     of New Mexico Press, August 1976), p. 9.

(4) The Committee for the Evaluation of Secondary Legislation related to
     Water Pricing (Ministry of Agriculture, August 1971) (Hebrew). Referred
     to by name of chairman of the committee, Knesset member Gad Jacobi,
     i. e. Jacobi Committee or Jacobi Report.

(5) Guidelines for the Determination of Water Policy (Tel Aviv: Water
     Commission, Ministry of Agriculture, October 9, 1974).

(6) Pohoryles, p. 66.

(7) Ibid.

(8) Ibid., p. 145.

(9) Tariffs for Discharge of Industrial Wastewater: Report and Recommen-
     dations of the Committee for the Evaluation of the Economic Aspects of
     Effluent Charges for Industrial Sewage (Water Commission, December
     1975) (Hebrew).

(10) Dan Region Wastewater Project, Vol. III, Design Report (Tel Aviv:
     Dan Region Association of Towns Sewage and Tahal, 1974).

(11) Martin Lang, Wilbur N. Torpey, and G. J. Stander, "Report on the Dan
     River Soreq Project to the General Directors of the Ministries" (unpub-
     lished).

(12) "Dynamic Optimization Models of Israel's Water Resources System,
     Interim Conclusions on its Operation and Development" (Tahal 01/76/54)
     (Hebrew).

(13) Guidelines for the Determination of Water Policy (Tel Aviv: Water Commission, Ministry of Agriculture, October 9, 1974).

(14) Menahem Kantor, Israeli Water Commissioner, Principles and Points of Emphasis in Reorganization of Israel's Water System (Water Commission, 1974) (Hebrew).

11

16

The Future of Arid Lands

Allen V. Kneese and Jennifer E. Zamora

*University of New Mexico, Albuquerque, New Mexico
and Resources for the Future, Washington, D.C.*

Introduction

For many of us who have spent major parts of our lives in them, the arid lands have an appeal that is naggingly there no matter how long or far we may have been away from them. At the same time we are aware that even though they are the sites where civilization was spawned they present many severe problems for the populations that currently inhabit them. Moreover, even those persons with a rather casual knowledge of these lands have come to realize that for various reasons they are currently suffering enormous stresses and strains, alas, in many instances not for the first time in their history.

In this chapter we try to provide a broad perspective on the situation of the world's arid lands, the trends affecting them, and possible future developments. The reader will find that the tone of this chapter is rather pessimistic. This is not congenial to us, and we hope that events will prove us wrong in those instances where we see strong grounds for concern.

The first substantive section of this chapter is a modest statistical analysis of some published data. It is aimed at exploring two major hypotheses. The first is that climate as such, when other influences are accounted for, tends to affect per capita income and that aridity, in particular, affects per capita income negatively. The second is that arid regions that are hinterlands of more humid regions are in quite a different situation economically than those that are not. Other hypotheses concerning the influence on income of the age structure of the population, education levels, and so on, are also tested. Our main interest in these, however, is to assure that we have identified them and adjusted for their effect so that the influence of the factors of primary interest can be identified. We then

379

go on to explore further the arid hinterlands type of situation and to a (necessarily) more qualitative and anecdotal discussion of other tendencies influencing the arid lands and their economic development.

Statistical Analysis

Data Collection and Procedures

Per capita income data for 118 countries were obtained for the year 1963 from U.N. Statistical Office sources.[1] The sample excludes Communist countries because, although data were available from the United Nations and other sources, it was felt that the possible effects of climate differences could be obscured or distorted in centrally planned economies.

1963 was chosen because it was the year for which the United Nations had per capita income figures for the largest number of countries. 1963 data were also gathered from U.N. sources for such socioeconomic variables as population, rate of population increase, age distribution of the population, life expectancy at birth, education levels, and urban population. Other economic variables for which data were collected included agricultural land as a percentage of total land area, and level of foreign aid received.

A climate classification was devised by collapsing Trewartha's classification into six major types: desert, steppe, tropical, mediterranean, humid subtropical, and humid continental. Each country in the sample was classified into one of the six types according to its predominant climate type. A second more aggregative classification of arid versus nonarid countries was made in which the countries classified as either desert or steppe were reclassified as arid and the countries in the other four climate types were designated as nonarid. Finally, arid lands as a percentage of total land area was estimated for each country, again using desert and steppe climate areas together as the definition of arid lands. A subset of the original sample was then created, composed of each country that had some proportion of arid land, however small, within its borders. The arid lands subset had 53 countries.

A simple linear regression model was used to estimate several equations formulated to determine if differences in economic well-being among countries, as denoted by the level of per capita income, can be attributed in part to climate differences in general and to aridity in particular. The equations were also designed to attempt to eliminate the influence of some of the variables that one would expect to have a significant effect on per capita incomes. In the following

---

[1] All data sources are listed in the Appendix to this chapter.

section the hypotheses and equations being tested are set out in more detail and the results of the statistical anaysis are presented.

Results of Statistical Analysis

Climatic Hypotheses

It was hypothesized that there would be significant differences in per capita income among groups of countries as a result of climate differences. To test this hypothesis two regression equations were estimated. The first was used to estimate the effect on per capita income of seven socioeconomic variables:

$$P_i = \beta_0 + \beta_1 R_i + \beta_2 PF_i + \beta_3 I_i + \beta_4 FA_i + \beta_5 LE_i + \beta_6 AL_i + \beta_7 PL_i \qquad (1)$$

where
P   = per capita income
R   = rate of population increase
PF   = percentage of population under age 15
I   = illiteracy rate of population over age 15
FA   = foreign aid received
LE   = life expectancy at birth
AL   = arable land as a percentage of total land area
PL   = pasture land as a percentage of total land area
i   = number of countries (118)
The second equation was estimated including dummy variables for the six major climate types used:

$$P_i = \gamma_0 + \beta_1 R_i + \beta_2 PF_i + \beta_3 I_i + \beta_4 FA_i + \beta_5 LE_i + \beta_6 AL_i + \beta_7 PL_i + \gamma_1 D_1$$
$$+ \gamma_2 D_2 + \gamma_3 D_3 + \gamma_4 D_4 + \gamma_5 D_5 \qquad (2)$$

The two equations were estimated, the variables whose coefficients were not significant at the 0.90 level of confidence were discarded, and the equations were estimated again using only the significant independent variables. An F-statistic was calculated to test the null hypothesis that there is no significant difference between the intercept of Eq. (1) and the intercepts of the six lines represented in Eq. (2).

Climate differences do have a significant impact on per capita income since the results of the estimate and F-test given in Table 1 allow the null hypothesis to be rejected. These influences, however, are not as strong an explantory factor as might have been expected, as indicated by the low R^2 values obtained for each equation. However, this may be accounted for by problems of data comparability over such a wide sample of nations. The fact that a significant

Table 1 Climate and Aridity Effects on per Capita Income: Results of Estimating Regression Equations

Variable	Equ. (1)	Eq. (2)	Eq. (3)	Eq. (4)	Eq. (5)	Eq. (6)	Eq. (7)	Eq. (8)	Eq. (9)
Dependent Constant	p = 685.54 (2.325)[a]	p = 223.53 (0.567)	p = 1939.5 (9.585)	p = 1850.1 (9.114)	p = 1837.2 (9.089)	p = 370.19 (1.359)	p = 464.35 (1.623)	p = 315.72 (1.192)	p = 472.56 (1.735)
PF	− 23.999 (5.303)	− 20.625 (4.1941)	− 39.33 (7.103)	− 33.273 (5.33)	− 32.834 (5.327)	− 13.933 (2.971)	− 14.518 (3.079)	− 13.318 (2.929)	− 14.485 (3.152)
LE	12.303 (3.693)	9.243 (2.373)				9.045 (2.873)	8.743 (2.77)	9.384 (3.077)	8.831 (2.867)
AL	− 0.0026 (1.45)	− 0.0017 (0.996)	− 0.004 (1.631)	0.0038 (1.5682)	− 0.0044 (1.81)	− 0.0023 (1.73)	− 0.0025 (1.904)	− 0.0034 (2.441)	− 0.0029 (2.169)
FA						0.367 (1.381)	0.412 (0.153)	0.345 (1.339)	0.434 (1.653)
D1		374.54							
D2		362.66							
D3		470.99							
D4		761.43							
D5		352.04							
PA				− 2.995 (1.948)			− 0.994 (1.065)		

DA					−278.41				
HT1								227.13	
HT2									− 122.54
R^2	0.3724	0.4504	0.4653	0.4976	0.5043	0.3147	0.3309	0.3719	0.3585
SSR	21,420,000	18,760,000	12,400,000	11,650,000	11,500,000	28,810,000	28,130,000	26,400,000	26,970,000
DF	114	109	60	59	59	48	47	47	47

F-test for Eqs. (1) and (2) = 3.091[b]
F-test for Eqs. (3) and (4) = 3.798[c]
F-test for Eqs. (3) and (5) = 4.617[b]
F-test for Eqs. (6) and (7) = 1.136[d]
F-test for Eqs. (6) and (8) = 4.291[b]
F-test for Eqs. (6) and (9) = 3.207[c]

[a] Absolute values of t-values are given in parentheses below the coefficients t > 1.289 significance at the 90% confidence level.
[b] Significant at 95% confidence level.
[c] Significant at 90% confidence level.
[d] Nonsignificant.

effect can be attributed to climate differences is interesting. Another observation which can be made by examining Table 1 is that although percentage of arable land (AL) was a significant explanatory variable in Eq. (1), its effect is greatly reduced in Eq. (2) when climate differences are taken into account. This suggests that this variable was actually masking climatic effects in the first equation.

Socioeconomic Variables

The results in Table 1 also provide a test for other hypotheses regarding the effect of several socioeconomic variables. We report these and give the rationale for using the ones we did but reiterate that our primary interest is in the climatic variables. We must also caution that the data on the socioeconomic variables are often of very poor quality and are sometimes highly intercorrelated. We hope, however, that their influence as a group of variables will have been adequately accounted for in the equations estimated.

Population Change. The hypothesis that rapid rates of population growth tend to be associated with low per capita income is not borne out statistically in this analysis. However, the correlation between the rate of population growth and other independent variables such as percentage of population under age 15 (PF) was relatively high (0.52). (The correlation matrix for the independent variables for which data were gathered is given at the end of the Appendix to this chapter). Since (PF) was a significant explanatory variable in the first estimation of Eq. (1), it was felt that it probably included the population growth factor and, therefore, R was eliminated.

Population Age. A rapidly increasing population will usually be a young population, which implies that a relatively small proportion of the population will be involved in the labor force. This would be expected to have a depressing effect on per capita income, regardless of whether the country is predominantly arid or humid. This conjecture is supported by the statistical analysis; percentage of population under age 15 (PF) is a significant variable in both equations and, as explained above, most likely accounts for some of the variation expected as a result of differences in the rate of population growth.

Level of Education. It was hypothesized that low levels of education in a country would be related to low levels of per capita income without reference to climatic conditions. Although the analysis did not indicate education level, as measured by the rate of illiteracy, as a significant variable, this may be due to the fact that illiteracy may not be the proper measure of education level to use. Perhaps some other measure, such as median years of school completed for various age segments of the population, would produce better results; however, these data were not available for enough countries in the sample to permit this supposition to be tested.

Health. It was hypothesized that the health of a country's citizens as measured by life expectancy at birth would be positively related to per capita income. This conjecture was supported by the analysis as demonstrated in Table 1. Life expectancy is a significant explanatory variable in both equations, although in Eq. (2) its t-value is somewhat lower as a result of the inclusion of direct climatic effects.

Arable Land. The percentage of arable land (AL) in a country can be taken as a measure of potential agricultural productivity. We expected this variable to be positively related to per capita income, but, in all of the equations we estimated, this variable, whether significant or not, showed a negative relationship' to per capita income. After some reconsideration we realized that although agriculture is an important industry in most countries, it is also one of the lowest in value added in production per value of productive inputs. The negative coefficients obtained in Eqs. (1) and (2) imply that, in general, an increase in arable land will actually have a depressing effect on per capita income. In other words, the resources required to bring more land under cultivation are greater than the addition to national income from the increased agricultural production. This situation may be aggravated by the heavy subsidization of agriculture in many countries.

The results in Table 1 show that the initial significance of the arable land variable in Eq. (1) is actually in response to climatic differences. When these differences are accounted for in Eq. (2), the general effect of (AL) is decreased although still negative. This implies that the significance in Eq.(1) was due to larger negative effects of AL for climate extremes.

The other variables in the first formulation of Eqs. (1) and (2) were nonsignificant and/or highly correlated with some other independent variables and were, therefore, eliminated from the analysis.

Aridity Hypotheses

Two additional equations were formulated to determine if aridity, in and of itself, has a significant influence on per capita income. Equation (4) is designed to test the hypothesis that the percentage of arid land area in a country is inversely related to per capita income, whereas Eq. (5) is designed to test for significant differences in per capita income between predominantly arid and nonarid countries. We felt that perhaps the full sample should not be used to test the impact of aridity on per capita income level because predominantly tropical countries also had very low per capita incomes and it was expected that this would obscure the aridity effects. Therefore, a subsample of 62 countries was constructed that excluded tropical countries. The estimates of Eqs. (3), (4), and (5) in Table 1 give the results of testing the aridity hypotheses with this "nontropical" sample. Equation (3) is the hypothesis equation without a climate variable, whereas Eqs. (4) and (5) include the two aridity variables:

PA = percentage of arid lands in a country

DA = a dummy variable denoting countries with 50% or more arid land area

The results of the estimation show that when tropical countries are excluded from the sample, the aridity hypotheses are supported. The t-value for percentage of arid land (PA) in Eq. (4) was significant at the 0.95 level and produced a substantial increase in the R^2 value. The F-statistics for comparing Eqs. (3) and (4) and Eqs. (3) and (5) were significant, indicating that conditions of aridity do have a significant impact on per capita income differences between countries.

Arid Hinterlands Hypotheses

The main hypothesis here was that those arid lands that are hinterlands of a more humid region, that is, located in a nation in which less than 40% of the land area is arid, will have a higher per capita income than those not so located. We want to test the notion that arid hinterlands can serve a number of useful purposes for a prosperous humid region and thereby enjoy relatively high per capita incomes, but that when nearly the entire country is arid there will not be a basis for this higher level of income.

To test this and other hypotheses, a set of equations was formulated and estimated using the original variables with the arid countries subsample of 53 countries. The equations were estimated, the nonsignificant variables discarded, and the final equations subjected to further statistical testing. The variables in these equations have all been identified previously with the exception of (HT_1), which is a dummy variable for countries with arid hinterlands defined as countries having between 25 and 40% arid lands, and (HT_2), which is a dummy variable for those countries having 75% or more arid land area.

The results shown in Table 1 support the hypothesis concerning arid hinterlands. An F-statistic calculated to compare Eqs. (6) and (8) was significant at the 0.95 level of confidence, which indicates that among countries with arid lands those that have an arid hinterland as defined previously also have significantly higher per capita incomes than those without.

The hypothesis that, among arid countries, the percentage of arid land area in a country would negatively influence per capita income is borne out to some extent. The coefficient for the (PA) variable is negative as predicted, although the t-value for the variable and the F-test between Eqs. (6) and (7) are nonsignificant. This appears to be at odds with the results in Table 1, but it must be recalled that no attempt was made to control for the influences of tropical countries in this sample.

Another test for aridity effects among arid countries is a comparison between Eqs. (6) and (9). The dummy variable (HT_2) was added to test the hypothesis that countries which are predominantly arid (75% or more) have lower per capita incomes, and the results support this contention.

General Results

The general result of the statistical analysis presented in this chapter supports our basic hypotheses about the effects of climate and arid climates in particular on the level of per capita incomes among countries. Climate differences in general are a significant explanatory factor of the variation in per capita incomes among countries. The effect of aridity on per capita income is generally negative; the more arid land a country has, the more likely it is to have a low per capita income. However, among countries with arid lands there is some relatively low proportion of arid land area that enhances the economic condition of these countries in relation to other arid countries. The next section of this chapter deals with a more detailed explanation of the concept and significance of "arid hinterlands."

Arid Hinterlands

The statistical analysis just presented suggests that the presence of an arid hinterland within a more humid nation does not have a depressing effect on per capita income, indeed may even increase it. Here we discuss the nature and uses of hinterlands in a little more detail.

One may regard arid hinterlands as being made up of essentially two types: first, those that are de facto hinterlands of other nations even though they are not politically part of them, and second, those situations where the hinterland function can be served effectively only if in fact the arid land is located within the more humid political jurisdiction.[2] The first category includes activities such as the following.

Recreation. A good instance of this is the North African beaches heavily used by European tourists. The excellent beaches with warm and dry climates of many coastal arid areas are an attraction to visitors, and political boundaries may have little influence on this attractiveness. Spain, vis-a-vis the rest of Europe, is an excellent illustration.

Winter Crops. Since most arid areas, aside from the polar ones, are located near the equator, they tend to have relatively warm climates. In many

---

[2] In the former case arid hinterlands may coincide with arid countries and the statistical analysis of the previous section is not applicable.

cases this means that high-value winter crops can be grown. The supplying of fruits and vegetables from several Middle Eastern countries to Northern Europe is a case in point.

Archeological Interest. Since (as we discuss below) the world's major civilizations and cultures arose in more arid climates, and because cultural artifacts persist much longer in arid than in humid climates, many arid areas are of archaeological interest. Again, this is true of the Middle East and China, and of Latin America and, to a somewhat lesser degree, the southwestern parts of the United States.

Astronomical Observations The clear atmosphere of many arid areas has made them outstanding for purposes of astronomical observation. The presence of observatories in arid mountain regions in various parts of the world attests to this. Because of the lack of conflict with other land uses, installations that are not particularly dependent on aridity as such are frequently located in arid areas (e.g., large radio telescopes).

This discussion is by no means meant to imply that the indicated activities are not also heavily conducted in areas where arid lands are hinterlands of more humid areas in the same political jurisdiction. The United States provides an excellent case illustrating this whole range of activities in a single political jurisdiction containing arid hinterlands. The only point is that these particular activities do not appear to be so highly dependent on location in the same political jurisdiction as some others discussed below. Except for the first two, recreation and winter crops, these activities are unlikely to have a large effect on per capita income.

It is possible, however, to think of a number of man's activities where having the location of both the arid and humid regions in the same political jurisdiction is very important.

Military Installations. Because of considerations of both weather and remoteness, many major military installations throughout the world are located in arid regions. This is particularly so of those requiring aircraft operations. In addition, availability of land and relative ease of securing installations have promoted their development in arid regions. Associated research activities are often large enough to be of economic significance. Installations of this nature are a major source of income in a number of arid regions, perhaps most strikingly in the western United States.

Residential Choice. For well-known reasons some arid areas are regarded as highly desirable places of residence. Although there are many instances of persons establishing residences in political jurisdictions outside the one in which they hold citizenship, for example, many people from the United States retire in Mexico, and from other parts of Europe in Spain, there are still in general fairly strong reasons for selecting a place of residence inside one's own country. These have to do with language, customs, legal rights, taxation, and a variety of other considerations. Perhaps the outstanding example of choice of arid areas as a place of residence within a hinterlands type of situation, is, once again, in the United States. People have moved in large numbers to southern California and are doing so increasingly to other states in the American Southwest. Over and above this, an enormous amount of land sales have occurred. Should all the plots that have been sold be occupied, the population of the area would be multiplied.

Footloose Industry. A number of modern industries are relatively free of direct ties to raw materials supplying locations or to markets. This is particularly true of industries in the electronics field, for example. To a considerable extent, these footloose industries locate in areas that are regarded as environmentally desirable, including arid areas in the United States and other countries. The possibility of living in a desirable environment has become increasingly important to many persons, and industries located in such environments may have a strong recruiting advantage for highly trained personnel.

The presence of arid lands within a more humid nation, may, for these reasons, be of substantial benefit to the nation as a whole. Since some of the benefits from using the arid lands have the nature of public goods type environmental assets, not all of the beneficial effects are recorded in per capita income. One may expect that as income continues to grow in a number of the more developed countries in the world, the desirability of arid lands as hinterlands will grow as well and in many regions this will be a source of sustenance and exert an upward influence on per capita income. Our statistical analysis tends to indicate, however, that aridity *as such* is a substantially negative factor in per capita income. Indeed, as one looks at developments in the arid countries, one can see a number of long-term, relatively irreversible tendencies that will work further in the direction of hindering their economic development.

Tendencies That Will Adversely Affect the Future of the Arid Lands

Desertification

Grazing and the search for fuels and additional farmland are denuding vast areas of North Africa, the Middle East, and the Indian subcontinent. Deforestation in India and Pakistan is forcing the use of dung for fuel and is depriving land of a natural source of fertility.[3] In papers prepared for the U.N. Conference on the Human Environment,[4] many countries documented this phenomenon of

---

[3] Lester Brown, *Population and Affluence, Growing Pressure on World Food Resources*, Population Reference Bureau, Washington, D.C., 1973, p. 11.
[4] *The Human Environment*, Vol. 2, Summaries of National Reports on Environmental

increasing desertification of semiarid and steppe areas. Israel, in its country report, pointed out that much of the Negev is a man-made desert, the product of ancient intensive grazing and wood gathering, which finally denuded the land and caused subsequent wind erosion, precluding the possibility of natural regeneration. It was pointed out that to return this land to any kind of useful status would require an enormous investment if it is possible at all. In addition, the modern return to this land has increased the tendency for erosion by disturbing the equilibrium established over past centuries of very slight human activity.[5] Iran's foreage-producing areas, which have also been grazed by domestic livestock since ancient times, are to a large extent rather marginal in quality. Iran's country paper reported that population growth and the rise of the standard of living there (which may or may not be sustainable when the oil runs out) have increased the demand on livestock production, while the amount of foreage space has been reduced, the number of animals has doubled in 20 years and is clearly in excess of the feed potential.[6] The forested areas of Iran have been greatly diminished in the last 50 years. Main factors have been charcoaling, shifting cultivation, and overgrazing, especially by goats. There are now some efforts to bring the situation under control. The country paper of Morocco reported that the soil is becoming degraded there in an alarming fashion. Mountain areas are highly populated and land clearing is pushed insistently, often without the most elementary precautions, leading to the loss of arable soil to erosion and floods. The livestock population is large; overgrazing and pasture degradation causes erosion and converts arid zones into desert. The forest area in Morocco has also been greatly reduced. Only about 5 million hectares remain, and these are continually subjected to invasion and depletion by agriculture.[7] Nigeria reports that soil depletion and erosion are continuing apace. The Enugu region is said to provide a striking example of gully erosion. Population pressure has reduced the former fallow periods of from 10 to 15 years to 1 to 2 years, resulting in serious soil degradation. Senegal reports that the activities of man are compounded by unfavorable climatic conditions in the intertropical areas. Charcoal is produced at an enormous rate, and annual brush fires destroy natural growth and wildlife. Thousands of hectares have been reduced to sand by overgrazing and subsequent abandonment.[8] These are only a few of the many examples that one can draw from the U.N. Reports, showing that the process of desertification is going on at a rapid rate and has been stemmed in only a few locations, if in fact, anywhere.

Problems 1972, Woodrow Wilson International Center for Scholars, Washington, D.C., March 1972.

[5] Ibid., p. 49

[6] Ibid., p. 43.

[7] Ibid., p. 63.

[8] Ibid., p. 79.

The Deterioration of Mountain Environments

Nearly all the world's high mountain environments adjacent to arid areas are suffering rapid deterioration.[9] The causes are very similar to those affecting the arid lands themselves—primarily population pressure leading to efforts to extract more production from these lands than they can sustain with the technologies being applied. The results are erosion, floods, siltation of reservoirs, and migration of mountain people to already poverty-stricken cities in search of work. In these ways millions of people residing in adjacent lower lands are affected. UNESCO has reported accelerating damage to the basic life support systems today in practically every mountainous region of Asia, Africa, and Latin America.

Eckholm has stated the situation well:

> When the environment starts to deteriorate on steep mountain slopes, it deteriorates quickly—far more so than on gentler slopes and on plains. And the damage is far more likely to be irreversible. The mountain regions are not only poor in economic terms; many areas are rapidly losing any chance of ever prospering as their thin natural resource base is washed away. Degenerating economic and ecological conditions in the mountains, in turn, often push waves of migrants into the lowlands, leaving behind an aged, dispirited population incapable of reversing the negative spiral.[10]

General Environmental Disruption

The environmental media—atmosphere, water, and the land—are usually very sensitive to human interventions in arid areas. Because of frequency of inversions, air pollution easily becomes a serious problem. Severe air pollution already exists in most of the world's large arid-zone cities, where growth in population and economic activity continues apace.

Salt

The salinity of several of the great river systems that feed the agriculture and other activities of the arid zones has increased markedly in recent decades and will continue to do so. An important case is the Colorado River in the

---

[9] See Eric P. Eckholm, The deterioration of mountain environment, Science, September 5, 1975.
[10] Ibid., p. 764.

United States, where salinity has been on the increase for some time in the lower reaches, which also are the most productive for agriculture. Further upstream, development threatens to aggravate this problem considerably in the next two decades. A similar, but perhaps less well-known situation exists in the River Murray in Australia. This river deteriorates progressively. In the upper reaches it has less than 30 mg/liter filterable residue but at Waiderin in South Australia it exceeds 600 mg/liter for much of the irrigation season during low flow periods.[11] Numerous other instances could be cited.

There is every reason to suppose that the water resources of arid lands will become increasingly saline. The manifest pressures of scarcity of food supply plus the availability of large amounts of capital in some arid countries may be expected to give rise to intense efforts to increase irrigation and in consequence to permit less and less fresh water to drain into the seas. This will be pushed by the introduction of crop varieties that both need and respond effectively to irrigation. Less salt will tend to be "flushed" from the continents through surface and subsurface channels, and the salinity of waters in arid areas accordingly will tend to increase. In Israel, for example, the coastal plain has been developed to the point of a "closed" water system, and little flushing to the sea takes place any longer. Since a high level of salt is the deadly enemy of many crops, this tendency, which is already so evident in areas developed for intensive agriculture, is distressing.

Fortunately some technological "helps," if not solutions, exist. In some instances it is possible to control relatively concentrated natural sources of salinity which contribute to the problem. For instance, it was possible to divert salt springs flowing into the Kinneret, the main reservoir in Israel's water system, and thereby reduce the delivering of salt to the lake by some 50%. Presently there are plans to try to control several major sources of salt loadings in the Colorado River system in the United States.

Furthermore, it is possible to reduce, or sometimes reverse, the adverse effects of salinity on crop production by selecting and breeding salt-tolerant species of crops and by modifying the technology of delivering water to the plants. For example, it appears from recent experiments conducted in several countries that drip systems of irrigation are substantially more amenable to the use of saline water than the conventional flooding and sprinkler systems.

Unfortunately, these methods for dealing with salinity normally require heavy, although perhaps cost-effective, investments. Moreover, adaptation to salinity rather than control of it greatly reduce the flexibility with which the affected water can be used.

---

[11] *Water for the Human Environment*, Proceedings of the First World Congress on Water Resources, Vol. 2, Country Reports, published by the International Water Resources Association, Chicago, 1973.

Groundwater Problems

Groundwater overdraft and quality deterioration are very substantial in many areas. Perhaps the most spectacular incidence of groundwater overdraft is found in the southwestern United States, where many millions of acres of irrigated land are supported by wells drawing upon limited amounts of fossil groundwater. This resource is diminishing and is doing so irreversibly. Another serious instance of groundwater overdraft is in the Cuyo region of Argentina. This region is one of the world's major producers of wine grapes and is wholly dependent on a depleting irrigation water supply for its economic existence.[12] Other problems associated with groundwater overdraft are subsidence in some urban areas and, in the coastal zones, intrusion of salty water into the groundwater aquifers. In Israel, for example, the coastal aquifer has been pumped much in excess of natural replenishment, especially in the 1950s and 1960s. Water levels have been lowered substantially. The fresh water-seawater interface, the location of which was originally seaward of the coastline, has intruded inland. In the Tel Aviv area, all city wells located within 2 to 3 km of the coast had to be abandoned in the late 1950s because of seawater intrusion. In some areas, especially north of Tel Aviv, seawater intrusion is still continuing. Intrusion of salty water into an aquifer is again a change that is reversible only to a limited extent.[13] Water quality in aquifers may also be otherwise affected by a variety of human activities, including in some instances the purposeful discharge of waste materials. In heavily irrigated areas using applications of nitrate fertilizers, nitrates may penetrate the aquifer. Once, again, to cite the case of Israel, a rather steep ascent of the nitrate content in the groundwater below the most populated areas of the coastal plain has been found. Causes are both fertilizer and sewage water infiltration. Some wells have passed the limit of allowable nitrate concentration for drinking water and have had to be used for agricultural purposes only, or closed entirely.[14] As the Green Revolution penetrates to additional areas, groundwater problems associated with the heavy application of fertilizers and pesticides can be expected to increase.

---

[12] A detailed examination of this case is found in Kenneth P. Frederick, *Water Management and Agricultural Development*, John Hopkins University Press, Baltimore, 1975.

[13] *Water for the Human Environment*, Vol. 2, p. 226.

[14] Nitrate levels of more than 100 ppm are frequently found in wells in agricultural parts of the country. The drinking water limit in the United States is 50 ppm. See Ralph Mitchell, Environmental deterioration, *Selected Papers on the Environment in Israel*, No. 3, Jerusalem, 1975.

Siltation of Scarce Reservoir Sites

Reservoir sites for water storage for various uses are a scarce resource. In many river basins, large-scale development of these sites has already taken place and they are in the process of being destroyed by siltation at a greater or lesser rate. Brown[15] cites the instance of a large irrigation reservoir built in Pakistan, which was originally expected to have a lifetime of 100 years but is now expected to last only half that long because of the siltation problems. Eckholm also reports many instances of reservoirs silting up with startling rapidity (in as little as 7 years) because of the deterioration of mountain environments discussed earlier.[16] If one looks at this matter in a larger time scale, it may well be that suitable reservoir sites in the world will have been used up and many will have become useless in the next century or so.

Decreasing Quality of the Marine Environment

Coastal arid regions are frequently highly dependent on the marine environment; most obviously perhaps for fish as a source of protein-short lands, but also on the magnificent beaches that are often found in arid areas and are a salable resource for recreation. Fishing has been greatly disturbed in many areas because of oil pollution in the rich coastal waters and, in the case of the eastern Mediterranean, the effect of the Aswan Dam on the amount of nutrients in the coastal waters. In addition, enormous spans of beach have been polluted by oil and other types of waste materials, greatly reducing their wholesomeness and attractiveness. Once again, this situation is richly reflected in the country reports for the U.N. Environmental Conference. Morocco reports, for example, that the major source of coastal water pollution is urban sewage. Existing services are overaged and inadequate and drain without any treatment into the sea and cause pollution of beaches.[17] Israel reports that oil pollution is visible along all its beaches, and that it is not yet clear what percentage is due to spill at terminals and ports and what to general contamination of the Mediterranean. The Mediterranean, it might be noted, has perhaps the most valuable beaches in the entire world. There is little or no effort made to protect them, and they are universally becoming seriously contaminated. Kuwait reports that marine pollution is an outstanding environmental problem, damaging coastal recreation areas and adversely affecting the fishing industry which supplies the local market and supports specialized industries. The sources of marine pollution are oil, oily

---

[15] Ibid., p. 12
[16] Ibid.
[17] Ibid., p. 63.

mixtures from ships and tankers, industrial effluents, and raw sewage discharged to the sea.[18] One of the most extraordinary cases of beach pollution is found in Spain. An enormous number of large hotels have been built along the Spanish Mediterranean since World War II. All of them discharge raw sewage to the ocean close to the beaches. In fact, we do not know of more than a few waste water treatment facilities along the entire Mediterranean coast.

Declining Quality and Quantity of Wildlife Populations

Population pressures that, as noted above, are contributing to desertification of vast areas and the massive deterioration of mountain environments are also leading to the diminution of numbers and diversity of wildlife. In many cases extinction is near at hand. Pressures to increase agricultural productivity are leading to heavy applications of pesticides, frequently of persistant varieties. The combination can be devastating to wildlife. Biocides are likely to become increasingly important as the Green Revolution spreads. The most diverse and many would say the most interesting wildlife populations in the world exist in Africa. In addition to whatever inherent interest their existence may have, they have also become an important source of income for several African countries. The country report for the U.N. Conference on Environment from Kenya is therefore of particular interest. It indicated that the main environmental problems connected with wildlife are conflicts in land use and threats directly to the wildlife resource and/or to its habitat. The report notes that these over-lapping problems together are liable to lead to a general deterioration of the natural environment. The serious threat that extending cultivation in marginal areas poses for wildlife populations is especially insidious when it occurs in areas peripheral to sanctuaries or across traditional migration routes. Population pressures make settlement within game reserves an increasingly pressing issue, requiring early resolution by the government if the original purpose of these areas is to be preserved. The disruption to wildlife in these cases is out of all proportion to the area settled and is the present major cause of wildlife elimination.[19] Judging by reports by other arid and semiarid countries, the situation in Kenya can by no means be regarded as the worst one.

The Viability of Nomadic Cultures

Through ages of evolution, nomadic cultures have arisen in most arid areas.

---

[18] Ibid., p. 58.
[19] Ibid., p. 57.

Their willingness to follow opportunity wherever it leads is the reason why some production useful for human beings is possible from many arid areas. The nomadic peoples are those that today are furthest removed from modern life in countries in which they exist. The Bedouin in Israel and the Navajo in the southwestern United States are enormously removed from the contemporary cultures within which these groups exist as human enclaves. Whether or not such societies are viable in these circumstances and can continue to make their far-flung harvest from the dry lands of the world is very much an open question. The ethics of the policies of dominant cultures with respect to these people is a matter of debate in many countries. If the nomadic way of life could persist, it is possible that modern science could be helpful in making it more productive. The camel, for example, is the most highly adapted to arid conditions of the large mammals. If it could be bred in such a manner as to be more generally useful, say for fiber and meat, its ability to range far from watering places might greatly increase the productivity of the desert lands ranged by the nomads. Similar results might possibly be achieved by increasing the number of watering places. But recent experience in the Sahel region of central Africa suggests that this approach would have to be used with great caution. A case (*Science Magazine*) has been made that a tube-well program to produce watering places, which was conducted under French auspices, made an important contribution to the desertification of much of the Sahel region in recent times. By permitting a great increase in the number of cattle and changing traditional migratory patterns, the program is said to have increased pressure on the land and possibly made as much of a contribution to the recent troubles in the Sahel as did the drought.[20] It seems likely, however, that the nomadic cultures will find it impossible to exist for many generations more if they are in contact with technologically more sophisticated societies, which in almost all cases they are. Their disappearance would tend to have a depressing effect on production from the arid regions.

Future Development

The previous section has indicated that there are a number of significant adverse tendencies insofar as the future of the arid lands is concerned. Most of these are not new, but some of them have intensified in the last few decades, particularly those related to population pressures. On the other hand, there has been a more or less continuous, if slow, increase in per capita income in most of these countries over a rather long period of time. This seems to have been the result of a

---

[20] Sahelian drought: No victory for Western aid, Science, July 1974.

number of influences, including some temporary ones such as the large-scale exploitation of mineral resources, especially energy, in some of them and an increased agricultural productivity resulting from the application of higher-technology methods in agriculture in others. A certain amount of industrialization has also been carried out in a number of arid countries. It was pointed out earlier that if per capita incomes continue to rise in the more humid regions, the hinterland influences on the arid regions may be expected to accelerate. However, the adverse developments in the environmental resource situation that we have indicated above and that it appears are nowhere near being brought to a halt, could have a severely dampening effect in the absence of some sort of bonanza resulting from mineral discoveries, and to counter depressing influences, the future of living standards in most arid regions appears to be heavily dependent on the improved use of scarce water resources, especially in agriculture.

Large-scale water transfers and the desalting of seawater, which are often looked to as ways of "making the deserts bloom," do not appear to have any decisive potential in this direction. Enormous schemes for transferring water have been proposed in several countries. There is what is referred to as the North American water and power alliance. There is a proposal for a large-scale divergence of waters from the Mississippi River to the high plains of Texas. The Soviet Union has put forward a scheme for reversing the flow of the Siberian rivers and irrigating millions of acres in central Asia.[21] All of these proposals are subject to serious criticisms on ecological and economic grounds, and they appear not to be in the picture, at least for a longer period into the future; and in any case they would not help the poorer countries. Desalting and delivery of water to points of use are likely to be too expensive in the foreseeable future to be justified for agriculture or to be justified for industrial or municipal uses if water supplies can be acquired from agriculture. Estimates of the cost of desalted water in the near term seem to converge to around 5.3 to 6.6 cents (1970 prices) per cubic meter. Even this near-term figure is speculative, and is reached only in conjunction with production of electric power with a large-scale nuclear plant. There is no reason, therefore, to expect that in the near future desalting offers much likelihood of substantially improving the economies of the less developed arid countries through expanded agriculture, unless it is undertaken and supported as a gift. But were this to be done it is likely that a gift of such magnitude would contribute far more to the recipients' economic welfare if it were made in some other form.[22]

---

[21] Our information on the Soviet scheme comes from personal discussion with Igor Belyaev.

[22] For additional discussion see Nathaniel Wollman, Economics of Land and Water Use. In Harold E. Dregne (ed.), *Arid Lands in Transition*, Pub. No. 90, American Association for the Advancement of Science, Washington, D.C., 1970.

It appears, therefore, that future gains in agricultural production must be based on improved use of existing water resources. The literature can leave little doubt that there is a very large scope for such improvements. Crosson's study of Chilean agriculture showed that a 30% increase in investment in irrigation works had little effect on total output, whereas an equivalent expenditure on fertilizer and pesticides would have yielded substantial results. He found that agricultural labor was not educated adequately enough to make efficient use of modern inputs and that irrigated land was not a limiting factor but that other inputs were.[23]

For most of the countries in the arid zones of the world, the scattered and incomplete evidence that is available indicates that output could be doubled or tripled with the same water base if more contemporary farming methods were adopted, including associated heavy capital and operating costs. Gains of this magnitude appear to be possible even if the "miracle grains" are neglected. But, as indicated further below, tradition, lack of education, costs, and environmental effects make rapid introduction of such methods on a worldwide scale unlikely.

Also, the widespread crop failures of the early 1970s served to remind us that the Green Revolution has thus far not made us disaster-proof. Actually, the Green Revolution has been much more limited in its impact than many people suppose. This is to a considerable measure due to the limited area it has actually effected. High-yielding varieties of rice have thus far been semidwarf and suitable for shallow-water regions comprising only 25 to 30% of the world's total rice lands. Furthermore, such dwarf varieties are particularly sensitive to flooding. The International Rice Research Institute in the Philippines is working on new varieties suitable for deeper-water conditions, and researchers there believe that rice production could be doubled throughout the world in the next 15 years. One promising line of development is work on varieties that elongate and thereby survive floods. The Institute is also working on drought- and insect-resistant varieties and adaptability to saline and nutrient-poor soil. The importance of progress in these areas is underlined by the fact that about one-third of mankind, or roundly 1,300,000,000 people, depend on rice for more than one-half their food.[24]

One must recall, however, that achieving the enormous gains in production that the Rice Institute foresees as necessary and possible will require gigantic investments in capital, education, and operating costs. This is especially so since the increase in energy prices has raised the cost of fertilizer, pesticides, and mechanical power inputs to agriculture. Whether or not it would be possible to make these investments quickly enough to avert disaster in the arid regions

---

[23] See Pierre R. Crosson *Agricultural Development and Productivity*, Johns Hopkins University Press, 1970.
[24] David Spurgeon, Up-dating the Green Revolution, Nature *254*, April 24, 1975.

experiencing rapid population growth is a very open question, it seems to us. Furthermore, the environmental impact of applying the vast amounts of fertilizer and pesticides that would be needed are still of somewhat unknown dimension but will no doubt contribute to some of the deterioration tendencies discussed earlier. It is perhaps unlikely that contamination by either will pose any acute threat to human life, but they could deal the death blow to many other life forms and lead to more rapid eutrification of major water bodies. Given the race between population growth and food production, such considerations are likely to receive scant attention except perhaps in some cases, such as parts of Africa, where wildlife is a major attraction and a substantial source of income.

In recent years the large exploitation of mineral resources, especially petroleum, has taken on major importance in the development plans of several arid countries. Since minerals are exhausting resources, their boosting effect on the economy is necessarily more or less temporary. In the case of petroleum income the effect will probably last less than half a century. Coal and nonfuel minerals may last somewhat longer. Many nations obtaining this type of income (including the Navajo nation in the arid hinterland of the United States as well as some Middle Eastern countries) are attempting to use the bonanza to provide a longer-term economic base for their countries. To do this successfully will require imagination and planning of a high order. In mineral-rich countries where irrigation is important, there are fairly straightforward opportunities for increasing agricultural efficiency through education and technological improvement. Industrialization is another matter. Renewable and other nonrenewable resources are often scarce; more often than not the location of arid lands (because they were not previously the locus of large-scale development) is poor with respect to markets and existing transportation routes. In some cases the recreational hinterland status of an arid nation may offer attractive opportunities for investment and development. But no instances in which this type of development has by itself provided a basis for generally high per capita income come to mind. High mineral incomes and large foreign exchange earnings do provide a unique opportunity for "a giant step forward," but how to make the step successfully is usually a very difficult question.

Epilogue

It seems rather anomalous that most of the arid regions of the world appear to be facing such a severely difficult future when they were also the areas where civilization first arose. What this suggests, however, is that such regions are fertile ground for the development of civilization and its (necessarily) rather sophisticated economic base, but that the level and magnitude of development that can be attained is somehow inherently limited. If this is true, it would follow that, up to a point, aridity, with some external source of river or spring water, usually from mountain ranges, is an advantage, but that the advantage is circumscribed. The favorable growing conditions typical of many arid regions, including long warm seasons and relative immunity of crops from natural disasters, mean that a surplus of food can be grown, sometimes year-round and without prodigous labor, if the population is small.[25] At the same time conditions for plant growth are not so favorable, as in the tropics or the coast of California, for example, that essentially no cultivation is needed. The Southern California Indians could go naked all year and pick berries and never develop any high order of culture. The forests of the north harbored animals to hunt, and the combination of weather and forest made primitive methods of cultivation rather unrewarding there. The need to cultivate in arid lands, and to move water, was a natural incentive to take an interest in mechanical things and physical principles. Because irrigation societies are necessarily settled societies of some size, there is a need to develop both permanent structures and enduring institutions. This reinforces the stimulus to develop engineering and naturally arouses an interest in human relationships and such matters as ethics and justice. Early arid lands civilizations have also usually been strong in astronomy and mathematics. It does not stretch the imagination to think that the clear skies and angularity of countryside and structures in arid lands have something to do with this.

Societies of gatherers, hunters, and nomads (other early forms for organizing economic activity) seem to lack one or more of the ingredients for generating a high level of civilization. Once the basis for civilization in mathematics, science, the arts, and human organizations has been laid, it does, however, seem to have high transfer value and to be able to achieve a self-generating dynamic of it own. Given the enormous flows of renewable resources and the more or less continuous development of technology (with a giant step up during the industrial revolution), the more humid lands have been able to develop their economies and their (to a large extent derivative) civilizations to unprecedented scales. Aridity has, however, held the development of the dry lands on a much tighter leash. At the same time, especially in the most recent times, population has grown enormously. The combination, plus many other complicating factors including those discussed in this chapter, has prevented most of the truly arid nations from rising up out of poverty. In some cases the question seems to be not population control but the much more difficult one of *reducing* the population to get it into a sustainable balance with available resources.

---

[25] This, of course, does not apply to nonirrigated semiarid areas, which contain probably the highest-risk agriculture in the entire world.

Acknowledgments

We wish to thank Nathaniel Wollman, Dean of the College of Arts and Sciences, The University of New Mexico, for many helpful comments on this chapter. Dr. Kneese also wishes to thank the International Institute for Applied Systems Analysis in Laxenburg, Austria, for support during the summer of 1975, part of which was directed toward the production of this chapter.

Appendix

Full Sample–118 Countries

Africa
  Algeria
  Angola
  Burundi
  Cameroon
  Central African Republic
  Chad
  Congo (Brazzaville)
  Congo, Democratic Republic of the
  Dahomey
  Ethiopia
  Gabon
  Gambia
  Ghana
  Guinea
  Ivory Coast
  Kenya
  Liberia
  Libya
  Malagasy Republic
  Malawi
  Mali
  Mauritania
  Morocco
  Mozambique
  Niger
  Nigeria
  Senegal
  Sierra Leone

  Somalia
  South Africa
  Southern Rhodesia
  Sudan
  Tanzania, United Republic of
  Togo
  Tunisia
  Uganda
  United Arab Republic
  Upper Volta
  Zambia

North America
  Canada
  United States

Central and South America
  Argentina
  Barbados
  Bolivia
  Brazil
  British Honduras
  Chile
  Columbia
  Costa Rica
  Dominican Republic
  Ecuador
  El Salvador

Guatemala	Middle East
Guyana	Iraq
Haiti	Israel
Honduras	Jordan
Jamaica	Kuwait
Mexico	Lebanon
Netherlands Antilles	Saudi Arabia
Nicaragua	Southern Yemen
Panama	Syria
Paraguay	
Peru	Europe
Surinam	Austria
Trinidad & Tobago	Belgium
Uruguay	Cyprus
Venezuela	Denmark
	Finland
	France
	Germany, Federal Republic of
Asia	Greece
Afghanistan	Iceland
Burma	Ireland
Cambodia	Italy
Ceylon	Luxembourg
China (Taiwan)	Malta
Hong Kong	Netherlands
India	Norway
Indonesia	Portugal
Iran	Spain
Japan	Sweden
Korea, Republic of	Switzerland
Laos	Turkey
Malaysia	United Kingdom
Nepal	
Pakistan	
Philippines	Oceania
Singapore	Australia
Thailand	Fiji
Vietnam, Republic of	New Zealand

Natural Resource Economics

Arid Sample—53 Countries

Africa
- Algeria
- Angola
- Chad
- Congo (Brazzaville)
- Dahomey
- Ethiopia
- Gambia
- Ghana
- Kenya
- Libya
- Malagasy Republic
- Mali
- Mauritania
- Morocco
- Mozambique
- Niger
- Nigeria
- Senegal
- Somalia
- South Africa
- Southern Rhodesia
- Sudan
- Tanzania
- Togo
- Tunisia
- United Arab Republic
- Upper Volta
- Zambia

North America
- Canada
- United States

Central and South America
- Argentina
- Brazil
- Chile
- Ecuador
- Mexico
- Paraguay
- Peru
- Venezuela

Asia
- Afghanistan
- India
- Iran
- Pakistan

Middle East
- Iraq
- Israel
- Jordan
- Kuwait
- Saudi Arabia
- Southern Yemen
- Syria

Europe
- Portugal
- Spain
- Turkey

Oceania
- Australia

Nontropical Sample—63 Countries

Africa
    Algeria
    Chad
    Ethiopia
    Kenya
    Libya
    Mali
    Mauritania
    Morocco
    Niger
    Senegal
    Somalia
    Southern Rhodesia
    Sudan
    Tunisia
    United Arab Republic
    Upper Volta

North America
    Canada
    United States

Central and South America
    Argentina
    Chile
    Mexico
    Paraguay
    Peru
    Uruguay

Asia
    Afghanistan
    Taiwan
    Hong Kong
    Iran
    Japan
    Korea, Republic of
    Nepal

    Pakistan

Middle East
    Iraq
    Israel
    Jordan
    Kuwait
    Lebanon
    Saudi Arabia
    Southern Yemen
    Syria

Europe
    Austria
    Belgium
    Cyprus
    Denmark
    Finland
    France
    Germany, Federal Republic of
    Greece
    Iceland
    Ireland
    Italy
    Luxembourg
    Malta
    Netherlands
    Norway
    Portugal
    Spain
    Sweden
    Switzerland
    Turkey
    United Kingdom

Oceania
    Australia
    New Zealand

Data Sources

Food and Agriculture Organization of the United Nations (1967). *Production Yearbook 1966*, FAO, Rome, Table 1, "Land use," pp. 3-8.

Espenshade, E.B. (ed.), *Goode's World Atlas*, 13th ed., Rand McNally, Chicago, pp. 12-13.

United Nations (1965). *Statistical Yearbook 1964*, New York, Table 187, "Illiteracy rate among population 15 years of age and over, by sex," pp. 694-697.

United Nations (1968). *Statistical Yearbook 1967*, New York, Table 185, "Estimates of total and per capita national income and gross domestic product at factor cost," pp. 576-580; Table 200, "Net official flow of external resources to individual developing countries from developed market economies and from multi-lateral agencies," pp. 692-695.

United Nations (1971). *Demographic Yearbook 1970*, New York, Table 20, "Expectation of life at specified ages for each sex: latest available year," pp. 710-728.

United Nations (1968). *Demographic Yearbook 1967*, New York, Table 2, "Population by sex, rate of population increase, area and density for each country of the world: latest census and mid-year estimates for 1963 and 1967"; Table 5, "Population by age, sex, and urban/rural residence: latest available year 1955-1967."

Correlation Matrix

	P	R	PF	I	FA	LE	AL	PL	PA
P	1.00	−0.34	−0.54	−0.31	−0.08	0.46	−0.07	−0.06	−0.23
R	−0.34	1.00	0.52	0.35	0.11	−0.25	−0.06	−0.06	0.28
PF	−0.54	0.52	1.00	0.42	0.12	−0.39	−0.05	−0.07	0.15
I	−0.31	0.35	0.42	1.00	0.23	−0.39	0.04	−0.08	0.22
FA	−0.08	0.11	0.12	0.23	1.00	−0.09	0.54	0.00	0.18
LE	0.46	−0.25	−0.39	−0.39	−0.09	1.00	0.06	0.10	−0.25
AL	−0.07	−0.06	−0.05	0.04	0.54	0.06	1.00	0.45	0.10
PL	−0.06	−0.06	−0.07	−0.08	0.00	0.10	0.45	1.00	0.23
PA	−0.23	0.28	0.15	0.22	0.18	−0.25	0.10	0.23	1.00

PART III

Environmental Economics and Policy

[12]

BACKGROUND FOR THE ECONOMIC ANALYSIS OF ENVIRONMENTAL POLLUTION

Allen V. Kneese*

Resources for the Future, Inc., Washington, D.C., USA

Summary

Relevant and useful work on economic aspects of environmental problems requires some knowledge of the scientific and technological aspects of these problems. This article provides a summary of the latter. Global effects of environmental pollution, like effects on climate and large ecological systems, are reviewed first. Then, smaller-scale but severe "regional" problems are addressed. These include air and water pollution and solid wastes disposal. Sources and type of pollutants are identified, their effects on nature and human receptors are discussed, and available control technologies are reviewed. Finally, a more coherent view of the whole set of problems is provided by means of a "materials balance" approach.

Introduction

Economic theory has provided a conceptual structure indispensable for understanding contemporary environmental problems and for formulating effective and efficient policy approaches toward them. Concepts like external diseconomies and public goods provide enormously useful insights. But economic theorizing and research that take place without being well informed about the substantive character of the problems under study is in danger of being somewhat arid because of extreme abstraction or of expending scarce energy and talent in the pursuit of relatively unimportant matters. The objective of the present essay is to provide an introduction to the substantive aspects of one of the major environmental problems facing both developed and some developing economies—environmental pollution.

Environmental pollution has existed for many yers in one form or another. It is an old phenomenon,[1] and yet in its contemporary forms it seems to have

---

* I wish to thank my colleagues Blair Bower, Clifford Russell, and Walter Spofford for assistance in the preparation of this paper.
[1] Many accounts attest that severe environmental degradation has existed for a long time in the western countries. In fact, the immediate surroundings of most of mankind in this part of the world were much worse a century ago than they are now. The following account of statements from an address of Charles Dickens may be interesting in this connection, especially to those who know contemporary London: "He knew of many places in it [London] unsurpassed in the accumulated horrors of their long neglect by the

2 *Background for the economic analysis of environmental pollution*

crept up on governments and even on pertinent professional disciplines such as biology, chemistry, most of engineering,[1] and, of course, economics. A few economists, such as Pigou, wrote intelligently and usefully on the matter a long time ago, but generally even that subset of economists especially interested in externalities seems to have regarded them as rather freakish anomalies in an otherwise smoothly functioning exchange system. Even the examples commonly used in the literature have a whimsical air about them. We have heard much of bees and apple orchards and a current favorite example is sparks from a steam locomotive—this being some eighty years after the introduction of the spark arrester and twenty years after the abandonment of the steam locomotive.

Moreover, air and water continued until very recently to serve the economist as examples of free goods. A whole new set of scarce environmental resources presenting unusually difficult allocation problems seems to have appeared on the scene with the profession having hardly noticed. Fortunately, this situation is changing fast and much good work is appearing in the current economics literature as the papers in this issue amply demonstrate.

Substantial and thoughtful attention from economists is especially needed because the economic and institutional sources of the problem are either neglected or thoroughly misunderstood by most of those currently engaged in the rather frantic discussion of it.

I. "Global" Problems

I will begin this discussion of the substantive aspects of pollution problems by concentrating first on those problems, or potential problems, which affect the entire planet. Thereafter I will focus on "regional" problems. By regional I mean all those other than global. One must use a word like regional rather than terms pertaining to political jurisdictions such as nations, states, or cities because the scale of pollution resulting from the emissions of materials and energy follows the patterns, pulses, and rhythms of meteorological and hydrological systems rather than the boundaries of political systems—and therein lies one of the main problems.

The global problems to be discussed here pertain largely to the atmosphere because the marks of man have already been seen on that entire thin film of

---

dirtiest old spots in the dirtiest old towns, under the worst old governments of Europe." He also said that the surroundings and conditions of life were such that "infancy was made stunted, ugly and full of pain—maturity made old—and old age imbecile." These statements are from *The Public Health a Public Question: First Report of the Metropolitan Sanitary Association*, address of Charles Dickens, Esq., London,1850. Great achievements in the elementary sanitation of the close-in environment have been made as well as impressive gains in public health. The distinguishing feature of contemporary environmental pollution seems to be the large-scale and subtle degradation of common property resources. This point is developed in the text below.

[1] There has been a relatively small group of sanitary engineers that has given close attention to environmental problems for a long time. I am here referring to the mainstream of work in these professions.

life-sustaining substance. It seems to have come as something of a shock to the natural science community that man not only can, *but has*, changed the chemical composition of the whole atmosphere.[1] Other large-scale problems, or potential problems, particularly those related to the "biosphere" will be discussed more briefly.

Before proceeding to what may be real global problems, it will be desirable to dispose of one red herring. One of the spectres raised by the more alarmist school of ecologists is that man will deplete the world's oxygen supply by converting it into carbon dioxide in the process of burning fossil fuels for energy. This idea has now been thoroughly discredited by two separate pieces of evidence. The first is measurement of .changes in the oxygen supply over a period of years. There is currently *one* monitoring station in the world whose objective it is to identify long-term changes in the atmosphere. The station is operated at a high elevation in Hawaii by the U.S. Weather Bureau. Observations there have shown the oxygen content of the atmosphere to be remarkably stable. The other piece of evidence—perhaps more persuasive—is in the form of a "gedankenexperiment". If one burns, on paper, the entire known world supply of fossil fuels and all the present plant biomass, the impact on the oxygen supply is to reduce it by about 3 %. This is much too small to be noticed in most areas of the earth.

Potentially real effects on the atmosphere and climate are thought to be connected with changes in carbon dioxide and particulate matter (including aerosols) in the atmosphere, petroleum in the oceans, waste energy rejection to the atmosphere, and the widespread presence of toxic agents in the coastal waters and oceans. I will discuss each of these briefly in turn.

The production of carbon dioxide is an inevitable result of the combustion of fossil fuels. In contrast to O_2, the relative quantity of CO_2 in the atmosphere has increased measurably. The possible significance of this is that CO_2 absorbs infrared radiations and therefore an increasing concentration of it in the atmosphere would tend to cause the surface of the earth to rise in temperature.[2] Some estimates have put the possible increase in CO_2,[3] if present rates of increase in the combustion of fossil fuel continue, at about 50 % by the end of the century. An increase of this amount could raise the world's mean surface temperature several degrees with attendant melting of ice caps, inundation of seacoast cities, and undesirable temperature increases in densely inhabited areas. Estimates made in the summer of 1970 suggest, however, that the CO_2 increase will only be about 20 % by the end of the century with lesser

---

[1] The fullest discussion of the range of problems considered in this section will be found in *Man's Impact on the Global Environment: Assessment and Recommendations for Action.* M.I.T. Press, Cambridge (Mass.), 1970.

[2] Most incoming radiation is in the form of visible light, while most outgoing energy is in the form of infrared radiation.

[3] Conservation Foundation, *Implications of Rising Carbon Dioxide Content of the Atmosphere,* New York, 1963.

4   Background for the economic analysis of environmental pollution

potential effects on climate.[1] The difference in estimates is accounted for by
the newly recognized fact that less of the CO_2 generated by combustion is
staying in the atmosphere than was previously supposed. Apparently one or
more of the "sinks" for CO_2 is responding to the increased concentration, or
possibly even a third force is leading to greater absorption. The main sinks for
CO_2, or more specifically carbon, are solution in the oceans and conversion
by the flora of the earth. Perhaps carbon is limiting to growth in some of these
plant populations, and they are responding to its increased availability from
the atmosphere.[2] Another possibility is less reassuring. Somewhat anomalously
the mean temperature of the earth's surface has been falling over the past
couple of decades according to Weather Bureau observations. As is true of
many gases, the solubility of CO_2 in water increases when water temperature
falls. Maybe that's where some of the CO_2 went.

But this brings us to another possible effect of man's activity on world climate. Some meteorologists—especially Bryson[3]—believe that man's industrial
and agricultural activities are causing the world to cool off. The suspected
mechanism is an increase in particulates and aerosols which, they think, are
increasing the earth's albedo (ability to reflect incoming solar radiation).
Farming and other activities in arid areas and the combustion of fuels send
immense amounts of particulates and fine water vapors (aerosols) into the
atmosphere each day. This is an undisputed fact although observations indicate that a worldwide increase in particulate matter cannot yet be identified.[4]
What is in dispute is the effect of the man-generated increase. Some not only
believe this effect is significant, but that it may be sending us rather rapidly
toward an ice age—perhaps the final ice age resulting in a perpetually frozen
planet. Other factors might lead in the same direction as we shall see subsequently. The freeze-up hypothesis is, however, disputed by those other meteorologists who regard it as important to recognize the difference between particulates of different types and at different elevations in the atmosphere. Mitchell
has pointed out that there has been a large amount of volcanic activity in
recent years which has deposited great quantities of particulates at high
elevations in the atmosphere.[5] The net effect of these is fairly clearly to reflect
more energy away from the earth, and this could well be responsible for the
observed temperature decline. On the other hand, he points out that particulates deposited at relatively low altitudes, such as those generated by man,

---

[1] *Man's Impact on the Global Environment* ... etc., *op. cit.*
[2] With higher concentrations of CO_2 in the atmosphere, one would naturally expect
some increase in absorption by the oceans, since CO_2 solubility is a function of the partial
pressure of CO_2.
[3] R. A. Bryson and J. T. Peterson: Atmospheric aerosols: Increased concentrations during
the last decade. *Science 162*, 3849 (Oct. 1968), pp. 120–21.
[4] It should be noted that this is a somewhat controversial conclusion.
[5] J. M. Mitchell, Jr.: A preliminary evaluation of atmospheric pollution as a cause of the
global temperature fluctuation of the past century. In *Global Effects of Environmental
Pollution* (ed. Singer) pp. 97–112. Reidel, Holland, 1970.

could well have the reverse effect because they reflect energy back toward earth as well as away from it. Mitchell's calculations tend to show that the former effect outweighs the latter.[1] Thus, when the effect of the volcanic particulates wears off over a period of years, the lower altitude particulates could begin to reinforce CO_2 as a factor leading to rising world temperatures.

An additional, and possibly reinforcing factor, is the release of energy to the atmosphere due to the energy conversion activities of man. A large proportion of the energy from fuels man uses is transferred directly to the atmosphere —as, for example, the energy converted in automobile engines. Another large proportion is initially tranferred to water—as, for example, when condensers in electric power plants are cooled with water. But this too is rather quickly rejected to the atmosphere by induced evaporation in watercourses or wet-cooling towers. Essentially, all of the energy converted from fuels is transferred to the atmosphere as heat. Because this is so, it is possible to make a rather precise estimate of this transfer by calculating the energy value of the fuels used in the world. On this basis there is an average emission of about 5.7×10^{12} watts of energy from human conversion.[2] What does one make of such a monstrous number? More understandable perhaps is the statement that this is about $1/15\,000$ of the absorbed solar flux. That doesn't seem like much, but another important element in the picture is the fact that energy conversion is a rapidly growing activity all over the world. The most spectacular example is conversion to electric power which in the United States has been proceeding at a doubling time of ten years and even faster in one or two other large economies. Worldwide energy conversion (by far the largest proportion of which is from fossil fuels) as a whole has been proceeding at a growth rate of about 4 % a year. If we project this growth rate for 130 years, we will reach a rate of energy rejection of about 1 % of the absorbed solar flux. This is enough, some meteorologists believe, to have a substantial effect on world climate. If we proceed at the 4 % growth rate for another 120 years, we will have reached 100 % of the absorbed solar flux. This would be a total disaster. The resulting mean increase in world temperature would be about 50°C—a condition totally unsuitable for human habitation. We will never reach such a situation, but the important question is what circumstances will prevent us from so doing.

If one is given to apocalyptic visions, he can readily imagine a situation in which CO_2, particulates, and energy conversion reinforce each other and will, after a short reprieve from the volcanoes, make the earth into a kind of mini-hell.

But other things may happen too. For one thing, we are annually spilling on the order of 1.5×10^6 tons of oil directly into the oceans with perhaps another 4×10^6 tons being delivered by terrestrial streams. This may be enough "oil on

---

[1] Personal communication to William Frisken.
[2] W. R. Frisken, "Extended Industrial Revolution and Climate Change," unpublished report prepared while he was a visiting scholar at RFF, July, 1970.

6　*Background for the economic analysis of environmental pollution*

troubled waters", some scientists believe, to smooth the sea surface sufficiently to cause its reflectivity to be increased significantly.[1] Again, the associated albedo effect would tend to cause cooling. But at the same time the reduction in the atmosphere–ocean interface would tend to diminish the absorption of CO_2 and thus possibly tend toward a warming condition.

And then there is the matter of the SST. The European Concorde and the Russian SST have already flown, and it looks as though the U.S. version will also fly one day. Aside from the major question of sonic booms, the emissions from SSTs may have substantial effects on the upper atmosphere. SSTs would fly at 65 000–70 000 feet and the atmosphere is very different up there. It is extremely dry and the layers at that elevation do not seem to mix much with the lower atmosphere. Five hundred SSTs might be in operation by the mid-1980s. If these were the American type, their emissions might cause an increase of water vapor in the upper atmosphere of 10 % globally and possibly 60 % over the North Atlantic where most of the flights would occur.[2] This could give rise to large-scale formations of very persistent cirrus cloud. Furthermore, the emissions of soot, hydrocarbons, nitrogen oxides, and sulfate particles could cause stratospheric smog. The effects of all this would be somewhat uncertain but presumably not unlike those produced by particulates deposited into the upper atmosphere by volcanoes—in other words, increased albedo and consequent cooling at the earth's surface.

A final category of substances of possibly global significance are persistent organic toxins. DDT is a good example of these and has been found in living creatures all over the world. How it got to remote places like the Antarctic is still somewhat mysterious, but apparently substantial amounts are transmitted through the atmosphere as well as through the oceans. Aside from possible large-scale effects on ecological systems, these persistent toxins could affect the O_2–CO_2 balance by poisoning the phytoplankton which are involved in one of the important CO_2–O_2 conversion processes. We do not know whether this is happening or not.

Clearly, we are operating in a context of great uncertainty. Equally clearly, man's activities now and in the relatively near-term future may affect the world's climatic and biological regimes in a substantial way. It seems beyond question that a serious effort to understand man's effects on the planet and to monitor those effects is indicated. Should we need to control such things as the production of energy and CO_2 in the world, we will face an economic and political resource allocation problem of unprecedented difficulty and complexity.

The discussion of global effects of pollution was necessarily somewhat

----

[1] Oil also may affect phytoplankton and other species directly.
[2] L. Machta, "Stratospheric Water Vapor," a working paper written for the 1970 Summer Study on Critical Environmental Problems, sponsored by the Massachusetts Institute of Technology and held at Williams College in Williamstown, Massachusetts, July 1970.

speculative, but now we turn to problems on a less grand scale. These regional problems are clear and present. A discussion is first presented under the traditional categories of waterborne, airborne, and solid residuals.[1] In the final section, I point explicitly to the interdependencies among these residuals streams and the implications of this for economic analysis. Unfortunately, most of the numbers given are from the United States. This is because I am simply not familiar with the data from other countries. The relationships in the United States may, however, be reasonably representative of those found in other industrialized countries.

II. Waterborne Residuals

Degradable residuals

A somewhat oversimplified but useful distinction for understanding what happens when residuals are discharged to watercourses is between *degradable* and *non-degradable* materials. The most widespread and best known degradable residual is domestic sewage, but, in the aggregate, industry produces greater amounts of degradable organic residuals almost all of which is generated by the food processing, meat packing, pulp and paper, petroleum refining, and chemicals industries. Some industrial plants are fantastic producers of degradable organic residuals: a single uncontrolled pulp mill, for example, can produce wastes equivalent to the sewage flow of a large city.

When an effluent bearing a substantial load of degradable organic residuals is expelled into an otherwise "clean" stream, a process known as "aerobic degradation" begins immediately. Stream biota, primarily bacteria, feed on the wastes and break them down into their inorganic forms of nitrogen, phosphorous, and carbon, which are basic plant nutrients. In the breaking down of degradable organic material, some of the oxygen which is dissolved in any "clean" water is utilized by the bacteria. But this depletion tends to be offset by reoxygenation which occurs through the air–water interface and also as a consequence of photosynthesis by the plants in the water. If the waste load is not too heavy, dissolved oxygen in the stream first will drop to a limited extent (say, to 4 or 5 parts per million from a saturation level of perhaps 8–10 ppm, depending upon temperature) and then rise again. This process can be described by a characteristically shaped curve or function known as the "oxygen sag". The differential equations which characterize this process were first introduced by Streeter and Phelps in 1925 and are often called the Streeter-Phelps equations.

If the degradable organic residual discharged to a stream becomes great enough, the process of degradation may exhaust the dissolved oxygen.

---

[1] Due to limitations of space, I will concentrate on material residuals as sources of environmental pollution. There is some discussion of energy residuals—especially where they interact in important ways with material residuals. Noise, an important energy residual, is not treated at all. A good introductory discussion of noise can be found in chapter 1 of the *Handbook of Noise Control* (ed. Cyril M. Harris). McGraw-Hill, New York, 1957.

8 _Background for the economic analysis of environmental pollution_

In such cases, degradation is still carried forward but it takes place anaerobically, that is, through the action of bacteria which do not use free oxygen
but organically or inorganically bound oxygen, common sources of which are
nitrates and sulphates. Gaseous by-products result, among them carbon
dioxide, methane, and hydrogen sulfide.

Water in which wastes are being degraded anaerobically emits foul odors,
looks black and bubbly, and aesthetically is altogether offensive. Indeed,
the unbelievably foul odors from the River Thames in mid-nineteenth century
London caused the halls of Parliament to be hung with sheets soaked in quick-
lime and even induced recess upon occasion when the reek became too
suffocating. So extreme a condition is rarely encountered nowadays, although
it is by no means unknown. For example, a large lake near São Paulo, Brazil, is
largely anaerobic, and most of the streams in the Japanese papermaking city
Fuji are likewise lacking in oxygen. Other instances could be mentioned. But
levels of dissolved oxygen low enough to kill fish and cause other ecological
changes are a much more frequent and widespread problem.

High temperatures accelerate degradation. They also decrease the saturation level of dissolved oxygen in a body of water. So a waste load which would
not induce low levels of dissolved oxygen at one temperature may do so if
the temperature of the water rises. In such circumstances, heat may be considered a pollutant. Moreover, excess heat itself can be destructive to aquatic
life. Huge amounts of heat are put into streams by the cooling water effluents
of electric power plants and industry.

There is, in fact, increased concern about the impacts of heat residuals,
particularly from power generation, in the face of the incessantly increasing
demand for electric power already described and the development of nuclear
power, the present "generation" of which requires more heat disposal per kwh
generated than fossil fuel plants. Increasing use of cooling towers has been
one response to this situation. But the use of cooling towers represents
basically a transfer of the medium into which to reject the residual heat
energy, that is, to the air instead of temporarily to the water. One author in
the United States has discussed some aspects of what would happen over the
central region of the United States under the alternative procedure, i.e., use
of once-through cooling with discharge of waterborne heat to the main streams
of the area, the Missouri and the Mississippi. About 540 million kilowatts of
fossil fuel burning capacity are assumed installed and operating in this region
by the year 2000. He writes:

Imposing the requirement of at least 10 miles separation between stations and
noting that such a generating capacity will raise the water temperature by about
20 deg F, we find approximately 3 000 miles of river spreading over the central
region of the United States with a temperature 20 deg F higher than normal.[1]

---

[1] S. M. Greenfield: *Science and the Natural Environment of Man*, p. 3, RAND Corporation, California, February 17, 1969.

Of course the ecological effects which would accompany such a large-scale heat discharge to our streams can only be speculated about at this time. If there were a substantial discharge of degradable organic residuals to these streams at the same time, they would almost certainly become anaerobic in the summer time. The freshwater life forms we are accustomed to would be lost.

A conventional sewage treatment plant processing degradable organic residuals uses the same biochemical processes which occur naturally in a stream, but by careful control they are greatly speeded up. Under most circumstances, standard biological sewage treatment plants are capable of reducing the BOD (biochemical oxygen demand) in waste effluent by perhaps 90 %. As with degradation occurring in a watercourse, plant nutrients are the end-product of the process.

Stretches of streams which persistently carry less than 4 or 5 ppm of oxygen will not support the higher forms of fish life. Even where they are not lethal, reduced levels of oxygen increase the sensitivity of fish to toxins. Water in which the degradable organic residuals have not been completely stabilized is more costly to treat for public or industrial supplies. Finally, the plant nutrients produced by bacterial degradation of degradable organic residuals, either in the stream or in treatment plants, may cause algae blooms. Up to a certain level, algae growth in a stream is not harmful and may even increase fish food, but larger amounts can be toxic to fish, produce odors, reduce the river's aesthetic appeal, and increase water supply treatment problems. Difficulties with algae are likely to become serious only when waste loads have become large enough to require high levels of treatment. Then residual plant nutrient products become abundant relative to streamflow and induce excessive plant growth.

Problems of this kind are particularly important in comparatively quiet waters such as lakes and tidal estuaries. In recent years certain Swiss and American lakes have changed their character radically because of the buildup of plant nutrients. The most widely known example is Lake Erie, although the normal "eutrophication" or aging process has been accelerated in many other lakes. The possibility of excessive algae growth is one of the difficult problems in planning for pollution control—especially in lakes, bays, and estuaries, for effective treatment processes today carry a high price tag.

In the United States, currently, BOD discharges by industry are apparently about twice as large as by municipalities. How fast BOD discharges grow depends on how effectively industrial wastes are controlled and municipal wastes treated. If current rates continue, BOD may grow about $3\frac{1}{2}$% per year with plant nutrient discharges growing even faster.

Bacteria might also be included among what we have called the degradable pollutants since the enteric, infectious types tend to die off in watercourses, and treatment with chlorine or ozone is highly effective against them. Because of water supply treatment, the traditional scourges of polluted water—

10   *Background for the economic analysis of environmental pollution*

typhoid, paratyphoid, dysentery, gastroenteritis—have become almost unknown in advanced countries. One might say that public concern with environmental pollution peaked early in this century with the rapid spread of these diseases. But public health engineers were so successful in devising effective water supply treatment that attention to water pollution lapsed until its recent upsurge.

A model for the analysis of bio-degradable residuals

I turn here to a brief description of a model which was used to analyse water quality improvement alternatives in the Delaware estuary area. I will linger over this model a while because it is an ingenious linking of an economic optimization (linear programming model) and a model of the residuals transport and degradation phenomena in the estuary. Analogous models have now been used for the economic analysis of water quality management problems in several other instances. What is illustrated here is one way of linking a diffusion model to an economic optimization model. Other ways have also been developed.[1]

The estuary was divided into 30 reaches, and the Streeter-Phelps oxygen balance equations previously mentioned were adapted and applied to these interconnected segments. This led to a system of linear first-order differential equations. The transfer functions, which related the change in segment i to an input of waste in segment j,[2] fortunately simplify to a set of linear relationships if steady-state conditions are assumed, i.e., if it is assumed that the discharge rate is constant and temperature and river flow are taken as parameters. In fact, the transfer functions can be represented by a matrix.[3]

This result is very fortunate because it means that these coefficients can readily be incorporated into a linear set of constraints which fit the linear programming format quite straightforwardly.

Assume that the watercourse consists of m homogeneous segments and c_i represents the improvement in water quality required to meet the D.O. target in segment i. The target vector c of m elements can be obtained by changes

---

[1] See, for example, the papers by K.-G. Mäler and C. S. Russell, below.

[2] The transfer relations are fairly complicated because the degradation of degradable organic residuals in the watercourse consumes D. O., whereas aeration, or movement of oxygen across the interface between air and water, tends to counteract this effect. Important variables that affect the oxygen balance for a given waste discharge are temperature and various characteristics of the watercourse.

[3] This result is explained by Sobel as follows: "The transfer function for D. O. response in segment i due to an input of frequency ω in segment j is:
$\Phi_{ij}(\omega) - a_{ij}(\omega) \exp. z\theta_{ij}(\omega)$
where $\theta_{ij}(\omega)$ is the phase shift, $a_{ij}(\omega)$ is the amplitude attenuation, and $z = \sqrt{-1}$. It can be shown that $\theta_{ij}(\omega)$ is an arctangent function whole value $\to 0$ as $\omega \to 0$; as $\omega \to 0$, $\Phi_{ij} \to a_{ij}(0)$. $a_{ij} \equiv a_{ij}(0)$ is the D.O. response in segment i per unit of steady-state input in segment j." Sobel attributes the development of this result to V. V. Solodovnikov, *Introduction to the Statistical Dynamics of Automatic Control Systems* (Dover Publications, New York, 1960). The discussion in this section is based on Matthew J. Sobel, "Water Quality Improvement Programming Problems," *Water Resources Research*, Fourth Quarter, 1965.

of inputs to the water resource from combinations of the m segments. Define a program vector $\mathbf{x} = (x_j, x_1, ..., x_n)$ in which the values of x refer to the volume of waste discharges in each of the estuary reaches. In a feasible solution, these values represent the waste discharges at the various points which meet the target vector c. This vector generates D.O. changes through the mechanism of the constant coefficients of the linear system already described—$a_{ij} =$ D.O. improvement in segment i per unit of x_j, $i = 1, ..., m$; $j = 1, ..., n$; and, of course, $x_j > 0$.

If we let A be the $m \times n$ matrix of a_{ij} coefficients, then $A\mathbf{x}$ is the vector of D.O. changes corresponding to $\mathbf{x}$.

Now, recalling that c is the vector of target improvements, we have two restrictions on $\mathbf{x}$, namely, $A\mathbf{x} \geqslant c$ and $x \geqslant 0$. The reader will have noticed that mathematically these are sets of linear constraints such as those found in a standard linear program. All we need is an objective function to complete the problem. Let d be a row vector where $d_j =$ unit cost of x_j, $j = 1, ..., n$. Notice that this assumes linear (or piece-wise linear) cost functions.[1] We can now write the problem as a standard linear program,[2]

min $\mathbf{dx}$

s.t. $A\mathbf{x} \geqslant c$

$\mathbf{x} \geqslant 0$

Of course the transfer coefficients (a_{ij}) relate to a steady-state condition and to specified conditions of stream flow and temperature. Thus the model turns out to be totally deterministic, and the variability of conditions is handled in this analysis by assuming extreme conditions usually associated with substantial declines in water quality. This model was used to analyze the costs of alternative treatment strategies for water quality improvement in the estuary.

Similar models can be devised for the other waterborne residuals to be discussed shortly. Usually the transfer coefficient matrices are much simpler to calculate for non-degradable residuals. In fact, such models can be built for a wide variety of residuals which are degraded or diluted in nature. They go under the general title of "diffusion models" and play an important role in the contemporary economic analysis of environmental quality problems. For example, such models are used in the Russell-Spofford procedure discussed in a paper in this volume.[3]

---

[1] Programs with linear constraints and non-linear objective functions can usually be solved if the non-linear function is not too complicated. So this condition would not necessarily have to hold.

[2] The actual programs needed to solve the problem encountered in the Delaware Estuary were somewhat more complicated. The reader interested in the details should consult the paper by Sobel, op. cit.

[3] See C. S. Russell, "Models for the Investigation of Industrial Response to Residuals Management Actions," in this volume.

12 *Background for the economic analysis of environmental pollution*

Non-degradable pollution

BOD serves as a good indicator of pollution where one aspect is concerned—the degradable residuals. But many residuals are non-degradable. These are not attacked by stream biota and undergo no great change once they get into a stream. In other words, the stream does not "purify itself" of them. This category includes inorganic substances—such materials as inorganic colloidal matter, ordinary salt, and the salts of numerous heavy metals. When these substances are present in fairly large quantities, they result in toxicity, unpleasant taste, hardness, and, especially when chlorides are present, in corrosion. These residuals can be a public health problem—usually when they enter into food chains. Two particularly vicious instances of poisoning by heavy metals have stirred the population of Japan. These are mercury poisoning through eating contaminated fish (Minimata disease) and cadmium poisoning through eating contaminated rice (Itai Itai disease). Several hundred people have been affected and more than a hundred have died. At the present time the Canadian government has forbidden the consumption of fish from both Lake Erie and Lake St. Clair because of feared mercury poisoning, and mercury has been discovered in many rivers in the United States.

Persistent pollutants

There is a third group of pollutants, mostly of relatively recent origin, which does not fit comfortably into either the degradable or non-degradable categories. These "persistent" or "exotic" pollutants are best exemplified by the synthetic organic chemicals produced in profusion by modern chemical industry. They enter watercourses as effluents from industrial operations and also as waste residuals from many household and agricultural uses. These substances are termed "persistent" because stream biota cannot effectively attack their complex molecular chains. Some degradation does take place, but usually so slowly that the persistents travel long stream distances, and in groundwater, in virtually unchanged form. Detergents (e.g., ABS), pesticides (e.g., DDT), and phenols (resulting from the distillation of petroleum and coal products) are among the most common of these pollutants. Fortunately, the recent development and successful manufacture of "soft" or degradable detergents has opened the way toward reduction or elimination of the problems associated with them, especially that of foaming. However, another problem associated with dry detergents has not been dealt with. These detergents contain phosphate "fillers" which may aggravate the nutrients problem.

Some of the persistent synthetic organics, like phenols and hard detergents, present primarily aesthetic problems. The phenols, for example, can cause an unpleasant taste in waters, especially when they are treated with chlorine to kill bacteria. Others are under suspicion as possible public health problems and are associated with periodic fish kills in streams. Some of the chemical insecticides are unbelievably toxic. The material endrin, which until recently was commonly used as an insecticide and rodenticide, is toxic to fish in minute concentrations. It has been calculated, for example, that 0.005 of a pound of endrin in three acres of water one foot deep is acutely toxic to fish.

Concentrations of the persistent organic substances have seldom if ever risen to levels in public water supplies high enough to present an *acute* danger to public health. The public health problem centers around the possible *chronic* effects of prolonged exposure to very low concentrations. Similarly, even in concentrations too low to be acutely poisonous to fish, these pollutants may have profound effects on stream ecology, especially through biological magnification in the food chain; higher creatures of other kinds—especially birds of prey—are now being seriously affected because persistent pesticides have entered their food chains. No solid evidence implicates present concentrations of organic chemicals in water supplies as a cause of health problems, but many experts are suspicious of them.

The long-lived radio-nuclides might also be included in the category of persistent pollutants. They are subject to degradation but at very low rates. Atomic power plants may be an increasingly important source of such pollutants. Generation of power by nuclear fission produces fission waste products which are contained in the fuel rods of reactors. In the course of time these fuels are separated by chemical processes to recover plutonium or to prevent waste products from "poisoning" the reactor and reducing its efficiency. Such atomic waste can impose huge external costs unless disposed of safely. A large volume of low-level waste resulting from the day-to-day operation of reactors can for the time being be diluted and discharged into streams, although the permissible standards for such discharge have recently been severely questioned in the United States, both outside and inside the Atomic Energy Commission.

"Hot" waste, containing long-lived substances such as radioactive strontium, cesium, and carbon, is in a different category from any other pollutant. So far, the only practical disposal method for high-level wastes is permanent storage. The "ultimate" solution to this contamination problem may be fusion energy which leaves no residuals except energy. But while some promising developments have occurred recently—especially in the Soviet Union—its development (if even possible) is, at least, decades away.

The range of alternatives

One of the most important features of the waterborne residuals problem, from the point of view of economic analysis, is the wide range of technical options which exist both for reducing the generation and discharge of wastes and for improving the assimilative capacity of watercourses. In industry, in addition to treatment, changes in the quality and type of inputs and outputs, the processes used, and by-product recovery are important ways of reducing residuals discharge. The capability of watercourses to assimilate residuals can often be

14   *Background for the economic analysis of environmental pollution*

Table 1. *Summary of gaseous residuals from energy conversion, 1965 (million tons)*

Energy user	Carbon monoxide (CO)	Hydro- carbons (HC)	Sulfur dioxide (SO$_2$)	Oxides of nitrogen (NO$_x$)	Particu- lates
Utility power	1	neg.	13.6	3.7	2.4
Industry and households	5	neg.	8.4	7.0	7.0
Transportation	66	12	0.4	6.0	0.2
Total	72	12	22.4	16.7	9.6

neg.: Negligible.
Source: U.S. Public Health Service.

increased by using releases from reservoirs to regulate low river flows and by the direct introduction of air or oxygen into them by mechanical means.[1]

III. Airborne Residuals[2]

Types, sources, and management alternatives

There is virtually an infinity of airborne residuals that may be discharged to the atmosphere, but the ones of central interest and most commonly measured are carbon monoxide, hydrocarbons, sulfur dioxide, oxides of nitrogen, and particulates. The quantities and main sources of these in the United States are shown in the following table.

In the United States, by far the greatest tonnage of airborne residuals comes from the transportation sector, and virtually all of this is from internal combustion engines. They are especially important sources of carbon monoxide, hydrocarbons, and oxides of nitrogen. There are a number of ways in which emissions can be reduced from internal combustion engines, and some of these have been implemented. Carbon monoxide and hydrocarbons can be controlled to some extent by various means of achieving more complete combustion of the fuel delivered to the fuel tank. Oxides of nitrogen are much harder to deal with because they are not a result of incomplete combustion but are synthesized from atmospheric gases when combustion takes place under high temperatures and pressures. It is now thought that the best way to control these would be through catalytic afterburners which, however, could add substantially to the cost and complexity of engines. Many people

---

[1] A fairly extensive discussion of technical options can be found in A. V. Kneese and B. T. Bower. *Managing Water Quality: Economics, Technology, Institutions.* The Johns Hopkins Press, Baltimore, 1968.
[2] In preparing the section on air pollution, I have benefitted from an unpublished memorandum by Blair Bower and Derrick Sewell, 1969.

outside the automobile industry believe that large reductions in emissions can be effectively and economically achieved by abandoning the internal combustion engine in favor of other engine types (such as steam and electric) and heavier reliance on mass transit.[1]

Stationary sources (utility power, industry and households) are the main sources of sulfur oxides, particulates, and oxides of nitrogen. Control of emissions from these sources is a large and complex subject, but the main possibilities can be grouped into four categories: (1) fuel preparation (such as removing sulfur-bearing pyrites from coal before combustion), (2) fuel substitutions (such as substituting natural gas and low-sulfur oil and coal for high-sulfur coal), (3) redesigning burners (for example, in oil-burning furnaces two-stage combustion can reduce oxides of nitrogen), and (4) the treatment of stack gases (for example, stack gases can be scrubbed with water or dry removal processes can extract sulfur and particulates).[2]

Of course, all of these control technologies are likely to involve net costs even when they result in usable recovered materials. Furthermore, none of these processes inherently results in a reduction of CO_2. The possible significance of this was discussed in the opening section.

Assimilative capacity of the atmosphere

The capacity of the atmosphere to assimilate discharges of residuals varies with time, space, and the nature of the materials being discharged. From a resources management point of view it is necessary to be able to translate a specified time and location pattern of discharges of gaseous residuals into the resulting time and spatial pattern of ambient (environmental) concentrations, because in most cases there are multiple sources of discharge. With variations in type, quantity, and time pattern of discharge, the problem is compounded in complexity. However, imaginative applications of atmospheric diffusion models analogous to the water diffusion models described earlier have been used to help define "air sheds" for analysis of air quality management strategies.[3]

Another complication in environmental modeling results from the interactions between gaseous residuals and water quality. Such interactions can involve large geographic areas. For example, atmospheric scavenging—particularly washout by precipitation—appears to be becoming an increasing problem. High stacks are often used to reduce the local impact of air pollution, but they result in spreading the residual more thinly over larger areas.

---

[1] R. U. Ayres and R. P. McKenna: *Alternatives to the Internal Combustion Engine: Impacts on Environmental Quality*. The Johns Hopkins Press, Baltimore, 1971.

[2] A good source on the technology of pollution control from stationary sources is Arthur B. Stern (ed)., *Air Pollution*, vols. I, II, III. Academic Press, New York, 1968.

[3] A. A. Teller: The Use of Linear Programming to Estimate the Cost of Some Alternative Air Pollution Abatement Policies", *Proceedings* of the IBM Scientific Computing Symposium on Water and Air Resource Management, held on Oct. 23–25, 1967, at the Thomas J. Watson Research Center, Yorktown, Heights, N.Y.

16   *Background for the economic analysis of environmental pollution*

Thus, high stacks on power plants in England are said to be causing "acid rain" in Scandinavia.

Precipitation is the primary cleansing mechanism for airborne gases and fine particles. Since sulfur dioxide is highly soluble in water, the washout process involves the absorption of the gas by drops of rain (or flakes of snow) as they fall through the gaseous discharge from a stack. Where the washout occurs over a body of water, adverse effects on water quality can occur. For example, atmospheric scavenging is believed to be contributing to deterioration of water quality in the Great Lakes Basin, at least with respect to the presence of trace elements in the lakes.

The areal extent of the atmospheric scavenging phenomenon is illustrated by data from the atmospheric chemical network stations in Europe relating to the acidity and sulfur contents of precipitation and the consequences on soils, surface waters, and biological systems. In 1958, pH values (pH is a measure of acidity—the lower the pH, the higher the acidity) below 5 were found only in limited areas over the Netherlands. In 1966, values below 5 were found in an area that spreads over Central Europe, and pH values in the Netherlands were less than 4.

Impacts of gaseous residuals on receptors
Perhaps of most immediate concern are direct effects on people, ranging in severity from the lethal to the merely annoying. Except for extreme air pollution episodes, fatalities are not, as a rule, traceable individually to the impact of air pollution, primarily because most of the effects are synergistic. Thus, air pollution is an environmental stress which, in conjunction with a number of other environmental stresses, tends to increase the incidence and seriousness of a variety of pulmonary diseases, including lung cancer, emphysema, tuberculosis, pneumonia, bronchitis, asthma, and even the common cold. Clearly, however, acute air pollution episodes have raised death rates. Such occurrences have been observed in Belgium, Britain, Mexico, and the United States, among others. But the more important health effects appear to be associated with persistent exposure to the degraded air which exists in most cities.

The preponderance of evidence suggests that the relationship between such pollutants as SO_2, CO, particulates, and heavy metals and disease is real and large.[1] But one should not underrate the difficulties of establishing such relationships in an absolutely firm manner.

Direct effects on humans have parallels in the animal and plant worlds. Animals of commercial importance (livestock) are not located to any appreciable extent within cities, so effects on them are usually minor. Effects on pets (dogs, cats, and birds) almost certainly exist, although they have not been much documented.

---

[1] L. B. Lave and E. P. Seskin: Air pollution and human health. *Science 169*, no. 3947 (Aug. 1970).

As far as plants are concerned, much the same situation holds. Crops are mostly some distance away from cities, and hazards are likely to be rather special in nature (e.g., fluorides from superphosphate plants, or sulfur oxides from copper smelters). However, there are some districts where truck crops— mostly fruits and vegetables—are grown in close juxtaposition to major cities and substantially affected by air pollution. In suburban gardens and city parks, there are deletrious effects on shrubs, flowers, shade trees, and even on forests in the air sheds of cities.

Damage to property

A third category of effects comprises damage to property. Here again, sulfur oxides and oxidants are perhaps equally potent. Sulfur oxides combine with water to form sulfurous acid (H_2SO_3) and the much more corrosive sulfuric acid (H_2SO_4). These acids will damage virtually any exposed metal surface and will react especially strongly with limestone or marble (calcium carbonate). Thus many historic buildings and objects (like "Cleopatra's Needle" in New York) have suffered extremely rapid deterioration in modern times.

Sulfur oxides will also cause discoloration, hardening and embrittlement of rubber, plastic, paper, and other materials. Oxidants such as ozone will also produce the latter type of effect. Of course, the most widespread and noticeable of all forms of property damage is simple dirt (soot). Airborne dirt affects clothing, furniture, carpets, drapes, exterior paintwork, and automobiles. It leads to extra washing, vacuum cleaning, dry-cleaning, and painting; and, of course, all of these activities do not entirely eliminate the dirt, so that people also must live in darker and dirtier surroundings.

A few comments comparing air and water pollution problems

There are important parallels and contrasts between the effects and possible modes of management of water and air pollution.

1. In the United States and abroad, air pollution is heavily implicated as a factor affecting public health. Water pollution may be more costly in terms of non-human resources, but the current link of water pollution to public health problems on any large scale in advanced countries is a matter of suspicion concerning chronic effects rather than of firm evidence. Much stronger evidence links air pollution to public health problems.

2. As in the case of water pollution, a great many of the external costs imposed by air pollutants would appear to be measurable, but very little systematic measurement has yet been undertaken. The more straightforward effects are, for example, soiling, corrosion, reduction in property values, and agricultural losses.[1]

3. Current technology apparently provides fewer classes of means of dealing

---

[1] Some efforts to provide economically useful estimates of damages are discussed elsewhere in this volume.

with air pollution than with water pollution. In part this is because it is easier for man to control hydrological events than meteorological events. The assimilative capacity of the air mantle cannot be effectively augmented. In part it is because air is not delivered to users in pipes as water frequently is, so that it is only to a limited extent that polluted air is treatable before it is consumed. Therefore, we are in somewhat the same position in regard to polluted air as the fish are with polluted water. We live in it. Furthermore, it is also more difficult and costly to collect gaseous residuals for central treatment. Accordingly, control of air pollution is largely a matter of preventing pollutants from escaping from their source, eliminating the source, or of shifting location of the source or the recipient. Water pollution, on the other hand, is in general subject to a larger array of control measures. Nevertheless, both present intricate problems of devising optimal control systems.

4. To the extent that air sheds are definable, air shed authorities or compacts of districts are conceivable and may be useful administrative devices. In the United States the current federal policy approach points strongly in this direction and in this respect (but not others) is more advanced than the water pollution control programs.

IV. Solid Residuals

Just about every type of object made and used by man can and does eventually become a solid residual. Some of the main categories of importance are organic material, which includes garbage, and industrial solid wastes, such as from the canning industry, for example. Newspapers, wrappings, containers, and a great variety of other objects are found in household, commercial, office, industrial solid wastes. A very important source of solids in the United States is automobiles which will be discussed separately, further on. In the United States, about 5 lb. per day of solid wastes are collected of which about three are household and commercial. Industrial, demolition, and agricultural wastes constitute most of the other. Altogether the United States generates (exclusive of agricultural wastes) each year approximately 3–5 billions tons of solid residuals from household, commercial, animal, industrial, and mining activities and spends about 4–5 billion dollars to handle and dispose of them.[1] In addition, there is a large amount of uncollected solids which litter the countryside.

The disposal of solid wastes can have a number of deleterious effects on society. Littering, dumps, and landfills produce visual disamenities. The disposal of solid wastes can cause adverse effects on air and water quality. Incineration of solid wastes is an obvious source of air pollution in many areas, as are burn-

---

[1] R. Black, A. Muhich, A. Klee, H. Hickman and R. Vaughn: *The National Solid Waste Survey*. U.S. Department of Health, Welfare, and Education, 24 Oct. 1968. Also W. O. Spofford, Jr. Solid waste management: Some economic considerations. *Natural Resources Journal*, vol. 11 (forthcoming: 1971).

ing dumps. Dumps tend to catch fire by spontaneous combustion unless they are relatively carefully controlled. Furthermore, drainage from disposal sites can reduce water quality in watercourses, and the sites may also provide a habitat for rodents and insect vectors. The disposal of collected solid wastes (which excludes much industrial waste, automobiles, and all of agricultural waste) in the United States is roughly in the following proportions: about 90 % goes into landfill operations of one kind or another; another 8 % is incinerated; and a small amount, about 2 %, goes into hog-feeding and miscellaneous categories. Landfill can be an effective and low external cost way of disposing of wastes. However, many landfills are poorly operated and impose external costs via effects on the air, water, and landscapes.

As previously mentioned, automobiles are a special problem. Of the 10–20 million junk cars in existence at any one time in the United States, about 73 % are in the hands of wreckers, in other words, in junk yards; about 6 % in the hands of scrap processers; and about 21 % abandoned and littering the countryside. Recovery could be made much more economical by slight design changes, but presently there are no incentives to do so. Furthermore, unless it is managed to avoid them, the recycle or "secondary materials" industry itself can cause substantial external costs. For example, automobiles are usually burned prior to being prepared for scrap metal, and this can be an important source of local air pollution. Some of the processes involved in recycling automobiles have very high noise levels. While it seems clear that recycle of materials is underused under present circumstances, suffering as it does from tax, labelling, and other disadvantages with respect to new materials, it is also true that it is not a total panacea as one might gather from some of its more ecstatic adherents. For example, the paint on automobiles could not be recycled except at the expense of immense quantities of energy and other resources. Moreover, some materials such as paints, thinners, solvents, cleaners, fuels, etc., cannot perform their functions without being dissipated to the environment.

V. The Flow of Materials[1]

To tie together some of the points made in previous sections, it is useful to view environmental pollution and its control as a materials balance problem for the entire economy. Energy residuals could be treated in an entirely parallel fashion, but I will not discuss this here.[2]

The inputs to the system are fuels, foods, and raw materials which are

---

[1] This section is based heavily on R. U. Ayres and A. V. Kneese: "Production, consumption, and externalities." *American Economic Review 59*, no. 3 (June 1969).

[2] While very little direct exchange between material and energy occurs, it is important to note that there are significant tradeoffs between these residuals streams. For example, an effort to achieve complete recycle with present levels of materials flow would require monstrous amounts of energy to overcome entropy.

20 *Background for the economic analysis of environmental pollution*

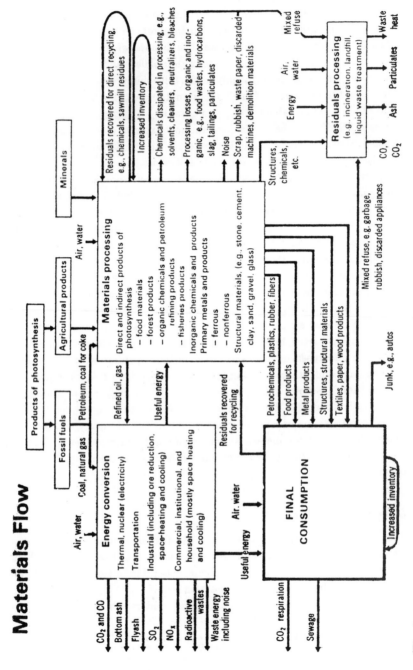

Fig. 1.

partly converted into final goods and partly become residuals. Except for increases in inventory, final goods also ultimately enter the residuals stream. Thus goods which are "consumed" really only render services temporarily. Their material substance remains in existence and must either be reused or discharged to the environment.

In an economy which is closed (no imports or exports) and where there is no net accumulation of stocks (plant, equipment, inventories, consumer durables, or residential buildings), the amount of residuals inserted into the natural environment must be approximately equal to the weight of basic fuels, food, and raw materials entering the processing and production system, plus gases taken from the atmosphere. This result, while obvious upon reflection, leads to the at first rather surprising corollary that residuals disposal involves a greater tonnage of material than basic materials processing, although many of the residuals, being gaseous, require no physical "handling."

Fig. 1 shows a materials flow of the type I have in mind in a little greater detail and relates it to a broad classification of economic sectors. In an open (regional or national) economy, it would be necessary to add flows representing imports and exports. In an economy undergoing stock or capital accumulation, the production of residuals in any given year would be less by that amount than the basic inputs. In the entire U.S. economy, accumulation accounts for about 10–15 % of basic annual inputs, mostly in the form of construction materials, and there is some net importation of raw and partially processed materials amounting to 4 or 5 % of domestic production. Table 2 shows estimates of the weight of raw materials produced in the United States in several recent years, plus net imports of raw and partially processed materials.

Of the active inputs,[1] perhaps three-quarters of the overall weight is eventually discharged to the atmosphere as carbon (combined with atmospheric oxygen in the form of CO or CO_2) and hydrogen (combined with atmospheric oxygen as H_2O) under current conditions. This results from combustion of fossil fuels and from animal respiration. Discharge of carbon dioxide can be considered harmless in the short run, as we have seen, but may produce adverse climatic effects in the long run.

The remaining residuals are either gases (like carbon monoxide, nitrogen dioxide, and sulfur dioxide—all potentially harmful even in the short run), dry solids (like rubbish and scrap), or wet solids (like garbage, sewage, and industrial wastes suspended or dissolved in water). In a sense, the dry solids are an irreducible, limiting form of waste. By the application of appropriate equipment and energy, most undesirable substances can, in principle, be removed from water and air streams[2]—but what is left must be disposed of in solid form, transformed, or reused. Looking at the matter in this way

---

[1] See footnote to Table 2.
[2] Except CO_2, which may be harmful in the long run, as noted.

22 *Background for the economic analysis of environmental pollution*

Table 2. *Weight of Basic Materials Production in the United States, plus Net Imports, 1963–65 (million tons)*

	1963	1964	1965
Agricultural (incl. fishery and wildlife and forest) products			
Food and Fiber			
Crops	.350	358	364
Livestock and diary	23	24	23.5
Fishery	2	2	2
Forestry Products			
Forestry Products (85% dry wt. basis)			
Sawlogs	107	116	120
Pulpwood	53	55	56
Other	41	41	42
Total	576	596	607.5
Mineral Fuels			
Total	1 337	1 399	1 448
Other Minerals			
Iron ore	204	237	245
Other metal ores	161	171	191
Other non-metals	125	133	149
Total	490	541	585
Grand Total[a]	2 403	2 536	2 640.5

[a] Excluding construction materials, stone, sand, gravel, and other minerals used for structural purposes, ballast, fillers, insulation, etc. Gangue and mine tailings are also excluded from this total. These materials account for enormous tonnages but undergo essentially no chemical change. Hence, their use is more or less tantamount to physically moving them from one location to another. If these were to be included, there is no logical reason to exclude material shifted in highway cut-and-fill operations, harbor dredging, landfill plowing, and even silt moved by rivers. Since a line must be drawn somewhere, we chose to draw it as indicated above.

Source: R. U. Ayres and A. V. Kneese: Environmental Pollution. In *Federal Programs for the Development of Human Resources*, a Compendium of Papers submitted to the Subcommittee on Economic Progress of the Joint Economic Committee, United States Congress, Vol. 2. Government Printing Office, Washington, 1968. Some revisions have been made in the original table.

clearly reveals a primary interdependence among the various residuals streams which casts into doubt the traditional classification, which I have used earlier in this article, of air, water, and land pollution as individual categories for purposes of planning and control policy.

Residuals do not necessarily have to be discharged to the environment. In many instances, it is possible to recycle them back into the productive system. The materials balance view underlines the fact that the throughput of new materials necessary to maintain a given level of production and consumption decreases as the technical efficiency of energy conversion and materials utilization and reutilization increases. Similarly, other things being equal, the longer cars, buildings, machinery, and other durables remain in service, the fewer new materials are required to compensate for loss, wear, and obsolescence—although the use of old or worn machinery (e.g., automobiles) tends to increase other residuals problems. Technically efficient combustion of (desulfurized) fossil fuels would leave only water, ash, and carbon dioxide as residuals, while nuclear energy conversion need leave only negligible quantities of material residuals (although thermal pollution and radiation hazards cannot be dismissed by any means).

Given the population, industrial production, and transport service in an economy (a regional rather than a national economy would normally be the relevant unit), it is possible to visualize combinations of social policy which could lead to quite different relative burdens placed on the various residuals-receiving environmental media; or, given the possibilities for recycle and less residual-generating production processes, the overall burden to be placed upon the environment as a whole. To take one extreme, a region which went in heavily for electric space heating, electric transportation systems, and wet-scrubbing of stack gases (from steam plants and industries), which ground up its garbage and delivered it to the sewers and then discharged the raw sewage to watercourses, would protect its air resources to an exceptional degree. But this would come at the sacrifice of placing a heavy residuals load upon water resources. On the other hand, a region which treated municipal and industrial waste water streams to a high level and relied heavily on the incineration of sludges and solid wastes would protect its water and land resources at the expense of discharging waste residuals predominantly to the air. Finally, a region which practiced high-level recovery and recycle of waste materials and fostered low residual production processes to a far-reaching extent in each of the economic sectors might discharge very little residual waste to any of the environmental media.

Further complexities are added by the fact that sometimes it is, as we have seen, possible to modify an environmental medium through investment in control facilities so as to improve its assimilative capacity. The easiest to see but far from only example is with respect to watercourses where reservoir storage can be used to augment low river flows that ordinarily are associated with critical pollution (high external cost situations). Thus, internalization of external costs associated with particular discharges, by means of taxes or other restrictions, even if done perfectly, cannot guarantee Pareto optimality. Collective investments involving public good aspects must enter into an optimal solution.

To recapitulate the main points these considerations raise for economic analysis briefly: (1) Technological external diseconomies are not freakish anomalies in the processes of production and consumption but an inherent and normal part of them. Residuals generation is inherent in virtually all production and consumption activities, and there are only two ways of handling them—recycle, or discharge into environmental media without or with modifications. (2) These external diseconomies are apt to be quantitatively negligible

24   *Background for the economic analysis of environmental pollution*

in a low-population or economically undeveloped setting, but they become progressively (nonlinearly) more important as the population rises and the level of output increases (i.e., as the natural reservoirs providing dilution and other assimilative properties become exhausted). (3) They cannot be properly dealt with by considering environmental media, such as air and water, in isolation. (4) Isolated and ad hoc taxes and other restrictions are not sufficient for their optimum control, although taxes and restrictions are essential elements in a more systematic and coherent program of environmental quality management. (5) Public investment programs, particularly including transportation systems, sewage disposal systems, and river flow regulation, are intimately related to the amounts and effects of residuals and must be planned in light of them. (6) There is a wide range of (technological) alternatives for coping with the environmental pollution problems stemming from liquid, gaseous, and solid residuals. Economic tools need to be selected and developed which can be used to approximate optimal combinations of these alternatives.

Production, Consumption, and Externalities

By ROBERT U. AYRES AND ALLEN V. KNEESE[*]

"For all that, welfare economics can no more reach conclusions applicable to the real world without some knowledge of the real world than can positive economics" [21].

Despite tremendous public and governmental concern with problems such as environmental pollution, there has been a tendency in the economics literature to view externalities as exceptional cases. They may distort the allocation of resources but can be dealt with adequately through simple *ad hoc* arrangements. To quote Pigou:

When it was urged above, that in certain industries a wrong amount of resources is being invested because the value of the marginal social net product there differs from the value of the marginal private net product, it was tacitly assumed that in the main body of industries these two values are equal [22][1].

And Scitovsky, after having described his cases two and four which deal with technological externalities affecting consumers and producers respectively, says:

The second case seems exceptional, because most instances of it can be and usually are eliminated by zoning ordi-

nances and industrial regulations concerned with public health and safety. The fourth case seems unimportant, simply because examples of it seem to be few and exceptional [25].

We believe that at least one class of externalities—those associated with the disposal of residuals resulting from the consumption and production process—must be viewed quite differently.[2] They are a normal, indeed, inevitable part of these processes. Their economic significance tends to increase as economic development proceeds, and the ability of the ambient environment to receive and assimilate them is an important natural resource of increasing value.[3] We will argue below that

[*] The authors are respectively visiting scholar and director, Quality of the Environment Program, Resources for the Future, Inc. We are indebted to our colleagues Blair Bower, Orris Herfindahl, Charles Howe, John Krutilla, and Robert Steinberg for comments on an earlier draft. We have also benefited from comments by James Buchanan, Paul Davidson, Robert Dorfman, Otto Eckstein, Myrick Freeman, Mason Gaffney, Lester Lave, Herbert Mohring, and Gordon Tullock.

[1] Even Baumol who saw externalities as a rather pervasive feature of the economy tends to discuss external diseconomies like "smoke nuisance" entirely in terms of particular examples [3]. A perspective more like that of the present paper is found in Kapp [16].

[2] We by no means wish to imply that this is the only important class of externalities associated with production and consumption. Also, we do not wish to imply that there has been a lack of theoretical attention to the externalities problem. In fact, the past few years have seen the publication of several excellent articles which have gone far toward systematizing definitions and illuminating certain policy issues. Of special note are Coase [9], Davis and Whinston [12], Buchanan and Stubblebine [6], and Turvey [27]. However, all these contributions deal with externality as a comparatively minor aberration from Pareto optimality in competitive markets and focus upon externalities between two parties. Mishan, after a careful review of the literature, has commented on this as follows: "The form in which external effects have been presented in the literature is that of partial equilibrium analysis; a situation in which a single industry produces an equilibrium output, usually under conditions of perfect competition, some form of intervention being required in order to induce the industry to produce an "ideal" or "optimal" output. If the point is not made explicitly, it is tacitly understood that unless the rest of the economy remains organized in conformity with optimum conditions, one runs smack into Second Best problems" [21].

[3] That external diseconomies are integrally related to economic development and increasing congestion has been noted in passing in the literature. Mishan has commented: "The attention given to external effects in

282

the common failure to recognize these facts may result from viewing the production and consumption processes in a manner that is somewhat at variance with the fundamental law of conservation of mass.

Modern welfare economics concludes that if (1) preference orderings of consumers and production functions of producers are independent and their shapes appropriately constrained, (2) consumers maximize utility subject to given income and price parameters, and (3) producers maximize profits subject to the price parameters; a set of prices exists such that no individual can be made better off without making some other individual worse off. For a given distribution of income this is an efficient state. Given certain further assumptions concerning the structure of markets, this "Pareto optimum" can be achieved via a pricing mechanism and voluntary decentralized exchange.

If waste assimilative capacity of the environment is scarce, the decentralized voluntary exchange process cannot be free of uncompensated technological external diseconomies unless (1) all inputs are fully converted into outputs, with no unwanted material residuals along the way,[4] and all final outputs are utterly destroyed in the process of consumption, or (2) property rights are so arranged that all relevant environmental attributes are in private ownership and these rights are exchanged in competitive markets. Neither of these conditions can be expected to hold in an actual economy and they do not.

Nature does not permit the destruction of matter except by annihilation with anti-matter, and the means of disposal of unwanted residuals which maximizes the internal return of decentralized decision units is by discharge to the environment, principally, watercourses and the atmosphere. Water and air are traditionally examples of free goods in economics. But in reality, in developed economies they are common property resources of great and increasing value presenting society with important and difficult allocation problems which exchange in private markets cannot resolve. These problems loom larger as increased population and industrial production put more pressure on the environment's ability to dilute and chemically degrade waste products. Only the crudest estimates of present external costs associated with residuals discharge exist but it would not be surprising if these costs were in the tens of billions of dollars annually.[5] Moreover, as we shall emphasize again, technological means for processing or purifying one or another type of waste discharge do not destroy the residuals but only alter their form. Thus, given the level, patterns, and technology of production and consumption, recycle of materials into productive uses or discharge into an alternative medium are the only general options for protecting a particular environmental medium such as water. Residual problems must be seen in a broad regional or economy-wide context rather

---

the recent literature is, I think, fully justified by the unfortunate, albeit inescapable, fact that as societies grow in material wealth, the incidence of these effects grows rapidly . . . " [21]; and Buchanan and Tullock have stated that as economic development proceeds, "congestion" tends to replace "co-operation" as the underlying motive force behind collective action, i.e., controlling external diseconomies tends to become more important than cooperation to realize external economies [7].

[4] Or any residuals which occur must be stored on the producer's premises.

[5] It is interesting to compare this with estimates of the cost of another well known misallocation of resources that has occupied a central place in economic theory and research. In 1954, Harberger published an estimate of the welfare cost of monopoly which indicated that it amounted to about .07 percent of GNP [15]. In a later study, Schwartzman calculated the allocative cost at only .01 percent of GNP [24]. Leibenstein generalized studies such as these to the statement that " . . . in a great many instances the amount to be gained by increasing allocative efficiency is trivial . . . " [19]. But Leibenstein did not consider the allocative costs associated with environmental pollution.

than as separate and isolated problems of disposal of gas, liquid, and solid wastes.

Frank Knight perhaps provides a key to why these elementary facts have played so small a role in economic theorizing and empirical research.

> The next heading to be mentioned ties up with the question of dimensions from another angle, and relates to the second main error mentioned earlier as connected with taking food and eating as the type of economic activity. The basic economic magnitude (value or utility) is service, not good. It is inherently a stream or flow in time . . . [18].[6]

Almost all of standard economic theory is in reality concerned with services. Material objects are merely the vehicles which carry some of these services, and they are exchanged because of consumer preferences for the services associated with their use or because they can help to add value in the manufacturing process. Yet we persist in referring to the "final consumption" of goods as though material objects such as fuels, materials, and finished goods somehow disappeared into the void—a practice which was comparatively harmless so long as air and water were almost literally free goods.[7] Of course, residuals from both the production and consumption processes remain and they usually render disservices (like killing fish, increasing the difficulty of water treatment, reducing public health, soiling and deteriorating buildings, etc.) rather than services. Control efforts are aimed at eliminating or reducing those disservices which flow to consumers and pro-

ducers whether they want them or not and which, except in unusual cases, they cannot control by engaging in individual exchanges.[8]

I. *The Flow of Materials*

To elaborate on these points, we find it useful initially to view environmental pollution and its control as a materials balance problem for the entire economy.[9] The inputs to the system are fuels, foods, and raw materials which are partly converted into final goods and partly become waste residuals. Except for increases in inventory, final goods also ultimately enter the waste stream. Thus goods which are "consumed" really only render certain services. Their material substance remains in existence and must either be reused or discharged to the ambient environment.

In an economy which is closed (no imports or exports) and where there is no net accumulation of stocks (plant, equipment, inventories, consumer durables, or residential buildings), the amount of residuals inserted into the natural environment must be approximately equal to the weight of basic fuels, food, and raw materials entering the processing and production system, plus oxygen taken from the atmosphere.[10] This result, while obvious

---

[6] The point was also clearly made by Fisher: "The only true method, in our view, is to regard uniformly as income the *service* of a dwelling to its owner (shelter or money rental), the *service* of a piano (music), and the *service* of food (nourishment) . . . " (emphasis in original) [14].

[7] We are tempted to suggest that the word consumption be dropped entirely from the economist's vocabulary as being basically deceptive. It is difficult to think of a suitable substitute, however. At least, the word consumption should not be used in connection with goods, but only with regard to services or flows of "utility."

[8] There is a substantial literature dealing with the question of under what conditions individual exchanges can optimally control technological external diseconomies. A discussion of this literature, as it relates to waterborne residuals, is found in Kneese and Bower [17].

[9] As far as we know, the idea of applying materials balance concepts to waste disposal problems was first expressed by Smith [26]. We also benefitted from an unpublished paper by Joseph Headley in which a pollution "matrix" is suggested. We have also found references by Boulding to a "spaceship economy" suggestive [4]. One of the authors has previously used a similar approach in ecological studies of nutrient interchange among plants and animals; see [1].

[10] To simplify our language, we will not repeat this essential qualification at each opportunity, but assume it applies throughout the following discussion. In addition, we must include residuals such as NO and NO_2 arising from reactions between components of the air itself but occurring as combustion by-products.

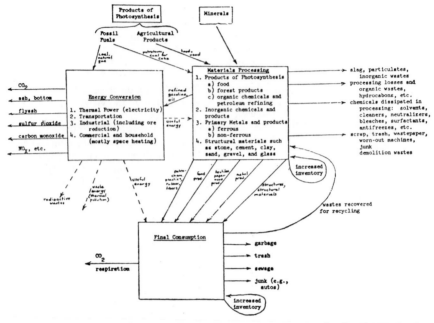

FIGURE 1.—MATERIALS FLOW

upon reflection, leads to the, at first rather surprising, corollary that residuals disposal involves a greater tonnage of materials than basic materials processing, although many of the residuals, being gaseous, require no physical "handling."

Figure 1 shows a materials flow of the type we have in mind in greater detail and relates it to a broad classification of economic sectors for convenience in our later discussion, and for general consistency with the Standard Industrial Classification. In an open (regional or national) economy, it would be necessary to add flows representing imports and exports. In an economy undergoing stock or capital accumulation, the production of residuals in any given year would be less by that amount than the basic inputs. In the entire U.S. economy, accumulation accounts for about 10–15 percent of basic annual inputs, mostly in the form of

construction materials, and there is some net importation of raw and partially processed materials amounting to 4 or 5 percent of domestic production. Table 1 shows estimates of the weight of raw materials produced in the United States in several recent years, plus net imports of raw and partially processed materials.

Of the active inputs,[11] perhaps three-quarters of the overall weight is eventually discharged to the atmosphere as carbon (combined with atmospheric oxygen in the form of CO or CO_2) and hydrogen (combined with atmospheric oxygen as H_2O) under current conditions. This results from combustion of fossil fuels and from animal respiration. Discharge of carbon dioxide can be considered harmless in the short run. There are large "sinks" (in the form of vegetation and large water bodies,

[11] See footnote to Table 1.

TABLE 1—WEIGHT OF BASIC MATERIALS PRODUCTION IN THE UNITED STATES PLUS NET IMPORTS, 1963 (10^6 tons)

	1963	1964	1965
Agricultural (incl. fishery and wildlife and forest) products			
Food ⎰ Crops (excl. livestock feed)	125	128	130
Food ⎱ Livestock	100	103	102
Other products	5	6	6
Fishery	3	3	3
Forestry products (85 per cent dry wt. basis)			
Sawlogs	53	55	56
Pulpwood	107	116	120
Other	41	41	42
Total	434	452	459
Mineral fuels	1,337	1,399	1,448
Other minerals			
Iron ore	204	237	245
Other metal ores	161	171	191
Other nonmetals	125	133	149
Total	490	541	585
Grand total*	2,261	2,392	2,492

* Excluding construction materials, stone, sand, gravel, and other minerals used for structural purposes, ballast, fillers, insulation, etc. Gangue and mine tailings are also excluded from this total. These materials account for enormous tonnages but undergo essentially no chemical change. Hence, their use is more or less tantamount to physically moving them from one location to another. If this were to be included, there is no logical reason to exclude material shifted in highway cut and fill operations, harbor dredging, land-fill, plowing, and even silt moved by rivers. Since a line must be drawn somewhere, we chose to draw it as indicated above.

Source: R. U. Ayres and A. V. Kneese [2, p. 630].

mainly the oceans) which reabsorb this gas, although there is evidence of net accumulation of CO_2 in the atmosphere. Some experts believe that the latter is likely to show a large relative increase, as much as 50 per cent by the end of the century, possibly giving rise to significant —and probably, on balance, adverse— weather changes.[12] Thus continued com-

[11] See [30]. There is strong evidence that discharge of residuals has already affected the climate of individual cities; see Lowry [20].

bustion of fossil fuels at a high rate could produce externalities affecting the entire world. The effects associated with most residuals will normally be more confined, however, usually limited to regional air and water sheds.

The remaining residuals are either gases (like carbon monoxide, nitrogen dioxide, and sulfur dioxide—all potentially harmful even in the short run), dry solids (like rubbish and scrap), or wet solids (like garbage, sewage, and industrial wastes suspended or dissolved in water). In a sense, the dry solids are an irreducible, limiting form of waste. By the application of appropriate equipment and energy, most undesirable substances can, in principle, be removed from water and air streams[13]— but what is left must be disposed of in solid form, transformed, or reused. Looking at the matter in this way clearly reveals a primary interdependence between the various waste streams which casts into doubt the traditional classification of air, water, and land pollution as individual categories for purposes of planning and control policy.

Residuals do not necessarily have to be discharged to the environment. In many instances, it is possible to recycle them back into the productive system. The materials balance view underlines the fact that the throughput of new materials necessary to maintain a given level of production and consumption decreases as the technical efficiency of energy conversion and materials utilization increases. Similarly, other things being equal, the longer that cars, buildings, machinery, and other durables remain in service, the fewer new materials are required to compensate for loss, wear, and obsolescence— although the use of old or worn machinery (e.g., automobiles) tends to increase other residuals problems. Technically efficient combustion of (desulfurized) fossil fuels

[13] Except CO_2, which may be harmful in the long run, as noted.

would leave only water, ash, and carbon dioxide as residuals, while nuclear energy conversion need leave only negligible quantities of material residuals (although thermal pollution and radiation hazards cannot be dismissed by any means).

Given the population, industrial production, and transport service in an economy (a regional rather than a national economy would normally be the relevant unit), it is possible to visualize combinations of social policy which could lead to quite different relative burdens placed on the various residuals-receiving environmental media; or, given the possibilities for recycle and less residual-generating production processes, the overall burden to be placed upon the environment as a whole. To take one extreme, a region which went in heavily for electric space heating and wet scrubbing of stack gases (from steam plants and industries), which ground up its garbage and delivered it to the sewers and then discharged the raw sewage to watercourses, would protect its air resources to an exceptional degree. But this would come at the sacrifice of placing a heavy residuals load upon water resources. On the other hand, a region which treated municipal and industrial waste water streams to a high level and relied heavily on the incineration of sludges and solid wastes would protect its water and land resources at the expense of discharging waste residuals predominantly to the air. Finally, a region which practiced high level recovery and recycle of waste materials and fostered low residual production processes to a far reaching extent in each of the economic sectors might discharge very little residual waste to any of the environmental media.

Further complexities are added by the fact that sometimes it is possible to modify an environmental medium through investment in control facilities so as to improve its assimilative capacity. The clearest, but far from only, example is with respect to

watercourses where reservoir storage can be used to augment low river flows that ordinarily are associated with critical pollution (high external cost situations).[14] Thus internalization of external costs associated with particular discharges, by means of taxes or other restrictions, even if done perfectly, cannot guarantee Pareto optimality. Investments involving public good aspects must enter into an optimal solution.[15]

To recapitulate our main points briefly: (1) Technological external diseconomies are not freakish anomalies in the processes of production and consumption but an inherent and normal part of them. (2) These external diseconomies are quantitatively negligible in a low-population or economically undeveloped setting, but they become progressively (nonlinearly) more important as the population rises and the level of output increases (i.e., as the natural reservoirs of dilution and assimilative capacity become exhausted).[16] (3) They cannot be properly dealt with by considering environmental media such as air and water in isolation. (4) Isolated and *ad hoc* taxes and other restrictions are not sufficient for their optimum control, although they are essential elements in a more systematic and coherent program of environmental quality management. (5) Public investment programs, particularly including transportation systems, sewage disposal, and river flow regulation, are intimately related to the amounts and

[14] Careful empirical work has shown that this technique can fit efficiently into water quality management systems. See Davis [11].

[15] A discussion of the theory of such public investments with respect to water quality management is found in Boyd [5].

[16] Externalities associated with residuals discharge may appear only at certain threshold values which are relevant only at some stage of economic development and industrial and population concentrations. This may account for their general treatment as "exceptional" cases in the economics literature. These threshold values truly were exceptional cases for less developed economies.

THE AMERICAN ECONOMIC REVIEW

effects of residuals and must be planned in light of them.

It is important to develop not only improved measures of the external costs resulting from differing concentrations and duration of residuals in the environment but more systematic methods for forecasting emissions of external-cost-producing residuals, technical and economic trade-offs between them, and the effects of recycle on environmental quality.

In the hope of contributing to this effort and of revealing more clearly the types of information which would be needed to implement such a program, we set forth a more formal model of the materials balance approach in the following sections and relate it to some conventional economic models of production and consumption. The main objective is to make some progress toward defining a system in which flows of services and materials are simultaneously accounted for and related to welfare.

II. *Basic Model*

The take off point for our discussion is the Walras-Cassel general equilibrium model,[17] extended to include intermediate consumption, which involve the following quantities:

resources and services
$$r_1, \cdots \cdots \cdots, r_M$$

products or commodities
$$X_1, \cdots \cdots \cdots \cdots, X_N$$

resource prices
$$v_1, \cdots \cdots \cdots \cdots, v_M$$

product or commodity prices
$$p_1, \cdots \cdots \cdots \cdots, p_N$$

final demands
$$Y_1, \cdots \cdots \cdots \cdots, Y_N$$

[17] The original references are Walras [28] and Cassel [8]. Our own treatment is largely based on Dorfman *et al.* [13].

The M basic resources are allocated among the N sectors as follows:

$$r_1 = a_{11}X_1 + a_{12}X_2 + \cdots + a_{1N}X_N$$
$$r_2 = a_{21}X_1 + a_{22}X_2 + \cdots + a_{2N}X_N$$
$$\vdots$$
$$r_M = a_{M1}X_1 + a_{M2}X_2 + \cdots + a_{MN}X_N$$

(1a) or

$$(1a) \quad r_j = \sum_{k=1}^{N} a_{jk}X_k \qquad j = 1, \cdots . M$$

In (1a) we have implicitly assumed that there is no possibility of factor or process substitution and no joint production. These conditions will be discussed later. In matrix notation we can write:

$$(1b) \quad [r_{j1}]_{M,1} = [a_{jk}]_{M,N} \cdot [X_{k1}]_{N,1}$$

where $[a]$ is an $M \times N$ matrix.

A similar set of equations describes the relations between commodity production and final demand:

$$(2a) \quad X_k = \sum_{l=1}^{N} A_{kl}Y_l \qquad k = 1, \cdots, N$$

$$(2b) \quad [X_{k1}]_{N,1} = [A_{kl}]_{N,N} \cdot [Y_{l1}]_{N,1}$$

and the matrix $[A]$ is given by

$$(3) \qquad [A] = [I - C]^{-1}$$

where $[I]$ is the unit diagonal matrix and the elements C_{ij} of the matrix $[C]$ are essentially the well known Leontief input coefficients. In principle these are functions of the existing technology and, therefore, are fixed for any given situation.

By combining (1) and (2), we obtain a set of equations relating resource inputs directly to final demand, viz.,

$$r_j = \sum_{k=1}^{N} a_{jk} \sum_{l=1}^{N} A_{kl}Y_l = \sum_{k,l=1}^{N} a_{jk}A_{kl}Y_l$$
$$(4a)$$
$$= \sum_{l=1}^{N} b_{jl}Y_l \qquad j = 1, \cdots, M$$

or, of course, in matrix notation (4b).

(4b)
$$[r_{j1}]_{M,1} = [a_{jk}]_{M,N} \cdot [A_{kl}]_{N,N} \cdot [Y_{l1}]_{N,1}$$
$$= [b_{jl}]_{M,N} \cdot [Y_{l1}]_{N,1}$$

We can also impute the prices of N intermediate goods and commodities to the prices of the M basic resources, as follows:

(5a) $p_k = \sum_{j=1}^{M} v_j b_{jk}$ $k = 1, \cdots, N$

(5b) $[p_{1k}]_{1,N} = [v_{1j}]_{1,M} \cdot [b_{jk}]_{M,N}$

To complete the system, it may be supposed that demand and supply relationships are given, a priori, by Pareto-type preference functions:

(6) Demand: $Y_k = F_k(p_1, \cdots, p_N)$
                               $k = 1, \cdots, N$

(7) Supply: $r_k = G_k(v_1, \cdots. v_M)$
                               $k = 1, \cdots, M$

where, of course, the p_j are functions of the v_j as in (5b).

In order to interpret the X's as physical production, it is necessary for the sake of consistency to arrange that outputs and inputs always balance, which implies that the C_{ij} must comprise *all* materials exchanges including residuals. To complete the system so that there is no net gain or loss of physical substances, it is also convenient to introduce two additional sectors, viz., an "environmental" sector whose (physical) output is X_0 and a "final consumption" sector whose output is denoted X_f. The system is then easily balanced by explicitly including flows both to and from these sectors.

To implement this further modification of the Walras-Cassel model, it is convenient to subdivide and relabel the resource category into tangible raw materials $\{r^m\}$ and services $\{r^s\}$:

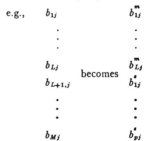

raw materials (units)

becomes

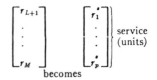

service (units)

becomes

where, of course,

(8) $L + P = M$

It is understood that services, while not counted in tons, can be measured in meaningful units, such as man-days, with well defined prices. Thus, we similarly relabel the price variables as follows:

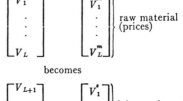

raw material (prices)

becomes

labor and service (prices)

The coefficients $\{a_{ij}\}$, $\{b_{ij}\}$ are similarly partitioned into two groups,

e.g., b_{1j} b_{1j}^m

           b_{Lj} becomes b_{Lj}^m
           $b_{L+1,j}$ b_{1j}^s

           b_{Mj} b_{pj}^s

These notational changes have no effect whatever on the substance of the model, although the equations become somewhat more cumbersome. The partitioned matrix notation simplifies the restatement of the basic equations. Thus (1b) becomes (9), while (5b) becomes (10).

$$
(9) \qquad M \left\{ \begin{bmatrix} \vdots \\ r \\ \vdots \end{bmatrix} \equiv \begin{bmatrix} & & \\ r^m & \} L \\ \cdots \\ r^s & \} P \end{bmatrix} = M \left(\overbrace{\begin{bmatrix} \} L & b^m \\ \cdots & Y \\ \} P & b^s \end{bmatrix}}^{N} \right\} N \right.
$$

$$
(10) \qquad [p_1, \cdots, p_N] = [v^m \!:\! v^s] \underbrace{\begin{bmatrix} b^m \\ \cdots \\ L \quad P \quad b^s \end{bmatrix}}_{M} M
$$

$$
= [\cdots v^m \cdots] \begin{bmatrix} \vdots & b^m & \vdots \\ \vdots & \cdots \cdots & \end{bmatrix} + [\cdots v^s \cdots] \begin{bmatrix} \vdots & b^s & \vdots \\ \vdots & \cdots \cdots & \end{bmatrix}
$$

The equivalent of (5a) is:

$$
(11) \qquad p_k = \underbrace{\sum_{j=1}^{L} b_{jk}^m v_j^m}_{\substack{\text{prices imputed} \\ \text{to cost of raw} \\ \text{materials}}} + \underbrace{\sum_{j=1}^{P} b_{jk}^s v_j^s}_{\substack{\text{prices imputed} \\ \text{to cost of} \\ \text{services}}}
$$

where $k = 1, \cdots, N$

We wish to focus attention explicitly on the flow of materials through the economy. By definition of the Leontief input coefficients (now related to materials flow), we have:

$C_{kj} X_j$ (physical) quantity transferred

from k to j

$C_{jk} X_k$ quantity transferred from j to k

Hence, material flows *from* the environment to all other sectors are given by:

$$
(12) \qquad \begin{aligned} \sum_{k=1}^{N} C_{0k} X_k &= \sum_{j=1}^{L} r_j^m = \sum_{j=1}^{L} \sum_{k=1}^{N} a_{jk}^m X_k \\ &= \sum_{j=1}^{L} \sum_{k=1}^{N} b_{jk}^m Y_k \end{aligned}
$$

using equation (1), as modified.[18] Obvi-

ously, comparing the first and third terms,

$$
(13) \qquad \underbrace{C_{0k}}_{\substack{\text{total material} \\ \text{flow (0 to } k)}} = \underbrace{\sum_{j=1}^{L} a_{jk}^m}_{\substack{\text{all raw materials} \\ (0 \text{ to } k)}}
$$

Flows into and out of the environmental sector must be in balance:

$$
(14) \qquad \underbrace{\sum_{k=1}^{N} C_{0k} X_k}_{\substack{\text{sum of all raw} \\ \text{material flows}}} = \underbrace{\sum_{k=1}^{N} C_{k0} X_0 + C_{f0} X_0}_{\substack{\text{sum of all return} \\ \text{(waste) flows}}}
$$

Material flows to and from the final sector must also balance:

$$
\begin{aligned} & \underbrace{\sum_{k=1}^{N} C_{kf} X_f}_{\substack{\text{sum of all} \\ \text{final goods}}} \\ (15) \quad & = \underbrace{\sum_{k=1}^{N} C_{fk} X_k}_{\substack{\text{sum of all} \\ \text{materials} \\ \text{recycled}}} + \underbrace{C_{f0} X_0}_{\substack{\text{waste residuals} \\ \text{(plus accumulation}[19])}} \end{aligned}
$$

[18] Ignoring, for convenience, any materials flow from the environment *directly* to the final consumption sector.

[19] For convenience, we can treat accumulation in the final sector as a return flow to the environment. In truth, structures actually *become* part of our environment, although certain disposal costs may be deferred.

Natural Resource Economics

Of course, by definition, X_f is the sum of the final demands:

$$(16) \qquad X_f = \sum_{j=1}^{N} Y_j$$

Substituting (16) into the left side of (15) and (2a) into the right side of (15), we obtain an expression for the waste flow in terms of final demands:

$$(17) \quad C_{f0}X_0 = \sum_{j=1}^{N} \sum_{k=1}^{N} (C_{jf} - C_{fj}A_{jk}) Y_k$$

The treatment could be simplified slightly if we assumed that there is no recycling per se. Thus, in the context of the model, we could suppose that all residuals return to the environmental sector,[20] where some of them (e.g., waste paper) become "raw materials." They would then be indistinguishable from new raw materials, however, and price differentials between the two would be washed out. In principle, this is an important distinction to retain.

III. *Inclusion of Externalities*

The physical flow of materials between various intermediate (production) sectors and the final (consumption) sector tends to be accompanied by, and correlated with, a (reverse) flow of dollars.[21] However, the physical flow of materials from and back to the environment is only partly reflected by actual dollar flows, namely, land rents and payments for raw materials. There are three classes of physical exchange for which there exist no counterpart economic transactions. These are: (1) private use for production inputs of "common property" resources, notably air, streams, lakes, and the ocean; (2) private use of the assimila-

tive capacity of the environment to "dispose of" or dilute wastes and residuals; (3) inadvertent or unwanted material inputs to productive processes—diluents and pollutants.

All these goods (or "bads") are physically transferred at zero price, not because they are not scarce relative to demand— they often are in developed economies— or because they confer no service or disservice on the user—since they demonstrably do so—but because there exist no social institutions that permit the resources in question to be "owned," and exchanged in the market.

The allocation of resources corresponding to a Pareto optimum cannot be attained without subjecting the above-mentioned nonmarket and involuntary exchanges to the moderation of a market or a surrogate thereof. In principle, the influence of a market might be simulated, to a first approximation, by introducing a set of shadow (or virtual) prices.[22] These may well be zero, where supply truly exceeds demand, or negative (i.e., costs) in some instances; they will be positive in others. The exchanges are, of course, real.

The Walras-Cassel model can be generalized to handle these effects in the following way:

1. One can introduce a set of R common-property resources or services of raw materials $\{r_1^{cp}, \cdots, r_R^{cp}\}$ as a subset of the set $\{r_j\}$; these will have corresponding virtual prices $\{v_j^{cp}\}$, which would constitute an "income" from the environment. Such resources include the atmosphere; streams, lakes, and oceans; landscape; wildlife and biological diversity; and the indispensable assimilative capacity of the environment (its ability to accept and neutralize or recycle residuals).[23]

---

[20] In calculating actual quantities, we would (by convention) ignore the weight of oxygen taken free from the atmosphere in combustion and return as CO_2. However, such inputs will be treated explicitly later.

[21] To be precise, the dollar flow governs and is governed by a combined flow of materials and services (value added).

[22] A similar concept exists in mechanics where the forces producing "reaction" (to balance action and reaction) are commonly described as "virtual forces."

[23] Economists have previously suggested generalization of the Walras-Cassel model to take account of public goods. One of the earliest appears to be Schles-

2. One can introduce a set of S environmental *disservices* imposed on consumers of material resources, by forcing them to accept unwanted inputs $\{r_1^u, \cdots, r_s^u\}$ (pollutants, contaminants, etc.); these disservices would have negative value, giving rise to *negative* virtual prices $\{u_j\}$.[24]

The matrix coefficients $\{a_{ij}\}$ and $\{b_{ij}\}$ can be further partitioned to take account of this additional refinement, and equations analogous to (9), (10), and (11) can be generalized in the obvious way. Equation (6) carries over unchanged, but (7) must be appropriately generalized to take account of the altered situation. Actually, (7) breaks up into several groups of equations:

$$(18) \qquad r_k^m = G_k^m(p_1, \cdots, p_N)$$
$$k = 1, \cdots, L$$

$$(19) \qquad r_k^s = G_k^s(p_1, \cdots, p_N)$$
$$k = 1, \cdots, P$$

However, as we have noted at the outset, the supplies of common-property resources and environmental services or disservices are *not* regulated directly by market prices of other goods and services. In the case of common-property resources, the supplies are simply constants fixed by nature or otherwise determined by accident or noneconomic factors.

The total value of these services performed by the environment cannot be

inger [23]. We are indebted to Otto Eckstein for calling our attention to this key reference.

[24] The notion of introducing the possibility of negative prices in general equilibrium theory has apparently been discussed before, although we are not aware of any systematic development of the idea in the published literature. In this connection, it is worth pointing out the underlying similarity of negative prices and effluent taxes—which have been, and still are being considered as an attractive alternative to subsidies and federal standard-setting as a means of controlling air and water pollution. Such taxes would, of course, be an explicit attempt to rectify an imbalance caused by a market failure.

calculated but it is suggestive to consider the situation if the natural reservoir of air, water, minerals, etc., were very much smaller, as if the earth were a submarine or "spaceship" (i.e., a vehicle with no assimilative and/or regenerative capacity). In such a case, all material resources would have to be recycled,[25] and the cost of all goods would necessarily reflect the cost of reprocessing residuals and wastes for reuse. In this case, incidentally, the ambient level of unrecovered wastes continuously circulating through the resource inventory of the system (i.e., the spaceship) would in general be nonzero because of the difficulty of 100 percent efficient waste-removal of air and water. However, although the quantity of waste products in constant circulation may fluctuate within limits, it cannot be allowed to increase monotonically with time, which means that as much material must be recycled, on the average, as is discarded. The value of common resources plus the assimilation services performed by the environment, then, is only indirectly a function of the ambient level of untreated residuals per se, or the disutility caused thereby, which depend on the cost efficiency of the available treatment technology. Be this as it may, of course, the bill of goods produced in a spaceship economy would certainly be radically different from that we are familiar with. For this reason, no standard economic comparison between the two situations is meaningful. The measure of worth we are seeking is actually the difference between the total welfare "produced" by a spaceship economy, where 100 percent of all residuals are promptly recycled, vis-à-vis the existing welfare output on earth, where resource inventories are substantial and

[25] Any consistent deviation from this 100 per cent rule implies an accumulation of waste products, on the average, which, by definition, is inconsistent with maintaining an equilibrium.

complete recycling need not be contemplated for a very long time to come.

This welfare difference might well be very large, although we possess no methodological tools for quantifying it. In any case, the resource inventory and assimilative capacity of the environment probably contribute very considerably to our standard of living.

If these environmental contributions were paid for, the overall effect on prices would presumably to be push them generally upward. However, the major *differential* effect of undervaluing the environmental contribution is that goods produced by high residual-producing processes, such as papermaking, are substantially underpriced vis-à-vis goods which involve more economical uses of basic resources. This is, however, not socially disadvantageous per se: that is, it causes no misallocation of resources unless, or until, the large resource inventory and/or the assimilative capacity of the environment are used up. When this happens, however, as it now has in most highly industrialized regions, either a market must be allowed to operate or some other form of decision rule must be introduced to permit a rational choice to be made, e.g., between curtailing or controlling the production of residuals or tolerating the effects (disservice) thereof.

It appears that the natural inventory of most common resources used as inputs (e.g., air as an input to combustion and respiratory processes) is still ample,[26] but the assimilative capacity of the environment has already been exceeded in many areas, with important external costs resulting. This suggests a compromise treatment. If an appropriate price could be charged to the producers of the residuals and used to compensate the inadvertent recipients—with the price determined by appropriate Pareto preference criteria—there would be no particular analytic purpose in keeping books on the exchange of the other environmental benefits mentioned, although they are quantitatively massive. We will, therefore, in the remainder of the discussion omit the common-property variables $\{r_j^{ep}\}$ and the corresponding virtual-price variables $\{v_j^{ep}\}$ defined previously, retaining only the terms $\{r_j^u\}$ and $\{u_{jk}\}$. The variable $\{r_j^u\}$ represents a physical quantity of the jth unwanted input. There are S such terms, by assumption, whose magnitudes are proportional to the levels of consumption of basic raw materials, subject to the existing technology. However, residuals production is not immutable: it can be increased or decreased by investment, changes in materials processing technology, raw material substitutions, and so forth.

At first glance it might seem entirely reasonable to assert that the *supplies* of unwanted residuals received will be functions of the (negative) prices (i.e., compensation) paid for them, in analogy with (7). Unfortunately, this assertion immediately introduces a theoretical difficulty, since the assumption of unique coefficients $\{a_{ij}\}$ and $\{C_{ij}\}$[27] is not consistent with the possibility of factor or process substitution or joint-production, as stated earlier. To permit such substitutions, one would have to envision a very large collection of alternative sets of coefficients: one complete set of a's and C's for each specific combination of factors and processes. Maximization of any objective function (such as GNP) would involve solving the entire system of equations as many times as there are combinations of factors and pro-

---

[26] Water is an exception in arid regions; in humid regions, however, water "shortages" are misnomers: they are really consequences of excessive use of watercourses as cheap means of waste disposal. But some ecologists have claimed that oxygen depletion may be a very serious long-run problem; see Cole [10].

[27] Or $\{b_{ij}\}$ and $\{A_{ij}\}$.

(21)
$$[r] = \begin{bmatrix} r^m \\ r^s \\ r^u \end{bmatrix} = M \underbrace{\left\{ \begin{bmatrix} a^m \\ \cdots \\ a^s \\ \cdots \\ a^u \end{bmatrix} \right] X \right\}}_{N} \quad N = \begin{bmatrix} b^m \\ \cdots \\ b^s \\ \cdots \\ b^u \end{bmatrix} Y$$

cesses, and picking out that set of solutions which yields the largest value. Alternatively, if the a's and C's are assumed to be continuously variable functions (of each other), the objective function could also, presumably, be parameterized. However, as long as the a's and C's are uniquely given, the supply of the kth unwanted residual is only marginally under the control of the producer, since it will be produced in strict relationship to the composition of the bill of final goods $\{Y_j\}$.

Hence, for the present model it is only correct to assume

(20) $r_k^u = G_k^u(Y_1, \cdots, Y_N)$

This limitation does not affect the existence of an equilibrium solution for the system of equations; it merely means that the shadow prices $\{u_{jk}\}$ which would emerge from such a solution for given coefficients $\{a_{ij}\}$, $\{b_{ij}\}$, and $\{C_{ij}\}$ might be considerably higher than the real economic optimum, since the latter could only be achieved by introducing factor and process changes.

Of course, the physical inputs are also related to the physical outputs of goods, as in (21).

Written out in full detail (21) is equivalent to:

(22) raw materials $r_k^m = \sum_{j=1}^{N} a_{kj}^m X_j = \sum_{j=1}^{N} b_{kj}^m Y_j$

$k = 1, \cdots, L$

(23) labor and technical services $r_k^s = \sum_{j=1}^{N} a_{kj}^s X_j = \sum_{j=1}^{N} b_{kj}^s Y_i$

$k = 1, \cdots, P$

(24) unwanted inputs $r_k^u = \sum_{j=1}^{N} a_{kj}^u X_j = \sum_{j=1}^{N} b_{kj}^u Y_j$

$k = 1, \cdots, S$

where, of course,

(25) $L + P + S = M$

The corresponding matrix equation for the prices of goods, in terms of production costs, is

(26)
$$[p_1, \cdots, p_N] = [v^m \vdots v^s \vdots u] \begin{bmatrix} b^m \\ \cdots \\ b^s \\ \cdots \\ b^u \end{bmatrix}$$

Written out in the standard form, we obtain

$$p_k = \underbrace{\sum_{j=1}^{L} b_{jk}^m v_j^m}_{\substack{\text{cost of raw} \\ \text{materials}}} + \underbrace{\sum_{j=1}^{P} b_{jk}^s v_j^s}_{\substack{\text{cost of labor} \\ \text{and technical} \\ \text{services}}}$$

(27)
$$+ \underbrace{\sum_{j=1}^{S} b_{jk}^u v_j^u}_{\substack{\text{cost (compensa-} \\ \text{tion) for pro-} \\ \text{viding environ-} \\ \text{mental disser-} \\ \text{vices}}}$$

$k = 1, \cdots, N$

Evidently, the coefficients b_{jk}^u are empirically determined by the structure of the regional economy and its geography. It is assumed that a single overall (negative) price for each residual has meaning, even though each productive sector—and even each consumer—has his own individual utility function. Much the same assumption is conventionally made, and accepted, in the case of positive real prices.

All of the additional variables now fit into the general framework of the original Walras-Cassel analysis. Indeed, we have $2N+2M-1$ variables (r_i, Y_i, p_i, v_i) (allowing an arbitrary normalization factor for the price level) and $2N+2M-1$ independent equations.[28] If solutions exist for the Walras-Cassel system of equations, the arguments presumably continue to hold true for the generalized model. In any case, a discussion of such mathematical questions would carry us too far from our main theme.

IV. *Concluding Comments*

The limited economics literature currently available which is devoted to environmental pollution problems has generally taken a partial equilibrium view of the matter, as well as treated the pollution of particular environmental media, such as air and water, as separate problems.[29] This no doubt reflects the propensity of the theoretical literature to view externalities as exceptional and minor. Clearly, the partial equilibrium approach in particular is very convenient theoretically and empirically for it permits external damage and control cost functions to be defined for each particular case without reference to broader interrelationships and adjustments in the economy.

[28] There is one redundant equation in the system, which expresses the identity between gross product and gross income for the system as a whole (sometimes called "Walras law").

[29] See, for example, the essays in Wolozin [29]

We have argued in this paper that the production of residuals is an inherent and general part of the production and consumption process and, moreover, that there are important trade-offs between the gaseous, liquid, or solid forms that these residuals may take. Further, we have argued that under conditions of intensive economic and population development the environmental media which can receive and assimilate residual wastes are not free goods but natural resources of great value with respect to which voluntary exchange cannot operate because of their common property characteristics. We have also noted, in passing, that the assimilative capacity of environmental media can sometimes be altered and that therefore the problem of achieving Pareto optimality reaches beyond devising appropriate shadow prices and involves the planning and execution of investments with public goods aspects.

We have exhibited a formal mathematical framework for tracing residuals flows in the economy and related it to the general equilibrium model of resources allocation, altered to accommodate recycle and containing unpriced sectors to represent the environment. This formulation, in contrast to the usual partial equilibrium treatments, implies knowledge of all preference and production functions including relations between residuals discharge and external cost and all possible factor and process substitutions. While we feel that it represents reality with greater fidelity than the usual view, it also implies a central planning problem of impossible difficulty, both from the standpoint of data collection and computation.

What, if any, help can the general interdependency approach we have outlined offer in dealing with pollution problems effectively and reasonably efficiently? A minimal contribution is its warning that partial equilibrium approaches, while more tractable, may lead to serious errors. Second, in projecting waste residuals for an economy—a regional economy would usually be the most relevant for planning and control—the inter-industry materials flow model can provide a much more conceptually satisfying and accurate tool for projecting future residuals production than the normal aggregative extrapolations.[30] The latter not only treat gaseous, liquid, and solid wastes separately, but do not take account of input-output relations and the fact that the materials account for the region must balance.

We think that in the next few years it will be possible to make improved regional projections of residuals along the lines sketched above. Undoubtedly, there will also be further progress in empirically estimating external costs associated with residuals discharge and in estimating control costs via various alternative measures. On the basis of this kind of information, a control policy can be devised. However, this approach will still be partial. Interrelations between the regional and national economy must be treated simplistically and to be manageable, the analysis must confine itself to a specific projected bill of goods.

The basic practical question which remains to be answered is whether an iterated series of partial equilibrium treatments—e.g., focusing on one industry or region at a time, *ceteris paribus*—would converge toward the general equilibrium

solution, or not. We know of no theoretical test of convergence which would be applicable in this case but, in the absence of such a criterion, would be willing to admit the possible relevance of an empirical sensitivity test more or less along the following lines: take a major residuals-producing industry (such as electric power) and parametrize its cost structure in terms of emission control levels, allowing all technically feasible permutations of factor (fuel) inputs and processes. It would be a straightforward, but complicated, operations research problem to determine the minimum cost solution as a function of the assumed (negative) price of the residuals produced. If possible industry patterns—factor and process combinations—exist which would permit a high level of emission control at only a small increase in power production cost, then it might be possible to conclude that for a significant range of (negative) residuals prices the effect on power prices —and therefore on the rest of the economy —would not be great. Such a conclusion would support the convergence hypothesis. If, on the other hand, electric power prices are very sensitive to residuals prices, then one would at least have to undertake a deeper study of consumer preference functions to try to determine what residuals prices would actually be if a market mechanism existed. If people prove to have a strong antipathy to soot and sulfur dioxide, for instance, resulting in a high (negative) price for these unwanted inputs, then one would be forced to suspect that the partial equilibrium approach is probably not convergent to the general equilibrium solution and that much more elaborate forms of analysis will be required.

[30] Some efforts to implement these concepts are already underway. Walter Isard and his associates have prepared an input-output table for Philadelphia which includes coefficients representing waterborne wastes (unpublished). The recent study of waste management in the New York Metropolitan region by the Regional Plan Association took a relatively broad view of the waste residuals problem [31]. Relevant data on several industries are being gathered. Richard Frankel's not yet published study of thermal power in which the range of technical options for controlling residuals, and their costs, is being explored is notable in this regard. His and other salient studies are described in Ayres and Kneese [2].

References

1. R. U. Ayres, "Stability of Biosystems in Sea Water," Tech. Rept. No. 142, Hudson Laboratories, Columbia University, New York 1967.

2. ―――― AND A. V. KNEESE, "Environmental Pollution," in U.S. Congress, Joint Economic Committee, *Federal Programs for the Development of Human Resources*, Vol. 2, Washington 1968.

3. W. J. BAUMOL, *Welfare Economics and the Theory of the State*. Cambridge 1967.

4. K. E. BOULDING, "The Economics of the Coming Spaceship Earth," in H. Jarrett, ed., *Environmental Quality in a Growing Economy*, Baltimore 1966, pp. 3–14.

5. J. H. BOYD, "Collective Facilities in Water Quality Management," Appendix to Kneese and Bower [17].

6. J. W. BUCHANAN AND WM. C. STUBBLEBINE, "Externality," *Economica*, Nov. 1962, *29*, 371–84.

7. ―――― AND G. TULLOCK, "Public and Private Interaction under Reciprocal Externality," in J. Margolis, ed., *The Public Economy of Urban Communities*, Baltimore 1965, pp. 52–73.

8. G. CASSEL, *The Theory of Social Economy*. New York 1932.

9. R. H. COASE, "The Problem of Social Cost," *Jour. Law and Econ.*, Oct. 1960, *3*, 1–44.

10. L. COLE, "Can the World be Saved?" Paper presented at the 134th Meeting of the American Association for the Advancement of Science, December 27, 1967.

11. R. K. DAVIS, *The Range of Choice in Water Management*. Baltimore 1968.

12. O. A. DAVIS AND A. WHINSTON, "Externalities, Welfare, and the Theory of Games," *Jour. Pol. Econ.*, June 1962, *70*, 241–62.

13. R. DORFMAN, P. SAMUELSON AND R. M. SOLOW, *Linear Programming and Economic Analysis*. New York 1958.

14. I. FISHER, *Nature of Capital and Income*. New York 1906.

15. A. C. HARBERGER, "Monopoly and Resources Allocation," *Am. Econ. Rev.*, Proc., May 1954, *44*, 77–87.

16. K. W. KAPP, *The Social Costs of Private Enterprise*. Cambridge 1950.

17. A. V. KNEESE AND B. T. BOWER, *Managing Water Quality: Economics, Technology, Institutions*. Baltimore 1968.

18. F. H. KNIGHT, *Risk, Uncertainty, and Profit*. Boston and New York 1921.

19. H. LEIBENSTEIN, "Allocative Efficiency vs. 'X-Efficiency,' " *Am. Econ. Rev.*, June 1966, *56*, 392–415.

20. W. P. LOWRY, "The Climate of Cities," *Sci. Am.*, Aug. 1967, *217*, 15–23.

21. E. J. MISHAN, "Reflections on Recent Developments in the Concept of External Effects," *Canadian Jour. Econ. Pol. Sci.*, Feb. 1965, *31*, 1–34.

22. A. C. PIGOU, *Economics of Welfare*. London 1952.

23. K. SCHLESINGER, "Über die Produktionsgleichungen der ökonomischen Wertlehre," *Ergebnisse eines mathematischen Kolloquiums*, No. 6. Vienna, F. Denticke, 1933.

24. D. SCHWARTZMAN, "The Burden of Monopoly," *Jour. Pol. Econ.*, Dec. 1960, *68*, 627–30.

25. T. SCITOVSKY, "Two Concepts of External Economies," *Jour. Pol. Econ.*, Apr. 1954, *62*, 143–51.

26. F. SMITH, *The Economic Theory of Industrial Waste Production and Disposal*, draft of a doctoral dissertation, Northwestern Univ. 1967.

27. R. TURVEY, "On Divergencies between Social Cost and Private Cost," *Economica*, Nov. 1962, *30*, 309–13.

28. L. WALRAS, *Elements d'economie politique pure*, Jaffé translation. London 1954.

29. H. WOLOZIN, ed., *The Economics of Air Pollution*. New York 1966.

30. CONSERVATION FOUNDATION, *Implications of Rising Carbon Dioxide Content of the Atmosphere*. New York 1963.

31. REGIONAL PLAN ASSOCIATION, *Waste Management*, a Report of the Second Regional Plan. New York 1968.

[14]

Measuring Social and Economic Change:
Benefits and Costs of Environmental
Pollution

ORRIS C. HERFINDAHL

AND

ALLEN V. KNEESE

RESOURCES FOR THE FUTURE, INC.

INTRODUCTION

Benefits and costs associated with the environment involve not only pollutants and their effects in the usual sense but psychic responses to features of the environment some of which may not even be describable in relevant quantitative terms. Our focus is on pollution in the narrow sense, however, not because the wider and less tractable issues are unimportant, but because of considerations of comparative advantage.

Of the many possible approaches to the measurement of benefits and costs connected with the environment, two are selected for examination here. One possibility is to approach the measurement problem within the framework of the national income accounts. Flows of environmental benefits or costs or responses to them are already partially reflected in the national accounts, and there is a possibility that present deficiencies in their treatment could be remedied. We consider this at some length, with results that are rather negative. Although change in the official definitions does not seem to be warranted, it probably would be useful to prepare some auxiliary series reflecting response to environmental change and control that users could combine with the official series.

NOTE: We are indebted to Henry Peskin, Robert A. Kelly, Clifford S. Russell, and Walter O. Spofford, Jr., for comments on an earlier draft.

Orris Herfindahl died on December 16, 1972, in Nepal, while on a hiking expedition in the Himalayas. This paper reflects the keen interest and concern he had for the natural environment.

442   *Amenities and Disamenities of Economic Growth*

Apart from the national accounts approach, a thoroughgoing application of which would involve estimates for the environment of various aggregates corresponding to the series already included—value of service flows, maintenance, environmental capital formation and depreciation (depletion?)—it may be possible to measure environmental benefits and costs on a more limited basis, say, in marginal terms, and this is the approach we have taken. We do not attempt any estimates of benefits and costs as such, but confine ourselves to some general observations on how such estimates might be made and what the data and information requirements are for some of the possible methods.

It is of central importance to any method being used to throw light on environmental benefits and costs that important real external effects are involved with no counterpart money flow. This is in strong contrast to the treatment of ordinary goods for which benefits and costs can be estimated on the basis of market prices. Similar estimates of the changes in environmental benefits and costs that would result from a specified change in pollutant output require the explicit use of a model which can take account of these real repercussions not reflected in market prices or costs or that would be reflected only under some different institutional arrangement.

Several models that can go some distance toward tracing the repercussions of control actions or that can contribute to decisions on the proper control action are discussed. Among these are the adaptation of the input-output scheme to the analysis of pollution problems and a conceptually more elaborate model containing an activity analysis model and other components designed to portray certain physical and biological events accompanying a change in pollution outputs.

The final question to be considered is the kinds of data and information needed for the design and administration of pollution control schemes. The data of the specific models examined in some detail provide substantial guidance here, but since our discussion is necessarily rather general, it has a wider applicability. In effect, the question considered is this: Given that there is to be a pollution control system, what kinds of data and information are needed to make it work? First, it is essential to have baseline or indicator data to know when things have changed for the worse or to get some indication of the possibility that it might be possible to improve things in city A in view of the fact that conditions are better in a similar city B. Second, control requires accurate and comprehensive information on pollutant flows. The possibility of assembling this information as a part of a comprehensive accounting for materials flows is examined. Finally, pollution control requires some change in the way things are now done, but what options are there? What parts of the production function would provide the best compromise between the demands standing behind pollution production and the demands of those who are injured by it, assuming that institutional arrangements permitted the change? The need for systematic information on production possibilities is often neglected, but in fact it is of strategic importance to the design of control schemes that pay at least some attention to the relevant benefits and costs.

I. SOCIAL ACCOUNTS AND ENVIRONMENTAL BENEFITS AND COSTS

The Nature of Social Accounts

An accounting system is a way of systematically describing what has happened between two points in time to the state of a certain group of objects in a system. Ordinarily what happens to the state of the different objects in the system will be associated with various types of flows during the period in question.

We speak of an accounting *system* because the entities involved in the state descriptions and the flows accounted for are members of a proper classification. There is no overlapping of entities or flows, there is some principle of closure which definitely circumscribes the group of entities and flows, and the flows and objects are related in a definite manner. Flows always come from and go to members of the group of entities, and in doing so they behave in accordance with certain relationships that can be specified.

The design of an accounting system requires a selection of the "objects of interest." What phenomena are we trying to account for? The answer to this question determines the nature of the classification of entities and flows. In any practical application of the system, there must be a determination of the boundaries of the system, and this will depend on the phenomena of interest.

One property of an accounting system with boundaries defined in spatial terms is that totals can be broken down by area, as with the income payments series, wealth estimates, and so on. This property is extremely useful if environmental resources are incorporated into an accounting framework, because our interest in these resources usually has a very strong locational component. Unlike, say, the monetary system, there are few aspects of any environmental resource the proper management of which is connected with national totals or any of their

444   *Amenities and Disamenities of Economic Growth*

national physical aspects. Much of our later discussion stresses the locational aspect.

Weight of flows of physical objects, like money flows between economic units, could form a suitable basis for an accounting system because its components add up to a definite total. While there is merit in an accounting system based on flows of mass—simply to provide an exhaustive means for tracing the flow of different substances—weight in fact may not be very closely connected with the true objects of our interest in connection with the natural environment. We would emphasize, however, the great importance of this exhaustive accounting device, at least for certain areas.

There is a possibility that many of the objects of interest may be such that a system of accounts—defined as above—could make only an indirect contribution to our understanding. For example, one of the things we are interested in is the effects of air pollutants on health—that is, effects on the feeling of well-being a person enjoys, on his performance, on sickness objectively viewed, and on age at death. To study these questions, we need to know the spatial and temporal distributions of concentrations of the different types of air pollutants and the temporal exposures of individuals to the various concentrations. It seems entirely possible, even likely, that the systematic series that we should like to see collected over time to facilitate study of the effects of air pollutants for the most part could not be combined in an accounting system apart from the aspect of mass. There is no point in adding concentrations at different locations, although their comparison in various ways may be of interest. Certain statistical operations can be viewed as the equivalent of adding together the exposures of different individuals at the same location, but there is little point in adding together the exposures of persons at different locations if exposures are different.

Considerations like these lead us to examine the possibility of thinking of social accounts in a looser way. We might, for example, think of social accounts as a systematic series of records over time that will aid us in "accounting" for what has gone on in a certain sphere of interest. Here we are thinking of "accounting" in the sense of describing or explaining rather than in the sense of identifying the numerical components of a total. In the case of the accounting system narrowly viewed, there is an additive unit of measurement which opens the possibility of forming a proper classification and specifying the boundaries of system and subsystem. With the looser system it is still possible to think of

Benefits and Costs of Environmental Pollution 445

system and subsystem, but perhaps with less precision, and the publicly additive property is not present. A weighted sum may be conceivable in certain cases, but the weights usually will be private and more or less subjective.

Series of this kind can be thought of as serving several purposes. They may provide summary indicators of tendencies, they may provide baseline information for future studies, or they may provide important inputs to research studies on specific problems. A major part of our discussion in part III concerns these matters.

Should GNP and NNP Be Modified to Account for Environmental Pollution and Its Control?

The question whether the aggregate output accounts—GNP and NNP —should be modified to reflect the growing generation, treatment, and discharge of residuals from production and consumption activities can be interpreted in two ways. First, should the official definitions be changed, and, second, should auxiliary modified series be presented along with the official series based on unchanged definitions? As a general matter, we feel that the official series should be continued on the basis of the present definitions, both because of the desirability of avoiding breaks in the series and because the advantages and significance of some of the changes that might be made are not yet completely clear. The discussion applies, then, to the second interpretation. Whenever we speak of the desirability of modifying GNP or NNP,[1] we refer not to the official series but to modified auxiliary series. Of course, experience with such series might later be thought to indicate the desirability of a change in the official definitions.

GNP is intended to measure the production of "final" goods and services in the economy. The final "consumers" of these goods and services are taken to be individuals and households (consumers in the traditional sense), government, and nonprofit institutions. It is assumed that these economic agents do not usually use inputs to provide intermediate services (such as, for example, a trucking company would), but rather that they "use up" the utility embodied in the goods and services which the economy produces. This is a working assumption which, in numerous particular instances, is highly debatable.

At any given time there exists a list of goods and services which is officially regarded as final. These goods and services are exchanged

[1] The discussion always refers to deflated, or "real," gross national product or net national product.

446   *Amenities and Disamenities of Economic Growth*

in markets [2] and therefore have market exchange determined prices attached to them in some base year as well as in the current period. As
time passes, new goods and services are often "wedged in" to help keep
the list more nearly complete. To calculate price-corrected or "real"
GNP, the changing amounts of physical units of the final goods and
services produced are multiplied by the unchanged base-period set of
prices—currently, 1958 prices are used. The system of accounts is of
the double entry type. In current prices the total of GNP calculated from
the product side must balance GNP calculated as the sum of values added
of all activities contributing to GNP. This is not true of real GNP,
however, because no deflator has been devised with which the value-
added side could be price corrected.[3] Thus, since we are here interested
in real GNP, we will refer exclusively to the product-side calculations.

If it were true that all salient goods and services were exchanged in
markets; that the degree of competition in these markets did not change;
that the programs of government and nonprofit institutions did not
change in such a way that they produced substantially altered welfare
relative to the final goods and services that they absorbed; that population stayed constant; and that the distribution of income did not change;
then alterations in real NNP (GNP minus capital consumption) could
be regarded as a good indicator of changes in the economic welfare of
the population.

This is an imposing string of assumptions, none of which is ever exactly met in reality. To the extent that they are not met, NNP diminishes
in usefulness as a welfare measure. In fact, the distance between reality
and these assumptions is large and significant in some cases, thus seriously reducing the practical usefulness of NNP as a welfare measure.

Of course the national accounts, which include much more than total
NNP, have been designed to serve a number of purposes. They are intended to provide information useful for economic stabilization policies
and programs, and they are meant to provide an estimate of the production of goods and services which the society has available to meet
alternative ends. The designers of the accounts thought that at best
they would serve to provide only a rough indicator of one dimension of
welfare.

But to divorce completely discussion of the accounts from broader
questions of welfare, as some would do, would be a serious mistake.

[2] In fact, some of these transactions are virtual or imputed. For example, the
value of owner-occupied housing is estimated by imputation.

[3] Deflated gross national product by industry is calculated by deflating industry
outputs and purchases separately and subtracting.

Benefits and Costs of Environmental Pollution 447

Whether originally intended or not, total NNP or GNP is often explicitly or implicitly viewed as an index of welfare change. Moreover, it is important to recognize explicitly that there are enormous flows of services and disservices, valued by people, which do not enter into the exchange system and therefore are not in the list of final goods and services. Unless care is taken to observe and analyze these flows, the real NNP may become grossly misleading even as to what is happening to production of potentially marketable goods and services in the economy. For example, should there be a large-scale shift from purchases of services (e.g., house painting, grass cutting, construction, household services) to self-provision of these services, the NNP would tend to fall although it would not necessarily be true that production had decreased. The reason that NNP would tend to fall is that the labor going into these self-provided services is not in the list of final products; consequently, working time shifted toward them "disappears" from the account. The reason they are not in the list is that the accountants have found them too difficult and costly to identify and evaluate—although there may be good reason to reconsider this position in view of contemporary techniques of data collection and handling.

It is highly illuminating to view objections of the "environmentalist" to the accounts as involving a question of what is or is not in the list of final products. When the environmentalist contends that GNP overstates growth, he implicitly incorporates in his list of final products many service flows which do not enter into market exchange and consequently are not in the official list. Moreover, he believes that the net effect of including the omissions would be to reduce real product. His list would include the life support, aesthetic, and convenience services of clean air, clean water, and spacious surroundings—all of which in some of their aspects are *common property* resources unsuited to private exchange. The only way a change in these service flows could influence the GNP and NNP as presently measured is if their changed quality or quantity made the production of items which are included in the list easier or more difficult. In reality, such feedbacks on the national accounts from altered quality of the common property resources are probably trivial, up to now, compared with alteration of service flows from these resources direct to final consumers. These are nowhere reflected as such in the list of final products, although they may affect some items that are. It is the marked deterioration of the environmental services not on the list that mainly concerns the environmentalist.

The exclusion of the services of clean air, clean water, space, etc., from the list of final goods probably is not the result of disagreement

448   *Amenities and Disamenities of Economic Growth*

that the services provided by nature are a factor in true welfare but rather of the judgment on the part of the income accountant that obtaining acceptable estimates for these values would be too difficult and costly. It is clear, however, that any reduction in the service flows of common property resources that is viewed as a loss in real product by consumers means that NNP overstates any increase in final product as compared with the total flow from the truly relevant and larger list of final goods and services. In the extreme case the "true" service flow could actually decrease while NNP rises. Some writers, like E. J. Mishan, believe that this is happening now.[4] This view seems a bit extreme, but whether it is or not is an empirical question.

That burdens on the service flows of common property assets tend to rise with increasing production unless effective, collectively imposed controls are undertaken is obvious from observation. There are also some reasons to believe that this rise will tend to be more than proportional to production growth in developed economies. Conservation of mass requires that all material resources used as inputs to the extractive, productive, and consumptive activities of the economy must appear as residuals which in some manner are returned to the environment—except for changes in the inventory of mass. If the use of material rises faster than production of final goods and services, so must the production of residuals. There are counteracting trends affecting materials use in the economy. However, as lower-quality ores are used greater quantities of unwanted material must be processed to get a given quantity of wanted material; as a result there appears a tendency for residuals to rise faster than final production of goods *and* services "embodying" materials. Also, energy usage recently has been rising faster than real NNP, and so long as it is obtained primarily from conversion of fossil fuels this implies a rapidly rising flow of residual materials and gases. In the absence of effective collective restriction on the use of common property resources like air and water they tend to become the receptacles into which residuals are discharged. Other sources of nonlinearities can be readily identified. Indeed, sometimes discontinuities or thresholds are encountered, as when a water body becomes anaerobic and its functioning changes dramatically for the worse so far as services like recreation and fishing are concerned.

There seems to be considerable agreement among those who have studied the matter that if it were practical to extend the list of final goods and services to include service flows from the natural environment

[4] See E. J. Mishan, *The Costs of Economic Growth*, London, Staples Press Ltd., 1967.

Benefits and Costs of Environmental Pollution 449

this should be done. But there also seems to be near universal hopelessness about the feasibility of doing it—at least for a long time to come. Accordingly it is often concluded that the best we can do in this respect is to supplement the real NNP with physical, chemical, or biological indicators of the state of the environment. We discuss this possibility in part III.

But are there any less ambitious adjustments that should be made? One possibility is to deduct consumer "defensive" expenditures from NNP. If environmental service flows remained constant, then "defensive" expenditures made voluntarily by consumers would be on the same footing as any other, being carried to the point where utility gained is equated with alternative cost in utility lost. It would make no difference if environmental service flows are included in the list of final products so far as indication of welfare changes over time is concerned.

If environmental service flows change, however, then it is clear that a list of final products that omits either these or the defensive consumer expenditures may give an incorrect indication of welfare change over time. If defensive expenditures were simply deducted from the present GNP, the necessary implicit assumption would be—if welfare change is to be correctly indicated—that the defensive expenditures exactly offset the decline in value of the environmental services that "ought" to but do not now affect the GNP. Even so, it probably would be of interest to try to estimate consumer defensive expenditures.

Defensive expenditures by industry are already appropriately treated from this point of view since they never appear in real NNP. We will not develop the rationale for these points here since it is quite analogous to that developed in some detail for residuals control expenditures, below.

Costs of meeting environmental standards. Up to this point we have been discussing common property environmental resources as though their use were completely unrestricted. In the United States, this was a fairly good approximation of reality until recently, but public policy development is now proceeding rapidly to regulate their use for residuals disposal. The policy path we are taking seems to be leading toward ambient *environmental* standards which are to be achieved by enforcement of *emission* standards or, in a few cases, through the incentives provided by emission charges or taxes. If these policies become effective they should give rise to large expenditures for the control of residuals generation and discharge. The time pattern these will follow is uncertain, but probably they will "hump" in the next five to ten years

450   *Amenities and Disamenities of Economic Growth*

during a clean-up phase, possibly then declining slightly for a time, following which they may tend to rise nonlinearly with increasing input. Table 1 gives some idea of the outlays which might be involved in the period 1970–75 if objectives are pursued very vigorously, although actual expenditures probably will be much less. The question arises, How should these expenditures be treated in the NNP?

Before trying to answer, we should review how such expenditures would be treated under present procedures. The fact is that they would be handled differently depending on whether they are incurred by consumers or government on the one hand or by industry on the other. In the following discussion we will neglect direct expenditures for pollution control by consumers, because we think they will be small (with one major exception which we discuss later), and in any case no different principles are involved.

The differential effect of industrial and governmental expenditures can easily be illustrated by a very simple example. Assume an economy in which only two commodities are produced in the base period, haircuts and bread (the citizens will be nude but well clipped). Accordingly the list of final products will consist of haircuts and bread (see Table 2). Let us assume that the production of haircuts generates no significant amount of residuals but that the production of bread does. Suppose also that barbers can be diverted to control residuals if that is desired (the bread can be produced with less waste if more labor is used).

In the base period there is a standard for the discharge of residuals, but the production of bread is just low enough to avoid violating it. In period 1, a change in family composition causes a shift in demand from haircuts to bread together with an increase in residuals. If there were no standard for discharge of residuals, the situation would be that labeled 1a. That is, $500 of productive services would have been diverted from the production of haircuts to bread, and residuals discharge would have increased.

There is a standard for residuals discharge, however, and it is not being met in situation 1a. If it is met by a diversion *within the industry* of barbers to residuals control, NNP will register a decline as compared with period 0, as shown by 1b. The decline in the flow of residuals is not recorded, of course. In contrast, if the government hires these same men to limit the discharge of residuals to the standard level, NNP will show no decline, as in 1c. The reason is that there is nothing in the list of final products corresponding to residual controls, and so the activities directed toward that end cannot be reflected in NNP evaluated

TABLE 1

A Collection of Rough Estimates of Increase in Costs to Achieve "Substantial" Reductions in Environmental Pollution, 1970–75

	Billions of Dollars [a]
Water	
Treating municipal sewage	12
Reducing nonthermal industrial wastes	6
Reducing thermal discharges	3
Sediment and acid mine drainage control	3
Reducing oil spills, water craft discharges, and other miscellaneous items	1
Added reservoir storage for low flow regulation	1
Separating storm and sanitary sewers	40
Total	66
Total without last item	26
Air	
Controls on stationary sources	5
Mobile sources	
To modify refining and distribution of gasoline	2
Engine modifications	2
Added fuel costs	1
Total	10
Solids	
Increased coverage of collection	1
Increased operating cost, including environmental protection costs	3
Total	4
Other	
Control of heavy metals (mercury, cadmium, etc.), stopping use of persistent pesticides, improving water treatment, control of pollutant-bearing soil runoff, control of feed-lot operations, etc.[b]	15
Grand total	
With storm-sewer separators (about 35 per cent increase of GNP)	95
Without storm-sewer separators (about 20 per cent increase of GNP)	55

SOURCE: Allen V. Kneese, "The Economics of Environmental Pollution in the United States," in Allen V. Kneese, Sidney E. Rolfe, and Joseph W. Harned, eds., *International Environmental Management: The Political Economy of Pollution*, Proceedings of Atlantic Council–Battelle Memorial Institute Conference of January 1971, Washington, D.C., forthcoming.

[a] Estimates include investment and operating costs.
[b] A sheer guess.

Natural Resource Economics

452 *Amenities and Disamenities of Economic Growth*

TABLE 2

The Haircuts and Bread Economy

		Q	P_0	NNP
Period 0	H	100	$10	$1,000
	B	100	10	1,000
				2,000
Period 1a	H	50	10	500
(as it would be without resid-	B	150	10	1,500
uals control)				2,000
Period 1b	H	25	10	250
(as it would be if industry	B	150	10	1,500
had to control residuals by				1,750
diverting 25 extra barbers)				
Period 1c	H	25	10	250
(as it would be if govern-	B	150	10	1,500
ment hired the extra bakers	G	25	10	250
and set them to controlling				2,000
residuals)				

H = haircuts.
B = bread.
G = government.

at base-year prices. However, since government is in effect regarded as a final consumer, its expenditure for the barbers (or rather residuals controllers) is included in NNP.[5]

Observations on Treating the Costs of Environmental Standards. If we visualize a situation in which the government establishes effective environmental standards which must be continuously met, the present NNP treatment of industry outlays to comply with them would seem to indicate welfare change more appropriately than the present treatment of similar governmental outlays. The reason is that the outlays made for residuals control can be viewed as simply being necessary to maintain, at some specified level, the service flow naturally provided by the common property assets. In that sense they are expenditures necessary to

[5] A more formal justification of these points is included in a forthcoming study by Karl-Göran Mäler of the Stockholm School of Economics.

Benefits and Costs of Environmental Pollution   453

maintain the unproduced capital stock. Failure to treat them this way could result in an anomalous situation in which a progressively larger share of production would have to be devoted simply to environmental quality maintenance with NNP continuing to rise. It would be hard to claim that this rise could in any way be regarded as indicating increased welfare. Viewed this way the appropriate procedure would be to treat industry outlays for control as at present and to change procedures so that government outlays for control could be treated similarly.[6] This would require identification of government expenditures for residuals control, which we think would not be too difficult, and their subtraction from the present NNP for presentation as an auxiliary series.

The one major exception to the view that consumer expenditures to control residuals will be small is in the control of emissions from automobiles. The approach adopted in the official series is essentially to add items called control devices to the list of final products. If this were not done, the price deflator would tend to indicate a reduced real production of automobiles.

The better approach, it seems to us, is to treat this case—again in an auxiliary series—symmetrically with the way industry is now treated. The consumer would be regarded as producing a service for himself, the production of which generates residuals. He is required in the interest of maintaining the service flow from common property assets to incur a cost. To add such costs to NNP over time would have the same anomalous results as already described in the case of industry.

As we have already indicated, our view appears to be contrary to the views of some experts in national income accounting. Their position apparently rests on two major considerations. The first reflects the special problem of dealing with a catch-up phase such as we are now experiencing in connection with the control of environmental pollution. When effective standards of higher than prevailing quality are first set, some of the expenditures made will result in actual improvements in environmental quality. Thus, the anomalous situation would arise that the population actually experiences an improvement in welfare while the associated influence on NNP is downward. To avoid this situation it has been proposed that the list of final products be expanded to include industrial outlays for residuals control. For reasons already explained we do not think this is the appropriate approach for the longer term welfare indicator. It would be preferable not to add the outlays but to

---

[6] We are still assuming, we think correctly, that consumer expenditures for residuals discharge control will be minor.

454 *Amenities and Disamenities of Economic Growth*

prorate them over a longer period of time, especially from earlier periods when NNP tended to be understated as an indicator of welfare.

The second argument relates to the accounts as measures of production. If it is argued that the GNP is an important measure of the production that might be diverted in periods of national emergency (wartime, for example) for overriding national ends, then the production going into residuals control should be included in GNP. This is because it could be diverted at the cost of permitting deterioration of the service flows from common property assets. In this sense it is quite analogous to running down private capital during such periods. But this does not argue that these expenditures should ever be included in NNP.

The argument is also made that not including production directed toward residuals control would distort labor productivity series which are obtained by dividing NNP by man-hours worked. One's point of view on this seems to be highly contingent on what one regards as measured by labor productivity. If one regards it as the output per man-hour net of the output needed to maintain the service flows of all assets—private and common—then it is wholly appropriate that productivity should tend to fall if a larger proportion of total effort has to go for meeting environmental standards. On the other hand if one regards productivity as pertaining only to conventional production processes, then one would wish activities devoted to environmental maintenance to be in the list of final goods.

Conclusions on national accounts. Since the character of the national product and income accounts is not directed very closely to the single objective of measuring changes in social welfare and uncertainty surrounds some of the changes that have been discussed—both as to implications and practicality—we feel that the official definitions should not be changed. However, series should be prepared that reflect, at least in part, the growth of activities that would indicate decreases in an idealized list of final products or that offset, at least to some degree, the apparent increases registered in, say, NNP.

To this end, we suggest the regular preparation and publication of the following series:

1. Industrial expenditures for residuals control;
2. Government expenditures for residuals control;
3. Consumer expenditures for residuals control;
4. Consumer, industry, and government defensive expenditures.

None of these is prepared currently, and all offer considerable difficulty. If they can be put together, however, the accounts could be ad-

Benefits and Costs of Environmental Pollution 455

justed to reflect various preferences and points of view. It probably would be desirable to publish auxiliary series modifying the official series. The following are some of the possibilities, with all series assumed to be price corrected:

1. GNP—including all residuals control in the list of final products;
2. NNP_1—GNP minus net depreciation of private assets;
3. NNP_2—GNP minus net depreciation of private assets and minus the nonindustry cost of residuals control and defensive expenditures (and in principle all other costs which may be induced by the growth process itself).

In no case, however, should the mistake be made of thinking that adjustments of these types can come very close to indicating changes in "true" welfare so far as flows of environmental services are concerned. The essential ingredient that is lacking is a valuation for the environmental services themselves and, on capital account, an expression for decreases or increases in the value of the corresponding natural assets.

Apart from this general caveat, the definition of some of the series is not very precise. This is especially true of industrial outlays made for pollution control to meet standards of environmental quality. This is evident immediately merely by considering the possible responses of industry to an increase in these standards. True, it may make some outlays, both capital and operating, which would be designated as pollution control outlays. These might include equipment for extracting substances from stack gases or fluid effluent, for example. There are other responses, however. A material may be substituted which is not regarded as a pollutant when emitted in gaseous, fluid, or solid waste. A basic process may be changed which cuts emission of pollutants. Total emission of pollutants may be cut by a combination of ordinary pollution control equipment which in turn causes a reduction in consumption of the article in question by increasing cost and price. There is little hope for estimating the latter types of response on any comprehensive basis.

Thus the whole problem cannot be solved. Even though the suggested adjustments are partial, however, they ought to be made, for they may permit some sharpening of conclusions on what has happened to real product.

II. MODELS FOR ACCOUNTING AND ANALYSIS

To go beyond the rather simpleminded compilation of series on expenditures made in connection with pollution change or control and estimate the net benefits associated with changes in pollutants emitted

456   *Amenities and Disamenities of Economic Growth*

requires the use of a model that will simulate, at least in part, the real repercussions that result from a change that is imposed. There are many models of widely varying degrees of complexity and adequacy that might be and are used for this task.[7] Several models have been presented in recent literature which lend themselves to rather detailed forecasting and policy analysis. They include rather straightforward extensions of open input-output models, analytical-type accounting models which balance materials flows as well as money flows, and activity analysis models embodying important features of natural environmental systems. In discussing them we will proceed from the simpler ones which are relatively easy to implement to those which encompass more significant elements of reality but are harder to implement. We discuss three, a national input-output model, models to account for all materials flows, and a linear programming model adapted to the analysis of regional pollution problems.

The National I-O Model

In recent papers, W. Leontief has proposed an extension of the basic national open I-O model which would permit forecasting of residuals emissons and of the effects of certain types of policy measures. The following exposition of his proposal is based on the mathematical appendix of Leontief's article in the *Review of Economics and Statistics*.[8] Although interpretation of the mathematics is rather straightforward, we shall describe the system in some detail because pollutants are handled somewhat differently from ordinary commodities and also because some readers may not be familiar with matrix representation of a system of equations.

The physical input-output balance with pollutants included in the system is shown by matrix equation (1) in Exhibit 1. We have m ordinary goods and $n - m$ pollutants, making a total of n inputs and outputs.

Each of the A matrices is a matrix of input-output coefficients. For example; a_{ij} is the amount of ith ordinary input required per unit of jth ordinary output (submatrix A_{11}); a_{ik} is the amount of ith ordinary input required to produce a unit of the kth pollutant reduction output (submatrix A_{12}); a_{ki} is the amount of the kth pollutant resulting from producing a unit of ith ordinary output (submatrix A_{21}); a_{kl} is the

---

[7] It is an interesting exercise to try to specify the model that is implicit in some of the current "analyses" of pollution problems.

[8] Wassily Leontief, "Environmental Repercussions of the Economic Structure: An Input-Output Approach," *Review of Economics and Statistics*, August 1970, pp. 262–271.

Benefits and Costs of Environmental Pollution 457

EXHIBIT 1

Physical Input-Output Balance

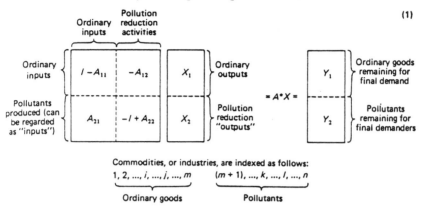

amount of the kth pollutant produced as a result of a unit reduction in the lth pollutant (submatrix A_{22}).

To see what is involved in this system of equations, let us separate out one of them and write it out in full. Assume that we have three ordinary commodities and two pollutant reduction activities,[9] a total of five outputs, or "inputs," in all. Take, for example, the first equation, (2), which is formed by multiplying each member of the first row of A^* by the corresponding members of the X vector of industry outputs and adding these products together, thereby obtaining the first member, y_1, of the vector of final outputs, Y:

$$[1 - a_{12} - a_{13} - a_{14} - a_{15}]\begin{bmatrix} x_1 \\ x_2 \\ x_3 \\ x_4 \\ x_5 \end{bmatrix} = y_1 \qquad (2)$$

or,

$$x_1 - a_{12}x_2 - a_{13}x_3 - a_{14}x_4 - a_{15}x_5 = y_1.$$

Note that in the matrices of input-output coefficients we have regarded a_{ii} and a_{kk} as zero so that industry output is always net of its own output that *it* uses.

[9] We speak of pollutant reduction activities rather than industries because in any application the pollutant reduction activities often will be a part of an ordinary industry. In some cases it may be desirable to account for these separately.

458 *Amenities and Disamenities of Economic Growth*

This equation simply says that the total output of the first commodity minus the amount used in the production of x_2, x_3, x_4, and x_5 is equal to the amount of the first commodity, y_1, going to final demanders. The last four terms account for all of the x_1 used in production, whether for ordinary goods or pollution reduction.

Now consider equation (3), in the bottom part of the square matrix, A^*, say the last one for the nth commodity, which is a pollutant. Note that since the output of the pollution-processing industry is here measured as pollution reduction, the signs of the elements of the two lower quadrants are reversed from those of the two upper ones:

$$[a_{51} + a_{52} + a_{53} + a_{54} - 1] \begin{bmatrix} x_1 \\ x_2 \\ x_3 \\ x_4 \\ x_5 \end{bmatrix} = y_5 \qquad (3)$$

or,

$$a_{51}x_1 + a_{52}x_2 + a_{53}x_3 + a_{54}x_4 - x_5 = y_5.$$

This says that the pollutant, which is commodity number five, that is generated in the production of x_1, x_2, x_3, and x_4 *minus* the amount by which this pollutant is reduced equals the amount which goes to final demanders.

Thus, in abbreviated matrix form, the physical input-output balance is $A^*X = Y$, where X and Y are vectors of industry outputs and deliveries of final goods, respectively. Industry outputs include pollutant reduction, and final goods include pollutants received.[10]

[10] So far, no account has been taken of pollutants generated by the final demand sector. To do so, form a "household" pollution generation matrix, A_y, of the coefficients a_{gy_i}, showing the amount of pollutant g generated per unit of commodity y_i consumed.

Then the vector of pollutants generated by household consumption will be, say, $Y_H = A_y Y_1$.

If Y_E is the vector of pollutants reaching the "environment," we have:

$$Y_E = \begin{bmatrix} A_{21} & \vdots & -I + A_{22} \end{bmatrix} \begin{bmatrix} X_1 \\ X_2 \end{bmatrix} + Y_H$$

$$= \underbrace{[A_{21} \quad A_{22}] \begin{bmatrix} X_1 \\ X_2 \end{bmatrix} + Y_H}_{\substack{\text{Total generated by industry} \\ \text{and households}}} \quad \underbrace{- X_2}_{\substack{\text{Pollutants} \\ \text{processed}}}$$

$$= Y_2 + Y_H.$$

[Cont. on p. 459]

Benefits and Costs of Environmental Pollution 459

EXHIBIT 2

Input-Output Balance Between Prices and Values Added

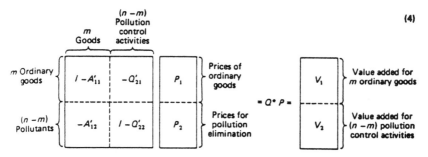

The system of equations, $A^*X = Y$, can be solved for the vector X, industry outputs, by premultiplying each side by the inverse of the matrix, $(A^*)^{-1}$, obtaining $X = (A^*)^{-1}Y$. Thus, if $(A^*)^{-1}$ has been calculated for a given industrial structure, the industry outputs, X, that would be associated with any specified bill of final goods, Y, can be calculated very easily, given, of course, the peculiar assumptions of the input-output scheme as commonly formulated. The main one is that the input coefficients, the a's, are fixed no matter what the size of an industry's output. That is, there is only one way to produce an output, a way that is completely described by one column of a coefficients. It is this assumption that facilitates calculation of economy-wide effects of certain policy changes or changes in final demands.

If the value added in the production of a unit of a commodity is known,[11] this schema can be used to calculate the prices of the commodities that will rule under certain specified conditions. First we express the input-output balance between prices and values added, as in equation (4) in Exhibit 2. P is a vector of prices of outputs, partitioned into ordinary goods and pollutants, as before, and V is a vector of values added, partitioned in the same way. The square matrix is different, however, in

[Cont. from p. 458]

Thus, if (1) is to hold, the lower part of the Y vector must be net of household pollution since these equations express relations between pollutants generated by industry, processed by industry, and delivered by industry to households:

$$\boxed{\begin{array}{c} Y_1 \\ \hline Y_z - Y_H \end{array}}$$

If $Y_H = 0$, this reduces to the original formulation with $Y_z = Y_z$.

[11] For example, if labor is the only factor input and the labor input coefficients, analogous to the input-output coefficients, a_{ij}, are known and a wage rate is specified, value added can be calculated for each good.

460   *Amenities and Disamenities of Economic Growth*

that A^* has been transposed, that is, its columns and rows have been interchanged so that, for example, element a_{ki} is now where element a_{ik} used to be.

In addition, the coefficients involving pollution generation [those in A_{21} and in $(-I + A_{22})$] have been modified. They have been reduced by a factor which reflects the proportion of pollutant generated by an industry the elimination of which is paid for by it. Thus, if industry i generates a_{ki} pollutant per unit of output (a_{ki} is in A_{ki}) and pays for the elimination of $100r_{ki}$ per cent of it, we replace a_{ki} by $q_{ki} = r_{ki}a_{ki}$. A similar modification is made for pollutants produced by the pollutant control industries, that is, of the a_{kl} found in the quadrant $(-I + A_{22})$.

After these modifications, A_{21} becomes $-Q_{21}$ and $(-I + A_{22})$ becomes $(I - Q_{22})$. Note that signs are changed in order to have the price of the product minus the sum of required inputs times their prices be equal to value added for each industry.[12]

In matrix form, the price–value-added balance is expressed as $Q^*P = V$. As before, we can premultiply both sides by $(Q^*)^{-1}$ and in this way determine the prices that must rule for a given set of values added *and* q's: $P = (Q^*)^{-1}V$. Note that if each industry pays for the

---

[12] Consider now an equation involving the top portion of the large square matrix, Q^*, in Exhibit 2, say the first. Assume a five-commodity economy as before.

Since A^* has been transposed (as indicated by the prime to the upper right of A_{11}, etc.), the first column of A^* is now the first row of Q^*, with the coefficients a_{ki} and a_{kl} modified as just explained. Thus the first equation, using *original* subscripts, is:

$$[1 - a_{21} - a_{31} - q_{41} - q_{51}] \begin{bmatrix} p_1 \\ p_2 \\ p_3 \\ p_4 \\ p_5 \end{bmatrix} = v_1$$

or,

$$p_1 - a_{21}p_2 - a_{31}p_3 - q_{41}p_4 - q_{51}p_5 = v_1.$$

This says that the price of commodity number one minus the cost of ordinary inputs numbers two and three minus that *portion* of the per unit cost of eliminating pollutants four and five generated in the production of good number one to be borne by industry number one is equal to the value added of industry number one. Similarly, the equation involving the last line of Q^* is:

$$-a_{1n}p_1 - a_{2n}p_2 - a_{3n}p_3 - q_{4n}p_4 + p_5 = v_n.$$

This says the same thing, with the industry in question a pollution control industry.

whole per unit cost of pollutants eliminated that it has produced (i.e., if r_{ki} and r_{kl} equal 1), then $Q_{21} = A_{21}$ and $Q_{22} = A_{22}$.

By using the relationships established in these equations, various interesting analyses can be performed. For example, calculations can now be made of changes in residuals resulting directly and indirectly from a change in final demand [13] or of the net increase in production needed to achieve a specified reduction in residuals while holding final goods production constant. This analysis accounts not only for the resources needed by the residuals control sector but the resources used indirectly to control residuals from the supplying industries.

Equation (4) and those derived from it balance the system in value terms and admit the possibility of some residuals being controlled by the manufacturing industries themselves (but still in activities separable from their normal production process) rather than only by the residuals control sector.

The appeal of the I-O approach as extended to include residuals generation and control lies in the ease with which it can be implemented. At least two efforts are already underway. Leontief reports on one in this volume, and at our own organization, Resources for the Future, an effort is being made to project resource use and residuals generation several decades into the future by means of a mathematical model which embodies a national input-output matrix.[14] This model contains techniques for projecting the "exogenous" final demands in the I-O model and also techniques for projecting the technical coefficients based on technological change and substitutions induced by relative price shifts. The model also projects residuals from government activities and final consumption.

The economy-wide I-O approach is best suited for residuals problems where location of discharge does not matter, or at least is not a dominant consideration, either for natural or policy reasons. For example, should the increase in atmospheric CO_2 become a problem of real concern, the I-O approach would permit testing the influence of different patterns of final demand on CO_2 discharge, given that the production technology of the economy did not change or changed in accordance with the projections of technical and residual coefficients. In this case the specific loca-

---

[13] When the change in final demand is a unit increase in the ith good or service, ordinary inputs required and residuals generated are the elements of the ith column of $(A^*)^{-1}$.

[14] This work is being conducted by Ronald G. Ridker and Robert U. Ayres.

462 *Amenities and Disamenities of Economic Growth*

tion of the discharge does not matter, because more or less uniform dilution occurs globally—at least in a given hemisphere.

In those cases where concentration, exposure, and assimilative capacity do vary with location, an "ideal" policy would take account of these differences, but certain considerations, cost of implementation, for example, may point to the desirability of national emission standards even in these cases. In this circumstance, the national I-O model will still be of some use. For example, the implications for residuals and industry outputs of alternative patterns of final demand and levels of residuals control can be played out, although the linkage with environmental effects must then be extremely loose.

As of September 1970, performance standards for new facilities had been established by the Environmental Protection Agency (EPA) for nitric acid plants, contact sulfuric acid plants, portland cement plants, large incinerators, and fossil fuel steam plants. In addition, emission standards applicable to all sources will shortly be established for asbestos, mercury, and beryllium.[15] The national I-O approach would be of considerable help in analyzing these and similar cases.

Another calculation that can be made is one in which patterns of final demand are projected under the assumption of no residuals control and with present or projected production technologies, including residuals generation coefficients, going into the future. One can get an impression of alternative possible futures by means of these "projections," as will be possible with the Ridker-Ayres model already mentioned.

The I-O approach as we have described it so far has some notable shortcomings, however:

1. The system as suggested up to this point is on a national scale whereas pollution "problem sheds" tend to be on a regional scale, and sometimes the region is quite small.

2. It has not accounted in a logically complete manner for the residuals generated in production and consumption in the initial attempts at application. In principle, however, the pollutant categories could be expanded to include *all* residuals. If the classification were rather detailed, there would be many pollution "control" industries with zero output.

3. It is usually not correct to think of residuals control as taking place in a separate residual control sector or even in separate residual control activities—especially in the case of industrial activities. In most indus-

[15] *Environmental Quality*, second annual report of the Council on Environmental Quality, August 1971, p. 9.

Benefits and Costs of Environmental Pollution 463

tries, process changes resulting in residual control and greater production of usable products are important alternatives to separate residual control activities either outside or within the industry. The only way such changes resulting either from new application of existing technology or development of new technology can be inserted into the I-O approach is by changing coefficients relating residuals generation to output. There is no internal optimizing method for selecting industrial processes in view of their residual generation characteristics and other economic attributes— unless I-O analysis is abandoned for activity analysis, its close relative.

4. The model focuses on residuals generation and discharge. It does not analyze what happens to residuals once they enter into the environment, nor does it incorporate any consideration of damages. The processes of transportation and transformation in the environment, as affected by hydrological, meteorological, biological, and other natural system conditions have a significant bearing on the damaging effects of a given amount of residuals discharge.

5. The model focuses on residuals control costs but gives no attention to the value of the loss in function of common property resources when their quality deteriorates due to the effects of residuals discharge.

Some of the deficiencies of the I-O approach as just described can be remedied within its framework, but only at the cost of considerable complication. For example, the limitation of national scale of the model immediately suggests regional I-O models. However, even this extension would leave two important limitations: the linearity of the system, which limits the extent of the changes with which it can deal, and the one-to-one relationship between process and product.

Regional and Interregional I-O Models

National boundaries seldom describe a satisfactory area for the analysis of pollution problems. They tend to conform more nearly to natural regions ranging from the entire globe (as with CO_2 and DDT) to small stretches of river or highly localized airsheds. In principle this fact could be accommodated in the I-O approach by developing a set of linked interregional models for the nation. There is not much logical or mathematical difficulty in converting the national to an interregional model. The extensions are straightforward, and consist primarily of adding rows and columns specifying imports to and exports from the various regions. The problem lies rather in data requirements.

There are many reasons for wishing to have a set of coherent I-O

464   *Amenities and Disamenities of Economic Growth*

models for subnational regions. Many tables have been constructed for individual states and regions, but no consistent set exists for the nation as a whole. The pollution issue adds another argument for developing such a system. We propose that discussions be initiated leading to the design of a national system of regional I-O models for analysis of various problems, including residuals generation and discharge.[16]

Accounting for Residuals in a Logically Complete Manner

The residuals generation aspect of the present I-O models does not completely account for all materials flows, including residuals, that are generated by the various parts of the real-world system. There is no environmental sector, and all residuals not processed are viewed as ending up in the final demand sector. Moreover, interdependencies among solid, liquid, and gaseous residuals in production, consumption, and transformation (treatment) processes are not identified or accounted for.

In a recent study by Ayres, d'Arge, and Kneese,[17] models have been explored which provide for a logically complete accounting of materials flowing into production and consumption processes in the economy and thence to the environment. The approach proceeds by specifying a set of equations representing materials balances in conjunction with the equations representing an interdependent economic system. We will treat it only briefly because so far it has had little empirical application. It has called attention to the importance of the conservation of mass in considering residuals processes—both as to the amounts produced and the limitations of treatment processes with respect to them. Essentially all raw materials (in terms of mass) which enter the extractive and materials-processing activities of the economy must be returned to the environment as residuals. This fact is not controverted by the application

[16] A substantial amount of work has already been done on regional environmental problems involving the I-O approach. See John H. Cumberland, "A Regional Interindustry Model for Analysis of Development Objectives," *Regional Science Association Papers*, 1966, pp. 65–94; Cumberland, "Application of Input-Output Technique to the Analysis of Environmental Problems," prepared for the Fifth International Conference on Input-Output Techniques, Geneva, January 11–19, 1971; and Walter Isard et al., "On the Linkage of Socio-Economic and Ecologic Systems," in *Regional Science Association Papers*, 1968, pp. 79–100.

[17] Allen V. Kneese, Robert U. Ayres, and Ralph C. d'Arge, *Economics and the Environment: A Materials Balance Approach*, Washington, D.C., Resources for the Future, Inc., 1971. For later comments on this approach, see Roger G. Noll and John Trijonis, "Mass Balance, General Equilibrium, and Environmental Externalities," *American Economic Review*, September 1971, pp. 730–735; and A. O. Converse, "On the Extension of Input-Output Analysis to Account for Environmental Externalities," *American Economic Review*, March 1971, pp. 197–198.

Benefits and Costs of Environmental Pollution 465

of treatment processes, since they only transform materials and do not destroy them. Some estimates of residuals generated in the U.S. economy have been made based on materials balance concepts, and other applications in analysis and forecasting are being explored.

The model developed by the above-mentioned authors is essentially an extension of the Walras-Cassel-Leontief general interdependency analysis with explicit introduction of the concept of mass balance. Theoretical welfare economic aspects of the model have also been examined, but these are of no particular interest to us here. Extensions of a model comparable to the one presented here have also been examined from a welfare economics point of view by Karl-Göran Mäler.[18]

There are a number of ways in which a comprehensive materials balance might be illustrated. Perhaps the simplest and most direct would be an adaptation of the activity analysis format, as in Exhibit 3. Row headings indicate particular goods or services. Activities (which could be industries but do not have to be) are indicated by column headings. Final consumption activities (here combined into one column) are also included in the format.

A negative entry in a cell indicates the quantity of the good (measured by weight except for services, which must be measured in conventional units) in that row that is used as an input by the corresponding activity. A positive entry in a cell indicates the amount of the good in that row that is produced by the corresponding activity.[19] For example, suppose that on row 3 a -22 appears in column 6 and a $+37$ in column 9. This would mean that 22 units of good 3 are used as an input to activity 6 and that 37 units of good 3 are produced by activity 9.

Resources coming from the environment are always inputs; hence the negative signs as indicated. Purely intermediate goods and services are used only within the industrial sector. Hence, all rows sum to zero for this sector.

Final goods and services have net positive balances for the industrial sector, but the totals for all economic units are zero, since goods and services going to the final consumption sector are regarded as inputs into the consumption activity.

Residuals may go into an activity that transforms them, perhaps producing some salable product (reclamation) along with other residuals or they may go to the environment. The destination might be indicated by a subscript, say A for atmosphere or W for water. In the case of

[18] *Op. cit.*
[19] All entries are per unit of time.

EXHIBIT 3
Format for Materials Balance

Outputs and/or Inputs	Industrial Activities 1	2	. . .	Total	Final Consumption Activities (e.g., households)	Total for All Economic Units	Total to Environment from: Industry	Total to Environment from: Final Consumption	Total from Environment to: Industry	Total from Environment to: Final Consumption
Resources 1. 2. .	–		–	–	–	–	0	0	–	–
Intermediate goods and services 1. 2. .	–	+	–	0	0	0	0	0	0	0
Final goods and services 1. 2. .	–	+		+	–	0	0	0	0	0
Residuals (including pollutants) 1. 2. .	–5 0	0 –2	+3I +2I+4A	0 or + –2 +4	0 or + +2I+3W +3A	0 if all is processed; + if not (some goes to environment) 7	4	3H 3		
Column total (excluding services)	0	0	0	0	0	0				

(Brackets: **B** spans the "Total to Environment from" columns; **C** spans the "Total from Environment to" columns.)

Benefits and Costs of Environmental Pollution 467

residual 1, for example, five units are "processed" by activity 1, of which three come from industry and two from households. These units contribute to the production of the outputs of activity 1, which may include other residuals. Households also discharge three units of residual 1 to water bodies.

In the case of residual 2, two units are used as input by activity 2, all of them coming from industrial activities. Industrial activities also discharge four units to the atmosphere along with three discharged by households.

Residual row totals for all activities will be zero if all of a given residual produced is processed. If not, the row total will be positive, with some of the residual going to the environment.

Neglecting inventory changes, column totals of tangibles should be zero for each activity, as should also the totals coming from and going to the environment ($B = C$).

Needless to say, the practical implementation of a materials balance accounting system would encounter a host of difficulties that have not been touched on here. This format is useful for thinking about pollution problems, however, since it provides the basis for viewing the choice of production and consumption activities and their levels as a programming problem that treats the production and processing of residuals as an integral part of the whole.

An interesting extension of the economic-materials balance model has been made by James E. Wilen.[20] The connecting link between Wilen's model and the economic-materials balance model is the r vector of resources inputs. In broadest overview, the linkage is as follows: via fixed coefficients, a Y vector of final demands determines the vector of resource materials (r) needed for their production. Next, a matrix D is defined such that $D^{-1}r$ yields a vector, m, of the mass and energy inputs necessary to produce r in nature. The use of these inputs to produce ecosystem products going to the economy (r) results in a reduction of ecosystem products available as production inputs into the ecosystem. This reduction is given by Cm, where C is a matrix converting mass and energy inputs into ecoproduct. The return of mass and energy from the economy to the ecosystems can be handled in an analogous fashion and a net impact on the ecoproduct derived.

This formulation is an interesting extension of the model in a highly

[20] James E. Wilen, "Economic Systems and Ecological Systems: An Attempt at Synthesis," paper presented at the Symposium on Economic Growth and the Natural Environment, April 26–28, 1971, University of California, Riverside.

468   *Amenities and Disamenities of Economic Growth*

desirable direction—the incorporation of the ecological impacts of production and consumption activities. However, the formulation does suffer from extreme abstraction and neglects the nonlinearities and interactions that are of central importance in ecological systems—as Wilen recognizes. The problem of linking ecological systems to economic systems will be pursued further in the discussion, below, of the Russell-Spofford model, which exhibits a somewhat greater concreteness and realism.

The Russell-Spofford Model

We have seen that in principle the interindustry-type models can be regionalized, made to account for materials flows to the environment in a logically complete fashion, and, at least in a rough way, to incorporate ecological impacts of production and consumption. We turn now to an operational model of quantitative residuals management devised by Russell and Spofford [21] which to some extent meets all five of the criteria implied by our above discussion:

1. It is regional and location-specific within the region. Its results can be translated into an accounting entity such as gross regional product. In this, it is similar to the I-O models.

2. It can account for residuals in a logically complete manner and does so in some of its submodels.

3. It can treat process, input, and product changes as well as residuals treatment in an integral manner.

4. It traces residuals discharged to the environment through processes of diffusion and degradation and specified concentrations of them at receptor locations. It incorporates an ecological model which translates these concentrations into impacts on higher organisms of direct interest to man.

5. It explicitly considers economic damages to receptors resulting from residuals discharge. In contrast to the I-O type models, it is an optimizing model which can be used to analyze a wide range of policy alternatives.

The Russell-Spofford model deals simultaneously with the three major general types of residuals—airborne, waterborne, and solid—and reflects the physical links among them. It "recognizes," for example, that the decision to remove waterborne organic wastes by standard sew-

[21] Clifford S. Russell and Walter O. Spofford, Jr., are the authors' associates at Resources for the Future, Inc.

Benefits and Costs of Environmental Pollution 469

age treatment processes creates a sludge which, in turn, represents a solid residuals problem; the sludge must either be disposed of on the land or burned, the latter alternative creating airborne particulates and gaseous residuals. Second, it can incorporate the nontreatment alternatives available (especially to industrial firms) for reducing the level of residuals generation. These include input substitution (as of natural gas for coal); change in basic production methods (as in the conversion of beet sugar refineries from the batch to continuous diffusion process —see Chart 1, below); recirculation or residual-bearing streams (as in recirculation of condenser cooling water in thermal-electric generating plants); and by-product recovery (as in the recovery and reuse of fiber, clay, and titanium from the white water "waste" of papermaking machines). Third, the model incorporates and can handle environmental simulation models if necessary, as well as analytical transformation functions which translate quantities of discharge (mass and energy— for example, heat) at particular (source) locations into concentrations at other (receptor) locations. Moreover, it incorporates an ecological model which translates residuals concentrations into impacts upon various species.

The model containing these features is shown schematically in Exhibit 4. The four main components of the over-all framework may be described as follows:

1. A linear programming interindustry model that relates inputs and outputs of selected production processes and consumption activities at specified locations within a region, including the unit amounts and types of residuals generated by the production of each product; the costs of transforming these residuals from one form to another (as of gaseous to liquid in the scrubbing of stack gases); the costs of transporting the residuals from one place to another; and the cost of any final discharge-related activity such as landfill operations.

The interindustry model permits choices among production processes, raw material input mixes, by-product production, recycling of residuals, and in-plant adjustments and improvement, all of which can reduce the total quantity of residuals generated; that is, the residuals generated are not assumed fixed either in form or in quantity. This model also allows for choices among treatment processes and hence among the possible forms of the residual to be disposed of in the natural environment and, to a limited extent, among the locations at which discharge is accomplished.

470 *Amenities and Disamenities of Economic Growth*

EXHIBIT 4

Schematic Diagram of Residuals—Environmental Quality Planning Model

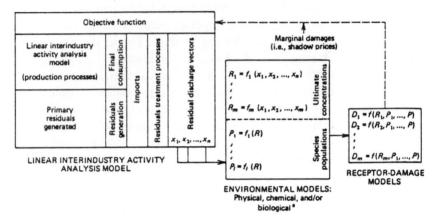

ª Linear and nonlinear analytical expressions as well as simulation models are implied by these expressions. For simplicity, the functions in the figure reflect only one type of pollutant.

2. Environmental diffusion models which describe the end of various residuals after their discharge into the physical environment. Essentially, these models may be thought of as transformation functions operating on the vector of residuals discharges and yielding another vector of ambient concentrations at specific locations throughout the environment. Between discharge point and receptor locations, the residual may be diluted in the relatively large volume of air or water in the natural world, transformed from one form to another (as in the decay of oxygen-demanding organics), accumulated or stored (as in the accumulation of organics in benthal deposits) and, of course, transported to another place. Fortunately, for many situations the equations characterizing the transformation of residuals between discharge and receptor locations reduce to simple linear forms for steady-state deterministic conditions so that the linkage sometimes can be made via a coefficient.[22]

3. Ecological models analogous to the more familiar physical diffusion models are models of ecological systems which reflect the changes (as through a food chain) following on the introduction of a particular

[22] It should be noted, however, that physical, chemical, and/or biological interactions among residuals in the environment cannot be handled quite so easily.

Benefits and Costs of Environmental Pollution 471

residual discharge or on moving to a different set of ambient concentrations. Instead of residuals concentrations as the end products of this type of model, we might obtain estimates of the populations of species of direct interest to man, such as sport fish or rare and endangered animals.

4. Ideally, a set of receptor-damage functions relating the concentration of residuals in the environment and the impact on species to the resulting damages, whether these are sustained directly by humans or indirectly through impacts on material objects or the medium of such receptors as plants or animals in which man has a commercial, scientific, or aesthetic interest. Ideally, the functions relating concentrations and impacts on species to receptor damage should be in monetary terms. Actually, adequate damage functions have not been estimated for any phase of the residuals problem. Consequently, in the computations so far, which have been aimed at testing the whole framework, it has been necessary to use arbitrary functions.

As an alternative to the use of damage functions in the analysis (or in their absence), constraints, or standards, could be specified for emissions or for concentrations at points where receptors are exposed to the pollutant. In practice, this will be a very important type of analysis because of the many difficulties in estimating damage functions.

The linkage between the components and the method of optimum-seeking may be explained in an illustrative way as follows. Solve the linear programming model initially [23] with no restrictions or prices on the discharge of residuals. Using the resulting initial set of discharges as inputs to the diffusion models and the resulting ambient concentrations as the arguments of the damage functions, the marginal damages can be determined (damage associated with a unit change in discharge). These marginal damages may then be applied as interim effluent charges on the discharge activities in the linear model, and that model solved again for a new set of production, consumption, treatment, and discharge activities. The procedure is repeated until the optimum is found.

This procedure can be looked at as a steepest ascent technique for solving a nonlinear programming problem. The objective function is linearized locally, using the provisional marginal damages as "fixed" residuals discharge prices. Because the constraint set is also linear, the resulting problem may be solved using standard linear programming

[23] There are a number of different ways in which the objective function and constraints might be formulated.

472 *Amenities and Disamenities of Economic Growth*

methods. This linearized subproblem is solved subject to suitable bounds on the allowable distance that a decision variable may move in a single iteration. The objective function is then linearized again around the new temporary solution point, and so on until a local optimum is reached.

The problem for which the model is intended to provide an approximate solution could also be stated in a completely general manner not suitable to numerical solution, as the above described version is, but perhaps easier to understand. The objective is to maximize, for a region, a complicated economic criterion function reflecting the costs of regional production, the benefits from regional consumption, the costs of residuals treatment, and the external damages resulting from residuals discharges, with allowance for the "assimilative" capabilities of the regional environment.[24] In this form, the regional residuals management problem is a general nonlinear programming problem, with both objective function and some constraints being nonlinear. But since the solution of a nonlinear problem as complicated as this one may be very difficult, if not impossible, it is useful to make the changes required to get rid of the nonlinearities. The problem then appears as sketched earlier.

The Russell-Spofford model was designed for the analysis of residuals management in regions where the scale and severity of the problems justify a considerable investment in data and analysis. The model is now in the process of being applied to the lower Delaware River basin. As a result, we shall know a good deal more about the precise form the model should take and about the volume and nature of the data required to provide a useful tool.

The model does not completely portray all aspects of the simultaneous economic production of goods and services and the handling of residuals. As it now stands, it does not incorporate adaptations at the consumer or household level. In principle, the consumer can be viewed as choosing among "consumption processes" to maximize utility in a manner entirely analogous to the choice among production processes that is an integral part of the solution of the linear programming part of the R-S model.[25] Specification of the consumption processes would

[24] For more detailed explanations of the model, see Clifford S. Russell and Walter O. Spofford, Jr., "A Quantitative Framework for Residuals Management Decisions," in Allen V. Kneese and Blair T. Bower, eds., *Environmental Quality Analysis: Theory and Method in the Social Sciences*, Baltimore, Johns Hopkins Press, 1971; and Clifford S. Russell, "Regional Environmental Quality Management: A Quantitative Approach," paper presented at the California Institute of Technology Conference on Technological Change and the Human Environment, October 19–21, 1970.

[25] See Kelvin Lancaster, "A New Approach to Consumer Theory," *Journal of Political Economy*, April 1966, pp. 132–157.

Benefits and Costs of Environmental Pollution   473

be enormously difficult, but the omission no doubt is quantitatively important for some problems. The cheapest way to reduce exposure to some pollutants is by substitution in the consumer budget.

Another partial limitation is the way in which the locational aspects of the problem are handled. As pointed out above, the model is location-specific in that locations of emission sources and receptors play an essential role in determining the concentrations to which receptors are exposed. The model does not optimize for location, however. That is to say, the effects of different specified locational configurations must be compared by successively solving models incorporating them. Apart from these limitations, the R-S model presents a pattern for considering analysis of environmental pollution problems that provides valuable guidance for the collection and organization of pertinent data.

III. DATA NEEDS SUGGESTED BY THE MODELS FOR ANALYSIS OF ENVIRONMENTAL POLLUTION

The models for analysis of environmental pollution discussed above could be implemented in various degrees of complexity and detail. They could be complicated or extended, as, for example, by a more elaborate treatment of the location factor or by giving direct attention to consumer response to changed conditions (including price changes) resulting from pollution controls.

Clearly, the types and depth of data that will be needed are going to depend on the particular forms of these and other possible models that will be found to be useful in grappling with pollution problems. Useful guidance for practical data decisions will be provided by efforts under way to implement the national I-O model, the Russell-Spofford model, and possibly others. Without waiting for substantial progress on these efforts, however, it is possible to make a few detailed suggestions for data on the basis of what we already know and to make a number of more general suggestions on types of data whose compilation should be initiated or expanded.

Our suggestions on needs for continuing data will be considered under two categories. First, baselines need to be established and maintained, the general idea being that departures from baselines serve as warning signals. Two types of baseline data will be considered: first, measures of a summary or indicator nature which will be useful for the general public, and, second, more detailed or sophisticated baselines useful to technicians. The second general category consists of data more directly needed for the design, analysis, and administration of pollution control schemes.

474   *Amenities and Disamenities of Economic Growth*

The idea behind use of the term "baseline" seems to be that in the absence of interference the system under examination—for example, an ecological system—continues to function in a manner approximating a steady state. This must be understood to include the case of nonexplosive oscillatory behavior, too. A definite departure from this baseline situation indicates that a new element has been introduced into the operation of the system. The resulting change may or may not be desirable with respect to human objectives. In any case, departure from the baseline calls for investigation. If the effect of the intrusion is benign, it would be good to know what has happened, for we might be able to turn the mechanism involved to our account. If the effect has been undesirable, we ought to understand what has happened, for the observed deterioration may presage more serious effects unless the disturbing factor is properly dealt with.

Baseline and Indicator Data for the Citizen

It is unlikely that any problem involving deterioration of the "environment" can be handled by public action unless a substantial part of the public understands that a particular type of deterioration actually has taken place. This is necessary if there is to be any consideration at all of the desirability of remedial action by members of the public and its elected representatives.

The general characteristics of baseline measures that might fill this need are suggested and limited by the level of technical understanding of the general public of the various physical and biological systems. Although the level of comprehension no doubt is rising gradually, the types of measures needed can best be characterized as indicators. The indicator itself may not be a part of the group of variables that are significant for control or manipulation of the system, although it will be closely associated with the variables that the expert might view as expressing best the state of the system in question.

With this in mind, it is possible to suggest some of the characteristics that a system of indicators useful to the general public should have. First, and very important, the number of indicators should be limited, for there is no useful result to be expected from asking the ordinary citizen to take the time to determine the significance of several hundred series even if he could. Indeed, even for the expert the very idea of changes in the state of a system that have significance for man seems to imply the view that there are some variables that perform the function of summarization. This function should be the main basis for choos-

Benefits and Costs of Environmental Pollution 475

ing the limited number of indicators. In systems with living organisms, the measure should be chosen with a view to its properties as an integrator of effects over time and over a variety of intrusions. This suggests that indicators probably should be chosen from the higher trophic levels of the various types of ecosystems in which we are interested, since in many cases substances are concentrated as the successive members of the food chain eat each other, thereby revealing adverse effects or intrusions more clearly.

To give concreteness to these general considerations, a few candidates for general indicators are suggested here. Our purpose is only to provide illustrations and not to suggest that these ought to be among the indicators that should be adopted, this determination being one that we gladly leave to the experts in these matters.

In the case of water bodies, changes in the various types of fish populations are a good summary indicator of changes in many aspects of the aquatic environment. The complete disappearance of certain types of fish is easily understood to signify a major change in the condition of the water body, perhaps a large change in dissolved oxygen content or the introduction of substances incompatible with the species in question.

In water bodies of various types, especially estuaries, changes in the distribution of the populations of different types of shellfish or in their density at particular locations can serve as summary indicators of effects flowing from a variety of sources.

A physical aspect of water bodies that is of direct concern to the nonexpert is turbidity, a quality that is measured in an easily understood standard way. Changes in turbidity—on the average, seasonal, after rains, etc.—may be caused by a variety of factors, which is the same as saying that this is an integrative indicator, a property we believe to be desirable. Note that the emphasis here is on changes in turbidity. In some cases natural conditions produce a permanently high but harmless level of turbidity.

Changes in bird populations are indicative of changes in soil and vegetation. That these changes can register effectively the introduction of pesticides into the soil and other parts of the environment (as, for example, with the introduction of the poison compound 1080 into carrion eaten by birds) is widely understood. The whole web of relations involved is very complex, of course, but the summarization of the effects on birds is just the kind of indicator that is needed to lead the nontechnician to an awareness that something important may be hap-

476   *Amenities and Disamenities of Economic Growth*

pening which will affect other things that may be more important to him than the birds themselves.[26]

In the case of the atmosphere, some of the pollutants that may have adverse effects on health are not visible nor do they have a distinctive odor. Still, because the presence of this type of pollutant is associated with the presence of other pollutants that are directly detectable by persons, an indicator of detectable pollutants can serve the double purpose of warning of the perceptible changes as well as those not directly accessible to human perception. What types of measure might qualify? There are various ways to measure haze, but many of the methods have no immediate significance for the nonexpert. Again, merely to indicate the *type* of measure needed, one possibility easily understood by the nonexpert would be an adaptation of a procedure used to test the quality of a camera lens. In this test a standard test card with various numbers of lines per inch on it is photographed under standard conditions (distance, light, etc.). Perhaps it would be possible to use a somewhat similar test to measure haze, for example, by photographing a test card under standard conditions at rather long distances. Whatever the method of measurement the technical expert might finally recommend, it is desirable that the procedure and the way in which the results of the test are expressed have a ready meaning for the ordinary person.[27]

The particulate content of the air is of rather direct significance for the nonexpert and would qualify as a suitable measure if translated into a form or forms with simple meaning, perhaps by a simple model of the respiration process or as calculated deposition per year under standard conditions.

Is the miner's canary the prototype of an indicator of the general severity of air pollution for health? Ideally several types of indicator, which might be insects, plants, or animals, would be useful. Some indicators are especially sensitive to particular pollutants, and the same indicator may not serve equally well to register acute episodes and longer-

[26] Leaving aside aesthetic or recreational interest in a wild animal or bird, the view of some—that extinction of a species is nothing very significant since extinctions have been occurring throughout all natural history—begs the question. This question is whether the observed imminent or actual extinction is the result of a change that will produce adverse effects in addition to the observed extinction.

[27] One of the authors was told of a similar and even simpler test conducted in Tokyo, Japan, over a period of many years. It appears that one gentleman kept a record each day of whether Mount Fuji could be seen or not. Over the period of rapid industrialization, the number of days per year on which it could be seen declined from about 90 to less than 1. What more dramatic indicator of air pollution for a Tokyo resident could be found?

Benefits and Costs of Environmental Pollution 477

term changes in pollutant levels. In any case, the desideratum is that a change in pollutant level increase mortality or produce other easily observable and quantifiable changes in appearance or function. Colonies of indicator plants, insects, or animals could be maintained in various cities and other environments with the members having a standard genetic composition and receiving standard care. The resulting data would serve as indicators of differences in pollution in time and space, thus suggesting when and where additional investigation should be undertaken.

Note that there is a locational aspect to all of the baseline indicators discussed to this point. Although some of them probably could be combined into state, regional, or national measures, there is little reason to do so. The effects are not national as are those, for example, of so many economic phenomena whose effects are dispersed and homogenized by the market mechanism. The appropriate remedies often appear to be mainly local, granted that it is possible and in some cases may be desirable to apply measures that require uniform action across the nation regardless of variation between locations in the damages produced and in the cost of reducing pollutants to reduce damages by a given amount.

Baseline and Indicator Data for the Experts

The rationale for baseline data useful to technical experts on various aspects of the physical environment is the same as that for indicators useful to the nonexpert. Movement of a measure outside the range of values it has taken in the past serves as a warning that something important may have happened. If the causative factor can be identified and its effect was adverse, it may be possible to develop corrective measures.

There is no need that data collected on a regular basis for possible use by experts have an immediate or obvious significance for the non-technical person. Nor is it necessary that all of them should be rather summary and/or integrative. Detail is no bar to data being useful to the expert, for if he truly is expert he will know how to use it and put it to work, but it is important to realize that he, too, can be overwhelmed by the enormously high rate at which some types of data can now be generated. This category of data should include a number of "basic" physical, chemical, and biological characteristics of the various environments.

Physical and chemical data. A good illustration of a data system for basic physical characteristics of an environment is provided by the pres-

478   *Amenities and Disamenities of Economic Growth*

ent data system for water quality in the United States. The label "water quality" is somewhat misleading, of course, since what is involved are characteristics which do not indicate generalized quality in and of themselves. This depends on the values attached to physical qualities by water users.

The water data system includes a large number of variables, generally expressed as concentrations, including several families of chemicals (e.g., phenols, chlorinated hydrocarbons), pH, individual metals (e.g., mercury, chrome, cobalt, lead), temperature, various aspects of flow behavior, and so on.

The system of baseline measurements for air pollution is far less well developed, reflecting in part the much shorter period over which interest has been strong enough to lead to formation of a measuring system. Pollutants are but part of a desirable system of atmospheric baselines; others include elemental and basic compound measurements and various meteorological characteristics such as cloud cover—a complex phenomenon in itself.

Baseline measures are needed for all the major natural systems, and in many areas systematic measures have been collected for a long time. What is needed at this time is to examine the scope and adequacy of the various systems of measurement to insure that important areas are not neglected and that the measurement programs meet proper sampling requirements.

Of what use are these seemingly isolated series, multiplied in number to a point that must seem otiose to the nontechnician? If a control system already exists or if the need for one should arise, these series very often will have a direct relevance for design or administration of the control system. More fundamental than this, research on the large-scale behavior of these systems cannot be very productive without data.

It ought to be possible to characterize the major changes in ways that would be meaningful to the nonexpert. Some small beginnings are made in the 1971 report to the Congress of the Council on Environmental Quality, but a larger effort is warranted. One essential is that the summary presentations contain references that will direct the interested person to the basic data sources for continuing series.

Biological data. Biological or ecological baseline data for expert use are needed, too. By and large, the detailed series that ought to be collected for different types of situations must be left to the experts for decision, just as in the case of the physical and chemical series on water quality and in other areas of interest. However, we venture to

Benefits and Costs of Environmental Pollution   479

suggest discussion of one type of more general series, namely, studies of ecosystems. The results of these studies should perhaps be included eventually in an augmented system of social accounts.

Studies of ecosystems. Every location in and bordering the country is a part of an ecosystem of one type or another. How can we get some indication that something important may have gone wrong with the way one of them functions, something that may have serious consequences for humans directly or indirectly? A possible method is a systematic program of repeated studies of different ecosystems at different locations in all parts of the country, including the study of populations of the different species and changes in their characteristics such as size, function, appearance, chemical composition, and so on. The discussion proceeds in terms of populations, since that is an aspect of the studies that is easily understood by the nonexpert.

By population study of an ecosystem we mean a study of the levels or densities of the populations (which could be measured by biomass) of the different species (or larger groups) of living beings in the system. We discuss first the general rationale of such a system and then the factors constraining its implementation.

The rationale of population studies of this type is simple. The basic ideas of ecology tell us that the size of an ecosystem—as expressed, say, by biomass—will depend on the energy and nutrients available to the system, other characteristics of the physical environment, and the species constituents. Ecology can be viewed as the study of the relations among energy, nutrients, and living things that determine the size of the system as measured by the rate of biomass production and the relative numbers (or masses) of the different species.

A fundamental concept here is that of the steady state. That is, if the system is subjected to a temporary disturbance, it will (usually) return to its original equilibrium position after a time. The equilibrium position might actually be one of nonexplosive continual oscillation, and these oscillations might be very complex. If the disturbance is permanent rather than temporary (for example, as with the continued inflow of a degradable pesticide into the system), the system will move to a *different* steady state characterized by a different total biomass and different relations among the numbers (or masses) of the various species originally present. Some may disappear altogether. In the larger and longer view, of course, the idea of a steady state to which ecosystems tend to return is bound to be erroneous because of the presence of natural forces producing progressive alteration of the system. Over

480 *Amenities and Disamenities of Economic Growth*

decades, ecological succession is a major changing force. On the evolutionary time scale, mutations are an important source of change. Our concern, however, is with shorter periods of time to which the concept of steady state has more relevance. Even from a shorter perspective, an "ecosystem" that is so small that it is not well separated from the influences of surrounding systems (that is, a system that is not large relative to the forces coming from the neighboring systems) is likely to evolve progressively, as may be the case, for example, with some of our national parks.

The steady state concept suggests that periodically collected population data for an ecosystem possibly could provide a comprehensive and sensitive indicator of the introduction of foreign substances and also of damage to some of the species therein, thereby indicating possible damage of significance to humans if we eat things related to the ecosystem, if we value it for its beauty or other qualities, or if we ingest things which, although not from this particular ecosystem, have been exposed to or contain the same substance. If the population census were quite detailed, it would direct our attention automatically to the most sensitive parts of the ecosystem, thereby increasing the probability of early warning. Whatever may be the species or group most susceptible to damage by, say, a pesticide, or whatever species that rapidly increases to fill the gap thus created, it would be forcefully brought to our attention by the change in its numbers. Furthermore, low concentrations of the foreign substance would in some cases be brought to our attention by being concentrated in organisms as it passes up the food chain. Some of these organisms near the end of the chain will be affected adversely. For example, reproduction may be impaired or death rates may rise. In other cases, however, the foreign substance may be concentrated in certain tissues without evident adverse effect.

Ideally, a system of population censuses like this would embrace all types of living things in the particular ecosystem including microorganisms, ranging from those on the surface, such as plants, mammals, or birds, those in the soil, those in water bodies, and those in the sediments underlying water bodies. In general, more frequent censuses would seem to be desirable where there already is a large flow of pollutants to an ecosystem, because the composition and quantity of the effluents could change over a comparatively short period of time. In certain cases where man's activities greatly simplify the "natural" ecosystem, as with agriculture, stability of the system is often diminished. It would be desirable that the censuses be more frequent in these cases, too. The period be-

Benefits and Costs of Environmental Pollution   481

tween studies would not have to be the same for every location, although a study ought to be made at the same time of year for a given location and probably should be made at the same time of year for the same type of ecosystem at different locations.

The difficulties. All of the above is a rather idealized version of how a system of studies of ecological systems might work. Unfortunately, there are many difficulties that prevent its realization, not the least of which is cost, which would rise rapidly as the attempt is made to cover each ecosystem site more completely and in more detail. After all, there are critters on critters, some critters have others inside them, and these have others on and in them—not ad infinitum, as a well-known limerick has it, but far enough in that direction to make the complex world of man-made objects seem simple by comparison.

The layman may believe that it is a simple matter to count the numbers of each species, but the unfortunate fact is that the biological world is not so simple nor is species identification or classification into higher groups an easy thing. Perhaps some 10,000 new species are found each year. Among large creatures that are abroad during the day, the number discovered each year is much less. Perhaps only some two or three are added to the list of birds (now about 8,600), but six to seven thousand insects are added each year to the present list of three-quarters of a million. Nor are species easy to identify. Some groups of organisms have no specialists currently studying them, for example.[28]

Having recognized the cost difficulty and the impossibility of taking a complete count by species, we encounter the fact that there is far from a consensus on classification or on what ought to be measured if budgets are limited. This has an important bearing on the effectiveness with which the diagnostic scheme outlined in the discussion of the idealized system can operate. In this case the detection of changes in the functioning of ecosystems depends on changes in relative populations, not of species—which would be too costly—but of larger groups. But the changes that are observed will depend on the type of measures and the classification used, and classification cannot be said to be the object of a very strong consensus. The difficulty is closely related to the problem of inferring changes in the stability of an ecosystem from changes in species diversity. As is so often pointed out, however, measures of species diversity are very sensitive to the particular scheme of classification that is used.

---

[28] See Philip Handler, ed., *Biology and the Future of Man*, New York, Oxford, 1970, p. 518ff.

482   *Amenities and Disamenities of Economic Growth*

Classification difficulties are but one of many in determining when a permanent change has taken place in the system. Populations of ecosystems do fluctuate. As one investigator states, "All populations of organisms fluctuate in size. For any population the only assertion that can be made about it with certainty is that its size will not remain constant." [29] For example, variations in weather affecting vegetal food supply are sufficient to induce changes in populations which will reverberate throughout the whole system, and these will be not only seasonal in nature but very likely annual, too, and of a rather complicated pattern.

In short, how is the usual noise of the system, consisting of fluctuations of populations within the range of past experience, to be distinguished from changes in populations that are associated with a genuine change in the structure of the system that determines its mode of functioning? Clearly there is a distinct possibility that a genuine change— perhaps one with ultimately important consequences—may be evidenced by population movements well within the range of fluctuations that have occurred in the past and that perhaps have been observed. More accurate interpretation of such fluctuations in populations will require much additional research on many aspects of the behavior of pertinent types of ecosystems.

These several difficulties diminish considerably the value that a system of ecosystem studies might at first sight appear to have, but they are far from sufficient to warrant an easy conclusion that a useful system cannot be formulated. What can be done?

One possibility would be to concentrate on some of the many known sensitive indicators.[30] Egg shells, for example, appear to be rather sensitive to the presence of certain pesticides in the environment. In addition, measurement might concentrate on those species or groups of species that are cheaper to identify, count, and/or weigh. Census efforts might be concentrated, for example, on the higher species. Birds would be preferred to mammals, the former being cheaper to count for various reasons. The principal species of fish, shellfish, and insects in an

[29] E. C. Pielou, *An Introduction to Mathematical Ecology*, New York, Wiley-Interscience, 1969, p. 7. Of course the sentences quoted were not intended to deny the existence of forces producing strong tendencies to equilibria.
This excellent work would be quite accessible to the economist with a modest preparation in mathematical statistics and matrix algebra.

[30] Dale Jenkins, director of the ecology program of the Smithsonian Institution, has provided a discussion of a possible biological environmental monitoring system in a paper entitled, "Biological Monitoring of the Global Chemical Environment," June 1, 1971 (processed). Many of the potential monitors are plants.

Benefits and Costs of Environmental Pollution   483

area might be included in the count. And of course in some cases important change may be reflected by an easily observable characteristic other than numbers or mass.

Every act of economy has its cost, of course, and a decision to concentrate on higher species or classes is no exception. It *is* possible that effects of the greatest significance to man would first and most clearly be evident in the detailed functioning of systems of microorganisms. Perhaps a suitable compromise in view of our great ignorance would be to make the censuses of a small number of systems rather complete, extending down to the important microorganisms of the system.

We advocate intense discussion looking forward to a larger, more systematic, and better integrated program of ecosystem studies. It would be extremely useful to have a more adequate system of biological indicators of a number of types in many different locations to give us warning of possible adverse changes that would be detected in other ways only with costly delay.

These suggestions—made very diffidently by nonspecialists—are put forward only to give other nonspecialists a sense of the potential usefulness that we feel such a system may have. Actually, the monitoring systems already in operation, both physical and biological, go a substantial distance in the directions suggested. Apart from the water and air quality systems mentioned earlier, a multiagency pesticide monitoring program has been in operation for a number of years under which residues in foods, feed, people, birds, animals, water, and soil have been measured. Many important changes—and decisions not to change—have been effected through these programs.

There is, of course, a multiplicity of monitoring programs. In the federal government alone, there are some 56 in sixteen agencies, costing about $40 million per year.[31] The mere multiplicity of programs raises the problem of coordination. While there may be good reasons for this multiplicity, it seems clear that the enormous quantity of data being generated is not being distilled into a form that will tell the interested layman what is happening. It ought to be possible for a citizen of, say, Washington, D.C., to find out what has happened to any of the various aspects of the environment in the area around his city over the last one, five, or ten years. At present he cannot possibly do this without calling on the services of not one but several specialists and even then will find many lacunae. To get out of the impasse will require an expanded monitoring effort on many fronts and a much

[31] Kneese and Bower, eds., *Environmental Quality*, p. 210.

484   *Amenities and Disamenities of Economic Growth*

stronger effort to convert the technical data into series that will speak to the nontechnician. The annual report of the Council on Environmental Quality would certainly seem to be the first point of reference. It does give some signs of eventually fulfilling this role.

Data for the Design, Analysis, and Administration of Control Schemes

When it becomes evident through the baseline-monitoring system or other means that something has gone wrong in the environment, the next question is whether remedial action is possible and should be taken. In short, what is needed to design a control scheme and to predict its operation in a way that will facilitate the decision to put it into operation? Three types of data are essential to this task: first, materials balance data; second, production function information—what types of action are possible; and, third, information on the benefits associated with the possible courses of action.

Materials balance accounts. One thing that seems to us to emerge rather clearly from the experience to date is the desirability of a genuinely complete accounting for material inputs and outputs of all economic units, including households, governmental units, and nonprofit institutions, measured in weight, and including those that are sold or paid for as well as those that are not. We discuss first the desirable characteristics of these data without reference to the current status of data collection efforts along these lines.

A materials balance accounting system certainly merits being called basic. These data are essential to almost any approach to the management of unsold residuals flowing from economic units. At a minimum, they permit the identification of sources and locations of emissions and provide the fundamental basis for estimates of transfer and ultimately of exposure. In those cases where a substance is suddenly recognized as an important and perhaps dangerous pollutant, the system would be of immense aid in tracking down the sources of emissions. Finally, if we do find it possible and desirable to move in the direction of models of the sort that have been discussed earlier, the process of implementing them could make very good use of such data. They would be essential for any calculations involving the national input-output system or regional systems that may be constructed in the future. This materials balance accounting system, therefore, should be integrable with the present I-O system, although in some cases a more detailed industrial classification would be desirable.

Classification of the noneconomic output (the residuals or effluents)

Benefits and Costs of Environmental Pollution   485

poses a very difficult problem, and here there is no escape from trying to anticipate later data needs. A considerable body of experience and thought on these matters is reflected in the current classifications of water and air pollution data that are now being collected on a regular basis. An important general question with respect to the classifications now used is whether in certain cases data should be gathered in more detail, as, for example, where one member of a family of pollutants is thought or known to have more serious effects than its relatives.

The products of economic units that are not sold include many things not included in the categories presently regarded as pollutants. One consideration relevant to their classification is the possibility that in the future the substance may be treated in some way (including reclamation) or that it may come to be recognized as a pollutant.

The materials balance accounting system would be more detailed than the I-O system in that discharge data would be for industry *by location*. A location tag for the discharges is an absolutely essential part of the system, although the degree of precision in the location designation need not be the same for all effluents. For those now regarded as important pollutants, the degree of required precision is very high, however. It would be advisable to record initial destination of the effluent in question—whether to an effluent-processing industry or to another disposal site such as atmosphere, water body, or land. In some cases it would be useful to have data not only on final discharges of effluents but also on certain pollutants produced in a plant and processed in that plant.

The data for such an accounting system would be organized by some type of geographical unit. The designation of geographical units should be such that county totals could be formed which could then be related to all the other data presently available on this basis. Probably the geographical unit should not be larger than the county in any case, but where an industrial complex is concentrated in an area, the basic geographical unit should be quite small.

The various censuses will be helpful in developing these balances, but where there are many similar firms in operation, sample coverage would be adequate. The required totals could be estimated on the basis of sample relations between the various materials flows and other variables which are already collected on a comprehensive basis.

Since so many other data with which materials balance data may be associated in the future are available on an annual basis, the calendar year seems to be the appropriate time unit for which the data should

486   *Amenities and Disamenities of Economic Growth*

be prepared for the system as a whole. In the case of many pollutants, however, there are strong seasonal, weekly, daily, or even hourly variations that carry important implications for measurement by control authorities and for the production of damages. Where sample inquiries are made, presumably of firms that emit important quantities of pollutants, it would be convenient simultaneously to collect more detailed data on the temporal variation in these flows. Existing knowledge is probably sufficient to allow a proper determination of firms falling in this category.

Use of a materials balance accounting system does not mean that every economic unit will literally have to weigh every transaction and split it into the various components dictated by the classification scheme. Although the system is an accounting system which in principle implies complete balance for each economic unit, for all subunits of the system, and for the system as a whole (just as is implied by the national income system), the basic data for the system could be built up from a variety of sources.

Emissions of residuals are currently the target of data collection programs of at least three federal agencies: the Water Quality Office and the Air Pollution Control Office of the Environmental Protection Agency [32] and the U.S. Army Corps of Engineers. The first two are using questionnaires and other means to assemble data on quantities and patterns of pollutant emissions. The Corps of Engineers is using the Refuse Act of 1899 (33 U.S. Code 407) as authorization to collect a quite elaborate body of data on industrial and various other discharges to navigable water bodies.

It is not yet clear just how extensive a body of data will result from these efforts, which are of course closely tied in with the current content of control programs in the case of the two EPA agencies. In any case, it seems clear that the existing programs will fall short of providing data by industry (i.e., all sectors of the economy) by location of pollutants emitted, let alone sufficient data to permit construction of a materials balance system of accounts.

It seems to us that the appropriate first step is to assign some statistical agency of the government the task of attempting to construct a system of materials flows on an annual basis. Only by making the attempt will it be possible to coordinate the pollution emission data activities already underway and to identify the gaps that must be filled

[32] Formerly Federal Water Quality Administration and National Air Pollution Control Administration.

Benefits and Costs of Environmental Pollution 487

before a complete set of accounts can be constructed. That the system of accounts be complete is not of importance in and of itself. The overwhelmingly important reason is that the possible repercussions of changes in residuals flows in one part of the system can be traced only if complete materials flow data are available on a rather detailed basis. This is true whether sufficiently detailed I-O systems are available for use or not. Any simpler procedures, such as catch-as-catch-can tracing of principal materials impacts, will require the same sort of data.

A possible result of the attempt to construct the complete system may be the integration of data-gathering activities directed principally at substances presently designated as pollutants. The cost of amplifying the body of basic data that will be available shortly to the point where a periodic accounting of the *whole* materials flow can be made may not be very great if the collection of the additional data needed is integrated with data generation activities already in existence.

Information on control techniques and costs. Historical I-O data, baseline data, and information on materials flows all have an important role to play in the comprehension and analysis of pollution problems, but they provide little direct help in deciding what, if anything, should be done. To make headway on this question, we need to know what options are open. For example, we need to know what the possibilities are for processing an effluent containing pollutants or for changing processes so as to alter the composition of effluents together with the costs associated with these different options. The question of what technical options are available arises not only in connection with industrial effluents, but also in connection with residuals coming from households. Similarly, we need also to know what technical options are available for intervention in a given type of environment to raise its assimilative capacity or to improve its condition and thereby the flow of service coming from it.

Assembly of information of this type does not necessarily entail going far beyond the range of experience. As is well-known, industrial processes often exhibit sizable geographical variations. The fact that processes are changing through time means that at any one time there will be processes recently adopted that may not be widely known. In many cases, it is possible to transfer or adapt processes from one industry or function to another, earlier conditions simply not having been such as to encourage the transfer. Thus there is often a rather wide range of choice simply from among already existing and quite well-known options.

488   *Amenities and Disamenities of Economic Growth*

Techniques and costs of controlling industrial residuals. Control of residuals may take a number of different forms. One possibility, perhaps the most obvious to the nontechnician, is to process the present flow of effluent, that is, to alter the composition of the final effluent so that it is less harmful. Additional inputs will be required, but whether the new effluent will be larger in mass than the old will depend on the extent to which salable products are recovered as a result of the new effluent treatment. In any case the main objective of effluent processing is to change the form of residuals so that they are less harmful or more concentrated and therefore more readily disposed of in comparatively harmless ways. Removal of sludge from sewage and putting it in land-fill is a good example.

Most of the estimates of the cost of pollution control one finds in official documents like *Clean Water* and *Clean Air* are based solely on the processing alternative and therefore tend, as we shall see below, to be too high. On the other hand they also tend to be low because they neglect the interrelations among liquid, solid, and gaseous residuals. A more integrated approach embracing a wider range of options is needed. This is illustrated below with a study of the beet sugar industry.

As just indicated, tacking on additional processes is only one of the possibilities. The composition and size of the effluent stream can also be changed by changing inputs (e.g., by substituting a nonpersistent for a persistent pesticide or by substituting low- for high-sulfur fuel) or by changing basic processes before the stage at which the present effluent is emitted. In addition, it may be possible to change the location of processes so that the concentration of the pollutant-reaching receptors is reduced. Finally, the quality characteristics of the final product can have a large bearing on the amount of residuals generated. For example, production of high brightness paper creates far more chemical residuals than that of low brightness paper.

The type of information on technical options and cost that is needed can be illustrated very forcefully by an examination of the operations of the beet sugar industry in the United States.[33] Here, as in many other industries, the most important of the possible responses to emissions control is not the adding on of separable effluent-processing devices, the technology conventionally considered by engineers and policy makers, but rather process change which results in fuller use of materials either

[33] The discussion in this section is based primarily on George O. G. Löf and Allen V. Kneese, *The Economics of Water Utilization in the Beet Sugar Industry*, Baltimore, Johns Hopkins Press for Resources for the Future, 1968. The materials balance described in later pages was calculated by George Löf.

Benefits and Costs of Environmental Pollution 489

by producing more of the primary product or by generating salable by-products.

As shown in Table 3, one of the major residuals causing water quality deterioration—the organic materials residuals load expressed in pounds of BOD (biochemical oxygen demand) per ton of beets processed—has been reduced greatly in the beet sugar industry as a whole in the last two decades by comparatively simple and economical alterations in processes. The main changes have been substituting beet pulp drying for storage of wet beet pulp in silos and the use of Steffens waste for the production of by-products. These changes reduce BOD generation by about 60 per cent. The other process change, i.e., a shift from cell type to continuous diffusers, is integrally related to recirculation of screen and press water. This further reduces the BOD generated by about 10 per cent.

Chart 1 indicates the main processing and waste water residuals streams in representative beet sugar plants. Chart 2 shows residuals streams in a plant practicing no material or by-product recovery and discharging all of its liquid residuals into a watercourse. A few cases approaching this still exist. Chart 3 shows a plant in which all water is fully recirculated, and there is no external discharge of waterborne residuals. There is one plant in the United States which uses basically this system; the others fall into intermediate positions. Charts 2 and 3 are not only helpful for understanding Table 3, but also the materials balance for a beet sugar plant, presented below.

It should be noted that the "closed" plant requires treatment (in the form of clarification) for its recirculating water stream, even though materials recovery and by-product production have greatly reduced water-borne residuals. Even where opportunities to utilize process changes and increase recovery are favorable, some residual material usually remains. The stream containing this residual may be treated, thus producing a solid or gaseous residual or changing the chemical composition of the waterborne residual. However, the treatment in this case is different from the usual add-on devices in the sense that it is an integral part of a re-circulating water stream which permits the external discharge of waste water to be closed off completely. Admittedly this is an extreme situation, but note that in this instance cost information about add-on devices would yield *no* information about what has been done to control residuals. On the other hand, attributing the cost of all process changes to residuals reduction would be erroneous because many valuable salable products have been generated as a result.

TABLE 3

Estimated Reduction of Biochemical Oxygen Demand (BOD) in Beet Sugar Processing, 1949 and 1962
(1,000 pounds per day)

Type of Waste	1949					1962				
	BOD Generated[a]	BOD Removed by Process Changes[b]	BOD Removed by Waste Treatment	Total BOD Removal	BOD Discharged	BOD Generated[a]	BOD Removed by Process Changes[b]	BOD Removed by Waste Treatment	Total BOD Removal	BOD Discharged
Flume and washer water	510	–	–	100	410	710	–	–	270	440
Cooling water and condensate	80	–	–	10[c]	70[c]	110	–	–	30	80
Pulp screen and press water	550	50	70	120	430	840	630	60	690	150
Silo drainage	1,390[d]	660[e]	140	800	590	1,940[d]	1,920[e]	10	1,930	10
Lime cake slurry	730	0	350	350	380	1,030	0	960	960	70
Steffens filtrate	610	160[f]	80	240	370	770	560[f]	160	720	50
Total BOD	3,870			1,620	2,250	5,400			4,600	800

Benefits and Costs of Environmental Pollution 491

Notes to Table 3

NOTE: Based on 158,000 tons of beets per day processed by 58 plants operating in 1962. In 1949, 113,000 tons per day were processed. To enable direct comparison, the data for 1949 were extrapolated to production of 158,000 tons per day, assuming constant proportions.

SOURCE: George O. G. Löf and Allen V. Kneese, *The Economics of Water Utilization in the Beet Sugar Industry*, Baltimore, Johns Hopkins Press for Resources for the Future, 1968.

[a] Based on BOD per ton of beets sliced in an "unimproved" plant, from U.S. Public Health Service, "Industrial Waste Guide to the Beet Industry," December 1950.

[b] By process changes and recirculation.

[c] Based on estimated 10 per cent reuse as diffuser make-up water.

[d] BOD which would be generated if all spent pulp were handled in silos, i.e., no pulp drying.

[e] BOD not generated because of use of pulp driers.

[f] By recycle-to-production process and production of concentrated Steffens filtrate.

To conclude this section we present a detailed materials balance calculation for two beet sugar production processes. One of these we term "high residual" and the other "low residual." Charts 4 and 5, showing the materials flow and residual materials, correspond to Charts 2 and 3 above, which show the water circulation streams. In a wet-process industry like beet sugar the two are closely related. Table 4 summarizes a few salient figures from the materials balance.

It will be noted from the table that a large reduction in organic residuals was purchased at the expense of a comparatively small increase in potentially harmful gas and inert solids. The interdependence among the residual waste streams going to different environmental media is revealed by these calculations. Considering the environmental circumstances in which most beet sugar factories operate—away from large cities but near small streams with very limited capacity to assimilate organic wastes—the trade-off shown is probably favorable, a conclusion that would not be evident if emission control policies for different media are considered in isolation, as has been the conventional practice.

To sum up, this example illustrates that control of emissions to one environmental medium may come at the expense of increased discharges to another. Consequently, an adequate study of the technology and costs of residuals control must consider the *sets* of emissions levels of interest as being simultaneously imposed for each type of stream. In this case, as probably in others, adjustment to emissions control would also result in greater production of salable output, and the value of this output must be subtracted from the expenditure to get a net cost of control.

Several studies of industrial residuals control taking these factors into account are now in process at Resources for the Future.

CHART 1

Main Processes in a Beet Sugar Plant

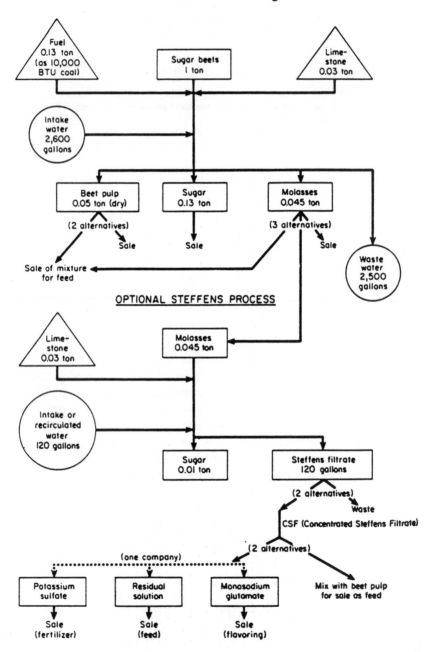

SOURCE: Allen V. Kneese, Robert U. Ayres, and Ralph d'Arge, *Economics and the Environment: A Materials Balance Approach,* Baltimore, Johns Hopkins Press for Resources for the Future, 1970.

Benefits and Costs of Environmental Pollution 493

CHART 2

High Residual Beet Sugar Production Process

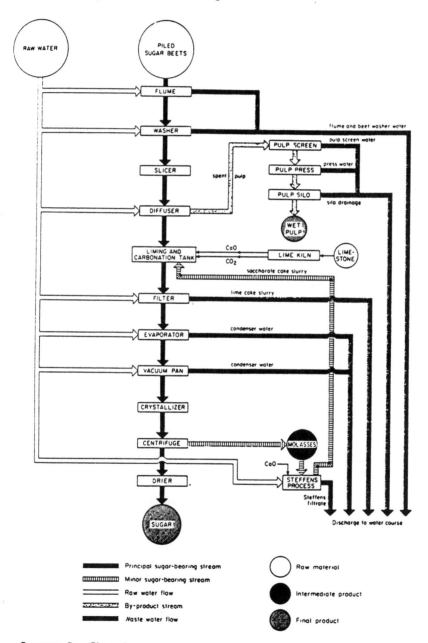

SOURCE: See Chart 1.

494   *Amenities and Disamenities of Economic Growth*

CHART 3

Low Residual Beet Sugar Production Process

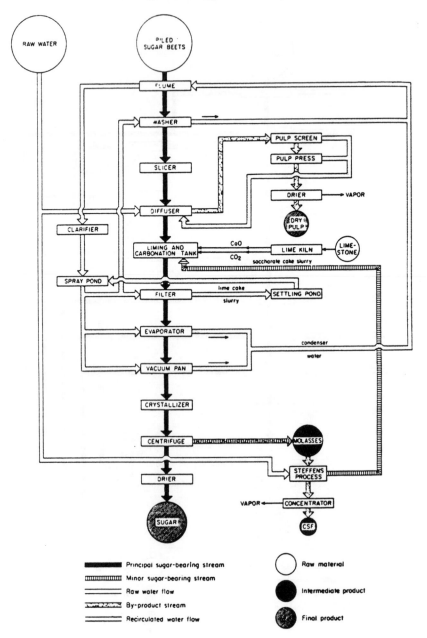

SOURCE: See Chart 1.

CHART 4

High Residual Beet Sugar Production Process Without Recirculation (in pounds per ton of beets processed except where otherwise stated)

Intake: 5,250 gallons per ton of sliced beets—regular; 175 gallons per ton of sliced beets—Steffens additional.

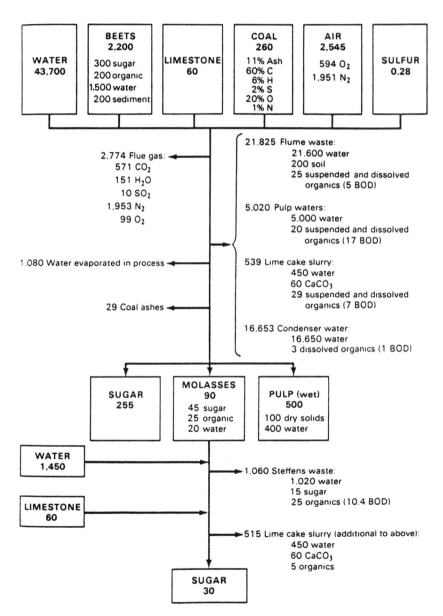

CHART 5

Low Residual Beet Sugar Production Process with Extensive Recycling (in pounds per ton of beets processed except where otherwise stated)

Intake: 270 gallons per ton of sliced beets—regular; 128 gallons per ton of sliced beets—Steffens.

Coal quantity based on 200 for simple plant plus 60 for pulp drying plus 25 for CSF production (evaporation). Coal assumed 10,000 Btu per pound, 11 per cent ash, 60 per cent carbon, 6 per cent hydrogen, 20 per cent oxygen, 2 per cent sulphur, 1 per cent nitrogen. Coal assumed to provide all the plant heat requirements, including pulp drying.

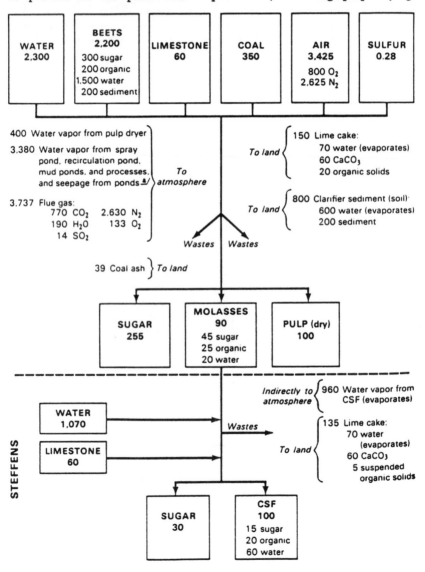

Benefits and Costs of Environmental Pollution 497

TABLE 4

Selected Figures from Materials Balance for
Two Beet Sugar Processes
(pounds per ton of beets processed)

Inputs and Outputs	High Residual Process	Low Residual Process
Raw material inputs		
Beets	2,200	2,200
Limestone	60	60
Coal	260	350
Sulfur	0.28	0.28
Product outputs		
Sugar	285	285
Pulp	100 [a]	100 [b]
Concentrated Steffens filtrate [c]	0	100
Waste residuals		
SO_2	10	14
$CaCO_3$	120	120
Coal ashes	29	39
Organics	122	25
Soil	200	200

SOURCE: Allen V. Kneese, Robert U. Ayres, and Ralph C. d'Arge, *Economics and the Environment: A Materials Balance Approach*, Johns Hopkins Press for Resources for the Future, 1970.

[a] Dry weight of wet pulp.
[b] Dry.
[c] Used for stock feed to recover monosodium glutamate and potassium sulfate.

It seems clear that information on alternative processes is a *sine qua non* for evaluating the implementation of any control scheme, whether this involves effluent charges, emission standards, or outright prohibitions.

Technical options and costs: household residuals and alteration of environmental states. Household residuals are on a par with industrial wastes as regards the need to know the technical options for management. The quantities of such residuals moving into sewers and into present channels of solid waste disposal are very large. Household consumption activities are an important direct contributor to air pollution since transportation, consisting primarily of passenger automobiles, is

498　*Amenities and Disamenities of Economic Growth*

the main source of carbon monoxide, hydrocarbons, and nitrous oxides sent to the atmosphere (71, 53, and 47 per cent, respectively).[34] Large quantities of waste heat are discharged in connection with home heating and cooling. A variety of effluents not entering the usual disposal channels comes from numerous consumption activities, an especially important one for water bodies being oil from motor boats with two stroke motors.

In general terms, the options available for the control and management of household effluents are similar to those for industrial effluents. It is possible to add on treatment devices at the effluent end, as is usually done with domestic sewage and solid waste. Other options are just as important, however, as in the case of industrial effluents. That is, "consumption processes" can be altered and inputs can be changed in ways that will alter the composition of effluents in a less harmful direction and perhaps reduce their quantity. Changes of this type are well illustrated by those already introduced for automobile motors, including closed crankcase ventilation circuits, which result in a more complete burning of hydrocarbons, elimination of atmospheric venting of gasoline tanks and carburetors, the use of unleaded gas with associated changes in motors (such as fuel injection), and alteration of timing in the tuning of motors.

A more fundamental process change would be to abandon the internal combustion engine altogether and substitute for it an inherently low emission engine type like the Rankine cycle. This looks like an option that should be taken very seriously.[35]

Another shift of inputs is exemplified by the changes that have taken place in the last few years in the types of household detergents used.

Clearly there is a need for a large body of up-to-date information on the options available for the management and processing of household discharges to sewers, for gathering, transporting, and processing or disposing of solid wastes, and for discharges going directly to the atmosphere from consumption activities.

Almost needless to say, this type of information on technical options and costs at both the levels of the firm and household is also essential for the effective application of analytical models such as those discussed in part II above. In fact, the building of these models and efforts

---

[34] Kneese and Bower, eds., *Environmental Quality*, p. 212.

[35] See Robert U. Ayres and Richard P. McKenna, *Alternatives to the Internal Combustion Engine: Impacts on Environmental Quality*, Baltimore, Johns Hopkins Press, forthcoming.

Benefits and Costs of Environmental Pollution   499

to bring them to empirical application has probably been the chief stimulus and guidance for structuring the proper approaches to information gathering. The research and information-gathering efforts in this area are, however, tiny in relation to our need to know. Leaving aside scientific and engineering work on details, they amount to no more than a few hundred man-years per year.

The "environment," or particular environments, are the final place for disposal of effluents. Here, too, there are options for control that should be available for consideration. In some cases it may be possible to alter the state of a particular environment so as to increase its assimilative capacity or to reduce adverse effects flowing from it to receptors. Perhaps the most familiar example is the augmentation of low-stream flows through releases from reservoir storage to increase the assimilative capacity of streams. Artificial stream aeration has a similar objective and has proved to be practical in some cases. Another example—not yet brought to fruition—is provided by the schemes that have been proposed to break up temperature inversions in the Los Angeles basin. Sometimes ecological systems can be altered in favorable ways as with the introduction of the coho salmon in the Great Lakes.

Amount and value of damages from different levels of residuals in the environment. It is not enough to know that a pollution control scheme will produce certain physical results at a specified cost. The decision to adopt it or reject it ought to be based on a more or less definite answer to the further question of what difference the change makes to the people concerned. The question we should like to have answered is: How much would the beneficiaries be willing to pay for the change (with what income constraint?) if they understood its nature and significance and if they had the opportunity to buy it? Failing estimates of the value of the change to them, it would be desirable to describe the impact of the change on humans in quantitative or otherwise communicable terms so that some judgment can be made on the desirability of the change. In many cases, it will be found that some of the effects of the change can be quantified and perhaps that values can be attached to them, but some of the effects will not permit this, in which case reliance must be had on a reaction to the proposal based on experience with similar conditions in other areas.

Note that a serious complicating factor is that the damage (or benefit) functions are often not linear, that is, the value of a marginal unit of reduction in a pollutant is not constant, since the initial reductions from a very undesirable situation are more significant than similar

500   *Amenities and Disamenities of Economic Growth*

changes initiated from an already favorable situation. While this characteristic of damage functions means that there will be many cases in which it can be demonstrated that a certain proposed change should be made since it may be possible to establish that the benefits are likely to be much greater than the costs, the question of the extent to which pollution control should be carried requires more precise estimates of the damage functions.

This is in full recognition of the fact that the final decisions concerning the use of common property resources must and should be made through our processes of collective choice, i.e., political processes. The effectiveness with which these work to aggregate preferences is itself an important topic for research and data collection.[36] The collective choice-making process cannot proceed rationally unless usable information about benefits and costs can be made available to it.

Of all the types of information required for formulation of a rational control scheme, the benefit functions are probably in the worst state. Without at least rough estimates of them, there is danger that control measures costing substantial sums will be introduced with little or no benefit, or, on the other side, that we will fail to take relatively cheap steps that could produce benefits far in excess of cost.

The work of Lave and Seskin provides an indication of the state of affairs in one sphere, namely, air pollution.[37] Limiting themselves to the effects of air pollution on human health, they surveyed a large number of studies attempting to relate air pollution to health (mainly epidemiological studies), reworked some of these, and also did a cross-sectional study of mortality, air pollution, and certain socioeconomic factors in 114 standard metropolitan statistical areas. Their summary conclusions are that the evidence is extremely good for association between air pollution and bronchitis and lung cancer but only suggestive for other ailments such as cardiovascular diseases and nonrespiratory tract cancers. They estimate that a 50 per cent reduction in air pollution might produce a 25 to 50 per cent reduction in morbidity and mortality from bronchitis at a saving in cost (direct earnings forgone) of $250 million to $500 million per year; lung cancer mortality would be reduced by 25 per cent with a saving of $33 million per year; all respiratory disease would be reduced by 25 per cent with a saving of $1,222 million per year. In sum, a 50 per cent reduction in air pollution levels in

[36] See Edwin T. Haefele, "Environmental Quality as a Problem of Social Choice," in Kneese and Bower, eds., *Environmental Quality*.

[37] Lester B. Lave and Eugene P. Seskin, "Air Pollution and Human Health," *Science*, August 21, 1970, pp. 723–733.

major urban areas might save about $2 billion per year. Whatever the particular costs assigned, they estimate that 4.5 per cent of the morbidity and mortality associated with air pollution would be saved by a 50 per cent reduction.

Their estimates are significant in indicating the importance of the air pollution problem, and if one believes the coefficients they have estimated, the equations can be applied to local and regional areas, but what is mainly of interest here are the limitations of the estimates. While two major classes of pollutants are distinguished in the Lave-Seskin study (particulates and sulfates), more detailed information would be very useful. A general difficulty afflicting most of the studies examined is the approximate nature of the exposure assigned to the individuals in the samples, the major weakness generally being the implicit assumption that the residents of an area have experienced the current levels of air pollution—as measured—for a long period of time. In fact, even within a city there are often significant variations in exposure. Finally, the availability of data for making such studies is revealed by the fact that they had to limit their own estimates to mortality, although morbidity and other loss of function are probably even more important. There is a great need for a program to generate health statistics that are truly usable for this type of problem.

While we are far from being completely at sea about the costs of air pollution, a great deal more work is warranted to provide more precision, greater detail, and a larger body of evidence. The need is fully as great for other types of pollution control.

IV. CONCLUSIONS

The national accounts approach for measuring benefits and costs resulting from environmental pollution was the first to be considered. While the treatment of industrial outlays for pollution control or defensive expenditures in the present official series is reasonably satisfactory, the consumer end of the problem is not. The difficulty lies in our inability to provide estimates of the value of environmental service flows, positive or negative, not reflected in ordinary transactions, and until this is done, any attempts to doctor the official series are likely to produce new errors to replace those corrected. However, outlays for pollution control and defensive expenditures are of interest in their own right and should be assembled. It can do no harm to see what the official series would look like if they were modified by these series in various ways.

502 *Amenities and Disamenities of Economic Growth*

If benefits and costs from environmental pollution cannot be estimated in the national accounts framework, it is possible to get at them
in a marginal sense. Indeed, estimates of this sort are needed to determine when, where, and how pollution should be controlled.

This line of investigation requires the use of some sort of model to
portray the effects that would result from the institution of different
types of control measures. Several models designed to aid in the analysis of these problems were examined, among them the national I-O
model and the Russell-Spofford model, which is a linear programming
model that can go some distance toward optimizing while taking into
account process options available, transport of pollutants, exposures of
receptors, damages suffered or avoided, and also prediction of changes
in some aspects of the environments involved.

We then examined briefly some of the data and information needed
to apply these models (or any model) to the design of pollution control
schemes. Comprehensive information on materials flows is essential,
and it must be linked with location. A serious problem in the implementation of a materials balance accounting system which we have
only pointed out is that of classification. On the one hand, great detail
is needed because of the specific effects and sources of many pollutants,
but the same degree of detail cannot be carried into all parts of the accounting system. Detail is most important for the flows from economic
units to the environment.

The need for a large body of information on alternative processes
bearing on pollution reduction was emphasized. This is required for
three areas: industrial processes, handling and processing of final consumer effluents, and alteration of environmental states.

Finally, pollution control can come close to its target only if usable
estimates of effects on receptors are available. These should be expressed in money terms if possible. The need for information of this
kind in a form useful to the design of pollution control measures is
pressing.

In sum, progress in measuring the benefits and costs from environmental pollution will depend on the efforts of a very large group of
people with diverse skills. The problem is rendered complex not only
by the physical and biological aspects of the systems involved but also
because pollution problems generally are location-specific. An emission
that has no adverse effects in one area may be a great danger in
another.

We have been able only to allude to the pressing need for estimates of

Benefits and Costs of Environmental Pollution 503

damages suffered from various levels of pollutants in the environment. The desirability of expressing these damages in monetary form, if possible, has been emphasized, although many effects of environmental pollution are psychic. This does not mean that they cannot be related to sums of money, but in many cases this will be very difficult.

The fact that many features of the environment which do not lend themselves very readily to quantitative description may nevertheless be of great importance to many persons greatly complicates the task of comprehensive estimation of benefits and costs from environmental pollution.

COMMENT

WILLIAM VICKREY, Columbia University

I find myself in such close general agreement with what Herfindahl and Kneese present in their paper that I hope I may be forgiven for taking this opportunity to make a few remarks prompted primarily by some of the preceding papers.

Mancur Olson's characterization of governments as generally inefficient has, I think, to be considered in the light of the fact that the activities involved are of a type which, when they are carried on by private enterprise, are to varying degrees carried on by a monopoly, and that these monopolies themselves are often considered to be less efficient than their competitive counterparts. There is a considerable body of opinion, for example, holding that the pricing policies, at least, of publicly owned electric power distribution systems have been more conducive to efficiency than those of privately owned systems. In the case of telephone service, again, many major innovations, among them the combination hand set, direct distance dialing, and free emergency calls from public telephones, were common practice in publicly operated services considerably before they were general in private systems. And while some claims have been made that the quality of service offered tended to be higher in private systems, it is at least arguable that this quality of service might well have been excessive in consideration of its greater cost, motivated by the closer association of private telephone managements with business and higher-income consumers whose preferences for a higher grade of service, even at a higher cost, may have been given rather more weight than might be considered appropriate on an over-all basis. In the field of pricing, especially, public enterprise seems

504　*Amenities and Disamenities of Economic Growth*

to have been more daring than private monopoly: witness the off-peak passenger fare schemes of the Canadian National Railways, the promotional electricity rates of the Tennessee Valley Authority, and the low prices offered by many public telephone systems for very' brief long-distance calls. It is at least dangerous to attempt to judge performance of public enterprise by the financial standards used in the competitive areas of the economy. To the extent that the New Jersey Turnpike is a financial success, for example, it is an economic failure in that such success necessarily entails an impaired performance in relieving congestion on U.S. 1.

There is, to be sure, a "succession problem" that is more severe in government, especially where political parties alternate frequently in power, than in private industry. Private management tends to be judged rather critically in terms of the future prospects of the firm as viewed, at the time the management leaves office, by fairly sophisticated investors. This judgment tends to be reflected fairly conspicuously in the quoted prices of the shares of the company. Government administrations are under a much greater temptation to resolve current issues in an atmosphere of *après moi le déluge* by planting time bombs under the desks of their successors, for example, in the form of labor dispute settlements by which government officials, in collusion with the older and more influential members of the labor unions, provide for large benefits in the form of liberal pension provisions which will constitute substantial windfalls to the older union members, while meaning relatively little in terms of discounted present value to the younger union members and which will constitute a relatively small immediate burden on the public budget, especially if the benefits are unvested or unfunded or both. If bonds can be floated for the financing of non-self-liquidating public works, and sometimes even for current operating expenses that can be capitalized by relabeling as capital improvements what should properly be called maintenance or replacement, there is a grave temptation for incumbents to try to claim the credit for such expenditures, while leaving to their successors the onus of levying the taxes. In extreme cases the resulting policy of "billions for construction, but not one cent for operations" can lead to serious inefficiency, as happened, for example, with the New York Transit Authority, where this general tendency was reinforced, for the period 1951 to 1967, by a legislative mandate that required fares to be raised to cover operating expenses but not capital charges. When to this is added the temptation to favor the construction of enduring monuments to which commemorative

Benefits and Costs of Environmental Pollution   505

plaques and names can be attached, the cumulative bias can be substantial.

I find I am intrigued by Olson's discussion of measurement possibilities in the field of broadcasting. Some aspects of the quantity of the product consumed are measured, at considerable expense, by the Nielson and other ratings, and the price, in terms of involuntary attention to commercials, can be expressed in terms of the ratio of programming to commercial time. As Olson indicates, this is a very high price indeed, the high price being a reflection of the fact that broadcast advertising is intrusive in a way that the classified ads, or even the display ads, in printed media are not. While the price thus exacted is subject to some degree of downward pressure from vague threats of license withdrawal by the FCC, and there is some degree of competition among stations and networks, "price" competition in terms of reducing the proportion of advertising seems to be minimal, with the result tending toward the shared monopoly solution of maximizing total "revenue," interpreted as prices times quantity, or in this case, the aggregate amount of man-hours spent by the the audience listening to or watching commercials. While there may be a modicum of information conveyed in this way, it seems to be far outweighed by misinformation, contained especially in advertisements for drugs of various kinds ranging from caffeine and aspirin to alcohol, the nicotine complex, and narcotics ("sleeping pills") (and then we wonder why we have a drug problem!).

There are interesting ramifications in Olson's suggestion for investigating the more directly monetary aspects of relating demand to a money measure by picking out a sample who would be required to pay a cash price for the reception of each program. It is worth noting that he deems it necessary that those picked out for the sample be compensated by some form of lump sum payment, in contrast to the procedure of drafting men for military service according to their dates of birth without any compensations. It may be hoped that arrangements would be made for appropriately reduced payments if the listener turns the program off in disgust halfway through. It is interesting to consider the application of this technique in another context, that of attempting to evaluate the benefits from an increased frequency of bus service. For example, in a small town the optimal long-run fare for a bus service may well be clearly zero, but whether a 10-minute or a 20-minute service should be operated may be less obvious. One could, experimentally, operate a 10-minute service with alternate buses designated "red" and

506   *Amenities and Disamenities of Economic Growth*

"green" and similarly alternate bus stops designated "red" and "green." Then a suitable sample, say those who cannot show evidence that they were not born on the day of some month corresponding to the current dates would be required to pay an extra fare for boarding a bus of a color not corresponding to the stop they board at. By varying the extra fare and observing how many wait for the succeeding bus rather than pay the extra fare, the value of the more frequent service can be estimated.

Of course, any evaluation of this kind has a cost in that during the evaluation the members of the sample, at least, will not be making optimal use of the service being provided. Moreover, to the extent that the individuals concerned are aware that the results of the measurement will be used to determine whether or not they will get the improved bus service, they may be tempted to bias their behavior according to whether or not they individually prefer the better service, together with whatever share of the added tax burden they expect to have to bear in order to finance it. This bias, moreover, will be the greater the smaller the sample. This can, perhaps, be considered an instance of what might be termed the Acton-Heisenberg principle: "Every use of a measure for a socially important purpose corrupts the measurement, and the worse the measure to begin with or the more important the use, the greater the corruption."

Turning to the Herfindahl-Kneese paper, my chief concern is with the concept that in the long run it is appropriate as a first approximation to assume that environmental services are constant, and that hence a correct welfare concept requires that outlays to control pollution or defend against its presence are not to be considered a part of the final product. While this is a convenient convention that at least reduces a part of the bias inherent in treating as final product outlays that merely preserve the status quo, it introduces an awkward distinction between the accounting procedure deemed appropriate for long-term purposes and that obviously required to account for the impact of short-run variations in antipollution efforts, not related to variations in pollution-producing activity. But although some such convention does represent a compromise, albeit arbitrary, between considering that environment has improved and that it has deteriorated, it does not in principle solve the problem inherent in this appraisal. Impact on the environment is only one of the many aspects of the problem of dividing the product of government activity between final product and intermediate product. If air pollution is a negative, final by-product of industry, to the extent that

Benefits and Costs of Environmental Pollution   507

it is not controlled, do we not also have to consider jails as a negative, final by-product of the government's production of security? It is difficult enough to determine whether even over past history the environment has improved or worsened, considering, for example the impact of DDT on malaria on the one hand and on the peregrine falcon on the other, or the increased pollution of streams vis-à-vis the reduced incidence of typhoid fever on the other; determining what is currently happening, on balance, to the environment, or what environmental trend might be considered optimal is even harder. We have already for a long time been guilty of ignoring the fact that much government output is intermediate product on any reasonable definition. Perhaps in the course of trying to deal with the problem of environmental change we can be brought to face the entire problem of the welfare impact of the government sector more realistically, even at the expense of some accuracy of computation.

In any case it seems a natural extension of the idea of incorporating environmental impacts in an input-output model, whether in terms of economic values or materials balances, that the dynamic aspects not be overlooked, and that distinctions be made between the treatment accorded short-lived pollution, such as that of streams, and of sulphur and nitrogen compounds in the air, and that accorded long-term and in some cases irreversible changes such as the dispersion of heavy metals, the accumulation of carbon dioxide in the atmosphere, or the extinction of species or the introduction of new predators.

Finally, it is perhaps worthwhile pointing out that while when considered in isolation the control of pollution at the household level through effluent charges may appear to involve disproportionately high costs, if such control is considered in conjunction with other costs, such as, in the case of the automobile, congestion and accident costs, the prospects may be considerably brighter. Indeed, if a system of congestion charges were to be instituted, the superposition of charges reflecting marginal pollution costs would be a fairly simple matter, involving chiefly a periodic rating of the individual automobiles, following which charges could be imposed that would take into account such factors as the time and place at which the vehicles are operated, and even, if desired, weather conditions. Such charges would have a salutary role to play especially during periods of transition from more to less pollution-prone vehicles, providing an equitable sharing of the burden between those using the new and those retaining the old vehicles, as well as providing appropriate incentives for the relegation of the pol-

508 *Amenities and Disamenities of Economic Growth*

lution-prone vehicles to types of use where the pollution produced would have less impact. The required mechanism consists merely of some optical or electronic identifier device on each vehicle which will enable it to be identified each time it passes scanning stations located along various screen lines. From the records thus generated and the recorded characteristics of the car, the appropriate charge could be computed and billed to the owner, and would represent the contribution that operation of the vehicle makes to congestion costs, pollution costs, and possibly accident hazard. A cost of assessing and collecting the charge which might be considered excessive for one of these elements separately may become a relatively minor drawback when applied to all three purposes at once.

[15]

From *The United States in the 1980s*, Peter Duignan and Alvin Rabushka, editors

Environmental Policy
Allen V. Kneese

X

That environmental problems are not new is shown by environmental conditions in relatively modern and even medieval cities. The history of the city of London is especially well documented. In the fourteenth century, butchers had been assigned a spot at Seacoal Lane near Fleet prison. A royal document reports: "By the killing of great beasts, from whose putrid blood running down the streets and the bowels cast into the Thames, the air in the city is very much corrupted and infected, whence abominable and most filthy stinks proceed, sickness and many other evils have happened to such as have abode in the said city, or have resorted to it."[1] Five centuries later, Charles Dickens reported, "He knew of many places in it unsurpassed in the accumulated horrors of their long neglect by the dirtiest old spots in the dirtiest old towns, under the worst old governments of Europe."[2]

It seems clear that in developed countries environmental conditions that directly and immediately affect the daily lives of the mass of citizens have improved immensely—at least until the middle of the twentieth century. Why then has environmental pollution become one of the most important problems of the day for many people? Several factors appear to be involved.

First, immense increases in industrial production and energy conversion have occurred in recent decades. The associated flow of materials and energy from concentrated states in nature to dispersed states in the environment have begun to alter the physical, chemical, and biological quality of the atmosphere and hydrosphere on a truly massive scale. Furthermore, we now have the means to detect even small changes in these natural systems.

Second, exotic materials are being introduced into the environment. Applications of modern chemistry and physics have exposed the world's biological systems to strange materials to which they cannot adapt (at least not quickly) or to which adaptation is highly specific among species and therefore disruptive.

Third, the mass of people have come to expect standards of cleanliness, safety, and healthfulness in their surroundings that were the exclusive province of the well-to-do in earlier times.

These considerations also suggest the increasing importance of viewing environmental issues as part of the general natural-resources problem rather than in isolation. In this context the present state of our natural resources policy is, to say the least, not encouraging.

I will return to this theme in a moment, but first, a few comments on the structure of this essay. The next section discusses the nature of environmental problems in the context of broader natural-resources issues. Following that I will review briefly the policies we have developed in the United States to try to deal with our environmental problems. Next, an alternative set of policies is presented, discussed, and evaluated. To this point I will be discussing the "mass" pollutants (for example, oxygen-demanding organic residuals in water and sulfur compounds in the air). These have received by far the greatest amount of legislative and administrative attention. But as the decade closes, efforts to deal with substances in the environment that are small in amount but highly toxic are moving to the center of attention and will greatly challenge our ability to manage the environment over the next several years. The essay concludes with a discussion of policy with respect to this new set of environmental problems.

NATURAL RESOURCES POLICY AND ENVIRONMENTAL ISSUES*

In my view the present state of natural resources in the United States, including policy at the national level with respect to them, is a matter for deep concern. Our policies are fragmented, suffering from multiple schizophrenia, and grossly overdependent upon direct regulation rather than on modification of the defective system of economic incentives, which is a primary source of our resource problems in the first place. To begin to remedy the deficiencies of our resource policies it is necessary to understand that our resource problems, from the energy crunch to the state of our watercourses, from landscapes shattered by surface mining to the often deplorable quality of our urban air, are interrelated issues. To

---

*This section draws heavily on Allen V. Kneese, "Natural Resources Policy 1975–85," *Journal of Environmental Economics and Management* 3, no. 4 (Dec. 1976): 253–288.

come to grips with this web of national problems we need a coherent program of resource policies rather than the scattershot, one-resource-at-a-time approach to legislation that exists today.

To some extent the present situation results from the fact that our policymaking processes are in a state of transitional stress. Policy artifacts such as depletion allowances and many other favorable tax treatments of extractive industries are remnants of a time when encouragement of rapid use of our natural resources was regarded as unquestionably desirable and the discharge of residuals to the environment could be, or at least was, neglected. We have federal oil and gas price regulations that reflect the abundance of another day. At the same time we ration the end uses of some of our fuels. We have in our legal and regulatory structure a number of biases against recycling, but we also have on the books laws that, if successfully implemented, would place strict controls on the use of environmental resources. Our policymakers are trying to come to grips with an inherited policy structure that, although fragmented and often internally contradictory, was largely constructed in an era of resource abundance. For the most part it reflects that context, but it now contains bits and pieces that mirror more recent events.

One aspect of the situation is more distressing, however. Current policy efforts, especially at the congressional level, do not give any evidence of a clear understanding of the basic nature of our resource problems and the associated integration and redirection of policies and modification of the policymaking process that they demand. Nothing could illustrate this more clearly than Congress' confused attempts to develop an energy policy over the past few years. At the most basic level, many of our most severe problems stem from several kinds of failures in the set of incentives that our market system, as it presently functions, generates. In more than a few instances, these misdirected incentives are further aggravated by public policies. Rather than altering perverse incentives, the inclination of Congress has been to move steadily in the direction of establishing more and more complex regulations. Many of these regulations are now coming to be widely recognized as arbitrary and capricious in application. Moreover, they usually fail to achieve their objectives, or if they do achieve them they do so only at great, and often unnecessary, cost.

I will elaborate on this theme. But first it will be helpful to take a look at what economic theory sees as the operation of an ideal market and what the most salient departures of actual markets, especially with respect to environment-resource issues, are from the functioning of this model. This brief digression will provide a somewhat abstract but reasonably coherent framework for the development of a broad perspective on our environmental problems.

The Ideal Market

When economists speak of the market they usually have in mind a particular type of intellectual construct. This conceptual model is the product of an evolutionary intellectual process going back at least as far as Adam Smith's *The Wealth of Nations*. The model grew out of the observation of a very special phenomenon. Economic activities—farming, mining, industrial production, selling, and finance activities—were unplanned and, on the surface at least, seemed entirely uncoordinated, and yet in the end order could be seen in the results. Smith saw with great clarity that the powerful signaling and incentive forces of prices determined by free exchange in markets were at the core of the process that, via many independent economic units, transformed resources into products and distributed them to consumers in accordance with their demands. Hence, his famous phrase "the invisible hand of the market."

In usual circumstances markets do produce an orderly and directed production process. But economic theorists have also been very interested in finding out whether this order was just orderly or whether it might have other desirable or normative properties. Theorists found that the results of an ideal market process may be regarded as desirable or normative if a basic value judgment is accepted and if the market-exchange economy displays certain structural characteristics.

The value judgment is that the personal wants and preferences of the individuals who constitute the present members of a society should guide the use of that society's resources. This is also the premise that is at the root of Anglo-American political theory.

The three structural characteristics are:

—All markets are competitive; this means that no specific firm or individual can influence any market price significantly by decreasing or increasing the supply of goods and services offered by that specific economic unit. A good example is an individual farmer. He can sell or hold his crop as he wishes and yet affect the market price for corn not at all. Competition must extend to all markets, including those for money.

—All participants in the market are fully informed as to the quantitative and qualitative characteristics of goods and services and the terms of exchange among them.

—All valuable assets in the economic system can be individually owned and managed without violating the first assumption—that is, that of perfect competition (this has usually been implicit). Individual ownership of all assets plus competition implies that all costs of production and consumption are borne by the producers and consumers directly involved in economic exchanges. A closely related requirement is that there must be markets for all possible claims. This becomes particularly pertinent when one considers questions on conservation and the role of future markets. I will discuss this matter in a little more detail later in connection with policies regarding nonrenewable natural resources.

If all these conditions hold, it can be concluded that the best social solution to the problem of allocating the society's scarce resources is to limit the role of government to deciding questions of equity in income distribution, providing rules of property and exchange, enforcing competition, and allowing the exchange of privately owned assets in markets to proceed freely.

Market exchange, with each participant pursuing his own private interest, will then lead to a "Pareto optimum" (named after Vilfredo Pareto [1848–1923], a prominent Italian economist and social theoretician). The proof that ideal markets can achieve a Pareto optimum may be regarded as one of the basic theorems of modern theoretical economics. Perhaps the most straightforward way of intuitively grasping the meaning of a Pareto optimum is to regard it as a situation in which all possible gains from voluntary exchange of goods and services have been exhausted and no participant is willing to make further exchanges at the terms of trade that have come to exist. Money is the medium of exchange and prices are the terms of exchange, but behind them lie exchanges of real goods and services of all kinds. Under the conditions postulated, an exchange takes place only when both parties feel they benefit by it. When no more beneficial exchanges can be made, the economic welfare of one individual cannot be improved without damaging that of another—in other words, unless a redistribution of assets favorable to him occurs. When no one can be better off without someone else being worse off, Pareto optimality has been reached. In economic parlance, an efficient balance has been obtained.

The connection between such a market exchange and the real working economy has always been tenuous at best. But the idealized model has served as a standard against which an actual economy could be judged as a resource-allocation mechanism for meeting consumer preferences. I shall use it in this way in considering the current state of our resource problems and policies, especially with respect to environmental resources. But, as I hope this discussion will make clear, questions of resource supply are closely interlaced with environmental considerations. The connection is revealed by considering the conservation of mass.

Pollution Problems in a Market System

With this background, it is easy to see the nature of the malfunction of real markets vis-à-vis the workings of the ideal market: the fundamental cause of pollution problems in market systems. We start with a simple concept from physics.

When materials—minerals, fuels, gases, and organic material—are obtained from nature and used by producers and consumers, their mass is essentially unaltered. Material residuals generated in production and consumption activities must therefore be about equal in mass to the materials initially extracted from nature. Similarly, all energy converted in human activities is discharged to the atmosphere or watercourses.

Conservation of mass-energy, taken together with the peculiar characteristics of environmental resources, has important implications for the allocation of resources in a real market system as contrasted with the ideal one. Although most extractive, harvesting, processing, and distributional activities can be conducted relatively efficiently through the medium of exchange of private ownership rights as the idealized market model envisages, the process of returning the inevitable residuals generated by production and consumption activities makes heavy use of common-property resources.

The term common-property resources refers to those valuable natural assets that cannot, or can only imperfectly, be held in private ownership and that therefore cannot be exchanged in markets like ordinary commodities. Important examples are the air mantle, watercourses, large ecological systems, landscapes, and the auditory and electromagnetic spectrums. When open and unpriced access to such resources is permitted, it is apparent what must happen. Careful study of particular common-property or common-pool problems such as oil pools and ocean fisheries has shown that unhindered access to such resources leads to overuse, misuse, and degradation of quality. Environmental degradation takes the form of discharges of large masses of materials and energy to watercourses and the atmosphere, lowering their quality. The less massive but highly destructive dispersal of litter and junk into urban and rural landscapes stems from the same roots. Furthermore, resource-extraction processes themselves can cause visual and other forms of pollution: clear-cut forests, mine tailings, unreclaimed strip-mine land, and acid mine drainage are just a few examples.

Costs associated with the destructive effects of these situations are of no consequence to the enterprises involved because they are imposed on, or transmitted through, common-property resources. The impacts of these effects, referred to as external costs, are imposed on society as a whole. Pareto optimality is not gained through exchange because private ownership of natural assets must be incomplete. Without ownership, the market can generate no incentive to protect environmental resources.

Conservation of mass-energy tells us that as economic development proceeds and as the flow of the mass of material and energy through the economy increases, provided that environmental resources remain in their common-property status, environmental conditions must display a tendency to get systematically worse as the economy grows.

Another result of looking at environmental pollution problems in terms of the concept of mass balance is that it reveals the interdependencies that must exist among different streams of residuals. For example, treatment of a residual does not reduce its mass: indeed, mass is increased because the treatment process itself requires the input of materials whose mass is also conserved. The result is that pollution control programs aimed at reducing the pollution in one medium often aggravate the problem in another. The incineration of sludge from waste-water treatment plants and the emission of additional gases into an already polluted urban atmosphere is a classic example. Wise environmental policy must provide some means of dealing with quality problems in all the media simultaneously.

As I have indicated, the main source of our environmental problems is the inability of market exchange as it is presently structured to allocate environmental resources efficiently—that is, to price their destructive use appropriately. But if we could stretch our minds and envisage a situation where these common-property resources could be reduced to private ownership in pieces small enough to be exchanged in competitive markets, then, distributional issues aside, the market could function just as efficiently to allocate them as it can to distribute any other resource. Prices would be generated, for example, for the use of air and water for the (usually destructive) activity of waste disposal. These prices would be signals and incentives reflecting the cost of the opportunity to use these resources for waste disposal and would affect the whole complex of decisions about their use—the design of industrial processes and the kinds of raw materials used, the nature of the final products produced, and the modification (not elimination—conservation of mass and energy prevents this) of streams of residuals before the purchaser paid for the privilege of discharging what was left. Conservation would suddenly become good business.

Instead, I have already shown, throughout history these resources have largely remained as open access common property. Moreover, it is so difficult to define rights to environmental resources that the desirable effects of market exchange affecting them must remain merely theoretical. However, explicit pricing of these resources through the medium of government administration could go far toward making environmental protection more efficient and effective than do the policies we now have. Before developing this theme, let us look more explicitly at what the ideas developed so far suggest in terms of the interrelationships between problems in the use of environmental and other resources.

Environmental Market Failure and Resource Commodities

The combination of two simple but illuminating concepts introduced in the previous section, conservation of mass and common-property resources, provides considerable insight into the basic nature of environmental-pollution problems in a market system. But the implications are not limited to environmental matters. When the use of certain (environmental) resources is not priced, the entire price structure gets distorted. Thus the prices of extractive resource commodities, which are exchanged in markets, deviate substantially from the actual social costs of their use. This comes about in two main ways.

First, the removal and processing of extractive resource commodities involve particularly heavy use of environmental resources. Strip mining, the processing of copper, the conversion of coal, the making of steel, and the refining of oil are obvious examples. In the ordinary course of market exchange the social costs associated with any damage to these environmental resources are not reflected in the costs incurred by the private producers of resource commodities and by the ultimate users of the products produced from them.

Second, when such commodities are devoted to their end uses they further generate social costs that the market does not reflect. Junkyards, litter in the countryside, and the combustion of fuel in automobile engines are obvious examples.

Thus the unfettered market generates a systematic bias, the result of which is essentially to subsidize the production of extractive resource commodities. The larger the impact on environmental resources in the extraction, processing, and use of resource commodities, the larger the subsidy. Furthermore, as environmental resources become increasingly scarce and valued, and as the production of environmentally destructive resource commodities increases, the societal subsidy to such production correspondingly increases.

The natural tendency of markets to work in this unfortunate manner is bad enough. But policies formed to stimulate the production of resource commodities during the euphoria of extreme abundance and in the interest of rapid economic growth aggravate the situation. Special tax treatment of extractive industries in relation to ordinary industries abounds. Depletion allowances, capital gains treatment, and expensing of various kinds of capital investments and operating expenditures are obvious examples. Superimposed on all this are policies that favor production from virgin materials rather than use of secondary materials. Railroad rate discrimination and discriminatory labeling requirements are often-cited examples.

The ultimate result of malfunctioning of the market and the biases of policy is excessive use of materials and energy in general, excessive use of virgin materials in particular, too little recovery and reuse of materials and energy, and excessive environmental deterioration. These miscarriages are not isolated and random events: they are a systematic result of the way our market and governmental institutions have operated.

In the context of the conceptual framework I have just developed, I will briefly review pertinent aspects of our efforts to deal with environmental problems in the United States.

Evolution of Environmental Policy

Over the post–World War II period, at all levels of government in the United States, numerous laws have been passed attempting to come to grips with the degradation of environmental quality. The rationale for such laws has been totally unrelated to the concepts I have developed in previous sections of this essay. In this process of policy formation, the role of the central government has gradually become increasingly dominant. It is worth reviewing the history of federal legislation in a little detail because it clearly highlights the pitfalls of exclusive reliance on efforts to impose direct regulations and on subsidy approaches. A summary review of the complete set of air and water laws is found in Table 1. I will select some of the more pertinent acts for brief discussion in the text.[3]

With respect to both air and water, the early federal legislation (in the 1950s) established enforcement action against individual sources of residuals discharges as the principal policy tool for controlling those discharges. These actions could be brought by the federal authorities against residuals dischargers if specific interstate damage could be demonstrated to have resulted directly from discharges at a particular

TABLE 1

Outline of Major Federal Legislation on Air and Water Pollution Control

Date of Enactment	Popular Title and Official Citation	Key Provisions
	Water	
March 3, 1899	1899 Refuse Act (30 Stat. 1152)	Required permit from chief of engineers for discharge of refuse into navigable waters.
June 30, 1948	Water Pollution Control Act (62 Stat. 1155)	Gave the federal government authority for investigation, research, and surveys; left primary responsibility for pollution control with the states.
July 9, 1956	Water Pollution Control Act Amendments of 1956 (70 Stat. 498)	Established federal policy for 1956–1970 period. Provided 1) federal grants for construction of munici-pal water treatment plants; and 2) complex procedure for federal enforcement actions against individual dischargers. (Some strengthening amendments were enacted in 1961.)
October 2, 1965	Water Quality Act of 1965 (79 Stat. 903)	Sought to strengthen enforcement process; pro-vided for federal approval of ambient standards for interstate waters. (Minor strengthening amendments were enacted in 1966 and 1970.)
October 18, 1972	1972 Water Pollution Act Amendments (86 Stat. 816)	Set policy under which federal government now operates. Provided 1) fed-eral establishment of effluent limits for individual sources of pollution; 2) issuance of discharge per-mits; and 3) large increase in authorized grant funds for municipal waste treatment plants.
	Air	
July 14, 1955	1955 Air Pollution Control Act (69 Stat. 322)	Authorized, for the first time, a federal program of research, training, and demonstrations related to air pollution control. (Ex-tended for four years by the amendments of 1959.)

TABLE 1 (continued)

Date of Enactment	Popular Title and Official Citation	Key Provisions
December 17, 1963	Clean Air Act (77 Stat. 392)	Gave the federal government enforcement powers over air pollution through enforcement conferences—a method similar to 1956 approach for water pollution control.
October 20, 1966	Motor Vehicle Air Pollution Control act (79 Stat. 992)	Added new authority to 1963 act, giving the Department of Health, Education, and Welfare power to prescribe emissions standards for automobiles as soon as practicable.
November 21, 1967	Air Quality Act of 1967 (81 Stat. 485)	1) Authorized HEW to oversee establishment of state standards for ambient air quality and of state implementation plans; and 2) for the first time, set national standards for automobile emissions.
December 31, 1970	Clean Air Amendments of 1970 (84 Stat. 1676)	Sharply expanded the federal role in setting and enforcing standards for ambient air quality and established stringent new emissions standards for automobiles.

SOURCE: Allen V. Kneese and Charles L. Schultze, *Pollution, Prices, and Public Policy* (Washington, D.C.: The Brookings Institution, 1975) p. 31–32.

source. Laws providing for modest federal subsidies for construction of municipal waste-water treatment plants and for certain water quality planning activities were also introduced early in the postwar period. It is now generally agreed that these first federal legislative enactments had little or no positive effect on the quality of the nation's environment.

Succeeding legislation was passed in an effort to strengthen enforcement provisions of earlier laws and, in a series of steps, the number of federal subsidies authorized for construction of municipal waste-water treatment plants was increased. Beginning in the mid-1960s, in the Water Quality Act of 1965, Congress began trying to circumvent the necessity for showing actual interstate damage in federal enforcement actions in the water quality area. This was to be accomplished by requiring the states to set water quality standards for interstate and boundary waters and to develop plans for attaining these standards. After many delays, the states finally complied in the late 1960s.

264   /   ENVIRONMENTAL POLICY

Watercourse standards were set by the state agencies on the basis of more- or (usually) less-informed consideration of potential water uses. The idea embodied by the law was that violations of water quality standards as a result of failure by a discharger to conform to the plan were to be regarded as prima facie evidence of interstate impact, without the necessity to show that direct damage had resulted in one state from a specific discharge in another.

A similar approach was legislated a few years later for air quality. But in this case nationally uniform ambient standards were set that were supposed to represent a threshold below which no health damage would occur—a politically convenient fiction. In addition, new sources of atmospheric emissions were supposed to be equipped with the best available control technology, and federal law, following the lead of California, began to specify stringent effluent limitations on automobile emissions.

The ambient standards implementation plan was no more effective as an approach to the water quality problem than the previous law had been. By the end of the 1960s it became apparent that nearly all the implementation plans were so loosely related to the water quality standards that the law would be unenforceable. Furthermore, the subsidy programs for the construction of waste-water treatment plants not only had been relatively ineffective but also had resulted in serious inefficiencies of various sorts. I will return to this point a bit later. At about the same time, an ancient piece of water legislation, the 1899 Refuse Act, was rediscovered. This law required that all industrial waste dischargers have permits from the U.S. Army Corps of Engineers. The provision was clearly intended to protect navigation, but it was now interpreted to extend to all forms of residuals discharged to watercourses. Enforcement of the law was started, and the Corps of Engineers received a large number of applications and began to issue some permits. But shortly before the process of issuing permits began, Congress passed another environmental law, the National Environmental Protection Act (NEPA). This law, among its various provisions, required that all federal, and federally supported, actions having a potentially significant impact on the environment must be preceded by an environmental impact statement. The courts ruled that permit-issuing activities of the Corps of Engineers fell under the provisions of the act. Consequently, the corps abandoned the hopeless task of issuing permits for which tens of thousands of environmental impact statements would be needed.

Following these events, Congress passed a new water quality law in

1972. Among its provisions was the requirement that permits be issued for all point-source waste discharges to watercourses. This time the permit issuing was not subject to the provisions of the NEPA and was to be done by the Environmental Protection Agency (EPA) and the states. Although the current law is notoriously ambiguous, the intent of its supporters seems to have been to make uniform across the nation the permit requirements for particular industries and municipalities. These requirements are to be based primarily on considerations of technical feasibility rather than on the uses to which receiving waters are to be put. However, stream standards established under the 1965 act are still to be the controlling ones if discharges under the permit system should result in poorer water quality than they required (one-third to one-half the stream miles in the country may fall into this category). The permit stipulations are also intended to become stricter in a succession of steps until a national goal of zero discharge is achieved in 1985. Subsidies for construction of municipal waste-water treatment plants were increased mightily by the 1972 laws, and under provisions of other laws, industries can benefit from rapid write-off of pollution control equipment against taxes and from low-interest municipal bond funding of facilities.

The pattern then, applying to both air and water and culminating in the most recent water quality legislation, has been toward increasingly heavy federal subsidization of certain kinds of pollution control facilities, greater and greater centralization of control efforts increasingly based on emission standards that are in turn based on some sort of concept of technical feasibility, and an effort to make emission standards as uniform nationally as possible.

There are several reasons for having deep reservations about the pollution control program that has evolved in the United States. The federal subsidies that have been provided bias the choice of control technologies toward end-of-the-pipe treatments rather than toward the use of processes that reduce the generation of waste in the first place. In practice, the municipal subsidies have tended to slow down construction as municipalities have queued up to await federal funds whose availability has always been less than authorized, or, more recently, as municipalities have striven to obey the letter of the law in planning requirements.

The imposition of uniform standards (for instance, among waste dischargers)—the objective of the federal legislation—implies that discharges from sources where control costs are high have to be controlled as much as those from sources where control costs are low. Accordingly, any level of ambient environmental quality attained is accompanied by higher costs (research suggests that these are higher by a multiple) than would be associated with a least-cost set of control efforts. Specifying particular "best available" technologies to be used in pollution control may have a serious dampening effect on the development of new pollution control technology. It puts firms in a quandary: if they innovate, they hand the regulatory authorities the means of imposing on them new and more stringent standards of pollution control. With respect to automobile emissions, for example, present control efforts appear to have locked us into a technology (reliance on modification of the internal combustion engine) that many scientific reports conclude is a very poor long-run approach to the problem.

Finally, the history of efforts to enforce the federal government's pollution laws, together with the vast short-term cost implications of recent legislation (should it be successfully implemented), elicit deep doubts about whether the federal program can ever be effectively enforced, much less whether it can produce efficient results. Even though an objective of recent legislation, especially of the Water Quality Act, was to make enforcement easier and more effective, there is still room in the actual statutes for staggering amounts of litigation and all the attendant delays. Large-scale litigation is in process. Many informed students of the permit-issuing process believe that the result will be to force permit requirements, for those permits that are issued, down to the lowest level of accepted practice, and that substantial environmental improvement will not be the result. Legislation for control of air pollution from stationary sources is still largely untested, but there are some major cases in the courts, and those reductions in emissions that have occurred by means of fuel substitution show signs of disappearing in the wake of the energy crisis as the nation shifts to greater emphasis on the utilization of coal. The automotive emissions provisions of the Clean Air Act have produced tinkering with the standard internal combustion engine rather than a shift to basically low-emission engine technologies.

A basic problem with the present program is that enforcement, especially since it involves criminal penalties, must leave ample room for due process: this means that there are many possibilities for delays or variances while the free-of-charge use of common-property resources continues. The economic incentive for users is to hire lawyers rather than to get on with discharge control. The recent report of the National Commission on Water Quality is implicitly a devastating indictment of the regulatory approach by a commission and commission staff basically sympathetic to that approach.[4]

ALTERNATIVE STRATEGIES

In this section I examine alternative strategies based explicitly upon the recognition that pollution problems, at their core, result from the failure of the market system to generate the proper incentives for the allocation and management of a particular type of resources: those with common-property characteristics. I begin with water and air pollution and then consider the failure of incentives in environmental management in general.

Effluent Charges and Cost Minimization

The overall costs of control are minimized by concentrating the reduction in pollution most heavily among those firms and activities whose costs of reduction are least.* An efficient approach to pollution control, therefore, requires different firms to reduce pollution by differing amounts, depending on their costs of reduction. Moreover, besides applying conventional waste treatment methods, each firm should take advantage of a wide range of control alternatives—modifying its production processes, recycling its by-product wastes, and using raw materials and producing varieties of its product that cause less pollution.

In theory, a regulatory agency could devise an efficient regulatory plan for reduction of pollution. Effluent limitations for each type of polluting activity could be designed to achieve the minimum-cost solution. In practice, however, the need to tailor limits to each firm and to consider for each the cost and effectiveness of all of the available alternatives for reducing pollution would be an impossible task. There are up to 55,000 major sources of industrial water pollution alone. A regulatory agency cannot know the costs, the technological opportunities, the alternative raw materials, and the kinds of products available for every firm in every industry. Even if it could determine the appropriate reduction standards for each firm it would have to revise them

---

*This is an oversimplification. The impact on water quality from the wastes of any firm depends on the firm's location along the river basin and on the hydrology of the stream. A least-cost solution for achieving any given level of ambient water quality would therefore have to take into account both these factors. Each firm's effluent would have to be weighted according to its impact on water quality along particular reaches of the watercourse. In a least-cost solution, each firm would then have to cut back its effluent to the point where its marginal cost per weighted unit of effluent reduction was the same as that for every other firm. But a study of the Delaware Estuary performed in the mid-1960s by the federal government shows that a fairly simple system of effluent charges could come close, in terms of costs, to the more complicated least-cost solution for the whole system.

frequently to accommodate changing costs and markets, new technologies, and economic growth.

Effluent charges, on the other hand, tend to elicit the proper responses even in the absence of an omniscient regulatory agency. Each source of pollution would be required to pay a fee for every unit of pollutant it discharged into the air or water. Faced with these effluent charges, a firm would pursue its own interest by reducing pollution by an amount related to the cost of reduction.

Each firm would be faced with different removal costs, depending on the nature of its production processes and its economic situation. For any given effluent charge, firms with low costs of control would remove a larger percentage of pollution than would firms with high costs—precisely the situation needed to achieve a least-cost approach to reducing pollution for the economy as a whole. Firms would tend to choose the least expensive methods of control, whether these involved treatment of wastes, modification of production processes, or substitution of raw materials that had less serious polluting consequences. Furthermore, products whose manufacture entailed a lot of pollution would become more expensive and would carry higher prices than those that generated less, so consumers would be induced to buy more of the latter.

The effluent-charge approach has another characteristic that makes it superior to the regulatory approach. Under the present system a firm has no incentive to cut pollution further once it has achieved the effluent limitation specified by regulation. Indeed, it has a positive incentive not to do so, since the additional reduction is costly and lowers profits. Because under the effluent-charge plan penalties would have to be paid for every unit of pollution firms had not removed, they would have a continuing incentive to devote research and engineering talent to finding less costly ways of achieving still greater reductions. This continuing incentive is important. The quantity of air and water available to the nation is fixed, roughly speaking. But as economic activity grows over time the volume of pollution discharged into the air and water will rise unless an ever-increasing percentage of pollutants is removed.

Economic research has tended to support the practical value and effectiveness of an effluent charge or tax approach. In the most pertinent case study, it was found that effluent charges could achieve a given water quality objective in the Delaware Estuary area for about half the cost of a regulatory approach aimed at uniform reductions. The efficacy of charges is also supported by the response of industrial firms when they become subject to municipal sewer surcharges, geared to the pollution content of waste waters. Even though such charges were much lower than a true effluent charge would be, the amount of wastes discharged to the municipal sewer system usually fell dramatically.[5]

Regulation versus Effluent Charges

Governmental folklore has it that regulation and enforcement are direct, effective, and dead-sure means for attacking market failures. Studies of how the regulatory process has worked in general, coupled with the earlier review of its operation with respect to pollution problems, reveal that it is instead cumbersome, corruptible, and arbitrary and capricious in its impact.

Lawmakers have exhibited skepticism about the effectiveness of market-like devices such as effluent charges. But the knowledge we have about the impacts of price changes, and the limited evidence specifically about effluent charges, provides strong arguments for their superiority over regulation. They constitute a relatively neutral device whose enforcement could be incorporated into the body of precedent and experience already surrounding the nation's tax laws. The imposition of charges or taxes would require that effluents be metered at each outfall. But regulations also call for metering. From that point on, the payment and collection of effluent taxes involve no major administrative burdens; more important, they raise no specter of court battles such as the case-by-case struggles over regulatory decisions. (Even though there is much tax litigation, the great bulk of taxes—especially excise taxes, which most resemble effluent charges—are paid without legal struggles.)

Effluent charges have another strong advantage over regulation, one that is especially important in times like the present when much of the national program of air pollution control seems to be falling victim to the energy crisis. That advantage is that the responses they call for can be flexible, but they always call for some sort of response. When tough restrictions are relaxed or eliminated, the continuing social costs of the pollutant discharges are in no way reflected in the discharger's decision making. He is "home free." Furthermore, whatever effectiveness the enforcement approach may have is entirely dependent on constant, vigorous enforcement, which can easily give way before the shifting enthusiasms, fears, and perceptions of problems by the public and its representatives. In a government that proceeds from crisis to crisis, as ours often does, this is an extremely important problem for the enforcement approach.

Instituting Effluent Charges

Despite the apparently compelling reasons for favoring a system of effluent charges as one of the cornerstones of effective and efficient national and regional water quality management, it would be difficult for particular states and regions to pioneer such a marked departure from previous practice. Indeed, as I showed in previous sections, states may find it difficult or impossible to institute even the more conventional controls. Although several states and regions have taken initiatives recently, the federal government's greater insulation from powerful local interests gives it the opportunity for leadership.

There is much to recommend a national minimum charge that would establish the principle universally and blunt industry's threats to move to more permissive regions. Moreover, the charge could provide an immediate across-the-board incentive to reduce discharges into the nation's watercourses. Unlike the strategy embodied in the 1972 amendments, such a charge would affect every waste discharger immediately, unavoidably, and equitably. Had such a charge been levied at an adequately high level when it was first seriously proposed to Congress in the sixties there would surely have been a great improvement in water quality nearly everywhere, rather than the stabilization or continued deterioration that has actually occurred.

The national charge could be considered a minimum that could be exceeded by state and regional agencies responsible for water quality management at their discretion and according to their own objectives. Revenues obtained by the federal government could supplement funds from general tax sources and be made available for financing the federal program, with the excess turned over to other governments of general jurisdiction. As an illustrative calculation, if the charge for BOD (biochemical oxygen demand) was set at 30 cents per pound (a strong incentive to reduction because it is well above the costs of higher-level treatment except at the smallest outfalls, and far above the cost of process changes in many industries), the annual revenues would be about $4 billion to $6 billion. On the assumption that charges for other substances would yield similar amounts, total annual revenues would be $8 billion to $12 billion.[6] But the amount would fall rapidly once the incentive took effect, probably to less than $1 billion after several years. Also, it might be preferable to implement the charges in stages, increasing them annually until they reach full scale.

In emphasizing effluent charges, I do not mean to imply that administrative rulings and legal remedies are unimportant in water quality management. Indeed, as I discuss in the concluding section, the discharge of some substances (primarily heavy metals and persistent organics) should probably be prohibited entirely; Joseph Sax, among others, has suggested ways in which the courts could take a more constructive part in environmental management.[7] But I am persuaded that economic incentives and regional management are the central elements in effectively and efficiently coming to grips with the problem of water quality management, in the long term as well as the short term.[8]

Air Pollution Alternatives

Just like the formation of national policy, economic research in the air pollution area and policy proposals stemming from it lagged behind similar activities related to water pollution by several years. The central ideas, methodology, and main results of the research were quite similar in the two areas. The efficiency advantages of emissions charges, and of greater or lesser degrees of regional planning and management, turned out to be even more spectacular for air than for water. The first such study, in the Memphis metropolitan area, compared the uniform-cutback approach with the cost-minimizing systems that would be induced by emissions charges, and found the latter method significantly less costly.[9] A later notable study, in preparation for the president's proposal of what was to become the Air Quality Act of 1967, involved construction of a composite model embodying elements from several major U.S. cities that had severe problems associated with the discharge of sulfur oxides and particulates. It was found that cost-minimizing programs could achieve the same environmental objectives with only 10 percent of the costs of the uniform-cutback method.[10] These results do not even include the more indirect efficiency effects, which I have discussed in connection with water and are equally valid here.

Sulfur Oxides Tax.   After further study by the Council on Environmental Quality, the Treasury Department, and the EPA, these considerations of efficiency, efficacy, and equity led President Nixon to propose the Pure Air Tax Act of 1972 in February 1972. The president had great difficulty in getting congressional attention for the resulting bill, but he supported it again in his 1973 environmental message. A strong approach was especially needed in this area because some studies had shown severe health implications of discharges of sulfur oxides.

To date, the switch from high- to low-sulfur fuels has been the primary reason for reduced emissions of sulfur oxides. As the events of late 1973 amply demonstrated, such a switch can readily be reversed—and its gains easily lost—especially if no economic penalties remain for emitting large quantities of sulfur oxides. The technologies for removing sulfur from fuels (especially coal) before burning, or from the exhaust streams, are on the drawing boards, but the past five years have seen little movement toward development of these alternatives. Here is a situation ripe for the application of a strategy based on economic incentives.

The bill proposed by President Nixon would have levied a charge beginning with calendar year 1976 on emissions of sulfur into the atmosphere. The initial tax rate was calculated to induce curtailment of sulfur emissions sufficient to meet the 1975 air quality standards established by the Clean Air Amendments. In the years after 1976 the tax rate would depend on the quality of a region's air in the preceding year; it would be fifteen cents and ten cents per pound, respectively, where primary and secondary standards were violated, and zero where all standards were met.

One problem with this proposal is that it would encourage existing firms to move operations from "dirty" regions to "clean" ones, and new plants to settle there in the first place, to avoid paying a charge. In time, therefore, shifts in industrial location would degrade the quality of air in the cleaner regions and bring the entire country down to the lowest common denominator.

This problem is at least partially dealt with in identical bills later proposed by Rep. Les Aspin (H.R. 10890) and Sen. William Proxmire (S. 3057) that would levy a flat national tax. Three main points of these bills are particularly worth noting. First, a target level of twenty cents per pound of sulfur would have been reached in five cent increments between 1972 and 1975. The target charge was greater than the then-estimated costs of high-level abatement but less than the estimated average cost of damages across the nation (put by EPA at about thirty cents per pound). Second, the tax would be uniform across the nation, both to insure administrative simplicity and to avoid creating havens for polluters. Finally, because Congress rather than an agency would set the level of the tax, the debate would be out in the open. Since these proposals were made, the only major action taken to levy emissions fees has been by the Navajo tribe. In 1977 the Tribal Council enacted a sulfur-emissions fee. The resulting legal situation is considerably more complex than it would be with respect to a national or state fee, and the matter is now in litigation.

Alternatives for Automobile Pollution.   Even with today's relatively simple systems, maintenance of pollution control devices on automobiles is a very serious problem. Cars are tested before they are sold to see that they meet the emissions standards already imposed on the manufacturer; but no follow-up assures that they continue to meet the standards, though a number of studies have shown that few can do so after as little as 10,000 to 15,000 miles of use. For example, results released by EPA in 1973 showed that more than half the vehicles tested after on-the-road service had higher emissions than the standards applicable to their model years permitted.[11]

How can we solve the twin problems of insuring maintenance and stimulating technology? Twenty years ago economists at Rand Corporation proposed an answer—a smog tax.[12] In one possibly very powerful version of this tax, cars would be tested periodically and assigned a smog rating, indicated by a seal or coded device attached to the car. Then, when the driver purchased gasoline, he would pay a tax, over and above the basic gasoline taxes, that would vary with his smog rating. The virtue of levying the tax at the level of the individual automobile is that it can elicit responses all the way from the driver (by driving less) to the manufacturer (by manufacturing cars that pollute less).

I feel that a scheme of this type has many attractive features and should be tried. But short of its full implementation, some of its incentives could be incorporated into the present law.

A study by Henry Jacoby and others recommends one way of accomplishing this goal that would essentially extend the deadline for achieving emissions-reduction goals and apply an economic incentive to innovation in the interim.[13] It would preserve the pre-1975 standards, which are essentially the same as those still in effect, and postpone the mandatory incorporation of stricter standards for several years. A fine equivalent to 5 to 10 percent of a car's cost would be levied on a model whose emissions fell between interim standards and the final goals.

I would propose to make different changes in the present law. The first would be a slight reduction in the existing standards so that no catalytic converters would be needed to achieve it. Then I would institute a smog tax on automobiles that would increase progressively over the remainder of this decade and into the next until in the mid-1980s the rate for a car still emitting at the 1974 new-car level would exceed the several hundred dollars per car associated with the catalytic system. A few urban areas with severe smog problems would be targeted for special treatment. I believe this strategy would almost certainly lead to the large-scale introduction of inherently low-emission and thermally efficient engines within the next few years.[14] It would clearly be second best since it would not influence behavior the way an emissions tax levied on the motorist would; but I believe it would be a vast improvement over the current system.

Fees for Atmospheric Emissions.   Emissions fees would have to be set on a number of different air pollutants. In calculating the appropriate fees it would be important to set them in the proper relationship to each other, to prevent the adoption of processes that reduce one type of pollutant only to increase another. One such scheme is the "pindex" method of weighting according to toxicity; a sample fee has been determined for California on this basis.[15] It starts with a fee calculated on the basis of an estimate of damage or the control cost to reach a target level of removal, and it deduces, on the basis of their relative toxicity, the implied fees for other substances for which no direct measures of harmfulness have been calculated.

Concluding Comments on Effluent Fees

Enough work has been done on the use of effluent fees and regional management devices for water and air quality management to provide a firm basis for a strategic alternative to the way we have been attacking these problems at the national level. Although any practicable program will necessarily contain many crudities and arbitrary elements, I feel that workable legislation based on this alternative not only is possible, but also would be much more efficient, equitable, and effective—in both the short run and the long run—than the legislation Congress has adopted. The proposals I have reviewed share the difficulty of the present approach in that they treat closely related problems in isolation, but they would mark a start toward the comprehensive and effective environmental management that we must ultimately achieve as part of a coherent natural resources policy.

TOWARD AN ENVIRONMENTAL-NATURAL RESOURCES POLICY FOR MASS RESIDUALS

As I indicated earlier in this essay, the conservation of mass implies that all of the materials and energy flowing through the economy must show up as residuals to be returned to the various environmental media. Accordingly, efforts to reduce discharges into one medium will increase the burden on others unless the processes used permit the material to be recycled. For example, the sludge from waste water treated in the usual kind of plant is often incinerated, and a favorite way of removing particulates from stack gases is to scrub them with a stream of water. These considerations suggest the need simultaneously to bring all the various residuals under management in an integrated, coherent program. These relationships present tangled complexities for any approach to emissions-control policy.

At the moment, economists and engineers are actively developing comprehensive models of a residuals management program that systematically deals with all the major residuals from production and consumption activities.[16] Until such models become routinely applicable, and until appropriate regional institutions can be created to use them for formulating fully coherent management programs for all the media simultaneously, it is highly important that our national legislation at least recognize the basic nature of the problem.

A systematic attack on perverse incentives should proceed on two fronts. First, we should remove the incentives that have been built into our system to aid rapid exploitation of virgin materials; they have encouraged excessive use of materials in general and attached false economic advantages to the use of virgin as opposed to recycled materials.

Removing these incentives will mean higher prices, but these should be carefully distinguished from inflationary increases. They reflect the embedding in prices of the social costs of particular goods and services—costs that now fall upon consumers whether they consume the polluting commodities or not.

The most important area for such reform is depletion allowances. Producers of most mineral products, such as lead, zinc, copper, and bauxite, can deduct from their gross incomes a substantial allowance for depletion, thereby reducing the effective tax rate they pay. This practice provides a major subsidy to producers in the form of lower prices of a number of resources, and thus encourages the excessive use of virgin materials as well as of all other materials. It appears not only that depletion allowances are entirely inappropriate to our current circumstances, but also that much can be said for federal efforts to strengthen the hands of the states in instituting or raising severance taxes.

To open a second front in the war on perverse incentives, we should directly and systematically encourage conservation of environmental media. As I have indicated, a fully coherent set of effluent charges is not possible at the moment, but levying such charges on a broad front would recognize the interdependencies among the environmental media and promote processes that consume fewer materials or that are more conducive to recycling, as well as treatment of residual materials where appropriate.

A very promising start in this direction was contained in a bill several years ago by Rep. John H. Heinz III of Pennsylvania. The bill would amend the Internal Revenue Code to levy "a tax on the discharge of taxable items . . . by any stationary or non-stationary source of pollution into the atmosphere or into or upon the navigable waters of the United States, adjoining shorelines, the contiguous zone, or the ocean."[17] The bill sets up a procedure for determining the tax rates to be set by Congress and calls for review at intervals. While it needs considerable elaboration, its direction is clearly right.

Eliminating subsidies for exploiting virgin materials and imposing across-the-board effluent charges could have a powerful effect on conservation of resources and improvement in environmental quality. Such actions would also have the desirable efficiency effects that I have previously discussed.

Present legislation tries to deal with all these problems, and to influence the whole vast array of decision makers involved, solely through direct regulation and subsidies. If this approach stands, it will, I believe, open a field day for lawyers, result in heavy costs, require a huge bureaucracy to give it any chance of success, impose ad-hoc and capricious impacts, and involve far-reaching intrusion of the government into decisions about the design of industrial processes.

I do not suggest that an incentive-oriented approach alone could deal with all of the sticky problems that arise in achieving environmental control objectives. As I discuss in the next section, the discharge of highly toxic substances would still have to be prohibited by law and prevented through regulation. Schedules of effluent and emissions charges that truly minimized the costs of pollution control would be too complex for practical application; the consequent simplified schedules would inevitably introduce some inefficiencies into the system. Because current production techniques and locations of industrial firms are based on a world in which effluent and emissions charges do not exist, the introduction of charges would probably have to be gradual to avoid excessive disruption. Some allowance for temporary relief might be needed for hardship cases; thus decisions of a regulatory type might have to be reintroduced during an interim period.

The advantage of the incentive approach is not that it is free of administrative problems nor that it can fully duplicate a theoretical least-cost solution, but that it is, in my judgment, far superior to the regulatory alternative on both of these counts.

THE PROBLEM OF HAZARDOUS MATERIALS

So far I have discussed what might be called the mass pollutants. These are the voluminous residuals produced by human activities of production and consumption. The concepts of mass balance and common-property resources are quite illuminating with respect to the origin of, and possible remedies for, pollution from these types of residuals. In addition the appropriate role of changes in economic incentives as part of the policy structure to deal with them seems clear.

There is however, another class of pollutants, some of which are deliberately introduced into the human food chain as additives; for these such concepts are less revealing and economic incentive changes are possibly less pertinent. These are materials emitted into the environment that are generally small in quantity but present large, although usually very uncertain, threats to human health or life-support systems. These are what are often referred to as hazardous materials.

The dangers of man-made hazardous materials in the environment and their potential impacts both on life-support systems and directly on human health represent the new generation of environmental problems. These problems present one of the most important and complex sets of public-policy issues currently facing modern society. Hundreds of new chemicals are introduced each year for beneficial use in society, but their adverse impacts on the environment and on human health are virtually unknown and may remain highly uncertain for many years to come. Other potentially serious problems include the hazards associated with nuclear power, coal combustion, coal gasification and liquefaction, carcinogens in drinking water, ozone depletion, the buildup of carbon dioxide, pesticides, and toxic chemicals generally.

Clearly, all of the foregoing problems pose some, mostly unknown, risks to human health. But the alternatives of reducing substantially or even stopping all technological progress until we are certain of all the impacts, or of drastically reducing consumption with no concomitant changes in technology, would impose enormous costs on society both now and in the future. Thus, the heart of the public-policy issue is how to strike an appropriate balance between, on the one hand, ways of providing the needed goods and services to human society, including the use of new technology and the development of new products, and, on the other, ways to eliminate or reduce the environmental and health risks associated with the use of these products and their processes of production. The policies that have so far been developed depend upon direct regulation to try to achieve this objective. Some regulation is essential in this field, but even here the possible important role of changes in economic incentive has largely been ignored. I will return to this topic after a brief review of the various laws pertaining to that set of hazardous materials usually referred to as toxic substances.[18]

Hazardous-Materials Legislation

Federal Water Pollution Control Act.   The federal Water Pollution Control Act contains a section specifically about the control of toxic pollutants. Under section 307 the administrator is directed to compile a list of "toxic pollutants or combination(s) of such pollutants," to publish proposed effluent standards for the pollutants within 180 days, and to publish final standards within another 180 days of the proposal of such standards and the hearings that follow them.

While EPA has issued no final effluent standards for hazardous pollutants as defined in section 307, the standards, when designated, will be based on best-available technology—to be determined on an industry-by-industry basis. Discharge standards have been proposed for the pesticides aldrin, dieldrin, and DDT and for endrin, toxaphene, benzidine, and PCBs.

Section 208 of the act requires area-wide planning for the control of water pollution. In principle this includes planning and associated regulation for control of non-point sources such as pesticide residues in agricultural runoff.

Federal Insecticide, Fungicide, and Rodenticide Act.   Pesticide laws initially were designed to insure honesty in packaging and safety in use, but they have evolved to enhance environmental quality and protect public health as well. The Federal Insecticide, Fungicide, and Rodenticide Act (FIFRA) and the Federal Environmental Pesticide Control Act that amended it now provide, among other things, for the registration of all pesticides and the uses to which they are put, the certification of individuals who apply certain restricted pesticides, and premarket testing of all new pesticides.

All pesticide registrations expire every five years and must be renewed. If the registration of a particular pesticide or pesticide use is denied, the administrator of EPA must publish reasons for denial in the federal register. The EPA has suspended the registrations of all crop uses of DDT, aldrin, and dieldrin, and most uses of heptachlor and chlordane because of evidence of their carcinogenicity as well as their persistence in the environment. Recently, EPA has also moved against pesticides containing kepone, chloroform, endrin, and chlorobenzilate.

Toxic Substances Control Act.   The Toxic Substances Control Act (TOSCA) became law in 1976. Generally speaking, it is intended to fill the gap between the regulation of pesticides by EPA under FIFRA (as amended) and the regulation of food, drugs, and cosmetics by the Food and Drug Administration. It is expected to play a major role in federal toxic-substance policy.

The TOSCA gives EPA the following wide authority: to require testing of any new chemical or new use of an existing chemical when it "may present an unreasonable risk of injury to health or the environment" (the cost of the tests are borne by the manufacturer); to control the manufacturing, distribution, and sale of chemical substances through sanctions ranging from relatively mild labeling requirements through strict prohibitions and extending to seizure or recall of "imminently hazardous" substances; and to require proponents of a new chemical to provide information on that chemical's name, properties, structure, intended levels of production and use, and by-products created. The EPA is directed to carry out research, testing, and monitoring necessary to implement the provisions of the act; this is to include the development of a system by which data on toxic substances are collected and can be retrieved and under which government research and information on toxics—from whatever source—are coordinated.

Resource Conservation and Recovery Act.   Subtitle C of the Resource Conservation and Recovery Act of 1976 deals with hazardous-waste management. Because this act, like TOSCA, is so new, the government has had little experience with toxic-substance control under this subsection of the law. Nevertheless, many feel that the act may play an important role in toxic-substance policy.

Section 1004 (5) of the act defines hazardous waste as ". . . a solid waste, or combination of solid wastes, which because of its quantity, concentration, or physical, chemical, or infectious characteristics may a) cause, or significantly contribute to an increase in mortality or an increase in serious irreversible, or incapacitating reversible, illness; or b) pose a substantial present or potential hazard to human health or the environment when improperly treated, stored, transported, or disposed of, or otherwise managed."

Within eighteen months of passage of the act, the administrator of EPA was to have established standards governing the generation, transportation and treatment, storage, and disposal of hazardous wastes. These guidelines have now been published.

Clean Air Act.   That portion of the Clean Air Amendments most relevant to the control of chronically toxic substances is section 112, which provides for national emissions standards for hazardous air pollutants to which no ambient air quality standard is applicable.

The administrator of EPA is directed to issue a list containing each hazardous pollutant for which he intends to publish standards; he is then to publish the proposed emissions standards for each pollutant and hold hearings on them within 180 days from the time they are put on the list. The final standard is to be published within another 180 days unless the hearings provide information that convinces the administrator that the pollutant is not hazardous.

Transportation Regulation*

Transportation regulation lags behind even the regulation of other sources of toxic materials. The main reason is the fragmentation and lack of clarity of the present statutory and administrative program. The ambiguity of the situation can hardly be overemphasized. Practically speaking, existing rules under the Occupational Safety and Health Act (OSHA) and the Clean Air Act apply to transportation of toxic materials only while rail tank cars, tank trucks, or tank vessels are on the premises of industrial plants for loading and unloading. Five statutes apply to the control of risks from transportation of toxic materials outside the plant premises: the 1975 Hazardous Materials Transportation Act, the 1972 Ports and Waterways Safety Act, the Dangerous Cargo Act, the Federal Railroad Safety Act, and OSHA. The first four statutes are administered by agencies within the Department of Transportation, and the last by OSHA, in the Department of Labor. Some modes of transport are potentially subject to more than one statute. Although the scope of some of these statutes is well defined, it is unclear whether several others authorize regulations meant to protect transportation workers alone, only the general public, or both.

Economic Incentives and
Hazardous-Materials Policy

The set of laws pertaining to toxic-substance regulation requires the generation of an enormous amount of information by both industry and the government and massive bureaucratic interventions into the market. The problem of regulation in this area is shot through with uncertainties of all sorts, and the magnitude of the task seems appalling when one considers the thousands of new substances advertently and inadvertently introduced into the environment each year.

Although there is no evidence that Congress specifically considered the role of changes in the economic incentive system when it enacted the existing set of laws to regulate toxic substances, in practice, the alteration of incentives associated with these laws may be their most important impact over the long run. For example, the expenses required by the reporting and premarket-testing provisions of TOSCA will significantly increase the cost of introducing a new substance that is potentially hazardous. Similarly, certification requirements for applications of certain pesticides that are considered dangerous but have no known good substitute will increase the cost of using those pesticides.

---

*For a more complete discussion see David D. Doniger, *The Law and Policy of Toxic Substances Control* (Baltimore: Johns Hopkins Press for Resources for the Future, 1979).

Another legal area that affects economic incentives is liability rules. Although liability is often hard to establish in the area of environmental risk, there has been a tendency in the past to bail out those who have engaged in an activity that later turns out to have produced such risk, and the well-known Price Anderson Act, which limits liability of utilities in the event of nuclear accident, is still on the books. In the past it was perhaps justifiable for the public to assume some of the liability for the environmental risks produced, since because of lack of testing and information generation risks were often discovered long after the fact. The Price Anderson Act was part of a program—misguided in the view of some, including myself—to introduce quickly a large new technology that might have some rather extreme environmental risks associated with it. But in the new situation, where testing is done to try to anticipate possible ill effects, a clear imposition of liability on the entity introducing the substance should go far to assure that the tests are done carefully and the results interpreted cautiously.

Another type of incentives policy that might produce better results than regulation in some instances is the imposition of a tax or fee on the potentially hazardous substance. In the case of pesticides, for example, Congress has chosen, or gives the EPA administrator discretion to choose, in certain instances, to require certification of applicators and restrictions on the kinds of crops to which a pesticide may be applied. It is at least arguable that a stiff fee on such a pesticide would result in the use of that pesticide only for purposes where there is no substitute of lesser hazard, and in its careful application. This would avoid most of the cost of the present approach, and it might be more effective, since the present provision would seem, on the face of it, to present very difficult enforcement problems.

One cannot say that study of the role of economic incentives in hazardous-materials policy is in its infancy: it is not yet born. It is, however, one of the most important, even urgent, areas for research by environmental economists.

NOTES

1. Quoted in B. Lambert, *History and Survey of London*, vol. 1 (London, 1806).

2. These statements are from *The Public Health as a Public Question: First Report of the Metropolitan Sanitary Association* (address of Charles Dickens, Esq., London, 1850).

3. For a relatively full discussion of the history of federal environmental legislation see Allen V. Kneese and Charles L. Schultze, *Pollution, Prices, and Public Policy* (Washington, D.C.: Brookings Institution, 1975).

4. *Staff Draft Report: National Commission on Water Quality* (Washington, D.C.: U.S. Government Printing Office, April 1976).

5. Further discussion of these results and citations is found in Allen V. Kneese and Blair T. Bower, *Managing Water Quality: Economics, Technology, Institutions* (Baltimore: Johns Hopkins Press, 1968).

6. BOD has been emphasized here because it is the single most common water-borne waste material and often a good indicator of other pollutants; but other substances should also be included in the charges scheme. Various weighting methods to establish equivalences have been suggested, but perhaps the best starting point would be the systems that have long been in effect in the Ruhr. See Kneese and Bower, *Managing Water Quality.*

7. Joseph L. Sax, *Defending the Environment: A Strategy for Citizen Action* (New York: Alfred A. Knopf, 1971).

8. The engineering, legal, and political aspects of charges systems are explored in depth in Frederick R. Anderson et al., *Environmental Improvement Through Economic Incentives* (Baltimore: Johns Hopkins Press, 1978).

9. See Azriel Teller, "Air-Pollution Abatement: Economic Rationality and Reality," *Daedalus* 96 (Fall 1967): 1082–1098.

10. See Jack W. Carlson's "Discussion" of a paper by Allen V. Kneese entitled "Environmental Pollution: Economics and Policy," both appearing in American Economic Association, *Papers and Proceedings of the Eighty-third Annual Meeting, 1970, American Economic Review* 61 (May 1971): 153–166, 169–172. A more complete discussion is found in U.S. Department of Health, Education, and Welfare, Office of the Assistant Secretary (Planning and Evaluation), "An Economic Analysis of the Control of Sulphur Oxides Air Pollution" (HEW, 1967, mimeograph).

11. CALSPAN Corporation, *Automobile Exhaust Emission Surveillance: A Summary,* APTD-1544 (Research Triangle Park, N.C.: U.S. Environmental Protection Agency, Air Pollution Technical Information Center, 1973) pp. 4–40.

12. D. M. Fort et al., "Proposal for a Smog Tax," reprinted in *Tax Recommendations of the President, Hearings before the House Committee on Ways and Means,* 91st Cong., 2d sess., 1970, pp. 369–379.

13. Henry D. Jacoby et al., *Clearing the Air: Federal Policy on Automotive Emissions Control* (Cambridge, Mass: Ballinger, 1973).

14. Such engines can almost certainly be developed. See, for example, Graham Walter, "The Stirling Engine," *Scientific American* 229 (August 1973): 80–87.

15. See A. M. Schneider, "An Effluent Fee Schedule for Air Pollutants Based on Pindex," *Journal of the Air Pollution Control Association* 23 (June 1973): 486–489.

16. See Clifford S. Russell and Walter O. Spofford, Jr., "A Quantitative Framework for Residuals Management Decisions," in *Environmental Quality Analysis: Theory and Method in the Social Sciences,* ed. Allen V. Kneese and Blair T. Bower (Baltimore: Johns Hopkins Press for Resources for the Future, 1972). See also Allen V. Kneese, Robert U. Ayres, and Ralph C. d'Arge, *Economics and the Environment: A Materials Balance Approach* (Baltimore: Johns Hopkins Press for Resources for the Future, 1970).

17. U.S. Congress, H.R. 635, January 1973.

18. For a more complete discussion see Paul R. Portney, "Toxic Substances Policy and the Protection of Human Health," in *Current Issues in U.S. Environ-Environmental Policy*, ed. Paul R. Portney (Baltimore: Johns Hopkins Press for Resources for the Future, 1978).

[16]

STATE LIABILITY FOR INTERNATIONAL ENVIRONMENTAL DEGRADATION: AN ECONOMIC PERSPECTIVE

RALPH C. d'ARGE* and ALLEN V. KNEESE**

INTRODUCTION

State responsibility and liability are not clearly defined with respect to environmental degradation. But a limited number of cases and declarations by international tribunals do point in a definable direction. In the famous *Trail Smelter Case,* the tribunal declared: "A State owes at all times a duty to protect other states against injurious acts by *individuals* from within its jurisdiction."[1] The Organization for Economic Cooperation and Development (OECD) adopted the "polluter pays" principle (PP) in 1972, which states that the waste discharger must pay for any ameliorating measures which are caused to be undertaken.[2] This principle does not apply to any residual damages which may remain. However, the German government has recently issued an interpretation which requires payment of an effluent charge which presumably, in some manner, is meant to reflect remaining damages within German territory.[3] The Stockholm Declarations could also be interpreted as placing responsibility upon those undertaking the actions which result in environmental degradation, although the emphasis is upon "common action" among states.[4] The tendency then is to interpret state responsibility as requiring that states within whose boundaries harmful actions occur must pay or cause to be paid the cost of ameliorating those actions and, possibly, must pay for the remaining damages as well.

In this paper, we shall define and analyze four major principles of assigning state responsibility and discuss the economic meaning of those principles. The first principle is that each state is responsible for all waste discharge control costs internally and externally but is not responsible for compensation of remaining damages following

*John S. Bugas Distinguished Professor of Economics, University of Wyoming.
**Senior Fellow, Resources for the Future, Inc., Washington, D.C.

1. Trail Smelter Case (United States v. Canada), 3 R. Int'l Arb. Awards 1905, 1963 (1935) (emphasis added).
2. ORGANIZATION FOR ECONOMIC COOPERATION AND DEVELOPMENT, POLLUTER PAYS PRINCIPLE (1975).
3. *See* A. KNEESE & B. BOWER, MANAGING WATER QUALITY: ECONOMICS, TECHNOLOGY, INSTITUTIONS (1968).
4. U.N. Stockholm Conference on the Human Environment, Declaration on the Human Environment, U.N. Doc. A/CONF. 48/4 (1972).

installation of the agreed-upon controls. This is a variant of the OECD principle cited above in that we apply it, as an area of major concern, to transfrontier pollution problems; application of the principle to such problems was explicitly excluded by OECD member nations. The second major principle is the full costing principle (FC), which requires the state responsible for waste discharge to pay compensation for remaining damages as well as control costs. The third principle is the "victim pays" principle (VP), which requires the affected state to compensate the affecting state (or internal parties creating harmful residuals) for all costs of control and to absorb all residual damages after controls are implemented. The fourth principle, in its simplest form, requires the establishment of an internal or international autonomous agency to regulate the joint use of common property resources by individual or multiple states. In the international case, the various states would give powers to the agency to regulate waste discharges into the commonly shared environment. For lack of a better description, we term this principle of responsibility the common property resource institution principle (CPRI).[5]

With the exception of certain studies on economic warfare in international trade, the international economics literature appears devoid of analyses encompassing non-aggressive involuntary exchanges that are international in scope.[6] This is in contrast to the very substantial literature on such exchanges internal to a sovereign nation. Environmental interdependencies among sovereign nations, not regulated *a priori* by international market or other forms of transactions, can be viewed as one type of or cause for involuntary exchange.[7] For example, when one nation's industry emits water-borne residuals which influence the productivity or utility of another nation's citizens, then

---

5. A fifth principle developed by OECD personnel and consultants is called the "mutual compensation" principle: each country contributes to the solution of the problem by sharing control costs and/or damages. Because of the diversity of possible economic outcomes from this type of principle, it will not be examined in detail here.

6. *See* M. KEMP, PURE THEORY OF INTERNATIONAL TRADE ch. 4 (1964); H. Wan, A Contribution to the Theory of Trade Warfare (1961) (unpublished doctoral thesis, Massachusetts Institute of Technology). On transnational public goods problems two enlightening papers by Michael B. Connolly have appeared. Connolly, *Trade in Public Goods: A Diagrammatic Analysis,* 86 Q.J. ECON. 61 (1972); Connolly, *Public Goods, Externalities, and International Relations,* 78 J. POLITICAL ECON. 279 (1970). (Since this paper was written and circulated, a number of economic studies on transfrontier pollution have been written. *See* ORGANIZATION FOR ECONOMIC COOPERATION AND DEVELOPMENT, PROBLEMS OF TRANSFRONTIER POLLUTION (1974); I. WALTER, INTERNATIONAL ECONOMICS OF POLLUTION (1976).)

7. It must be kept in mind in a historical evolutionary context that externalities and especially diseconomies in social relationships are perhaps one major reason for the existence of discrete nations and the role of national sovereignty as the dominant consideration in world politics.

in effect there is an involuntary exchange of wealth among nations.

External diseconomies in the domestic economy have been characterized as perceptible non-market interdependencies among economic units that arise inadvertently, without anticipation, or with
inadequate information by one or more of the parties involved. The
externality event is unforeseen as to its effects or not adequately
anticipated before occurrence. Coase, Buchanan, Kneese, and
Mishan, among others, have explicitly or implicitly applied this characterization.[8] In what follows we shall adhere to this characterization
and omit consideration of involuntary international exchanges which
arise by design (i.e., assertion of power and threat of warfare). Thus,
the class of problems we wish to address is unanticipated involuntary
international exchanges involving environmental interdependencies
among nations that lack markets or exchange processes of any kind
prior to their appearance.

From an economic perspective, there are two major issues in the
interpretation of international doctrines or laws applicable to transnational environmental problems. The first relates to prohibitions on
domestic activities affecting other nations, and the second to explicit
financial responsibility for harmful effects. There is a body of international law concerned with constraints on a nation's activities which
prescribes certain doctrines of behavior. The common maxim applicable as a constraint is: *use your own property so as to not injure
your neighbor's* and *every state's obligation [is to] not allow knowingly its territory to be used for acts contrary to other states.*[9] These
general principles delineate both constraints to activities and asser-
tions of responsibility. Note, however, that they are implicit with
regard to specification of property ownership, and the allocation of
common property resource ownership, or jointly used resources, is
not identified. Further, the bulk of common law on oceans, the
major common property resource of recognized importance thus far,
is concerned with the establishment of principles of access and the
"right of use" but not with constraints on use. The precedent-setting
Trail Smelter Case between the United States and Canada in 1935
established that "under the principles of international law . . . , no
State has the right to use or permit the use of its territory in such
manner as to cause injury by fumes in or to the territory of another

8. Buchanan & Stubblebine, *Externality,* 29 ECONOMICA 17 (n.s. 1962); Coase, *The
Problem of Social Cost,* 3 J.L. & ECON. 1 (1960); Mishan, *The Postwar Literature on
Externalities: An Interpretative Essay,* 9 J. ECON. LITERATURE 1 (1971).
    9. *See* C. BRAMSEN, TRANSNATIONAL POLLUTION AND INTERNATIONAL LAW
(OECD restricted series, Aug. 1972); C. JENKS, THE COMMON LAW OF MANKIND
(1958).

or the properties or persons therein, when the case is of serious consequence and the injury is established by clear and convincing evidence."[10] More recently, the United Nations General Assembly passed a resolution that each nation has the sovereign right to formulate its own environmental policies, provided "in the exercise of such right and in the implementation of such policies due account must be taken of the need to avoid producing harmful effects on other countries."[11] The U.N. Stockholm Conference Declaration went even further in stating that nations have "the responsibility to ensure that activities within their jurisdiction or control do not cause damage to the environment of other States or of areas beyond the limits of national jurisdiction."[12] The Stockholm Declaration begins to introduce a more encompassing criterion of responsibility by referring to all areas beyond jurisdictional limits. Also, instead of "due account" being taken of damages to other countries, the specification is made that no damages be caused.

To summarize this very brief discussion, existing common law and United Nations declarations appear to prohibit domestic activities which cause environmentally harmful effects to other countries. In so doing, this body of law implicitly provides constraints to potential actions within countries but does not provide meaningful economic guidelines of responsibility. Implicitly the responsible country is the one *initiating* the activity that causes damages.

The initiating country, however, may be hard to discover. The following cases illustrate this point: (1) a country's tanker spills oil and damages the coastline of a second country; (2) a country's residents undergo a shift in preferences (due to rising income and affluence) and begin to suffer aesthetic damages due to previously unrecognized air pollution from an adjacent country; (3) a downstream country decides to expand irrigated agriculture onto desert lands where salt flushing is required but finds that an upstream country is contributing salts into return flows to the common river, precluding flushing and efficient production in the downstream country; (4) one downstream country decides to use internal resources—i.e., rivers and airsheds—as total waste disposal resources and common property rivers as predominantly recreational resources.

In the first example, responsibility is quite clearly delineated. But in the other examples, responsibility is imperfectly clear. Certainly in

---

10. Trail Smelter Case (United States v. Canada), 3 R. Int'l Arb. Awards 1905, 1965 (1935).

11. U.N. Doc. A/RES.2849(XXVI) at 2 (1971).

12. U.N. Stockholm Conference on the Human Environment, Declaration on the Human Environment, U.N. Doc. A/CONF. 48/4, at 4 (1972).

the fourth case there is an element of monopoly of the downstream country working to require the upstream country, provided it is identified as being responsible, to pay for controls exceeding what it would normally need to pay. International doctrines have provided direction on assigning responsibility for external diseconomies and in establishing constraints on *knowingly* initiating activities which create damages transnationally. However, as was argued earlier, externalities have been viewed as inadvertent actions resulting from inadequate prior information and negotiation by the parties involved. The "laws" do not specify which is the responsible country or how such responsibility should be determined.

The classical economic solution to externality problems is to "internalize" them either by developing a well-defined market for the "spillovers" or by controlling them through collective provision of regulations. Neither of these possibilities appears easily amenable to the problem of transnational externalities in general and environmental externalities in particular. First, environmental externalities have arisen because most dimensions of the natural environment on a regional or global scale are resources without defined ownership rights or rights of use. The oceans, stratosphere, and electromagnetic spectrum are examples. These resources are viewed as being commonly owned or not owned at all. A nation that agrees to a particular pattern of ownership could potentially lose some of its implicitly controlled resources and thereby decrease its national wealth.[13] As long as international entitlements are obscure, any nation can lay implicit claim to the common property resource exceeding any equitable share it may presume to receive if entitle-

---

13. Christy has emphasized that a major element in the common property problems of oceans is differences in perceived entitlement and consequent wealth of the common property users. Christy also draws a distinction between the production of wealth and the distribution or ownership of wealth with regard to ocean fisheries: the first concept involves issues of access and free use, while the second involves specification of shares. The discussion in this paper will be centered on distributional as opposed to use or access issues. It appears that the issue of open access in fisheries competition and regulation is the polar opposite of transnational external diseconomies, but it has implications for management not highly dissimilar. The distinguishing feature appears to be that with fisheries there are incentives for rapid exploitation if non-coordination prevails between countries. Alternatively, with environmental diseconomies that are reciprocal between countries, there appear to be "built in" incentives for unilateral control in that such control implies at least a small amount of environmental improvement. This idea was first expressed, to our knowledge, by Anthony Scott. However, if one country perceives that regardless of what its actions are, other countries will treat a common property resource as a sewer, it is hard to imagine it would do otherwise. *See* Christy, *Fisheries: Common Property, Open Access, and the Common Heritage,* in E. BORGESE, PACEM IN MARIBUS 183 (1972); Scott, *The Economics of International Transmission of Pollution,* in ORGANIZATION FOR ECONOMIC COOPERATION AND DEVELOPMENT, PROBLEMS OF ENVIRONMENTAL ECONOMICS (1972).

ment were made explicit. This is not to say that, once some other nation impinges on a nation's implicit entitlement, it will not find a negotiated settlement and explicit entitlement to be superior to an implicit one. However, the affected nation, in negotiating, must revise downward its own perception of ownership of the common property resource. In consequence, proceeding from a situation of implicit entitlement of common property resources to explicit regulation and thereby ownership implies that some (or all) nations must reduce their perception of national wealth.

A second aspect of major importance arises from the concept of national sovereignty. Like consumer sovereignty as conceptualized by economists, national sovereignty involves the idea that governments, acting in their own interest, will, omitting considerations of deviation in power or information, achieve the greatest welfare for themselves by independently pursuing autonomous goals and interacting through organized international markets. The belief in national sovereignty and independent decision-making as an ideal is so embedded that it seems impractical to presume it will be given up easily.[14]

In the remainder of this paper we examine assignments of polluter responsibility under the four principles cited earlier, and one perhaps more immediately realizable alternative, in terms of their implications for efficiency of the international economy. We also comment on some related matters—predominantly equity implications and enforceability. In doing so we find it useful to discuss several kinds of case situations separately, since they carry different interpretations for the matters of interest here. First we briefly introduce each of the cases and then discuss each one in more detail.

TAXONOMY OF SITUATIONS

Direct "Technological Externalities"

The archetype of an international environment problem is where activities in one country have a direct (non-market) impact on production or consumption activities in another country. This occurs via some common environmental medium such as a watercourse, the common air mantle, or a large ecological system. Such impacts may

---

14. This is not to suggest that governments through cooperation or by forming coalitions embodying common interests do not attempt to internalize externalities of a positive sort. NATO, EEC, LAFTA, and EFTA are just a few counterexamples. The important distinction, however, is that each country is not bound irrevocably to accept decisions unfavorable to it or even to continue participation in such collective arrangements. This is demonstrated by the recent discussion on the possible United States withdrawal from several U.N. agencies because of foreign domination of their administrative structures.

be bilateral or multilateral, unidirectional or reciprocal, or various combinations of these. Salt pollution of the Rio Grande is a unidirectional-bilateral case with water as the medium. Destruction of wildfowl habitat in Canada is unidirectional-multilateral (affecting the U.S. and Mexico) with an ecological system as the medium. Pollution of the Baltic Sea is multilateral-reciprocal, again with water as the medium. It is readily seen that these cases vary greatly in both structure and complexity and may have differing implications for a concept of state responsibility.

Effects on a Universal Common Property Resource

Excessive environmental degradation results from adverse impacts on a common property resource (CPR)—that is, one in regard to which market exchange does not function or functions only very imperfectly. Thus the Rhine River and the stratosphere are CPRs because they cannot be easily parcelled into units suitable for exchange in domestic and international markets. But defined state sovereignties do cover their entire reach. The deep oceans and the atmosphere over them are CPRs in an even more far-reaching sense, since they are not even covered by state jurisdiction. We term them *universal* CPRs.

One example of why this situation is important may be helpful. In the case where national sovereignties are directly involved, at least one sovereignty (the damaged one) will have an incentive to generate information and even take action (bribe polluters to reduce waste discharges). Where national sovereignties over the resource are not defined, such incentives are absent until pronounced feedback effects reach a national sovereignty. Accordingly, it is quite possible for an activity (say dumping of high-level radioactive wastes in eventually corrodable containers) to reach a potentially catastrophic level with the only limiting direct incentive being the fear of feedback effects on the party doing the activity. This may not in principle be different from the previous case in terms of ultimate state responsibility. It is importantly different in terms of the indirectness of effects and the different context of incentives within which such responsibility occurs.

Preferences for Fixed Site Environmental Features in Another Sovereignty

Many market-type goods can be produced in one sovereignty and not another and yet be desired there—e.g., Mandarin oranges in England. This fact plus differences in the comparative advantage of producing other goods are the sources of international trade. But some goods which cannot be exported are produced by nature in certain jurisdictions. Examples are unique biological amenities (those of the Serengeti) and unique geomorphological features (Murchison Falls). The only way citizens of another sovereignty can directly experience their benefits is to travel greater or lesser distances to observe them. Thus the market can function, at least if there are no travel restrictions. But the market does not by any means function perfectly. Since many persons are uncertain whether they will ever experience such attractions, but would like to, an option demand not expressed through markets may exist. Moreover, there seem to be many persons who care greatly about the existence of such amenities even though they never expect, or even hope, to experience them. In principle, the destruction or diminution of such features is a technological externality quite like the direct technological externalities discussed above. They are of the type where an activity in one country enters directly into the welfare of individuals in another. But the often irreversible nature of the destruction of such amenities, the difficulty of evaluating them, and the fact that they are usually located in developing countries while preferences for them are strongest in developed countries have unique implications for state responsibility.

Problems Associated with International Trade

A conclusion derived from economic theory is that if all markets, domestic and international, are competitive and if free trade exists, the processes of exchange will normally generate a Pareto optimum— that is, a situation in which there are no further gains from trade and consumer preferences are fulfilled to a maximum, given the resource endowments of nations and the distribution of resources within and among them. A usually unstated but implied assumption is that there are no CPRs. The theory can be extended to conclude that such an optimum could be achieved anyway if a public agency priced all CPRs in such a way as to obtain a Pareto optimum in their use as well. But even without direct international technological externalities, differences in the way CPRs are handled internally in the various trading nations can cause distortions in the international economy which lead to transitional problems or a permanently less-than-optimal use of global resources. If one country prices CPRs (say by levying effluent charges) and another subsidizes industries to induce them to control use of CPRs, there will be a shift in the international relative costs not adequately reflecting real differences in factor endowments, including CPRs. Even if all countries wish to "internalize" external costs by using similar policy tools, they may hesitate to act unilaterally for fear of adjustment impacts such as temporary unemployment or balance of payments disequilibrium.

Special Problems Associated with Particular Entities

Developing Countries. In principle, both developing countries and developed countries should act on the same principles with respect to transnational aspects of environment, since both presumably have a common interest in the efficiency of the international system. As a practical matter there are many difficulties. Since technology transfer is, in general, one-directional from the more developed to the less developed world, the former may inadvertently, or by design, create for the developing countries a technology requiring too high a cost for environmental protection given their circumstances and preferences. Also, the developing countries have been the recipients of unilateral financial transfers from the developed world (at least at the governmental level), and they fear that emphasis on environmental improvement in the latter may cut back on these transfers. The ability of developing countries to analyze and monitor adverse environmental effects is vastly less than that of developed countries where, needless to say, it is none too adequate.

Multinational Corporations. In recent years, multinational corporations have grown rapidly; they now conduct much of the business of the international economy. They have the advantage of relatively easy information and experience transfer among countries and may be able to adapt more readily to environmental policies than their domestic counterparts. On the other hand, their vast capacity to generate technological and economic information (or perhaps misinformation) could be used to intimidate local authorities. Similarly, the greater international factor mobility they are said to represent may make them less dependent on specific national locations and may improve their bargaining power with states beyond that of their domestic counterparts. Again new facets of state responsibility show themselves.

DISCUSSION OF SITUATIONS

Direct Technological Externalities

The Bilateral Case. We have mentioned four possible principles of state responsibility in the introduction. There are a number of variants of these basic principles. For example, one may have a "polluter pays" principle where paying for pollution is acceptable only through reducing emissions in the polluting country. Or the emitter country may be responsible for damage compensation to receptor countries while the receptors are responsible for paying control costs to the emitting country in addition to their own defensive expenditures.

The current implied legal doctrine that each country must pay for transnational pollution by ceasing activities that cause it may for various reasons (including the difficulty of estimating damages, especially internationally) be adopted as the best practical type of polluter pays principle, but it can be shown to be inefficient in many instances. Let us suppose that agriculture in Arizona is very much more productive than downstream in Mexico and that the only way to reduce salt content downstream is to take land out of cultivation upstream. Then the current legal doctrine offers the following choice: let the Mexicans continue to suffer uncompensated losses or take more productive land out upstream and replace it with less productive land downstream. Other considerations aside, a PP principle with compensatory flexibility would be more efficient, since agricultural production across both countries could be maintained at a higher level and the parties involved could share the gain through compensation arrangements to the betterment of both.

Under certain simplified conditions, it can be shown that the VP and PP principles applied to transnational pollution problems both produce Pareto efficiency in the short run and the long run if consumers and factors of production are immobile internationally.[15] The only difference between the two is in the international distribution of income. This result might lead one to favor the VP principle for the simple reason that it can be implemented without international enforcement machinery which in the past has proved so intractable. The damaged party has an incentive both to get information and to bargain with the sovereignty within which the offending activity is taking place. The principle also has the advantage that the willingness of the affected sovereignty to pay for reduction provides a quantitative estimate of the damage loss, which might otherwise be very hard to calculate. But aside from the fact that most people would probably consider the arrangement quite inequitable, it has another basic flaw. If the VP principle is applicable, the exter-

15. *See* R. d'Arge, On the Economics of Transnational Environmental Externalities (1972) (paper presented at the Conference on Economics of the Environment, sponsored by Universities-National Bureau Committee for Economic Research and Resources for the Future, Chicago).

nality-generating country may threaten (by giving high estimates of future loads) to discharge materials as an incidental aspect of the production of other goods simply to obtain compensation for not doing so. One may hypothesize that polluting material could be produced at low cost. Thus, if the VP principle were to be applied, an aspect of state responsibility would have to be structured to remove the incentives underlying "pollution for profit."

Of course, under the PP or FC principles, the injured country could also exaggerate its losses, but it is not in the superior position which would permit it to exact retribution if its demands are not met. Thus, there seem to be significant preliminary grounds for preferring the FC or PP principles for both efficiency and equity reasons.

Before turning to the multilateral case, we should point out that the theoretical symmetry among the PP, FC, and VP principles indicated above is dependent upon the assumption (usually made in the classical international trade literature) that resources are immobile internationally. If this is not the case, capital or labor movements will cause the outcomes of the principles to differ.

We now proceed to a rather technical discussion of the efficiency properties of the various principles in the context of an international economy. The most efficient operation, use, or allocation of a common property resource (CPR), be it national or international in impact, is to design a management-ownership-rights solution which will operate to maximize global rent of the CPR. A full costing principle means that there is a payment between emitter and receptor countries, with the normal presumption that the emitter country will tax (and/or require emissions contracts from) internal polluters and the receptor country will provide payment to the internal damaged parties. In this case, the countries act as neutral (and presumed costless) allocators of funds, but in so doing they perpetrate international inefficiencies unless one or both governments take additional control measures. The inefficiency occurs because other governments or private negotiators are not directly and competitively involved to remove the distorting impact on profit rates of firms or consumer prices. In consequence, with resources internationally mobile, resources will be inefficiently allocated in a global context.

A rigorous proof of this assertion is given elsewhere.[16] What we wish to do here is provide a heuristic argument justifying this conclusion for the bilateral case where emissions from the emitter country's

---

16. *See id.*

firms raise production costs in the receptor country. To make the case simple and tractable, we shall omit considerations of control costs for the emitter country or defensive expenditures by the receptor country. Thus, reduction in damage can only come about through reduced production in either the emitter or receptor country. We shall also assume that damage costs increase at an increasing rate with increased output of firms in the emitter country for any positive and constant level of output by firms in the receptor country.

If the firms in the emitter country are taxed by their government according to total damages, total damage payments will be less than optimal damage payments because of the assumption of increasing marginal damages with increasing output. The net effect is to decrease the average cost in the emitter industry below that of the optimum but above average cost without compensation. Thus, at the zero profit point for each firm where average costs are minimized, output per firm is necessarily lower than the optimum, while price is also lower. Both price and output per firm are below what is optimum for the emitter country, and this implies that total output is too large for the industry taken as a whole. This result occurs because price for the country's output can only be lower than the optimum if industry output is larger than the optimum, given that market price falls with greater quantity delivered to the market. Thus in the emitter country the price of the domestic product is too low and production is excessive, which means, if there is international mobility of resources, that too many resources will be utilized there. A parallel situation arises in the receptor country. Since all firms are now *totally* compensated for damages, average costs are lower than they would be if payments were made contingent on marginal damages. The net effect is to cause firms to produce at a lower price and lower output, but by the arguments given above, total output in the receptor country must be excessive. In consequence, there is an overallocation of international resources to the receptor country as well. What we observe is a distortion in the international flow of resources resulting from an implied non-competitive use of the CPR linking the emitter and receptor counties.

The FC principle could be made efficient, allowing for international mobility of resources, if the emitter country taxed its own firms according to marginal damages and then refrained from paying the receptor country, or if for some reason the receptor country's government was convinced that damage payments would not be rebated to the internally affected industry. It might be easier in an international context to get agreement on the FC principle if a stipulation of no transfer of funds among states was accepted.

With the PP principle, we observe international distortions with mobility of resources even if the level of emissions is agreed upon in advance. Here average costs of the emitting firm rise by less than the optimum, since residual damages are not compensated. The net effect is likely to be a less-than-optimal price and output per firm in the emitting country and thus excess international resources committed in the long run. The receptor country's firms have reduced damages but are not compensated for residual damage. In consequence, average costs will decrease but it is uncertain whether the decrease will be greater or less than what is globally optimal.

Under the victim pays principle, average costs of emitters are below the optimum and, through higher short term profits, entry of new firms will be encouraged. With international resource mobility, new firms will continue to enter until excess profits are eliminated. But as the number of firms expands and prices decline, the amount the receptor country's firms pay will increase to the point where profits are negative or at least not excessive. The long-run adjustment therefore should generally lead to excessive resources being committed to the emitter country and too few resources to the receptor country. Such a situation may also not be stable, since at equilibrium firms in the receptor country must make excess profits to pay compensation, and without further governmental regulation it will be advantageous for individual firms at the margin to break away from the coalition and not pay their share of the compensation. This condition occurs because, with increasing marginal damages, the amount paid by any one firm will exceed its losses at the margin by being subject to an additional amount of waste discharge.

The Multilateral Case. With multi-country environmental problems, assessment of the efficiency of the previously stated principles in allocating global resources is much less clear than in the bilateral case just analyzed. As an example, consider one upstream country with waste discharges affecting two downstream countries. With the FC principle, there is the problem of arriving at an agreement between the downstream countries about which is damaged the most and which should consequently be compensated the most. The PP principle contains similar problems in that there must be joint agreement on acceptable levels of upstream control. Finally, the VP principle is fraught with so-called "free-rider" problems in that, if one country provides a substantial amount of the necessary controls, the second downstream country receives reduced damages at no cost. If, in general, there are more receptor countries than emitters, then it will be more difficult, in terms of coordination, for a solution to emerge under the VP principle than under the FC principle. This result follows because the agreement on compensation requires a greater number of sovereignties arranging to make a payment, which inherently seems more difficult to negotiate than those same sovereignties agreeing to *receive* a payment.

Summary. The various principles of state responsibility have substantially different impacts on the global efficiency of resources unless there are no transfers of resources among nations. With no transfers or movements, the various principles tend to affect only the distribution of wealth among nations. In terms of allocative efficiency, the "best" principle would be one of converting all CPRs to internationally operated and regulated resources. But such a conversion may imply substantial changes in wealth and therefore may be unacceptable. The principle with the most desirable efficiency properties would appear to be a modified FC principle where the emitter country's government taxed internal firms according to receptor country damages but did not provide compensation to the receptor country.

Solutions for Universal Common Property Resources

It appears that the principle of common ownership among nations of universal common property resources can be presumed. Without offensive actions or viable non-market threats, it is unreasonable to conclude that any single nation could openly appropriate a universal CPR or that it would be in the national interest of any sovereignty to exclude itself voluntarily from ownership. However, the central issue on the efficient use of universal CPRs concerns the right of access and use, as has been demonstrated by the various coastal boundary disputes. A single nation with access to a common property resource has economic incentives to utilize it inefficiently, not unlike a petroleum firm pumping from a common pool. The petroleum firm will pump more than is optimal because if it does not, some other firm will reduce its share. Again, the economic principle which will lead to greatest global efficiency is likely to be the common property resource institution rule (CPRI) cited earlier, which allocates the CPR according to highest-valued use. But such a principle appears absurd in view of national sovereignty and the character of universal CPRs. For example, it seems ludicrous to presume that any nation would formally and voluntarily relinquish allocative choice-making for the

stratosphere and its *services* over the country.[17] None of the bilateral principles for adjudicating economic responsibility appears to
offer meaningful guidelines for universal CPRs. However, with a few
notable exceptions, the FC principle is the principle of state responsibility with the most desirable economic efficiency characteristics
where universal CPRs are not directly regulated by supra-national
organizations.[18] This is because the degree of distortion between
domestic-international prices and domestic social costs is then minimized. In application it could, at best, resemble the theoretical ideal
only crudely because of great difficulties of evaluation and enforcement. There is at present no body of international law that could
make the principle enforceable in practice. The same can be said
about the less efficient PP principle. Without some substantial innovations and revisions in the international order, we will be stuck,
de facto, with the VP principle as the main device for dealing with
universal CPR problems.

One variant of the CPRI principle which may merit discussion
because of its incentive structure and resulting efficiency properties,
and which might possibly be practical, is the establishment of an
international fund into which each country would automatically pay
some proportion of its GNP or a sum related to its actual use of
universal CPRs. The fund would be administered by an international
body having two major responsibilities: to concern itself with universal common property resources and to act as an international tribunal
awarding compensation to sovereignties that suffer damages from
transnational externalities. An example of the first kind of responsibility would be cleaning up or controlling an oil spill occurring in
international waters. Costs would be assessed against that portion of
the fund supplied by the country under whose flag the ship sailed.
That country presumably would have an incentive to shift all or at
least some of this cost back to the company owning the tanker and
thereby provide an incentive for safer operations. In its second role,
the agency would hear claims for damages resulting from transnational externalities. The victim's sovereignty could confront the
active party, or in reciprocal cases, the parties could confront each

---

17. It might be noted that in the case of atomic weapons testing and space vehicular
travel, involuntary allocation has already occurred. However, the ban on intra-continental
travel of SST-type planes is an example of a case where potential involuntary allocation of
stratospheric services is at least partially controllable.

18. The main exceptions are the situation of preferences for fixed site assets in another
sovereignty and the principle of multilateral action with respect to international trade
aspects.

other, in what would amount to an adversary proceeding. After hearing evidence, the international tribunal would make awards, taking the necessary funds from that portion of the fund contributed by the nation judged responsible for the damage. If such damages were of a continuing variety rather than once and for all, the payments would be assessed at an annual rate to be diminished or terminated upon demonstration that ameliorating measures had been taken. The important characteristic of this variant of the CPRI rule is that it provides a form of insurance to nations damaged by use of universal CPRs by other nations, and thus to some extent it recognizes implicit entitlement to universal CPRs. And this "insurance" need not necessarily be contingent on identifying the CPR user nation(s), though for global efficiency in most cases such identification is necessary.

Preferences for Fixed Site Environmental Features in Another Sovereignty

Not infrequently, unique or rare natural environments are destroyed or blemished because of the inability of a state to regulate its internal industrial, mining, or agricultural activities or to foresee the future value of these resources. No doubt there is widespread regret that the Hetchy Valley in California has been devoted to a water supply reservoir and that uranium mining was permitted on the rim of the Grand Canyon. In the discussion that follows, we assume away internal enforcement problems and short sightedness, although these are no doubt important determinants of what is happening to the natural world.

The case we consider here is this: a state within which a unique or rare natural feature resides does not accord it sufficiently high value to wish to preserve it in the face of development pressure, but the residents of another state do value it enough that, if their preferences counted, the feature would be preserved. There are many cases which may fall into this category, and they are often characterized by considerable urgency in terms of a rational decision.

A case in point is Kenya, which occupies some of the best of the East African wildlife country. The net growth rate of population approaches 3.5 percent per year, the highest in the world, and it may remain very high for a long time to come because about half the present population is under 16 years old. Kenya's population is expected to double in less than 20 years. Population pressure has caused a spillover of the human population into drier game-supporting Savannah lands. The time is rapidly approaching when, unless major new lands are brought into cultivation, there will be less than one acre of arable land per person. Some of the best remaining agricultural lands are in Mosail and on the borders of the Mara game reserve. It is to these lands that 1,500,000 wild beasts, zebras, and gazelles from the Serengeti Park come during their seasonal migration. The results of dense human settlement in this area and of farmers protecting their crops can readily be imagined. Similar situations exist with respect to other African parks.[19] Many visitors, potential visitors, viewers of African films and TV shows, and readers of natural history all over the world must deeply regret the impending damage to, or ultimate destruction of, one of the world's great natural spectacles. Ecologists tell us that the associated loss of genetic information will be irreversible.

In principle, this situation is similar to the technological externality situation discussed earlier. One could readily make an argument for applying the FC or PP principle—i.e., the East African countries should bear the cost of maintaining this international treasure and compensate the rest of the world for damaging it. The situation is not different from that of one country polluting a river and causing environmental degradation in another without regard to the values it destroys.

In practice, however, this type of argument would prove unacceptable. To begin with, the evaluation problems associated with option demands and preferences of citizens of various culturally diverse countries are almost certainly unique and intractable. These problems are vastly complicated by the huge differences in value systems and preferences among countries and the associated complexities in making interpersonal comparisons. Secondly, the distributional implications are so extreme that, even in the absence of any clear criterion of justice for international income distribution, most people would rebel at the thought of wealth transfers from the poorest people on earth to the richest.

It seems that in this case state responsibility consists of accepting the VP principle or some limited form of the PP principle under which the developing country is partially responsible for control costs and other countries bear all residual damages. Since the site is fixed geographically with no non-market environmental dependencies, there are no problems of an efficiency character in its use under a VP principle so long as external values for its use are completely represented when decisions are made. But unless this principle is accepted on a multinational basis and the negotiation-arbitration costs of

---

19. *See* Myers, *The People Crunch Comes to East Africa*, 82 NAT. HIST. 10 (1973).

multinational action can be overcome, other nations may suffer a highly regrettable irreversible loss. The essential problem to solve here is the development of an international agency that can facilitate implementation of the VP principle. Limited organizations for specific sites such as the Nubian monuments have already emerged. But a much more encompassing institution subsidized by the common nations appears to be needed. Furthermore, as in all applications of the VP principle, there is the potential for extortion. But in this case, it is more self-limiting than in the case of actual transnational pollution. The maximum the "polluter" country can do in this case is to destroy the internationally valued resource, or threaten to do so.

Problems of International Trade

If external diseconomies associated with waste disposal occur wholly within the boundaries of a single country with no impact on external preferences, national efficiency in production-consumption can be achieved by that country by applying the various principles of individual or state responsibility described earlier, as long as resources are immobile internally or the state provides additional restraints on relocation of internal resources. From the global efficiency perspective, however, such autonomous decisions on internal waste discharge controls may lead to inefficiencies by distorting international prices and creating a comparative advantage among countries. Consider, for example, two countries, one accepting the FC principle internally and the other the VP principle internally. Even though the first country may have a distinct comparative advantage in producing waste-intensive commodities (i.e., commodities that have relatively high waste discharges associated with their production), it will be induced, through profit disadvantages in terms of international trade, to produce commodities with relatively less waste discharge. In effect, there is a loss in world income because of the shift away from comparative advantage of the two countries in providing waste-intensive and extensive commodities. If resources are mobile internationally, the loss in comparative advantage is even more pronounced since resources will move in response to incorrect profit signals. In the long run, the country with a comparative advantage in producing waste-intensive commodities and adopting the FC principle without other controls will lose resources from this sector to the country imposing the VP principle.

To achieve global efficiency in resource use thus necessarily requires harmonization of internal principles of responsibility among nations. The adoption of various principles without harmonization results in distortions in international trade highly similar to tariffs and export subsidies: relative costs are not reflected internationally in relative prices. It should be pointed out that this is not a direct problem with external preferences for a fixed, unique site except through potential distortions in travel, an increasingly important component of international trade and payments among countries.

While the concept of harmonization of internal principles of responsibility may be important in the long run, it might be difficult to achieve now because of the short-term effects on the balance of payments, national income, and employment. It would appear very useful in an international context for nations to agree to a general principle and then allow flexibility in the timing of implementation to compensate for short-term social effects.

It is important, however, that there be consistency between the principles of responsibility adopted internally by countries and those adopted for external responsibility. To see why this is important, consider the types of incentives that would emerge if a country adopted an FC principle internally but a VP principle as regards state responsibility. Firms within that country would then have incentives to locate and pollute on the boundaries of the country even though this might not result in efficient use of internal or common property resources.

Solutions for Developing Countries and Multinational Corporations

The developing countries exhibit a great range of environmental problems, attitudes, and preferences. National sovereignty requires that developing countries, as well as all others, be given the maximum scope to design their own environmental policies and standards with respect to their internal environments. Still, it would be closing one's eyes to reality not to admit that they will have some special problems in doing so in a way that maximizes the welfare of their populations. Moreover, population pressures and the quest for rapid economic development may induce them to use technologies which produce quick payoffs at the expense of grave, longer term costs to other nations' environments as well as their own.

One of the most striking aspects of environmental problems in developing countries is the rate at which they are getting worse—especially in the rapidly urbanizing areas. In Sao Paulo, huge costs must be incurred soon to try to improve a potentially disastrous water quality situation. Similar situations appear to prevail in many other locations. To some extent this is the result of a conscious policy of delaying expenditures on environmental improvement while economic development proceeds. But it also reflects the almost complete absence of analytical and planning capabilities with respect to the environment, as well as the primitive state of public policy and public administration in many developing nations.

Accordingly, state responsibility in the more technically advanced countries would seem to involve development of a benign paternalism to replace the often exploitative paternalism of the past and present. Some possible components of this new attitude would be a system of environmental impact statements to accompany and ideally to influence the evaluation and design of projects financed by foreign aid programs. In a primitive way, a program of this kind is already getting underway under World Bank auspices.

Various types of technical assistance can also be imagined. The U.N. agencies might be an especially appropriate medium for a program which could include training as well as the provision of technical personnel to help develop local competence in environmental analysis and planning. Subventions might be provided to make such a program more attractive.

Finally, several of the more developed countries in which the major multinational corporations have their headquarters could use whatever control they have over these corporations in the interest of at least minimal environmental protection in developing countries where these corporations also operate. It is known from a number of studies that rather far-reaching environmental protection designed into a new facility when it is just in place will increase its cost very little. It is often the last 10 or 20 percent of protection which becomes very costly. Also, going back and retrofitting existing installations is usually much more costly because of disruptions and because the range of available technical options is then considerably restricted. Consequently, an arrangement whereby multinational corporations agreed, or were required, to design at least minimal protection into their facilities in developing countries would probably be highly beneficial.

THE PROBLEM OF INFORMATION AND TRANSACTIONS COSTS OUTLINED

Economists have recognized for a long time that one of the major impediments to efficient solutions of common property resource problems is the costs associated with obtaining information, achieving agreement by all interested parties, and maintaining or enforcing the resulting agreements. These costs are all grouped under the term "transactions costs"—the cost of successful negotiation per se. In this section we briefly outline the ramifications of the various economic principles of state responsibility when transactions costs are a significant barrier in resolving problems of CPRs.

As discussed earlier, there are three major types of externalities. One involves preferences for resource conservation outside one's sovereignty; another, direct environmental linkages among countries; the third, indirect environmental linkages via distortions in trade prices and patterns. Here we shall only examine the impact of transactions costs where direct environmental linkages appear in the bilateral nation case. It must be emphasized that preferences for fixed site resource in other countries offer many unique and difficult problems where information costs are high and there is no incentive to pay for them because of lack of information initially. For example, a country may decide to assert that a particular national treasure is being preserved when in fact it is being degraded, as long as information on the resource is not readily available to the citizens of other countries. The current exploitation of the Amazon jungle is a case in point.

There appear to be four cases regarding transactions costs for transnational externalities: (1) where transactions costs are always or nearly zero between emitter and receptor countries; (2) where transactions costs are positive and significant both before and after emergence of an externality; (3) where transactions costs are positive before the externality appears but zero thereafter; and (4) where transactions costs are zero before the externality appears but positive and perceptively significant thereafter. Case (1) can be easily disposed of as one which rules out the existence of externalities that are not *a priori* resolved by market or internationally public negotiations. The Coase proposition on the neutrality of property rights is a special case of (3).[20] Case (4) appears to be logically unreasonable. Finally, case (2) is the important one taxonomically for analyzing "real world" problems. An important subset of cases under case (2) arises where transactions costs are different for the two countries either independent of or dependent upon the prevailing rules for state responsibility and liability.

Transactions costs may affect negotiations in a multitude of ways, depending on their source. These include: uncertainty and information gaps (or costs); known or unknown contracting or negotiation costs; cost associated with organizing and sustaining negotiations between countries, including dissemination of information; and enforcement costs for existing contracts. Of these different types of transactions costs we shall concentrate briefly only on two types—

---

20. Coase, *The Problem of Social Cost*, 3 J.L. & ECON. 1 (1960).

those associated with confronting an uncertain prospect of a future environmental externality and those associated with negotiation once the externality has occurred.

A realistic case is one where, under the FC principle, the receptor country incurs negotiation costs, and under the VP principle, the emitter country pays such costs. Thus, those who potentially gain are assumed to initiate negotiation and underwrite the cost of negotiation. Positive negotiation costs, regardless of whether the FC or VP rule is adopted, will impede negotiation so that the optimal level of environmental damage activity *with* zero negotiation costs is never achieved; the cost of additional accuracy of information, monitoring precision, etc., at some point will make it not worthwhile to be closer to this optimum. Costly negotiation where one country incurs these costs may lead to a case where an FC or PP rule results in a higher level of externality-generating activity than a VP rule. This outcome can be induced by differences in marginal utility of income between the emitter and receptor countries as well as a large number of assumptions on initial endowments and preferences. The important point here is that it cannot be *a priori* determined that FC or PP principles will reduce transnational external diseconomies by a greater amount than no such principles when negotiation costs are introduced and must be paid by the country initiating negotiation. If negotiation costs are different for the two countries, the outcome is even less clear. It often has been contended, however, that emitters must have lower negotiation or organization costs than receptors, since receptor countries generally are numerous while the emitter often is viewed as a single country—suggesting that an FC or PP principle might yield a greater reduction in environmentally harmful effects than a VP principle. Whether this greater reduction is globally more efficient cannot be established except by individual case. Under FC or PP rules, the receptor country must undertake negotiation costs since there is no incentive for the emitter to do so unless some provision for punitive damage payments could be agreed upon and enforced. Alternatively, under VP there is an incentive for both nations to undertake negotiations and incur such costs. Thus, with regard to incentives to "discover" the extent of environmental harm, the VP principle appears more efficient. What is important from the above very brief statements is that FC or PP principles or lack of them, with transactions costs, requires for allocative efficiency an additional international rule specifying who must incur these costs. For example, if the FC principle is adopted but there is a negative differential between such costs for emitter and receptor, efficiency is not obtained if the receptor must always pay them. Without such an international rule, negotiation in some instances may be completely stopped and inefficiencies will result.

SUMMARY AND CONCLUSIONS

We have attempted to demonstrate that there is no overarching principle of state responsibility such as "the polluter pays" which is politically or economically (in the efficiency sense) applicable to the entire spectrum of transnational environmental problems. In bilateral cases of transnational pollution, the adoption of a full costing principle by all nations appears to be relatively efficient if the emitter country does not compensate the receptor and the receptor country does not utilize the payments by the emitter country to compensate firms (or individuals) for damages. In multilateral cases, the FC principle also appears to be the most efficient if the number of receptor countries is large relative to the number of emitters, because negotiation costs can be expected to be lower. It should be noted that in both cases, if negotiation or other transactions costs are significant, a viable internationally agreed-upon rule for identifying who must incur these costs and setting penalties for not doing so needs to be specified.

No nation will easily accept international agreement on entitlements of universal common property resources without compensating payments to retain its perception of national wealth. In consequence, the classical answer to externality problems—internalizing the decision-making process for the resource—is not easily transferable to these transnational problems. A new overriding element of distributional gains and losses must be simultaneously included in efficiency considerations. We suggest that with universal CPRs a special environmental insurance fund be set up under international auspices, with an agency empowered to allocate such funds to damaged nations and limited authority to establish annual payments or rebates.

In the case of fixed site preferences in other sovereignties, efficiency is achieved by adoption of either the full costing or victim pays principle. In consequence, the particular principle of state responsibility is not of major concern as long as all diverse interests in the use of the resource are represented. This can be most easily resolved with the VP principle, provided the requisite information and mechanisms for negotiation are available. Here we recommend the creation of an international agency with the explicit duty of facilitating information flow and possibilities for negotiation.

Finally, for global efficiency in the utilization of internal as well as common property resources, we find that the principles of state responsibility internally need to be harmonized with external principles.

[17]

BRIBES AND CHARGES IN POLLUTION CONTROL: AN ASPECT OF THE COASE CONTROVERSY

ALLEN V. KNEESE° and KARL-GÖRAN MÄLER°°

In his invitation to contribute to this symposium on the Coase controversy, the editor of this journal remarked, ". . . Coase initiated a very intensive debate on the neutrality of property rights as regards resource allocations in 1960." This is indeed true and as it happened, a fairly casual set of remarks in a publication by one of the present authors (Kneese) became one epicenter of this debate. The remarks were contained in a publication considering, among other things, the traditional Pigovian solution of taxing an externality-causing activity, in this case the discharge of water pollutants. The question arose as to whether a system of subsidy payments (later termed bribes in the literature) could be made equivalent to charges or taxes as regards allocative effects.[1]

This question has some pertinence since many governments have displayed a fondness for subsidizing pollution control activities. In terms of property concepts, the tax solution could be taken to imply that rights to the waste assimilative capacity of the environment are publicly held and subsidies that they are privately held by the waste dischargers. The equivalence is not exact since in the bribes and charges case there is no exchange of money between the dischargers and specific receptors. In the charges case payments go to the "public in general" rather than to specific receptors. In the bribes case money to make the payment comes from "the general fund." Accordingly, if we wish to relate these schemes to property concepts, we must in the case of charges conceive of the general public, rather than specific users owning the resources. In the bribes case the dischargers can be thought of as owning the resource and the government acting in behalf of other users.

It was concluded that in principle bribes could be so arranged that the effects on *opportunity* costs and hence on allocative decisons would be similar to those of taxes. The procedure would be to make payments to the waste discharger per unit of reduction of waste discharge. But it was pointed out that the required payments scheme bore little resemblance to the subsidy programs actually undertaken by governments and that the information requirements of an optimal

°Director, Quality of the Environment Program, Resources for the Future, Inc., Washington, D. C.

°°Professor of Economics, University of Stockholm.
1. A. Kneese, The Economics of Regional Water Quality Management (1964).

payment system were so extreme as to make it little more than an intellectual curiosum. Specifically, it was said that:

> . . . finally, and most important, the payments procedure encounters particularly difficult administrative problems. For one thing, an industrial enterprise may find it profitable to adopt processes which generate much waste in order to be able to accept payment for reducing discharge. Problems are compounded when industrial location decisions or decisions to enter or leave an industry are involved. Payments would have to be continued to a firm even if it chose going out of business as the best means of reducing its waste discharge. Furthermore, payments would have to be made to firms who would locate in the region if the payment were not available.[2]

Since the bribes approach was regarded as essentially impossible to implement, the remainder of the discussion focused mostly on effluent charges and direct government investment as means of managing water quality efficiently.

But the statements made about the bribes-versus-charges question subsequently stimulated considerable comment in the literature. A major article by Kamien, Schwartz, and Dolbear[3] further developed the matter of how bribes might be arranged when the administrative authority does not know how much would in fact have been discharged if no bribe had been paid—a matter raised in the above quotation. They referred to it as the "zero point question." Without knowledge of what discharges would have been in the absence of intervention, they assume that the control agency bases its payment on the amount by which the waste producer reduces his discharge below the waste *actually* produced, rather than the amount he *would have* produced in the absence of intervention. The authors show by a detailed and rigorous analysis that this payments scheme will induce the profit-maximizing waste producer to produce more waste than he would have under the correctly specified charge scheme (i.e., one based upon the amount he would have produced in the absence of intervention) and that he may produce more than he would have in the absence of any intervention. They conclude that this is a basic asymmetry between bribes and charges.

The Kamien, Schwartz, and Dolbear contribution was a useful elaboration of one of the points raised in the above quotation. But other commentators claimed that there is a more fundamental asymmetry between bribes and charges which was overlooked in the

---

2. *Id.* at 58.

3. Kamien, Schwartz, & Dolbear, *Asymmetry Between Bribes and Charges*, 2 Water Resources Research 147-57. (1966).

above cited book and that the conclusion about symmetry stated there was consequently wrong.[4]

Bramhall and Mills make the point succinctly, and a quote from their article serves well to put the critics' case:

> The point that is important for long run analysis is that the resulting profit levels . . . differ. . . . Under the payments scheme, profits will be larger than they would have been in the absence of intervention, and under the fee scheme profits will be smaller than in the absence of intervention. On the usual assumptions about entry and exit, entry will take place in the former case and exit in the latter case. Entry will lower the price of his product relative to prices of other products, and exit will raise it. Thus, relative prices will, in the long run, be different under the payments scheme rather than under the charge scheme. Since relative prices will differ, the choice between the two schemes is partly a matter of efficiency and not, as Kneese concludes, entirely a matter of equity.[5]

Since the critics made quite a point of the assertion that the analysis neglected differences in profit levels (i.e., impacts on average costs of actual, potential, and past producers in the industry), an effort was made to elaborate the exposition in a subsequent revision of the book in which the symmetry argument was originally made.[6] After supplying a graphical and numerical description of how marginal costs are affected by bribes and charges, it was pointed out explicitly that average cost would be affected similarly by bribes and charges because both become an opportunity cost of production—but only if the bribes system is designed in a very particular way.

We think it will be helpful to the reader to reproduce the pertinent text, leaving out the numerical example.[7]

> We believe that a system of payments, or "bribes" as they have recently been termed in the literature, could in principle achieve the same result as an optimal charges scheme, despite some recent statements to the contrary.
>
> Assume that a profit-maximizing firm has an incremental production cost curve as indicated by *MC* in Figure 16, that the price at which the firm can sell the commodity it produces is given, as indicated by the curve *D*, that the *only* way the firm can

---

4. *See, e.g.,* Bramhall & Mills, *A Note on the Asymmetry Between Fees and Payments,* 2 Water Resources Research 615-16 (1966); Freeman, *Bribes and Charges: Some Comments,* 3 Water Resources Research 287-98 (1967).

5. Bramhall & Mills, *supra* note 4.

6. A. Kneese and B. Bower, Managing Water Quality: Economics, Technology, Institutions (1968).

7. *Id.* at 101-04.

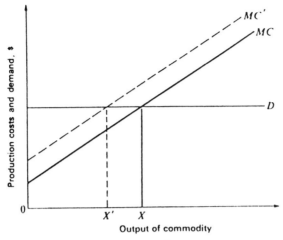

Figure 16

diminish the amount of a residual substance which it discharges
into a stream is to reduce production, and that residual waste per
unit of output is a constant. If a regulatory authority imposes a
unit charge on the effluent of the firm, the incremental production
cost function will shift upward by the amount of the charge per
unit of output (i.e., charge per unit of effluent times effluent per
unit of output) from *MC* to *MC'*.

On the other hand, if the regulatory authority offers to pay the
same amount per unit for reducing waste discharge, the incremental cost function will still be *MC'*. A firm rationally trying to
maximize its profits will view the payment as an opportunity cost
of production because waste discharge is, by assumption, a
straightforward function of production.†

. . . .

The question may well be raised whether in terms of longer-
term adjustments, i.e., a firm's decision to enter or leave an
industry or to expand or contract production capacity, the effect
may not be different. The answer is in principle "no," but great
informational and administrative difficulties emerge if the payments route is adopted. These are discussed later.

In Figure 17, *AC* indicates the long-run average cost curve of a
plant. This curve indicates the average costs of producing various
levels of output (including an average return on investment) under
conditions where a plant can be designed to produce a given
output at least overall cost. If the price is as indicated by *D*, the
firm would construct a plant for which costs were lowest at output
level *X*. This is the relationship which would tend to prevail in

---

†The assumption that waste discharge is a linear function of output was released in later parts
of the text, but this is not necessary for present purposes.

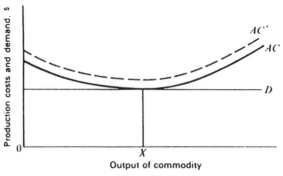

Figure 17

equilibrium in a competitive industry. A charge on effluent per unit would raise the average cost function by the same amount for each unit of output. Consequently, the new average cost curve would be a simple vertical displacement of the old, as shown by AC'. A payment would have the same effect because it is an opportunity cost. The price of output must be high enough to cover the amount of the available payment as well as costs of production (including a normal return on investment), if it is to be worthwhile for the firm to produce an additional unit. In effect, the plant's cost curve (reflecting the value of all foregone opportunities if production is carried on) is raised by the amount of the payment if the payment is available to it whether it is producing or not.

. . . .

The effects of waste disposal costs on prices, location, and decisions to enter or leave an industry will usually be small, because these costs are generally quite low relative to other costs of production and because the firm has the option of treating or otherwise modifying final waste output.

Decisions on location and/or industry entry or exit, however, have a major effect on the administration of a system of payments. Payment must be continued after shutdown of a plant, if the procedure is to have the desired results. While this might be manageable, serious problems would occur if a shift in demand for the product should increase the potential profitability of the plant, or if other dynamic adjustments should take place. Moreover, plants might introduce processes that produce a greater quantity of waste in order to obtain payment for reducing waste.

Even more perplexing would be the handling of proposals for new industrial locations. The administrative authority would have to stand ready to make payments to industrial plants which never do locate in the area but which would do so if a payment reflecting the costs their effluents would impose were not made. Payments on this basis would of course be an open invitation to extortion. If charges were levied, however, the authority would only have to provide the prospective firm with an estimate of the unit charge to be placed on its effluent.

As this quotation implies but perhaps does not point out clearly enough, the central problem is how to make the "shadow" average costs of potential and past producers in an industry (region) reflect the external costs of production. If one sticks to a pure bribes scheme, this can be done only by arrangements whereby the bribe is not made contingent on actual participation in the industry (region). A consequence of this (plus the "zero point" problem) is that an optimal bribes scheme would require information about the full general equilibrium solution for the entire economy. Several authors have demonstrated that under some plausible conditions much less information than that is needed to implement a charges system.[8]

We could let the matter rest here except that we are apparently far from having convinced everyone. In both conversation with other economists and in the literature, the complaint is still voiced that the argument is invalid in the long run, because it neglects effects on average costs and profits. For example, Lambelet has written about the above reproduced discussion: "The source of confusion seems to be that they disregard the fact that a subsidy lowers the average total cost curve while a tax increases it. . . ."[9]

RESULTS FROM A GENERAL EQUILIBRIUM MODEL

We might be forgiven for accusing, in a peevish mood, some of the critics of the symmetry argument of reading what is in their head, not what is on the paper. But more soberly, it is clear that the assumptions have not yet been set out straightforwardly enough, and the argument has yet to be stated with sufficient clarity and rigor. We try to do this in the appendix of this paper. The device used is a simple general equilibrium model of a competitive economy. While simple, it contains all the main relationships usually included in such models and does not require any unusually strong assumptions.

As we mentioned, the details of the model are presented in the appendix but we do want to state the main conclusions here. With the

---

8. For an excellent recent discussion *see* Baumol, *On Taxation and the Control of Externalities*, 62 Am. Econ. Rev. 307 (1972).

9. Lambelet, Recent Controversies Over Environmental Policies, University of Pennsylvania, Department of Economics, Discussion Paper No. 237 (May, 1972); *see also* Tybout, *Pricing Pollution and Other Negative Externalities*, 3 The Bell J. of Econ. & Management Sci. 252-65 (1972); The Instruments for Environmental Policy, a paper presented by W. Baumol & W. Oates at the Conference on Economics of the Environment sponsored by the Universities–National Bureau Committee for Economic Research and Resources for the Future, Inc. in Chicago, Nov. 10-11, 1972.

help of the model three different types of situations are examined: (1) a pure charges strategy, (2) a mixed strategy involving both bribes and charges, and (3) a pure bribes strategy. It is shown that all three can be made equivalent in terms of allocative effects. In the case of the mixed strategy, taxes are levied on new firms entering an industry (region) and subsidies are paid to those already in it. But for this strategy to be equivalent to the pure tax strategy the subsidy must continue to be paid to firms who leave because of the internalization of opportunity cost, but who would not do so if payment were made contingent upon continuing in the activity. In the pure bribes case, bribes must be extended symmetrically to firms which do not enter but would do so if payments of the bribe were made contingent on entry. These are the same results previously deduced from a less rigorous analysis.

CONCLUSION

If we have finally convinced our readers that one can envision conditions in which bribes and charges achieve a similarly efficient result, we nevertheless regard it as rather a hollow victory. The information needed to administer an optimal system of bribes, or some reasonable approximation of it is, for all practical purposes, impossible to get. The main practical purpose for going through such an exercise as we have just done is to reveal how far short the actual subsidy schemes adopted by many governments fall from being able to achieve an efficient allocation of resources. All the subsidy arrangements with which we are familiar provide support for the construction of waste treatment facilities and do not make payments for the actual reduction of waste discharges. By itself, such support provides no incentive at all to reduce waste discharges. Even if the government paid the entire cost of building a waste treatment facility, the discharger would still be indifferent as to whether to use it if there is no penalty for the discharges he actually makes. Accordingly, the subsidies must be accompanied by an elaborate enforcement system.

Furthermore, subsidies for waste treatment plant construction bias the selection of technologies in a particular way. In most industrial processes, by-product recovery and other process adjustments can greatly reduce waste generation and usually curb discharges at lower cost than exclusive reliance on treatment. But the provision of subsidies for treatment biases the cost comparison.

To move the subsidy schemes which now exist in the direction of efficiency would require, to begin with, rewarding the actual reduction of waste discharge in a technologically neutral way. Then one could worry about distorting long-run effects on profit margins. But in terms of attaining efficiency in an actually functioning program, the results of more than a decade of theoretical and empirical research since Coase's article appear to point right back to the Pigovian approach.

APPENDIX

A GENERAL EQUILIBRIUM MODEL FOR ANALYSIS OF BRIBES AND CHARGES

The model economy is assumed to be perfectly competitive. There are n different commodities and services. The set of potential producers is denoted by Λ, and each producer is denoted by an index k. The price vector is p. The set of producers actually operating in a market when the price vector is p is denoted by $K(p)$.

We assume that all individual production sets are strictly convex so that the supply functions are indeed functions and not correspondences.[10] We follow the usual convention and regard outputs (including waste products as positive quantities and inputs as negative quantities. The supply function of producer k is written $x^k(p)$. The total supply is

$$x(p) = \sum_{k \in K(p)} x^k(p).$$

The profit for producer k is

$$p^T x^k(p), \qquad (p^T x \text{ denotes the inner product of } p \text{ and } x)$$

There are H consumers in the economy. Each consumer owns a vector of resources w^h and a share in firm k's profit α_k^h. The wealth of consumer h is then

$$R^h = p^T w^h + \sum_{k \in K(p)} \alpha_k^h p^T x^k(p).$$

Utility maximization gives the demand functions (we assume strictly quasi-concave utility functions so that no correspondences will appear)

---

10. Baumol and Bradford have shown that externalities between different production activities will in general create non-convexities in the aggregate production set. Baumol & Bradford *Detrimental Externalities and Non-Convexity of the Production Set*, Economica (May, 1972). This does not apply to our model because the externalities considered here affect only the consumers. Moreover, Starrett has pointed out that even if there are negative externalities between different producers, the production sets that are relevant to a discussion of charges and bribes are still convex. D. A. Starrett, Harvard Institute of Economic Research Discussion Paper No. 115.

$$D^h(p, R^h, Y),$$

where Y is a vector of environmental qualities (if environmental quality affects not only the satisfaction of consumers but also the production possibilities of the firms, then Y should also appear as an argument in the supply functions, whereupon convexity may be violated. If it is not, the following argument applies.).

The total demand is then

$$\sum_{h=1}^{H} D^h(p, R^h, Y).$$

Private equilibrium is defined by

$$z = \sum_{k \in K(p)} x^k(p) + \sum_{h=1}^{H} w^h - \sum_{h=1}^{H} D^h(p, R^h, Y) \geq 0$$

$$K(p) \subset \left\{ k \in \Lambda;\ p^T x^k(p) \geq 0 \right\},\quad \Lambda/K(p) = \left\{ K \in \Lambda;\ p^T x^k(p) \leq 0 \right\}$$

(The symbol A/K(p) denotes the set theoretical difference between A and K(p).)

$$R^h = p^T w^h + \sum_{k \in K(p)} \alpha_k^h p^T x^k(p),\quad h = 1, ..., H.$$

The first condition is the short-run equilibrium condition that the excess demand for no service and no commodity must be positive. The second condition is that no firm operating in any market has a negative profit and that no potential producer can make positive profit by entering some market. The third condition is simply the definition of the wealth of consumer h.

For some commodities the excess supply will be strictly positive, and this excess supply must be disposed of by discharging it into the environment. This is in particular true for waste products for which there are no demands at all. This use of the environment as a dumping ground will deteriorate the quality of the environment. We assume that the relation between the environmental qualities and the discharge of residuals (or excess supplies) is given by the environmental interaction function

$$Y = F(z).$$

Next, assume that the society has an objective to prevent the vector of environmental qualities to fall below certain ambient standards, $\overline{Y}$:

$$Y \geq \overline{Y}.$$

In order to achieve this objective, the society may impose effluent charges given by the vector q. For most goods the corresponding components in q will be zero, but for residuals which are harmful to the environment the corresponding components will be positive. The effluent charges will change the price vector from p to p – q, meaning that commodities which in private equilibrium have a zero price now have a negative price. The proceeds from the charges are assumed to be distributed in a lump sum manner to the consumers.

The public equilibrium is defined by

$$z = \sum_{k \in K(p\text{-}q)} x^k(p\text{-}q) + \sum_{h=1}^{H} w^h - \sum_{h=1}^{H} D^h(p\text{-}q, R^h, Y) \geq 0$$

$$K(p\text{-}q) = \left\{ k \in A; \ (p\text{-}q)^T x^k(p\text{-}q) \geq 0 \right\}, \ A/K(p\text{-}q) \left\{ k \in A; \ (p\text{-}q)^T x^k(p\text{-}q) \leq 0 \right\}$$

$$R^h = (p\text{-}q)^T w^h + \beta^h q^T z + \sum_{k \in K(p\text{-}q)} \alpha_k^h (p\text{-}q)^T x^k(p\text{-}q), \quad h = 1, ..., H$$

$$F(z) \geq \overline{Y}$$

The first condition says, as before, that excess demand must be non-positive. The second condition is exactly as in private equilibrium. The third condition now defines wealth as the value of resources, the share of profits and lump sum transfers or the proceeds from the effluent charges. The last condition is simply that the ambient standards must be met. We know that this public equilibrium has certain normative properties, in particular that the ambient standards are met at least social cost.

Let us now introduce bribes or subsidies. We will consider the following scheme for subsidizing the polluters. For each agent a vector of commodities and services is determined, and the agent is paid in accordance with the amount he is able to reduce his supplies in comparison to this vector. For a firm k there is thus determined a vector $\overline{z}_k$ and the firm is paid $q^T(\overline{z}_k - x^k)$ where x^k is the firm's actual supply vector (q is equal to the vector of effluent charges considered above). For commodities that are not in excess supply the charge is zero, and consequently the firm is not subsidized for reducing the supply of such commodities. The same is true for commodities that, even if they are in excess supply, are not harmful to the environment. It is natural to assume that $\overline{z}_f^k = 0$ for potential firms not operating in a market. If such a firm enters a market, it will not be subsidized but has to pay effluent charges $q^T x^k$. It is possible, however, to imagine situations where new firms should also be subsidized, but in these cases the subsidy must not be contingent upon participation in the industry.

Similarly for consumers. The net supply of consumer h is $w^h - D^h$, and if the vector $\bar{z}_c^h$ is determined for him, he will be paid $q^T(\bar{z}_c^h - w^h + D^h)$. The total expenditures for this scheme are

$$S = \sum_{k \in K'} q^T(\bar{z}_f^h - x^k) + \sum_{h=1}^{H} q^T(\bar{z}_c^h - w^h + D^h)$$

$$= q^T \left[\sum_{k \in K'} \bar{z}_f^k + \sum_{h=1}^{H} \bar{z}_c^h - \sum_{k \in K'} x^k - \sum_{h=1}^{H} w^h + \sum_{h=1}^{H} D^h \right]$$

$$= q^T \left[\sum_{k \in K'} \bar{z}_f^k + \sum_{h=1}^{H} \bar{z}_c^h - z \right],$$

where K' is the set of firms actually operating in a market with this subsidy scheme (K' will be defined more precisely below). These expenditures are financed by lump sum transfers from the consumers, so that consumer h pays $\beta^h S$.

The wealth (or lump sum income) of consumer h is then

$$R^h = p^T w^h + \sum_{k \in K'} \alpha_k^h \Pi^k + x - \beta^h S,$$

where Π^k is the profit of firm k:

$$\Pi^k = p^T x^k + q^T(\bar{z}_f^k - x^k) = (p-q)^T x^k + q^T \bar{z}_f^k$$

It is clear from this that if the firm is producing something, then its supply is determined from the same supply function as above, that is

$$x^k(p-q)$$

Obviously the same is true for the consumers, so that their behavior can be described as maximization of utility with prices p-q and lump sum income

$$R^h + q^T \bar{z}_c^h$$

The short-run equilibrium can now be characterized by

$$z = \sum_{k \in K'} x^k(p-q) + \sum_{h=1}^{H} w^h - \sum_{h=1}^{H} D^h(p-q, R^h + q^T \bar{z}_c^h, Y) \geq 0.$$

The set K' depends on the precise way the subsidies are administered. If the subsidy ends if firms stop production, then there are incentives for the firms to remain producing and K' will contain more producers than the corresponding set $K(p-q)$ when effluent charges are used. In this case, the two approaches will differ with respect to resource allocation, and since the effluent charges scheme is efficient, bribes cannot be efficient.

On the other hand, if the subsidies continue after the firms have stopped production (as transfers equal to $q^T \bar{z}_f^k$ to the old owners), the subsidy will not have any effects on the incentives to stop production, and the outcome is the same as when effluent charges are used, except that the income distribution is different (it is however possible to choose the shares β^h in such a way that the income distribution is the same in the two cases).

We have thus shown that it is possible to construct a scheme of subsidies that is equivalent to effluent charges. This scheme consists of a subsidy per unit of waste discharge reduction in comparison to a predetermined level for agents that already are polluters and effluent charges for new firms. The subsidy must however continue to the owners of firms even after the firms have stopped their operations.

Moreover, if exclusive reliance is placed on subsidies, all potential entrants to the industry which would enter the industry if they had to do so to obtain the subsidy have to be subsidized. This includes firms which never come into being but would if the subsidy were made contingent on actually producing the product (i.e., discharging waste materials). In addition, if dynamic adjustments in demand or supply can occur, the condition becomes even more restrictive. In that case, subsidies must be paid to all firms which would come into being under all alternative price structures if the subsidy were contingent upon participation in the industry.

[18]

POLLUTION, PRICES, AND PUBLIC POLICY

Allen V. Kneese and Charles L. Schultze

SO FAR, this book has been a rather long, but we hope not tedious, account of the failures and continuing problems of federal environmental policy in the United States. In this chapter we examine alternative strategies based explicitly upon the recognition that, at their core, pollution problems result from the failure of the market system to generate the proper incentives for the allocation and management of a particular type of resources—those with common-property characteristics. We begin with water and air pollution and then consider the failure of incentives in environmental management in general.

A Decade of Research

To understand the importance of some ten years of accumulated research on the economics of water quality management, one must recognize that sanitary engineers (until recently the only profession giving any real attention to pollution) and public policy makers in the United States have seen the problem almost entirely in terms of the treatment of municipal and industrial wastewaters. Historically, they have given scant attention to technologies other than treatment plants and have utterly ignored the economic incentives bearing on the generation and discharge of residual materials.

About a decade ago, an economic paradigm was proposed for research in the area of water quality.[1] This was the concept of a hypothetical "basin-wide firm." The river basin or other watercourse was viewed as an asset that could produce many services—high-quality water for drinking, recreation, and wildlife; stream flow

1. Allen V. Kneese, *Water Pollution: Economic Aspects and Research Needs* (Resources for the Future, 1962).

From Allen V. Kneese and Charles L. Schultze, *Pollution, Prices, and Public Policy* (Brookings stitution, 1975), pages 85-111. Copyright 1975 by Brookings Institution.

for navigation; and a sink for human and industrial wastes. Each of these uses has a value for society, but they compete with each other. Using the stream as a sink reduces its value for recreation; holding pollution to a minimum raises costs for the firms and municipalities along the river. If a single firm (or government) were charged with managing the asset for society's benefit, it would seek to allocate the uses and deal with the wastes so as to gain the greatest possible net value for society.

In designing an optimum management system to meet this goal, the basin-wide firm would have to depart from society's traditional ways of coping with water management problems. First, since polluting wastes lower the quality of the asset that the firm is charged with managing, it would have to treat such wastes as costs, just as real as any other costs of operation and just as important to minimize.

Second, in addition to treatment of wastewater, an optimum management system for the basin-wide firm would have to include such alternatives as regulation of stream flow; a variety of measûres for the improvement of in-stream water quality; the diversion of wastewaters from sensitive areas; their use for irrigation; short-term, high-level treatment measures; and a revision of the incentive system bearing on the generation and disposal of wastewaters. None of these technological and policy options was, strictly speaking, new. Most of them had found application in isolated instances. But they had not generally been regarded as possibilities to be systematically and routinely considered along with waste treatment in water quality management and, of course, the market provided no incentive for their use.

Finally, an optimal management system would not impose a uniform reduction of wastes on each industrial activity, municipality, and other source. Rather, it would adjust the degree of pollution removal required of each activity so as to minimize the total cost of cleanup for the river basin as a whole.

Based on this framework, a series of case studies was launched to test the applicability of this approach to water quality management in real situations. They provide compelling evidence that a system of regional water quality management, using a wide range of technologies for improving water quality and employing economic incentives to encourage their adoption in the optimum combination, would be far superior in both cost and effectiveness to the present legalistic approach, which emphasizes treatment technology and a regulatory approach to effluent standards and enforcement.

The Evidence

Studies of the Potomac River Basin, the Delaware Estuary area, the San Francisco Bay, the Raritan Bay, the Miami River Basin in Ohio, and the Wisconsin River Basin, among others, leave hardly any doubt about the general validity of this conclusion.[2] Each of these studies analyzed alternative approaches to achieving a specified set of water quality standards. In every case, the best alternative included a combination of techniques ranging from the mechanical reaeration of river basins to the pumping of groundwater for low-flow augmentation. Compared to the conventional approach, which relies on uniform treatment of all wastes, the superior alternatives offered sharply lower costs. Moreover, as we remarked in chapter 2, such regional measures may be the only way of dealing with nonpoint sources of pollution such as agricultural runoff.

Even more important than the exploration and implementation of a wide range of technical options is the use of economic incentives as a device to achieve pollution control. Economic incentives, in the form of taxes or "effluent charges" levied on each unit of pollution discharged into the watercourse, have three advantages: First, the imposition of effluent charges encourages a pattern of waste management among different firms and municipalities that tends to minimize the costs of control for the river basin as a whole. Second, charges are much more likely to be enforceable than is the chief alternative, the setting of effluent limits on individual firms and municipalities by a regulatory agency. Third, charges provide a continuing incentive to adopt improved technology as it comes along.

Effluent Charges and Cost Minimization

The overall costs of control are minimized by concentrating the reduction in pollution most heavily among those firms and activities

---

2. The reader can find a reasonably current review of the results of the pertinent research, including most of the cases mentioned in this section, in Allen V. Kneese and Blair T. Bower, *Managing Water Quality: Economics, Technology, Institutions* (Johns Hopkins Press for Resources for the Future, 1968).

whose costs of reduction are least.[3] An efficient approach to pollution control, therefore, requires that different firms reduce pollution by differing amounts, depending on the costs of reduction. Moreover, besides applying conventional waste treatment, each firm should take advantage of a wide range of control alternatives— modifying its production processes, recycling its by-product wastes, and using raw materials and producing varieties of its product that cause less pollution.

In theory, a regulatory agency could devise an efficient plan for uniform reduction of pollution. Effluent limitations for each type of polluting activity could be designed to achieve the minimum-cost solution. In practice, however, the need to tailor limits to each firm, and to consider for each the cost and effectiveness of all of the available alternatives for reducing pollution, would be an impossible task. There are up to 55,000 major sources of industrial water pollution alone. A regulatory agency cannot know the costs, the technological opportunities, the alternative raw materials, and the kinds of products available for every firm in every industry. Even if it could determine the appropriate reduction standards for each firm, it would have to revise them frequently to accommodate changing costs and markets, new technologies, and economic growth.

Effluent charges, on the other hand, tend to elicit the proper responses even in the absence of an omniscient regulatory agency. Each source of pollution would be required to pay a tax on every unit of pollutant it discharged into the air or water. Faced with these effluent charges, a firm would pursue its own interest by reducing pollution by an amount related to the cost of reduction.

An example of pollution removal costs for a hypothetical firm helps make the point:

Percentage of BOD removed	Cost of removing an additional pound of BOD (cents)
40	2
60	4
80	7
90	10
95	15
99	40

3. This is an oversimplification. The impact on water quality from the wastes of any firm depends on the firm's location along the river basin and the hydrology

In these circumstances, if an effluent charge of 10 cents were imposed on each pound of biological oxygen demand (BOD) discharged, the firm would find it profitable to remove 90 percent of the BOD from its effluent because the cost of removal is less than the effluent charge up to that point. The firm would choose to discharge the remaining 10 percent of BOD, however, since the cost of removing it would be greater than the effluent charge. If the charge were raised to 15 cents, the firm would now find it profitable to remove 95 percent of the BOD. In other words, an effluent charge can be set high enough to accomplish any desired degree of pollution removal.

Each firm would be faced with different removal costs, depending on the nature of its production process and its economic situation. For any given effluent charge, firms with low costs of control would remove a larger percentage than would firms with high costs —precisely the situation needed to achieve a least-cost approach to reducing pollution for the economy as a whole. Firms would tend to choose the least expensive methods of control, whether treatment of wastes, modification in production processes, or substitution of raw materials that had less serious polluting consequences. Further, the kinds of products whose manufacture entailed a lot of pollution would become more expensive and would carry higher prices than those that generated less, so consumers would be induced to buy more of the latter.

The effluent-charge approach has another characteristic that recommends it over the regulatory approach. A firm has no incentive to cut pollution further once it has achieved the effluent limitation specified by regulation. Indeed, it has a positive incentive *not* to do so, since the additional reduction is costly and lowers profits. Because effluent charges must be paid for every unit of pollution firms have not removed, they would have a continuing incentive to de-

---

of the stream. A least-cost solution for achieving any given level of ambient water quality would, therefore, have to take into account both the firm's location and the stream's hydrology. Each firm's effluent would have to be weighted by its impact on water quality along particular reaches of the watercourse. In a least-cost solution, each firm would then have to cut back its effluent to the point where its marginal cost per *weighted* unit of effluent reduction was the same as that for every other firm. But the Delaware study, reviewed below, shows that a fairly simple system of effluent charges could come close, in terms of costs, to the more complicated least-cost solution for the whole system.

vote research and engineering talent to finding less costly ways of achieving still further reductions. This continuing incentive is important. The quantity of air and water available to the nation is fixed, roughly speaking. But as economic activity grows over time, the volume of pollution discharged into the air and water will rise unless an ever-increasing percentage of pollutants is removed.

Economists have long advocated, in abstract terms, a tax or charge on activities like pollution that impose costs on society but are not recognized in the accounting that underlies business decisions. Such a tax would automatically force each decision maker to reckon the social costs of his activities. This approach was foreign to the engineering profession, however, and to those most responsible for public policy in this area; and, until quite recently, they have usually greeted it with skepticism when they became aware of it. Even some of those—including some economists—who acknowledge its theoretical merit have been dubious of its practicability. Others have felt that it would elicit little response from polluters, who would simply pass the cost on to consumers and proceed as before.

Economic research has tended to support the practical value and effectiveness of an effluent-charge or tax approach. In the most pertinent case study, it was found that effluent charges could achieve a given water quality objective in the Delaware Estuary area at about half the cost of a regulatory approach aimed at uniform reductions. The efficacy of charges is also supported by the response of industrial firms when they become subject to municipal sewer surcharges, geared to the amount of pollution content of wastewaters. Even though such charges were much lower than a true effluent charge would be, the amount of wastes discharged to the municipal sewer system usually fell dramatically.

Finally, the effectiveness and efficiency of a regional approach to water quality management are supported by study of the successful programs developed over seventy years by agencies in the Ruhr area of West Germany (which includes several river basins other than the Ruhr). These agencies were granted broad authority; and the principles of water quality laid down for them in their basic charter included a broad range of technological options which they systematically combined according to economic criteria. As a result, they have evolved an approach, and a set of policies and facilities, in which economic incentives play an important role. In

general they resemble those that a hypothetical basin-wide firm
might adopt when charged with maximizing the net value to society
of the services provided by the basin.

Enforceability: Regulation versus Effluent Charges

Governmental folklore has it that regulation and enforcement are
direct, effective, and dead-sure means for attacking market failures.
Studies of how the regulatory process has worked in general,
coupled with our review in chapter 5 of its operation with respect to
pollution problems, reveal that it is instead cumbersome, corruptible, and arbitrary and capricious in its impact.

The regulatory approach suffers from an inescapable dilemma. If
the system is simple enough to be handled by a central bureaucracy,
as one might have thought was true for the uniform treatment
strategy in effect before 1972, it is bound to be very inefficient. But
if it seeks to accommodate the tremendous diversity of the economy, and tries to devise effluent standards that minimize costs, the
regulatory task becomes insurmountable. The resulting—and unavoidable—arbitrariness and inequity will in turn make the enforcement of regulatory limits in the courts difficult, time-consuming, and
ultimately ineffective. Furthermore, even if the program were successfully administered, dischargers would undoubtedly view the greatly
differing limits they faced as highly inequitable.

Law makers have exhibited skepticism about the effectiveness of
market-like devices such as effluent taxation. But what we know
about the impacts of price changes, and the limited evidence specifically about effluent taxes, provides strong arguments for their
superiority over regulation. They constitute a relatively neutral device whose enforcement could be incorporated into the body of
precedent and experience already surrounding the nation's tax laws.
The imposition of charges or taxes would require that effluents be
metered at each outfall. But regulations also call for metering.
From that point on, the payment and collection of effluent taxes
involve no major administrative burdens; and, more important, they
raise no specter of court battles over case-by-case regulatory decisions. While there is much tax litigation, the great bulk of taxes—
especially excise taxes, which most resemble effluent charges—are
paid without legal struggles.

Effluent charges have another strong advantage over regulation, especially important in times like the present, when much of the national program of air pollution control seems to be falling victim to the energy crisis. That advantage is that the responses they call for can be flexible, but they always call for some sort of response. When "tough" restrictions are relaxed or eliminated, the continuing social costs of the pollutant discharges are in no way reflected in the discharger's decision making. He is "home free" so to speak. Furthermore, whatever effectiveness the enforcement approach may have is entirely dependent on constant, vigorous enforcement, which can easily give way before the shifting enthusiasms, fears, and perceptions of problems by the public and its representatives. In a government that proceeds from crisis to crisis, as ours often does, this is an extremely important problem for the enforcement approach.

Other Advantages of an Effluent-Charge Strategy

To the extent that the subsidy-regulatory system is effective in reducing discharge, it tends to bias choice toward the less efficient control techniques. Only treatment plants qualify for subsidies; and treatment processes are likely to be emphasized because they are easy to identify and to specify in regulations based on the status of technology. Such is the strategy in the 1972 water quality legislation. This strategy promotes the construction of waste treatment facilities by industry, although in many, if not most, cases other approaches would be cheaper. Effluent charges, on the other hand, are neutral: they do not favor waste treatment or any other single technique, but induce firms to reduce pollution by the most economical means.

The 1972 water quality legislation does reduce the bias toward waste treatment embodied in earlier policy. Previously, industrial firms whose wastes were processed by municipalities had an advantage from the heavy subsidization of the treatment plants by federal construction grants. Even if the municipalities charged firms enough to cover municipal costs, the fees were still lower than full economic costs. The 1972 amendments required industrial firms to pay a fee reflecting their appropriate share of the full costs of the municipal plant. But the provisions of the tax code that allow firms an accelerated writeoff of waste treatment facilities remain in force, and provide a biased subsidy for one form of pollution control. Furthermore, tax-exempt bond financing for industrial pollution abatement facilities has expanded rapidly. In 1973 such financing rose to nearly $1.8 billion, from zero in 1971. A recent survey indicates that, exclusive of tax-exempt bank loans, which are unreported, it could total $2.9 billion in 1974, or about 40 percent of industry's own reported plans for spending on air and water pollution control during the year.[4] This subsidy (since it is for separate pollution control facilities) has the same technological bias as tax writeoffs and grants.

An additional advantage of effluent charges lies in the fact that they yield revenue rather than straining an already seriously overextended tax system. This revenue can be put to useful public purposes, including improvements in the quality of our environment. From the point of view of fiscal policy, the ideal tax base is an activity that generates social costs. Taxes on such activities not only yield revenue but, if properly designed, improve the allocation of resources by moving private costs closer to social costs. This is important because most conventional taxes tend to distort resource use in one way or another.

Industry has been emphasized so far in this discussion of charges, but municipalities too are paying only part of the social costs associated with the wastewaters they generate, and what they pay is capriciously distributed depending on how much treatment they have implemented and whether they waited for federal subsidies. Effluent charges would give these municipalities reasons to proceed expeditiously with the effective treatment of waste, which would reduce the charges they have to pay. Moreover, this system focuses on what is put in the stream and thereby offers an incentive for effective operations of existing facilities—a matter of great importance, as we saw in chapter 3. Finally, about half the residuals treated in municipal plants come from industrial sources. Thus, a charge on municipal discharges, passed back to these industrial sources, is necessary to motivate firms to curb generation of residuals.

4. See John J. Winders, "Tax-Exempt Anti-Pollution IRBs Level Off in Volume in 1st Half," *The Money Manager,* Vol. 3 (July 15, 1974), p. 48. A good discussion of such financing is found in Edward F. Renshaw, "Should the Federal Government Subsidize Industrial Pollution Control Investments?" *Journal of Environmental Economics and Management,* Vol. 1 (May 1974), pp. 84–88.

Some Equity Aspects

Public policy should be effective and efficient, but it should also meet our society's criteria of equity. Unfortunately, these criteria are not well defined. But they seem to say that we want to avoid worsening the distribution of personal income and to avoid imposing costs and requirements on some persons and industries that others similarly situated escape.

In general, by far the best way to meet equity criteria for personal income is to redistribute income directly, and a considerable amount (if, in our view, not enough) of this is done by progressive taxation and payments to poor people. A particularly bad way would be to let social costs like pollution go unpaid in order to keep prices down. Effluent charges, together with the internal controls they induce, bring private costs more in line with social costs; but whether the effect on prices would be greater or less than that of an enforcement program alone is unclear. The greater efficiency of the charges scheme could well wipe out any tendency for charges plus control costs to outweigh control costs alone under an enforcement scheme. In the Delaware case the two amounts were about the same, but the scheme of charges required only about half the cost in real resources—the remainder being revenue available for other governmental purposes.

Viewed by the waste dischargers themselves, effluent charges have desirable equity features. First, the sort of scheme we envisage would affect all waste dischargers at the same time, avoiding the erratic distribution of effects created by the permit-issuing–enforcement–appeals process. Second, the combination of charges paid and internal control costs incurred tends to be more evenly distributed among dischargers than the costs associated either with uniform cutbacks or with the minimum-cost strategy imposed through direct regulation.

While there are strong economic reasons for applying an effluent charge system to municipal waste discharges, formidable political objections would be raised against any proposals under which the federal government or regional water management bodies imposed taxes on "financially hard-pressed" local governments. To reduce these obstacles, the effluent charges paid by municipalities might be channeled into a special fund, to be redistributed to local governments (perhaps in inverse relation to their per capita pollution levels). They would then have substantial incentives to manage their wastes properly.

How to Institute Effluent Charges

Despite the apparently compelling reasons for favoring a system of effluent charges as one of the cornerstones of effective and efficient national and regional water quality management, it would be difficult for particular states and regions to pioneer such a marked departure from previous practice. Indeed, as we saw in the previous chapters, states may find it difficult or impossible to institute even the more conventional controls. Although several states and regions have taken initiatives recently, the federal government's greater insulation from powerful local interests gives it the opportunity for leadership.

There is much to recommend a national minimum charge that would establish the principle universally and blunt industry's threats to move to more permissive regions. Moreover, the charge could provide an immediate across-the-board incentive to reduce discharges into the nation's watercourses. Unlike the strategy embodied in the 1972 amendments, such a charge would affect every waste discharger immediately, unavoidably, and equitably. Had such a charge been levied at an adequately high level when it was first seriously proposed to the Congress in the sixties, there would surely have been a large improvement in water quality nearly everywhere rather than the deterioration that has actually occurred.

The national charge could be considered a minimum that, at their discretion, could be exceeded by state and regional agencies having responsibility for water quality management, according to their own objectives. Revenues obtained by the federal government could supplement funds from general tax sources and be made available for financing the federal program, with the excess turned over to other governments of general jurisdiction. As an illustrative calculation, if the charge for BOD were set at 15¢ per pound (a strong incentive to reduction, because it is well above the costs of higher-level treatment except at the smallest outfalls, and far above the cost of process changes in many industries), the annual revenues would be about $2 billion to $3 billion. On the assumption that charges for other substances would yield similar amounts, total annual revenues would be $4 billion to $6 billion.[5] But the amount would fall rapidly once the incentive took effect, probably to less than $1 billion after several years. Also it might be preferable to implement the charges in stages, increasing them annually until they reach full scale.

Regional Water Quality Management Agencies

The revenues from effluent charges could be used to help establish regional water quality management agencies, which are the other element in our proposed alternative strategy. One way for the federal government to encourage regional agencies would be to establish incentives and guidelines for their organization and operation, either under state law (where appropriate, these agencies could be the states themselves) or through interstate arrangements. An agency with adequate authority to plan and implement a regional system would be eligible for grants to pay staff and to make the first data collections, analyses, and formulation of specific measures for water quality management. Some of the money would also be made available for retraining some of the scientists and engineers now in surplus to do this work.

If the federal government is satisfied that the proposed regional program and the plan for its implementation meet criteria for effective and efficient operation, the agency might be eligible for a grant to assist it with actual construction and operating expenses. Such grants might appropriately be limited to the early implementation stage—say, five years. During this period, longer-term arrangements for financing the agency would have to be worked out, in which the revenues from the effluent charges could play a major role. Administration of the charges system would be turned over to the regional agencies with the federal level of charges as a baseline. In this manner, the same measures that financed the management of

5. BOD has been emphasized here because it is the single most common waterborne waste material and often a good indicator of other pollutants; but other substances should also be included in the charges scheme. Various weighting methods to establish equivalences have been suggested, but perhaps the best starting point would be the systems that have long been in effect in the Ruhr. See Kneese and Bower, *Managing Water Quality*.

the common-property asset on a regional scale would serve as incentives to waste dischargers to cut back on their emissions. Special provisions might be included in the federal law to protect marginal industrial plants in which there is a broad social interest; the adjustment provisions of our international trade law offer a pattern here. In these efforts, special attention should be given to assisting in the reemployment of labor, perhaps through retraining and subsidized movement. Assistance to the firms themselves is less desirable, because any plant that would shut down under the pressure of the program outlined here is probably in deep trouble anyway.

In emphasizing effluent charges, we do not mean to imply that administrative rulings and legal remedies are unimportant in water quality management. Indeed, the discharge of many substances (primarily heavy metals and persistent organics) should probably be prohibited entirely; Sax, among others, has suggested ways in which the courts could take a more constructive part in environmental management.[6] But we are persuaded that economic incentives and regional management are the central elements in effectively and efficiently coming to grips with the problem of water quality management, in the long term as well as the near term.[7]

Many of the elements of this alternative strategy were embodied in a bill introduced by Senator William Proxmire and a number of prominent cosponsors late in 1969; Congressman Lee H. Hamilton and others introduced identical legislation in the House.[8] These bills would have established a national effluent charge (unfortunately, for presumed reasons of political necessity, excluding municipalities) and provided incentives for the creation of regional agencies along the lines outlined above. As the reader will infer from the discussion in chapters 3 and 4, the bill was introduced at a time when strategic reconsideration of the approach embodied in earlier legislation should have been possible. Moreover, committees of the National Academy of Sciences, the Urban Coalition, and various consumer groups, among others, had gone on record supporting the incentives approach. Despite these facts and strong efforts by Senator Proxmire

6. Joseph L. Sax, *Defending the Environment: A Strategy for Citizen Action* (Knopf, 1971).
7. The engineering, legal, and political aspects of charges systems are explored in depth in a forthcoming Resources for the Future book.
8. S. 3181, November 1969; H.R. 12304, December 1971.

and others to get the Public Works Committee to take it seriously, the approach was virtually ignored in the deliberations leading up to the 1972 amendments.[9]

As an interesting sidelight, however, we note that, over roughly the same period, the major European countries were working out strategies much more in keeping with the economic and technological realities of the problem. In some respects the most interesting case is West Germany, where a standards-permits-enforcement strategy has been in effect since 1957. There is now a detailed proposal for a national effluent-charges law, a brief discussion of which is presented in the appendix to this chapter. Approaches incorporating effluent charges and regional management have also been put into effect or are being developed in France, Great Britain, Holland, and Czechoslovakia.

Air Pollution Alternatives

Just like the formation of national policy, economic research in the air pollution area, and policy proposals stemming from it, lagged similar activity concerning water by several years. The central ideas, methodology, and main results of the research were quite similar in the two areas. The efficiency advantage of emission charges, and of greater or lesser degrees of regional planning and management, turned out to be, if anything, more spectacular for air than for water. The first such study, in the Memphis metropolitan area, compared the uniform-cutback approach with the cost-minimizing systems that would be induced by emission charges, and found the latter significantly less costly.[10] A later notable study, in preparation for the President's proposal of what became the Air Quality Act of 1967, involved construction of a composite model embodying elements from several major U.S. cities with severe problems

9. One can envisage a strategy that would incorporate the incentives-regional approach and some of the better elements of the 1972 amendments. This could include strengthened planning and support for institution building, with emphasis shifted to the regional scale; improved legal standing accorded interested parties; control of toxic substances along the lines of the amendments; a permit program for screening new industrial plants to ensure that their performance on residuals generation matched that of, say, the top 25 percent of existing plants; and a national program of stiff effluent fees.

10. See Azriel Teller, "Air-Pollution Abatement: Economic Rationality and Reality," *Daedalus*, Vol. 96 (Fall 1967), pp. 1082–98.

associated with the discharge of sulfur oxides and particulates.[11] It was found that cost-minimizing programs could achieve the same environmental objectives at only 10 percent of the costs of the uniform-cutback method.[12] These results do not even include the more indirect efficiency effects, discussed in connection with water and equally valid here. Also equally valid are the equity and efficacy elements considered above.

Sulfur Oxides Tax

After further study by the Council on Environmental Quality, the Treasury Department, and the EPA, these considerations of efficiency, efficacy, and equity led President Nixon to propose the Pure Air Tax Act of 1972 in February 1972. The President had great difficulty in getting congressional attention for the resulting bill, but supported it again in his 1973 environmental message. A strong approach was especially needed in this area because of the severe health implications of sulfur oxides discharges.

To date, the switch from high- to low-sulfur fuels has been the primary reason for reduced emissions of sulfur oxides. As the events of late 1973 amply demonstrated, such a switch can readily be reversed—and its gains easily lost—especially if no economic penalties remain for emitting large quantities of sulfur oxides. The technologies for removing sulfur from fuels (especially coal) before burning, or from the exhaust streams, are on the drawing boards, but the past five years have seen little movement toward development of these alternatives. Here is a situation ripe for the application of a strategy based on economic incentives.

Levying a per-pound charge on the sulfur emitted by power plants and other industrial firms would elicit a variety of economic responses resulting in improved air quality.

1. The potential cost saving would lend a strong impetus to the development and installation of effective systems for sulfur removal.

11. See p. 17 above on the use of such models.
12. See Jack W. Carlson, "Discussion" of paper by Allen V. Kneese, "Environmental Pollution: Economics and Policy," both appearing in American Economic Association, *Papers and Proceedings of the Eighty-third Annual Meeting, 1970 (American Economic Review*, Vol. 61, May 1971), pp. 153–66, 169–72. A fuller discussion is found in U.S. Department of Health, Education, and Welfare, Office of the Assistant Secretary (Planning and Evaluation), "An Economic Analysis of the Control of Sulphur Oxides Air Pollution" (HEW, 1967; processed).

2. Confronted with a charge on high-sulfur fuels, users of coal and oil with a range of fuel options would choose the low-sulfur fuels voluntarily, even though they are now more expensive.

3. By creating an economically based demand for low-sulfur fuels, the charge on sulfur oxide emissions would provide oil refiners with the strong incentive they now lack to remove sulfur in the refining process and to develop techniques for doing it less expensively. The sulfur content of coal can also be reduced by processing.

4. The emission charge would tend to divert consumers to commodities with less serious environmental effects by raising the prices of those whose production processes employ coal and oil for combustion.

The bill proposed by President Nixon would levy a tax, beginning with calendar year 1976, on emissions of sulfur to the atmosphere. The initial tax rate was calculated to induce curtailment in sulfur emissions sufficient to meet the 1975 air quality standards established by the Clean Air Amendments. In years after 1976, the tax rate would depend on a region's air quality in the preceding year; it would be 15¢ and 10¢ per pound, respectively, where primary and secondary standards were violated, and zero where all standards were met.

One problem with President Nixon's proposal is that it would encourage existing firms to move operations from "dirty" regions to "clean" regions, and new plants to settle there in the first place, to avoid paying a charge. Therefore, in time, shifts in industrial location would degrade the quality of air in the cleaner regions and bring the entire country down to the lowest common denominator.

This problem is at least partially dealt with in identical bills later proposed by Congressman Les Aspin (H.R. 10890) and Senator Proxmire (S. 3057), which would levy a flat national tax. Three main points of these bills are particularly worth noting. First, a target level of 20¢ per pound of sulfur would be reached in 5¢ increments from 1972 to 1975. The target is greater than the estimated costs of high-level abatement but less than the estimated average cost of damages across the nation (put by EPA at about 30¢ per pound). Second, the tax would be uniform across the nation, both to ensure administrative simplicity and to avoid creating havens for polluters.

Finally, because Congress, rather than an agency, would set the level of the tax, the debate would be out in the open.[13]

Automobiles

Even with today's relatively simple systems, maintenance of pollution control devices on automobiles is a very serious problem. Cars are tested before they are sold to see that they meet the emission standards already imposed on the manufacturer; but no follow-up assures that they continue to meet the standards, though a number of studies have shown that few can do so after as little as 10,000 to 15,000 miles of use. For example, results released by EPA in 1973 showed that over half of the vehicles tested after on-the-road service had higher emissions than the standards applicable to their model years.[14] Responding to the importance of maintenance and tuning, the 1970 law required manufacturers, starting with the 1975 models, to guarantee that their cars will continue to meet emission standards for 50,000 miles or five years—bringing on the technological and enforcement problems we have already reviewed.

How to solve the twin problems of ensuring maintenance and stimulating technology? Fifteen years ago economists at Rand Corporation proposed the answer—a smog tax.[15] In one, possibly very powerful, version of this tax, cars would be tested periodically and assigned a smog rating, indicated by a seal or coded device attached to the car. Then, when the driver purchased gasoline, he would pay a tax, over and above the basic gasoline taxes, that would vary with his smog rating.

An individual could reduce his smog tax bill in several ways.

1. Tuning up or overhauling his engine to reduce emissions and obtain better gas mileage would be an economical alternative to paying the tax. Recently established emission standards for cars regis-

13. As an interesting sidelight, two of three American Nobel Prize winners in economics joined many others in publicly favoring this proposal (the third did not comment). See Coalition to Tax Pollution, "The Sulfur Tax" (Washington: The Coalition. May 25, 1972; processed).

14. CALSPAN Corporation, *Automobile Exhaust Emission Surveillance: A Summary*, APTD-1544 (Research Triangle Park, N.C.: U.S. Environmental Protection Agency, Air Pollution Technical Information Center, 1973), pp. 4, 40.

15. D. M. Fort and others, "Proposal for a Smog Tax," reprinted in *Tax Recommendations of the President*, Hearings before the House Committee on Ways and Means, 91 Cong. 2 sess. (1970), pp. 369–79.

tered in New Jersey are less stringent for earlier than for more recent model years. In a pilot study, 45 percent of the cars failed the state standards. But more important, almost every car that failed could pass after a regular "emission tune-up" by a trained mechanic at an average cost of about $20.[16] The New Jersey work demonstrated that vehicles can be efficiently tested (it takes about 35 seconds) and that engine condition, including the recency and quality of tune-up, is extremely important to emissions.

2. A car owner has many options that would allow him to drive fewer miles per year—living closer to his job, using mass transit, or participating in car pools. Standards based on emissions per vehicle-mile do nothing whatsoever about miles driven, but the smog tax would affect this extremely important variable, as well as emissions per mile.

3. Control devices could be installed on older cars. In 1970, in a market test, General Motors offered control kits for pre-1968 models at about $20 installed; but no one bought them. Clearly, it was nonsensical to expect anyone to make this investment since, without assurance that others would make it, any one person's effect on the situation would be negligible. Similarly, no one would buy the kit if he were sure that everyone else would so do: his air would be equally clean whether he bought the kit or not—so why bother? This is the "free rider" problem in the economic theory of "public goods." A smog tax would introduce a new and persuasive element into this calculation.

4. Because consumers would demand them, manufacturers would have an incentive to design automobiles that had better smog ratings not only when they rolled off the assembly line but throughout their lifetimes. In the long run this is probably the most important incentive effect of all.

Only the first of these four ways to reduce one's smog tax is relevant to the question of who should be responsible for the continued attainment of emission standards. But the New Jersey study suggests the practicability of placing the responsibility on owners and backing it up with appropriate economic incentives. The tax elicits other desirable responses from drivers, such as the last three

16. New Jersey Department of Environmental Protection, Bureau of Air Pollution Control, "Motor Vehicle Tune-up at Idle," The New Jersey REPAIR Project (The Department, no date; processed).

alternatives, and its incentives apply to owners of pre-1968 cars that have no control systems, but whose emissions can often be cut substantially by better maintenance and certain retrofitted devices. The smog tax could be varied seasonally; and it could be raised in critical areas—for example, those with unworkable urban transit plans—as a powerful spur to car pooling, reduction in frivolous driving, use of available mass transit, and demand for more.

The gasoline surcharge is also adaptable to reflecting other external costs associated with the use of automobiles, such as highway and street congestion, and uncompensated social costs imposed by the manufacture of certain fuels. Size and fuel consumption variables could govern the amount of tax per gallon. The incentives to manufacturers to develop efficient low-emission technologies are obvious, and no deadline would act to freeze in a technology. For engine types that are inherently and dependably very low in emissions (such as Rankine engines), the smog tax might be canceled entirely.

We feel that a scheme of this type has many attractive features and should be tried. But, short of its full implementation, some of its incentives could be incorporated into the present law.

The Jacoby study recommends one way of doing this that would essentially extend the deadline and apply an economic incentive to innovation in the interim.[17] It would preserve the pre-1975 standards, and postpone the mandatory incorporation of the 1975–76 standards until 1981. A fine equivalent to 5 to 10 percent of its cost would be levied on a model that fell between interim standards and the full 1975–76 goals. In 1981 the full $10,000 fine would be levied on vehicles that did not meet the 1975–76 standards.

We would adapt the present law somewhat differently. The first element would be a slight reduction in the 1975 standard (now delayed) so that no catalytic converters would be needed to achieve it. Then we would institute a smog tax on automobiles progressively over the remainder of the decade until in 1981 the rate for a car still emitting at the 1974 new-car level would exceed the several hundred dollars per car associated with the catalytic system. A few urban areas with severe smog problems would be targeted for special treatment. We believe this strategy would almost certainly

17. Henry D. Jacoby, John D. Steinbruner, and others, *Clearing the Air: Federal Policy on Automotive Emissions Control* (Ballinger, 1973).

lead to the large-scale introduction of inherently low-emission and thermally efficient engines before the end of the decade.[18] It would clearly be second best since it would not influence behavior the way an emission tax levied on the motorist would; but it would be, we think, a vast improvement over the current system.

A Coherent Set of Fees for Atmospheric Emissions

Emission fees would have to be set on a number of different air pollutants. In calculating the appropriate fees, it would be important to set them in the proper relationship to each other, to prevent the adoption of processes that reduce one type of pollutant only to increase another. One such scheme is the "pindex" method of weighting according to toxicity; a sample fee has been calculated for California on this basis.[19] It starts with a fee calculated on the basis of an estimate of damage or control cost for a target level of removal and, on the basis of their relative toxicity, deduces the implied fee for other substances for which no direct measures of harmfulness have been calculated.

Concluding Comments on Effluent Fees

Enough work has been done on the use of effluent fees and regional management devices for water and air quality management to constitute a firm basis for a strategic alternative to the way we have been attacking these problems at the national level. While any practicable program will necessarily have many crudities and arbitrary elements, we feel that workable legislation based on this alternative not only is possible but also would be much more efficient, equitable, and effective—in both the short and the long run—than the legislation Congress has adopted. While the proposals we have reviewed share the difficulty of the present approach by treating closely related problems in isolation, they would mark a start toward the comprehensive and effective environmental management that we must ultimately achieve.

18. Such engines can almost certainly be developed. See, for example, Graham Walker, "The Stirling Engine," *Scientific American*, Vol. 229 (August 1973), pp. 80–87.

19. See A. M. Schneider, "An Effluent Fee Schedule for Air Pollutants Based on Pindex," *Journal of the Air Pollution Control Association*, Vol. 23 (June 1973), pp. 486–89.

Toward a Comprehensive Environmental Policy

The conservation of mass implies that the entire flow of materials and energy through the economy must show up as residuals to be returned to the various environmental media. Accordingly, efforts to reduce discharges into one medium will increase the burden on others unless the processes used permit the material to be recycled. For example, the sludge from wastewater treated in the usual plant is often incinerated, and a favorite way of removing particulates from stack gases is to scrub them with a stream of water. These considerations suggest simultaneously bringing all the various residuals under management in an integrated, coherent program. These relationships present tangled complexities for any approach to emissions control policy.

At the moment, economists and engineers are actively developing comprehensive models of residuals management that systematically embody all the major residuals from production and consumption activities.[20] Until such models become routinely applicable, and until appropriate regional institutions can be created to use them to formulate fully coherent management programs for all the media simultaneously, it is highly important that our national legislation at least recognize the basic nature of the problem.

A systematic attack on perverse incentives should proceed on two fronts. First, we should remove the incentives that have been built into our system to aid rapid exploitation of virgin materials; they have encouraged excessive use of materials in general and lent false economic advantages to virgin as opposed to recycled materials.

Removing these incentives will mean higher prices, but these should be carefully distinguished from inflationary increases. They reflect the embedding in prices of the social costs of particular goods and services, which now fall upon consumers.

20. See Clifford S. Russell and Walter O. Spofford, Jr., "A Quantitative Framework for Residuals Management Decisions," in Allen V. Kneese and Blair T. Bower (eds.), *Environmental Quality Analysis: Theory and Method in the Social Sciences* (Johns Hopkins Press for Resources for the Future, 1972). See also Allen V. Kneese, Robert U. Ayres, and Ralph C. d'Arge, *Economics and the Environment: A Materials Balance Approach* (Johns Hopkins Press for Resources for the Future, 1970).

The most important area for such reform is depletion allowances. Producers of most mineral products, such as lead, zinc, copper, and bauxite, can deduct from their gross incomes a substantial allowance for depletion, thereby reducing the effective tax rate they pay. This practice provides a major subsidy to the price of a number of resources, and thus encourages the excessive use of virgin materials as well as all materials generally. It appears not only that depletion allowances are entirely inappropriate to our current circumstances but also that much can be said for federal efforts to strengthen the hands of the states in instituting or raising severance taxes.

To open a second front in the war on perverse incentives, we should directly and systematically encourage conservation of environmental media. A fully coherent set of effluent charges is not possible at the moment, but levying such charges on a broad front would recognize the interdependencies among the environmental media and promote processes that consume fewer materials or that are more conducive to recycling, as well as treatment of residual materials where appropriate.

A very promising start in this direction is contained in a bill recently introduced by Congressman John H. Heinz III of Pennsylvania. The bill would amend the Internal Revenue Code to levy "a tax on the discharge of taxable items . . . by any stationary or nonstationary source of pollution into the atmosphere or into or upon the navigable waters of the United States, adjoining shorelines, the contiguous zone, or the ocean."[21] The bill sets up a procedure for determining the tax rates to be set by Congress and calls for review at intervals. While it needs considerable elaboration, its direction is clearly right.

Eliminating subsidies for exploiting virgin materials and imposing across-the-board effluent charges could have a powerful effect on conservation of resources and improvement in environmental quality. Such actions would also have the desirable efficiency effects that we have previously discussed.

Present legislation tries to deal with all these problems, and to influence the whole vast array of decision makers involved, through direct regulation and subsidies. If this approach stands, it will, we believe, open a field day for lawyers, incur heavy costs, require a

21. H.R. 635, January 1973.

huge bureaucracy to give it any chance of success, impose ad hoc and capricious impacts, and involve far-reaching intrusion of the government into decisions about the design of industrial processes.

We do not suggest that an incentive-oriented approach could deal alone with all of the sticky problems that arise in achieving environmental control objectives. As we have pointed out, the discharge of highly toxic substances would still have to be prohibited by law and regulation. Schedules of effluent and emission charges that truly minimized the costs of pollution control would be too complex for practical application; the consequent simplified schedules would inevitably introduce some inefficiencies into the system. Because the current production techniques and locations of industrial firms are based on a world in which effluent and emission charges do not exist, the introduction of charges would probably have to be gradual to avoid excessive disruption. Some allowance for temporary relief might be needed for hardship cases, thus reintroducing regulatory-type decisions during an interim period.

The advantage of the incentive approach is not that it is free of administrative problems nor that it can fully duplicate a theoretical least-cost solution. But on both of these counts it is superior to the regulatory alternative.

A Positive Program

We conclude with a list of steps the federal government could take on the road to effective, efficient, and continuous management of our environmental resources. A few of these steps are partially embodied in current legislation.

1. Eliminate the artificial price advantage that virgin materials now enjoy vis-à-vis recycled materials. Doing so would also tend to damp excessive materials use. Consider reversing the relative exploitation of these materials by the systematic use of severance taxes.

2. Develop a list of possibly deleterious substances in effluents that is as complete as practical. Require all who discharge substantial amounts to sample their effluents and report them to a special data center operated by the Environmental Protection Agency or some other suitable agency.

3. Develop a list of substances whose discharge is forbidden because it has deleterious effects that clearly outweigh its cost-saving

benefits. Toxic persistent organics and heavy metals would be prime candidates. Those toxic substances whose use cannot be practicably forbidden should be taxed at a high rate on the input side to make throwing them away very costly.

4. On substances whose discharge is not absolutely forbidden, or whose use is not controlled by input taxes, levy national effluent or emission taxes at levels that provide a genuine incentive for control. Special provision could be made to assist firms that suffer particularly adverse effects that they can demonstrate. Where emission taxes cannot practically be collected, taxes should fall on inputs leading to discharge of deleterious substances. It must be recognized, however, that placing the tax on anything but the pollutant itself narrows the range of possible responses.

5. Increase the burden of proof on producers of new products or processes to identify and report any substances associated with them that might have adverse effects on health or on the ecological system.

6. Use the proceeds of the emission taxes and, if necessary, other appropriated federal funds to encourage the establishment of pollution management agencies that cover whole regions. These might be states, where appropriate, and they could be defined in terms of environmental media such as air, water, and land; but requirements should be laid down to assure that interdependencies among airborne, waterborne, and solid wastes are appropriately recognized, and that efficient regional programs of control can be pursued. Once regional agencies are duly established, the task of collecting emission taxes would be turned over to them, and the proceeds made available to them. They would be permitted to raise some or all of the emission taxes but not to reduce them below the national level.

7. Enact national legislation, such as that passed in Michigan, repealing the public-nuisance doctrine which effectively prohibits suits by individuals against general "public nuisances" like air and water pollution.[22] Thus, legal approaches would have the benefit of a second line of defense against the inevitable failures of management agencies.

22. Sax, *Defending the Environment*, pp. 247–52.

8. Improve understanding of the functioning of natural systems affected by residuals discharge through research, models of the environment, and monitoring. The activities of the Environmental Protection Agency and the National Oceanic and Atmospheric Administration should be greatly extended in these areas.

9. Strongly support the development of national indicators that accurately reflect real changes in the state of the environment and the quality of life.

Appendix: A New Water Quality Law for West Germany

In the fall of 1973, a new water quality law was to be presented to the Parliament of the Federal Republic of Germany. The following paragraphs present the highlights of a discussion of the proposed law issued by the German Interior Ministry in July 1973.

The document discussed the advantages of a charges system over the permit and enforcement system that had been in effect in West Germany since 1957. Of special importance was the tendency of the proposed system to minimize costs by concentrating reductions where costs are lowest and by encouraging the development and installation of low-discharge technologies in industry. The potential result was the rationalization of the price structure that, under the previous system, favored processes that make heavy use of common-property resources by failing to exact payment for them.

The continuing decline in water quality in the Federal Republic lends even more weight to the new scheme, for it can be highly effective as well as efficient. The scheme levies fees on dischargers in accordance with the damaging effect of their waste waters, and sets the fees so that they will provide a strong stimulus to reducing waste discharges to watercourses. The choice of technologies for reducing or eliminating waste water discharges is to be left to the discharger. In other words, the system is designed to be technologically neutral and to motivate research and development for improved processes generating fewer residual materials.

Payments are to be made by all public and private dischargers of waste water to surface waters and coastal waters without regard to the legality of the discharge, or to the size or quality of the watercourses to which discharges are made.

The institution of treatment or other processes for controlling waste water can reduce the payment; but as long as there is any discharge, no matter how small, some payment must be made. Two reasons underlie this requirement: One is to maintain an incentive to the development of low-discharge technologies. The second is that otherwise the system, besides being inefficient, would be regarded as unfair to small dischargers; the residual waste material from a large enterprise might be larger than the total discharge from a small enterprise, and yet the larger and more destructive discharge would incur no penalty.

The level of the charge is to be uniform throughout the Federal Republic in an effort to make broad progress on reducing water pollution. Background material presented in the early part of the draft indicates that despite the existence of a permit and enforcement technique in the Federal Republic, discharges of waste water have continued to climb significantly. Also, uniform charges discourage industries from migrating from dirtier to cleaner areas, where the charges would otherwise be lower.

For an interim period of four years, the charge will be 25 German marks per population equivalent. This level of charge is regarded as just sufficient to spur construction of treatment plants at larger sources, although the stimulus to process change might be considerable even at smaller sources. Following this interim period, the level will rise to 40 marks per population equivalent, which would strongly stimulate the construction of full biological treatment plants for even small, or otherwise high-cost, discharge points.

The charge is suspended for a period keyed to the average time needed to construct a treatment plant. If the plant is constructed by that time, the charge will apply only to the remaining discharge. If it is not, the charge is to apply retroactively to the entire discharge.

The charges are to be based on reports by the dischargers themselves on their own discharges, supplemented by random checks. The proceeds will go to the Länder for improving water quality or diminishing the damages of waste discharges. The Bund and the Länder themselves will be charged for any discharges from facilities they operate.

The draft law also contains an appendix in which the formula for determining population equivalent is given. It resembles closely the formulas now used by the Genossenschaften to levy charges on waste dischargers in the Ruhr region. It weighs suspended material of both mineral and organic type with amounts of both biochemical and chemical oxygen demand. The appendix in the draft law does not include any toxic materials or pH in the formula. However, formulas discussed in earlier documents do include such factors. It is possible that the formula has not been settled at this point.[23]

23. A fairly full discussion of the Genossenschaft formulas is found in Kneese and Bower, *Managing Water Quality.*

[19]

The economy of the earth: Philosophy, law, and the environment. By MARK SAGOFF. Cambridge Studies in Philosophy and Public Policy series. Cambridge, New York and Melbourne: Cambridge University Press, 1988. Pp. x, 271. $29.95. ISBN 0-521-34113-2.

JEL 89-0031

The avowed objective of the philosopher author of this book is to "bury" environmental and natural resources economics. The take off point for his critique is Congressional testimony I gave nearly twenty years ago (prepared statement of Dr. Allen V. Kneese, "The Environmental Decade" *Hearings Before a Subcommittee of the Committee on Government Operations*, House of Representatives, 91st Congress 2nd sess., 1970). Since there are other negative references to my work throughout the book, there is a temptation to take his remarks personally. However, I shall not do that since the book is a frontal attack on resources and environmental economics and all of its many practitioners, not on me personally.

In the testimony I gave, delivered before most of our national environmental legislation was enacted, I stated that I shared many of the environmentalists' values which I characterized as concern for the natural, the tranquil, the beautiful, and the very long run. But I argued that it was not necessary to wait for a new morality or environmental ethic to develop and be widely accepted before legislation on environmental protection is enacted because there are sound economic reasons for protecting environmental resources. These reasons I based on the familiar concepts of economic efficiency, external costs, common property resources, and observation of what was happening to the environment.

But Professor Sagoff, in common with many environmentalists, does not *want* environmental regulation to be justified on economic grounds. He wants it to be based on moral considerations.

In this connection he makes two distinctions, and an interpretation of the political process in the United States, that are central to his argument. The first distinction is that between a person as a consumer and a person as a citizen. In the former role, self-interest is assumed and individual preferences count. In the latter role, Sagoff contends, moral considerations are paramount. The second distinction is that between economic legislation and regulation on the one hand and social regulation on the other. In the former, say, for example, regulation as practiced by the Federal Trade Commission, consideration of economic efficiency is admissible while in the latter it is not. Social legislation, which includes all environmental regulation, should be grounded on moral considerations according to the author.

Related to these distinctions are his views on the nature of the political process. First, in accordance with the above distinctions the political process reflects the votes of moral citizens. In addition, representative government seeks morality—not preference aggregation—and produces endogenous "virtue" not restricted by exogenous criteria like economic efficiency. The process is viewed as an open one that envelopes all interests and considerations [1674] and produces results that can be characterized by terms like noble, just, and virtuous.

With respect to the distinction between a person as a consumer and/or a citizen: In my judgment, while certainly all persons carry some ethical concerns into the polling booth, the best working assumption for both economic and political analysis is that persons by and large act in their own self-interest as they perceive it. This does not foreclose them from acting collectively on common problems; the classic work on this is Mancur Olson's *The Logic of Collective Action* (Cambridge, MA: Harvard U. Press, 1965). More recently, such arrangements have been couched in the language of game theory.

As to the author's view of the political process, I will comment on that after some discussion of a mode of applied economic analysis to which he is particularly opposed, benefit-cost analysis. He cites, for example, well-known problems with the Kaldor Hicks criterion with respect to distributional considerations. Economists have expressed various views about the importance of these problems. But this is not his main point, which is, to repeat, that it is inappropriate to apply economic analysis to what he perceives to be a moral question.

In this connection it is to be noted that much of the important work of economists on environmental problems has involved cost-effectiveness analysis rather than cost-benefit analysis. This was either because of perceived difficulties in measuring benefits, because objectives had already been set by legislation, or because the economists themselves had conceptual difficulties with applying the concept (of cost-benefit analysis) in particular contexts (see Allen V. Kneese and William D. Schulze, "Ethics and Environmental Economics," *Handbook of Natural Resource and Energy Economics*, Vol. 1. Eds.: Allen V. Kneese and James Sweeney. Amsterdam: North Holland, 1985, pp. 191–200).

But economists do have a problem with setting levels of environmental protection solely on moral grounds. Sagoff himself finally admits that there is a problem with this when, on page 80, he writes

> we must acknowledge, however idealistic we may be, that clean air, work place safety, and the like have a price, and at some point the additional amount of cleanliness or safety may be grossly disproportionate to the goods and services we must forego in order to pay for it.

That indeed is the problem, how to compare costs and benefits. The author sees two possible solutions:

The first involves economic benefit estimation—the "willingness to pay" approach that has been under rapid development by economists. He says public officials might commission economists to develop the necessary information. The fact, of which the author is either unaware or chooses to ignore, is that in a number of very important instances public officials have done so. The Flood Control Act of 1936 required that projects to protect against this environmental hazard must have benefits to "whomsoever they accrue" that exceed costs. This provision, which is still in effect, is consistent with the Kaldor-Hicks criterion, and sophisticated methods for estimating flood control benefits have been in use for many years. Since about 1975, the U.S. Environmental Protection Agency has been supporting a large program to improve methods for estimating benefits from environmental improvement. Executive

Order 12291, signed by President Reagan in 1981, requires that all of EPA's (and other agencies') major regulatory actions be subject to a cost-benefit analysis. The Superfund Act of 1980 introduces the concept of damages to natural resources. Such damages are to be quantified in economic terms, a challenging task which the community of environmental and resource economists is now actively addressing.

Clearly, this approach is not the one favored by Sagoff. But what to do? He leaves the choice of the level of environmental protection to political representatives acting without information on benefits. On page 113 he writes, "We expect our political representatives, therefore, to deliberate over these questions and to make wise and virtuous decisions on scientific, moral, aesthetic, economic, and legal grounds." This may be what he expects but if he believes representative government actually operates that way, I think I have a bridge to sell him. The efforts by Congress and the Department of Energy to site a high level nuclear waste repository or the defense appropriation process (aimed at providing that most public of public goods) might reward a little study in that regard. [1675]

Ironically, and perhaps more on point, I had occasion to observe closely the process leading to one of our most basic pieces of environmental legislation, the 1972 Water Pollution Control Act Amendments. That legislation was the product of an exceedingly closed process that purposely excluded much information, especially on costs, not the open enveloping process Sagoff describes. The committee staff never seriously sought information on alternative strategies despite strong advocacy by many prominent individuals and institutions. The real political process is fully as often about excluding information as it is about including it (see Allen V. Kneese and Charles L. Schultze, *Pollution, Prices, and Public Policy*. Washington, DC: Brookings, 1975, pp. 56 and 57).

Nor is it necessarily proper or desirable to have our representatives decide what is virtuous. Many a foul deed has been done in the name of virtue. In a pluralistic society, it seems reasonable to want a collective choice process that aggregates preferences, gives weight to the intensity of preferences, and reflects minority views. Economists as well as philosophers and political scientists understand that, in the final analysis, in a democracy, choices about the level of provision of public goods must be made politically. But in this process, cost is always important and benefit information, where it can usefully be developed, is also important, especially since we appear to be on the steep slope of the marginal cost curve for many of our environmental programs. In this context, environmental and natural resource economics seems more relevant than ever, not irrelevant as the author claims to have shown.

It should be noted in passing that while the author makes this broad claim, resource and environmental economics is a large field containing many important areas of work the author does not even mention. For example, the *Handbook* cited above contains long essays on forty different topics, only one of which is benefit-cost analysis.

I do feel, however, that the profession needs to consider ethical aspects of environmental and natural resource problems more explicitly than it has, interest itself more in collective choice problems, and develop more sophisticated theories and data about consumer demand formation and attitudes, especially in risky situations. In the meantime, the reader interested in applied welfare economics would be better served by examining the more rigorous critiques which have emanated from economists over the years (for example, I.M.D. Little, *A Critique of Welfare Economics*, 2nd ed. Oxford University, 1957; and more recently, Amartya Sen, *Choice, Welfare, and Measurement*. Cambridge: MIT Press, 1982).

ALLEN V. KNEESE
Resources for the Future   [1676]

Name index

Aaron, H. 97
Abramovitz, M. 26
Anderson, F.R. 404
Aristotle 33
Arkwright 86
Arrow, K. 24, 104–5
Aspin, L. 394, 457
Ayers, R.U. 12, 24, 27, 63, 87, 281, 285, 288, 295, 305, 327, 330, 358, 363–4, 404, 462

Back, W.D. 158, 174, 183
Barnett, H. 5–6, 27
Bauman, D. 198
Baumol, W. 15, 435, 437
Bell, F.W. 196
Bentham, J. 32–3
Black, R. 284
Bonem, G. 139, 143
Borgese, E. 410
Boulding, K.E. 62–3, 88, 293
Bower, B.T. 193, 267, 280, 293, 338, 349, 364, 404, 406, 432, 444, 453, 462, 468
Bowes, M. 9
Boyd, J.H. 295
Bradford 437
Bramhall 432
Bramsen, C. 408
Brown, F.L. 183
Brown, L. 248, 253
Brown, R.E. 66
Brozenski, F.R. 194
Bryson, R.A. 270
Buchanan, J. 291–2, 408
Burton, I. 197
Bush, D. 152
Byron, Lord 44

Carlson, J.W. 404, 456
Carter, President 131
Cartwright, E. 86
Cassel, G. 297

Chevalier, M. 85
Christy 410
Cicchetti, C.J. 194
Ciriacy-Wantrup, S.V. 20, 43
Clausius, R. 28
Coase, R.H. 291, 408, 426, 430, 437
Cole, G.D.H. 86
Cole, L. 302
Connolly, M.B. 407
Converse, A.O. 330
Crompton 86
Crosson, P.R. 257
Cumberland, J.H. 330

D'Arge, R. 24, 330, 358, 363, 404, 415, 462
Davidson, P. 291
Davis, O.A. 291
Davis, R.K. 146–7, 296
Day, J.C. 150
Debreu, G. 24
Dewling, R.T. 194
Dickason, C. 150–51
Dickens, Charles 267–8, 375, 403
Dolbear 431
Domar, E.D. 27
Doniger, D.D. 402
Dooley 129
Dorfman, R. 193, 200, 291
Dracup, J.A. 179, 184
Dregne, H.E. 256
Dupuit, J. 17, 34, 127

Eckholm, E.P. 250, 253
Eckstein, O. 18, 35, 129, 291, 301
Edgeworth, F. 48
Einstein, A. 28
Eisenhower, President 129
Ely, N. 174
Engelbert, E.A. 182
Espenshade, E.B. 264

Fabricant, S. 26

Faustmann, M. 8–9
Feinberg, J. 40
Fisher, A.C. 194
Fisher, I. 293
Fort, D.M. 404, 458
Frankel, R. 305
Frederick, K.D. 150, 153, 182–3, 252
Freeman, M. 291
Frisken, W.R. 81, 271

Gaffney, M.M. 9, 291
Gallatin, A. 17, 34, 127
Georgescu-Roegen, N. 12, 24
Gibbons, D.C. 147
Gillespie, W.C. 184, 196
Goeller, H.E. 11
Goodpaster, K.E. 39–40
Gordan, H.S. 196
Gray, E.D. 37
Gray, L.C. 7
Greenfield, S.M. 274

Haefele, E.T. 189, 199–200, 366
Hamilton, L.H. 454
Handler, P. 347
Hanke, S.H. 146–8
Hansen, T. 196
Hanson, J.C. 150, 153
Harberger, A.C. 292
Hare, R.M. 39
Harned, J.W. 317
Harris, C.M. 273
Harrod, R.F. 26–7
Headley, J. 293
Heinz, J.H. III 397, 463
Herfindahl, O. 291, 307, 369, 372
Hickman, H. 284
Hicks, Sir John 86–7
Hirschleifer, J. 18, 35, 129
Hite, J.C. 196
Hiyakawa, Senator 50
Hoch, I. 94
Holburt, M. 167, 183
Hoover, H. 171
Horner, G.L. 150
Hotelling, H. 7
Howe, C.W. 147, 291
Hundley, N. 158, 165, 170–71, 183
Hunt, W.M. 40–41
Huntsman, B. 86

Ingram, H. 182
Isard, W. 305, 330

Jackson, C. 35

Jacobi, G. 236
Jacoby, G.C. Jr 140, 166
Jacoby, H. 193, 200, 395, 404, 460
Jaffe, A.B. 130
Jefferson, President 17, 34, 103, 127
Jelesnianski, Dr C. 197
Jenkins, D. 348
Jenks, C. 408
Johnson, E. 193

Kamien 431
Kammerer, J.C. 139, 182
Kant, E. 38–9
Kantor, M. 203, 236–7
Kapp, K.W. 291
Kapp, W. 15
Kates, R.W. 197
Kelly, R.A. 193, 307
Kelman, S. 33, 56–9
Kemp, M. 407
Kendrick, J. 26
Kennedy, President 129
Keynes, J.M. 10
King, L.B. 154
Klee, A. 284
Klein, L. 10
Kneese, A.V. 20, 23–4, 63, 139, 143,
    183, 189, 193, 199, 236, 260, 280,
    285, 288, 293, 295, 305, 317, 330,
    338, 349, 354, 357–8, 363–4, 369,
    372, 376, 385, 403–4, 406, 408, 430,
    432, 442, 444, 453, 456, 462, 468–9,
    471–2
Knight, F. 293
Krutilla, J.V. 9, 194, 291

Lamb, B.L. 160
Lambelet 435
Lambert, B. 403
Lancaster, K. 338
Landsberg, H. 6
Laney, N. 156, 183
Lang, M. 229, 236
Larsen, Commissioner 118
Lave, L.B. 282, 291, 366
Leibenstein, H. 292
Lekson, S. 184
Leontief, W. 322, 327
Leopold, A. 41
Leopold, L. 167
LeVeen, E.P. 154
Linaweaver, F.P. 147
Little, I.M.D. 473
Locke, J. 44
Löf, G.O.G. 354, 357

Lowry, W.P. 295
Lytle, J.S. 196

Maass, A. 18, 35
Macaulay 105
Machta, L. 272
MacIntyre, A. 33, 42, 43
MacKichan, K.A. 139, 182
Madison 104
Mäler, K.-G. 276, 318, 331
Malthus, T. 5–6, 86
Marietta, D.E. 36
Marshall, A. 5, 14, 17
Martin, W.E. 149
Marx, K. 42
McGuire, M.C. 94, 97, 100–102, 199
McKenna, R.P. 281, 364
Mead, W.J. 194
Mencken, H.L. 99
Meshorev, H. 160
Mill, J. 32, 105
Miller, P. 41
Mills 432
Mishan, E.J. 291, 314, 408
Mitchell, J.M. Jr 270
Mitchell, R. 252
Mohring, H. 291
Morse, C. 5, 27
Moss 156, 175
Muhich, A. 284
Murray, C.R. 139, 182
Myers 422

Nair, K. 194
Nietzsche, F. 50
Nihoul, Prof. C.J. 193
Nixon, President 393–4, 456–7
Noll, R.G. 330
Nozick, R. 23, 51

Oates, W. 435
O'Connor, D.J. 193
Olsen 110
Olson, M. 369, 371, 470
Orbell, J.M. 107

Page, T. 20, 22, 33, 43–7
Pareto, V. 379
Passmore 33
Patten, B.C. 193
Pauly, P.V. 99
Peskin, H. 307
Peterson, J.T. 270
Phelps 273
Pickles, L.M. 196

Pielou, E.C. 348
Pigou, A.C. 15, 47–8, 54, 268, 291
Pohoryles, S. 236
Portney, P.R. 94, 405
Powers, R. 184
Price, M. 159, 183
Prigogine, I. 25, 28
Proxmire, W. 394, 454, 457

Quirk, J.P. 196

Rawls, J. 21, 33, 44–5, 49–50
Reagan, President 18, 131, 472
Reeves, E.B. 139, 182
Reid, K. 182
Reinsberg, M. 94
Renshaw, E.F. 450
Reynolds, S.E. 157, 184
Ricardo, D. 5, 86
Ridker, R.G. 68, 327
Robinson, J. 32
Rolfe, S.E. 317
Rolston, H. 41
Rothenberg, J. 99–100
Russell, C.S. 94, 200, 267, 276–7, 307,
    334, 338, 404, 462

Sagoff, M. 469–72
Saliba, B. 152
Samuelson, P.A. 9
Sax, J.L. 108, 392, 404, 454, 465
Schaefer, M.B. 195
Scherer, D. 41
Scheuring, A.F. 182
Schlesinger, K. 300–301
Schmookler, J. 82
Schneider, A.M. 404, 461
Schultze, C.L. 385, 403, 442, 472
Schulze, W. 20, 23, 27, 471
Schwartz 431
Schwartzman, D. 292
Schweitzer, A. 37
Scitovsky, T. 291
Scott, A. 196, 410
Sen, A. 473
Seskin, E.P. 282, 366
Sewell, D. 280
Shupe, S.J. 152
Shute, S. 37
Sims, J.H. 198
Singer 270
Sloggett, G. 150–51
Smith, A. 13, 24, 378
Smith, F. 293
Smith, V.L. 196

Snead, R. 197
Sobel, M.J. 276–7
Soddy, F. 24
Solley, W.B. 139, 150
Solow, R. 10, 11, 26
Sorensen, P.E. 194
Spofford, W.O. Jr 200, 267, 284, 307, 334, 338, 404, 462
Sporhase 156–7, 168, 174–5, 184
Spurgeon, D. 257
Stander, G.J. 229, 236
Starrett 437
Steinberg, R. 291
Stengers, I. 25, 28
Stern, A.B. 281
Stockton, C.W. 140, 166
Streeter 273
Streinbruner, J.D. 460
Stubblebine, W.C. 291, 408
Sweeney, J. 471

Tamerlane 91, 119
Taylor, J.S. 158, 174, 183
Teller, A.A. 281, 404, 455
Thomann, R.V. 193
Thomas, H.A. 193, 200
Tiebout, C.M. 100–101
Torpey, W.N. 229, 236
Trewartha 239
Trijonis, J. 330
Truman, President 129

Tullock, G. 291–2
Turvey, R. 196, 291
Tybout 435

Uno, T. 107

Vaughn, R. 284
Von Neumann, J. 27

Wahl, R.W. 134, 146–7, 153–4, 157
Walker, G. 461
Walker, K.H. 194
Walras, A. 24
Walras, L. 297
Walter, G. 404
Walter, I. 407
Wan, H. 407
Warnock, G.J. 39
Watson, R.A. 37–9
Weatherford, G.D. 159, 182–3
Weinberg, A. 11, 89, 92, 114, 118, 120
Whinston, A. 291
White, G.F. 197
Wiener 214
Wilen, J.E. 333–4
Winders, J.J. 450
Winters 158, 170–71, 173
Wollman, N. 256, 260
Wolozin, H. 304
Wray, J.D. 66

Zamora, J. 149